THE AMERICAN NEGRO

HIS HISTORY AND LITERATURE

THE
NEGRO IN CHICAGO
A STUDY OF RACE RELATIONS
AND A RACE RIOT IN 1919

ARNO PRESS and THE NEW YORK TIMES

NEW YORK 1968

General Editor
WILLIAM LOREN KATZ

THE MASS MIGRATION OF NEGROES FROM THE RURAL SOUTH TO the urban North, begun during World War I, transformed the "Negro Question" from a regional to a national issue; and in the process it opened a new era of conflict and development for the Negro people and the nation.

The Negro new-comers, repelled by racial oppression in the South and attracted by enlarged economic, educational and political opportunities in the North, settled in cities whose white populations were quite unprepared to receive them. Friction developed, especially over housing as the migrants came to "invade" white neighborhoods, and over jobs as the post-war lay-offs began. Seemingly minor incidents led to bloody anti-Negro riots in northern cities, and they were paralleled by similar developments in the South. Between 1917 and 1921, there were a series of major lynchings and riots by whites against Negroes—notably in Chester and Philadelphia, Pennsylvania; Washington, D.C.; Omaha, Nebraska; Charleston, South Carolina; Longview, Texas; Chicago, Illinois; Knoxville, Tennessee; and Tulsa, Oklahoma.

Unlike the "civil disorders" in northern Negro ghettos during the 1960's, they were racial massacres similar to European pogroms—against which, of course, the Negroes fought back.

Chicago, main northern port-of-entry for Negro migrants from the central South, experienced the worst of these anti-Negro riots —a week of killing and maiming and burning in the summer of 1919. Immediately thereafter, the Governor of Illinois was petitioned by representatives of civic, business and professional organizations to appoint a committee to study the causes and conditions underlying the riot and "to make such recommendations as will tend to prevent a recurrence of such conditions in the future." Within three weeks the Governor complied by appointing the Chicago Commission on Race Relations, whose exhaustive report, *The Negro in Chicago*, is here reproduced.

In introducing the Commission's report to the public, the Governor expressed the opinion that action upon its recommendations would "make impossible . . . a repetition of the appalling tragedy which brought disgrace to Chicago in July of 1919." The hopes here implicit, as the 1968 Report of the President's Commission on Civil Disorders makes clear, were not soon to be fulfilled.

Doxey A. Wilkerson,
ASSOCIATE PROFESSOR OF EDUCATION
YESHIVA UNIVERSITY

THE NEGRO IN CHICAGO

THE UNIVERSITY OF CHICAGO PRESS
CHICAGO, ILLINOIS

———

THE BAKER & TAYLOR COMPANY
NEW YORK

———

THE CAMBRIDGE UNIVERSITY PRESS
LONDON

THE MARUZEN-KABUSHIKI-KAISHA
TOKYO, OSAKA, KYOTO, FUKUOKA, SENDAI

THE MISSION BOOK COMPANY
SHANGHAI

THE NEGRO IN CHICAGO

CHICAGO RACE RIOT—BEGINNING OF THE RIOT

WHITES AND NEGROES LEAVING TWENTY-NINTH STREET BEACH AFTER THE DROWNING OF EUGENE WILLIAMS

THE NEGRO IN CHICAGO

A STUDY OF RACE RELATIONS
AND A RACE RIOT

BY

THE CHICAGO COMMISSION ON
RACE RELATIONS

THE UNIVERSITY OF CHICAGO PRESS
CHICAGO ILLINOIS

Composed and Printed By
The University of Chicago Press
Chicago, Illinois, U.S.A.

TABLE OF CONTENTS

LIST OF ILLUSTRATIONS

LIST OF MAPS

FOREWORD

There is no domestic problem in America which has given thoughtful men more concern than the problem of the relations between the white and the Negro races. In earlier days the colonization of the Negro, as in Liberia, was put forward as a solution. That idea was abandoned long ago. It is now recognized generally that the two races are here in America to stay.

It is also certain that the problem will not be solved by methods of violence. Every race riot, every instance in which men of either race defy legal authority and take the law into their own hands, but postpones the day when the two races shall live together amicably. The law must be maintained and enforced vigorously and completely before any real progress can be made towards better race relations.

Means must be found, therefore, whereby the two races can live together on terms of amity. This will be possible only if the two races are brought to understand each other better. It is believed that such understanding will result in each having a higher degree of respect for the other, and that such respect will form the basis for greatly improved relations between the races.

The Commission on Race Relations, composed of distinguished representatives of both races, has made the most thorough and complete survey of the race situation that I have seen anywhere. While its field of study was necessarily limited to Chicago, the conditions there may be regarded as fairly typical of conditions in other large cities where there is a large colored population.

The report does not pretend to have discovered any new formula by which all race trouble will disappear. The subject is too complex for any such simple solution. It finds certain facts, however, the mere recognition of which will go a long way towards allaying race feeling. It finds that in that portion of Chicago in which colored persons have lived longest and in the largest numbers relatively there has been the minimum of friction. This is a fact of the first importance. For it tends to show that the presence of Negroes in large numbers in our great cities is not a menace in itself.

There is one recommendation (No. 31) to which I desire to call special attention: that a permanent local commission on race relations be created. When as Governor of Illinois I withdrew troops from Chicago after the riots, I was not at all persuaded that all danger of their recurrence was past. I kept observers from the Adjutant General's office on the ground to watch for any signs of fresh trouble. The Commission on Race Relations was appointed, and conditions at once began to improve. The activities of this Commission, composed of the best representatives of both races, were, as I believe, the principal cause for this improved condition.

Causes of friction, insignificant in themselves, but capable of leading to serious results, were discovered by the Commission and by its suggestion were removed in time to avoid grave consequences. Gross exaggerations of some fancied grievance by either the one race or the other were examined into and were found to rest upon nothing else than idle rumor or prejudice. In the light of truth which the Commission was able to throw upon the subject, these grievances disappeared. In other words, misunderstanding, which had been so prolific a source of trouble between the races, was greatly reduced.

The report contains recommendations, which, if acted upon, will make impossible, in my opinion, a repetition of the appalling tragedy which brought disgrace to Chicago in July of 1919.

Men may differ as to some of the conclusions reached, but all fair-minded men must admit, I think, that the report of the Commission on Race Relations is a most important contribution to this important subject.

FRANK O. LOWDEN

INTRODUCTION

On Sunday, July 27, 1919, there was a clash of white people and Negroes at a bathing-beach in Chicago, which resulted in the drowning of a Negro boy. This led to a race riot in which thirty-eight lives were lost—twenty-three Negroes and fifteen whites—and 537 persons were injured. After three days of mob violence, affecting several sections of the city, the state militia was called out to assist the police in restoring order. It was not until August 6 that danger of further clashes was regarded as past.

To discuss this serious situation and means of preventing its recurrence, a group of eighty-one citizens, representing forty-eight social, civic, commercial, and professional organizations of Chicago, met on August 1, 1919, at the Union League Club. Mr. Charles W. Folds, president of the Club, presided. Brief addresses were made by Mr. H. H. Merrick, president of the Chicago Association of Commerce, Dr. Graham Taylor, Miss Harriet Vittum, Major John S. Bonner, Mr. Charles J. Boyd, and Rev. William C. Covert.

Resolutions were passed and given to the press, and the following letter to the Governor of Illinois was authorized:

To His Excellency, Frank O. Lowden
Governor of Illinois

DEAR SIR: A meeting was held today at the Union League Club to take up the matter of the present race riots.

This meeting was attended by 81 representatives of 48 prominent civic, professional and commercial organizations, such as Chicago Medical Association, Chicago Bar Association, Federation of Churches, Association of Commerce, Packing House Industries, Urban League, Woman's City Club, Chicago Woman's Club, Foreign Language Division, representing foreign-born population, etc.

A resolution was adopted unanimously, appointing the undersigned as a committee to wait upon you and ask that you appoint at your earliest convenience an emergency state committee to study the psychological, social and economic causes underlying the conditions resulting in the present race riot and to make such recommendations as will tend to prevent a recurrence of such conditions in the future.

The committee would welcome an opportunity to meet you at any time convenient to yourself and to talk over with you details and give you such information as has been gathered through these various organizations.

Respectfully,

CHARLES W. FOLDS
GRAHAM TAYLOR
WILLIAM C. GRAVES
HARRIET E. VITTUM
T. ARNOLD HILL
FELIX J. STREYCKMANS

In response to this and other urgent requests by various citizens and organizations, and pursuant to his personal knowledge of the situation derived from investigations made by him in Chicago during the period of the riot, Governor Lowden announced on August 20, 1919, the appointment of a Commission on Race Relations, consisting of twelve members, six from each race, as follows—Mr. Bancroft being designated by him as chairman:

Representing the white people: Edgar A. Bancroft, William Scott Bond, Edward Osgood Brown, Harry Eugene Kelly, Victor F. Lawson, Julius Rosenwald.

Representing the Negro people: Robert S. Abbott, George Cleveland Hall, George H. Jackson, Edward H. Morris, Adelbert H. Roberts, Lacey Kirk Williams.[1]

In announcing the appointment of this Commission, Governor Lowden made public the following statement:

I have been requested by many citizens and by many civic organizations in Chicago to appoint a Commission to study and report upon the broad question of the relations between the two races. These riots were the work of the worst element of both races. They did not represent the great overwhelming majority of either race. The two are here and will remain here. The great majority of each realizes the necessity of their living upon terms of cordial good will and respect, each for the other. That condition must be brought about.

To say that we cannot solve this problem is to confess the failure of self-government. I offer no solution of the problem. I do know, however, that the question cannot be answered by mob violence. I do know that every time men, white or colored, take the law into their own hands, instead of helping they only postpone the settlement of the question. When we admit the existence of a problem and courageously face it, we have gone half-way toward its solution.

I have with the utmost care, in response to the requests above set forth, appointed a Commission to undertake this great work. I have sought only the most representative men of the two races. I have not even asked them whether they had views as to how the question could be met. I have asked them only to approach the difficult subject with an open mind, and in a spirit of fairness and justice to all. This is a tribunal that has been constituted to get the facts and interpret them and to find a way out. I believe that great good can come out of the work of this Commission.

I ask that our people, white and colored, give their fullest co-operation to the Commission. I ask, too, as I have a right to ask, that both races exercise that patience and self-restraint which are indispensable to self-government while we are working out this problem.

During an absence of the chairman, due to ill health, Governor Lowden requested Dr. Francis W. Shepardson, director of the State Department of Registration and Education, to serve as acting chairman. On Mr. Bancroft's return and at the Commission's request, the Governor appointed Dr. Shepardson a member and vice-chairman of the Commission.

[1] For biographical data see p. 652.

The Commission's first meeting was held on October 9, 1919. Nine other meetings were held during the remainder of that year to canvass the possible fields of inquiry, and to provide for the organization of studies and investigations.

The Commission was seriously handicapped at the outset by a complete lack of funds. The legislative session of 1919 had ended before the riot, and the next regular session was not to convene until January, 1921. The Commission felt that it could not with propriety seek to raise funds on its own appeal. To meet this situation a group of citizens offered to serve as a co-operating committee to finance the Commission's inquiry and the preparation and publication of its report. This Committee, consisting of Messrs. James B. Forgan, chairman, Abel Davis, treasurer, Arthur Meeker, John J. Mitchell, and John G. Shedd, gave effective aid, being most actively assisted by Messrs. R. B. Beach and John F. Bowman, of the staff of the Chicago Association of Commerce. Without the co-operation of these gentlemen and the resulting financial assistance of many generous contributors the Commission could not have carried on its work. It here expresses its most grateful appreciation.

The Commission organized its staff, inviting Mr. Graham Romeyn Taylor, as executive secretary, and Mr. Charles S. Johnson, as associate executive secretary, to assume charge of the inquiries and investigations under its direction. They began their work on December 7, 1919.

While the Commission recognized the importance of studying the facts of the riot, it felt that even greater emphasis should be placed on the study and interpretation of the conditions of Negro life in Chicago and of the relations between the two races. Therefore, after a brief survey of the data already collected and of the broad field for its inquiries, it organized into six committees, as follows: Committee on Racial Clashes, Committee on Housing, Committee on Industry, Committee on Crime, Committee on Racial Contacts, Committee on Public Opinion.

Along all these lines of inquiry information was sought in two general ways: through a series of conferences or informal hearings, and through research and field work carried on by a staff of trained investigators, white and Negro. Thus both races were represented in the membership of the Commission, in its executive secretaries, and in the field and office staff organized by the executive secretaries.

It is not without significance that in securing office quarters the Commission found several agents of buildings who declined to make a lease when they learned that Negroes as well as whites were among the prospective tenants. They stated their objections as based, not upon their own prejudices, but upon the fear that other tenants would resent the presence of Negroes. Office space at 118 North La Salle Street was leased to the Commission by the L. J. McCormick estate, beginning February 1, 1920. When these offices were vacated, May 1, 1921, the agents of the estate informed the Commission that no tenant of the building had complained of the presence of Negroes.

By March 1, 1920, the staff of investigators had been organized and was at work. The personnel was recruited as far as possible from social workers of both races whose training and experience had fitted them for intelligent and sympathetic handling of research and field work along the lines mapped out by the Commission.[1]

The period of investigations and conferences or informal hearings lasted until November, 1920. The work of compiling material and writing the various sections of the report had begun in October, 1920. Including its business meetings and thirty conferences the Commission held more than seventy-five meetings; forty of these were devoted to the consideration of the text of the report.

The executive secretaries with their staff collected the materials during 1920, and soon after presented the first draft of a report. This was considered and discussed by the Commission in numerous sessions, and the general outlines of the report were decided upon. Then a second draft, in accordance with its directions, was prepared by subjects, and a copy was submitted to each member of the Commission for suggestions and criticisms. Afterward the Commission met and discussed the questions raised by the different members, and determined upon the changes to be made in substance and form. After the entire report had been thus revised, the Commission in many conferences decided what recommendations to make. These recommendations, with a summary of the report, were then prepared, and were reviewed by the Commission after they had been sent to each member. After full consideration they were further revised and then adopted by the Commission. In all these conferences upon the report, all of the Commissioners, with one exception, conferred frequently and agreed unanimously. Mr. Morris, on account of his duties as a member of the Constitutional Convention, did not attend any of these conferences upon the report, summary, or recommendations, and does not concur in them.

The Commission received the cordial assistance of many agencies, organizations, and individuals. The Chicago Urban League placed at its disposal a large amount of material from its files. It also gave a leave of absence to the head of its Department of Research and Investigation, Mr. Charles S. Johnson, the Commission's associate executive secretary. Many citizens, representing widely divergent lines of interest, who were invited to attend conferences held by the Commission, gave most generously of their time and knowledge. The L. J. McCormick estate donated three months' office rent. Messrs. George C. Nimmons & Company, architects, contributed valuable services, including study and supervision by Frederick Jehnck of their office,

[1] The members of this staff, with the previous training and experience of each, are listed in the Appendix, p. 653.

in preparing maps and charts designed to present most effectively data collected by the Commission. The Federal Bureau of the Census made available advanced data from the 1920–21 censuses. Superintendent Peter A. Mortensen and many principals and teachers in the Chicago public schools co-operated in the extensive studies of race relations in the schools; and the Committee of Fifteen provided a report showing important facts in the study of environment and crime. The various park boards, many municipal, county, and state officials, superintendents and others connected with industrial plants, trades-union officers, and leaders in many civic and social agencies greatly facilitated investigations in their respective fields. To all these the Commission returns sincere thanks. But, perhaps, the greatest debt of gratitude is due Mr. Ernest S. Simpson, who generously and devotedly gave his spare time for many months to the editing of this report.

The Commission's letter to Governor Lowden summarizing its work, and his answer follow:

January 1, 1921

Honorable Frank O. Lowden
Governor of Illinois

Sir: Following the race riot in Chicago in July and August, 1919, in which fifteen white people and twenty-three Negroes were killed and very many of both races were injured, you appointed us as a Commission on Race Relations "to study and report upon the broad question of the relations between the two races." We have completed the investigations planned as a basis for this study, and are now preparing a final report of our findings, conclusions and recommendations. This report will soon be ready.

The Commission began its work in October, 1919, and for eleven months has had a staff of investigators assisting it in its activities. While devoting much effort to the study of the Chicago riot as presenting many phases of the race problem, the Commission has placed greater emphasis upon the study of the conditions of life of the Negro group in this community, and of the broad questions of race relations. It therefore organized itself into six committees on the following subjects: Racial Clashes, Housing, Industry, Crime, Racial Contacts, and Public Opinion.

In these fields the Commission's work has been done along two main lines:

(*a*) a series of conferences, at which persons believed to have special information and experience relating to these subjects have been invited to give the Commission the benefit of their knowledge and opinions;

(*b*) research and field work by a trained staff of investigators, both white and Negro, to determine as accurately as possible, from first-hand evidence, the actual conditions in the above fields.

The series of conferences, numbering thirty, covered a wide range of topics, such as: the race riot of 1919 as viewed by the police, the militia, the grand jury, and state's attorney; race friction and its remedies; contacts of whites and Negroes in public schools and recreation places; special educational problems of Negro children; Negro housing, its needs, type, and financing, and its difficulties in mixed areas; Negro labor in relation to employers, fellow-workers, and trade unions; Negro women in industry; the Negro and social agencies; Negro health; Negroes and whites in the courts and in correctional institutions; and the Negro and white press in relation to public opinion on race relations.

Of two hundred and sixty-three persons invited, one hundred and seventy-five attended these conferences and presented their information and views. They represented both races and various groups and viewpoints; they included educators and teachers, real estate men, bankers, managers of industrial plants, housing experts, trades-union leaders, social workers, physicians, park and playground directors, judges, clergymen, superintendents of correctional and other institutions, police, militia, and other public officials, and newspaper editors.

The research and field work done by the staff of investigators covered in general the same broad range. The character is indicated by a bare outline of the work in the six main fields:

Racial Clashes: 1919 Chicago riot, seventeen antecedent clashes; three minor clashes in 1920; brief comparative study of Springfield riot in 1908 and East St. Louis riot in 1917.

Racial Contacts: In schools, transportation lines, parks, and other recreation places; contacts in mixed neighborhoods; adjustment of southern Negro families coming to Chicago; survey of Negro agencies and institutions.

Housing: Negro areas in Chicago and their expansion 1910–1920; 274 family histories showing housing experience, home life, and social back-ground, including families from the South; 159 blocks covered in neighborhood survey; financing Negro housing; depreciation in and near Negro areas; 52 house bombings, 1917–1920.

Industry: Data covering 22,448 Negroes in 192 plants; 101 plants visited; quality of Negro labor; the widening opportunities and chance for promotion studied; special study of trades unions and the Negro worker.

Crime: Police statistics of arrests and convictions of Negroes and selected nationalities compared and analyzed for six years[1]; also juvenile court cases; 698 cases (one month) in three police courts studied, including detailed social data on Negro cases; also 249 sex cases (two years) in criminal court; record of eleven penal institutions; environmental survey of Negro areas.

Public Opinion: Files of white and Negro newspapers studied to analyze handling of matters relating to race relations; study of rumor and its effects, and of racial propaganda of white and Negro organizations.

We believe that the large volume of information collected will prove, when properly set forth, of great value not only in Chicago but in other communities where public-spirited citizens are endeavoring to establish right relations between the two races. This end can be attained only through a more intelligent appreciation by both races of the gravity of the problem, and by their earnest efforts toward a better mutual understanding and a more sympathetic co-operation.

Hoping that our appreciation of the trust you have reposed in us may appear in some measure in the aid our report may give toward working out better race relations, we are, Very respectfully yours,

(Signed by members of the Commission and its Executive Secretaries)

[1] In the final revision of the report, the Commission decided that the police statistics were, as a rule, too unreliable to be made a basis of conclusions.

STATE OF ILLINOIS
OFFICE OF THE GOVERNOR
SPRINGFIELD

January 3, 1921

MY DEAR MR. BANCROFT:

I have received and read with great interest your letter of January 1st transmitting to me a detailed statement of the work of the Chicago Commission on Race Relations appointed by me after the race riot in Chicago in 1919, which is signed by yourself as chairman and by the other members of the Commission.

I am greatly pleased to know that the Commission has been able to accomplish so much through its investigations and that there has been such hearty co-operation on the part of many citizens to make the inquiry in this important field as valuable as possible.

I shall look forward with more than ordinary interest to the appearance of the completed report in printed form. I suggest that the Commission arrange for its publication as soon as possible in order that your findings and recommendations may be made available to all students of race relations in our country.

I desire to express to you and through you to the members of the Commission my great appreciation of the service which you have rendered to the people of Chicago and of Illinois in connection with the Commission. I have been advised from time to time of your continuing interest, your fidelity in attendance upon the meetings of the Commission, and your earnest desire to render as accurate a judgment as possible.

Yours very sincerely,

(Signed) FRANK O. LOWDEN

HON. EDGAR A. BANCROFT
Chairman, Chicago Commission on Race Relations

In accordance with Governor Lowden's suggestion the Commission herewith presents its report, with findings and recommendations, hoping that it may prove of service in the efforts to bring about better relations between the white and Negro races.

THE PROBLEM

The relation of whites and Negroes in the United States is our most grave and perplexing domestic problem. It involves not only a difference of race—which as to many immigrant races has been happily overcome—but wider and more manifest differences in color and physical features. These make an easy and natural basis for distinctions, discriminations, and antipathies arising from the instinct of each race to preserve its type. Many white Americans, while technically recognizing Negroes as citizens, cannot bring themselves to feel that they should participate in government as freely as other citizens.

Countless schemes have been proposed for solving or dismissing this problem, most of them impracticable or impossible. Of this class are such proposals as: (1) the deportation of 12,000,000 Negroes to Africa; (2) the establishment of a separate Negro state in the United States; (3) complete separation and segregation from the whites and the establishment of a caste system or peasant class; and (4) hope for a solution through the dying out of the Negro race. The only effect of such proposals is to confuse thinking on the vital issues involved and to foster impatience and intolerance.

Our race problem must be solved in harmony with the fundamental law of the nation and with its free institutions. These prevent any deportation of the Negro, as well as any restriction of his freedom of movement within the United States. The problem must not be regarded as sectional or political, and it should be studied and discussed seriously, frankly, and with an open mind.

It is important for our white citizens always to remember that the Negroes alone of all our immigrants came to America against their will by the special compelling invitation of the whites; that the institution of slavery was introduced, expanded, and maintained in the United States by the white people and for their own benefit; and that they likewise created the conditions that followed emancipation.

Our Negro problem, therefore, is not of the Negro's making. No group in our population is less responsible for its existence. But every group is responsible for its continuance; and every citizen, regardless of color or racial origin, is in honor and conscience bound to seek and forward its solution.

Centuries of the Negro slave trade and of slavery as an institution have created, and are often deemed to justify, the deep-seated prejudice against Negroes. They placed a stamp upon the relations of the two races which it will require many years to erase. The memory of these relations has profoundly affected and still affects the industrial, commercial, and social life of the southern states.

The great body of anti-Negro public opinion, preserved in the literature and traditions of the white race during the long, unhappy progress of the Negro from savagery through slavery to citizenship, has exercised a persistent and powerful effect, both conscious and unconscious, upon the thinking and the behavior of the white group generally. Racial misunderstanding has been fostered by the ignorance and indifference of many white citizens concerning the marvelous industry and courage shown by the Negroes and the success they have achieved in their fifty-nine years of freedom.

The Negro race must develop, as all races have developed, from lower to higher planes of living; and must base its progress upon industry, efficiency, and moral character. Training along these lines and general opportunities for education are the fundamental needs. As the problem is national in its scope and gravity, the solution must be national. And the nation must make sure that the Negro is educated for citizenship.

It is of the first importance that old prejudices against the Negroes, based upon their misfortunes and not on their faults, be supplanted with respect, encouragement, and co-operation, and with a recognition of their heroic struggles for self-improvement and of their worthy achievements as loyal American citizens.

Both races need to understand that their rights and duties are mutual and equal, and that their interests in the common good are identical; that relations of amity are the only protection against race clashes; that these relations cannot be forced, but will come naturally as the leaders of each race develop within their own ranks a realization of the gravity of this problem and a vital interest in its solution, and an attitude of confidence, respect, and friendliness toward the people of the other race.

All our citizens, regardless of color or racial origin, need to be taught by their leaders that there is a common standard of superiority for them all in self-respect, honesty, industry, fairness, forbearance, and above all, in generous helpfulness. There is no help or healing in appraising past responsibilities, or in present apportioning of praise or blame. The past is of value only as it aids in understanding the present; and an understanding of the facts of the problem—a magnanimous understanding by both races—is the first step toward its solution.

CHAPTER I

THE CHICAGO RIOT
July 27–August 2, 1919

Thirty-eight persons killed, 537 injured, and about 1,000 rendered homeless and destitute was the casualty list of the race riot which broke out in Chicago on July 27, 1919, and swept uncontrolled through parts of the city for four days. By August 2 it had yielded to the forces of law and order, and on August 8 the state militia withdrew.

A clash between whites and Negroes on the shore of Lake Michigan at Twenty-ninth Street, which involved much stone-throwing and resulted in the drowning of a Negro boy, was the beginning of the riot. A policeman's refusal to arrest a white man accused by Negroes of stoning the Negro boy was an important factor in starting mob action. Within two hours the riot was in full sway, had scored its second fatality, and was spreading throughout the south and southwest parts of the city. Before the end came it reached out to a section of the West Side and even invaded the "Loop," the heart of Chicago's downtown business district. Of the thirty-eight killed, fifteen were whites and twenty-three Negroes; of 537 injured, 178 were whites, 342 were Negroes, and the race of seventeen was not recorded.

In contrast with many other outbreaks of violence over racial friction the Chicago riot was not preceded by excitement over reports of attacks on women or of any other crimes alleged to have been committed by Negroes. It is interesting to note that not one of the thirty-eight deaths was of a woman or girl, and that only ten of the 537 persons injured were women or girls. In further contrast with other outbreaks of racial violence, the Chicago riot was marked by no hangings or burnings.

The rioting was characterized by much activity on the part of gangs of hoodlums, and the clashes developed from sudden and spontaneous assaults into organized raids against life and property.

In handling the emergency and restoring order, the police were effectively reinforced by the state militia. Help was also rendered by deputy sheriffs, and by ex-soldiers who volunteered.

In nine of the thirty-eight cases of death, indictments for murder were voted by the grand jury, and in the ensuing trials there were four convictions. In fifteen other cases the coroner's jury recommended that unknown members of mobs be apprehended, but none of these was ever found.

The conditions underlying the Chicago riot are discussed in detail in other sections of this report, especially in those which deal with housing, industry, and racial contacts. The Commission's inquiry concerning the facts of the riot included a critical analysis of the 5,584 pages of the testimony taken by the coroner's jury; a study of the records of the office of the state's attorney; studies of the records of the Police Department, hospitals, and other institutions with reference to injuries, and of the records of the Fire Department with reference to incendiary fires; and interviews with many public officials and citizens having special knowledge of various phases of the riot. Much information was also gained by the Commission in a series of four conferences to which it invited the foreman of the riot grand jury, the chief and other commanding officers of the Police Department, the state's attorney and some of his assistants, and officers in command of the state militia during the riot.

Background of the riot.—The Chicago riot was not the only serious outbreak of interracial violence in the year following the war. The same summer witnessed the riot in Washington, about a week earlier; the riot in Omaha, about a month later; and then the week of armed conflict in a rural district of Arkansas due to exploitation of Negro cotton producers.

Nor was the Chicago riot the first violent manifestation of race antagonism in Illinois. In 1908 Springfield had been the scene of an outbreak that brought shame to the community which boasted of having been Lincoln's home. In 1917 East St. Louis was torn by a bitter and destructive riot which raged for nearly a week, and was the subject of a Congressional investigation that disclosed appalling underlying conditions.

This Commission, while making a thorough study of the Chicago riot, has reviewed briefly, for comparative purposes, the essential facts of the Springfield and East St. Louis riots, and of minor clashes in Chicago occurring both before and after the riot of 1919.

Chicago was one of the northern cities most largely affected by the migration of Negroes from the South during the war. The Negro population increased from 44,103 in 1910 to 109,594 in 1920, an increase of 148 per cent. Most of this increase came in the years 1916–19. It was principally caused by the widening of industrial opportunities due to the entrance of northern workers into the army and to the demand for war workers at much higher wages than Negroes had been able to earn in the South. An added factor was the feeling, which spread like a contagion through the South, that the great opportunity had come to escape from what they felt to be a land of discrimination and subserviency to places where they could expect fair treatment and equal rights. Chicago became to the southern Negro the "top of the world."

The effect of this influx of Negroes into Chicago industries is reviewed in another section of this report.[1] It is necessary to point out here only that friction in industry was less than might have been expected. There had been a few strikes which had given the Negro the name of "strike breaker." But the demand for labor was such that there were plenty of jobs to absorb all the

[1] Pages *infra.*

white and Negro workers available. This condition continued even after the end of the war and demobilization.

In housing, however, there was a different story. Practically no new building had been done in the city during the war, and it was a physical impossibility for a doubled Negro population to live in the space occupied in 1915. Negroes spread out of what had been known as the "Black Belt" into neighborhoods near-by which had been exclusively white. This movement, as described in another section of this report, developed friction, so much so that in the "invaded" neighborhoods bombs were thrown at the houses of Negroes who had moved in, and of real estate men, white and Negro, who sold or rented property to the newcomers. From July 1, 1917, to July 27, 1919, the day the riot began, twenty-four such bombs had been thrown. The police had been entirely unsuccessful in finding those guilty, and were accused of making little effort to do so.

A third phase of the situation was the increased political strength gained by Mayor Thompson's faction in the Republican party. Negro politicians affiliated with this faction had been able to sway to its support a large proportion of the voters in the ward most largely inhabited by Negroes. Negro aldermen elected from this ward were prominent in the activities of this faction. The part played by the Negro vote in the hard-fought partisan struggle is indicated by the fact that in the Republican primary election on February 25, 1919, Mayor Thompson received in this ward 12,143 votes, while his two opponents, Olson and Merriam, received only 1,492 and 319 respectively. Mayor Thompson was re-elected on April 1, 1919, by a plurality of 21,622 in a total vote in the city of 698,920; his vote in this ward was 15,569, to his nearest opponent's 3,323, and was therefore large enough to control the election. The bitterness of this factional struggle aroused resentment against the race that had so conspicuously allied itself with the Thompson side.

As part of the background of the Chicago riot, the activities of gangs of hoodlums should be cited. There had been friction for years, especially along the western boundary of the area in which the Negroes mainly live, and attacks upon Negroes by gangs of young toughs had been particularly frequent in the spring just preceding the riot. They reached a climax on the night of June 21, 1919, five weeks before the riot, when two Negroes were murdered. Each was alone at the time and was the victim of unprovoked and particularly brutal attack. Molestation of Negroes by hoodlums had been prevalent in the vicinity of parks and playgrounds and at bathing-beaches.

On two occasions shortly before the riot the forewarnings of serious racial trouble had been so pronounced that the chief of police sent several hundred extra policemen into the territory where trouble seemed imminent. But serious violence did not break out until Sunday afternoon, July 27, when the clash on the lake shore at Twenty-ninth Street resulted in the drowning of a Negro boy.

The beginning of the riot.—Events followed so fast in the train of the drowning that this tragedy may be considered as marking the beginning of the riot.

It was four o'clock Sunday afternoon, July 27, when Eugene Williams, seventeen-year-old Negro boy, was swimming offshore at the foot of Twenty-ninth Street. This beach was not one of those publicly maintained and supervised for bathing, but it was much used. Although it flanks an area thickly inhabited by Negroes, it was used by both races, access being had by crossing the railway tracks which skirt the lake shore. The part near Twenty-seventh Street had by tacit understanding come to be considered as reserved for Negroes, while the whites used the part near Twenty-ninth Street. Walking is not easy along the shore, and each race had kept pretty much to its own part, observing, moreover, an imaginary boundary extending into the water.

Williams, who had entered the water at the part used by Negroes, swam and drifted south into the part used by the whites. Immediately before his appearance there, white men, women, and children had been bathing in the vicinity and were on the beach in considerable numbers. Four Negroes walked through the group and into the water. White men summarily ordered them off. The Negroes left, and the white people resumed their sport. But it was not long before the Negroes were back, coming from the north with others of their race. Then began a series of attacks and retreats, counter-attacks, and stone-throwing. Women and children who could not escape hid behind débris and rocks. The stone-throwing continued, first one side gaining the advantage, then the other.

Williams, who had remained in the water during the fracas, found a railroad tie and clung to it, stones meanwhile frequently striking the water near him. A white boy of about the same age swam toward him. As the white boy neared, Williams let go of the tie, took a few strokes, and went down. The coroner's jury rendered a verdict that he had drowned because fear of stone-throwing kept him from shore. His body showed no stone bruises, but rumor had it that he had actually been hit by one of the stones and drowned as a result.

On shore guilt was immediately placed upon a certain white man by several Negro witnesses who demanded that he be arrested by a white policeman who was on the spot. No arrest was made.

The tragedy was sensed by the battling crowd and, awed by it, they gathered on the beach. For an hour both whites and Negroes dived for the boy without results. Awe gave way to excited whispers. "They" said he was stoned to death. The report circulated through the crowd that the police officer had refused to arrest the murderer. The Negroes in the crowd began to mass dangerously. At this crucial point the accused policeman arrested a Negro on a white man's complaint. Negroes mobbed the white officer, and the riot was under way.

One version of the quarrel which resulted in the drowning of Williams was given by the state's attorney, who declared that it arose among white and Negro gamblers over a craps game on the shore, "virtually under the protection of the police officer on the beat." Eyewitnesses to the stone-throwing clash appearing before the coroner's jury saw no gambling, but said it might have been going on, but if so, was not visible from the water's edge. The crowd undoubtedly included, as the grand jury declared, "hoodlums, gamblers, and thugs," but it also included law-abiding citizens, white and Negro.

This charge, that the first riot clash started among gamblers who were under the protection of the police officer, and also the charge that the policeman refused to arrest the stone-thrower were vigorously denied by the police. The policeman's star was taken from him, but after a hearing before the Civil Service Commission it was returned, thus officially vindicating him.

The two facts, the drowning and the refusal to arrest, or widely circulated reports of such refusal, must be considered together as marking the inception of the riot. Testimony of a captain of police shows that first reports from the lake after the drowning indicated that the situation was calming down. White men had shown a not altogether hostile feeling for the Negroes by assisting in diving for the body of the boy. Furthermore a clash started on this isolated spot could not be augmented by outsiders rushing in. There was every possibility that the clash, without the further stimulus of reports of the policeman's conduct, would have quieted down.

Chronological story of the riot.—After the drowning of Williams, it was two hours before any further fatalities occurred. Reports of the drowning and of the alleged conduct of the policeman spread out into the neighborhood. The Negro crowd from the beach gathered at the foot of Twenty-ninth Street. As it became more and more excited, a group of officers was called by the policeman who had been at the beach. James Crawford, a Negro, fired into the group of officers and was himself shot and killed by a Negro policeman who had been sent to help restore order.

During the remainder of the afternoon of July 27, many distorted rumors circulated swiftly throughout the South Side. The Negro crowd from Twenty-ninth Street got into action, and white men who came in contact with it were beaten. In all, four white men were beaten, five were stabbed, and one was shot. As the rumors spread, new crowds gathered, mobs sprang into activity spontaneously, and gangs began to take part in the lawlessness.

Farther to the west, as darkness came on, white gangsters became active. Negroes in white districts suffered severely at their hands. From 9:00 P.M. until 3:00 A.M. twenty-seven Negroes were beaten, seven were stabbed, and four were shot.

Few clashes occurred on Monday morning. People of both races went to work as usual and even continued to work side by side, as customary, without signs of violence. But as the afternoon wore on, white men and boys living between the Stock Yards and the "Black Belt" sought malicious amusement in directing mob violence against Negro workers returning home.

Street-car routes, especially transfer points, were thronged with white people of all ages. Trolleys were pulled from wires and the cars brought under the control of mob leaders. Negro passengers were dragged to the street, beaten, and kicked. The police were apparently powerless to cope with these numerous assaults. Four Negro men and one white assailant were killed, and thirty Negro men were severely beaten in the street-car clashes.

The "Black Belt" contributed its share of violence to the record of Monday afternoon and night. Rumors of white depredations and killings were current among the Negroes and led to acts of retaliation. An aged Italian peddler, one Lazzeroni, was set upon by young Negro boys and stabbed to death. Eugene Temple, white laundryman, was stabbed to death and robbed by three Negroes.

A Negro mob made a demonstration outside Provident Hospital, an institution conducted by Negroes, because two injured whites who had been shooting right and left from a hurrying automobile on State Street were taken there. Other mobs stabbed six white men, shot five others, severely beat nine more, and killed two in addition to those named above.

Rumor had it that a white occupant of the Angelus apartment house had shot a Negro boy from a fourth-story window. Negroes besieged the building. The white tenants sought police protection, and about 100 policemen, including some mounted men, responded. The mob of about 1,500 Negroes demanded the "culprit," but the police failed to find him after a search of the building. A flying brick hit a policeman. There was a quick massing of the police, and a volley was fired into the Negro mob. Four Negroes were killed and many were injured. It is believed that had the Negroes not lost faith in the white police force it is hardly likely that the Angelus riot would have occurred.

At this point, Monday night, both whites and Negroes showed signs of panic. Each race grouped by itself. Small mobs began systematically in various neighborhoods to terrorize and kill. Gangs in the white districts grew bolder, finally taking the offensive in raids through territory "invaded" by Negro home seekers. Boys between sixteen and twenty-two banded together to enjoy the excitement of the chase.

Automobile raids were added to the rioting Monday night. Cars from which rifle and revolver shots were fired were driven at great speed through sections inhabited by Negroes. Negroes defended themselves by "sniping" and volley-firing from ambush and barricade. So great was the fear of these raiding parties that the Negroes distrusted all motor vehicles and frequently opened fire on them without waiting to learn the intent of the occupants. This type of warfare was kept up spasmodically all Tuesday and was resumed with vigor Tuesday night.

At midnight, Monday, street-car clashes ended by reason of a general strike on the surface and elevated lines. The street-railway tie-up was complete for the remainder of the week. But on Tuesday morning this was a new source of terror for those who tried to walk to their places of employment. Men were killed en route to their work through hostile territory. Idle men congregated on the streets, and gang-rioting increased. A white gang of soldiers and sailors in uniform, augmented by civilians, raided the "Loop," or downtown section of Chicago, early Tuesday, killing two Negroes and beating and robbing several others. In the course of these activities they wantonly destroyed property of white business men.

Gangs sprang up as far south as Sixty-third Street in Englewood and in the section west of Wentworth Avenue near Forty-seventh Street. Premeditated depredations were the order of the night. Many Negro homes in mixed districts were attacked, and several of them were burned. Furniture was stolen or destroyed. When raiders were driven off they would return again and again until their designs were accomplished.

The contagion of the race war broke over the boundaries of the South Side and spread to the Italians on the West Side. This community became excited over a rumor, and an Italian crowd killed a Negro, Joseph Lovings.

Wednesday saw a material lessening of crime and violence. The "Black Belt" and the district immediately west of it were still storm centers. But the peak of the rioting had apparently passed, although the danger of fresh outbreaks of magnitude was still imminent. Although companies of the militia had been mobilized in nearby armories as early as Monday night, July 28, it was not until Wednesday evening at 10:30 that the mayor yielded to pressure and asked for their help.

Rain on Wednesday night and Thursday drove idle people of both races into their homes. The temperature fell, and with it the white heat of the riot. From this time on the violence was sporadic, scattered, and meager. The riot seemed well under control, if not actually ended.

Friday witnessed only a single reported injury. At 3:35 A.M. Saturday incendiary fires burned forty-nine houses in the immigrant neighborhood west of the Stock Yards. Nine hundred and forty-eight people, mostly Lithuanians, were made homeless, and the property loss was about $250,000. Responsibility for these fires was never fixed. The riot virtually ceased on Saturday. For the next few days injured were reported occasionally, and by August 8 the riot zone had settled down to normal and the militia was withdrawn.

Growth of the riot.—The riot period was thirteen days in length, from Sunday, July 27, through Thursday, August 8, the day on which the troops were withdrawn. Of this time, only the first seven days witnessed active rioting. The remaining days marked the return toward normal. In the seven active days, rioting was not continuous but intermittent, being furious for hours, then fairly quiescent for hours. The first three days saw the most acute disturbance, and in this span there were three main periods: 4:00 P.M. Sunday till 3:00 A.M. Monday; 9:00 A.M. Monday till 9:00 A.M. Tuesday; noon Tuesday till midnight. This left two long intervals of comparative quiet, six hours on Monday and three hours on Tuesday. On the fourth day, Wednesday, there were scattered periods of rioting, each of a few hours' duration. Thus Monday afternoon to Tuesday morning was the longest stretch of active rioting in the first four days.

For the most part the riot was confined to the South Side of the city. There were two notable exceptions, the district north and west of the south branch of the Chicago River and the "Loop" or downtown business district. A few isolated clashes occurred on the North Side and on the extreme West Side, but aside from these the area covered was that shown on the accompanying outline map.

For the purposes of discussion it is convenient to divide the riot area into seven districts. The boundaries in some instances are due to the designation of Wentworth Avenue by the police as a boundary west of which no Negroes should be allowed, and east of which no whites should be allowed.

I. "Black Belt." From Twenty-second to Thirty-ninth, inclusive; Wentworth Avenue to the lake, exclusive of Wentworth; Thirty-ninth to
Fifty-fifth, inclusive; Clark to Michigan, exclusive of Michigan.

II. Area contested by both Negroes and whites. Thirty-ninth to Fifty-fifth,
inclusive; Michigan to the lake.

III. Southwest Side, including the Stock Yards district; south of the Chicago
River to Fifty-fifth; west of Wentworth, including Wentworth.

IV. Area south of Fifty-fifth and east of Wentworth.

V. Area south of Fifty-fifth and west of Wentworth.

VI. Area north and west of the Chicago River.

VII. "Loop" or business district and vicinity.

In the district designated as the "Black Belt" about 90 per cent of the Negroes live. District II, the "contested area," is that in which most of the bombings have occurred. Negroes are said to be "invading" this district. Extension here instead of into District III, toward the Stock Yards neighbor-hood, may be explained partly by the hostility which the Irish and Polish groups to the west had often shown to Negroes. The white hoodlum element of the Stock Yards district, designated as III, was characterized by the state's attorney of Cook County, when he remarked that more bank robbers, pay-roll bandits, automobile bandits, highwaymen, and strong-arm crooks come from this particular district than from any other that has come to his notice during seven years of service as chief prosecuting official.[1]

In District IV and V, south of Fifty-fifth Street, Negroes live in small communities surrounded by white people or are scattered through white

---

[1] Carl Sandburg, *The Chicago Race Riots*, chap. i, p. 1. Harcourt, Brace & Howe.

inside it. Neither motorman nor conductor took names of witnesses or attempted to fix a description of the assailants in mind.

When B. F. Hardy, a Negro, was killed on a street car at Forty-sixth Street and Cottage Grove Avenue, the motorman and conductor offered no resistance and did not get names or descriptions.

The testimony of the conductor and motorman on a car attacked at Thirty-eight Street and Ashland Avenue was clear and showed an attempt to get all information possible. They secured names of witnesses. One member of the crew had been in the service of the Chicago Surface Lines for ten years, and the other for twelve years.

The tie-up of the street railways affected the riot situation by forcing laborers to walk, making them more liable to assault in the hostile districts, by keeping many workers from jobs, turning out on the streets hundreds of idle men, and by increasing the use of automobiles.

Tuesday morning two white men were killed while walking to work through the Negro area, and two Negroes were killed while going through the white area.

Curiosity led the idle to the riot zone. One such was asked on the witness stand why he went. "What was I there for? Because I walked there—my own bad luck. I was curious to see how they did it, that is all."

Under cover of legitimate use gangs used motor vehicles for raiding. Witnesses of rioting near Ogden Park said trucks unloaded passengers on Racine Avenue, facilitating the formation of a mob. On Halsted Street crowds of young men rode in trucks shouting they were out to "get the niggers." An automobile load of young men headed off Heywood Thomas, Negro, and shot him, at Taylor and Halsted streets, as he was walking home from work.

Beside daily routine and the street-car situation, the weather undoubtedly had an influence in the progress of the riot. July 27 was hot, 96 degrees, or fourteen points above normal. It was the culmination of a series of days with high temperatures around 95 degrees, which meant that nerves were strained. The warm weather of Sunday, Monday, and Tuesday also kept crowds on the streets and sitting on doorsteps until late at night. Innocent people trying to keep cool were injured when automobiles raced through the streets, the occupants firing to right and left. Wednesday night and Thursday it rained. Cool weather followed for the rest of the week.

Gangs and "athletic clubs."—Gangs and their activities were an important factor throughout the riot. But for them it is doubtful if the riot would have gone beyond the first clash. Both organized gangs and those which sprang into existence because of the opportunity afforded seized upon the excuse of the first conflict to engage in lawless acts.

It was no new thing for youthful white and Negro groups to come to violence. For years, as the sections of this report dealing with antecedent clashes and with recreation show, there had been clashes over baseball grounds, swimming-pools in the parks, the right to walk on certain streets, etc.

Gangs whose activities figured so prominently in the riot were all white gangs, or "athletic clubs." Negro hoodlums do not appear to form organized gangs so readily. Judges of the municipal court said that there are no gang organizations among Negroes to compare with those found among young whites.

The Stock Yards district, just west of the main Negro area, is the home of many of these white gangs and clubs; it is designated as District III in the discussion of the riot growth. The state's attorney, as already indicated (see p. 8), referred to the many young offenders who come from this particular district. A police detective sergeant who investigated the riot cases in this district said of this section, "It is a pretty tough neighborhood to try to get any information out there; you can't do it." A policeman on the beat in the district said, "There is the Canaryville bunch in there and the Hamburg bunch. It is a pretty tough hole in there."

There was much evidence and talk of the political "pull" and even leadership of these gangs with reference to their activities in the riot. A member of "Ragen's Colts" just after the riot passed the word that the "coppers" from downtown were looking for club members, but that "there need be no fear of the coppers from the station at the Yards for they were all fixed and told to lay off on club members." During the riot he claimed they were well protected by always having a "cop" ride in one of the automobiles so everything would be "O.K." in case members of the gang were picked up. Another member of the club said he had been "tipped off by the police at the Yards to clean out and keep away from the usual hangouts because investigators were working out of Hoyne's and out of Brundage's offices, and were checking up on the activities of the 'Ragen's' during the riot."

The foreman of the August grand jury which investigated the riot cases said in testifying before the Commission:

The lead we got to investigate the Forty-seventh Street district was from an anonymous letter stating that Ragen had such influence in the Forty-seventh Street police station that these individuals were allowed to go without due process of law.

I didn't believe that was a fact in this particular instance. We did learn that Ragen was a great power in that district and at the time of our investigation we learned that some of the "Ragen's Colts" had broken into the police station and pried open a door of a closet where they had a good deal of evidence in the nature of weapons of prisoners concealed, and they got all of this evidence out of there without the police knowing anything about it.

The station referred to is at Forty-seventh and Halsted streets. Gangs operated for hours up and down Forty-seventh Street, Wells, Princeton, Shields, and Wentworth avenues and Federal Street without hindrance from the police.

A judge of the municipal court said in testimony before the Commission: "They seemed to think they had a sort of protection which entitled them to go out and assault anybody. When the race riots occurred it gave them something to satiate the desire to inflict their evil propensities on others."

Our Flag Club is located farther east on Forty-seventh Street near Union Avenue. When John Mills was dragged from a street car at this point and killed, a policeman recognized several of the club's members in the crowd, but vouchsafed the opinion that they were not part of the aggressive mob, "for they did not run as did the others when the patrol came down the street." Another policeman said he had never had any trouble with the club.

Eight members of the Sparklers' Club were seen at the fire at 5919 Wentworth Avenue, a building in which two Negro families lived. The arson is reported to have been planned in a neighboring cigar store. One of the boys put waste soaked in gasoline under the porch and ran. Two of them threw oil in the building and two others lit it. It took three attempts to make a fire at this place. Each time it was started the Fire Department put it out. Two of the boys are declared to have stolen phonograph records and silverware from the house. A lad not a member of the club was with them at the fire. Afterward one of the boys warned him, "Watch your dice and be careful or you won't 'see your home any more." Six boys were held for arson, in connection with this affair; one was discharged in the boys' court, and the cases of two others were nolle prossed. In connection with their arrest the *Chicago Tribune* of August 15, 1919, said:

Evidence that organized bands of white youths have been making a business of burning Negro dwellings was said to have been handed to Attorney General Brundage and Assistant State's Attorney Irwin Walker. . . . . Chief of Police Garrity, also informed of the Fire Marshal's charges, declared several so-called athletic clubs in the Stock Yards district may lose their charters as a result.

A report about the Aylward Club was to the effect that as the Negroes came from the Stock Yards on Monday, a gang of its members armed with clubs was waiting for them and that each singled out a Negro and beat him, the police looking on.

The names of a number of gang ringleaders were reported by investigators. For illustration, L. Dennis, a Negro of 6059 Throop Street, was attacked on the night of Monday, July 28, by a mob led by three roughs whose names were learned and whose loafing place was at Sixty-third Street and Racine Avenue. A mob of thirty white men who shot Francis Green, Negro, eighteen years old, at Garfield Boulevard and State Street had a club headquarters in the vicinity of Fifty-fourth Street and their "hangout" was at the corner of Garfield Boulevard and State Street.

Other clubs mentioned in riot testimony before the coroner's jury, but not in connection with riot clashes, are the Pine Club, the Hamburgers, the Emeralds, the White Club, Favis Grey's, and the Mayflower. The police closed the clubs for a period of several months after the riot. There were then in existence a number of Negro gambling clubs, and the state's attorney declared that it was the colored gamblers who "started this shooting and tearing around town," and that "as soon as they heard the news that the boy

Williams was drowned, they filled three or four machines and started out to shoot."

A saloon-keeper near Wabash Avenue and Fifty-fifth Street, one of the leaders of these colored gamblers, was identified by a white woman as being in an automobile with five other Negroes exhorting colored men to riot after the drowning of Williams. The next day he was arrested in an automobile with other colored men who were said to be shooting into the homes of white people. They were arrested but were discharged by Judge Barasa at the Stock Yards court.

Police raids were made on some of the "Black Belt" clubs on August 23. At the Ranier Club, 3010 South State Street, two revolvers, one razor, one "black-jack," seven cartridges, one cattle knife, and one ordinary knife were found. At the Pioneer Club, 3512 South State Street, eight guns, four packages of cartridges and twenty-four knives were taken. A raid at 2700 South State Street netted four guns, one hunting-knife, and fifty-eight cartridges and bullets.

The foreman of the grand jury which investigated the riots discussing the "athletic" and "social" clubs before the Commission, said:

Most of them were closed immediately after the riots. There were "Ragen's Colts," as they were known, concerning whom the grand jury were particularly anxious to get something concrete, although no evidence was presented that convicted any of the members of that club. There were the Hamburgers, another athletic club, the Lotus Club, the Mayflower, and various clubs. These were white clubs.

Asked if they really were athletic clubs, he replied:

I think they are athletic only with their fists and brass knuckles and guns. We had Mr. Ragen before the grand jury, and he told us of the noble work that they were doing in the district, that Father Brian, who had charge of these boys, taught them to box and how to build themselves up physically, and they were doing a most noble work, and you would think that Ragen was a public benefactor. During the deliberations of this grand jury a number of anonymous letters were written with reference to "Ragen's Colts," and most of the explanations of the fact that they failed to put their names on these letters were that they were afraid they would lose their lives.

The grand jury included in its report this reference to the gang and club phase of the riot:

The authorities employed to enforce the law should thoroughly investigate clubs and other organizations posing as athletic and social clubs which really are organizations of hoodlums and criminals formed for the purpose of furthering the interest of local politics. In the opinion of this jury many of the crimes committed in the "Black Belt" by whites and the fires that were started back of the Yards, which, however, were credited to the Negroes, were more than likely the work of the gangs operating on the Southwest Side under the guise of these clubs, and the jury believes that these fires were started for the purpose of inciting race feeling by blaming same on the blacks. These gangs have apparently taken an active part in the race riots, and no arrests of their members have been made as far as this jury is aware.

SCENES FROM FIRE IN IMMIGRANT NEIGHBORHOOD "BACK OF THE YARDS"

NEGROES UNDER PROTECTION OF POLICE LEAVING WRECKED HOUSE
IN RIOT ZONE

The coroner's jury which conducted inquests into the thirty-eight riot deaths said:

The suggestion has also been made that race hatred and tendency to race rioting had its birth and was fostered in the numerous social and athletic clubs made up of young men and scattered throughout the city. We doubt this, but if in part true, it calls for the inspection and control of such clubs. These clubs are here, they are popular, they take the place of the disappearing saloon and poolroom. Properly governed and controlled, they should be encouraged and fostered and, when necessary, disciplined.

Hoodlums are the nucleus of a mob—the young, idle, vicious, and in many instances degenerate and criminal, impatient of restraint of law, gather together, and when fortified by sufficient numbers, start out on a mission of disorder, law-breaking, destruction, and murder. Mobs, white or colored, grow about a nucleus of this character.

Types of clashes.—Racial outbreaks are often characterized by hangings, burnings, and mutilations, and frequently the cause given for them is a reported Negro attack upon a white woman. None of these features appeared in the Chicago riot. An attempted hanging was reported by a white detective but was unsubstantiated. A report that Joseph Lovings, one of the Negroes killed in the riot, was burned, was heralded abroad and even carried to the United States Senate, but it was false. The coroner's physicians found no burns on his body.

Reports of assaults upon women were at no time mentioned or even hinted at as a cause of the Chicago riot, but after the disorder started reports of such crimes were published in the white and Negro press, but they had no foundation in fact.

Of the ten women wounded in the Chicago riot, seven were white, two were Negroes, and the race of one is unknown. All but one of these ten injuries appears to have been accidental. The exception was the case of Roxy Pratt, a Negro woman who, with her brother, was chased down Wells Street from Forty-seventh by gangsters and was seriously wounded by a bullet. No cases of direct attacks upon white women by Negro men were reported.

The Commission has the record of numerous instances, principally during the first twenty-four hours, where individuals of opposing races met, knives or guns were drawn, and injury was inflicted without the element of mob stimulus.

On Monday mobs operated in sudden, excited assaults, and attacks on street cars provided outstanding cases, five persons being killed and many injured. Nicholas Kleinmark, a white assailant, was stabbed to death by a Negro named Scott, acting in self-defense. Negroes killed were Henry Goodman at Thirtieth and Union streets; John Mills, on Forty-seventh Street near Union; Louis Taylor at Root Street and Wentworth Avenue; and B. F. Hardy at Forty-sixth Street and Cottage Grove Avenue. All died from beatings.

Crowds armed themselves with stones, bricks, and baseball bats and scanned passing street cars for Negroes. Finding them, trolleys were pulled off wires and entrance to the cars forced. Negroes were dragged from under car seats and beaten. Once off the car the chase began. If possible, the vanguard of the mob caught the fleeing Negroes and beat them with clubs. If the Negro outran the pursuers, stones and bricks brought him down. Sometimes the chase led through back yards and over fences, but it was always short.

Another type of race warfare was the automobile raids carried on by young men crowded in cars, speeding across the dead line at Wentworth Avenue and the "Black Belt," and firing at random. Crowded colored districts, with people sitting on front steps and in open windows, were subjected to this menace. Strangely enough, only one person was killed in these raids, Henry Baker, Negro.

Automobile raids were reported wherever colored people had established themselves, in the "Black Belt," both on the main business streets and in the residence sections, and in the small community near Ada and Loomis streets in the vicinity of Ogden Park.

These raids began Monday night, continued spasmodically all day Tuesday, and were again prevalent that night. In spite of the long period, reports of motorcycle policemen show no white raiders arrested. One suspected raiding automobile was caught on State Street Tuesday night, after collision with a patrol wagon. One of the occupants, a white man, had on his person the badge and identification card of a policeman assigned to the Twenty-fourth Precinct. No case was worked up against him, and the other men in the machine were not heard of again in connection with the raid.

Most of the police motorcycle squad was assigned to the Stanton Avenue station, which was used as police headquarters in the "Black Belt." Several automobile loads of Negroes were arrested, and firearms were found either upon their persons or in the automobile.

In only two cases were Negroes aggressively rioting found outside of the "Black Belt." One of these was the case of the saloon-keeper already mentioned, and the other was that of a deputy sheriff, who, with a party of other men, said they were on the way to the Stock Yards to rescue some beleaguered members of their race. It is reported that they wounded five white people en route. Sheriff Peters said he understood that the deputy sheriff was attacked by white mobs and fired to clear the crowd. He was not convicted.

"Sniping" was a form of retaliation by Negroes which grew out of the automobile raids. These raiding automobiles were fired upon from yards, porches, and windows throughout the "Black Belt." One of the most serious cases reported was at Thirty-first and State streets, where Negroes barricaded the streets with rubbish boxes. Motorcycle Policeman Cheney rammed through and was hit by a bullet. His companion officer following was knocked from his machine and the machine punctured with bullets.

After the wounding of Policeman Cheney and Sergeant Murray, of the Sixth Precinct, policemen made a thorough search of all Negro homes near the scene of the "sniping." Thirty-four Negroes were arrested. Of these, ten were discharged, ten were found not guilty, one was given one day in jail, one was given five days in jail, one was fined and put on probation, two were fined $10 and costs, one was fined $25; six were given thirty days each in the House of Correction, and one, who admitted firing twice but said he was firing at one of the automobiles, was sentenced to six months in the House of Correction. His case was taken to the appellate court.

Concerted retaliatory race action showed itself in the Italian district around Taylor and Loomis streets when rumor said that a little Italian girl had been killed or wounded by a shot fired by a Negro. Joseph Lovings, an innocent Negro, came upon the excited crowd of Italians. There was a short chase through back yards. Finally Lovings was dragged from his hiding-place in a basement and brutally murdered by the crowd. The coroner reported fourteen bullet wounds on his body, eight still having bullets in them; also various stab wounds, contusions of the head, and fractures of the skull. Rumor made the tale more hideous, saying that Lovings was burned after gasoline had been poured over the dead body. This was not true.

This same massing of race against race was shown in a similar clash between Italians and Negroes on the North Side. The results here, however, were not serious. It was reported in this last case that immediately after the fracas the Negroes and Italians were again on good terms. This was not true in the neighborhood of the Lovings outrage. Miss Jane Addams, of Hull-House, which is near the scene of Lovings' death, testified before the Commission that before the riot the Italians held no particular animosity toward Negroes, for those in the neighborhood were mostly from South Italy and accustomed to the dark-skinned races, but that they were developing antipathy. In the September following the riot, she said the neighborhood was still full of wild stories so stereotyped in character that they appeared to indicate propaganda spread for a purpose.

The gang which operated in the "Loop" was composed partly of soldiers and sailors in uniform; they were boys of from seventeen to twenty-two, out for a "rough" time and using race prejudice as a shield for robbery. At times this crowd numbered 100. Its depredations began shortly after 2:00 A.M. Tuesday. The La Salle Street railroad station was entered twice, and Negro men were beaten and robbed. About 3:00 A.M. activities were transferred to Wabash Avenue. In the hunt for Negroes one restaurant was wrecked and the vandalism was continued in another restaurant where two Negroes were found. One was severely injured and the other was shot down. The gangsters rolled the body into the gutter and turned the pockets inside out; they stood on the corner of Wabash Avenue and Adams Street and divided the spoils, openly boasting later of having secured $52, a diamond ring, a watch, and a brooch.

Attacks in the "Loop" continued as late as ten o'clock Tuesday morning, Negroes being chased through the streets and beaten. Warned by the Pinkerton Detective Agency, business men with stores on Wabash Avenue came to protect their property. The rioting was reported to the police by the restaurant men. Policemen rescued two Negroes that morning, but so many policemen had been concentrated in and near the "Black Belt" that there were only a few patrolmen in the whole "Loop" district, and these did not actively endeavor to cope with the mob. In the meantime two Negroes were killed and others injured, while property was seriously damaged.

Tuesday's raids marked the peak of daring during the riot, and their subsidence was as gradual as their rise. For the next two days the gangs roamed the streets, intermittently attacking Negro homes. After Tuesday midnight their operations were not so open or so concerted. The riot gradually decreased in feeling and scope till the last event of a serious nature occurred, the incendiary fires back of the Stock Yards.

While there is general agreement that these fires were incendiary, no clue could be found to the perpetrators. Negroes were suspected, as all the houses burned belonged to whites. In spite of this fact, and the testimony of thirteen people who said they saw Negroes in the vicinity before or during the fires, a rumor persisted that the fires were set by white people with blackened faces. One of the men living in the burned district who testified to seeing a motor truck filled with Negroes said, when asked about the color of the men, "Sure, I know they were colored. Of course I don't know whether they were painted." An early milk-wagon driver said that he saw Negroes come out of a barn on Forty-third Street and Hermitage Avenue. Immediately afterward the barn burst into flames. He ran to a policeman and reported it. The policeman said he was "too busy" and "it is all right anyway." One of the colonels commanding a regiment of militia said he thought white people with blackened faces had set fire to the houses; he got this opinion from talking to the police in charge of that district.

Miss Mary McDowell, of the University of Chicago Settlement, which is located back of the Yards, said in testimony before the Commission:

I don't think the Negroes did burn the houses. I think the white hoodlums burned them. The Negroes weren't back there, they stayed at home after that Monday. When we got hold of the firemen confidentially, they said no Negroes set fire to them at all, but the newspapers said so and the people were full of fear. All kinds of mythical stories were afloat for some time.

The general superintendent of Armour & Company was asked, when testifying before the Commission, if he knew of any substantial reason why Negroes were accused of setting fires back of the Yards. He answered:

That statement was originated in the minds of a few individuals, radicals. It does not exist in the minds of the conservative and thinking people of the community, even those living in back of the Yards. They know better. I believe it goes without saying that there isn't a colored man, regardless of how little brains he'd have, who would attempt to go over into the Polish district and set fire to anybody's house over there. He wouldn't get that far.

The controlling superintendent of Swift & Company said he could not say it from his own experience, but he understood there was as much friction between the Poles and Lithuanians who worked together in the Yards as between the Negroes and the whites. The homes burned belonged to Lithuanians. The grand jury stated in its report: "The jury believes that these fires were started for the purpose of inciting race feeling by blaming same on the blacks."

The methods of attack used by Negroes and whites during the riot differed; the Negroes usually clung to individual attack and the whites to mob action. Negroes used chiefly firearms and knives, and the whites used their fists, bricks, stones, baseball bats, pieces of iron, hammers. Among the white men, 69 per cent were shot or stabbed and 31 per cent were beaten; among the Negroes almost the reverse was true, 35 per cent being shot and stabbed and 65 per cent beaten. A colonel in charge of a regiment of militia on riot duty says they found few whites but many Negroes armed.

Arms and ammunition.—The foregoing figures and statements gave some color to the belief persistent during and after the riot that Negroes had stores of arms and ammunition. A lieutenant of police testified before the coroner's jury that he had known in advance that the riot was coming because "there were guns in every house out there; I knew they were there for a purpose." He said he had heard that Negroes had been advised to arm themselves and defend their homes, that the Constitution of the United States provided for that. The state's attorney said before the Commission that prior to the riot he had received reports from detectives of private agencies stating the same thing. He was informed that Negroes readily got firearms from Gary, Indiana, and that porters on the Pullman trains brought them in from outside places. He further stated: "I am very definitely assured of the fact that they were arming and that there were more arms and weapons grouped in that general district loosely termed the 'Black Belt' than any place else, and my information is that conditions are that way now."

During the riot there were frequent rumors that Negroes had broken into the Eighth Regiment Armory for guns and ammunition, but all these rumors were proved false.

Since the riot many tales have been told of stores of arms brought in by Pullman porters and by white prostitutes. Mexicans were reported to be assisting Negroes in the manufacture of bombs and hand grenades. Lists of addresses where ammunition was being stored have been gathered by detectives, but not verified.

The same sort of rumors are found circulating among the Negroes in regard to the arming of whites. It is said that such and such white men have great boxes of guns and ammunition in the cellars of their homes, and that white men are forming shooting clubs for the purpose of attacking Negroes in the event of another riot.   There are also widely believed stories that a department store sold guns to white people before the riot but refused to sell to Negroes.   It was said that pawn shops sold to white people without permits from the police.

Crowds and mobs.—It may be observed that a crowd is merely a gathering of people while a mob is a crowd with its attention so strongly fixed upon some lawless purpose that other purposes are inhibited and it acts along the line of the one purpose.   During the riot many crowds of curiosity seekers were transformed into vicious mobs when exciting rumors circulated and the suggestion of vengeance was made by leaders.   Such suggestion was frequently accompanied by some daring act, stimulated by the excitement.

The mob in its entirety usually did not participate actively.   It was one in spirit, but divided in performance into a small active nucleus and a large proportion of spectators.   The nucleus was composed of young men from sixteen to twenty-one or twenty-two years of age.   Sometimes only four would be active while fifty or 150 looked on, but at times the proportion would be as great as twenty-five in 200 or fifty in 300.   Fifty is the largest number reported for a mob nucleus.   This was in the case of John Mills and five other Negroes who were beaten, dragged off a Forty-seventh Street car and chased, Mills being killed.   Here there were three degrees of crowd formation.   First came the nucleus of fifty active men who did the beating, chasing, and killing. Closely aiding and abetting them were 300 or 400 others.   After the Negroes had been forced off the car and were being hunted through the neighborhood a crowd of about 2,000 gathered and followed the vanguard of attackers and spectators.   These were present out of morbid curiosity, but sufficiently imbued with the spirit of the mob not to interfere with the outrages.

The fact that children were frequently a part of mobs is one of the thought-provoking facts of the Chicago riot.   Psychologists say that impressions made upon the child mind are forces which mold adult character to a great extent. A number of children, some not more than four or five years old, swarmed in front of the Forty-seventh Street car in the John Mills case and effectively blocked it while men climbed aboard and sought out the Negroes.   Children, often witnesses of mob brutality, ran to where Negro victims had fallen and pointed them out to the policemen who came up after the mobs had dispersed.

There were others, still children in mind, Negro boys of fifteen, accused of murders.   The enormity of their acts faded in the joy of describing their weapons.   "Fat had a club; it looked like a police club," said one, "it had leather on it."   "And the gun had a little picture of an owl on the side of it," said another describing a patched-up weapon that brought down a white laboring-man who left a widow and eight children.

Among the spectators of mob violence were men, women, and children of all ages; they included tradesmen, craftsmen, salesmen, laborers.   Though the spectators did not commit the crimes, they must share the moral responsi-

SCENES FROM FIRE IN IMMIGRANT NEIGHBORHOOD "BACK OF THE YARDS"

SCENE FROM FIRE IN IMMIGRANT NEIGHBORHOOD "BACK OF THE YARDS"

bility. Without the spectators mob violence would probably have stopped short of murder in many cases. An example of the behavior of the active nucleus when out of sight of the spectators bears this out. George Carr, Negro, was chased from a street car. He outstripped all but the vanguard of the mob by climbing fences and hiding in a back yard. This concealed him from the rest of the crowd, who by that time were chasing other Negroes. The young men who followed Carr left him without striking a blow, upon his mere request for clemency. In regard to the large non-active elements in the crowds, the coroner said during the inquest, "It is just the swelling of crowds of that kind that urges them on, because they naturally feel that they are backed up by the balance of the crowd, which may not be true, but they feel that way." Juror Ware said, "If sightseers were lending their aid and assistance—" Juror Dillon interrupted and finished, "they ought to be punished."

Often the "sightseers" and even those included in the nucleus did not know why they had taken part in crimes the viciousness of which was not apparent to them until afterward. A mere attempt to cover up participation would have called forth excuses in testimony, but their answers show irritation at the questioning, an inability to appreciate the situation, or complete bewilderment. These excerpts from the testimony before the coroner's jury are examples:

Henry Woodman, in the mob at Sixtieth and Ada streets: "I don't know. I didn't have any grudge against them [the Negroes]. But they [the mob] seemed to have it in for the colored people. That is all."

Edward Klose, in the mob in front of 1021 South State Street: "I followed the crowd, and I was in there because I was in there; they all bunched around and what could I do?"

One of the boys in the mob at Forty-third Street and Forrestville Avenue: "I just wanted to see how things were getting along. We wanted to see what the riot looked like."

Another of this same crowd: "I was following the rest. I wanted to see what they were going to do."

Another from the same mob: "When they started to grab them [the Negroes] in the lot, I rushed over directly to the conflict, by the colored men, thinking I would see more on that side."

Mobs got under way for the commission of atrocities by having the direct suggestion put to them by one of the leaders. With minds already prepared by rumors circulating wherever crowds gathered, it was easy to arouse action. A street car approaching and the cry, "Get the niggers!" was enough. Prompt action clinched the idea, and the emotion of the attack narrowed the field of consciousness. War cries aided in keeping emotion at fever heat. "Get the nigger!" "Kill the black —— of a ——!" "Kill him!" These were always an incident of mob action.

Counter-suggestion was not tolerated when the mob was rampant. A suggestion of clemency was shouted down with the derisive epithet, "Nigger lover!" Silenced objectors made no further effort to thwart mob action. There are no records of such persons notifying the police or persisting in their remonstrances. Those whose objections took the form of action against the mob met with violence. A white man, an instructor in music at the University of Chicago, saw several white men attack a Negro who was waiting for a street car at Sixty-third Street and Cottage Grove Avenue. Without trying verbal remonstrance he struck out at them. His glasses were knocked off, and he was thrown into the middle of the street and left unconscious.

Not only did action once under way make interference hazardous, but it brought into the mob circle a greater number of participants and increased its energy. Five men jerked a trolley from the wires; ten men boarded the car; twenty-five men chased and beat the routed Negroes. The mob action grew faster than the increase in numbers. Ideas suggested by individual members were quickly carried out in the action of all. The mob as a whole and the individuals in it increased in fury, and a normal street crowd was often turned from peaceful assemblage to brutal murder.

A sharp diversion of attention sometimes caused the dispersal of mobs. An unexpected revolver shot was the most effective means of such diversion. Here are some instances:

When Thomas Joshua, a Negro boy, was shot by Police Lieutenant Day, a throng of Negroes came on the run from State Street. The officers, terrified, escaped in a taxi, leaving their own automobile behind. The mob attempted to make this car suffer vicariously for the escaped police officers. Other policemen on the scene had difficulty in holding them back. Two shots were heard on Federal Street. Immediately the crowd ceased its clamoring, left the automobile, and apparently lost all thought of Lieutenant Day and ran to Federal Street.

In the first mob of the riot, that at Twenty-ninth Street and Cottage Grove Avenue, Negroes and policemen were struggling in a mass in the middle of the street. A shot was fired by James Crawford, and the mob dispersed from that corner.

A mob chased a Negro off a street car on Thirty-ninth Street near Wallace. A policeman with presence of mind followed the group into the alley, fired a few shots in the air, and the crowd ran.

In no case where an unexpected shot was fired did it fail to scatter the mob, but shooting which was part of the mob's own action did not seem to have the same effect.

The course of one riotous mob can be traced in the activities of a certain group of five white boys who linked up with the riot excitement. They met at the corner of Sixty-third Street and Ingleside Avenue at 8:30 Monday evening. While they were trying to decide which movie to attend, a taxi driver informed them of a riot at Forty-seventh Street. They took the "L" to Forty-seventh Street and joined the mob. From then until 2:00 A.M. they were active in mobs which assaulted Negroes at several points. Two were beaten at Forty-seventh Street and the elevated railway. The mob then proceeded to Fifty-first Street, but the police drove it back and it moved on to Indiana Avenue and Forty-third Street, where a deputy sheriff held it off. Returning here later it attacked a street car, beat a Negro, and then moved south on Indiana Avenue, jerking trolleys from wires and assaulting passengers. At Forty-fifth Street a shot fired by a police sergeant scattered it toward Forty-third Street.

There the mob met Lieutenant Washington, a Negro ex-soldier, who, with five Negro companions, was obliged to walk across town because car service had been discontinued on account of the rioting. Lieutenant Washington, testifying before the coroner's jury, gave this account of the affair:

After we crossed Grand Boulevard I heard a yell, "One, two, three, four, five, six," and then they gave a loud cheer and said, "Everybody, let's get the niggers! Let's get the niggers," and we noticed some of them crossed the street and walked on up even with us. The rest of them were about ten or fifteen feet north . . . . there were about between four and six men . . . . crossed the street and got in front of us . . . . just before we got to Forrestville Avenue, about twenty yards, they swarmed in on us.

After this attack, in which Lieutenant Browning was shot, and Clarence Metz, a white boy, was killed by a stab wound inflicted by Lieutenant Washington in self-defense, the mob moved on to Grand Boulevard, preceded by the rumor that it intended to attack the homes of Negroes. A shot from a house grazed a white lad, and the crowd went on, leaving the police to come and arrest the Negroes who had fired.

Mob action in planned attacks was more daring, but not more dangerous. Robbery was occasionally an accompaniment of spontaneous attack, but arson never. Whether or not some of the organized raids could readily have been stopped by the police, and the mobs dispersed, remains unproved. No attempt was made either in the "Loop" district, in the Forty-seventh and Wells streets districts or in the Sixty-ninth and Elizabeth streets district to check the depredations.

Rumor.—Rumor was often the first step in crowd formation and often opened the way for the sharp transformation of a crowd into a mob. The circulation of rumors was partly due to natural repetition, often with increasing embellishment, by one person to another of what he had heard or read. The desire to tell a "big story" and create a sensation was no doubt an important factor. With so much bitter feeling there was also considerable conscious effort to provoke vengeful animosity by telling the worst that the teller had heard or could imagine about the doings of the opposite race. The latter type of rumor circulation especially fed the riot from the beginning to the final clash. It continues to be a constant menace to the friendly relations of the races.

Newspapers were often supplied a source of rumor material through mistake in fundamental facts, due either to misinformation or exaggeration.

In considering the newspaper handling of riot news, it should be borne in mind that the task was most difficult during a period of such excitement and such crowding of events. Further it must be considered that white reporters might very justifiably avoid the risk of seeking news where crowds of Negroes had been roused to a high pitch of resentment against whites. There were doubtless instances in which news was secured from sources ordinarily trustworthy, but inaccurate during the riot. On the other hand, it must be recognized that in a time of such excitement the effect of sensational news on the popular mind is generally accentuated, and the responsibility for careful handling of news is correspondingly greater. Where bias is as pronounced as in a race riot it is of the utmost importance that essential facts be stated correctly.

TABLE I

DATE	NUMBER OF INJURED AS REPORTED BY THE "TRIBUNE" AND "HERALD-EXAMINER" DURING THE FIRST FOUR DAYS OF RIOT			FACTS AS LATER OBTAINED FROM POLICE, STATE'S ATTORNEY, HOSPITAL REPORTS, AND OLIVET BAPTIST CHURCH, COVERING EACH DAY			
	White	Negro	Total	White	Negro	Unknown	Total
July 27................................	29	19	48	10	31	5	46
July 28................................	64	60	124	71	152	6	229
July 29................................	62	72	134	55	80	4	139
July 30................................	40	21	61	20	20	2	42
Total..........................	195	172	367	156	283	17	456
Percentage of total..............	53	47	100	34	62	4	100

Reports of numbers of dead and injured tended to produce a feeling that the score must be evened up on the basis of "an eye for an eye," a Negro for a white, or vice versa. A most unfortunate impression may be made upon an excited public, Negro and white, by such erroneous reporting as the following, in which newspapers, although they understated rather than exaggerated the number of injuries, reported that 6 per cent more whites were injured than Negroes, when the fact was that 28 per cent more Negroes were injured than whites.

The *Tribune* of July 29 in a news item said that before 3:00 A.M., July 29, twenty persons had been killed, of whom thirteen were white and seven colored. The truth was that of twenty killed, seven were white and thirteen colored.[1]

[1] Figures compiled from police reports, state's attorney reports, hospital reports, and Olivet Baptist Church reports.

The *Daily News* of July 29 gave the starting-point of t
clash, referring to it as "the center of the trouble." The
the spread to the Stock Yards district. The fact was t
street cars in the Stock Yards district Monday after
further brutalities there helped to start the Angelus riot

The *Tribune* of July 30 stated that "the Black Belt
center of conflict." Up to July 30 the "Black Belt"
injuries, while the district west of Wentworth Avenue had had 139. For the
entire riot period the "Black Belt" furnished 34 per cent of the total number
of injuries, and the district west of Wentworth Avenue 41 per cent.

Exaggeration in news reports, when popular excitement is at a high pitch,
is peculiarly dangerous. For the very reason that the essential fact seems
authenticated by the simultaneous appearance of the gist of the report in
several papers, the individual reader is the more inclined to believe such
exaggerations as may appear in his favorite journal.

Cases of exaggeration could be adduced from every Chicago newspaper,
but a typical one is the report in the *Chicago Daily News* of July 29 concerning
the killing of Harold Brignadello, white. This item said:

Four women and nine men are held at the South Clark Street Station after their
arrest at 1021 South State Street, where they had a formidable arsenal.

Harry Signadell [*sic*], 35, white, died on the way to St. Luke's Hospital shortly
before noon after his bullet-riddled body had been picked up by the police in front of
1021 South State Street, where a colored woman and 20 other Negroes had barricaded
themselves and were shooting at all whites who passed the place.

Other persons arrested included Kate Elder, 26 years old, who gave her home as
the State Street address. In all, four women and nine men were made prisoners at
the raid on the place which was found to be an arsenal for the Negro rioters. Two
revolvers, two rifles, an axe, several knives, and several hundred rounds of ammunition, including 38 and 48 [*sic*] calibre cartridges, were discovered piled up near the
window from which the Negroes had been shooting.

Patrolman John Hayes, of the South Clark Street Station, heard the shots fired
by the Negroes who were firing from the house and saw the spurts of fire from their
rifles and revolvers whenever whites ventured to pass the place. An unknown white
man, a victim of the Negroes' bullets, was found lying on the sidewalk. He was
rushed to St. Luke's Hospital where he died.

The facts of this case, as reported by the coroner's jury are as follows:

. . . . Harold Brignadello . . . . came to his death on the 29th day of July,
A.D. 1919, at St. Luke's Hospital from shock and hemorrhage due to a bullet wound
in the chest cavity.

[NOTE.—"*a* bullet wound," not "bullet-riddled."]

We find the deceased while standing at the southwest corner of State and Taylor . . . . was shot and wounded by a bullet fired from the revolver held in the hand
of one Emma Jackson who was standing at an open window on the second floor of
the premises at 1021 South State Street.

¹ Testimony before the coroner's jury.

Testimony shows that just prior to the shooting, said premises had been stoned by a mob of white men.

We, the jury, recommend that the said Emma Jackson, said Kate Elder, said John Webb, said Ed. Robinson, and said Clarence Jones be held to the grand jury upon a charge of murder until discharged by due process of law.

[NOTE.—Two women and three men, not "four women and nine men," nor yet "a colored woman and 20 other Negroes." They were indicted by the grand jury but found not guilty.]

We believe from the evidence that the police have sufficient information as to the identity of some of said white men to warrant arrest, and we recommend such action be taken.

[NOTE.—No arrests of men in the white mob were made.]

The testimony further showed that there were 150 white men in the mob grouped in front of 1021, and four of the men were stoning the house at the time Emma Jackson fired into their midst.

Only one gun was found and no stores of ammunition, instead of "a formidable arsenal," or a "barricade" or "an arsenal for Negro rioters," or "two revolvers, two rifles, an axe, several knives, and several hundred rounds of ammunition, including 38 and 48 [sic] calibre cartridges . . . . piled up near the window from which the Negroes had been shooting." The one gun was hidden in a niche in the skylight.

Following are examples of rumors current during the riot and disseminated by the press and by word of mouth, grouped on the basis of the emotions which they aroused—vengeful animosity, fear, anger, and horror:

Daily News, July 30. Subheadline: "Alderman Jos. McDonough Tells How He Was Shot at on South Side Visit. Says Enough Ammunition in Section to Last for Years of Guerrilla Warfare":

[NOTE.—The reference in the headline to the large amount of ammunition is repeated in the text, but not elaborated or explained.]

An alderman in an account of his adventures says the Mayor contemplates opening up 35th and 47th streets in order that colored people might get to their work. He thinks this would be most unwise for, he states, "They are armed and the white people are not. We must defend ourselves if the city authorities won't protect us." Continuing his story, he describes bombs going off, "I saw white men and women running through the streets dragging children by the hands and carrying babies in their arms. Frightened white men told me the police captains had just rushed through the district crying, 'For God's sake, arm. They are coming, we cannot hold them.'"

The point here is not whether the alderman was correctly quoted, but the effect on the public of such statements attributed to him. There is no record in any of the riot testimony in the coroner's office or in the state's attorney's office of any bombs exploded during the riot, nor of police captains warning white people to arm, nor of any fear on the part of whites of a Negro invasion. In the Berger Odman case before the coroner's jury there is a statement that

WRECKED HOUSE OF A NEGRO FAMILY IN RIOT ZONE

NEGROES AND WHITES LEAVING THE STOCK YARDS

a police sergeant warned the Negroes of Ogden Park to arm and to shoot at the feet of rioters if they attempted to invade the few blocks marked off for Negroes by the police.

Herald-Examiner, July 28.   Subheadline: "Negroes Have Arms":

A man whose name is withheld reported to the *Herald-Examiner* that Negroes had more than 2,000 Springfield rifles and an adequate supply of soft-nosed bullets. R. R. Jackson, alderman from the second ward, brands the story as untrue.

This statement is not substantiated.

Herald-Examiner, July 29:

Several thousand men stoned the old Eighth Regiment Armory in the heart of the riot zone, doors were burst in, and hundreds of guns with ammunition taken by the mob.   Police rushed to the scene firing into the mob and finally drove it from the armory.   According to reports more than 50 persons were shot or otherwise injured.

Refutation of this statement is found in the testimony of Police Captain Mullen before the coroner's jury in the Eugene Williams case:

I received a rumor that the soldiers [referring to Negro soldiers of the Eighth Regiment] had gone over to the armory for the sole purpose of breaking in and getting rifles.   I dispatched two patrol wagons full of men; after arriving there, we found out they had been there and broke some windows, but they found out there were no weapons in there.

Another type of fear-provoking rumor current in street crowds reported the force and the aggressive plans of the opposing race.   Some of these rumors, current among Negro crowds, were to the effect that a white mob was gathering on Wentworth Avenue ready to break into the "Black Belt"; that a white mob was waiting to break through at Sixtieth and Ada streets; that a white mob was ready to advance upon Twenty-seventh and Dearborn streets.   The first of these rumors had its effect upon the inception of the Angelus riot, and the second so aroused the fears of Negroes that when a white mob led by young white boys did step over the "dead-line" boundaries established by the police, guns were immediately turned upon them, and one of the invaders was killed. Of the third rumor, Police Lieutenant Burns said:

. . . . an old colored man came to me . . . . and said that the colored people on Dearborn Street in the 2800 block were moving out in fear of a white mob coming from across the tracks from across Wentworth Avenue. . . . . On the southwest corner of Twenty-eighth and Dearborn I found a number of colored men standing in front of a building there.   They had pieces of brick and stone in their pockets and were peering around the corner west on Twenty-eighth Street apparently in great fear.

Among the whites fear was not so prevalent.   A fear-producing rumor was revealed, however, in the examination of two deputy sheriffs who fired on a Negro.   The deputies had heard that Negroes were going to burn up or blow up factories in the district which they were patrolling.   When a dark form was seen in an alley, panic seized both deputies, and they emptied their revolvers at an innocent Negro who lived in the adjoining house.

Chief among the anger-provoking rumors were tales of injury done to women of the race circulating the rumor. The similarity of the stories and their persistence shows extraordinary credulity on the part of the public. For the most horrible of these rumors, telling of the brutal killing of a woman and baby (sometimes the story is told of a Negro woman, sometimes of a white) there was no foundation in fact. The story was circulated not only by the newspapers of both races, but was current always in the crowds on the streets. Here is the story as told in the white press:

Chicago Tribune, July 29:

There is an account of "two desperate revolver battles fought by the police with colored men alleged to have killed two white women and a white child."

It is reported that policemen saw two Negroes knock down a woman and child and kick them. The Negroes ran before the police could reach them.

Herald-Examiner, July 29:

Two white women, one of them with a baby in her arms, were attacked and wounded by Negro mobs firing on street cars. . . . .

A colored woman with a baby in her arms was reported at the Deering Police Station, according to this item, to have been attacked by a mob of more than 100 white men. When the mob finally fled before the approach of a squad of police both the woman and child were lying in the street beaten to death, "it is said."

Daily News, July 29:

Another man is held at the Stock Yards station charged with the murder of a white woman in West 47th Street and Wentworth. . . . .

The Negroes, four in number, were arrested at East 39th and Cottage Grove Avenue, this afternoon by the detective. They are believed to be the ones who seriously wounded Mrs. Margaret Kelley, white woman, at W. 47th and Wentworth. She was shot in the back and may die. The names of those under arrest were not given out.

[NOTE.—"Murder" changed to "seriously injured" in the main story. Mrs. Mary Kelly was shot in the arm according to the police report and not in the back.]

The men arrested for the shooting were Henry Harris and Scott Brown, deputy sheriffs, and four others according to the records of the state's attorney. Sheriff Peters says of the case, that Harris was charged with shooting someone, but when the case came up the charge was dropped. Sheriff Peters was convinced that Harris was innocent.

Daily News, July 29. Headline, given place of first importance in the pink section: "Women Shot as Riots Grow." Columns 7 and 8 of first-page white section are headed, "Attack White Women as Race Riots Grow. Death Roster Is 30."

The item reads: "Race rioters began to attack white women this afternoon according to report received at the Detective Bureau and the Stock Yards Police Station." The article continues, that Swift & Company had not received any such reports of attacks on their women employees. But farther on the item gives an account of a Swift & Company truck filled with girl employees fired upon by Negroes at Forty-seventh Street and the Panhandle railroad. The driver was reported killed and several of the girls injured.

The juxtaposition of "Death roster is 30" and "Attack white women" gives a wrong impression. The "several girls injured" at Forty-seventh Street evidently refers to the case of Mrs. Mary Kelly. The records of the state's attorney's office also show that Josephine Mansfield was supposed to have been wounded by Harris, *et al.*, but the charge was dropped. She was wounded in the shoulder, according to the police report.

Daily News, July 30:

Alderman McDonough described a raid into the white district the night before by a carload of colored men who passed Thirty-fifth Street and Wallace "shouting and shooting." The gunmen shot down a woman and a little boy who stood close by.

[NOTE.—No record of such a case.]

Here is the "injury done to women" story as it appeared in the Negro press: *Chicago Defender*, August 2:

An unidentified young woman and three-months-old baby were found dead on the street at the intersection of Forty-seventh and Wentworth. She had attempted to board a car there when the mob seized her, beat her, slashed her body to ribbons, and beat the baby's brains out against a telegraph pole. Not satisfied with this one rioter severed her breasts and a white youngster bore it aloft on a pole triumphantly while the crowd hooted gleefully. The whole time this was happening several policemen were in the crowd but did not make any attempt to make a rescue until too late.

Concerning all of these stories it may be stated that the coroner had no cases of deaths of women and children brought before him. There was nothing in the police reports or the files of the state's attorney or hospital reports or the reports of Olivet Baptist Church, which would give any foundation for reports of the killing of a woman and child, white or Negro.

There were other rumors which had the same anger-producing effect as reports of attacks on women. A notable case of this kind was the fatal clash at the Angelus, an apartment house for white people at Thirty-fifth Street and Wabash Avenue, on Monday, July 28 (see p. 6). The trouble here grew from four o'clock in the afternoon until it culminated in the shooting at 8:00 P.M. The excitement was stimulated by the rapid spread of various rumors. It was said that a white mob was gathering at Thirty-fifth Street and Wentworth Avenue, only a few blocks from the colored mob which was massed on Thirty-fifth Street from State Street to Wabash Avenue. The rumor was that the white men are armed and prepared to "clean up the 'Black Belt.'" Another rumor had it that a Negro's sister had been killed while coming home from the Stock Yards where she worked. Finally came the rumor that a white person had fired a shot from the Angelus building, wounding a colored boy. The rumor quickly went through the crowd swarming around the building, but no one heard or saw the shooting. A search of the

building disclosed no firearms.   Police Sergeant Middleton, Negro, described
the situation as "everybody trying to tell you something and you couldn't
get anything."   Another Negro policeman said it was "just a rumor that
went around through the crowd and everybody was saying, 'He shot from
that window'; I would go to that window and the crowd would say, 'That is
the window over there.'"

The anger-provoking power of rumor was seen in the ensuing clash.   About
1,500 Negroes massed on one corner of Thirty-fifth Street and Wabash Avenue,
and about 100 policemen grouped themselves at the intersection of the two
streets.   At the sight of a brick flying from the Negro mob the police fired a
volley into the midst of the mob.   More shots came quickly from both sides.
Four Negroes were killed, and many were injured, among both the Negroes
and the police.

The Angelus rumor appeared as follows in a Negro newspaper, the *Chicago
Defender*, August 2:   "White occupants of the Angelus apartments began
firing shots and throwing missiles from their windows.   One man was shot
through the head but before his name could be secured he was spirited away."

In the case of Joseph Lovings, a Negro killed by an Italian mob, press
reports that were entirely false tended strongly to provoke the anger of Negro
mobs.   For example:

Herald-Examiner, July 30:   "He had been shot, stabbed and gasoline had
been thrown on his body which had been set afire.   The police extinguished
the fire and took the body to the County Morgue."

Tribune, July 30:   "This report says that he was stabbed and shot sixteen
times, then his body saturated with gasoline and set afire."

The coroner's jury in commenting on this rumor said: "It gives us satisfaction to say that this rumor, from our investigation, is false and unsubstantiated."

Among the horror rumors one finds such examples as the story of the white
man who stood at the entrance to Exchange Avenue and knocked down half
a dozen Negroes as they came by.   This was current in the Stock Yards and
was told by one of the workers at the inquest on the body of William Dozier,
Negro, killed in the Yards.   Another rumor had it that a Negro woman
nicknamed "Heavy" had partly slashed off the head of a white man.   This
was picked up by a detective circulating among white people living in the
"Black Belt."

But chief among horror rumors was the Bubbly Creek rumor, which took
this form in the press:

Daily News, July 29.   Subheadline: "Four Bodies in Bubbly Creek."
The article does not give details but says, "Bodies of four colored men were
taken today from Bubbly Creek in the Stock Yards district, it is reported."

This was one of the most persistent rumors of the riot, and intelligent men
were found repeating it in half-credulous tones.   A meat curer, talking in the

superintendent's office of Swift & Company, said: "Well, I hear they did drag two or three out of Bubbly Creek. . . . . Dead bodies, that is the report that came to the Yards, but personally I never got any positive evidence that there was any people who was found there."

A juror on the coroner's panel said: "A man told a friend of mine—I can furnish the name of that man—a man told him that he saw fifty-six bodies taken out of Bubbly Creek. They made a statement they used a net and seine to drag them out."

Mr. Williams, Negro attorney, said he was told that the bodies of 100 Negroes had been found in Bubbly Creek.

In its final report, the coroner's jury made this conclusive statement regarding the Bubbly Creek rumor:

Bubbly Creek has been the favorite cemetery for the undiscovered dead, and our inquiry has been partly directed to that stream. In our inquiry we have been assisted by the Stock Yards officials and workers, by adjacent property owners and residents, by private detective bureaus, the Police Department, Department of Health, State's Attorney's office, by observing and intelligent colored citizens, and by other agencies, and we are firmly of the opinion that these reports, so widely circulated, are erroneous, misleading, and without foundation in fact, the race riot victims numbering thirty-eight, and no more, nor are there any colored citizens reported to us as missing.

Rumor, fermenting in mobs, prepares the mob mind for the direct suggestion impelling otherwise law-abiding citizens to atrocities. Another more insidious and potentially more dangerous result is the slow accumulation of feeling which builds between the white and Negro the strongest barrier of race prejudice.

Police.—There has been much criticism of the manner in which the riot was handled by the authorities, but it may be pointed out that the riot was not quelled until at least four groups of peace guardians had taken part in handling it. The two most important groups were the police and the militia; the others were composed of deputy sheriffs and Negro ex-soldiers.

Testimony before the coroner's jury and in hearings before this Commission throws considerable light on the actions of the Police Department as a whole during the riot, its methods in meeting the unusual situation, and on the conduct of individual policemen. First-hand information and opinion was obtained from Chief of Police Garrity and State's Attorney Hoyne.

The police had two severe handicaps at the outset of the rioting. The first, as declared by Chief Garrity, was lack of sufficient numbers adequately to cope with the situation. The coroner's jury found that "the police force should be enlarged. It is too small to cope with the needs of Chicago." The grand jury added: "The police force is also inadequate in numbers, and at least one thousand (1,000) officers should be added to the existing force." This number approximates the need urged by Chief Garrity, who, when asked before the Commission as to the sufficiency of his force, answered: "No. I haven't sufficient force. I haven't got a sufficient force now to properly police the city of Chicago by one-third." Militia officers and other police officials held the same general opinion.

The second handicap, distrust of white policemen by all Negroes, while implied and not admitted by Chief Garrity, was frankly explained by State's Attorney Hoyne. He said before the Commission: "There is no doubt that a great many police officers were grossly unfair in making arrests. They shut their eyes to offenses committed by white men while they were very vigorous in getting all the colored men they could get."

Leaders among the Negroes clearly indicate that discrimination in arrest was a principal cause of widespread and long-standing distrust. Whether justified or not, this feeling was actual and bitter. This distrust had grown seriously during the six months preceding the riot because no arrests were made in bombing cases. State's Attorney Hoyne said before the commission: "I don't know of ·a single case where the police have apprehended any man who has blown up a house."

Charles S. Duke, a well-educated and fair-minded Negro, gave his reaction to the bombings when he said that he did not "believe a Negro would have been allowed to go unpunished five minutes." Mrs. Clarke, Negro, said her house was bombed three times, once while a plain-clothes policeman was inside waiting for bombers, but no arrests were made. One suspect was put under surveillance but was not held.

The trial of the three Negro policemen before the Merit Committee of the Police Department because they refused to use the "Jim Crow" sleeping-quarters in a police station doubtless added to race feeling, particularly in view of the publicity it received in the "Black Belt."

Negro distrust of the police increased among the Negroes during the period of the riot. With each clash a new cause for suspicion seemed to spring up. The most striking instance occurred on the first afternoon when Policeman Callahan refused to arrest the white man whom the Negro crowd accused of causing the drowning of Williams, the Negro boy. This refusal has been called the beginning of the riot because it led to mob violence of grave consequences. However that may have been, the fact remains that this refusal was heralded broadcast by the Negroes as the kind of action they might expect from the police.

Typical of the minor tales which laid the foundation for the Negroes bitterness toward this white policeman are the following:

1. Kin Lumpkin, Negro, was beaten by a mob on the "L" platform at Forty-seventh Street, as he was going home from work. The policeman arrested Lumpkin and had him booked for rioting. No other arrests were made. Lumpkin was held from July 28 to August 1.

2. Two policemen, one of them Officer McCarty of the Twenty-sixth Precinct, witnessed the beating of Wellington Dunmore, Negro, of 4120 South Campbell Avenue, but, according to the victim, refused to assist him.

NEGROES BEING ESCORTED BY POLICE TO SAFETY ZONE FROM THE
NEIGHBORHOOD OF FORTY-EIGHTH STREET AND
WENTWORTH AVENUE

SEARCHING NEGROES FOR ARMS IN POLICE STATION

3. John Slovall and brother, Negroes, were beaten and robbed by whites in sight of a white policeman. No arrests were made. The officer did not even call for aid.

4. While looking for his mother at Thirty-first and State streets on Tuesday, July 29, Wm. F. Thornton, Negro, 3207 South Park Avenue, asked a policeman to take him home. The officer took him to the police station and locked him up. Another Negro applied for protection, but the police searched him, clubbed him, and when he ran, the sergeant told another policeman to shoot him. The policeman obeyed and the man fell under the "L" station. He was picked up by the same patrol wagon that took Thornton to the Cottage Grove Police Station. The officer, Bundy, arrested Thornton.

A report on 229 Negroes and whites accused of various criminal activities disclosed the fact that 154 were Negroes and seventy-five were whites. The state's attorney reported eighty-one indictments against Negroes and forty-seven against whites after all riot cases were cleared up. These figures show that twice as many Negroes appeared as defendants and twice as many were indicted as whites.

At first glance these figures indicate greater riot activity on the part of Negroes, and therefore one would expect to find twice as many whites injured as Negroes. But out of a total of 520 injured persons whose race was definitely reported, 342 were Negroes and 178 whites. The fact that twice as many Negroes appeared as defendants and twice as many were injured as whites suggests the conclusion that whites were not apprehended as readily as Negroes.

Herman M. Adler, state criminologist of Illinois, testifying before the Commission, expressed the belief that the police showed much more readiness to arrest Negroes than whites because the officers thought they were "taking fewer chances if they 'soaked' a colored man."

Negro distrust of police and courts seems to have been confirmed by the action of the state's attorney's office in bringing only Negro riot cases before the grand jury. This body, however, took a stand for fair play and justice for both sides, and though its action may have been novel, it was effective. In its final report, the grand jury said:

This jury has no apology to offer for its attitude with reference to requesting the state's attorney to supply it with information of crimes perpetrated by whites against blacks before considering further evidence against blacks. This attitude gave rise to the reports in the press that this grand jury "had gone on a strike." As a matter of fact, its position was merely a suspension of hearing further cases of crimes committed by blacks against whites until the state's attorney submitted evidence concerning the various crimes committed by whites against blacks. The reason for this attitude arose from a sense of justice on the part of this jury. It is the opinion of this jury that the colored people suffered more at the hands of the white hoodlums than the white people suffered at the hands of the black hoodlums. Notwithstanding this fact, the cases presented to this jury against the blacks far outnumber those against the whites.

State's Attorney Hoyne justified this action by saying that the Police Department brought in Negroes only, and until they arrested whites, he was limited to proceedings against Negroes.

The coroner's jury on November 3, 1919, reported as follows:

Our attention was called strikingly to the fact that at the time of race rioting, the arrests made for rioting by the police of colored rioters were far in excess of the arrests made of white rioters. The failure of the police to arrest impartially, at the time of rioting, whether from insufficient effort or otherwise, was a mistake and had a tendency to further incite and aggravate the colored population.

This seeming discrimination in arrests naturally deepened Negro distrust and lack of confidence in the police. Testimony was taken by the Commission on the plans and action of the Police Department during the riot period, since the Commission felt that the distribution of forces and the methods used by the department to meet such an emergency were matters of first importance.

Chief of Police Garrity testified that there were 3,500 policemen in the department at the time of the riot, and that he had "practically every policeman in the city of Chicago down there," indicating Thirty-fifth Street and Rhodes Avenue as "practically in the heart of the district where the most trouble was." The widest distribution from that center, he said, was over an area bounded by Lake Michigan, Ashland Avenue, Van Buren Street, and Sixty-ninth Street.

The heaviest concentration of police, however, was in the "Black Belt." The Stanton Avenue Police Station at Thirty-fifth Street and Rhodes Avenue is at about the center of the most congested Negro residential area. Asked how many policemen were assigned to that vicinity (the area from Twenty-second to Thirty-ninth streets), Chief Garrity said, "We had in the neighborhood of 2,800 men in that territory." Later the chief said only "the necessary sergeants and one or two men at each station were held back for emergency calls" in all other parts of the city. This means that four-fifths of the total police force was concentrated there.

Although there is no direct testimony as to the existence of flying squadrons of police, yet such bodies appear to have been operating. Probably the most important of these was the patrol under Police Captain Mullen, who said that his territory extended from Twenty-second to Thirty-ninth streets and from the lake to the Rock Island tracks, or roughly the "Black Belt." Chief Deputy Alcock[1] sent eighty-eight policemen into this district on Sunday afternoon, twenty-five more at midnight, and fifty more on Monday morning.

In describing the disposition of police details, Chief Garrity said: "They were routed by him [Alcock] according to conditions existing in different districts. Some districts might have a hundred men in the block and in the next block there might be only ten, according to what conditions were."

[1] Chief of Police Garrity was out of the city at the time the riot began on Sunday, but returned on Monday.

Forces were moved from one point of disturbance to another by means of patrol wagons on request of local commanders.

The 2,800 policemen in the "Black Belt" were under the command of Chief Deputy Alcock with headquarters in the Stanton Avenue Station. He "used his discretion in the number of men assigned to the different points and the handling of them in the different territories."

Riot orders were given by Chief Garrity as follows: "Wherever possible suppress the riot and restore peace"; "the second day I ordered a dead line on Wentworth Avenue and Twenty-second Street to, I think, Sixty-third Street"; "instructions were that 'you will allow no colored people to go across to the west and no white people to go across to the east.'" Cabarets, saloons, and public places were ordered closed, and all large gatherings of either whites or Negroes were prohibited from Van Buren to Sixty-ninth streets and from Ashland Avenue to the lake. The chief added, "Closing clubrooms and everything in the district west of Wentworth Avenue as well as east of it." A general policy was adopted of search and seizure of persons suspected of carrying weapons on the street, and of houses from which firing came. Captain Mullen testified before the coroner's jury at the Eugene Williams inquest that on July 29 Chief Deputy Alcock lined up the policemen in front of the Stanton Avenue Station and gave them their orders. They were told to "preserve the peace; that was all."

Police records of clashes were incomplete and often inaccurate. This was in part due, and naturally so, to the stress of the moment. In many cases the station lists of injured were far from complete and in few instances were the names of witnesses given. Even the dates and hours of clashes were loosely recorded. Persons arrested were frequently not booked at all, while on the other hand it was not uncommon to find innocent persons charged with serious offenses. Henry Scholz, policeman of the Twenty-sixth Precinct, threw much light on police records while being examined in connection with certain automobile arrests:

They were all discharged, booked for "disorderly," because we couldn't find the guns in the mix-up. It was the first or second day down there and they were bringing them in right and left, and I suppose in the mix-up they mislaid the guns, or put them away somewhere, or booked them to someone else. We held them about a week trying to find the guns and trying to find the officers that got the guns.

It is important to know how the distribution and routing of police affected the general riot situation. As already shown four-fifths of the police forces were concentrated in the "Black Belt." This undoubtedly both weakened police forces elsewhere and also prevented or delayed reinforcements in outside districts. Only 34 per cent of the total number of reported injuries occurred in the area of concentration. Negro hatred of the police is worth mentioning again here, especially since many of the deaths and injuries occurred during clashes between white policemen and Negro mobs.

That other districts where danger existed were poorly protected is shown by the fact that fatal clashes occurred there without interruption by the police. The most conspicuous case is noted in the "Loop" atrocities on July 29, where two Negroes, Hardwick and Williams, were killed, several were injured and robbed, and business property of whites was damaged. A police sergeant said that only three officers and one sergeant were in the district on the night of July 28–29. In the Stock Yards district, where 41 per cent of the injuries and several deaths occurred, there is no record of an attempt by the police to increase the riot forces. In this district gang raids by whites were practically beyond control. On July 28 B. F. Hardy, a Negro, was killed at Forty-sixth Street and Cottage Grove Avenue. Sergeant Clancy later testified that there were no policemen in this district until after the trouble. The foreman of the grand jury investigated the activities of the Deering Street Station under Police Captain Gallery. He says: "They didn't have a sufficient number of policemen to handle the situation. If I remember correctly, he had eight patrolmen covering a district of any number of square miles."

In spite of the concentration of police in the "Black Belt" some parts of that area seem at times not to have been properly guarded. Several serious clashes occurred there after the police arrived in force. Theodore Copling, Negro, was shot to death at Thirtieth and State streets in the heart of the "Black Belt" on July 30. This had been a riotous corner for three days, yet no policemen were at hand. The nearest was a detective sergeant on Twenty-ninth Street between Federal and State streets. Samuel Banks, Negro, was shot and killed near the corner of Twenty-seventh and Dearborn streets on July 30 at 11:00 P.M., yet Lieutenant Burns, in charge of this district, testified at the inquest that twelve to fourteen officers were at Twenty-seventh and Dearborn streets immediately before the shooting.

It was undoubtedly the relatively large number of clashes which the police were unable to prevent that led the coroner's jury to recommend that "(6) there should be organization of the force for riot work for the purpose of controlling rioting in its incipient stages."

The conduct of individual policemen received much adverse criticism from the Negroes. This was to be expected in the circumstances, but disregarding the general prejudice of which white officers were accused, certain cases of discrimination, abuse, brutality, indifference, and neglect on the part of individuals are deserving of examination.

Abusive and brutal treatment was complained of by Horace Jennings, 3422 South Aberdeen Street. He reported to the state's attorney's office that Policeman G—, of the Grand Crossing Station, approached him, as he lay wounded by a mob attack, with the words, "Where's your gun, you black —— of a ——? You damn niggers are raising hell"; that the officer hit him on the head, and he did not regain consciousness until some time later in the

Burnside Hospital; and he further charged that Gallagher took a purse containing $13 when he searched him.

Three Negroes were rescued by the police from a white mob of twenty-five or thirty men. Scott, one of the Negroes, was taken from the street car on which all three were riding, by the command of a policeman to "come out of there, you big rusty brute, you. I ought to shoot you," and was given a blow on the head. According to a witness he was again struck by the policeman as he was pushed into the patrol wagon. He was subjected to rough treatment at the jail and was kept incommunicado from July 28 to August 4, not being permitted to notify his wife or an attorney. None of the twenty-five or thirty white rioters was arrested. There was some evidence of fear on the part of the police to arrest rioting whites.

Fear by policemen of Negroes is also disclosed. George Crumm, white, 124 East Forty-sixth Street, informed the state's attorney's office that he was beaten by a Negro mob, got police assistance, and pointed out the rioters, but the police "didn't seem to want to interfere any."

On several occasions policemen left the scene of riots on questionable excuses while the rioting was in progress. Of the three mounted policemen at Thirty-fifth Street and Wabash Avenue who rushed to the spot where a mob was attacking Otterson, two accompanied the automobile of Otterson to the hospital. The mob was not quelled or dispersed. When the house of William O'Deneal, Negro, 4742 Wells Street, was attacked, the police took O'Deneal to the station and left the mob to sack and burn his house. At the killing of William Dozier, Negro, all three police officers who responded to notice of an attack by a white mob of 300 or more, left in the same patrol wagon. The names of witnesses were not taken. It was the custom for all to accompany the wagon, according to Officer McDonough.

Political "pull" exercised with the police on behalf of rioters has been indicated. It was noted that one of "Ragen's Colts" said an officer of the Stock Yards Station "tipped them off" to stay away from their club because Attorney General Brundage's office was out investigating them.

Indifference both to extreme lawlessness during the riot and to the procedure of the inquest marked the examination of Captain of Police Mullen before the coroner's jury. He was in command of twelve mounted men and between sixty-three and 100 men on foot at Thirty-fifth Street and Wabash Avenue when a clash between the police and a Negro mob occurred. While it appears to be the fact that he left just before the heavy firing to telephone from a saloon one block away, yet the building he was in was struck by bullets. The following excerpt from the inquest speaks for itself:

Q.: What time did the shooting take place at the building known as the Angelus Building? What time did that occur? Was there any shooting at that building?

Mullen: Not that I heard.

Q.: Had there been any shooting done there that evening around . . . . before you left?

Mullen: Not to my knowledge.

Q.: When was the shooting done, and where were you?

Mullen: What do you mean shooting?

Three men were killed and many injured at Thirty-fifth Street and Wabash Avenue at this time. Firing broke out near-by almost immediately.

Q.: There were some shots fired at Thirty-fifth and State, Captain, at eight that night, right after the volley was fired, we have absolute evidence.

Mullen: Well, you may have, but I have not.

Yet Captain Mullen was in command of the police who killed two more men and inflicted other wounds when the Negroes ran before the police advance.

Militia.—The rapid growth of the riot both in violence and territorially created such alarm among the authorities and the public that the question of its control became a matter of paramount concern to the community. Before twenty-four hours had elapsed requests were made to the local authorities for the militia. The representations were based on insufficiency of police forces and were strongly urged before the chief of police.

Chief Garrity steadily refused to ask for troops, in spite of his repeated statement that the police force was insufficient. He gave as his reason the belief that inexperienced militiamen would add to the deaths and disorders. Mayor Thompson supported the chief's refusal until outside pressure compelled him to ask the governor for aid. On the other hand the chief deputy of police was quoted by State's Attorney Hoyne as having said at the outbreak of the riot that the police would not be able to handle the situation, and that troops were needed. In this he was supported by Mr. Hoyne. From observation of conditions on the first three days of the riot, the chief of staff of the troops, Colonel Ronayne, concluded that the police were insufficient in numbers, that no improvement was apparent in the general situation, and that therefore the troops were necessary. He saw no reason, however, for putting the city under martial law. Other military men were of the same opinion.

During all of this time Governor Lowden kept in close touch with the situation from his quarters at the Blackstone Hotel. When the riot appeared to be subsiding he started to keep an appointment out of town but, on hearing that there was a renewal of violence, returned to the city on a special train. When the request was made for the active co-operation of the troops he acted with promptness.

The troops themselves were clearly of high caliber. For the most part they were in home service during the war and were older men than are ordinarily found in militia organizations. They "usually came from the higher type of business men, men of affairs, men that knew how to think," as one of their commanding officers described them. They were all American-born.

NEGROES UNDER PROTECTION OF POLICE AND MILITIA BUYING PRO-
VISIONS BROUGHT INTO THEIR NEIGHBORHOOD IN WAGONS

THE MILITIA AND NEGROES ON FRIENDLY TERMS

The militia discipline was of the best. Not a single case of breach of discipline was reported to the regimental commanders. No guardhouse was necessary during the riot, a remarkable commentary on troop conduct.

The militia had been given special drills in the suppression of riots and insurrections for a year and a half previous to this occasion, and were, in the estimation of their commanding officer, "probably better prepared for riot drill than any troops ever put on duty in the state."

The activities of the militia did not begin as early as many citizens wished. Though troops began to mobilize in the armories on Monday night, July 28, they were not called to actual duty on the streets until 10:30 P.M., Wednesday, July 30. When called to active duty they were distributed in the areas of conflict. Between 5,000 and 6,000 troops were called out. This number was made up entirely of white troops from the Ninth, Tenth, and Eleventh Infantry, Illinois National Guard, and from the First, Second, Third, and Fourth Reserve Militia regiments of the militia. Colored troops who had composed the Eighth Regiment were not reorganized at that time, and therefore none participated.

Distribution of troops was determined not by the militia command but by the police, because the city was not under martial law, the civil authority being merely insufficient, not broken. The Third Infantry covered the territory from Thirty-first to Thirty-eighth streets and from State to Halsted streets; Eleventh Infantry from Thirty-ninth to Forty-seventh streets, and from State to Halsted streets; Tenth Infantry from Forty-eighth to Fifty-fifth streets (later extended to Sixty-third Street by details from the First Infantry), and from Cottage Grove to Stewart avenues. The First, Fourth, and Ninth Infantry were held in reserve. Detachments responded to calls from the chief of police in districts outside these areas. Headquarters for the commanding general and his chief of staff were in the Congress Hotel at the northern boundary of the riot zone.

The orders under which the militia operated did not have the authority of martial law. The purpose of the orders was to effect a thorough co-operation with the police only, and not to take over any duties other than the preservation of law and order. Except in this respect, civilian routine remained undisturbed. The method of co-operation put the commanding officer of a regiment in absolute control, within the limits above described, in his district. The police reduced their number to normal requirements by removing their reserves as soon as the militia moved in. The patrolmen then went about on ordinary duties in the districts. Persons arrested by the militia were turned over to the police.

Responsibility for the preservation of law and order rested on the regimental commanders. Careful instructions were given troops for preventing violence: they were to act as soldiers in a gentlemanly manner; they were furnished with arms to enable them to perform their duties; they were to use the arms only when necessary; they were to use bayonet and butt in preference to firing, but if the situation demanded shooting, they were not to hesitate to deliver an effective fire. Above all, the formation of mobs was to be prevented.

The manner in which the militia was received by various elements in the communities where stationed is illuminating. Police officers were glad that the troops came to relieve them. Two policemen on duty with a patrol exclaimed, when they heard the militia had come in force, "Thank God! We can't stand up under this much longer!" The police at Cottage Grove Avenue said, "We are tickled to death to see you fellows come in; you have never looked so good to us before!" A regimental commander said his organization was "welcomed into the zone, of course, by everybody, and I'd say especially by the colored people." A similar report came from another regimental commander.

But there was some show of hostility to the troops. Hoodlums fired on some detachments when they first came in, and Colonel Bolte reported a hatred for the troops by "the Hamburg Athletic Club, the Ragen's, and the Emeralds, and a whole bunch of them over there who didn't like to be controlled!" Volunteer ex-service men with no legal status, but who aided the police at the time, and deputy sheriffs with overseas training ridiculed the militia with such taunts as, "Tin soldiers!" The effect of this attitude on the populace necessitated the arrest of some disturbers and the removal of unauthorized persons from the streets.

It is a singular fact that militia activities were principally against gangs of hoodlums, and the majority of these gangs were composed of white youths. Said one commander, "Rowdies of the white population tried to get through the lines and had to be arrested." "At one time a heavy truck or two loaded with white gangsters attempted to break through the militia but was checked." Plenty of trouble "with the Ragen's and other similar organizations" was reported by yet another commander.

The militia unquestionably prevented mob formations, raids, and "sniping." They checked marauders still in search of prey. In many cases they prevented the initial moves of lawlessness by taking stations at critical points long before raiders arrived.

There was a marked contrast between the militia and the police. The troops were under definite orders; commanders had absolute control of their forces and knew at all times where and how many effectives were available. Precision and promptness of movement was the rule. Reserves were always at hand. Discipline was always good. Only one person, a white man, was killed by the troops. Whatever other restraining causes contributed, it is certain that the riot was not revived after the troops were posted.

Most of the troops were withdrawn on August 8.

Volunteers.—Many Negro ex-service men, formerly members of the old Eighth Regiment (Negro) of the Illinois National Guard, donned their uniforms, armed, and offered their services to the police and militia. The militia on duty found that these Negro volunteers had no authority or military status and consequently ordered them to disband, which they did.

Before the troops were called out, however, a determined effort was made by one Britton, white police reserve, to organize ex-soldiers for volunteer service. He said as many as thirty-five joined him. They were denied permits to carry weapons but are reported to have done so. It was these men who used an automobile, driven with the mufflers open, to clear the streets.

Evidence of the use of liquor was noticed among these men during their active period. Some were involved in the killing of Samuel Banks, Negro; some in the robbery of a restaurant and in misdeeds of a minor character. Following the implication of individuals among them in these crimes, numbers of the ex-soldiers were arrested by the police, but were released by order of Chief Garrity on account of the assistance many of them had rendered the department and because of representations of business men who felt that the arrests were unjust.

Deputy sheriffs.—In addition to police, militiamen, and volunteers, another group composed of specially recruited deputy sheriffs, appeared in the riot zone as preservers of the peace. They were sworn in by Sheriff Peters, of Cook County, after citizens had appealed to him, he said, to quell the riot. In regard to their formation, numbers, orders, and duties, the sheriff had this to say:

I advertised for ex-service men to serve as deputy sheriffs. A thousand or more applied. They were all men who had returned from the war and were out of work. I hired 500 of them, kept them in the army uniforms, and instructed them to shoot to kill any disturbers or rioters. The presence of these men and the show of authority thereby made was effective, and the riot was quelled.

Fifteen thousand dollars was spent on this force.

It appears that these deputies came on the scene toward the end of the riot week and at once fell into disfavor with the militia, whom they ridiculed as "tin soldiers" in much the same manner as did the volunteers. Two regimental commanders of militia said the special deputies "did not behave in a very pleasant manner" and "in the majority of instances were no good." The sheriff was notified to call them in and they soon disappeared. There is no record of organized methods of procedure or of their activities.

Restoration of order.—Long before actual hostilities ceased, and even before the arrival of the militia, various agencies, in addition to the police, were at work trying to hold lawlessness in check and restore order. Efforts of citizens of both races helped greatly in bringing about peace. As long as the rioting was in progress thousands of Negroes were cut off from their employment. The Stock Yards workers especially were affected, since Negroes living east of Wentworth Avenue would have been forced to go to work on foot through the district in which the worst rioting occurred. The hostilities also cut off the food supply in the main riot areas. The dealers in the "Black

Belt," principally Jewish merchants, became alarmed lest temporary lack of funds due to the separation from work and wages should lead Negroes to loot their stores.

On August 1, the various packing companies made the unpaid wages of Negro employees available for them by establishing pay stations at the Chicago Urban League at 3032 Wabash Avenue, the Wabash Avenue Young Men's Christian Association at 3763 Wabash Avenue, the South Side Community Service House at 3201 South Wabash Avenue, and the Binga State Bank, Thirty-eighth and State streets. Approximately 6,000 employees were paid in this way. Banks within the district made small temporary loans to stranded persons, sometimes without security. The cashier of the Franklin State Bank at Thirty-fifth Street and Michigan Avenue said that he had made loans of more than $200 to Negroes in sums of $2 and $3 on their simple promise to pay, and that every dollar had been repaid.

All the local newspapers in their editorial columns took a vigorous stand against disorder, urged the people to be calm and avoid crowds, and were insistent that those responsible for rioting should be brought to justice. The *Tribune*, for example, published editorials under the following captions: "Regain Order and Keep It," "Sane Men and Rioters," "This Is No Holiday," "The Facts of the Riot," and "Penalties for Rioters." All of these articles were calm appeals for tolerance, sanity, and dispassionate inquiry for the facts. The *Evening American*, in an editorial entitled "This Is Chicago's Crisis; Keep a Cool Head," said:

Chicago is facing its crisis today.

In one great section of the city law and order for the time being seem to have been flung to the four winds. White men and colored men are shooting one another down in the streets for no earthly cause except that the color of their faces differs.

These mobs are not representative of whites or blacks. They are the hoodlums of both races. But the law abiding whites and blacks are innocent victims.

Hotheads and smoking gun barrels have almost wrested the rule from the keepers of the peace.

It is worse than a calamity, this race rioting. It is a deadly, ghastly scourge, a dire contagion that is sweeping through a community for no reason except that mob violence is contagious.

It is up to the cool-headed men of Chicago to settle the great difficulty. It is up to the serious-minded business men of the city to get together and find a *solution* to a problem which has become so serious.

To meet violence with violence is but making matters worse. Gun toting at a time like this only adds fuel to the fire already raging.

Reason is the solution. It is mightier than the six-gun. How it is to be exerted is for the level-headed citizenry to decide, and decide at once.

Hardly an hour passes that more names are not added to the already long list of slain in the South Side rioting.

There is no time to be lost. Other matters must be put aside for the moment and a solution reached for Chicago's greatest problem.

NEGRO STOCK YARDS WORKERS CUT OFF FROM WORK RECEIVING WAGES

Photograph taken at temporary pay station established at the Y.M.C.A. by packing companies

BUYING ICE FROM FREIGHT CAR SWITCHED INTO NEGRO RESIDENCE AREA

Labor unions also took a hand in the efforts toward peace. Unionists of both races were exhorted to co-operate in bringing about harmonious relations, and meetings for this purpose were planned by trade-union leaders, as described in the section of this report dealing with the Negro in industry. Probably the most effective effort of union labor was the following article in the *New Majority*, the organ of the Chicago Federation of Labor, prominently displayed:

FOR WHITE UNION MEN TO READ

Let any white union worker who has ever been on strike where gunmen or machine gun have been brought in and turned on him and his fellows search his memory and recall how he felt. In this critical moment let every union man remember the tactics of the boss in a strike when he tries by shooting to terrorize striking workers into violence to protect themselves.

Well, that is how the Negroes feel. They are panic-stricken over the prospect of being killed.

A heavy responsibility rests on the white portion of the community to stop assault on Negroes by white men. Violence against them is not the way to solve the vexed race problem.

This responsibility rests particularly heavy upon the white men and women of organized labor, not because they had anything to do with starting the present trouble, but because of their advantageous position to help end it. Right now it is going to be decided whether the colored workers are to continue to come into the labor movement or whether they are going to feel that they have been abandoned by it and lose confidence in it.

It is a critical time for Chicago.

It is a critical time for organized labor.

All the influence of the unions should be exerted on the community to protect colored fellow-workers from the unreasoning frenzy of race prejudice. Indications of the past have been that organized labor has gone further in eliminating race hatred than any other class. It is up against the acid test now to show whether this is so.

Various social agencies took steps to help in the emergency and restore order. The American Red Cross has a branch at Thirty-fifth Street and Michigan Avenue. As soon as the rioting became serious a special relief headquarters was established here, and food was distributed to needy families cut off from work. The Urban League was used as a headquarters for the distribution of food.

The Urban League had for several years, through its employment bureau, handled a large proportion of the city's Negro labor supply and was conversant with difficulties likely to result from the rioting. It made food surveys of the entire Negro area, printed and distributed thousands of circulars and dodgers urging Negroes to stay off the streets, refrain from dangerous discussions of the riot, and co-operate with the police in every way to maintain order. The League sent telegrams to the governor and mayor suggesting plans for curbing disorder, organized committees of citizens to aid the authorities in restoring order, and served as a bureau of information and medium of communication between the white and Negro groups during the worst hostilities.

The Young Men's Christian Association was similarly active within the area of its efforts. Religious bodies, ministers' associations, and individual ministers exerted their influence over their respective groups by advising the citizens to "keep cool," "hold their heads," and generally to let the authorities settle the riot. Negro business men and one Negro alderman sent wagons through the streets bearing large signs which advised Negroes not to congregate on streets, engage in arguments, or participate in any way in the disorders. The signs further stated that people would be advised when it would be safe to return to work. Other persons went about speaking on street corners urging co-operation with the police and militia. Appeals by officials and leading citizens were published in the white and Negro papers, carrying similar advice. During the riot a committee of citizens representing forty-eight social, civic, commercial, and professional organizations met at the Union League Club and petitioned the governor to take steps to quiet the existing disorder and appoint a commission to study the situation with a view to preventing a repetition of it. As a result of this appeal followed by similar urgings by many committees, the present Chicago Commission on Race Relations was appointed and began its work.

Aftermath of the riot.—After the restoration of order community activities were superficially the same as before the riot, but under the surface there remained a deepened bitterness of race feeling which spread far beyond the time and territorial limits of the riot itself.

All the deep-seated causes of friction which had developed so largely the failure to work out an adjustment of the increased Negro population due to the migration were and are still present, undiminished in influence. Consciousness of racial difference and more or less unconscious fear and distrust were increased and spread by the riot. Among the whites this was evidenced by the general belief that Negroes were gathering stores of arms and ammunition. Among the Negroes a growing race solidarity has been marked. There is a greater lack of confidence in the white man's law and machinery of protection. Continued bombings of Negro houses in mixed areas and failure to apprehend the culprits no doubt strengthen this attitude.

Reports of various Negro gatherings held soon after the riot show this to be the case. Many Negroes frankly urged their brothers that they must arm themselves and fight if attacked. At one meeting a Negro is reported to have said:

The recent race riots have done at least one thing for the colored race. In the past we Negroes have failed to appreciate what solidarity means. We have, on the contrary, been much divided. Since the riot we are getting together and devising ways and means of protecting our interests. The recent race riots have convinced

us that we must take steps to protect ourselves. Never again will we be found unprepared. It is the duty of every man here to provide himself with guns and ammunition.
I, myself, have at least one gun and at least enough ammunition to make it useful.

The riot furnished the gang and hoodlum element a chance to indulge in
lawlessness. Fear of death and injury may help to hold that element in check.
But it cannot be argued that fear of punishment is much of a factor, for very
few convictions of rioters were secured.

Quick justice would have been a salutary means of curbing tendencies to
riot, according to both the coroner's jury and the grand jury. The coroner's
jury said: "One remedy for race rioting is a speedy conviction and punishment
of those guilty, regardless of race or color, giving all concerned a fair and
impartial hearing." Its eighth recommendation reads: "Above all, a strict
enforcement of the law by public officials, fair and impartial, will do more
than any other agency in restoring the good name of Chicago, and prevent
rioting from any cause from again disturbing the peace of our city."

The August, 1919, grand jury said: "This jury feels that in order to allay
further race prejudice and to prevent the re-enactment of shameful crimes
committed during the recent riots, efficient, prompt, and fearless justice on
the part of the judiciary be meted out to the guilty ones, whether they be white
or black."

In a fair consideration of whether swift and impartial justice was meted
out, it must be noted that it was extremely hard to secure evidence sufficient
for successful prosecution. Police attention upon arriving at the scene of a
clash was directed more to removing the injured than apprehending the
guilty. Where attempts were made to search out the offenders, it was next
to impossible to get results on account of the keen race consciousness which
made Negroes disclaim knowledge of Negro culprits and white people deny
seeing specific white men act aggressively. Many of the crowds were neighborhood gatherings and leaders were often the sons of neighbors.

In most of the riot cases brought before the state's attorney's office the
same difficulty was experienced. Whole blocks of residents were subpoenaed
and accurately described the assaults, but failed entirely to recognize any of
the assailants. The grand jury found the same obstacle. The foreman,
referring to the kind of testimony brought before that body by Negroes on
complaints against whites, said: " . . . . they [the grand jury] usually found
it to be hearsay testimony. Some other individual told them about So-and-So.
That a crime had been committted there was no question, but to get at the
root of it was absolutely impossible."

In spite of these difficulties, those familiar with the riot situation believe
that more arrests of active rioters might have been made and more convictions
obtained. A study of the riot deaths shows that justice failed to be as swift
and sure as the coroner's and grand juries recommended. The blame for
this failure is variously placed on the police, state's attorney, judge, or jury,

according to the prejudice of the one attempting to fix blame, or his connection with any of these agencies. The fact remains that the punitive results of the legal processes were too negligible to furnish a proper deterrent to future rioters.

Of the thirty-eight persons whose death constituted the riot's principal toll—

Fifteen met death at the hands of mobs. The coroners' jury recommended that the members of the unknown mobs be apprehended. None were ever found.

Six were killed under circumstances establishing no criminal responsibility: three white men were killed by Negroes in self-defense, and three Negroes were shot by policemen in the discharge of their duty.

Four Negroes lost their lives in the Angelus riot. The coroner made no recommendations, and the cases were not carried farther.

Four cases—two Negro and two white—led to recommendations from the coroner's jury for further investigation of certain persons, but sufficient evidence was lacking for indictments.

Nine cases resulted in indictments, four of which led to convictions.

Thus in only four cases was criminal responsibility for death fixed and punishment meted out to the guilty.

Indictments and convictions are divided according to the race of the persons criminally involved as follows:

	NEGRO		WHITE	
	Cases	Persons	Cases	Persons
Indictments*........	6	17	3	4
Convictions.........	2	3	2	2

*For brief description of cases see Appendix.

There is evidence that the riot of 1919 aroused many citizens of both races to a quickened sense of the suffering and disgrace which had come and might come again to the community, and developed a determination to prevent a recurrence of so disastrous an outbreak of race hatred. This was manifest, as another section of this report shows, in the courage and control which people of both races displayed on at least two occasions in 1920 when confronted suddenly with events out of which serious riots might easily have grown.

This examination of the facts of the riot reveals certain outstanding features, as follows:

1. The riot violence was not continuous, hour by hour, but was intermittent.

2. The greatest number of injuries occurred in the district west of Wentworth Avenue, inclusive of Wentworth, and south of the Chicago River to

MILK WAS DISTRIBUTED FOR THE BABIES

PROVISIONS WERE SUPPLIED BY THE RED CROSS TO HUNDREDS
OF NEGRO FAMILIES

Fifty-fifth Street, or, broadly speaking, in the Stock Yards district. The next greatest number occurred in the so-called "Black Belt," Twenty-second to Thirty-ninth streets, inclusive, Wentworth to the lake, exclusive of Wentworth; Thirty-ninth to Fifty-fifth streets, inclusive, Clark Street to Michigan Avenue, exclusive of Michigan.

3. Organized raids occurred only after a period of sporadic clashes and spontaneous mob outbreaks.

4. Main thoroughfares witnessed 76 per cent of the injuries on the South Side. The streets which suffered most severely were State, Halsted, Thirty-first, Thirty-fifth, and Forty-seventh. Transfer corners were always centers of trouble.

5. Most of the rioting occurred after working hours. This was particularly true after the street-car strike started.

6. Gangs, particularly among the young whites, formed definite nuclei for crowd and mob leadership. "Athletic clubs" supplied the leaders of many gangs.

7. Whites usually employed fists and clubs in their attacks upon Negroes; Negroes used firearms and knives in their attacks.

8. Crowds and mobs engaged in rioting were usually composed of a small nucleus of leaders and an acquiescing mass of spectators. The leaders were young men, usually between sixteen and twenty-one. Dispersal was most effectively accomplished by sudden, unexpected gun fire.

9. Rumor kept the crowds in an excited, potential mob state. The press was responsible for wide dissemination of much of the inflammatory matter in spoken rumors, though editorials calculated to allay race hatred and help the forces of order were factors in the restoration of peace.

10. The police lacked sufficient forces for handling the riot; they were hampered by the Negroes' distrust of them; routing orders and records were not handled with proper care; certain officers were undoubtedly unsuited to police or riot duty.

11. The personnel of the militia employed in this riot was of an unusually high type. This unquestionably accounts for the confidence placed in them by both races. Riot training, definite orders, and good staff work contributed to their efficiency.

12. The machinery of justice was affected by prejudices and political rivalries.

From their reviews of the evidence brought before them, the coroner's jury and the grand jury presented analyses of the riot, and each made recommendations of a remedial sort. These recommendations follow:

CORONER'S JURY RECOMMENDATIONS

1. We believe that a representative committee of white and colored people, working together, could suggest and bring about the necessary and advisable changes.

2. In specifically attacking the housing situation: The correction of the evil by enlarging the living quarters and placing them in a better sanitary state would in

part solve the difficulty. We believe voluntary segregation would follow and to a considerable extent remove one cause of unrest.

This is a matter that might well be considered by the Real Estate Board and by improvement clubs and organizations of property owners in the South Division, and by the Health Department.

3. In regard to the "athletic clubs": Properly governed and controlled they should be encouraged and fostered and, when necessary, disciplined.

4. Hoodlumism evokes this comment: Citizens of Chicago, make your hoodlum element amenable to law, break up and destroy hoodlumism as you would a pestilence. It is our belief that this element can be brought under control of the law, and it must be done if we are to remove the danger of rioting from any cause. Vicious hoodlumism, entirely aside from race hatred, was present in practically all of the thirty-eight killings, known as race riots.

5. We earnestly urge that fathers and mothers teach their children the lesson of remaining at home when rioting occurs, and furthermore, they should be kept occupied, as idleness and bad association often cause young people to become bad men and women.

6. One remedy for race rioting is a speedy conviction and punishment of those guilty, regardless of race or color, giving all concerned a fair and impartial hearing.

7. Tolerance must be practiced between both white and colored in the discussion of the race problem, practiced in our everyday intercourse, in public conveyances, and in meetings of all kinds.

8. Our attention was called strikingly to the fact that at the time of race rioting the arrests made for rioting by the police of colored rioters were far in excess of the arrests made of white rioters. The failure of the police to arrest impartially at the time of rioting, whether from insufficient effort or otherwise, was a mistake and had a tendency to further incite and aggravate the colored population.

9. In cases of murder it is of the utmost importance that expert criminologists should arrive on the scene at the earliest possible moment, and that a complete examination may be made of the scene of the murder before the body is removed or handled, and while the necessary evidence for conviction may be obtained, which otherwise may be lost or destroyed. We have found in the riot cases many instances where the removal of bodies by inexperienced men, in some cases police officers, destroyed valuable evidence.

We heartily concur with Coroner Hoffman as to the fact that Chicago badly needs a permanent murder-investigation squad, which the coroner planned and has so persistently advocated in the past. We believe that this squad should be equipped with motor vehicles and subject to call at any hour of the day or night. This squad should consist of six or more trained policemen, working in relays of eight hours, a photographer, a finger-print expert, a coroner's physician and chemist, the coroner or deputy coroner, and a state's attorney. In addition thereto, two trained policemen from the police department precinct wherein the murder occurred, and a representative of the City News Bureau. This squad should be available for immediate service, and it should be the duty of the police at the scene of the murder to allow no one to handle the body or enter premises where murder occurred until the arrival of the squad.

10. The police force should be enlarged. It is too small to cope with the needs of Chicago, and under the present living conditions the policeman's pay is entirely inadequate and should be substantially increased.

Superannuated and incapacitated members of the police force should be retired under a proper and satisfactory pension system.

There should be organization of the force for riot work, for the purpose of controlling rioting in its incipient stages.

GRAND JURY RECOMMENDATIONS

1. It is reasonable to believe that the colored people, if provided with proper housing facilities and an area sufficient in extent, would voluntarily segregate themselves. The present neighborhood known as the "Black Belt" could, by reasonable public improvement, assisted by our leading public citizens, be made a decent place to live in for a much larger population than it now accommodates. . . . . This movement should enlist the financial and moral support of the industries employing large numbers of the black race.

2. Facilities for bathing, playgrounds, police protection, better housing and neighborhood conditions, are matters deserving the earnest attention of the proper authorities.

3. The employment of the colored people is imperative to the welfare of this community. Discriminating against the Negro, or, in other words, failure to give him an opportunity to make an honest livelihood after having induced him to migrate to this section of the country, simply adds to the already far too great number of hoodlums that infest our city.

4. This jury feels that in order to allay further race prejudice and to prevent the re-enactment of shameful crimes committed during the recent riots, efficient prompt, and fearless justice on the part of the law-enforcing officers, as well as on the part of the judiciary, be meted out to the guilty ones, whether they be white or black.

5. . . . . There is a lack of co-operation and harmony among the agencies of law enforcement, which impairs their efficiency, leads to miscarriages of justice, and wastes the public funds.

6. The parole law should be amended so that a criminal once paroled and subsequently arrested may not a second time be paroled.

7. The efficiency of the police force would be further greatly increased by the co-operation of the judiciary in refusing to grant wholesale continuances without carefully scrutinizing the results thereof when members of the police force are required to act as witnesses.

8. The police department is in need of a thorough house-cleaning. Every officer, no matter what his position is, who fails in his full duty should be dismissed. Grafters and those who allow themselves to be dominated by political influences, who are paid to protect the lives and property of our citizens, should be dismissed and punished to the fullest extent of the law.

9. It is the opinion of this jury that the police force is also inadequate in numbers, and at least one thousand (1,000) officers should be added to the existing force.

10. Policemen who have arrived at the age where their usefulness is a matter of the past should be pensioned, notwithstanding their present number, and notwithstanding the fact that the pension fund is already taxed to its utmost. The needed funds for this purpose should be provided.

11. . . . . payment of salaries to public officers commensurate with the increased cost of living.

12. The authorities employed to enforce the law should thoroughly investigate clubs and other organizations posing as athletic and social clubs which really are organizations of hoodlums and criminals formed for the purpose of furthering the interest of local politics.

13. The jury also finds that vice of all kinds is rampant in the "Black Belt," and a thorough cleaning up of that district is absolutely essential to the peace and welfare of the community.

14. Political influence to a large extent is responsible for the brazenness with which the Chicago bum, pickpocket, and gun and hold-up man operates. It is also the opinion of the jury that the indeterminate-sentence law frequently operates in a miscarriage of justice, and it is our opinion that the court should fix the sentence of offenders at the time of their conviction.

15. Because of the large number of young boys involved in the rioting, the jury recommends the resumption of the activities of the Y.M.C.A., the Knights of Columbus, and Salvation Army, as well as other similar organizations. . . . .

CHAPTER II

OTHER OUTBREAKS IN ILLINOIS

I. Minor Clashes in and near Chicago

1. Clashes in Chicago Preceding the Riot of 1919

The race riot of 1919 in Chicago was preceded by a long series of more or less serious clashes between whites and Negroes. Some of these are discussed in the section of this report dealing with contacts in recreation. Others are here described to show the development of friction and conflict leading up to the 1919 riot. Two brutal and unprovoked murders of Negroes by gangs of white hoodlums preceded the riot by only a few weeks.

In many of the antecedent clashes a conspicuous part was played by gangs or clubs of white boys and young men. These operations frequently showed organization, and the gangsters were often armed with brass knuckles, clubs, and revolvers.

Some of the earlier clashes, however, did not have their origin in gang activities. For instance, it may be that the resentment by whites of the coming of Negroes into their neighborhood inspired the crowd of boys between twelve and sixteen years of age who, in February, 1917, stoned a four-flat building at 456 West Forty-sixth Street. Two Negro families moved into the two second-floor flats of this building. The next afternoon about 100 boys from nearby schools stoned the building. The two Negroes attempted to remonstrate but were driven back. One of them reached the office of the agent of the building, who notified the police. A patrol wagon responded, but the boys had disappeared. After it had gone the boys reappeared and renewed the stoning. Every window in the upper part of the building was broken. On a second riot call Captain Caughlin and Lieutenant James McGann and a squad of police rescued the Negroes, who shortly afterward sought other quarters.

Detectives learned the identity of thirty of the boys, some of whom confessed. With their parents they were compelled to appear at the Stock Yards police station and pay for the damage inflicted.

The death of a white man, wrongly thought to have been murdered by Negroes, led to rioting on the night of July 3, 1917, in which a party of white men in an automobile fired upon a group of Negroes at Fifty-third and Federal streets. Apparently no one was hit. Earlier in the evening Charles A. Maronde, a saloon-keeper at 5161 South State Street, had been found dead following an altercation with Negroes whose passage through his premises had irritated him. Two shots were fired, but it was not proved whether by

Maronde or by the Negroes. A coroner's jury found that he had died of heart disease.

In July and August, 1917, there were minor outbreaks of trouble between Negroes and naval recruits from the Great Lakes Naval Training Station. In some instances recruits and in others Negroes were reported to be the aggressors.

When organized gangs took part in clashes the results were more serious. A typical case started in the Kohler saloon at South State and Fifty-first streets on May 27, 1919, two months before the riot.

A group of about ten white men entered the saloon together. When a Negro came in and called for a drink, one of the whites knocked him down and kicked him out of the front door. Arming himself with brickbats, the Negro called on the whites to come out. The gang crossed to another saloon on the opposite corner, and when they left it shortly afterward, they carried revolvers. They then beat the Negro, cutting his head. Dr. Homer Cooper, whose office is above the Kohler saloon, and one of his patients, Michael Pantaliono, witnessed the affray.

Roscoe C. Johnston, a Negro plain-clothes man who had been on the police force only four days, was told of the trouble by a citizen and found the gang in the second saloon. As he approached, Mart. Flannigan drew a revolver. Johnston called two plain-clothes men, who chanced to be outside, to summon a patrol wagon, then followed the gang back to the Kohler saloon and disarmed and arrested Flannigan. Johnston found three automatic revolvers behind the bar in the saloon and arrested three more of the men for carrying concealed weapons. Later six more of the men were taken when the patrol wagon returned to Kohler's, including Patten, the bartender.

The cases of these ten men were dismissed when they came to trial a week later before Judge Grant; lack of evidence was the reason given. Flannigan explained that he carried the gun to protect himself while taking money to the bank. These young men were said by onlookers to be members of "Ragen's Colts."

"Ragen's Colts" were frequently identified with lawlessness and specific clashes before and during the riot. They are typical of the gangs and "athletic clubs" which were responsible for much disorder, including attacks upon Negroes. This organization was sponsored by Frank Ragen, a politician whose record and methods have long offended the decent citizenship of Chicago. As a member of the Board of Cook County Commissioners, he allied himself with a spoils-seeking majority against which two or three public-spirited members waged a courageous struggle. His participation in the Board's deliberations was marked by such conduct as the hurling of a large record book and inkwells at members who opposed the "ring."

As part of his political following he gathered about him the young hoodlums who make up an important element of the club on which he bestowed his name.

Ragen's influence has often been able to protect the "Colts" from punishment for criminal acts, including the persecution of Negroes.

Other "athletic" and "social" clubs, though not so notorious, have been of a like nature. Miss Mary McDowell, head resident of the University of Chicago Social Settlement, told the Commission that she knew of five such clubs composed of young men between seventeen and twenty-two:

Especially before the war they were always under obligation to some politician for renting a store and paying the initial expenses of their clubs. That's what started them, and it has come to be quite the fashion to get an empty store with big panes of glass on which they like to put their names. I am speaking now of "back of the Yards" conditions.

The Ragen Club is mostly Irish-American. The others are from the second generation of many nationalities. I don't think they have deliberate criminal desires. I think they get into these ways, and then they are used and exploited often by politicians. . . . . It is about the most dangerous thing that we have in the city. Whether the police could not stop them at the time of the riot on the Monday when they went down Forty-seventh Street with firearms showing in their hands in autos (a young man living with us can give you his affidavit on it) and shouting as they went, "We'll get those niggers!" I don't suppose anybody would want to say, but the fact remains that nobody did stop them. They went across Halsted Street towards State Street. Four policemen were there and they never stopped them at all.

Miss Jane Addams, of Hull-House, also described to the Commission the way in which the ward politicians are responsible for these clubs. She said:

The politicians have had a new trick the last few years all over the city. They pay rent, as Miss McDowell said, for clubs of boys below the voting age. The politician used to take care of the young voter and the boy nearly a voter, but now he comes down to boys of thirteen and fourteen and fifteen and begins to pay their rent and give them special privileges and keeps the police off when they are gambling. The whole boy problem is very much more mixed up with these—I won't call them gangs, but they are clubs with more or less political affiliations. They are not always loyal to their political boss, but he expects them to be and they are, more or less.

The gangs and "athletic clubs" became more boldly active in the spring of 1919. On the night of June 21, five weeks before the riot, there were two wanton murders of Negroes by gangs of white hoodlums. One of the Negroes was Sanford Harris, the other Joseph Robinson. There is no evidence that either had been offensive in any way, yet they were deliberately killed by gangs. There is evidence that the gangs in the neighborhoods of these crimes had spread such fear among Negro residents that murders of this kind were not unexpected.

Harris lived on Dearborn Street between Fifty-sixth and Fifty-seventh streets. About 11:30 P.M. on June 21 he escorted from his home to a street car at State and Fifty-seventh streets a woman friend who had been calling on his wife. A Negro man, woman, and child alighted from this car, and Harris walked behind them west on Fifty-seventh Street on his way home. A number of white youths approached the man, woman, and child, one of the gang saying, "Let's get that nigger," referring to the man. Because of the child's presence they were allowed to pass unmolested.

Then the gang caught sight of Harris, who started to run across a vacant lot toward his home. A shot was fired and Harris fell after going a short distance. He died at the Cook County Hospital from peritonitis due to the bullet wound.

A woman living near Fifty-seventh and Dearborn streets caught hold of one of the gang who had a pistol in his hand. A plain-clothes policeman appeared, and she called upon him to arrest the gangster who, she said, had shot Harris. The detective merely asked how she was able to pick out the man who had fired the shot. Apparently he ignored the fact that the man held a revolver in his hand, nor does it appear that he even looked to see whether it had been recently discharged.

A Mrs. T—, who lived above the saloon at the northwest corner of State and Fifty-seventh streets, had witnessed the assault on Harris from her back porch. When other plain-clothes men came upon the scene, she told them that the gang had hidden under the viaduct on Fifty-seventh Street west of Dearborn, but there were no arrests and apparently no attempts to make any.

Earlier the same evening, an altercation had taken place between a number of white boys from sixteen to twenty years of age and Thomas Johnson, a Negro who, with a Mrs. Moss, conducted a store next to a saloon at State and Fifty-seventh streets. The boys had been loafing outside the door and using foul language. Johnson remonstrated with them and finally got a stick and started after them. A number of other Negroes aided in driving off the boys, who, as they left, threatened to "get a gang and come back and get you." It is thought that this was the gang that killed Harris.

Joseph Robinson, the other Negro killed that same night, had lived at 514 West Fifty-fourth Place. He was forty-seven years of age, a laborer for the Union Coal Company, and had a wife and six children, the oldest seventeen years of age. He was attacked by a gang at Fifty-fifth Street and Princeton Avenue, apparently without provocation, and received knife wounds in the back and left leg. He died from shock and hemorrhages on June 23.

A man named Morden, who lived at 5713 Drexel Avenue, testified at the Robinson inquest that he had met a gang of from fifteen to thirty men at Fifty-fifth Street and Shields Avenue about a block from Princeton Avenue. He said the gang was walking rapidly east and divided to pass him. He was not far away when Robinson was attacked. The Negro had evidently been coming in the opposite direction, west on Fifty-fifth Street (Garfield Boulevard) and the assault began the instant he met the gang. Morden heard a shot fired and saw Robinson stagger across the street to a candy store. He saw several men rush forward and help Robinson in the door as the gang scattered. Morden declared that several of the gang carried clubs, and that he saw several of these during the assault.

Nicholas Gianakas, who conducted the candy store at 5458 Princeton Avenue, into which the wounded man had run, testified that he heard the shot and saw people outside running in all directions. He saw Robinson coming in the door with blood running off him. Presently Robinson got up and went outside to sit on the curb. Gianakas called up the police station for an ambulance. He saw no weapons in the hands of any of the crowd outside and recognized none of them. He heard people saying that a mob had come from "the Yards."

Peter Paul Byrne, a patrolman, testified that he had been called from his beat at Fifty-fifth and State streets by a man in an automobile, who drove him to the candy store. There he also telephoned for an ambulance, then went out and rounded up "some kids" on suspicion. There was a big crowd around, he said, men, women, and children.

One man testified at the inquest that an acquaintance spoke of having seen a Greek run out of the candy store and hit Robinson on the head with a hammer or hatchet. But this acquaintance, when called to testify, denied the story.

Captain Caughlin, in charge of the police of that precinct, testified that a number of men had been arrested on suspicion, but all of them had been discharged because none of them knew anything about the matter. People had been running in every direction, he said, there had been a good deal of commotion, and he seemed to think it would have been virtually impossible for the police to find any of the guilty persons.

C. L. McCutcheon, a Negro railway postal clerk, living at 517 West Fifty-fourth Place, testified at the inquest that he had been threatened by mobs, that a gang over on the boulevard had so terrorized the fifteen or twenty "colored boys" in the neighborhood for a long time that none of them dared to go about alone; that he himself had two boys who would not go on Halsted Street for $10 a trip.

Following the killing of Harris and Robinson notices were posted along Garfield Boulevard and some neighboring streets saying that the authors of the notices would "get" all the "niggers" on July 4, 1919. These notices also called for help from sympathizers. They predicted that there would be a street-car strike on the appointed day, and that then they expected to run all Negroes out of the district. Some witnesses at the inquest stated that the Negroes of the district, who up to that time had done nothing to protect themselves, were advised by friendly whites to "prepare for the worst," as trouble could scarcely be avoided.

2. RACIAL OUTBREAK IN WAUKEGAN
May 31 and June 2, 1920

Waukegan, Illinois, thirty-six miles north of Chicago and near the Great Lakes Naval Training Station of the United States Navy, was the scene of two riotous attacks during the nights of May 31 and June 2, 1920, on a lodging-house for Negroes, by bands of recruits on leave from the Naval Training Station. No lives were lost, and only two persons were hurt, neither of them seriously.

These outbursts scarcely classify as race riots. The chief motive seems to have been a desire for excitement on the part of young and active naval recruits.

The Sherman House was a dilapidated place on Genesee Street, the main street of the town. It had been abandoned by whites and was run as a lodging-house for thirty or thirty-five unmarried Negroes, chiefly factory workers. On the first floor was a poolroom and soft-drink "parlor," which some of the naval recruits had patronized.

A mischievous Negro boy of ten years, George Taylor, was primarily responsible for the outbreaks. On the afternoon of May 31 he and his little sister had been throwing stones at passing automobiles in Sheridan Road. One of these missiles broke the wind shield of an automobile driven by Lieutenant A. F. Blazier, an officer at the Great Lakes Station, who allowed this fact to become known to some of the recruits at the station. Late that evening an unorganized mob of recruits assembled at the Sherman House and threw stones, breaking nearly all the windows. The mob was rushed by all the available police in Waukegan, who took six prisoners. One reported incident was the chasing of a Negro by half a dozen bluejackets and marines and his rescue by the police.

Provost guards from the Naval Station rounded up the rioters and took them back to Great Lakes, thus ending the outbreak.

Two nights later, or June 2, 150 boys on leave from the Naval Training Station renewed the attack. They gathered in a ravine near the hotel and at ten o'clock they poured forth, led by a sailor carrying an American flag. The police had been warned and were ready with reinforcements.

About seventy-five feet from the lodging-house the police ordered the attackers to halt; no attention was paid to the command, and they fired their riot guns in the air, wounding two marines who were some distance away. Hand-to-hand fighting ensued, during which the police seized the flag and arrested two marines. The Great Lakes boys gathered about the police station and demanded their comrades.

Commander M. M. Frucht, executive officer of the Naval Station, who had already been sent to Waukegan by Commandant Bassett, appeared at the door and quieted the crowd with a promise that all concerned would have a square deal. He also advised them to return at once to the Naval Station.

The police released the two prisoners and gave back the flag. Two hundred provost guards from the Naval Station arrived in motor trucks while the crowd was at the police station.

Waukegan youths, evidently banded together for the purpose, searched the house of Edward Dorsey, Negro, at 905 Market Street, on the night of June 5. Ten of them, ranging from seventeen to twenty-two years, were arrested. They said they had heard that five white persons were held prisoners in Dorsey's home and that it was their intention to effect a rescue. It was asserted that a number of provost guards accompanied the crowd to the Dorsey house.

The general spirit of the people of Waukegan regarding Negroes may be judged from a proclamation by Mayor J. F. Bidinger, in which he disclaimed for the people of the city any intention to harass the Negro. Referring to reports that some of the white people of the town had participated in the disturbances, the mayor said: "In the first they did not, and in the second in no great numbers. Hoodlums generally run true to form and seldom overlook ready-made opportunity to manifest their peculiar taste in deviltry. Hence the mixing of a few of them into these fracases signifies nothing in so far as our general public is concerned."

Observers agreed with the mayor that the disturbances were not race riots. In this connection his proclamation said:

Now it is a definitely ascertained fact that no adult Negro was even remotely connected with the first stone-throwing; that the colored people did not then retaliate and have not since sought to retaliate in even the smallest measure; and that all the episodes have consisted simply of an attack upon people who have been as inoffensive throughout the entire affair as they could well be. All of which I submit stamps this affair as an example of disorderly conduct indeed, but not as a race riot.

3. THE "ABYSSINIAN" AFFAIR

Sunday afternoon, June 20, 1920, a small group of Negroes styling themselves "Abyssinians" ended a parade of their "order" in front of a café at 209 East Thirty-fifth Street frequented by both whites and Negroes. After a brief ceremony one of the leaders produced an American flag and deliberately burned it. He then began to destroy a second flag in the same manner. Two white policemen remonstrated with the men but were intimidated by threats and a brandishing of revolvers. They left immediately to notify police headquarters. Patrolman Owens, Negro, arrived as a second flag was lighted. Rushing up to the leader who held the burning flag in his hands and remonstrating with the group for their disloyalty, he was immediately shot and wounded. Robert Lawson Rose, a sailor on leave from the Great Lakes Naval Training Station, protested against the destruction of the flag and he too was shot; he staggered into the doorway of a cigar store at 207 East Thirty-fifth Street. Some of the parade leaders got rifles from a closed automobile which had followed the parade and was standing near by, and fired into the cigar store. One of these bullets killed Joseph Hoyt, a clerk in the store. The sailor, Rose, also died from his wound. In all about twenty-five shots were fired during the fracas, and several persons were injured.

The men who did the shooting escaped but were arrested later. Crowds attracted by the demonstration quickly dispersed when the shooting began, and from then on there was virtually no disorder except for attacks at a railroad station on three Negro ministers who were returning to the city and knew nothing of the shooting. Nine Negroes were arrested and held to the grand jury. One of them was Grover Cleveland Redding, thirty-seven or thirty-eight years of age, who was the "prophet" of the "Abyssinian" order in Chicago. Redding, who had admitted the shooting of Rose, was held with Oscar McGavick for murder, and the others as accessories after the fact.[1]

The exact reason for this flag-burning has not been disclosed, although it was apparently intended to symbolize the feeling of the "Abyssinian" followers that it was time to forswear allegiance to the American government and consider themselves under allegiance to the Abyssinian government.

The guns used in the shooting were found by the police in a garage, together with the regalia of the "Abyssinians," and much of their printed matter and other effects.[2]

The "Abyssinian" affair might easily have been turned into another great outbreak such as that of July, 1919. But the police, profiting by their experience of the previous year, were vigilant. They had organized an emergency force which was quickly mobilized and put in service in the district. Moreover, there was evident such a feeling of restraint on the part of both whites and Negroes that they combined to hunt down the offenders.

Indicative of this spirit of co-operation to prevent racial conflict, and helpful to it, was the careful handling of the matter by the press. Practically every newspaper gave prominence to the way in which the two races worked together to this end, and all dwelt on the courageous action of the Negro policeman. A picture printed in the *Herald-Examiner* the following morning showed people of the two races fraternizing after the shooting. The *Daily News* in reporting the affray said that only the co-operation of the white and Negro merchants of the district stopped the disturbance; that rowdies in the neighborhood were ready for a fight, but that "the better class of whites and Negroes worked directly with the police to stop any such trouble as a recurrence of the rioting last summer, which occurred in the same neighborhood."

To understand the "Abyssinian" affair an acquaintance with other characters, certain group propaganda and movements, is necessary. The "Back to Africa" movement, which lent fervor and enthusiasm to the development of lawlessness and wanton killing by this group of unlettered Negroes, has been in progress for more than two years. The Black Star Steamship Line and the Universal Improvement Association, headed by a Negro, Marcus Garvey, a British subject, were organized to establish commercial relations

---

[1] Redding had admitted having shot Rose, and evidence against others for their participation in the killing, while not conclusive, was rather convincing.

[2] At the trial of these men six months later, Grover Cleveland Redding and Oscar McGavick were sentenced to hang for the murder of Rose and Hoyt. The others held for trial were released. Redding has since been hanged.

THE LION OF JUDAH

TREATY

BETWEEN THE

KING OF ETHIOPIA

AND THE

UNITED STATES

His Majesty Menelik II., King of Kings of Ethiopia
TO REGULATE

COMMERCIAL RELATIONS
BETWEEN THE TWO COUNTRIES

Signed at Addis-Ababa, December 27, 1903;
Ratification advised by the Senate, March 12, 1904;
Ratified by the President, March 17, 1904;
King of Ethiopia notified of Ratification, August 2, 1904
Proclaimed, September 30, 1904.
BY THE PRESIDENT OF THE UNITED STATES
OF AMERICA

A PROCLAMATION

WHEREAS a treaty of commerce between the United States of
America and His Majesty Menelik II., King of Kings of
Ethiopia, was concluded on the twenty-seventh day of December, one thousand nine hundred and three, the original of which treaty,
being in the Amharic and French languages, is word for word as
follows:

PROPAGANDA LITERATURE USED BY "ABYSSINIANS" IN RECRUITING
FOLLOWERS

with Africa. To arouse interest and secure funds for the enterprise, sentiment has been created among Negroes for the developing of sections of Africa where they may govern themselves and build up their own institutions and commerce. The movement has gained thousands of adherents; although the language of its appeals has frequently been extreme, it has engaged in no dangerous or unpatriotic activities. Its connection with the tragic incident lies in the implication that "Back to Africa" means away from the land of unfair treatment, and thus suggests contempt for the United States.

The "Star Order of Ethiopia and Ethiopian Missionaries to Abyssinia" appears to be an illegitimate offspring of the Universal Improvement Association and the Black Star Steamship Line. The visit of the Abyssinian Mission to this country a year ago to renew a treaty between their country and the United States probably served as an added suggestion. The leaders of the movement were Redding, secretary of the order; Joseph Fernon, called the "Great Abyssinian," and his son, "The Prince." Together with a "Dr." R. D. Jonas, a white man who for several years has engaged in sundry activities among Negroes, they organized this movement among a class of Negroes too ignorant to exercise restraint over their racial resentments.

Emotionalism was aroused and a semi-religious twist was given through their appeals, which played more or less injudiciously on the desire of Negroes to improve their economic status and to escape from what some of them regard as oppression, either in this or in other countries. One or two other similar organizations are making such an appeal, not only to Negroes in this country, but to other dark-skinned races throughout the world. It is sought to weld them all together into a great nation. Glittering promises are set before the illiterate element of the Negro race, which has responded sufficiently to fatten the purses of some, at least, of the "prophets."

Redding was one of these "prophets." He was influenced by the white man, "Dr." R. D. Jonas, and had purchased from him the robe or toga which he wore during the parade of June 20. According to those who knew both men, he had first "stolen Jonas' thunder" and the following out of which the "Star Order of Ethiopia" had been manufactured. Having lost this, Jonas was willing to sell the regalia.

Jonas, it appears, had been promoting one movement after another among illiterate Negroes for six or seven years. At one time he conducted a co-operative store on State Street, in which he sold shares. He was often an orator at street gatherings and had been arrested a number of times. When Alexander Dowie of Zion City died, Jonas is said to have attempted to put himself into the vacant position. After the East St. Louis riots he appeared in Chicago in an express wagon with signs indicating that he was collecting funds for the Negroes of East St. Louis.

During the afternoon of the shooting, Jonas had been the principal speaker at a small, orderly meeting of Negroes in Johnson's Hall, 3516 South State

Street, at which he had launched a campaign for Mayor Thompson as a third-party candidate for president of the United States. The Mayor, he said, was the only man who could be trusted "to carry out Roosevelt's work" and put through the treaty with Abyssinia which expired in 1917. He also referred to the efforts of the Jews to return to Palestine and of the Irish to free themselves from British domination, and suggested the desirability of a coalition of the Negro, Jewish, and Irish races. Redding's hold on many of the Negroes was partly due to the fact that he is a Negro and claims to be a native of Abyssinia, whereas Jonas is a white man.

Quite evidently the "Back to Abyssinia" movement was used as a means for exploiting credulous Negroes. For one dollar they could purchase an Abyssinian flag, a small pamphlet containing a prophecy relating to the return of the black-skinned people to Africa, a copy of a so-called treaty between the United States and Abyssinia, and a picture of the "Prince of the Abyssinians." Likewise when the propaganda had begun to take root, one might sign a blank form which would commit him to return to "my motherland of Ethiopia" in order that he might fill any one of forty-four positions, such as electrical engineer, mechanical draftsman, civil engineer, architect, chemist, sign-painter, cartoonist, illustrator, traffic manager, teacher, auto-repairing, agriculture, and poultry-raising. The blank itself was headed:

STAR ORDER OF ETHIOPIA

AND

THE ETHIOPIAN MISSIONARY TO ABYSSINIA

"A Prince shall come out of Egypt. Ethiopia shall soon stretch
out her hands to God."—Ps. 68:31.

This is to certify that my name was given to Elder Grover Redding, Missionary to Abyssinia, to show to my brothers in my motherland that I am with them, heart and soul.

Oh, Wonderful Land, God remembers Thee. He shall deliver Thee from under the heels of Thy Oppressors. He remembers when Asia condemned Him, and Europe put Him to death, and it was Africa who haven him until King Herod was dead. It was Africa's son who helped Bare his Cross up to Calvary. There was Africa's son the Apostle Phillip met, and he carried the Gospel to Thy land. It was Thee whose Queen came to King Solomon to prove him with hard questions. Ethiopia, Thou was first on Earth; Thou shall be last, for Jehova has spoken it. (See Scrip: Zeph. 3:8, 9, 10; Isa. 18 Chap.; Ps. 68:30, 31.)

STAR ORDER OF ETHIOPIA

AND

ETHIOPIAN MISSIONARY TO ABYSSINIA

This is to certify that I have signed my name as an Ethiopian in America in sympathy with our motherland Ethiopia. I henceforth denounce the name of Negro which was given me by another race.

At this point the applicant declares himself ready at any time needed to fill any of the positions in a list below, which he has checked and which he is qualified to fill. Blank space appears then for name, address, present occupation, city, state, and county. At the bottom appears the name of George Gabriel, described as "Abyssinian" linguist and native of Abyssinia, together with that of Grover C. Redding, secretary and missionary. The applicant is requested to mail the blank to 1812 Thirteenth Street, Washington, D.C., in care of Mrs. Dabney, or 115 W. 138th Street, New York City, care of Charles Manson, or Joseph Goldberg, Jaffa, Palestine.

The immediate inspiration of the Abyssinians, as previously suggested, was a visit to this country, more than a year before, of a delegation from Abyssinia, which had concerned itself with a renewal of the old treaty. It is pointed out that the chief reason why Negroes should be interested in this treaty is that they might use it to overthrow "Jim Crow" laws in certain states. Under this treaty Abyssinians had been guaranteed the right to travel at will in the United States under the protection of the federal government. Men like Redding had evidently interpreted this to mean that under such a treaty the United States would be bound to interfere in behalf of Abyssinians, if they should be discriminated against under a "Jim Crow" law.

Redding, however, had some sort of biblical interpretation for his movement. He maintained that his mission was indicated in the Bible. He quoted from the Scriptures these words: "So shall the King of Assyria lead away the Egyptian prisoners, the Ethiopian captives, young and old, to the shame of Egypt." Asserting that the Ethiopians do not belong here, and that they should be taken back to their own country, he construed a biblical passage as meaning that the time of their bondage in a foreign country should be the expiration of a 300-year period. This period, he said, began in 1619, when Negroes were first taken for purposes of slavery from Africa to America. He said that the burning of the flag was the symbol indicated to him through these biblical passages, and the sign that Abyssinians should no lónger stay in this country.

As to the flag of Abyssinia, he had interpreted it thus: "The red means the blood of Christ; the green, the grass on which he knelt for you and me; the yellow for the clay. The Ethiopian flag is better known as 'Calvary's flag.'"

Jonas, from whom Redding had obtained these ideas of a Negro Utopia in Africa, claimed that he had introduced to President Wilson the Abyssinian delegation which had come to this country. He claimed the credit for having taken Redding into his home and cared for him several years ago at the behest of Mrs. Jonas, who had told him that he was a "smart young fellow."

The ceremonies and manifestations of the "Abyssinians" were marked by such fanaticism that responsible Negroes repudiated them and condemned the leaders along with other criminals and exploiters of the ignorant Negroes. The *Negro World*, organ of the Universal Improvement Association and Black Star Line, carried the following article.

Appalled by the violence aroused on Sunday night, when an American flag was burned and two men were killed by the Abyssinian zealots, colored leaders of the Middle West have begun a systematic campaign to eliminate white exploitation among the Negroes and to bring about better racial co-operation.

The Chicago police announced today that all the men wanted in the case, except two, are under arrest. They also promised that the career of Grover Cleveland Redding, self-styled "Prince of Abyssinia," and identified as a ringleader in the affair, will enter a new phase tomorrow when the frock-coated suspect is formally charged with murder, accessory to murder and rioting.

Oscar McGavick, one of the men sought, was arrested in Pittsburgh today. "Bill" Briggs and Frank Heans were taken into custody here. This leaves the police list with only two names, the Fernons, father and son. "Dr." R. D. Jonas, known on the South Side as a professional agitator, was released today, no evidence having been found of his direct connection with the shooting. Federal officials are investigating him.

According to the opinions of some of the leaders among Chicago Negroes the "Abyssinian movement," from which Sunday night's trouble indirectly resulted, is a legitimate and valid enterprise. It is but one of the manifestations of that bubbling activity which today characterizes the colored people of America in their struggle for race progression.

The trouble lies, they claim, in a group of exploiters and mountebanks, who, unauthorized by real leaders in the movement, have seized upon it as a medium for personal gain. In Chicago two of these were Jonas and Redding, it is claimed.

Pertinent on this point also is the stand taken by the *Chicago Defender*, among the most influential of the Negro publications, concerning the Abyssinians, which said editorially:

We warn all agitators, whether they be white or black, that this paper, standing as it does for law and order, for justice to all men, for that brotherhood without which no country can long prosper, and for the better element of our twelve millions, that we condemn their disloyalty and will do all in our power to aid the constituted authorities in crushing them.

The burning of the American flag by a group of self-styled Abyssinians at 35th St. and Indiana Avenue last Sunday evening, as a means of showing their contempt for the United States, and the resultant murders that followed in the wake of this demonstration, instead of accomplishing the end desired by these malcontents, acted as a boomerang. Every black face portrayed indignation. Every black arm was lifted to strike a blow at these law-breakers. This is our home, our country, our flag, for whose honor and protection we will give our last drop of blood. With all our shortcomings it can never truthfully be said that we are disloyal or unpatriotic.

The real problem indicated by the "Abyssinian" affair is how to prevent self-seekers from playing upon the superstitions and emotions of ignorant Negroes, to the harm of others and the disturbance of the peace.

4. THE BARRETT MURDER

The murder of a white man, Thomas J. Barrett, by a Negro on September 20, 1920, is not particularly significant in itself. But it was committed in

AFTER THE "ABYSSINIAN MURDERS"

Photograph taken at Thirty-fifth Street and Indiana Avenue, where both races co-operated to maintain order

the heart of the district where some of the worst rioting took place in 1919, it created a situation which might easily have developed into another serious riot, and it affords an example of prompt and effective police handling.

Forty-seventh and Halsted streets is the intersection of two main thorough-fares used by Negroes returning home from work in the Stock Yards. The neighborhood is one where gangs of hoodlums have attacked Negroes, and is thickly settled with people who have shown considerable antagonism toward Negroes.

Barrett, who was a motorman on the Chicago surface lines, was killed shortly after seven o'clock in the evening. He had had his shoes shined at the stand of William Sianis, 4720 South Halsted Street, and had purchased a newspaper at Halsted and Forty-seventh streets at about 7:00 P.M. About the same time three Negroes came out of the yards of Ready & Callaghan on Halsted Street between Forty-sixth and Forty-seventh, and one of these Negroes went to the news stand seeking a newspaper in which to roll up his overalls. In an encounter with these Negroes, Barrett was fatally stabbed, dying before he reached a hospital. His head was nearly severed from his body.

The Negroes, pursued by a rapidly increasing crowd of whites, ran north nearly a block on Halsted Street. They turned into a vacant lot and went through alleys until they emerged on Forty-fifth Street near Emerald Avenue, evidently trying to work their way east to the main Negro neighborhood. The crowd, however, had thickened so rapidly that they took refuge in St. Gabriel's Catholic Church, just east of Lowe Avenue.

The mob was checked by the appearance and quieting remarks of Father Thomas M. Burke, pastor of the church. He told them that the Negroes had sought sanctuary, that there were laws to punish them, and that it was not the province of a mob to wreak summary vengeance.

Meanwhile the police were already arriving. A patrol wagon had left the Stock Yards station about seven o'clock, and followed the pursuing crowd. Acting Lieutenant Bullard telephoned at once to Chief Garrity, and extra police were quickly thrown into the neighborhood to control the crowd.

Samuel C. Rank, lieutenant of police at the Thirteenth Precinct station, Forty-seventh Place and Halsted Street, had received the alarm about seven o'clock. He sent five detectives and followed shortly after to the scene of the disturbance. He went into the church with Sergeant Brown and three detectives. Lieutenant Rank forced a number of the mob to leave the church and locked the doors. Captain Hogan, of the Tenth Police Precinct, and Chief Garrity arrived about this time. The three Negroes were taken through a rear entrance to a patrol wagon in the alley and removed to the Hyde Park police station, a considerable distance away.

The crowd in front of the church had grown by this time to 3,000 or 4,000. In order to quiet them they were again addressed by Father Burke, who told them the Negroes had been removed from the church. They dispersed about 10:30 P.M.

Profiting by the experience of 1919 Chief Garrity made prompt use of prearranged plans to check all such disorders in their incipiency. He immediately closed saloons and "clubs" in which young hoodlums were accustomed to gather. He had the police patrol the streets by twos. He drew a "dead line" to prevent Negroes from entering the district. With his forces well organized and distributed, he set up headquarters at the Stock Yards Precinct station and spent the night there, with Captain Westbrook, commander of the second battalion of police, Captain Hogan, and Lieutenant Ira McDonnell, of the Desplaines Street station. Street cars and automobiles approaching the police "dead line" were stopped and all Negro passengers warned off. Street gatherings were broken up and people were searched for weapons. People were also kept moving in the streets. This display of force undoubtedly had its quieting effect. Nevertheless, a stray Negro was here and there attacked despite the vigilance of the police.

During the five or six hours following the murder, racial street fights occurred at Forty-fifth Street and Wabash Avenue. A mob stormed a house at 229 East Forty-fifth Street, attempted to burn it and did considerable damage. Frank Gavin, a white man, 1509 Marquette Road, was shot in the back during the mobbing of a Negro at Fifty-third Street and Racine Avenue. Hoodlums pulled Negroes from street cars and beat them. A Negro who had been dragged from a car at Thirty-ninth and Emerald Avenue, was rescued by several white women after he had been severely beaten with clubs. A man and a small boy, Negroes, were attacked by a gang at Fuller Park, Forty-fifth Street and Shields Avenue. At Forty-seventh and Halsted streets three Negroes were taken from a car and slugged, and two others had a similar experience at Forty-seventh Street and Union Avenue. Frank Stevens, a white man, 3738 Langley Avenue, was badly injured by a crowd of Negroes at Thirty-ninth Street and Normal Avenue.

Precautions were continued next day for the protection of Negroes working in the Stock Yards, and frequenting the district where the disorders had occurred. This district ran as far west as Racine Avenue and as far east as Prairie; as far north as Thirty-second Street and as far south as Fifty-third Street. Negroes working at the Stock Yards had police escorts to and from their work, and the car lines on Halsted and Forty-seventh and Thirty-fifth streets, and on Racine Avenue, which are much used by the Negroes, were especially guarded. Only one clash was recorded the following day. By six o'clock Wednesday morning, thirty-seven hours after the murder, the special police concentration was discontinued.

Nine persons in all were reported injured during this disturbance. Nine men were arrested, including the three Negroes whom Barrett had encountered. These three were: Samuel Hayes, forty years old, 519 East Thirty-fifth

Street; Henry Snow, thirty-two years old, 517 East Thirty-fifth Street; and Frank Gatewood, forty-three years old, 3446 Prairie Avenue.

Witnesses at the inquest differed as to whether there was any provocation for the stabbing of Barrett. Only one of them testified that he heard any of the four persons say anything. This was Carl Duwell, a printer, 466 West Twenty-fourth Place, who had just alighted from a Halsted Street car. He said that Barrett was following the three colored men and seemed to be threatening them, saying "You want to fight?" One of the Negroes suddenly turned and struck at Barrett, slashing his throat. The Negroes had been walking fast, with Barrett following a few feet behind them. After he was struck, Barrett staggered a few feet to the curb and fell.

Barrett's widow said he was not in the habit of carrying weapons, but it was current talk that he had been arrested a number of times for street fights with Negroes. He had been a policeman in the service of the South Park Commission, and was an ex-soldier. William Sianis, at whose stand Barrett had his shoes shined just before the murder, said that Barrett was apparently sober. Neighborhood gossip was to the effect that Barrett had been drinking at McNally's saloon at Forty-seventh and Halsted streets. Also Duwell's testimony indicated that Barrett had been drinking.

According to Police Captain Hogan, when the Negroes were arrested in the church, knives were found on the persons of two of them. One of these, Sam Hayes, admitted to the police at that time that he had stabbed a white man at Forty-seventh and Halsted streets. His story was that when he asked the newsboy at the corner for a newspaper in which to wrap his overalls, Barrett threatened him and then struck him, and the stabbing followed.

During the night following the murder, Chief of Police Garrity issued a statement which was published conspicuously in the morning newspapers, and was most effectively worded to prevent misunderstanding of the incident and avert use of it to inflame racial hostility. The statement began:

There has been no race riot. The killing at Forty-seventh and Halsted streets was merely a street-corner fight. There was grave danger that it would be followed by serious trouble. Precautionary measures were taken at once to forestall the recurrence of the riots, with the destruction of life and property, of last summer.

This was followed by a detailed account of the special measures and distribution of police to handle the situation.

II. THE SPRINGFIELD RIOT
August 14-15, 1908

The race riot at Springfield, Illinois, in August, 1908, which cost the lives of two Negroes and four white men, is an outstanding example of the racial bitterness and brutality that can be provoked by unsubstantiated rumor or, as in this case, by deliberate falsehood. The two Negro victims were innocent and unoffending. They were lynched under the shadow of the capitol of

Lincoln's state, within half a mile of the only home he ever owned, and two miles from the monument which marks the grave of the great emancipator.

A second fundamental factor in the Springfield riot situation was the fertile field prepared by admittedly lax law enforcement and by tolerance in the community of vicious conditions, the worst of which were permitted to surround the Negro areas.

The spark which touched off the explosion was the old story of the violation of a white woman by a Negro, and not until the damage had been done was its falsity confessed by the woman who had told it.

On the night of Friday, August 14, 1908, according to her story, Mrs. H—, wife of a street-railway conductor, was asleep in her room. She was alone in the house. She declared that a Negro entered, dragged her from her bed to the back yard, and there committed the crime. She said she had attempted to scream but was choked by her assailant, who left her lying unconscious in the garden.

A Negro, George Richardson, who had been at work on a neighboring lawn the day before the attack, was accused by Mrs. H— and was arrested when he returned to work the next morning. He was placed in the county jail and on August 19 he was indicted.

During inquiry by a special grand jury certain facts were disclosed concerning Mrs. H—'s character, and she admitted that, though she had been brutally beaten by a white man on the night indicated, Richardson was not present and had no connection with the affair. She admitted that she had not been raped. For reasons known only to herself, she wished to keep the name of the real assailant a secret, and therefore she had accused Richardson. She signed an affidavit exonerating him. Richardson had no criminal record. He and two of his family were property owners in Springfield.

While Richardson was in custody and before he was exonerated, feeling against him was intensified because of the murder, three or four weeks before, of Clergy A. Ballard, a white man, by Joe James, a Negro tramp, who was a drug and whiskey addict. James had been taken from a freight train and placed in jail for thirty days and had been released on the night of the crime. He was charged with entering the room of Ballard's daughter, Blanche, at night. Ballard grappled with him, but James broke away and ran. In the struggle Ballard was mortally injured. James was found asleep in a park near the Ballard home about noon the next day, under the influence of a drug. He was tried and hanged, and his body was taken back to Mississippi by his mother for interment. Rev. Mr. Dawson, spiritual adviser of James, stated that James declared he had no knowledge of the crime.

Springfield was, therefore, in a receptive mood when, on the morning of Friday, August 15, it got the first rumors concerning the attack on Mrs. H— Richardson had been taken before her and partially identified. In the afternoon, when it became known that he had been arrested, crowds gathered about the jail. They seemed good-natured rather than blood-thirsty. It was also known that James, accused of the Ballard murder, occupied a cell in the jail. The sheriff preserved order through the afternoon, no effort being made to disperse the crowd of 300 or 400 persons. About five o'clock Richardson and James were taken in an automobile to Sherman, north of Springfield, and there they were transferred by train to Bloomington.

About 7:00 P.M. leadership began to develop in the mob about the jail. The leaders demanded the two Negroes, but were finally convinced by the sheriff that they were not in the jail. Then the story spread that Harry Loper, a restaurant keeper, had provided the automobile in which the men had been removed. The crowd rushed to the restaurant five blocks away. In response to the mob's hootings Loper appeared in the doorway with a firearm in his hand. About 8:30 P.M. someone threw a brick through a plate-glass window and in a few minutes the front of the restaurant had been smashed out. Then followed the complete wrecking of the restaurant, as well as the owner's automobile, which had been standing in front.

When the mob began to surge through the town the Fire Department was called to disperse it, but the mob cut the hose. Control having been lost by the sheriff and police, Governor Deneen called out the militia. The mob, by this time very much excited, started for the Negro district through Washington Street, along which a large number of Negroes lived on upper floors. Raiding second-hand stores which belonged to white men, the mob secured guns, axes, and other weapons with which it destroyed places of business operated by Negroes and drove out all of the Negro residents from Washington Street. Then it turned north into Ninth Street.

At the northeast corner of Ninth and Jefferson streets was the frame barber shop of Scott Burton, a Negro. The mob set fire to this building. From that point it went a block farther north to Madison Street and then turned east and began firing all the shacks in which Negroes and whites lived in that street.

Burton, the first victim of the mob's violence, was lynched in the yard back of his shop. The mob tied a rope around his neck and dragged him through the streets. An effort was then made to burn the body, which had been hung to a tree. This was at two o'clock in the morning.

About this time a company of militia arrived from Decatur, Illinois, and proceeded through Madison Street to Twelfth Street, where the mob was engaged in mutilating Burton's body, riddling it with bullets. The mob was twice ordered to disperse, and the militia fired in the air twice. The third time the troops fired into the ankles and legs of the mob. At least two of the men in the mob were wounded and the mob quickly gave way.

By this time the Negroes were badly frightened and began leaving town. Meanwhile, Governor Deneen had sent for more troops, including two regiments from Chicago. Before the rioting ended 5,000 militiamen were patrolling the streets of Springfield. On Saturday morning the militia began to arrive in force, including detachments from Chicago. This was a comparatively quiet day, but that night another Negro was lynched within a block of the State House. The mob gathered on the Court House Square and marched south on Fifth Street to Monroe, west on Monroe to Spring, and south on Spring to Edwards. At the southeast corner of Spring and Edwards streets a Negro named Donegan and his family had lived for many years. Donegan was eighty-four years old and owned the half-block of ground where he lived. He was found sleeping in his own yard and was quickly strung up to a tree across the street. Then his throat was cut and his body mutilated. The troops interfered at this point and cut down the man, taking him in an ambulance to the hospital, where he died the following morning. Donegan's only offense seems to have been that he had had a white wife for more than thirty years. He bore a good reputation, and the mob had found no reason for lynching him.

Abe Raymer, who was supposed to have been the leader of the mob, was charged with the murder of Donegan, but was released.

As an example of the disorder which occurred Friday evening, it is narrated that Eugene W. Chafin, Prohibition candidate for the presidency, was delivering an address on the east side of the public square. A Negro pursued by the mob ran toward the speaker's stand from Fifth and Washington streets, where he had been pulled from a street car. Two men helped him to the speaker's stand, while Chafin at the front of the platform threatened to shoot into the crowd. Although he had no revolver he made a motion toward his hip pocket. During the mêlée before gaining the platform the Negro drew a knife from his pocket and slashed several white men. When he had escaped from the rear of the platform, missiles flew in the direction of Mr. Chafin, one of them hitting him on the head.

Four men were rounded up who had been blacked up to resemble Negroes and had been firing on soldiers during the night in an effort to substantiate the assertion that the Negroes did not welcome the soldiers.

Sunday was quiet. No effort was made to reorganize the mob. The whole city was as if under martial law. The saloons were shut and every place of business was closed at 9:00 P.M.

The people who took part in the mob violence had no grievances against the Negroes. They were hoodlums and underworld folk. Many of the hoodlums, according to one observer, were less than twenty years old.

During the rioting four white men were killed. They were: Louis Johnson, of 1208 East Reynolds Street, whose body was found at the foot of the stairs leading to the barroom in Loper's restaurant. He was shot through the abdomen; John Colwell, of 1517 Matheny Street, who died at St. John's Hospital; J. W. Scott, of 125 East Adams Street, who was shot in the lungs; Frank Delmore, who was killed by a stray bullet.

Seventy-nine persons were injured. The property destroyed included Loper's restaurant and automobile, Scott Burton's barber shop, the Delmonico saloon, and one block of houses between Tenth and Eleventh streets, which were burned, with all their contents. Scores of families were left destitute. Many Negroes were severely beaten before they were able to escape from the district. Numbers of these homeless colored people swarmed to neighboring towns and to Chicago. Three thousand of them were concentrated at Camp Lincoln, the National Guard camp grounds. Some of the refugees were cared for at the arsenal.

Current comment concerning the riots suggested political corruption and laxity of law enforcement as important underlying causes of the riots. An assistant state's attorney in Springfield charged that saloons had long been violating the law, and that the law was not generally enforced as it ought to be. He cited these conditions as responsible in large measure for the rioting and murders. Pastors in their sermons on the riot focused attention on the way in which vicious elements were permitted to flout the law with impunity. This comment came so generally and insistently from those conversant with the situation that the *Chicago Daily News* was led to remark editorially upon the responsibility of the public authorities of Springfield. It said:

Vice and other forms of law breaking have been given wide latitude here. The notoriety of Springfield's evil resorts has been widespread.

A mob which murders, burns and loots, is a highly undesirable substitute even for a complacent city administration. It is a logical result, however, of long temporizing with vice and harboring of the vicious. When a mob begins to shoot and hang, to destroy and pillage, there is instant recognition on the part of responsible persons of the beauty of law enforcement and of general orderliness.

On the Sunday following the riots some Springfield saloon-keepers took advantage of the fact that large crowds of sight-seers had come to town to open their places, in violation of the order by Mayor Reece to remain closed. Some of them were arrested for defiance of the mayor's proclamation to remain closed until order had been restored.

By Monday or Tuesday order was pretty well restored in Springfield. Some of the National Guard troops were kept on duty for several days. Almost 100 arrests were made, and a special grand jury returned more than fifty indictments.

III. EAST ST. LOUIS RIOTS

May 28 and July 2, 1917

Following a period of bitter racial feeling, frequently marked by open friction, a clash between whites and Negroes in East St. Louis, Illinois, occurred on May 28, 1917, in which, following rumors that a white man had been killed by Negroes, a number of Negroes were beaten by a mob of white men. This outbreak was the forerunner of a much more serious riot on July 2, in which at least thirty-nine Negroes and eight white people were killed, much property was destroyed by fire, and the local authorities proved so ineffective and demoralized that the state militia was required to restore order. A Congressional Committee investigated the facts of the riot and the underlying conditions, which included industrial disturbances and shameful corruption in local government.[1]

The coroner of St. Clair County in which East St. Louis is situated, held thirty-eight inquests, as a result of which it was found that twenty-six of these deaths had been due to gun-shot wounds, four to drowning, four to burns, two to fractured skulls, one to hemorrhage of the brain, and one to pneumonia after a fracture of the thyroid cartilage. Hundreds of persons were estimated to have been more or less seriously injured, seventy having been treated in St. Mary's Hospital. It has been impossible to get an accurate accounting of the deaths and injuries. One man who had taken a deep interest in the situation estimated that from 200 to 300 Negroes were killed.

About 200 people were arrested. Some of these were released, some were charged with rioting and conspiracy, and others with arson. Two white women were tried for conspiracy and rioting, and fined $50.00. Ten Negroes were convicted of rioting and murder. Indictments of 104 white persons grew out of the immediate activities of the rioters. Three policemen were among those indicted for murder in connection with firing upon Negro bystanders. In this same group of assailants were seven soldiers who were court-martialed. No finding in their cases has been announced. Three white men were indicted for murder in connection with a raid upon a street-car load of Negro passengers in which a father and son were killed, a mother was wounded severely, and a little daughter escaped. Twenty-six men, two of them Negroes, were indicted for arson.

The effort to bring the guilty to justice was commented upon and summarized by this Congressional Committee as follows:

Assistant Attorney General Middlekauf had active charge of the prosecutions growing out of the riot, and he showed neither fear nor favor. Capable, determined, and courageous, he allowed neither political influence nor personal appeals to swerve him from the strict line of duty.

As a result of these prosecutions by the attorney general's office 11 Negroes and 8 white men are in the State penitentiary, 2 additional white men have been sentenced to prison terms, 14 white men have been given jail sentences, 27 white men, including the former night chief of police and three policemen, have pleaded guilty to rioting and have been punished.

[1] This statement is based mainly upon the report of this special committee appointed by Congress to investigate the East St. Louis riots and upon the stenographic report of the testimony taken by it. This testimony, comprising 6,000 typewritten pages, was placed at the disposal of the Commission through the courtesy of the chairman of the Committee, Representative Ben Johnson, of Kentucky, and the interest and co-operation of Representative James R. Mann, of Illinois.

These convictions were obtained in the face of organized, determined effort, backed with abundant funds, to head off the prosecutions and convictions. In the case of Mayor Mollman there seems to have been an open, paid advertising campaign to slander and intimidate the attorney general.

The burned area of the city was on Fifth Street, Broadway, Walnut Street, Eighth Street, Eleventh Street and Bond Avenue, as well as "the Flats" on Seventh Street, between Division and Missouri avenues. This latter area was that occupied by Negroes. There were 312 buildings and forty-four railroad cars totally or partially destroyed, with a total loss of $393,600.

The riots in East St. Louis may be traced, more or less directly, to a number of causes, the influence of each being apparent.

Without doubt conditions resulting from the migration of a large number of Negroes from the South, a movement which was more or less general at that time, account in large measure for the riots, but also involved in it all are the facts that there had been industrial friction, and that the city was flagrantly misgoverned.

The Congressional Committee observed an effort to shift the blame from one element to another. The labor interests sought to place responsibility for the riots upon the employers, who, they said, had brought great numbers of Negroes to East St. Louis in order that they might more readily dominate the employment situation. The employers, on the other hand, thought the blame rested upon the city and county administration because of laxity in law enforcement, exploitation of Negroes for political purposes, and all sorts of political corruption, including the "protection" of vice and crime. The political ring sought to dodge responsibility by emphasizing economic and industrial causes of the outbreak.

Whatever may have been the conditions resulting from the influx of Negroes, they were undoubtedly actuated by a desire to improve their condition. Some 10,000 or 12,000 Negroes had come to St. Clair County from the South during the winter of 1916–17. During the year and a half preceding the riot, the number of such migrants was estimated at 18,000, although it was reported that many had returned during the winter of 1916–17, because of the unaccustomed cold climate. It is certain that this influx severely taxed the housing accommodations of East St. Louis, which were of the insanitary and inadequate nature that so often characterizes urban districts in which the Negroes find that they must live. The report of the Congressional Committee on this point says:

It is a lamentable fact that the employers of labor paid too little heed to the comfort or welfare of their men. They saw them crowded into wretched cabins without water or any of the conveniences of life, their wives and children condemned to live in the disreputable quarters of the town, and made no effort to lift them out of the mire. The Negroes gravitated to the insanitary sections, existed in the squalor of filthy cabins and made no complaint, but the white workmen had a higher outlook, and failure to provide them with better homes added to their bitter dissatisfaction with the burdens placed upon them by having to compete with black labor.

It is likewise in evidence that special inducements were offered to the southern Negroes to come to East St. Louis, as well as to other industrial centers in the North. Advertisements were placed in southern newspapers, offering employment at wages far in excess of those paid in the South. Low railroad rates were offered, and in some instances during this general migration the railroads are said to have transported Negroes free in order that they might be employed by the railroads. Failures of crops in the South, floods and ill treatment of Negroes there, coupled with the hope that they would find fairer treatment in the North, as well as better wages and living conditions, were the direct causes of migration. After this had become fairly general it was further stimulated by Negroes who had come North, and who wrote home painting northern conditions in glowing colors.

From the industrial point of view it should be noted that in the summer of 1916 there had been a strike of 4,000 white men in the packing-plants of East St. Louis. It was asserted that Negroes were used in these plants as strike breakers. A report on the Negro migration by the United States Department of Labor states that when the strike was ended Negroes were still employed, and some of the white men lost their positions. It says further: "The white leaders undoubtedly realized that the effectiveness of striking was materially lessened by this importation of black workers."

Furthermore, it is stated in the report of the Congressional Committee that the Aluminum Ore Company, during a strike, brought hundreds of Negroes to the city as strike breakers in order to defeat organized labor, "a precedent which aroused intense hatred and antagonism, and caused countless tragedies as its aftermath. The feeling of resentment grew with each succeeding day. White men walked the streets in idleness and their families suffered for food and warmth and clothes, while their places as laborers were taken by strange Negroes who were compelled to live in hovels and who were used to keep down wages."

In May, 1917, a strike followed demands which had been made upon the Aluminum Ore Company by the "Aluminum Ore Employees' Protective Association." These related to alleged injustices and discriminations said to have been practiced against the employees. The company failed to comply with these demands, and a thousand white workers struck.

Closely related to this situation was a notice sent to the delegates of the Central Trades Labor Union by the secretary of the Union, dated May 23, which declared that the immigration of the southern Negro had reached a point where "drastic action must be taken if we intend to work and to live peaceably in this community." This notice declared that these men were being used "to the detriment of our white citizens by some of the capitalists and a few real estate owners." It called a meeting to present to the mayor and city council a demand for action to "retard this growing menace, and also devise a way to get rid of a certain portion of those who are already here." The notice read further: "This is not a protest against the Negro who has long been a resident of East St. Louis, and is a law abiding citizen."

This meeting was held on May 28 in the auditorium of the city hall and was attended not only by the labor men but also by a large number of other persons. The Congressional Committee refers to one of the speakers at this meeting as "an attorney of some ability and no character." The report of the Committee says that he virtually advised the killing of Negroes and burning of their homes. The report says further:

He was not authorized to speak for those who went there to protest against the lawlessness which disgraced the city and the presence of thousands of Negroes who it is claimed were taking the places of the white workmen, but his inflammatory speech caused many of his hearers to rush into the street and to resort to acts of violence. . . . . He was in full sympathy with the action of the mob. They followed his advice and the scenes of murder and arson that ensued were the logical result of his utterances.

That night, May 28, following the meeting, a crowd of white people assembled in front of the police station and clamored for Negro prisoners. A rumor circulated through the crowd that a white man had just been killed by Negroes, and parts of the crowd left, forming a mob which severely beat a number of Negroes whom it met. The situation was so serious that the mayor called for troops. The trouble subsided, however. It is important to note that from this time until the riot of July 1–2, no effort was made to strengthen the police force nor were any other steps taken to control the situation.

In connection with the industrial phase of the situation, it should be remembered that the war had cut off the normal supply of foreign labor, and that not a few white workers had left East St. Louis for other industrial centers. Most of the Negro migrants were unskilled workers, and their competition was, therefore, with the unskilled white workers. One witness before the Congressional Committee expressed the view that the labor shortage in East St. Louis prior to the riot certainly did not justify the great influx of Negroes, but it is of record that most of the newcomers got profitable employment in unskilled occupations.

The employers were fighting unions of any sort, whether of whites or Negroes. Unions were seeking membership of Negroes as well as whites in the hope that the use of Negroes as strike breakers might be prevented. Whether union men or not, the white workers resented the influx of Negro workers who might take their jobs. The inevitable consequence was friction between whites and Negroes.

The Congressional Committee laid great stress upon corrupt politics as the leading cause of the riots of July 2. It disclosed an almost unbelievable combination of shameless corruption, tolerance of vice and crime, maladministration, and debauchery of the courts. The report says that East St. Louis for many years was a plague spot, harboring within its borders "every offense in the calendar of crime" and committing openly "every lapse in morals and public decency." Politicians looted its treasury, gave away valuable franchises, and elected plunderers to high office. Graft, collusion with crime and vice, and desecration of office were openly and deliberately practiced. Criminals were attracted and welcomed, and the good people of the community were powerless. Owners of large corporations and manufacturers pitted white against black labor, giving no thought to their thousands of workmen living in hovels, the victims of "poverty and disease, of long hours and incessant labor."

The mayor, continues the report, was a tool of dishonest politicians, the electorate was "debauched," the police were a conscienceless bunch of grafters, and the revenue of the city was largely derived from saloons and dens of vice.

Several officials and politicians of high standing were singled out by the Committee for especial condemnation as the "brains of the city's corruption."

A great deal of the city's crime and vice was concentrated in what is known as "Black Valley." This was the section in which the Negroes lived, but much of the vice and crime was promoted and practiced by vicious whites. There was much mixing of whites and Negroes in the vilest practices.

Similar conditions existed in the town of Brooklyn near by, with about 3,000 people, of whom only about fifty were white. Its dens of iniquity were notorious and were the resort of many white people. So openly operated were these resorts that the Congressional Committee reported that in the Brooklyn high school "24 out of 25 girls who were in the graduating class went to the bad in the saloons and dance halls and failed to receive their diplomas."

Not only were conditions of this sort demoralizing and degrading for the decent Negroes, but the sanitary conditions were likewise extremely bad. Some of the houses in the Negro districts had not been painted for fifteen years and were in a state of great disrepair. Their setting consisted largely of pools of stagnant water and beds of weeds. At one period during the migration Negroes were coming in so fast that even these miserable housing conditions were inadequate, and some of them were forced to live in sheds. In one instance sixty-nine newcomers were found living in one small house. Whenever houses were vacated by white people and rented to Negroes, the rental price was largely increased, sometimes doubled.

After reviewing the corruption in East St. Louis, the report of the Congressional Committee discussed the riot. It described the condition of affairs on the night of July 1, 1917, when the second and most serious outbreak occurred. An automobile (some witnesses said two) went through the Negro section of the city, its occupants firing promiscuously into homes. This aroused fierce resentment among the Negroes, who organized for defense and armed themselves with guns. The ringing of the church bell, a prearranged signal for assembling, drew a crowd of them, and they marched through the streets ready to avenge the attack. A second automobile filled with white men crossed their path. The Negroes cursed them, commanded them to drive on, and fired a volley into the machine. The occupants, however, were not the rioters but policemen and reporters. One policeman was killed and another was so seriously wounded that he died later.

Thousands viewed the riddled car standing before police headquarters. The early editions of the newspapers gave full accounts of the tragedy, and on July 2 the rioting began. Negro mobs shot white men, and white men and boys, girls and women, began to attack every Negro in sight. News spread rapidly and, as excitement increased, unimaginable depredations and horrible tortures were committed and viewed with "placid unconcern" by hundreds. Negro men were stabbed, clubbed, and hanged from telephone poles. Their homes were burned. Women and children were not spared. An instance is given of a Negro child two years old which was shot and thrown into a doorway of a burning building.

On the night of July 1, Mayor Mollman telephoned to the Adjutant General of Illinois saying that the police were no longer able to handle the situation and requesting that the militia be sent. Both the police and the militia are severely censured by the Congressional report for gross failure to do their duty. The police, says the report, could have quelled the riot instantly, but instead they either "fled into the safety of cowardly seclusion or listlessly watched the depredations of the mob, passively and in many instances actively sharing in the work."

In all, five companies of the Illinois National Guard were sent to East St. Louis. Some of them arrived on the morning of July 2, the first at 8:40 A.M. These forces were in command of Colonel S. O. Tripp. Concerning the conduct of the militia, the Congressional Committee reported in strong terms, singling out Colonel Tripp for especial condemnation. It said that he was a hindrance instead of a help to the troops; that "he was ignorant of his duties, blind to his responsibilities and deaf to every intelligent appeal that was made to him."

The troops, in the estimation of the Committee, were poorly officered and in only a few cases did their duty. The report states that "they seemed moved by the same spirit of indifference or cowardice that marked the conduct of the police force. As a rule they fraternized with the mob, joked with them and made no serious effort to restrain them."

Many instances are given of active participation and encouragement of the mob in its murders, arson, and general destruction.

The only redeeming feature of the activities of the militia, according to the Congressional Committee, was "the conduct, bravery, and skill of the officer second in command, whose promptness and determination prevented the mob from committing many more atrocities."

By eight o'clock of the evening of July 2 there were seventeen officers and 270 men on duty, and by July 4 the force had increased to thirty-seven officers and 1,411 men. On the evening of July 2 the fury of the mob had spent itself, and the riot subsided.

The behavior of the troops was condemned not only by the Congressional Committee but by citizens generally, and a special inquiry was made into their conduct by the Military and Naval Department of the State of Illinois. Witnesses to dereliction on duty on the part of the soldiers were examined and commanding officers of troops were asked to testify and explain specific acts of violence and neglect of duty. In all seventy-nine persons were examined. Although the charges against the soldiers in a large number of cases were serious and sufficient to warrant the criticism which they received, identification of individuals guilty of these acts was difficult. This probably accounts for the fact that only seven court-martials resulted from the inquiry. The commanding officer, though severely censured by the Congressional Committee, was exonerated by this inquiry.

CHAPTER III

THE MIGRATION OF NEGROES FROM THE SOUTH

I. INTRODUCTION

During the period 1916–18 approximately a half-million Negroes suddenly moved from southern to northern states. This movement, however, was not without a precedent. A similar migration occurred in 1879, when Negroes moved from Mississippi, Louisiana, Texas, Alabama, Tennessee, and North Carolina to Kansas. The origin of this earlier movement, its causes, and manner resemble in many respects the one which has so recently attracted public attention.

The migration of 1916–18 cannot be separated completely from the steady, though inconspicuous, exodus from southern to northern states that has been in progress since 1860, or, in fact, since the operation of the "underground railway." In 1900 there were 911,025 Negroes living in the North, 10.3 per cent of the total Negro population, which was then 8,883,994. Census figures for the period 1900–1910 show a net loss for southern states east of the Mississippi of 595,703 Negroes. Of this number 366,880 are found in northern states. Reliable estimates for the last decade place the increase of northern Negro population around 500,000.

The 1910–20 increase of the Negro population of Chicago was from 44,103 to 109,594, or 148.5 per cent, with a corresponding increase in the white population of 21 per cent, including foreign immigration. According to the Census Bureau method of estimating natural increase of population, the Negro population of Chicago unaffected by the migration would be 58,056 in 1920, and the increase by migration alone would be 51,538.

The relative 1910–20 increases in white and Negro population in typical industrial cities of the Middle West, given in Table II, illustrate the effect of the migration of southern Negroes.

The migration to Chicago.—Within a period of eighteen months in 1917–18 more than 50,000 Negroes came to Chicago according to an estimate based on averages taken from actual count of daily arrivals. All of those who came, however, did not stay. Chicago was a re-routing point, and many immigrants went on to nearby cities and towns. During the heaviest period, for example, a Detroit social agency reported that hundreds of Negroes applying there for work stated that they were from Chicago. The tendency appears to have been to reach those fields offering the highest present wages and permanent prospects.

TABLE II

	Negroes		Percentage of Negro Increase, 1910-20	Percentage of White Increase, 1910-20
	1910	1920		
Cincinnati, Ohio.....	19,639	29,636	50.9	8.0
Dayton, Ohio.......	4,842	9,029	86.5	28.0
Toledo, Ohio........	1,877	5,690	203.1	42.5
Fort Wayne, Ind....	572	1,476	158.0	34.3
Canton, Ohio........	291	1,349	363.6	71.7
Gary, Ind..........	383	5,299	1,283.6	205.1
Detroit, Mich.......	5,741	41,532	623.4	106.9
Chicago, Ill.........	44,103	109,594	148.5	21.0

II. CAUSES OF THE MIGRATION

A series of circumstances acting together in an unusual combination both provoked and made possible the migration of Negroes from the South on a large scale. The causes of the movement fall into definite divisions, even as stated by the migrants themselves. For example, one of the most frequent causes mentioned by southern Negroes for their change of home is the treatment accorded them in the South. Yet this treatment of which they complain has been practiced since their emancipation, and fifty years afterward more than nine-tenths of the Negro population of the United States still remained in the South. "Higher wages" was also commonly stated as a cause of the movement, yet thousands came to the North and to Chicago who in the South had been earning more in their professions and even in skilled occupations than they expected to receive in the North. These causes then divide into two main classes: (1) economic causes, (2) sentimental causes. Each has a bearing on both North and South. The following statements are based on reports prepared by trustworthy agencies during the migration, on letters and statements from migrants, Negroes and whites living in the South and the North, and on family history obtained by the Commission's investigators.

I. ECONOMIC CAUSES OF THE MIGRATION

A. THE SOUTH

Low wages.—Wages of Negroes in the South varied from 75 cents a day on the farms to $1.75 a day in certain city jobs, in the period just preceding 1914. The rise in living costs which followed the outbreak of the war outstripped the rise in wages. In Alabama the price paid for day labor in the twenty-one "black belt" counties averaged 50 and 60 cents a day. It ranged from 40 cents, as a minimum, to 75 cents, and, in a few instances, $1.00 was a maximum for able-bodied male farm hands.[1]

A Negro minister, writing in the *Montgomery* (Alabama) *Advertiser*, said:

The Negro farm hand gets for his compensation hardly more than the mule he plows; that is, his board and shelter. Some mules fare better than Negroes. This,

[1] Negro migration in 1916-17, *U.S. Department of Labor Report*, p. 67.

TYPICAL PLANTATION HOMES IN THE SOUTH OF MIGRANTS TO CHICAGO

too, in spite of the fact that the money received for farm products has advanced more than 100 per cent. The laborer has not shared correspondingly in this advance.

High rents and low wages have driven the Negro off the farms. They have no encouragement to work. Only here and there you will find a tenant who is getting a square deal and the proper encouragement.

A white man, writing in the same paper, said:

There is an article in today's *Advertiser* headed "Exodus of the Negroes to Be Probed." Why hunt for a cause when it's plain as the noonday sun the Negro is leaving this country for higher wages? He doesn't want to leave here but he knows if he stays here he will starve. They have made no crops, they have nothing to eat, no clothes, no shoes, and they can't get any work to do, and they are leaving just as fast as they can get away. . . . . If the Negro race could get work at 50 cents per day he would stay here. He don't want to go. He is easily satisfied and will live on half rations and will never complain.

The *Atlanta Independent*, white, said:

If our white neighbors will treat the Negro kindly, recognizing his rights as a man, advance his wages in proportion as the cost of living advances, he will need no ordinance nor legislation to keep the Negro here. The South is his natural home. He prefers to be here, he loves its traditions, its ideals and its people. But he cannot stay here and starve. . . . .

When meat was 15 cents a pound and flour $8 a barrel, the Negro received from $4 to $8 a week. Now meat is 30 cents a pound and flour $16 a barrel, and the Negro is receiving the same wages. He cannot live on this and the white man cannot expect him to live in the South and live on the starvation wages he is paying him, when the fields and the factories in the North are offering him living wages.

The boll weevil.—In 1915 and 1916 the boll weevil cotton pest so ravaged sections of the South that thousands of farmers were almost ruined. Cotton crops were lost, and the farmers were forced to change from cotton to food products. The growing of cotton requires about thirty times as many "hands" as food products. As a result many Negroes were thrown out of employment. The damage wrought by the boll weevil was augmented by destructive storms and floods, which not only affected crops but made the living conditions of Negroes more miserable.

Lack of capital.—The "credit system" is a very convenient and common practice in many parts of the South. Money is borrowed for upkeep until the selling season, when it is repaid in one lump sum. The succession of short crops and the destruction due to the boll weevil and storms occasioned heavy demands for capital to carry labor through the fall and early winter until a new crop could be started. There was a shortage of capital, and as a result there was little opportunity for work. During this period many white persons migrated from sections of the South most seriously affected.

"Unsatisfactory" living conditions.—The plantation cabins and segregated sections in cities where municipal laxity made home surroundings undesirable have been stated as another contributing cause of the movement.

Lack of school facilities.—The desire to place their children in good schools was a reason often given by migrants with families for leaving the South. School facilities are described as lamentably poor even by southern whites. Perhaps the most thorough statement of these conditions is given in a *Study of Negro Education* by Thomas Jesse Jones, made under the direction of the federal Bureau of Education, and comparing provisions for white and Negro children in fifteen southern states and the District of Columbia. He states:

In the South they [Negroes] form 29.8 per cent of the total population, the proportion in Mississippi and South Carolina being over 55 per cent and ranging in the "black belt" counties from 50 to 90 per cent of the total population. Almost 3,000,000 are engaged in agricultural pursuits. They form 40.4 per cent of all persons engaged in these pursuits in the Southern States.

Though the United States census shows a decrease in illiteracy, there are still about 2,225,000 Negroes illiterate in the South, or over 33 per cent of the Negro population ten years of age and over.

TABLE III

	White	Colored
Total population...................................	23,682,352	8,906,879
Population six to fourteen years of age...............	4,889,762	2,023,108
Population six to fourteen*.......................	3,552,431	1,852,181
Teachers' salaries in public schools...................	$36,649,827	$5,860,876
Teachers' salaries per child six to fourteen.............	$10.32	$2.89
Per cent of illiteracy..............................	7.7	33.3
Per cent rural.....................................	76.9	78.8

* In 1,055 counties.

In the fifteen states and the District of Columbia for which salaries by race could be obtained, the public school teachers received $42,510,431 in salaries. Of this sum $36,649,827 was for the teachers of 3,552,431 white children and $5,860,876 for teachers of 1,852,181 colored children. On a per capita basis, this is $10.32 for each white child and $2.89 for each colored child.

TABLE IV

County Groups, Percentage of Negroes in the Population	White School Population	Negro School Population	Per Capita for White	Per Capita for Negro
Counties under 10 per cent..............	974,289	45,039	$ 7.96	$7.23
Counties 10 to 25 per cent..............	1,008,372	215,744	9.55	5.55
Counties 25 to 50 per cent..............	1,132,999	709,259	11.11	3.19
Counties 50 to 75 per cent..............	364,990	661,329	12.53	1.77
Counties 75 per cent and over..........	40,003	207,900	22.22	1.78

The supervisor of white elementary rural schools in one of the states recently wrote concerning the Negro schools:

"I never visit one of these [Negro] schools without feeling that we are wasting a large part of this money and are neglecting a great opportunity. The Negro school-houses are miserable beyond all description. They are usually without comfort, equipment, proper lighting, or sanitation. Nearly all of the Negroes of school age in the district are crowded into these miserable structures during the short term which the school runs. Most of the teachers are absolutely untrained and have been given certificates by the county board, not because they have passed the examination, but because it is necessary to have some kind of a Negro teacher. Among the Negro rural schools which I have visited, I have found only one in which the highest class knew the multiplication table."

A state superintendent writes:

"There has never been any serious attempt in this state to offer adequate educational facilities for the colored race. The average length of the term for the state is only four months; practically all of the schools are taught in dilapidated churches, which, of course, are not equipped with suitable desks, blackboards, and the other essentials of a school; practically all of the teachers are incompetent, possessing little or no education and having had no professional training whatever, except a few weeks obtained in the summer schools; the schools are generally overcrowded, some of them having as many as 100 students to the teacher; no attempt is made to do more than teach the children to read, write, and figure, and these subjects are learned very imperfectly. There are six or eight industrial supervisors financed in whole or in part by the Jeanes Fund; most of these teachers are stimulating the Negro schools to do very good work upon the practical things of life. A few wide-awake Negro teachers not connected with the Jeanes Fund are doing the same thing. It can probably be truthfully said that the Negro schools are gradually improving, but they are still just about as poor and inadequate as they can be."

Commenting on the cause of the migration, the *Atlanta Constitution*, a prominent southern white paper, says:

While mob violence and the falsehood which has been built upon that foundation constitutes, perhaps, a strong factor in the migration of the Negroes, there is scarcely a doubt that the educational feature enters into it. Negroes induced to go to the North undoubtedly believe they can secure better educational facilities there for their children, whether they really succeed in getting them or not.

Georgia, as well as other southern states, is undoubtedly behind in the matter of Negro education, unfair in the matter of facilities, in the quality of teachers and instructors, and in the pay of those expected to impart proper instruction to Negro children.

We have proceeded upon the theory that education would, in his own mind, at least, carry the Negro beyond his sphere; that it would give him higher ideas of himself and make of him a poorer and less satisfactory workman. That is nonsense. . . . .

B. THE NORTH

The cessation of immigration.—Prior to the war the yearly immigration to the United States equaled approximately the total Negro population of the North. Foreign labor filled the unskilled labor field, and Negroes were held closely in domestic and personal-service work. The cessation of immigration and the return of thousands of aliens to their mother-country, together with the opening of new industries and the extension of old ones, created a much greater demand for American labor. Employers looked to the South for Negroes and advertised for them.

High wages.—Wages for unskilled work in the North in 1916 and 1917 ranged from $3.00 to $8.00 a day. There were shorter hours of work and opportunity for overtime and bonuses.

Living conditions.—Houses available for Negroes in the North, though by northern standards classed as unsanitary and unfit for habitation, afforded greater comforts than the rude cabins of the plantation. For those who had owned homes in the South there was the opportunity of selling them and applying the money to payment for a good home in the North.

Identical school privileges.—Co-education of whites and Negroes in northern schools made possible a higher grade of instruction for the children of migrants.[1]

2. SENTIMENTAL CAUSES OF THE MIGRATION

The causes classed as sentimental include those which have reference to the feelings of Negroes concerning their surroundings in the South and their reactions to the social systems and practices of certain sections of the South. Frequently these causes were given as the source of an old discontent among Negroes concerning the South. Frequently they took prominence over economic causes, and they were held for the most part by a fairly high class of Negroes. These causes are in part as follows:

Lack of protection from mob violence.—Between 1885 and 1918, 2,881 Negroes were lynched in the United States, more than 85 per cent of these lynchings occurring in the South. In 1917, 2,500 Negroes were driven by force out of Dawson and Forsythe counties, Georgia.[2]

The Chicago Urban League reported that numbers of migrants from towns where lynchings had occurred registered for jobs in Chicago very shortly after lynchings. Concerning mob violence and general insecurity both whites and Negroes living in the South have had much to say. Their statements at the time of the migration are here quoted.

From the *Atlanta Constitution* (white), November 24, 1916:

Current dispatches from Albany, Georgia, in the center of the section apparently most affected, and where efforts are being made to stop the exodus by spreading correct information among the Negroes, say:

The heaviest migration of Negroes has been from those counties in which there have been the worst outbreaks against Negroes. It is developed by investigation that where there have been lynchings, the Negroes have been most eager to believe what the emigration agents have told them of plots for the removal or extermination of the race. Comparatively few Negroes have left Dougherty County, which is considered significant in view of the fact that this is one of the counties in southwest Georgia in which a lynching has never occurred.

These statements are most significant. Mob law as we have known in Georgia has furnished emigration agents with all the leverage they want; it is a foundation upon which it is easy to build with a well concocted lie or two, and they have not been slow to take advantage of it.

[1] See "Contacts in Public Schools."   [2] *Colored Missions*, January, 1921.

This loss of her best labor is another penalty Georgia is paying for her indifference and inactivity in suppressing mob law.

From the *Southwestern Christian Advocate* (Negro), April 26, 1917:

But why do they [the Negroes] go? We give a concrete answer: some months ago Anthony Crawford, a highly respectable, honest and industrious Negro, with a good farm and holdings estimated to be worth $300,000, was lynched in Abbeville, South Carolina. He was guilty of no crime. He would not be cheated out of his cotton. That was insolence. He must be taught a lesson. When the mob went for him he defended himself. They overpowered him and brutally lynched him. This murder was without excuse and was condemned in no uncertain words by the Governor, other high officials and the press in general of South Carolina. Officials pledged that the lynchers would be punished. The case went to the grand jury. Mr. Crawford was lynched in the daytime and dragged through the streets by unmasked men. The names of the leaders were supposed to have been known, and yet the grand jury, under oath, says that it could not find sufficient evidence to warrant an indictment. . . . .

Is any one surprised that Negroes are leaving South Carolina by the thousands? The wonder is that any of them remain. They will suffer in the North. Some of them will die. But Anthony Crawford did not get a chance to die in Abbeville, South Carolina. He was shamefully murdered. Any place would be paradise compared with some sections of the South where the Negroes receive such maltreatment.

From the *Savannah* (Georgia) *Morning News* (white), January 3, 1917:

Another cause is the feeling of insecurity. The lack of legal protection in the country is a constant nightmare to the colored people who are trying to accumulate a comfortable little home and farm. There is scarcely a Negro mother in the country who does not live in dread and fear that her husband or son may come in unfriendly contact with some white person as to bring the lynchers or the arresting officers to her door which may result in the wiping out of her entire family. It must be acknowledged that this is a sad condition. . . . .

The Southern white man ought to be willing to give the Negro a man's chance without regard to his race or color, give him at least the same protection of law given to anyone else. If he will not do this, the Negro must seek those North or West, who will give him better wages and better treatment. I hope, however, that this will not be necessary.

Injustice in the courts.—An excerpt from one of the newspapers of that period illustrates the basis of this cause:

While our very solvency is being sucked out from underneath we go out about affairs as usual—our police officers raid poolrooms for "loafing Negroes," bring in twelve, keep them in the barracks all night, and next morning find that many of them have steady, regular jobs, valuable assets to their white employers, suddenly left and gone to Cleveland, "where they don't arrest fifty niggers for what three of 'em done" [*Montgomery* (Alabama) *Advertiser* (white), September 21, 1916].

Inferior transporation facilities.—This refers to "Jim Crow cars," a partitioned section of one railway car, usually the baggage car, and partitioned sections of railway waiting-rooms, poorly kept, bearing signs, "For colored only." This dissatisfaction is expressed in part in the following comment of a Negro presiding elder, writing in the *Macon* (Georgia) *Ledger*, a white paper:

The petty offenses, which you mention, are far more numerous than you are aware of, besides other unjust treatments enacted daily on the streets, street cars and trains. Our women are inhumanly treated by some conductors, both on the street cars and trains. White men are often found in compartments for Negroes smoking, and if anything is said against it they who speak are insulted, or the car is purposely filled with big puffs of smoke and the conductor's reply is, "He'll quit to-rectly." Recently a white man entered a trailer for Negroes with two little dogs. One of the dogs went between the seats and crouched by a woman; she pushed him from her and the white man took both dogs and set them aside her and she was forced to ride with them. This is one of the many, many acts of injustice which often result in a row for which the Negro has to pay the penalty. These things are driving the Negro from the South.

Other causes stated are (*a*) the deprivation of the right to vote, (*b*) the "rough-handed" and unfair competition of "poor whites," (*c*) persecution by petty officers of the law, and (*d*) the "persecution of the Press."

III. BEGINNING AND SPREAD OF MIGRATION

The enormous proportions to which the exodus grew obscure its beginning. Several experiments had been tried with southern labor in the Northeast, particularly in the Connecticut tobacco fields and in Pennsylvania. In Connecticut, Negro students from the southern schools had been employed during summers with great success. Early in 1916, industries in Pennsylvania imported many Negroes from Georgia and Florida. During July one railroad company stated that it had brought to Pennsylvania more than 13,000 Negroes. They wrote back for their friends and families, and from the points to which they had been brought they spread out into new and "labor slack" territories. Once begun, this means of recruiting labor was used by hard-pressed industries in other sections of the North. The reports of high wages, of the unexpected welcome of the North, and of unusually good treatment accorded Negroes spread throughout the South from Georgia and Florida to Texas.

The stimuli of suggestion and hysteria gave the migration an almost religious significance, and it became a mass movement. Letters, rumors, Negro newspapers, gossip, and other forms of social control operated to add volume and enthusiasm to the exodus. Songs and poems of the period characterized the migration as the "Flight Out of Egypt," "Bound for the Promised Land," "Going into Canaan," "The Escape from Slavery," etc.

The first movement was from Southeast to Northeast, following main lines of transportation. Soon, however, it became known that the Middle West was similarly in need of men. Many industries advertised for southern Negroes in Negro papers. The federal Department of Labor for a period was instrumental in transporting Negroes from the South to relieve the labor shortage in other sections of the country, but discontinued such efforts when southern congressmen pointed out that the South's labor supply was being depleted.   It was brought out in the East St. Louis riot inquiry that plants there had advertised in Texas newspapers for Negro laborers.

Chicago was the logical destination of Negroes from Mississippi, Arkansas, Alabama, Louisiana, and Texas, because of the more direct railway lines, the way in which the city had become known in these sections through its two great mail-order houses, the Stock Yards, and the packing-plants with their numerous storage houses scattered in various towns and cities of the South. It was rumored in these sections that the Stock Yards needed 50,000 men; it was said that temporary housing was being provided by these hard-pressed industries.   Many Negroes came to the city on free transportation, but by far the greater numbers paid their own fare.   Club rates offered by the railroads brought the fare within reach of many who ordinarily could not have brought their families or even come themselves.   The organization into clubs composed of from ten to fifty persons from the same community had the effect, on the one hand, of adding the stimulus of intimate persuasion to the movement, and, on the other hand, of concentrating solid groups in congested spots in Chicago.

A study of certain Negro periodicals shows a powerful influence on southern Negroes already in a state of unsettlement over news of the "opening up of the North."

The *Chicago Defender* became a "herald of glad tidings" to southern Negroes.   Several cities attempted to prevent its circulation among their Negro population and confiscated the street- and store-sales supplies as fast as they came.   Negroes then relied upon subscription copies delivered through the mails.   There are reports of the clandestine circulation of copies of the paper in bundles of merchandise.   A correspondent of the *Defender* wrote: "White people are paying more attention to the race in order to keep them in the South, but the *Chicago Defender* has emblazoned upon their minds 'Bound for the Promised Land.'"

In Gulfport, Mississippi, it was stated, a man was regarded "intelligent" if he read the *Defender*, and in Laurel, Mississippi, it was said that old men who had never known how to read, bought the paper simply because it was regarded as precious.[1]

Articles and headlines carrying this special appeal which appeared in the *Defender* are quoted:

WHY SHOULD THE NEGRO STAY IN THE SOUTH?

WEST INDIANS LIVE NORTH

It is true the South is nice and warm, and may I add, so is China, and we find Chinamen living in the North, East, and West.   So is Japan, but the Japanese are living everywhere.

[1] Johnson, *Migration to Chicago.*

SCHOOL BOARDS BAD

While in Arkansas a member of the school board in one of the cities of that state (and it is said it is the rule throughout the South that a Race woman teacher to hold her school must be on friendly terms with some one of them) lived openly with a Race woman, and the entire Race, men and women, were afraid to protest or stop their children from going to school, because this school board member would get up a mob and run them out of the state. They must stomach this treatment.

FROZEN DEATH BETTER

To die from the bite of frost is far more glorious than that of the mob. I beg of you, my brothers, to leave that benighted land. You are free men. Show the world that you will not let false leaders lead you. Your neck has been in the yoke. Will you continue to keep it there because some "white folks Nigger" wants you to? Leave to all quarters of the globe. Get out of the South. Your being there in the numbers you are gives the southern politician too strong a hold on your progress.

TURN DEAF EAR

Turn a deaf ear to everybody. You see they are not lifting their laws to help you, are they? Have they stopped their Jim Crow cars? Can you buy a Pullman sleeper where you wish? Will they give you a square deal in court yet? When a girl is sent to prison, she becomes the mistress of the guards and others in authority, and women prisoners are put on the streets to work, something they don't do to a white woman. And your leaders will tell you the South is the best place for you. Turn a deaf ear to the scoundrel, and let him stay. Above all, see to it that that jumping-jack preacher is left at the South, for he means you no good here at the North.

GOOD-BYE, DIXIE LAND

One of our dear southern friends informs an anxious public that "the Negroes of the North seem to fit very well into their occupations and locations, but the southern Negro will never make a success in the North. He doesn't understand the methods there, the people and the work are wholly unsuited to him. Give him a home in the South where climatic conditions blend into his peculiar physical makeup, where he is understood and can understand, and let him have a master and you have given him the ideal home." There is the solution of the problem in a nutshell. This dear friend thinks that under a master back of the sugar cane and cotton fields, we might really be worth something to the world. How thoughtful to point out the way for our stumbling feet.

Those who live in the North presumably always lived there, and, like Topsy, they "just growed" in that section, so naturally fit well into their occupations. There is such a difference between the white man and the black man of the South; the former can travel to the North Pole if he chooses without being affected, the latter, "they say" will die of a million dread diseases if he dares to leave Dixie land, and yet the thousands who have migrated North in the past year look as well and hearty as they ever did. Something is wrong in our friend's calculations.

We hear again and again of our "peculiar physical makeup." Is there something radically different about us that is not found in other people? Why the constant fear of Negro supremacy if the white brain is more active and intelligent than the brain found in the colored man? A good lawyer never fears a poor one in a court battle—he knows that he has him bested from the start. The fact that we have made good wherever and whenever given an opportunity, we admit, is a little disquieting, but it is a way we have, and is hard to get out of. Once upon a time we permitted other people to think for us—today we are thinking and acting for ourselves, with the result that our "friends" are getting alarmed at our progress. We'd like to oblige these unselfish (?) souls and remain slaves in the South, but to other sections of the country we have said, as the song goes: "I hear you calling me," and boarded the train singing, "Good-by to Dixie-Land."

News articles in the *Defender* kept alive the enthusiasm and fervor of the exodus:

LEAVING FOR THE NORTH

Tampa, Fla., Jan. 19.—J. T. King, supposed to be a race leader, is using his wits to get on the good side of the white people by calling a meeting to urge our people not to migrate North.   King has been termed a "good nigger" by his pernicious activity on the emigration question. Reports have been received here that all who have gone North are at work and pleased with the splendid conditions in the North. It is known here that in the North there is a scarcity of labor, mills and factories are open to them. People are not paying any attention to King and are packing and ready to travel North to the "promised land."

DETERMINED TO GO NORTH

Jackson, Miss., March 23.—Although the white police and sheriff and others are using every effort to intimidate the citizens from going North, even Dr. Redmond's speech was circulated around, this has not deterred our people from leaving. Many have walked miles to take the train for the North. There is a determination to leave and there is no hand save death to keep them from it.

THOMAS LIKES THE NORTH

J. H. Thomas, Birmingham, Ala., Brownsville Colony, has been here several weeks and is very much pleased with the North. He is working at the Pullman shops, making twice as much as he did at home. Mr. Thomas says the "exodus" will be greater later on in the year, that he did not find four feet of snow or would freeze to death. He lives at 346 East Thirty-fifth St.

LEAVING FOR THE EAST

Huntsville, Ala., Jan. 19.—Fifteen families, all members of the Race, left here today for Pittsburgh, Pa., where they will take positions as butlers, and maids, getting sixty to seventy-five dollars per month, against fifteen and twenty paid here, Most of them claim that they have letters from their friends who went early and made good, saying that there was plenty of work, and this field of labor is short, owing to the vast amount of men having gone to Europe and not returned.

THEY'RE LEAVING MEMPHIS IN DROVES

Some are coming on the passenger,
Some are coming on the freight,
Others will be found walking,
For none have time to wait.

Other headlines read: "Thousands Leave Memphis"; "Still Planning to Come North"; "Northbound Their Cry." These articles are especially interesting for the impelling power of the suggestion of a great mass movement.

Denunciation of the South.—The idea that the South is a bad place, unfit for the habitation of Negroes, was "played up" and emphasized by the *Defender*. Conditions most distasteful to Negroes were given first prominence. In this it had a clear field, for the local southern Negro papers dared not make such unrestrained utterances. Articles of this type appeared:

EXODUS TO START

Forest City, Ark., Feb. 16.—David B. Smith (white) is on trial for life for the brutal murder of a member of the Race, W. H. Winford, who refused to be whipped like others. This white man had the habit of making his "slave" submit to this sort of punishment and when Winford refused to stand for it, he was whipped to death with a "black snake" whip. The trial of Smith is attracting very little attention. As a matter of fact, the white people here think nothing of it as the dead man is a "nigger."

This very act, coupled with other recent outrages that have been heaped upon our people, are causing thousands to leave, not waiting for the great spring movement in May.

The *Defender* had a favorite columnist, W. Allison Sweeney. His specialty was "breaking southerners and 'white folks' niggers on the wheel." One of his articles in the issue of June 23, 1917, was captioned: "A Chicago 'Nigger' Preacher, a 'Feeder,' of The 'Little Hells,' Springs up to Hinder Our Brethren Coming North."

A passage from this article will illustrate the temper of his writings. Aroused by what he calls a "white folks nigger," he remarks:

Such a creature has recently been called to my attention, and for the same reason that an unchecked rat has been known to jeopardize the life of a great ship, a mouse's nibble of a match to set a mansion aflame, I've concluded to carve a

"Slice of liver or two"

from that bellowing ass, who, at this very moment no doubt, somewhere in the South, is going up and down the land, telling the natives *why* they should be content, as the *Tribune*, puts it, to become "Russianized," to remain in that land—to them—of *blight;* of *murdered* kin, *deflowered* womanhood, *wrecked* homes, *strangled* ambitions, *make-believe* schools, *roving* "gun parties," *midnight arrests, rifled* virginity, *trumped up* charges, *lonely* graves, where owls hoot, and where friends dare not go! Do you wonder at the thousands leaving the land where every foot of ground marks a tragedy, leaving the grave of their fathers and all that is dear, to seek their fortunes in the North? And you who say that their going is to seek better wages are insulting truth, dethroning reason, and consoling yourself with a groundless allegation.

Retaliation.—In answer to the warnings of the South against the rigors of the northern winters, articles of this nature appeared:

FREEZING TO DEATH IN THE SOUTH

So much has been said through the white papers in the South about the members of the race freezing to death in the North. They freeze to death down South when they don't take care of themselves. There is no reason for any human staying in the Southland on this bugaboo handed out by the white press, when the following clippings are taken from the same journals:

AGED NEGRO FROZEN TO DEATH

Albany, Ga., Feb. 8.—Yesterday the dead body of Peter Crowder, an old Negro, was found in an out-of-the-way spot where he had been frozen to death during the recent cold snap [from the *Macon* (Georgia) *Telegraph*].

DIES FROM EXPOSURE

Spartanburg, Feb. 6.—Marshall Jackson, a Negro man, who lived on the farm of J. T. Harris near Campobello Sunday night froze to death [from the *South Carolina State*].

NEGRO FROZEN TO DEATH IN FIRELESS GRETNA HUT

Coldest weather of the last four years claimed a victim Friday night, when Archie Williams, a Negro, was frozen to death in his bed in a little hut in the outskirts of Gretna [from the *New Orleans Item*, dated Feb. 4th].

NEGRO WOMAN FROZEN TO DEATH MONDAY

Harriet Tolbert, an aged Negro woman, was frozen to death in her home at 18 Garibaldi Street early Monday morning during the severe cold [Atlanta (Ga.) *Constitution*, dated Feb. 6].

If you can freeze to death in the North and be free, why freeze to death in the South and be a slave, where your mother, sister, and daughter are raped and burned at stake, where your father, brother and son are treated with contempt and hung to a pole, riddled with bullets at the least mention that he does not like the way he has been treated?

Come North then, all of you folks, both good and bad. If you don't behave yourself up here, the jails will certainly make you wish you had. For the hard working man there is plenty of work—if you really want it. The *Defender* says come.

Still in another mood:

DIED, BUT TOOK ONE WITH HIM

Alexandria, La., Sept. 29.—Joe Pace (white) a southern workman, who had a way of bulldozing members of the Race employed by the Elizabeth Lumber Company, met his match here last Saturday night.

Pace got into one of his moods and kicked a fellow named Israel. Israel determined to get justice some way and knowing that the courts were only for white men in this part of the country, he took a shot at Pace and his aim was good.

Another type of article appeared. In keeping with the concept of the South as a bad place for Negroes, their escape from it under exceptional circumstances was given unique attention. Thus, there were reported the following kind of cases.

SAVED FROM THE SOUTH

Lawyers Save Another from Being Taken South

SAVED FROM THE SOUTH

Charged with Murder, but His Release Is Secured by Habeas Corpus

NEW SCHEME TO KEEP RACE MEN IN DIXIE LAND

A piece of poetry which received widespread popularity appeared in the *Defender* under the title "Bound for the Promise Land." Other published poems expressing the same sentiment were: "Farewell, We're Good and Gone"; "Northward Bound"; "The Land of Hope."

Five young men were arraigned before Judge E. Schwartz for reading poetry. The police claim they were inciting riot in the city and over Georgia. Two of the men were sent to Brown farm for thirty days, a place not fit for human beings. Tom Amaca was arrested for having "Bound for the Promise Land," a poem published in the *Defender* several months ago. J. N. Chislom and A. A. Walker were arrested because they were said to be the instigators of the movement of the race to the North, where work is plentiful and better treatment is given.

The "Great Northern Drive."—The setting of definite dates was another stimulus. The "Great Northern Drive" was scheduled to begin May 15, 1917. This date, or the week following, corresponds with the date of the heaviest arrivals in the North, the period of greatest temporary congestion and awakening of the North to the presence of the new arrivals. Letters to the *Chicago Defender* and to social agencies in the North informed them of many Negroes who were preparing to come in the "Great Drive." The following letter tells its own story:

April 24th, 1917

Mr. R. S. Abbot

SIR: I have been reading the *Defender* for one year or more and last February I read about the Great Northern Drive to take place May 15th on Thursday and now I can hear so many people speaking of an excursion to the North on the 15th of May for $3.00. My husband is in the North already working, and he wants us to come up in May, so I want to know if it is true about the excursion. I am getting ready and oh so many others also, and we want to know is that true so we can be in the Drive. So please answer at once. We are getting ready.

Yours,

———

Usually the dates set were for Wednesday and Saturday nights, following pay days.

It is probably no exaggeration to say that the *Defender's* policy prompted thousands of restless Negroes to venture North, where they were assured of its protection and championship of their cause. Many migrants in Chicago attribute their presence in the North to the *Defender's* encouraging pictures of relief from conditions at home with which they became increasingly dissatisfied as they read.

A NEGRO FAMILY JUST ARRIVED IN CHICAGO FROM THE RURAL SOUTH

NEGRO CHURCH IN THE SOUTH

IV. THE ARRIVAL IN CHICAGO

At the time of the migration the great majority of Negroes in Chicago lived in a limited area on the South Side, principally between Twenty-second and Thirty-ninth streets, Wentworth Avenue and State Street, and in scattered groups to Cottage Grove Avenue on the east.   State Street was the main thoroughfare.   Prior to the influx of southern Negroes, many houses stood vacant in the section west of State Street, from which Negroes had moved when better houses became available east of State Street.   Into these old and frequently almost uninhabitable houses the first newcomers moved.   Because of its proximity to the old vice area this district had an added undesirability for old Chicagoans.   The newcomers, however, were unacquainted with its reputation and had no hesitancy about moving in until better homes could be secured.   As the number of arrivals increased, a scarcity of houses followed, creating a problem of acute congestion.

During the summer of 1917 the Chicago Urban League made a canvass of real estate dealers supplying houses for Negroes, and found that in a single day there were 664 Negro applicants for houses, and only fifty houses available.   In some instances as many as ten persons were listed for a single house. This condition did not continue long.   There were counted thirty-six new neighborhoods, formerly white, opening up to Negroes within three months.

At the same time rents increased from 5 to 30 and sometimes as much as 50 per cent.   A more detailed study of living conditions among the early migrants in Chicago was made by the Chicago School of Civics and Philanthropy. The inquiry included seventy-five families of less than a year's residence. In the group were sixty married couples, 128 children, eight women, nine married men with families in the South.   Of these migrants forty-five families came from rural and thirty-two from urban localities.   The greatest number, twenty-nine, came from Alabama; twenty-five were from Mississippi, eleven from Louisiana, five from Georgia, four from Arkansas, two from Tennessee, and one from Florida.   Forty-one of these seventy-five families were each living in one room.   These rooms were rented by the week, thus making possible an easy change of home at the first opportunity.

It was at this period that the greatest excitement over the "incoming hordes of Negroes" prevailed.

A significant feature was the large number of young children found.   The age distribution of 128 children in these seventy-five families was forty-seven under seven years, forty-one between seven and fourteen years, and forty over fourteen years.

Most of these children were of school age and had come from districts in the South which provided few school facilities.   The parents were unaccustomed to the requirements of northern schools in matters of discipline, attendance, and scholarship.   Considerable difficulty was experienced by teachers, parents, and children in these first stages of adjustment.

V. ADJUSTMENTS TO CHICAGO LIFE

Meeting actual conditions of life in Chicago brought its exaltations and disillusionments to the migrants. These were reflected in the schools, public amusement places, industry, and the street cars. The Chicago Urban League, Negro churches, and Negro newspapers assumed the task of making the migrants into "city folk." The increase in church membership indicates prompt efforts to re-engage in community life and establish agreeable and helpful associations. It also reflects the persistence of religious life among the migrants. This increase is shown in Table V.

Adjustment to new conditions was taken up by the Urban League as its principal work. Co-operating with the Travelers Aid Society, United Charities, and other agencies of the city, it met the migrants at stations and, as far as its facilities permitted, secured living quarters and jobs for them. The churches took them into membership and attempted to make them feel at home. Negro

TABLE V

NAME OF CHURCH	INCREASE IN MEMBERSHIP DURING MIGRATION PERIOD	
	Number	Percentage
Salem........................	700	51
Olivet........................	5,543	80
South Park....................	2,425	1,872
St. Mark's....................	1,800	100
Hyde Park.....................	95	131
Bethel........................	650	800
Walters.......................	351	338

newspapers published instructions on dress and conduct and had great influence in smoothing down improprieties of manner which were likely to provoke criticism and intolerance in the city.

Individual experiences of the migrants in this period of adjustment were often interesting. The Commission made a special effort to note these experiences for the light they throw upon the general process. Much of the adjustment was a double process, including the adjustment of rural southern Negroes to northern urban conditions. It is to be remembered that over 70 per cent of the Negro population of the South is rural. This means familiarity with rural methods, simple machinery, and plain habits of living. Farmers and plantation workers coming to Chicago had to learn new tasks. Skilled craftsmen had to relearn their trades when they were thrown amid the highly specialized processes of northern industries. Domestic servants went into industry. Professional men who followed their clientèle had to re-establish themselves in a new community. The small business men could not compete with the Jewish merchants, who practically monopolized the trade of Negroes near their residential areas, or with the "Loop" stores.

Many Negroes sold their homes and brought their furniture with them. Reinvesting in property frequently meant a loss; the furniture brought was often found to be unsuited to the tiny apartments or large, abandoned dwelling-houses they were able to rent or buy.

The change of home carried with it in many cases a change of status. The leader in a small southern community, when he came to Chicago, was immediately absorbed into the struggling mass of unnoticed workers. School teachers, male and female, whose positions in the South carried considerable prestige, had to go to work in factories and plants because the disparity in educational standards would not permit continuance of their profession in Chicago.

These illustrations in Table VI, taken from family histories, show how adjustment led to inferior occupation.

TABLE VI

Occupation in South	Occupation on First Arrival in Chicago	Occupation One or More Years Later
Display man on furniture	Laborer	Laborer in factory
Stone mason	Laborer in coal yard	Laborer in Stock Yards
Proprietor of café	Laborer	Elevator man
Farmer	Laborer in Stock Yards	Laborer in Stock Yards
Coal miner	Porter in tailoring shop	Janitor
Proprietor of boarding-house	Laborer	Laborer in Stock Yards
Farmer	Factory worker	Factory worker
Barber	Painter	Janitor
Hotel waiter	Waiter	Porter in factory
Plasterer	Laborer in Stock Yards	Laborer in steel mill
Farmer	Hostler	Laborer in livery stable
Clergyman	Stationary fireman	Laborer in Stock Yards
Tinsmith	Waiter	Laborer
Farmer	Laborer in cement factory	Laborer in Stock Yards
Blacksmith	Barber	Janitor
Office boy	Porter	Laborer in Stock Yards

The following experiences of one or two families from the many histories gathered, while not entirely typical of all the migrants, contain features common to all:

The Thomas family.—Mr. Thomas, his wife and two children, a girl nineteen and a boy seventeen, came to Chicago from Seals, Alabama, in the spring of 1917.

After a futile search, the family rented rooms for the first week. This was expensive and inconvenient, and between working hours all sought a house into which they could take their furniture. They finally found a five-room flat on Federal Street. The building had been considered uninhabitable and dangerous. Three of the five rooms were almost totally dark. The plumbing was out of order. There was no bath, and the toilet was outside of the house. There was neither electricity nor gas, and the family used oil lamps. The rent was $15 per month. Although the combined income of the family could easily have made possible a better house, they could find none.

Mr. and Mrs. Thomas were farmers in the South. On the farm Mrs. Thomas did the work of a man along with her husband. Both are illiterate. The daughter had reached the fourth grade and the boy the fifth grade in school. At home they belonged to a church and various fraternal orders and took part in rural community life.

On their arrival in Chicago they were short of funds. Father and son went to work at the Stock Yards. Although they had good jobs they found their income insufficient; the girl went to work in a laundry, and the mother worked as a laundress through the first winter for $1 a day. She later discovered that she was working for half the regular rate for laundry work. Soon she went back to housekeeping to reduce the food bill.

All the family were timid and self-conscious and for a long time avoided contacts, thus depriving themselves of helpful suggestions. The children became ashamed of the manners of their parents and worked diligently to correct their manner of speech. The children attended Wendell Phillips night school in the hope of improving their community status.

The freedom and independence of Negroes in the North have been a constant novelty to them and many times they have been surprised that they were "not noticed enough to be mistreated." They have tried out various amusement places, parks, ice-cream parlors, and theaters near their home on the South Side and have enjoyed them because they were denied these opportunities in their former home.

The combined income of this family is $65 a week, and their rent is now low. Many of their old habits have been preserved because of the isolation in which they have lived and because they have not been able to move into better housing.

The Jones family.—Mr. Jones, his wife, a six-year-old son, and a nephew aged twenty-one, came from Texas early in 1919. Although they arrived after the heaviest migration, they experienced the same difficulties as earlier comers.

They searched for weeks for a suitable house. At first they secured one room on the South Side in a rooming-house, where they were obliged to provide gas, coal, linen, bedding, and part of the furniture. After a few weeks they got two rooms for light housekeeping, for $10 a month. The associations as well as the physical condition of the house were intolerable. They then rented a flat on Carroll Avenue in another section. The building was old and run down. The agent for the property, to induce tenants to occupy it, had promised to clean and decorate it, but failed to keep his word. When the Jones family asked the owner to make repairs, he refused flatly and was exceedingly abusive.

Finally Jones located a house on the West Side that was much too large for his family, and the rent too high. They were forced to take lodgers to aid in paying the rent. This was against the desire of Mrs. Jones, who did not like to have strangers in her house. The house has six rooms and bath and is in a state of dilapidation. Mr. Jones has been forced to cover the holes in the floor with tin to keep out the rats. The plumbing is bad. During the winter there is no running water, and the agent for the building refuses to clean more than three rooms or to furnish screens or storm doors or to pay for any plumbing. In the back yard under the house is an accumulation of ashes, tin cans, and garbage left by a long series of previous tenants. There is no alley back of the house, and all of the garbage from the back yard must be carried out through the front. Jones made a complaint about insanitary conditions to the Health Department, and the house was inspected, but so far nothing has been done. It was difficult to induce the agent to supply garbage cans.

Jones had reached the eighth grade, and Mrs. Jones had completed the first year of high school. The nephew had finished public-school grades provided in his home town and had been taught the boiler trade. He is now pursuing this trade in hope of securing sufficient funds to complete his course in Conroe College, where he has already finished the first year. The boy of six was placed in a West Side school. He was removed from this school, however, and sent back south to live with Mrs. Jones's mother and attend school there. Mrs. Jones thought that the influence of the school children of Chicago was not good for him. He had been almost blinded by a blow from a baseball bat in the hands of one of several older boys who continually annoyed him. The child had also learned vulgar language from his school associates.

The Jones family were leading citizens in their southern home. They were members of a Baptist church, local clubs, and a missionary society, while Jones was a member and officer in the Knights of Tabor, Masons, and Odd Fellows. They owned their home and two other pieces of property in the same town, one of which brought in $20 a month. As a boiler-maker, he earned about $50 a week, which is about the same as his present income. Their motive in coming to Chicago was to escape from the undesirable practices and customs of the South.

They had been told that no discrimination was practiced against Negroes in Chicago; that they could go where they pleased without the embarrassment or hindrance because of their color. Accordingly, when they first came to Chicago, they went into drug-stores and restaurants. They were refused service in numbers of restaurants and at the refreshment counters in some drug-stores. The family has begun the re-establishment of its community life, having joined a West Side Baptist church and taking an active interest in local organizations, particularly the Wendell Phillips Social Settlement. The greatest satisfaction of the Joneses comes from the "escape from Jim Crow conditions and segregation" and the securing of improved conditions of work, although there is no difference in the wages.

VI. MIGRANTS IN CHICAGO

Migrants have been visited in their homes, and met in industry, in the schools, and in contacts on street cars and in parks. Efforts have been made to learn why they came to Chicago and with what success they were adjusting themselves to their new surroundings.

Some of the replies to questions asked are given:
Question: Why did you come to Chicago?

Answers:
1. Looking for better wages.
2. So I could support my family.
3. Tired of being a flunky.
4. I just happened to drift here.
5. Some of my people were here.
6. Persuaded by friends.
7. Wanted to make more money so I could go into business; couldn't do it in the South.
8. To earn more money.
9. For better wages.
10. Wanted to change and come to the North.
11. Came to get more money for work.
12. To better my conditions.
13. Better conditions.
14. Better conditions.
15. Better living.
16. More work; came on visit and stayed.
17. Wife persuaded me.
18. To establish a church.
19. Tired of the South.
20. To get away from the South, and to earn more money.

Question: Do you feel greater freedom and independence in Chicago? In what ways?
Answers:
1. Yes. Working conditions and the places of amusement.
2. Yes. The chance to make a living; conditions on the street cars and in movies.
3. Going into places of amusement and living in good neighborhoods.
4. Yes. Educationally, and in the home conditions.
5. Yes. Go anywhere you want to go; voting; don't have to look up to the white man, get off the street for him, and go to the buzzard roost at shows.
6. Yes. Just seem to feel a general feeling of good-fellowship.
7. On the street cars and the way you are treated where you work.
8. Yes. Can go any place I like here. At home I was segregated and not treated like I had any rights.
9. Yes. Privilege to mingle with people; can go to the parks and places of amusement, not being segregated.
10. Yes. Feel free to do anything I please. Not dictated to by white people.
11. Yes. Had to take any treatment white people offered me there, compelled to say "yes ma'am" or "yes sir" to white people, whether you desired to or not. If you went to an ice cream parlor for anything you came outside to eat it. Got off sidewalk for white people.
12. Yes. Can vote; feel free; haven't any fear; make more money.
13. Yes. Voting; better opportunity for work; more respect from white people.
14. Yes. Can vote; no lynching; no fear of mobs; can express my opinion and defend myself.
15. Yes. Voting, more privileges; white people treat me better, not as much prejudice.

16. Yes.   Feel more like a man.   Same as slavery, in a way, at home.   I don't have to give up the sidewalk here for white people as in my former home.
17. Yes.   No restrictions as to shows, schools, etc.   More protection of law.
18. Yes.   Have more privileges and more money.
19. Yes.   More able to express views on all questions.   No segregation or discrimination.
20. Sure.   Feel more freedom.   Was not counted in the South; colored people allowed no freedom at all in the South.
21. Find things quite different to what they are at home.   Haven't become accustomed to the place yet.

Question: What were your first impressions of Chicago?
Answers:

1. I liked the air of doing things here.
2. A place of real opportunity if you would work.
3. Place just full of life.   Went to see the sights every night for a month.
4. I thought it was some great place but found out it wasn't.   Uncle told me he was living on Portland Avenue, that it was some great avenue; found nothing but a mud hole.   I sure wished I was back home.
5. When I got here and got on the street cars and saw colored people sitting by white people all over the car I just held my breath, for I thought any minute they would start something, then I saw nobody noticed it, and I just thought this was a real place for colored people.   No, indeed, I'll never work in anybody's kitchen but my own, any more, that's the one thing that makes me stick to this job.
6. Was completely lost, friend was to meet me but didn't and I was afraid to ask anyone where to go; finally my friend came; was afraid to sleep first night—so much noise; thought the cars would finally stop running so I could rest.
7. Liked the place.
8. Always liked Chicago, even the name before I came.
9. Liked it fine.
10. Good city for colored people.
11. Fine city.
12. Thought it the best place for colored people.
13. Thought it a good place for colored people to live in.
14. Very favorable, thought it the place to be for myself and family.
15. Didn't like it; lonesome, until I went out.   Then liked the places of amusement which have no restrictions.
16. Liked it fine, like it even better now.
17. Liked Chicago from the first visit made two years ago; was not satisfied until I was able to get back.
18. Think I will like it later on.

Question: In what respects is life harder or easier here than in the South?
Answers:

1. Easier.   I don't have to work so hard and get more money.
2. Easier in that here my wife doesn't have to work.   I just couldn't make it by myself in the South.
3. Living is much easier; chance to learn a trade.   I make and save more money.

4. Easier, you can make more money and it means more to you.
5. Easier to make a living here.
6. Easier, I get more money for my work and have some spare time.
7. Have better home, but have to work harder. I make more money, but spend it all to live.
8. Have more time to rest here and don't work as hard.
9. Find it easier to live because I have more to live on.
10. Earn more money; the strain is not so great wondering from day to day how to make a little money do.
11. Work harder here than at home.
12. Easier. Work is hard, but hours are short. I make more money and can live better.
13. More money for work, though work is harder. Better able to buy the necessities of life.
14. Easier; more work and more money and shorter hours.
15. Living higher, but would rather be here than in South. I have shorter hours here.
16. Don't have to work as hard here as at home. Have more time for rest and to spend with family.
17. Easier to live in St. Louis. More work here and better wages. Living higher here. Saved more there.
18. Must work very hard here, much harder than at home.
19. Harder because of increased cost of living.
20. The entire family feels that life is much easier here than at home. Do not find work as hard anywhere.

Question: What do you like about the North?
Answers:

1. Freedom in voting and conditions of colored people here. I mean you can live in good houses; men here get a chance to go with the best-looking girls in the race; some may do it in Memphis, but it ain't always safe.
2. Freedom and chance to make a living; privileges.
3. Freedom and opportunity to acquire something.
4. Freedom allowed in every way.
5. More money and more pleasure to be gotten from it; personal freedom Chicago affords, and voting.
6. Freedom and working conditions.
7. Work, can work any place, freedom.
8. The schools for the children, the better wages, and the privileges for colored people.
9. The chance colored people have to live; privileges allowed them and better homes.
10. The friendliness of the people, the climate which makes health better.
11. Like the privileges, the climate; have better health.
12. No discrimination; can express opinion and vote.
13. Freedom of speech, right to live and work as other races. Higher pay for labor.
14. Freedom; privileges; treatment of whites; ability to live in peace; not held down.

15. Freedom of speech and action.   Can live without fear, no Jim Crow.
16. More enjoyment; more places of attraction; better treatment; better schools for children.
17. Liberty, better schools.
18. I like the North for wages earned and better homes colored people can live in and go more places than at home.
19. Privileges, freedom, industrial and educational facilities.
20. The people, the freedom and liberty colored people enjoy here that they never before experienced.   Even the ways of the people are better than at home.
21. Haven't found anything yet to like, except wife thinks she will like the opportunity of earning more money than ever before.

Question: What difficulties do you think a person from the South meets in coming to Chicago?

Answers:

1. Getting used to climate and houses.
2. Getting accustomed to cold weather and flats.
3. Getting used to living conditions and make more money; not letting the life here run away with you.
4. Adjusting myself to the weather and flat life: rooming and "closeness" of the houses.
5. Getting used to flat conditions and crowded houses.
6. Getting used to living in flats, and growing accustomed to being treated like people.
7. Getting used to the ways of the people; not speaking or being friendly; colder weather, hard on people from the South.
8. Just the treatment some of the white people give you on the trains.   Sometimes treat you like dogs.
9. Know of no difficulties a person from the South meets coming to Chicago.
10. I didn't meet any difficulties coming from the South.   Know of none persons would likely meet.
11. Can think of no difficulties persons meet coming from the South to Chicago.
12. Adjustment to working conditions and climate.
13. Climatic changes.
14. Change in climate, crowded living conditions, lack of space for gardens, etc.
15. Change in climate, crowded housing conditions.
16. Coming without knowing where they are going to stop usually causes some difficulty.   Get in with wrong people who seek to take advantage of the ignorance of newcomers.
17. Becoming adjusted to climate.
18. If they know where they are going, when they come here.   The danger lies in getting among the wrong class of people.
19. Adjustment to city customs, etc.
20. If persons know where they are going and what they are going to do, will not have any trouble.   Must come with the intention of working or else expect many difficulties.
21. Know of no difficulties.

Question: Do you get more comforts and pleasures from your higher wages?

Answers:

1. Yes. Better homes, places of amusement, and the buying of your clothes here. You can try on things; you can do that in some stores in Memphis, but not in all.

2. Yes. Living in better houses, can go into almost any place if you have the money, and then the schools are so much better here.

3. Yes. I live better, save more, and feel more like a man.·

4. Yes. I can buy more, my wife can have her clothes fitted here, she can try on a hat, and if she doesn't want it she doesn't have to keep it; go anywhere I please on the cars after I pay my fare; I can do any sort of work I know how to do.

5. Yes. Go anywhere I please, buy what I please; ain't afraid to get on cars and sit where I please.

6. Well, I make more money. I can't save anything from it. There are so many places to go here, but down South you work, work, work, and you have to save, for you haven't any place to spend it.

7. Yes. Better homes. Spend money anywhere you want to, go anywhere you have money enough to go; don't go out very much but like to know I can where and when I want to.

8. Have chance to make more money, but it is all spent to keep family up.

9. At home did not earn much money and did not have any left to go what few places colored people were allowed to go. Here, Negroes can have whatever they want.

10. Don't have to worry about how you are going to live. More money earned affords anything wanted.

11. Have more comforts in the home that could not have at home; more conveniences here. Wages sons earn make it possible to have all that is wanted.

12. Yes. Better houses and more enjoyment.

13. Yes. I live in larger house and have more conveniences. Can take more pleasure; have more leisure time.

14. Yes. Better houses and more amusement. More time of my own, better furniture and food.

15. Yes. Better houses and furniture. More pleasures because of shorter hours of work, giving me more time.

16. What little was earned at home was used for food and clothing. Here, earn more, have more to spend; now and then put some in the bank, and can spend some for pleasure without strain or inconvenience.

17. Yes. More places to go, parks and playgrounds for children, and no difference made between white and colored. Houses more convenient here.

18. Have more money to spend but when you have to live in houses where landlord won't fix up you can't have much comfort. Go no place for pleasure, but enjoy the chance of earning more money.

19. No comment.

20. Have money to get whatever is desired. Live in a better house and can go places denied at home. All the family are perfectly satisfied and are happier than they have ever been.

21. Live in better house than ever lived in. Never had the comforts furnished here. Some houses there had no water closets; only had cistern and wells out in the yard.

Question: Are you advising friends to come to Chicago?
Answers:

1. Yes. People down there don't really believe the things we write back, I didn't believe myself until I got here.
2. No. I am not going to encourage them to come, for they might not make it, then I would be blamed.
3. Yes. If I think they will work.
4. Some of them, those who I think would appreciate the advantages here.
5. No. Not right now, come here and get to work, strikes come along, they're out of work. Come if they want to, though.
6. Yes. I have two sisters still in Lexington. I am trying to get them to come up here. They can't understand why I stay here, but they'll see if they come.
7. Yes. People here don't realize how some parts of the South treat colored folks; poor white trash were awful mean where we came from; wish all the colored folks would come up here where you ain't afraid to breathe.
8. Yes. Want friend and husband to come; also sister and family who want her to come back that they may see how she looks before they break up and come. Youngest son begs mother never to think of going back South. Oldest son not so well satisfied when first came, but since he is working, likes it a little better.

Only a few migrants were found who came on free transportation, and many of these had friends in Chicago before they came. Few expressed a desire to return.

VII.   EFFORTS TO CHECK MIGRATION

The withdrawal of great numbers of Negroes, both because of the migration and because of military service, left large gaps in the industries of the South dependent upon Negro labor. Thousands of acres of rice and sugar cane went to waste. The turpentine industry of the Carolinas and the milling interests of Tennessee were hard pressed for labor. Cotton-growing was much affected, especially in the delta region of Mississippi. The situation became critical, presenting a real economic problem. Organized efforts were made, and at times extreme measures were taken, to start a return movement. A report was circulated that on one day in the winter of 1919 in Chicago, 17,000 Negroes were counted in a bread line. The "horrors of northern winters" were played up as they had been during the migration.

The press throughout the country was used to spread broadcast the South's needs, its kind treatment of Negroes, its opportunities, and its growing change of heart on the question of race relations. Newspaper articles from sections of the North and South carried about the same story. The *Chicago Tribune* said in a conspicuous headline: "Louisiana Wants Negroes to Return." Other such headlines were: *Washington Post*—"South Needs Negroes. Try to Get Labor for Their Cotton Fields. Tell of Kind Treatment"; *New York Evening Sun*—"To Aid Negro Return"; *Philadelphia Press*—"South Is Urging Negroes to Return. Many Districts Willing to Pay Fare of Those

Who Come Back"; *Memphis Commercial Appeal*—"South Is Best for Negro, Say Mississippians.   Colored People Found Prosperous and Happy."

Though such reports were widely circulated throughout the North, the actual efforts of agencies from the South seeking the return of Negro labor centered around Chicago.   This was due largely to the fact that from the southern states most acutely in need the drift during the migration had been to Chicago, and because the increase of Chicago's Negro population had been so great.

Immediately following the riots in Chicago and Washington, rumors gained wide currency that hundreds of migrants were leaving for sections of the South.   So strong was the belief in the truth of this report that a Chicago newspaper telegraphed the governors of southern states inquiring the number of Negroes they needed.   Agents of the South, including representatives of the Tennessee Association of Commerce, the Department of Immigration of Louisiana, the Mississippi Welfare League, and the Southern Alluvial Land Association, visited northern cities with a view to providing means for the return of Negroes.   Although free transportation was offered, together with promises of increased wages and better living conditions, the various commissions were disappointed.

Their interviews with Negroes living in Chicago revealed a determination not to return to conditions they had left two years before.   To offset this objection, two Chicago Negroes and one white man were taken to Mississippi by a representative of the Mississippi Welfare League to make an investigation.   They visited several delta towns, traveling for the most part in automobiles and interviewing farmers and laborers.   They reported in substance as follows:

Railroad accommodations for Negroes were adequate and uniform, irrespective of locality;   treatment accorded Negro passengers by railroad officials was courteous throughout.   Public-school terms were nine months in the city and eight months in the country for white and colored alike, and the strongest possible human ties between planter and worker exist. . . . . In no instance were Negroes not given the freest use of sidewalks, streets, and thoroughfares and we were unable to find any trace of friction of any kind between the races.

An effort was then made by the Chicago Urban League to ascertain the precise state of affairs.   Its southern representative questioned hundreds of Negroes living in the South, regarding improved relationships.   Answers to this query were all about the same.   Some of them are quoted:

There has been no change.   Lincoln League organized in this city has been denounced by the white newspapers as a movement that will cause trouble, and the National Association for the Advancement of Colored People, and the Urban Leagues of various cities have been called "strife breeders and meddlers in southern affairs"; Jim Crow accommodations are just the same as ever.   If there is any change for the better, I can't see it.

It is ridiculous for any Negro to say he finds conditions better here. Don't you remember that Negroes answering an invitation to meet the Welfare Committee of white men not long ago were told as soon as they got into the meeting place that the Committee was ready to hear what Negroes wanted, but that the question of the Negro's right to exercise the right of voting would not be allowed to be discussed at all, and that that must be agreed to before any discussion whatever would be entertained, and that the Negroes left the meeting place without a chance to demand the one thing they wished to enjoy?

Some deceitful, lying Negro may say that times are better, but he would, at the same time, know that he was not telling the truth. Haven't you been hearing more reports of lynching of Negroes than you ever did in your life, since the war? Where, then, is there any improvement? Ain't all the judges, all the police and constables, all the juries as white man as ever? Does the word of a Negro count for more now than it did before the war? Don't white men insult our wives and daughters and sisters and get off at it, unless we take the law into our own hand and punish them for it ourselves, and get lynched for protecting our own, just as often as ever? How much more schooling from public funds do our children get now than they got before the war? How much more do we have to say now than we had to say before the war about the way the taxes we pay shall be spent for schools, or for salaries, or for anything connected with administration and government? Why, even the colored man in Caddo parish who subscribed for $100,000 in Liberty bonds and bought lots of War Savings stamps, and others who bought less, but in the hundreds, and thousands of the bonds and War Saving stamps, have no more to say about affairs now than they ever had. Where is the improvement?

The Urban League also made an inquiry into the numbers of Negroes leaving and arriving in the week following the riot, and when the strongest efforts were being made to induce a return of migrants. During this period 261 Negroes came to Chicago and 219 left the city. Of the 219 leaving, eighty-three gave some southern state as their destination. For the most part, they were persons returning from vacations in the North, and Chicago Negroes going South to visit or on business. Some were rejoining their families. Fourteen were leaving because of the riot. None, however, indicated any intention of going South to work.

It is clear that migrant Negroes are not returning South. On the contrary, there is a small but continuous stream of migration to the industrial centers of the North. No great number of Negroes returned to the South even during the trying unemployment period in the early part of 1921. Census figures for Chicago for 1920 show a number much smaller than the usual estimates of the size of the Negro population during the period of the heaviest migration. This may be accounted for by the fact that Chicago has been used as a re-routing point to other northern cities. The decrease from 1918 undoubtedly means that some returned to the South, but it is apparent that the great majority of the migrants remain, despite the hardships attending shortage of work.

CHAPTER IV

THE NEGRO POPULATION OF CHICAGO

A. DISTRIBUTION AND DENSITY

The Negro population of Chicago, as reported by the Federal Bureau of the Census, was 44,103 in 1910 and 109,594 in 1920. The increase during the decade was therefore 65,491, or 148.5 per cent. Negroes constituted 2 per cent of the city's total population in 1910 and 4.1 per cent in 1920. The increase in the white population during the decade was 450,047, or 21 per cent, bringing the white population up to 2,589,104 in 1920. The remainder of the population consisted of 3,007 Chinese, Japanese, and Indians, of whom there were 2,123 in 1910. Chicago's total population in 1920 was 2,701,705.

In order to indicate where the Negro population of the city lived in 1910 and in 1920, the Commission sought the co-operation of the Census Bureau. On the basis of a rough preliminary survey, certain areas in which it was evident that the main groups of Negroes lived were delimited, and liberal margins allowed to include scattered residents living near the main areas. For these areas the Census Bureau supplied figures showing the total and Negro population by census-enumeration districts. Since each enumeration district embraced from one or two to six city blocks in the more crowded portions of the city, the data thus made available enabled the Commission to prepare maps showing with a fair degree of accuracy where Negroes in Chicago lived in 1910 and in 1920, and also their proportion to the total population in these units of area.

The 510 enumeration districts covered for 1910 included 40,739, or 92.3 per cent of the 44,103 Negroes reported by the Census Bureau for that year; and the 730 enumeration districts covered for 1920 included 106,089, or 96.8 per cent of the 109,594 Negroes reported for that year. The small remaining number of Negroes scattered throughout the parts of the city not embraced in these areas in 1910 and 1920 included many janitors living in the buildings where they worked, and others employed in private homes and living on the premises, thus making their presence inconspicuous among white residents. The areas in which 40,739 Negroes were living in 1910 contained a total population of 657,044, the Negroes thus constituting 6.2 per cent of the total. The areas in which 106,089 Negroes lived in 1920 contained a total population of 779,279, the Negroes thus constituting about 13 per cent of the total.

The outstanding fact concerning these data for 1910 and 1920 is that the large increase in Negro population did not bring into existence any new large colonies but resulted in the expansion and increased density of areas in which groups of Negroes already lived in 1910.

RACIAL CONTACTS AMONG CHILDREN IN AN ADJUSTED NEIGHBORHOOD

Negro. This, however, is not the case. The area between Twelfth and Thirty-ninth streets, Wentworth Avenue and Lake Michigan, includes the oldest and densest Negro population of any section of its size in Chicago. However, the actual numbers of whites and Negroes living there are 42,797 and 54,906 respectively. In this area the Negro population has increased gradually and without disturbance for many years. Although for a long period Negroes were confined to the area bounded by State Street, Wentworth Avenue, Twelfth, and Thirty-ninth streets, their movement into the neighborhood east of State Street was ultimately looked upon as a natural and expected expansion. Within the whole of this territory a relationship exists, which, although perhaps not uniformly friendly, yet is without friction or disorder. During the riot few white persons living or engaged in business there were attacked by Negroes, who were in the majority in many parts of the area. Many whites remaining in the area, which was formerly all white, are small property owners who for sentimental reasons prefer to live there. Numbers of family hotels and large apartment houses there continue to be occupied by whites, who are apparently little affected by the presence of 10 per cent more Negroes than whites around them. Michigan Avenue and Grand Boulevard are the streets into which Negroes have moved most recently. The only recorded bombing within this area occurred on Grand Boulevard. The Grand Boulevard district is affiliated with the Kenwood and Hyde Park Property Owners' Association. Although the bombing was an expression of resentment against Negroes because they moved into this block, there are circumstances which indicate that the resentment did not come from the neighbors. For example, the wife of a Negro physician owning and living in a house in the same block was asked by her white neighbors to serve as chairman of a committee to keep up the property in the neighborhood.

The first Negro family to move into the Vernon Avenue block immediately south of Thirty-first Street bought its residence in 1911. It was five years before another Negro family came. White neighbors, who were and are very friendly, said this family's good care of its lawn was an example for the whole block.

When an apartment house in which a Negro family lived on South Park Avenue near Thirty-first Street was burned, white neighbors took them into their home and kept them until another house was secured. At a meeting of the City Club of Chicago a white man who had lived in this area for forty years thus characterized the relations between whites and Negroes living there:

Having lived on the South Side in what is now known as the "Black Belt" for forty years, I can testify that I have never had more honest, quiet, and law-abiding neighbors than those who are of the African race, either full or mixed blood. In the precinct where I live we have several families blessed with many orderly and well-behaved children, of Caucasian and African blood. They seem to get along nicely, and why should they not? . . . . There is no race question, it is a question of intelligence and morality, pure and simple.

Occasional minor misunderstandings have resulted from contacts in this area, but they have not been conspicuously marked by racial bitterness. Objections, sometimes expressed when the tradition of an "all white" neighborhood was first broken, disappeared as the neighbors came to know each other. Long residence is apparently one condition of the adjustment process.

Expansion and adjustment.—The first noticeable expansion of the Negro population following the migration in 1917 and 1918 was in the area extending south from Thirty-ninth Street to Forty-seventh Street on Langley, St. Lawrence, and Evans avenues. Negroes began moving into this area early in 1917, first a few and finally in large numbers. There is yet no compact group, for these Negro families, while numerous, are well distributed. The experiences of some of the first families there are interesting.

A Negro woman bought a piece of property on Langley Avenue, near Forty-third Street, when every other family in the block was white. The courtesy shown her by them was all that could be desired, she declares. There are still six or eight white families in the block, and they continue on the most friendly terms with her. A Negro woman in another block has white neighbors all around her, but there has been no racial objection or friction. Another, who owns her property on Evans Avenue, has had no trouble with white families that remain in the block. So with a Negro who rents from the Negro owner of a flat on East Thirty-sixth Street. A Negro who has bought a home on St. Lawrence Avenue near Forty-seventh Street declares that the white families living thereabouts "treat my family right." In one block on St. Lawrence Avenue a Negro family is surrounded by white neighbors, but no trouble has been experienced. In a block on Langley Avenue another family of Negroes has had no clashes with the white neighbors who compose most of the neighborhood.

A woman who built her home in the 4800 block on Champlain Avenue, when hers was the only Negro family there and has lived there ever since, had no trouble with neighbors until other Negroes moved in. Then a white woman circulated a petition for the purpose of compelling the Negroes to move out. This effort failed. In another block on East Forty-sixth Street a Negro family lives in a neighborhood which has a majority of whites, but the relations have been amicable. An apartment house on Champlain Avenue near Forty-sixth Street is occupied entirely by Negroes, though there are white families all through the neighborhood. One Negro who has lived there for three years says they have never been molested. A pioneer Negro family in a white block on Vernon Avenue near Thirty-ninth Street reports no trouble with the white neighbors.

Two women who were among the last of the whites to leave the Langley Avenue vicinity say they always found the Negroes to be kindly neighbors. A Negro family on Forty-first Street has been there a year without friction with white neighbors. In another block on East Forty-second Street a Negro woman reported that, though there are white people all through the neighborhood, the two races get along peaceably. In the 400 block of East Forty-sixth Street a similar report is given. In still another block on Champlain Avenue lives a woman who has been in the midst of white families for a number of years without experiencing animosity. On East Forty-second Street a Negro family has lived for three years in similar freedom from racial friction.

In another instance a pioneer Negro family in a block otherwise wholly white was well regarded by all except one of the neighbors. This white man who voiced loudly his objections to the "invasion" was one who, because of his drunken habits and troublesome nature, had long been considered an undesirable neighbor by other whites in the block.

Woodlawn.—Relations in Woodlawn, where the Negro population increase has been relatively large, are for the most part friendly. There is an association of Negro property owners interested in keeping up the physical appearance of their homes in the neighborhood. No clashes have been reported except one instance of a group of white boys from another neighborhood throwing stones at a building where they saw Negroes. Following the stirring up and organization of anti-Negro sentiment in Hyde Park, an attempt was made to organize white Woodlawn property owners against the invasion of the district by Negroes. This organization was not a great success. There have been no bombings in this district, and no concerted opposition to the presence of Negroes as neighbors. Long residence together and the good character and conduct of both Negroes and whites are probably important reasons for lack of friction.

2. THE WEST SIDE

A situation like that in the adjusted neighborhoods of the South Side exists in the district bounded by Washington and Kinzie, Ashland and California avenues, where there has been a settlement of Negroes for many years. Houses are cheaper than on the South Side, and although the general standard of workingmen's homes compares favorably with that on the South Side, few of the abandoned good residences formerly occupied by wealthy persons are available for Negroes. The densest and oldest settlement of Negroes is within the boundaries named, although the Negro residence area actually extends many blocks beyond them on all sides. There has been little friction, though the area has 9,221 whites and 6,520 Negroes. South of Washington Boulevard occasional difficulties have been met by the incoming Negro population, similar to those found in areas where the most congested Negro population on the South Side is spreading. On the West Side no bombings have occurred, although there have been frequent protests against the expansion. Some streets have come to be recognized as Negro streets.

In recent years many Negroes have bought homes on the West Side when they could not easily find living quarters in or near the older Negro residence areas on the South Side. Almost uniformly they keep their homes in good condition, which cannot be said of all the Negroes who settled early in this district. West Side Negroes, laborers for the most part, are generally home-loving, hard-working, and desirous of improving conditions for their children. Older settlers among them have been able to make their adjustments without great difficulty and with no marked antagonism from white neighbors.

Though occasionally trivial conflicts arise between Negro and white neighbors, the attitude of whites in nearby areas is customarily friendly if not cordial. For example, a Negro doctor has a considerable practice among nearby Italians in the vicinity of the Chicago Commons Social Settlement. At Chicago Commons itself no distinction is made with respect to the few Negro families which at times make use of the facilities. Children of these families have entered classes and clubs, and one of them became a leader of a group.

The Poles who mainly occupy the neighborhood around the Northwestern University Social Settlement are entirely friendly to Negroes. Three years ago an educated Negro was at the head of the boys' department of the settlement, and, with one exception, no one in that position has made more friends among the boys and their families.

On the West Side, as on the South and North sides, Negroes have established their own restaurants and barber shops and some groceries and delicatessen stores. There are several theaters whose patronage is largely Negro.

3. THE NORTH SIDE

On the North Side, Negroes live among foreign whites and near a residence area of wealthy Chicagoans. Their first appearance occasioned little notice or objection, since they were generally house servants living near their work. The largest numbers are to be found between Chicago Avenue and Division Street on North Wells, Franklin, and cross streets connecting them.

This neighborhood has experienced several complete changes in population. It was first occupied by Irish, then by Swedes, then by Italians. The present neighbors of Negroes are Italians. As indicated by the population changes, the neighborhood is old and run down, and the reasons given by Negroes for living there are low rents and proximity to the manufacturing plants where they work.

The Negroes there are renters, because the property, although undesirable for residence purposes, is valuable for business and too expensive for them to buy. The families are chiefly respectable, hard-working people. They have their own barber and tailor shops and similar business places. In social affairs they confine themselves largely to meetings, dances, and similar gatherings held exclusively for their own race. Formerly the second floor of a building on Division Street was frequently rented by the Negroes for church and other meetings, and dances. Recently they have found other meeting places, particularly for religious devotions. Some of their social gatherings and meetings take place at Seward Park.

They are welcomed not only in Seward Park, one of the city's recreation centers, but in the settlements. At Eli Bates House, 621 West Elm Street,

A SAVINGS BANK IN THE NEGRO RESIDENCE AREA ON SATURDAY EVENING

CHILDREN AT WORK IN A COMMUNITY GARDEN

for example, there has been a club of Negro young men, and applications have been received for admission of Negro children to some classes. The head resident of the settlement reports, however, that it has not had much contact with the Negro group. A few Negro children come to the kindergarten; a group of Negro boys makes use of the gymnasium, and some neighboring Negro families have asked settlement residents for advice.

In this neighborhood friendly relations exist between the Sicilians, who predominate, and their Negro neighbors. Some Negroes live harmoniously in the same tenements with the Sicilians. Their children play together, and some Negro children have learned Sicilian phrases, so that they are able to deal with the Sicilian shopkeepers.

Elsewhere on the North Side the feeling between Italians and Negroes is not so cordial. During the riot of 1919, serious trouble was averted on the North Side through prompt and effective efforts by the police and members of the community. It was reported throughout the district that automobiles loaded with armed Negroes were on their way from the South Side to "shoot up the North Side." The Italians immediately armed themselves and began to shoot recklessly. They were eventually quieted by the police and others, and there was no retaliation of the Negroes,

Many Negroes who have purchased homes and lived on the North Side for years report little opposition. One family on North Wells Street has lived there since 1888 and now owns several valuable pieces of property. The man had no trouble in buying property, and the whites have always been friendly to them and to all Negroes in that section. Another Negro family on North Wells Street, where Negroes first lived, had no difficulty in getting their flat sixteen years ago. This block is occupied by whites and Negroes without friction.

Minor expressions of antagonism attended the moving in of some Negro families, but after several months the white neighbors accepted them and now are on good terms with them.

II. NON-ADJUSTED NEIGHBORHOODS

Failure of adjustment between whites and Negroes has greatly accentuated the difficulties of the housing problem for Negroes. When a general shortage of housing is relieved there may still be a serious shortage for Negroes because of the hostility of white neighborhoods. The sentiment for "all-white" neighborhoods has grown with the increase in Negro population and the threatened occupancy in small or large degree by Negroes. These non-adjusted neighborhoods fall into distinct classes:

1. Neighborhoods of unorganized opposition. These are neighborhoods where few Negroes live. Though contiguous they are sharply separated from areas of Negro residence and are definitely hostile to Negroes, even those passing through the neighborhood going to and from work, but the hostility in them is unorganized.

2. Neighborhoods of organized opposition. (*a*) Neighborhoods in which no Negroes live but which are in the line of Negro expansion. Opposition to threatened invasion has been strong. As yet they are exclusively white, and every effort is being made to keep them so. They are illustratively treated here as "exclusive neighborhoods." (*b*) Neighborhoods in which the presence of Negro residents is hotly contested, by or〔　〕and unorganized efforts to oust them. These for convenience are〔　　　〕tested neighborhoods."

I.　NEIGHBORHOODS OF UN〔　　　　〕

In Certain West Side neigh〔　　　〕vners objected to the expansion of the n〔　　　　　　　　　〕ection.

The pasto〔　　　　　　　　　　〕ngton Boulevard, who can〔　　　　　　　　　　　〕2008 Washington Bouleva〔　　　　　　　　　　〕moved into one of them in〔　　　　　　　　　　〕er house received warning〔　　　　　　　　〕nces. The last of these wa〔　　　　　　　〕was paid to them.

Dur〔　　　　　　　　　　〕e Negroes in the West Side district, who generally remained in their own houses and neighborhoods. Some became involved in clashes on their way to or from work, but there was no serious clash.

The district west of Cottage Grove Avenue and south to Sixty-third Street in Woodlawn is rather sparsely built up, most of the buildings being one- and two-family houses. Numbers of white people in the neighborhood believe that the district has been blighted because of the occasional presence of Negroes.

On the North Side some hostility to Negroes was shown during the 1919 riot. One Negro, who had lived on North Franklin Street for five years and in Chicago for thirty years, told of having been spit at by rowdy Italians, and on another occasion threatened with shooting by young roughs in a passing automobile. White neighbors, however, intervened. Under pressure of the riot excitement, some Italian children pushed through windows and doors pictures of skulls and coffins inked in red. At the time of the riot Eli Bates House issued a circular deploring race hatred and appealing for order and fairness.

Although the few Negroes living in the Lake Park Avenue area[1] have experienced little opposition in their present homes, there has been no Negro expansion there. The colony, has in fact, dwindled in size since 1910. It is made up largely of Negroes who were house servants for white families near-by or worked in the hotels of the district.

Negroes of this colony are barred from all white restaurants in the district except one place conducted by a Greek. In three of the motion-picture houses

[1] See "Negro Population of Chicago," p. 107.

they are not allowed to sit in the best seats. In one of these theaters a sign reads, "We reserve the right to seat our patrons to suit ourselves." Negroes are permitted in the balcony or in the rear seats of the main floor.

On Langley, St. Lawrence, and adjoining streets south of Fifty-fifth Street there is considerable friction resulting from the presence of Negroes.

There are residence districts of Chicago adjacent to those occupied by Negroes in which hostility to Negroes is so marked that the latter not only find it impossible to live there, but expose themselves to danger even by passing through. There are no hostile organizations in these neighborhoods, and active antagonism is usually confined to gang lawlessness. Such a neighborhood is that west of Wentworth Avenue, extending roughly from Twenty-second to Sixty-third streets. The number of Negroes living there is small, and most of them live on Ada, Aberdeen, and Loomis streets, south of Fifty-seventh Street. In the section immediately west of Wentworth Avenue and thus adjoining the densest Negro residence area in the city, practically no Negroes live. In addition to intense hostility, there is a lack of desirable houses. Wentworth Avenue has long been regarded as a strict boundary line separating white and Negro residence areas. The district has many "athletic clubs."[1] The contact of Negroes and whites comes when Negroes must pass to and from their work at the Stock Yards and at other industries located in the district. It was in this district that the largest number of riot clashes occurred.[2] Several Negroes have been murdered here, and numbers have been beaten by gangs of young men and boys. A white man was killed by one of two Negroes returning from work in that district, who declared that they had been intimidated by the slain man. Speaking of this district, the principal of the Raymond School, a branch of which is located west of Wentworth Avenue, said that antagonism of the district against Negroes appeared to have been handed down through tradition. He said:

We get a good deal of the gang spirit in the new school on the other side of Wentworth Avenue. There seems to be an inherited antagonism. Wentworth Avenue is the gang line. They seem to feel that to trespass on either side of that line is ground for trouble. While colored pupils who come to the school for manual training are not troubled in the school, they have to be escorted over the line, not because of trouble from members of the school, but groups of boys outside the school. To give another illustration, we took a little kindergarten group over to the park. One little six-year-old girl was struck in the face by a man. A policeman chased but failed to catch him. The condition is a tradition. It is handed down.

2. NEIGHBORHOODS OF ORGANIZED OPPOSITION

"*Exclusive neighborhoods*."—In neighborhoods which are exclusive on the basis of social class, whose restrictions apply to Negroes and the majority of whites alike, the high price of property is a sufficient barrier against Negroes;

[1] See "Gangs" and "Clubs" under "Racial Clashes."
[2] See "Clashes."

it is in the neighborhoods where property values are within the means of Negroes that fears of invasion are entertained. In many new real estate subdivisions houses are sold on easy payments. Almost without exception these sections are exclusively for whites, and usually it is so stated in the prospectus. Other sections longer established come to notice when some incident provokes the expression of opposition already organized and awaiting it.

Such a section is the neighborhood known as Park Manor and Wakeford. This neighborhood lies between Sixty-ninth and Seventy-ninth streets, and Cottage Grove and Indiana avenues. It is newly built, chiefly with small dwellings, most of them not more than five years old. Many of the residents had lived in a neighborhood to the north, nearer Woodlawn, whose growth of Negro population had caused some of them to move. Park Manor and Wakeford were startled by the following advertisement in the *Chicago Daily News* in July, 1920:

For sale—Colored Attention: homes on Vernon, South Park and Indiana Aves. Sold on easy terms; come out and look this locality over; Protestant neighborhood, Park Manor and Wakeford; good transportation. Blair, 7455 Cottage Grove Avenue.

Blair, a real estate agent, denied all knowledge of the advertisement and attributed it either to an enemy or to a practical joker. He sent notices to be read the following day in the nine churches of the district, so stating, deploring the occurrence and pledging himself to aid the other residents in excluding Negroes and in hunting down the author of the advertisement.

Meanwhile the entire district had been aroused, and a meeting called for the evening of July 12, in front of a church at Seventy-sixth Street and St. Lawrence Avenue. About 1,000 people gathered for this meeting, which was conducted by the presidents of the South Park Manor and Wakeford Improvement Associations. The former announced that he had visited the *Daily News* and learned that the advertisement had been handed to a clerk in typewritten form and with a typewritten signature, and paid for in advance, whereas Blair's regular advertising was done on a charge account. This and other information tended to show that the agent was not responsible for the advertisement. In its issue of Monday, July 12, the *Daily News* printed an explanatory statement.

Other speakers at the meeting were a real estate dealer and an alderman. Considerable indignation was expressed over the false light in which the community had been placed. Even the suggestion that Negroes might by chance become a part of this community seemed to be abhorrent. As far as Negroes were concerned there was no excitement, but they resented being used to frighten white residents.

"*Contested neighborhoods.*"—The contested neighborhoods are by far the most important among the types of non-adjusted neighborhoods, both because of the actual presence in them of varying numbers of Negroes and their

Negro invasion of the district was the worst calamity that had struck the city since the Great Fire. A prominent white real estate man said: "Property owners should be notified to stand together block by block and prevent such invasion."

Distinctly hostile sentiments were expressed before audiences that came expecting to hear how their property might be saved from "almost certain destruction." A speaker at one of the meetings said in part:

We are taught that the principle of virtue and right shall be the rule of our conduct in all of our transactions with our fellow-men, and therefore it is our duty to help the Negro, to uplift him in his environment, mark you, not ours. But it is not our duty, now mark this, it is not our duty as I see it, nor is it according to the laws of nature for us to live with him as neighbors or on a social basis. There is an immutable, unchanging law that governs the distribution, association and conduct of all living creatures. Man is no exception to the universal rule. In every land and clime man obeys the second law of his nature and seeks his own kind, avoiding every other, and ever, ever is he warring with his unlike neighbor, families, classes, societies, tribes, and nations.

There are men who proclaim to the world and ourselves that the destiny of the black man and the white man is one. I do not believe it; I cannot believe it. Now, listen! As far back as September 18, 1858, in his famous joint debate with Stephen A. Douglas, Abraham Lincoln, that wonderful, Godlike man, the liberator of the slaves, said this (Now listen, 1858, over sixty years ago): "I am not nor ever have been in favor of bringing about in any way the social and political equality of the white and the black race. I am not nor ever have been in favor of qualifying them to intermarry with white people, and I will say in addition to this, that there is a physical difference between the white and black races living together on terms of social and political equality."

Other remarks of speakers at these meetings were:

The depreciation of our property in this district has been two hundred and fifty millions since the invasion. If someone told you that there was to be an invasion that would injure your homes to that extent, wouldn't you rise up as one man and one woman, and say as General Foch said: "They shall not pass"?

There isn't an insurance company in America that will turn around and try to buck our organization when we as one man give them to understand that it is dangerous to insure some people.

Why I remember fifteen or twenty years ago that the district down here at Wabash Avenue and Calumet was one of the most beautiful and highest-class neighborhoods of this great city. Go down there today and see the ramshackle broken-down and tumble-down district. That is the result of the new menace that is threatening this great Hyde Park district. And then tell me whether there are or not enough red-blooded, patriotic, loyal, courageous citizens of Hyde Park to save this glorious district from the menace which has brought so much pain and so much disaster to the district to the south of us.

You cannot mix oil and water. You cannot assimilate races of a different color as neighbors along social lines. Remember this: That order is heaven's first law.

Throughout the meetings, profession was made of friendliness toward the Negroes, together with a desire to serve their needs and accord them fair treatment. The *Property Owners' Journal*, published by the Association, was less guarded. While some of its columns made similar professions, its remarks in other columns were characterized by extreme racial bitterness and antagonism.

An apparently conciliatory attitude was also taken by speakers at meetings of the Hyde Park Association and its Grand Boulevard branch. In a meeting of the latter on January 19, 1920, the chairman declared that he wished to say for publication: "We have no quarrel with the colored people. We have no desire to intimidate them by violence." The mission of the organization, he said, was peaceable, and it was the purpose to proceed according to law and order. The Association, he averred, had been charged "by the colored press" with being parties to bombing outrages. He wanted it known that "we have denounced officially the action of anyone or any set of people who would indulge in a practice of that character." The story of the bombing campaign is given in another section of this report.

At another meeting it was asserted that the Kenwood and Hyde Park Association had a membership of 1,000 persons, and it was estimated that in the district to which it applied the investment in real estate was $1,000,000,000. The purpose of the organization was declared to be "to guard that $1,000,000,000 against depreciation from anything." One speaker said he did not believe there was a piece of property west of Cottage Grove Avenue in Hyde Park that was worth 33 cents on the dollar "as it stands now with this invasion." He said his home cost about $25,000, but he felt safe in saying that he could not then get $8,000 for it. A city alderman was one of the speakers at this meeting.

Most of the real estate dealers in the area were claimed as members of the Kenwood and Hyde Park Association or its Grand Boulevard branch. Special reference was made at various times and in scathing terms to dealers who declined to affiliate. At the meeting of the Grand Boulevard district on January 19, 1920, it was reported that the Executive Committee of the parent association had succeeded during the previous two or three months in educating real estate men. "The colored man," a speaker said, "would have never been in this district had not our real estate men in their ambition to acquire wealth and commissions, which is perfectly legitimate, put them here, although this action on their part has been very shortsighted, as some of them now admit." This speaker said also that the Association's "greatest successes" had been in getting all but five or six of the real estate men to sign a pledge thirty-two were exploded within the square bounded by Forty-first and Sixtieth streets, Cottage Grove Avenue and State Street. With an average of one race bombing every twenty days for three years and eight months, the police and the state's attorney's office succeeded in apprehending but two persons suspected of participation in these acts of lawlessness. One of these, James Macheval, arrested on the complaint of C. S. Absteson, a janitor, was released on a $500 bond. At the writing of this report, one year after the arrest, there has been no trial. Another man was apprehended, questioned, held under surveillance for two days by the police, and finally released.

News of threatened bombings in many cases was circulated well in advance of the actual occurrence. Negroes were warned of the exact date on which explosions would occur. They asked for police protection, and, in some instances where police were sent beforehand, their homes were bombed, and no arrests were made.

The persons directing these bombings did not limit their intimidations to Negro residents in white neighborhoods; residences of Negroes and white real estate men were bombed because they had sold or rented property in these exclusive areas to Negroes, and Negro bankers' houses were bombed because they made loans on Negro property and supported their mortgages.

These bombings increased rapidly in frequency and damaging effect. The six months' period ended October 1, 1920, witnessed as many bombings as the entire thirty-five months preceding. Prior to 1919 there were twelve bombings. Four of these were directed at properties merely held by Negro real estate men as agents, two of them in Berkeley Avenue just north of Forty-third Street, and near the lake. Five were in the 4500 block on Vincennes Avenue, two at 4200 Wabash Avenue, and one at 4732 Indiana Avenue.

Bombing of real estate men's properties appears to have been part of a general scheme to close the channels through which the invasion proceeded rather than a protest of neighbors. The four explosions in the 4500 block on Vincennes Avenue appear to have been deliberately aimed at the tenants. This block is at the center of the neighborhood most actively opposed to the coming in of Negroes. In January, 1919, a white and a Negro real estate agent were bombed; in March, Jesse Binga's real estate office at 4724 State Street and an apartment at 4041 Calumet Avenue were bombed. In April there were two more bombings, one of a realty office. Following a public meeting on May 5 to arouse white property owners of the Hyde Park district against Negro invasion, there were four bombings. Between January 1, 1920, and March 1, 1920, there were eight bombings in eight weeks. Responsibility for the creation of the sentiment thus expressed was in some instances assumed by organizations. For example the *Property Owners' Journal*, in its issue for February 1, 1920, said:

Our neighborhood must continue white. This sentiment is the outgrowth of the massmeeting of property owners and residents which was held Monday, January 19.

Mr. George J. Williams furnished the climax of the meeting when he informed the audience in terse, pithy language that "Hyde Park enjoys a reputation too splendid as a neighborhood of white culture to allow Negroes to use it as their door mat."

In the issue of December 13, 1919, white and Negro real estate men and owners selling property to Negroes in the district were "branded as unclean outcasts of society to be boycotted and ostracized in every possible manner," and W. B. Austin, white, was accused of violating a gentleman's obligation to his community in selling a home to a Negro. It was asserted falsely that the house which he had sold had been used during the race riots as a "rendezvous for Negroes who fired volleys of revolver shots from doors and windows at white boys in the street who, according to the testimony of neighbors, had not attacked the premises."

On December 26 the home of J. H. Coleman, a white real estate man who had sold a house to a Negro, was bombed. The transaction was not public, and occupancy was not to take place for five months. On December 27 the home of Jesse Binga, a Negro real estate man, was bombed. One week later, on January 6, came the bombing of W. B. Austin, on the North Side.

During 1919 and 1920 committees and delegations of whites and Negroes appealed to the chief of police, the mayor, State's Attorney Hoyne, and the press, but nothing was done. The mayor referred these matters to his chief of police. The police were unable to discover the bombers or anyone directing them. The state's attorney, in response to appeals, emphatically defined his duty as a prosecuting rather than an apprehending agent. All the while, however, the bombings continued steadily; no arrests except the two mentioned were made; and the Negro population grew to trust less and less in the interest of the community and the public agencies of protection.

I. TYPICAL BOMBINGS

The circumstances of the bombings were investigated by the Commission, and details of what happened in several typical cases are here presented.

Bombing of the Motley home.—In 1913 S. P. Motley, Negro, and his wife purchased a building at 5230 Maryland Avenue through a white agent, and on March 15, 1913, the family moved in. For four years they lived there without molestation save the silent resentment of neighbors and open objection to the presence of Negro children in the streets. On July 1, 1917, without warning or threat, a bomb was exploded in the vestibule of the house, and the front of the building was blown away. The damage amounted to $1,000. Police arrived from the station at Fifty-second Street and Lake Park Avenue ten minutes after the explosion. No clews were found and no arrests were made. The original owner of the building was bitterly opposed to Negroes and was a member of an organization which was seeking to keep Negroes out of the district.

Some time after this incident it was rumored that Motley was planning to purchase the building adjacent. At 4:00 A.M. June 4, 1919, a dynamite bomb was exploded under the front of the house adjacent and tore up its stone front. The neighbors

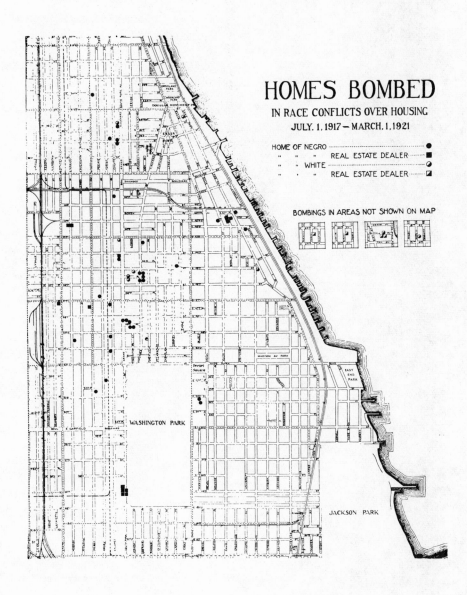

HOMES BOMBED
IN RACE CONFLICTS OVER HOUSING
JULY, 1, 1917 — MARCH, 1, 1921

HOME OF NEGRO .... ●
" " " REAL ESTATE DEALER .... ■
" " WHITE .... ◑
" " " REAL ESTATE DEALER .... ◪

BOMBINGS IN AREAS NOT SHOWN ON MAP

WASHINGTON PARK

JACKSON PARK

were in the street immediately after the explosion. No clews were found and no arrests were made. The Motley family on this occasion was accused of inviting another Negro family into the block. The new family in question negotiated for its own property, and before an actual settlement had been made, received numerous telephone messages and threats. It moved in, but was not bombed.

Bombing of Moses Fox's home.—Moses Fox, white, connected with a "Loop" real estate firm, lived at 442 East Forty-fifth Street. The house was too large, and he decided to move to smaller quarters. The building was sold through a real estate firm to persons whom he did not know. On March 10, 1920, a few days after the sale, he received a telephone call informing him that he must suffer the consequences of selling his home to Negroes. At 7:30 that evening an automobile was seen to drive slowly past his home three times, stopping each time just east of the building. On the last trip a man alighted, and deposited a long-fuse bomb in the vestibule. The fuse smoked for four minutes. Attracted by the smoke, Fox ran toward the front of the house. The bomb exploded before he reached the door. It was loaded with dynamite and contained slugs which penetrated the windows of buildings across the street. The evening selected for the bombing was the one on which Patrolman Edward Owens, Negro, was off duty and a white policeman was patrolling his beat. The bombing was witnessed by Dan Jones, a Negro janitor, and Mrs. Florence De Lavalade, a Negro tenant. The front of the building was wrecked and all the windows shattered. Damage amounting to $1,000 was done. No arrests were made.

Bombing of Jesse Binga's properties.—Jesse Binga is a Negro banker and real estate man. His bank is at 3633 State Street, his real estate office at 4724 State Street, and his home at 5922 South Park Avenue. He controls more than $500,000 worth of property and through his bank has made loans on Negro property and taken over the mortgages of Negroes refused by other banks and loan agencies.

On November 12, 1919, an automobile rolled by his realty office and a bomb was tossed from it. It left the office in ruins. The police were soon on the scene, but the car was well beyond reach by the time of their arrival. No clews to the bombers were found, and no arrests were made. It was the opinion of the police that white residents of the Hyde Park district resented Binga's handling of Negro property in that district.

Twenty-one days later an automobile drew up in front of Binga's home at 5922 South Park Avenue, and its occupants put a bomb under the front steps. It failed to explode. When the firemen arrived they found it sizzling in the slush beneath the porch. The police declared that this was an expression of racial feeling.

Twenty-five days later the bombers reappeared and left a third bomb. It tore up the porch of Binga's home. Again the police found that the explosion had been caused by "racial feeling," white men having said that "Binga rented too many flats to Negroes in high-class residence districts." The house was repaired and police provided to guard the house. At twelve o'clock each night the guard changed watch. On the night of February 28 the policeman on duty until twelve o'clock left a few minutes early, and the policeman relieving him was just a few minutes late. In this unguarded interval an automobile swung around the corner, and as it passed the Binga home a man leaned out and tossed a bomb into the yard. The bomb lit in a puddle of water and the fuse went out. It was found that the bomb had been made of black powder, manila paper, and cotton. The explanation of the attempt was that "his $30,000 home is in a white neighborhood."

A police guard was still watching the house on the night of June 18, 1920, when the bombing car appeared again. On this occasion neither policeman was in sight when the car drew up. A man alighted this time and carefully placed the bomb. The explosion that followed almost demolished the front of the house and smashed windows throughout the block. This last explosion damaged the home to the extent of $4,000. Binga offered a reward of $1,000 for the apprehension of those guilty of these repeated acts of lawlessness.

On November 23 Binga was bombed again. This time the bomb damaged his neighbors more seriously than it did Binga's property. No clews were found and no one was arrested.

Bombing of R. W. Woodfolk's home.—R. W. Woodfolk, Negro banker and real estate dealer, purchased a flat at 4722 Calumet Avenue. It was an investment of the Merchants and Peoples' Bank, 3201 South State Street, which he controlled. The building was occupied by one white and four Negro families. On the evening of February 1, 1920, a person with keys to the building locked the tenants in their apartments, sprung the locks of the doors leading to the street, and planted a bomb in the hallway. The explosion ripped up the hall and stairway, tore away the brick work around the entrance, and shattered the windows of adjacent buildings. The damage was estimated at $1,000. No arrests were made.

Bombing of the Clarke home.—Mrs. Mary Byron Clarke, Negro, purchased through W. B. Austin, a white banker and real estate man, properties at 4404 and 4406 Grand Boulevard, vacant for a year at the time of purchase, and previously used by prostitutes. A real estate dealer herself, she had frequently been assisted by Austin in financing her transactions, one of which was the sale to Negroes of Isaiah Temple, a Jewish synagogue at Forty-fifth Street and Vincennes Avenue.

The dwellings were renovated and she moved into one of them; the other she rented. During the riot of July, 1919, her home was attacked by a mob. When the police arrived in response to a call by the Clarkes, they battered in the doors at the demand of the mob and arrested Mr. and Mrs. Clarke. They were acquitted. On January 5, 1920, the house was bombed. The explosion caused $3,360 worth of damage. The building was again bombed February 12, 1920, this time with a dynamite bomb thrown through the plate-glass door in the hallway from a passing automobile. The stairway was knocked down and large holes blown in the wall. The police came, found no clews, and made no arrests. At the request of Mrs. Clarke a special policeman was detailed to guard the property.

Numerous threatening letters and telephone calls followed, all of which were reported to the police. There were threats of another bombing if she did not sell, and there were visits from representatives of real estate interests in Hyde Park making offers.

Tuesday evening, April 13, 1920, a third bomb was exploded in spite of the presence of the two special policemen. The bomb was thrown from the premises of Frederick R. Barnheisel, an immediate neighbor, a telephone wire deflected it, and it landed near the Clarke garage.

Mrs. Clarke made a statement concerning this bombing before the Commission in which she said:

"Wednesday [the day following the third bombing] we got a letter saying 'move out or sell, there is nothing else for you to do. We missed you last night but we will get you the next time. We are determined.' A letter prior to that stated if we did not get out they would 'get our hides.'

"There has been some sinister influence brought to bear on the insurance company since the riot and since the first bombing. We have had our house insured against bombing since the first bombing. The first damage of about $500 they paid and canceled the insurance on 4404 Grand Boulevard. The second bomb did damage to the extent of $3,360. They wrote saying they would cancel it, subject however to pending loss. There was a clause calling for settlement within sixty days. After sixty days we would have to enter suit to get it. The sixty days have passed, and there has been no attempt to settle. Some of the glass has been replaced. They have accepted it, and there has been no disposition on their part to settle.

"Berry, Johnston, & Peters, the men with whom we have had the most business dealings, have insisted that we sell the place. Mr. Peters said last week he could get a buyer from the Hyde Park–Kenwood Association people, also said if any indebtedness remained on the contract or deeds, that the money must first be paid to them, then to us. We have been careful not to let any indebtedness, even for ten days, come against 4406."

Bombing of Crede Hubbard's home.—Following is part of Hubbard's statement to the police immediately after the bombing of his home at 4331 Vincennes Avenue on the night of April 25, 1920:

"The day on which I had planned to move, a man who said he was Mr. Day, of the Hyde Park and Kenwood Association, telephoned me. He said: 'I hear you have acquired property and you are dissatisfied with it; we can take it off your hands—relieve you of it.' I replied that I didn't think I needed any help. He asked, 'What do you expect to do?' I said, 'I expect to move into it or sell it if I can get my price.' I moved on Tuesday and Wednesday he called in person. He said, 'I called to find out if you want us to sell or handle your property for you.' I told him I thought I could handle it, and that I was not anxious to sell but would consider selling if I could get an offer of say $11,000. He replied that his buyers were not able to go that far. He continued, 'The point is, I represent the Hyde Park–Kenwood Association. We have spent a lot of money and we want to keep this district white.' I asked him why they had not thought of buying the property before and told him that the house had been for sale for eight months. He replied that it was a lamentable fact that they had overlooked it. I told him that I heard the Hyde Park Association had a $100,000 slush fund out of which $100 was paid for each bombing. He said he would have some of his buyers come in and look over the property. Shortly afterward, Mr. Stephen D. Seman and another man came and represented themselves as buyers. They looked over the inside of the house. I only carried them through the halls. Mr. Seman said, 'You only paid $8,500 for this property.' I told him that he had been misinformed, I had paid $9,000. He said, 'I will give you $9,500 for it.' I refused. As they were leaving he added, 'You had better consider our offer.' Soon after that a man named Casson, real estate man, called. I would not let him in. When he asked me my price I told him $11,500.

"A week later a delegation from the Hyde Park Association called. The spokesman began: 'I am Mr. Austin. You understand the nature of our business with you, I suppose.' . . . . I told the chief clerk of the office of the Northwestern Railroad to inform you that we were coming to see you. We are the Hyde Park–Kenwood Association and you will understand that you are not welcome in this district. We want to know what can be done.' I replied that I didn't know what could be done unless they wanted to buy; otherwise I expected to live there, and my price was $11,500. They continued, 'Do you suppose if I moved into a black district where I wasn't wanted, that I would want to live there?' I said, 'If you had bought property there and liked the property, I don't see why you should move.' They said, 'Why do you persist in wanting to live here when you know you are not wanted?' I said, 'I have bought property here and I am expecting to live here.' Then they filed out of the door, and one of the members stated, 'You had better consider this proposition.'

"In the office of the Northwestern Railroad, Mr. Shirley called me in and read a letter to me which he had received from Mr. Austin. 'Murphy, his name is,' he said, 'I know him fairly well, and I simply want to make an answer to the letter. Don't think I am trying to influence you one way or the other. This is the letter: it goes about like this: "Crede Hubbard has purchased a three-flat building at 4332 Vincennes Avenue. Property values are always shot to hell when Negroes move in. Use whatever influence you have to induce him to sell and find out for us his lowest figures."' He added, 'Don't think I am trying to brow-beat you into selling this property.'"

"On the following Sunday night on my way back to Milwaukee, I read in the paper that my house had been bombed. My family was at home, my two boys sleeping about ten feet from the place that was most seriously damaged. The bomb was placed inside the vestibule. The girl there heard a taxicab drive up about twenty-five minutes to twelve and stop for a few minutes and start off again. About six minutes after the taxicab stopped, the explosion came, and in about five minutes there were not less than 300 people on the street in front of the place asking questions. There were a number of plain-clothes men in the crowd. I told my story to the chief of police and to a sergeant of the police and they said it was evidence enough to warrant the arrest of the officials of the Association named, but they also thought that it would do no good. . . . . 'The thing we will have to do is to catch somebody in the act, sweat him and make him tell who his backers are.'

"The police believe that the actual bombing is being done by a gang of young rough-necks who will stop at nothing, and they expect a pretty serious encounter if they are interfered with. A big automobile is being shadowed now by the police. It is used by this bunch of young fellows under suspicion, and it is thought that they keep the car well loaded with ammunition, and whoever attacks them must expect trouble. There are four plain-clothes men on guard in this district now. The police told me to get anything I want from a Mauser to a machine gun and sit back in the dark, and when anybody comes up to my hallway acting suspiciously to crack down on him and ask him what he was there for afterwards."

Bombing of the Harrison home.—Mrs. Gertrude Harrison, Negro, living alone with her children, contracted to buy a house at 4708 Grand Boulevard. In March, 1919, she moved in. She immediately received word that she had committed a grave error. She and her children were constantly subjected to the insulting remarks both of her immediate neighbors and passers-by.

DAMAGE DONE BY A BOMB

This bomb was thrown into a building at 3365 Indiana Avenue, occupied by Negroes. A six-year-old Negro child was killed.

On May 16, 1919, a Negro janitor informed her that neighbors were planning to bomb her house. She called up the Forty-eighth Street police station and told of the threatened danger. The officer answering the telephone characterized her report as "idle talk" and promised to send a man to investigate. The regular patrolman came in and promised to "keep an eye on the property," but there were ten blocks in his beat. A special guard was secured and paid by Mrs. Harrison when it was learned that one would not be furnished by the police.

The following night, May 17, her house was bombed while the patrolman was "punching his box" two blocks away and the special watchman was at the rear. A detail of police was then provided both at the front and rear. The following night a bomb was thrown on the roof of the house from the window of a vacant flat in the adjoining apartment house. The flat from which the bomb was thrown had been unlocked to admit the bombers and locked again. The police failed to question either the persons living in the apartment or those leaving it immediately after the explosion.

The first explosion blew out the front door and shattered the glass in the front of the house. The bomb was filled with gravel and bits of lead. The second was of similar character, but did not do as much damage. No arrests were made.

In all these fifty-eight bombings the police have been able to accomplish nothing definite. Practically every incident involved an automobile, descriptions of which were furnished by witnesses. The precautions taken to prevent bombings, even if they were well planned and systematically carried out, failed lamentably.

2. REACTION OF WHITES IN HYDE PARK

Increasing frequency of bombings, failure of the police to make arrests, and the apparent association of these acts of open violence with the white residents of Hyde Park drew out explanations.

Pastors of churches in the district who, it had been charged, helped to give circulation to printed sentiments of the organized opposition to the "invasion" were strong in their repudiation. The menace to law and order was definitely recognized and the public given to understand that neither the pastor nor his congregation had encouraged acts of lawlessness in any manner. In a statement to a Commission investigator, one of these pastors said, "I am not in sympathy with the methods and am very doubtful about the aims of the Property Owners' Association and have, therefore, been unable to join them or indorse their efforts."

A local paper, the *Real Estate News*, published a long article in February, 1920, on "Solving Chicago's Race Problem." It was directed at South Side property owners and carried a stern warning "against perils of boycott and terrorism being promoted by local protective associations." Referring to the bombing outrages, this paper, under the heading "Danger in Boycotts and Bombs," said:

In Kenwood and Hyde Park, particularly, a number of "protective associations" have been formed. Property owners have been urged to join these bodies, which, without attempt at concealment, advocate a boycott against all persons of a certain race. At meetings of these groups there has been open advocacy of violence. There has been incendiary talk. Bombs and bullets have been discussed, and speakers talking thus have been applauded. There have been repeated acts of violence. Night bombing of Negro homes and apartments has taken place. Bombing and shooting is increasing in frequency.

The time has come, we believe, for a word of solemn warning to all South Side property owners. It is: Keep out of those associations. If you are now in, get out! For you are in great danger of the penitentiary! You are in grave peril of losing your property by damage suits!

Another excerpt, under the heading "Perils of 'Protective' Organizations," said:

No one can justly criticize men for forming organizations to protect or advance their own interests lawfully. Property owners ought to unite wherever practicable for proper and lawful purposes beneficial to themselves. For such unions operate to the welfare of all.

Recently, however, a number of men have joined in forming and promoting organizations on the South Side which are perilous to themselves and to every property owner who joins them. Owners of real estate should be the last men in the world to get mixed up in movements involving violence, threats, intimidations, or boycotts. Because they are responsible. Their wealth cannot be concealed. Judgments against them are collectible.

Under the heading "Drastic Laws Forbid Conspiracies":

The law of conspiracy is drastic. Conspiracy is an association together of persons for the purpose of doing an unlawful thing in an unlawful way, or a lawful thing in an unlawful way, or an unlawful thing in a lawful way. Under the law, all persons in a conspiracy are equally guilty. One need not throw a bomb, or even know of the intent of throwing a bomb, to be found guilty. The act of one, no matter how irresponsible, is the act of all.

Any association formed in Chicago for the purpose of, or having among its aims, refusal to sell, lease or rent property to any citizen of a certain race, is an unlawful association. Every act of such an association for advancement of such an aim is an act of conspiracy, punishable criminally and civilly in the District Court of the United States. And every member of such an association is equally guilty with every other member. If one member hires a bomber, or a thug who commits murder in pursuance of the aims of the association, all the organization may be found guilty of conspiracy to destroy property or to commit murder, as the case may be.

This entire article was widely circulated in the disturbed neighborhoods by the Protective Circle, an organization of Negroes, 25,000 copies being mailed to residents of Hyde Park.

Residents of the district, stirred by the succession of bombings, began to protest. The paper of the Kenwood and Hyde Park Property Owners' Association reflected this feeling in a statement declaring that the Association had no connection with the bombings, and that its president was considering the advisability of assisting the authorities in apprehending these lawless individuals. On another occasion, this paper took pains to explain that the bombing of George A. Hyers' property on March 5 was an outgrowth of labor troubles and not of a property owners' organization recently formed in this community. At a meeting of the General Committee of the Property Owners' Association the following resolution was unanimously adopted:

WHEREAS, Our attention has been called to various explosions of bombs in our neighborhood at the houses of colored people living in this vicinity, and

WHEREAS, While we are anxious to persuade these people to move from this locality, we are opposed to violence of every description, therefore, be it

Resolved, That we condemn the action of anyone resorting to throwing of bombs or other methods not in accordance with reason, law or justice.

The attention of the city was directed to these unlawful happenings and protests from both white and Negro individuals made themselves heard. The bombings, however, did not abate in frequency. Neither were the police any more successful in locating their sources.

3. REACTION OF NEGROES

From the beginning Negroes were outspoken in their indignation over the bombings, but their protests had no apparent effect in checking the outrages.

The attacks, however, have made the Negroes firm in their stand. Mrs. Clarke was bombed four times; she still lives in the property and declares that she will not be driven out. Jesse Binga has been bombed six times but states he will not move. Only two of the forty Negro families bombed have moved; the others have made repairs, secured private watchmen or themselves kept vigil for night bombers, and still occupy the properties.

Following the bombing of Jesse Binga on June 18, 1920, the *Chicago Daily News* quoted him as saying to a policeman, "This is the limit; I'm going." When his attention was called to the statement he promptly replied:

Statements relative to my moving are all false. My idea of this bombing of my house is that it is an effort to retard the Binga State Bank which will take over the mortgages of colored people now buying property against which effort is being made to foreclose. I will not run. The race is at stake and not myself. If they can make me move they will have accomplished much of their aim because they can say, "We made Jesse Binga move; certainly you'll have to move," to all of the rest. If they can make the leaders move, what show will the smaller buyers have? Such headlines are efforts to intimidate Negroes not to purchase property and to scare some of them back South.

In February a group of Negroes formed themselves into a body known as the Protective Circle of Chicago, the purpose of which, as stated in its constitution, was "to combat, through legal means, the lawlessness of the Kenwood and Hyde Park Property Owners' Association and by organized effort to bring pressure to bear on city authorities to force them to apprehend those persons who have bombed the homes of twenty-one Negroes."

A mass meeting was held February 29, 1920, with 3,000 Negroes present. A popular appeal for funds for the purposes of this organization raised $1,000. Attacks were directed against the Kenwood and Hyde Park Property Owners' Association. A representative of the Protective Circle said in part:

The Hyde Park Property Owners' Association is not a new thing. It is more than eighteen years old. Eighteen years ago they proposed fourteen points as a platform for their Association. The thirteenth point was that they would keep out undesirables. All Negroes were classed as undesirables. Ten years ago Dr. Jenifer, a Negro minister, appeared before the Association and severely criticized the organization for its un-American policies. It is just recently that this organization has shown its hand openly, and the things that they have said and done are dangerously near to illegality. I have in my files this statement taken from a stenographic report of one of their meetings, made by the president of the Association: "If Negroes do not get out of Hyde Park, we will get Bolsheviks to bomb them out." The bombers of the homes of Negroes have been allowed to get away unpunished. Judge Gary hanged numbers of anarchists in the Haymarket riot for very much less complicity in bomb outrages than these men are guilty of. Hatred can never be counteracted by hatred. We cannot put any stop to the bombings of Negro homes by going out and bombing homes of white persons.

The Negro press severely condemned the bombings, and the Negro population in general felt that the apathy of city authorities and even the influential public was responsible for continuance of the outrages. Protests were sent to the governor of the state. The mayor, chief of police, and state's attorney were persistently importuned to stop the destruction of Negroes' property and remove the menace to their lives. Negroes pointed out, for example, that the authorities had shown ability to apprehend criminals, even those suspected of bomb-throwing. They cited the bombing of the home of a professional white "gunman," when eleven suspected bombers were caught in the dragnet of the state's attorney within thirty hours. Yet in fifty-eight bombings of Negro homes only two suspects were ever arrested.

In March, 1920, a Commission from the Chicago Church Federation Council sent a delegation to Mayor Thompson, Chief of Police Garrity, and State's Attorney Hoyne, to demand action on the bombing of Negroes' homes. Prominent white and colored men comprised this delegation. A prominent Negro, testifying before the Commission, said that he, with other Negroes, both from the local branch of the National Association for the Advancement of Colored People, and from other organizations, had carried their grievances to city officials. He said:

We have been to the mayor's office, we have been to the state's attorney's office we have sent representatives to both these offices, and nothing has been done— possibly something is being done, but nothing of great moment. I think that the colored people feel that they are so insecure in their physical rights that rather than take any chance they're going out and paying whatever the charge is for insurance against bombing.

Another delegation of Negroes in June, 1919, twice attempted to register a complaint with the mayor against bomb outrages. The mayor's secretary, however, refused them an audience with the mayor.

The editors of local daily papers have also been visited by mixed white and Negro delegations in an endeavor to arouse public opinion.

The effect of these delegations and protests has been small. One joint conference with the mayor, chief of police, and state's attorney brought out the information that it was beyond the state's attorney's province to make arrests. The mayor, after some discussion, instructed Chief of Police Garrity to do what he could toward putting a stop to the bombing of Negroes' homes. The chief of police, after explaining the shortage of patrolmen, said he would do so.

The bombing question began to figure in local politics. Charges were made before the primary election of September, 1920, that the city administration had not given Negroes the protection it had promised. The matter of apprehending the "nefarious bomb plotters" was included in the platforms of Negroes running for office, and in those of white candidates seeking Negro votes.

The Commission had neither authority nor facilities for accomplishing what all public agencies had signally failed to do. It could, however, and did, go over the trail of the bombers and collect information which shows that the sentiment aroused in the contested neighborhoods was a factor in encouraging actual violence. Whatever antagonisms there were before the agitation were held in restraint, even though Negroes were already neighbors. Other districts, like Woodlawn and sections of the North Side, undergoing almost identical experiences as those of Hyde Park, have had no violence; the absence of stimulated sentiment is as conspicuous as the absence of violence. In the Hyde Park district, between Thirty-ninth and Forty-seventh streets and State Street and Cottage Grove Avenue, four-fifths of the bombings occurred. All but three of those happening outside the district were against real estate men accused of activities affecting the Hyde Park District. It seemed, especially in the first bombings, that the bombers had information about business transactions which the general public could not ordinarily get. Houses were bombed in numbers of cases long before their occupancy by Negroes. Each of the bombings was apparently planned, and the opportune moment came after long vigil and, as it would seem, after deliberately setting the stage. The first bombing of Binga does not appear to have been the result of resentment of neighbors in the vicinity of his home, for it was his office on State Street that was bombed. His office is in a neighborhood around which there is no contest.

4. OTHER MEANS EMPLOYED TO KEEP OUT NEGROES

The Grand Boulevard Property Owners' Association officially decided that its object should be "the acquisition, management, improvement and disposition, including leasing, sub-leasing and sale of residential property to both white and colored people within the said district heretofore described." This district was to include the area from Thirty-fifth to Sixty-third streets, and from the Chicago and Rock Island Railroad tracks to Lake Michigan.

In August, 1920, the manager of the Association cited an instance in which it had functioned. On Vernon Avenue a white man had sold property direct to Negroes. The next-door neighbor had arranged a similar sale to potential Negro buyers. The neighbor next to him, a widow, loath to lose her home, appealed to the Association. After a conference with the possible Negro buyers, their money was returned to them, the Association purchased the house in question, and the whole matter was thus amicably arranged.

During April, 1920, inquiries were made by the Commission into the unrest caused by rumors that 800 Negro families intended to move into Hyde Park. It developed that May 1, the customary "moving day," was feared both by whites in Hyde Park and by Negroes in and out of Hyde Park. Negroes living there feared that an attempt would be made to oust them by canceling or refusing to renew their leases, and whites thought Negroes might get possession of some of the properties vacated on that date. The Commission found, however, only eighteen instances where leases were canceled on houses occupied by Negroes who were having difficulty in finding other places to live.

In the summer of 1920 the Kenwood and Hyde Park Property Owners' Association stated that sixty-eight Negro families had been moved through cancellation of leases and mortgage foreclosures.

Incidental to the general plan of opposition to the entrance of Negroes in Hyde Park was the sending of threatening letters. For example, in August, 1919, a leading Negro real estate agent and banker received this pen-printed notice by mail:

HEADQUARTERS OF THE WHITE HANDS
TERRITORY, MICHIGAN AVE. TO LAKE FRONT

You are the one who helped cause this riot by encouraging Negroes to move into good white neighborhoods and you know the results of your work. This trouble has only begun and we advise you to use your influence to get Negroes to move out of these neighborhoods to *Black Belt* where they belong and in conclusion we advise you to get off South Park Ave. yourself. Just take this as a warning. You know what comes next.

Respect.

WARNING COM.

This man's home and office have been bombed a number of times. Efforts were made to buy out individual Negroes who had settled in the district, as well as to cause renters to move out. There are numerous incidents of this nature, with indications of many others. A Negro woman who was living in the district, told one of the Commission's investigators that she and her husband had formerly lived in the 3800 block of Lake Park Avenue. White neighbors caused them so much trouble that they had moved and bought the apartment house in which they are now living, renting out the second and third flats. Almost immediately white people began to call and inquire whether she was the janitress, or whether she was renting or buying the place. When she gave evasive answers, letters began to arrive by mail. One letter was slipped under the door at night. These letters informed her that she was preventing the sale of the adjoining house because she would not sell and no white person would live next door to her. She was advised that it would be best for her to answer and declare her intentions. Two white women called and offered her $1,500 more than she had paid for the property. She refused and a few days later she received a letter demanding an immediate answer, to the Kenwood and Hyde Park Property Owners' Association.

Later three white men in overseas uniforms inquired as to the ownership of the property, asking if she was the janitress and if she knew who the owner was. She answered in the negative. One of the men tore down a "For Sale" sign on the adjoining property, and another informed her that it was the intention to turn the neighborhood back to white people and that all Negroes must go.

This woman is the president of a neighborhood protective league, including the Negroes in several of the blocks thereabouts. She received a letter from the Kenwood and Hyde Park Property Owners' Association asking the purposes and intentions of this league.

This woman also reported that a man had been going about the neighborhood under the pretext of making calling cards, advising Negroes to sell out and leave the neighborhood, as it was better not to stay where they were not wanted. Another white man who had been about the neighborhood selling wearing apparel, told her that two Negro families in the neighborhood would be bombed. She inquired how he knew this and was told to wait and see. Within two weeks these bombings had taken place.

IV. TREND OF THE NEGRO POPULATION

In considering the expansion of Negro residential areas, the most important is the main South Side section where more of the Negro population lives. This group is hemmed in on the north by the business district and on the west by overcrowded areas west of Wentworth Avenue, called in this report "hostile." During the ten years 1910–20 business houses and light manufacturing plants were moving south from the downtown district, pushing ahead of them the Negro population between Twelfth and Thirty-first streets. At the same time the Negro population was expanding into the streets east of Wabash Avenue. This extension was stopped by Lake Michigan, about eight blocks east. Negro families then began filtering into Hyde Park, immediately to the south.

In 1917 the Chicago Urban League found that Negroes were then living on Wabash Avenue as far south as Fifty-fifth street east of State Street, where they had moved from the district west of State Street. From Thirty-first to Thirty-ninth streets, on Wabash Avenue, Negroes had been living from nine to eleven years, and the approximate percentage of Negroes by blocks ranged from 95 to 100; from Thirty-ninth Street to Forty-seventh Street they had been living from one to five years and averaged 50 per cent. The movement had been almost entirely from the west and north.

On Indiana Avenue, from Thirty-first to Forty-second streets, a similar trend was revealed. In the 3100 block, Negroes had been living for eight years, in the 3200 block for fourteen years; in the more southerly blocks their occupancy had been much briefer, ranging down to five months. In the most northerly of these blocks Negroes numbered 90 per cent and in the most southerly only 2 per cent.

On Prairie Avenue, farther east, two Negro families bought homes in the 3100 block in 1911, but the majority of the Negroes had come in since 1916. The percentage of Negroes in that block was 50. From Thirty-second to Thirty-ninth Street the blocks were found to have more than 90 per cent Negroes. One family had been there five years and the average residence was one and one-half years. No Negroes were found from Fortieth to Forty-fourth Street on Prairie Avenue. There were two families in the 4500 block, and none south of that.

On Forest Avenue, from Thirty-first to Thirty-ninth Street, 75 per cent of the families were Negroes and had lived there less than six years.

On Calumet Avenue, the next street east of Prairie, Negroes had begun to live within four years. The population was 75 per cent Negro from Thirty-first to Thirty-ninth Street. None live south of Thirty-ninth Street, except at the corner, where they had been living for five months.

A similar situation was found on Rhodes Avenue, still farther east, from Thirty-first to Thirty-ninth Street. Negroes had lived in Vincennes Avenue, the next street east, less than two years, and in Cottage Grove Avenue, still farther east less than one year.

South Park Avenue and its continuation, Grand Boulevard (south of Thirty-fifth Street) was the most recent street into which Negroes had moved in large numbers. This had occurred within the years 1915–17. The first Negro families had moved into the 3400 block less than four years previously. The percentage of Negroes between Thirty-first and Thirty-fifth streets was less than 50. Within five months two Negro families had moved into the hitherto exclusively white 3500 block.

Few Negroes had moved from east of State Street to west of that street.

V. OUTLYING NEIGHBORHOODS

The Commission's investigation being confined to the city of Chicago, the growing Negro colonies in such suburbs as Evanston and Glencoe were not studied, but attention was given to two southwestern outlying neighborhoods

A NEGRO CHORAL SOCIETY

in the east part of Morgan Park, just inside the city limits, and the village of Robbins, wholly Negro, just outside.

1. MORGAN PARK

In 1910, 126 Negroes lived in Morgan Park, with a total population of 5,269. In 1920 the area had been incorporated in the city of Chicago, and there were 695 Negroes in a total population of 7,780 occupying approximately the same area.

In its early days Morgan Park was the site of a theological seminary, which in 1892 became part of the University of Chicago. The first Negroes there were servants, mostly from the South, working in the households of the professors. The colony remained, and its more recent increase was due in considerable measure to the influx of well-to-do Negroes from farther north in Chicago, many of whom bought houses. In some cases Negroes in congested Negro residential areas sold out to Negroes arriving in the migration and re-established themselves in much better dwellings and surroundings in Morgan Park.

Less prosperous Negroes also came, despite the feeling of some home owners that too great an influx of that type would injure property values and render the neighborhood less desirable. Many of these work in the South Chicago steel mills and the shops at Pullman. Some work in the Stock Yards.

A number of Negroes of Morgan Park are employed at the Chicago City Hall. Some are porters on Pullman cars. Only a small number are laborers. Many of the women sew or work as car cleaners and seem reluctant to do housework even at day wages.

Physically Morgan Park is attractive with comfortable homes and large grounds. Several churches, a number of schools, and an attractive park all add to the desirability of the place as a "home town." The lots are deep, affording plenty of space for gardens, and many vacant lots are cultivated. The opportunity for garden patches is an attraction for many Negroes. There are two Negro churches, Methodist and Baptist, and a Colored Men's Improvement Association which has provided a social hall for the Negro population.

School facilities are inadequate, and the buildings are old and overcrowded. Because of this congestion, it becomes necessary for children in the sixth and higher grades to go three miles to a school on Western Avenue. About twenty Negroes attend the high school. In the Esmond Street school approximately 25 per cent of the children are Negroes. The Negroes have repeatedly requested enlarged school facilities. They want a new building conveniently situated for their children.

The white people of Morgan Park are not unfriendly toward their Negro neighbors, though there seems to be a common understanding that Negroes must not live west of Vincennes Road, which bisects the town from northeast to southwest. A Negro once bought a house across the line but found he was so unwelcome that he promptly sold again.   More recently the owner of a three-story brick flat building rented to Negroes the twenty flats above his stores.   A protest was made by both white and Negro house owners, so that he was forced to eject the Negro tenants.

The demand for homes is shown in the numbers of Negroes who go to Morgan Park on Sundays by automobile, street car, and train.   In the spring of 1920 a number of houses were being erected for Negro occupancy in what is known in Morgan Park as "No Man's Land," east of Vincennes Road from 109th to 112th streets.   This swampy tract of land was being reclaimed. Streets had been surveyed and laid out, though with little paving.   Water, light, and gas were available, and some efforts at drainage had been made, leaving some stagnant pools.   Other plans involved the building of eighty five-room bungalows by a Chicago contractor.   Six of these were under construction at the time of the investigator's visit, and five had been sold, corner-lot houses at $4,550, houses on inside lots at $4,330.

Morgan Park Negroes appear to be progressing financially.   An officer of a local trust and savings bank said that they met their obligations promptly, only occasionally defaulting or suffering foreclosure and then only because of illness, death, or loss of employment.   The same officer said savings accounts of Negroes were increasing in number, though small in amount,

Whites and Negroes maintain a friendly attitude.   During the 1919 riots a number of conferences took place between Negroes and white people of Morgan Park.   The Negroes kept rather close to their own neighborhood, and the only difficulty the police had was in controlling rowdy white boys.

Younger children of the two races play together in the school yards.   A teacher in the Esmond Street school declared that no distinction was made between Negroes and whites in that school.   It was noted, however, that when games were played, this teacher directed the little Negroes to take little Negro girls as partners.   Some prejudice is discernible among whites in the community, but there is an evident desire to be fair and to give the Negroes every reasonable opportunity to exemplify good citizenship so long as they do not move from their own into the white neighborhoods.

Those familiar with the Morgan Park settlement believe that it offers unusual inducements as a home community for Negroes.   The contractor who is already building for Negroes there has confidence in the venture.   He has dealt before with Negroes and found them satisfactory clients.

2. ROBBINS

This village is the only exclusively Negro community near Chicago with Negroes in all village offices.

Robbins is not attractive physically.   It is not on a car line and there is no pretense of paved streets, or even sidewalks.   The houses are homemade, in most cases by labor mornings, nights, and holidays, after or before the day's wage-earning. Tar paper, roofing paper, homemade tiles, hardly seem sufficient to shut out the weather; older houses, complete with windows, doors, porches, fences, and gardens, indicate that some day these shelters will become real houses. In 1920 the village took out its incorporation papers, and while there are some who regret this independence and talk of asking Blue Island to annex it, in the main the citizens are proud of their village and certain of its future. There are 380 people all told, men, women, and children, living in something more than seventy houses. It is a long mile down the road to the street car, but daily men and women trudge away to their work, taking with them the feeling of home ownership, of a place for the children to play unmolested, of friends and neighbors.

These men and women find many kinds of work in the neighboring towns—at the mills, on the railroads, in the factories. Many of the women work in the factory of Libby, McNeil & Libby. Their wages go into payments for their homes. Men and women together are living as pioneer families lived—working and sacrificing to feel the independence of owning a bit of ground and their own house.

C. THE NEGRO COMMUNITY

I. THE BEGINNING OF THE NEGRO COMMUNITY

Negroes have been living in Chicago since it was founded. In fact, Jean Baptiste Point de Saible, a San Domingan Negro, was the first settler and in 1790 built the first house, a rude hut on the north bank of the Chicago River near what is now the Michigan Boulevard Bridge.

There are records of Negroes owning property in Chicago as early as 1837, the year of its incorporation as a city. In 1844 there were at least five Negro property owners and in 1847 at least ten. Their property was in the original first and second wards of the city, one on Lake Street, others on Madison, Clark, and Harrison, and Fifth Avenue. In 1848 the first Negro church property was purchased at the corner of Jackson and Buffalo streets, indicating the presence of the first colony of Negroes. In 1850 the passage of the Fugitive Slave Law caused many to flee for safety to Canada, many of the property owners disposing of their holdings at a great loss. In 1854 Negroes held two pieces of church property in the same general locality. Although the great majority lived on Clark and Dearborn streets north of Harrison Street, there was a tendency among the property-owning class to invest in outlying property. Some of them bought property as far south as what is now Thirty-third Street.

The year of the Great Fire, 1871, Negroes owned four pieces of church property. That fire stopped at Harrison Street and did not consume all of the Negro settlement. A second large fire in 1874 spread northeast and burned 812 buildings over an area of forty-seven acres. With the rebuilding of the city they were pushed southward to make room for the business district.

In 1900 the most congested area of Negro residence, called the "Black Belt," was a district thirty-one blocks long and four blocks wide, extending from Harrison Street on the north to Thirty-ninth Street on the south, between Wabash and Wentworth avenues. Although other colonies had been started in other parts of the city, notably the West Side, at least 50 per cent of the 1900 Negro population of 30,150 lived in this area. As this main area of Negro residence grew, the proportion of Negroes to the total Negro population living in it increased until in 1920 it contained 90 per cent of the Negroes of the city.

II. THE ORGANIZATION OF THE NEGRO COMMUNITY

In the discussion of race contacts attention is called to the peculiar conditions which compel Negroes of the city to develop many of their own institutions and agencies. Partly from necessity and partly from choice, they have established their own churches, business enterprises, amusement places, and newspapers. Living and associating for the most part together, meeting in the same centers for face-to-face relations, trusting to their own physicians, lawyers, and ministers, a compact community with its own fairly definite interests and sentiments has grown up.

The institutions within the Negro community that have been developed to aid it in maintaining itself and promoting its own welfare, are of four general types: (1) commercial and industrial enterprises; (2) organizations for social intercourse; (3) religious organizations; (4) agencies for civic and social betterment.

1. COMMERCIAL AND INDUSTRIAL ENTERPRISES

Commercial and industrial establishments conducted by Negroes are listed by Ford S. Black in his yearly *Blue Book*, which serves as a directory of Negro activities. They increased from 1,200 in 1919 to 1,500 in 1920. The compilation lists 651 on State Street, the main thoroughfare, 549 on principal cross streets, and more than 300 on other streets. The increase is strikingly shown in the following figures: In 1918 Negro business places on Thirty-first Street numbered nine and seventy-one in 1920; on Thirty-fifth Street there were forty-seven in 1918 and seventy-seven in 1920. On Cottage Grove Avenue, Negroes have only recently established themselves in large numbers, yet between Twenty-eighth and Forty-fifth streets there are fifty-seven Negro business places, including nine groceries, three drug-stores, and two undertaking establishments.

A partial list of business places as listed in Black's *Blue Book* is given:

Art stores	14	Barber shops	211
Automobile schools and repair shops	10	Baths	2
		Blacksmith shops	6
Bakeries, wholesale and retail	13	Book and stationery stores	6
Banks	2	Chiropodist	29

OLIVET BAPTIST CHURCH
The largest Negro church in Chicago (old building), at Twenty-ninth and Dearborn streets

ST. MARK'S M.E. CHURCH
Located at Fiftieth Street and Wabash Avenue, built by Negroes

OLIVET BAPTIST CHURCH

The largest Negro church in Chicago, larger and more modern building, Thirty-first Street and South Park Avenue, purchased recently by Negroes.

Cleaning, dyeing, and repairing establishments	68	Music and musical instruments	16
Clothing stores	8	Newspapers and magazines	13
Decorators	12	Musicians and music teachers	66
Dressmaking shops	32	Notions	25
Drug-stores	31	Optometrists	4
Electricians and locksmiths	9	Orchestras	1
Employment agencies	15	Photographers	4
Express and storage offices	71	Plumbers	4
Fish markets	7	Printers	20
Florists	5	Public stenographers	6
Furnace and stove repairing	6	Real estate offices	52
Groceries and delicatessens	119	Restaurants	87
Hairdressing parlors	108	Schools	4
Hotels	11	Shoemaking and repairing shops	33
Ice-cream and confectionery stores	7	Shoe-shining parlors	26
Insurance companies	3	Sign painters	4
Jewelers	5	Soft-drink parlors	11
Laundries	2	Tailors	62
Medicine specialists	9	Toilet articles	10
Millinery shops	15	Undertaking establishments	21
		Vending machines	2

2. ORGANIZATIONS FOR SOCIAL INTERCOURSE

Various organizations for social intercourse and mutual helpfulness have developed in the Negro community. Some are local lodges or branches of national organizations, and others are purely local and independent. Some are simply for social intercourse, and others have in addition benefit features, professional interests, etc. Frequent reference is made in the family histories given in this report to these various organizations.

Fraternal organizations.—Fraternal organizations are an old institution among Negroes. In the South they rank next in importance to the church; in the North they have considerable prestige. Membership is large and interest is strong. Following is a list of the most active in Chicago:

Elks, Great Lakes Lodge No. 43, I.B.P.O.	Masons
Elks of the World (an independent order of Elks)	Grand Court Heroines of Jericho of Illinois
Ancient Order of Foresters	Eastern Star
Catholic Order of Foresters	The Golden Circle
American Woodmen	Odd Fellows (G.U.O. of O.F.)
Builders of America	Royal Circle of Friends
Knights of Pythias	United Brotherhood of Friendship
Mosaic Templars of America	Sisters of the Mysterious Ten

All of these organizations, although having their own rituals, serve as a means of group control and of exchange of views and opinions. They are also a guaranty against absolute friendlessness, and that is perhaps one of the strongest motives for the establishment of the first organizations years ago. Much charitable and relief work is carried on by these fraternal bodies among their members.

Out of these associations have grown clubs with social activities among wider circles. There are, for example, the Easter Lily Club, the Mayflower Club, and the Masonic Progressive Club.

Social clubs.—Many of the clubs and societies with social, educational, or professional interests are modeled after those of the larger community. There are, for example, the Arts and Letters Society, the University Society, and Civic Study Club. There are also many smaller clubs organized for various purposes, but designed principally to serve the Negro community. There are more than seventy women's clubs, leagued in the Chicago Federation of Colored Women's Clubs. There are also the Art and Charity Club, Chicago Union Charity Club, Cornell Charity, Dearborn Centre, Diana Charity, East End 30th Ward, East Side Woman's Club, Eureka Fine Arts, Fideles Charity, Giles Charity, Hyacinth Charity, Ideal Embroidery Art, Ideal Woman's Club, Imperial Art, Kenwood Center, Mental Pearls, Mothers' Union, Necessity Club, New Method Industrial, North Shore, North Side Industrial, Motley Social Uplift, Phyllis Wheatley Club, Progressive Circle of Kings Daughters, 37th Ward Civic League, Volunteer Workers, West Side Woman's City Club, and the Woman's Civic League.

Among the exclusive social clubs, perhaps the most important is the Appomattox Club. Its membership includes the leading business and professional men, and it has a well-appointed club building. Its membership is limited and it carries civic and social prestige.

The Phalanx Club is an organization of government employees. Its membership is large, though limited by occupational restriction. Its interests are largely social. The Forty Club and Half Century Club are purely social and still more exclusive.

Negro professional societies, sometimes formed because of the objections of whites to the participation of Negroes in white societies of a similar nature, include the Lincoln Dental Association, Physicians, Dentists and Pharmacists' Association, a Bar Association, and a Medical Association.

3. RELIGIOUS ORGANIZATIONS

Negro churches.—The church is one of the first and probably one of the strongest institutions among Negroes. The importance of churches in the Negro community lies not only in their large membership and religious influence, but in their provision of a medium of social control for great numbers of Chicago Negroes, and in their great value in promoting the adjustment of newcomers.

In the South the churches are the principal centers for face-to-face relations. They serve as a medium for the exchange of ideas, making and maintaining friendships, community co-operation, collective striving, group competition, as well as for the dissemination of information, assistance and advice on practical problems, and the upholding of religious ideals. The pastors know the members personally, and the church exercises a definite control over individual behavior.

The church is often the only Negro social institution with an unhampered opportunity for development. In most southern cities, Negroes have no Y.M.C.A., public playground, welfare organizations, public library, gymnasium, orderly dance halls, public parks, or theaters. The church in a large degree takes the place of these and fills a vacancy created by the lack of the public facilities ordinarily found in white communities. In many instances it determines the social standing of the individual Negro. No one can escape the opprobrium attached to the term "sinner" if he is not a member of the church, however successful otherwise.

The minister is the recognized leader of the Negroes, and often their legal adviser and school teacher. He is responsible for the social good behavior of his people. No movement can get the support of the people unless it has his sanction.

In the North the function of both Negro church and pastor is different. Negroes can find other places than the church for their leisure time; numerous urban and civic organizations with trained workers look after their interests, probably better than the church. In the Y.M.C.A. they find religion related to the development of their bodies and minds. In northern cities enterprises and movements thrive without the good-will or sanction of the clergy, and even against their protest.

The field wholly occupied in the South by the church is shared in the North by the labor union, the social club, lectures, and political and other organizations. Some of the northern churches, realizing this, have established employment agencies and other activities of a more social nature in response to this new demand.

Social activities.—The churches in Chicago serve as social-contact centers, though not to the same extent as in the South. Frequently they arrange lectures, community programs, fêtes, and meetings. Many of them, seeking to influence the conduct of the group, have provided recreation and amusements for their members. Several churches have social-service departments, basket-ball teams, and literary societies. Olivet Baptist Church, with a membership of 9,069, maintains an employment department, rooming directory, kindergarten, and day nursery, and employs sixteen workers; in its social organization there are forty-two auxiliary departments. During the last five years it has raised $200,000, contributed $5,600 for charitable relief, and found jobs for 1,100 Negroes.

Unique among such developments is the People's Church and Metropolitan Community Center, organized by a group which withdrew from the Bethel

African Methodist Episcopal Church in October, 1920. Relying solely upon its membership, it raised $22,000 during its first five months. Six persons are employed to carry on the work, one a social-service secretary. Land for a church building has been purchased, and plans have been made to buy a community-center building to accommodate several thousand people.

Relief work.—The records of the United Charities, which assumes the care of dependent children of the juvenile court, show a much smaller proportion of appeals for aid from Negroes than might be expected. This is partly explained by the work of the churches in relieving Negro families. A very high proportion of families below the line of comfortable subsistence belong to the churches, the small "store-front" churches. The number and variety of denominational divisions and sects increases competition for membership and sends pastors and members out into the community to gather in the people. Forty-one churches, many of them small, reported a total of $15,038 distributed during 1920 for the relief of the sick and distressed.

Following is a summary of information collected by the Commission concerning the churches in the Negro community:

Number of churches, regular and "store-front"........	170
Number visited...................................	146
Number of churches owning their property............	49
Value of property owned...........................	$1,677,183
Indebtedness on church properties being bought.......	$325,895.91
Amount collected in 146 churches during 1919.........	$400,000.00
Membership of 62 of the 146 churches...............	36,856
Number in Sunday school in 57 of 146 churches.......	16,847
Number of persons in attendance in 64 of 146 churches	
Morning.......................................	20,379
Evening.......................................	13,806

In a very few cases, Negroes are found to be members of white churches, but the Negro churches have an entirely Negro membership with Negro pastors.

"Store-front" churches.—The "store-front" church membership is merely a small group which, for one reason or another, has sought to worship independently of any connection with the larger churches. The establishment of such a church may be the result of a withdrawal of part of the membership of a larger church. They secure a pastor or select a leader from their own number and continue their worship in a place where their notions are not in conflict with other influences. Most frequently a minister formerly in the South has come with or followed his migrant members and has re-established his church in Chicago. Or again a group with religious beliefs and ceremonies not in accord with those of established churches may establish a church of its own. The groups are usually so small and the members so poor as to make the purchase of a building impossible. The custom has been to engage a small store and put chairs in it. Hence the name "store-front" church.

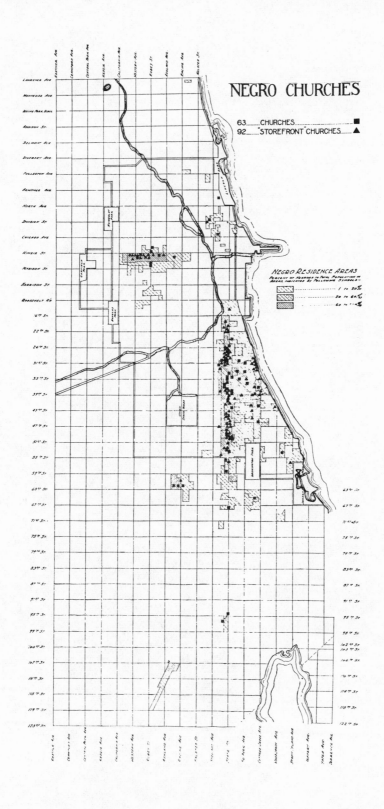

NEGRO CHURCHES

63 ___ CHURCHES ___ ■
92 ___ STOREFRONT CHURCHES ___ ▲

NEGRO RESIDENCE AREAS
PERCENT OF NEGROES TO TOTAL POPULATION OF
AREAS, INDICATED BY FOLLOWING SYMBOLS—

              1 TO 20%
              20 TO 60%
              60 TO 100%

Denominations.—The varieties of denominational divisions are wide and interesting. A classification on the basis of information collected by the Commission is given in Table VII.

TABLE VII

Denomination	Regular	"Store-Front"
Baptist:		
Missionary Baptist.....................	19	61
Free Will Baptist...........................	....	2
Primitive Baptist.........................	....	4
Methodist:		
Methodist Episcopal....................	6	....
African Methodist Episcopal.............	9	6
African Methodist Episcopal Zion.........	3	1
Colored Methodist Episcopal.............	3	....
Independent Methodist Episcopal.........	....	6
Presbyterian............................	2	2
Episcopal................................	1	....
Congregational.........................	1	....
Disciples of Christ......................	1	....
Saints, Holiness, and Healing Churches......	....	20
Total............................	45	102

The steady growth in the number of churches is shown in the dates of organization of sixty-five of them as given in Table VIII.

TABLE VIII

Year	Number
1825–50	2
1850–80	2
1880–90	5
1890–1900	5
1900–1910	5
1910–15	12
1915–16	4
1917	3
1918	15
1919	6
1920	6
Total	65

Church property.—It was not easy to determine the amount of money raised and handled by the Negro churches for any specific period, because only the better-organized churches keep accurate accounts.

The total value of the property holdings of twenty-six of the larger and better-organized churches is $1,677,183.02, with a total indebtedness on nineteen of them of $318,595.91. In twenty of the twenty-six annual collections aggregate $226,216.25.

Out of 100 "store-front" churches visited only seven own or are buying the property they use. The total value of the property of these seven churches is $44,300. Four of the seven have an indebtedness of $7,300; and the four that kept records showed a total annual collection of $5,170.

The pastors.—A sharp division both as to education and experience is found between the pastors of the regular churches and those of the "store-front" churches. Generally the larger churches have the better-trained, more experienced, and more highly salaried ministers. Exceptions are found in the case of one or two "holiness" churches.

The ministers in these various churches represent a range of training from that of such seminaries as Newton Theological and institutions like Yale University, University of Chicago, and Northwestern University, down to that of the sixth grade in grammar school. Some have had no schooling at all. The number of specially trained ministers totals twenty-one. Six of these are graduates of recognized northern institutions, while fourteen are graduates of recognized Negro institutions such as Lincoln University, Howard University, Virginia Union University, and Livingston College. Four are graduates of standard high schools and four of other high schools below the standard rating. The remainder fall below the sixth grade. Among this last group it is not unusual to hear that "God prepares a man to preach; he does not have to go to school for that. All he must do is to open his mouth and God will fill it. The universities train men away from the Bible."

The range of active service in the ministry is from two months to forty-four years. Here again the larger established churches have the ministers of longer service. Typical examples are found in churches like Bethel African Methodist Episcopal Church, whose pastor has had forty-four years of service; Shiloh, thirty-seven years; Bethesda Baptist Church, thirty-seven years; Grace Presbyterian Church, thirty-two years (all at this one church); Original Providence, thirty-five years; Berean Baptist Church, thirty years.

4. SOCIAL AND CIVIC AGENCIES

Social agencies in the Negro communities are an expression of group effort to adjust itself to the larger community. Within the Negro community there are two types, those especially for Negroes and those which are branches of the agencies of the larger community but located conveniently for use by Negroes.

A. AGENCIES ESPECIALLY FOR NEGROES

Chicago Urban League.—This organization is one of the thirty-two branches of the National Urban League whose headquarters are in New York City. It was established in Chicago in 1917 during the period of heaviest migration of Negroes to the city. The numerous problems consequent upon this influx guided the development of the League's activities. Its executive board and

TRINITY M.E. CHURCH AND COMMUNITY HOUSE

Located at Prairie Avenue near Thirty-first Street, purchased recently by Negroes

SOUTH PARK M.E. CHURCH

The congregation moved from a store-front church to this edifice at Thirty-second Street and South Park Avenue in less than three years after the church was established.

PILGRIM BAPTIST CHURCH

Located at Thirty-third Street and Indiana Avenue. Formerly a Jewish synagogue, purchased recently by Negroes.

officers are whites and Negroes of high standing and influence in both the white and Negro groups, and it is supported by voluntary subscriptions. Within four years this organization has taken the leading place among all the social agencies working especially among Negroes. It has a well-trained staff of twelve paid workers, and its work is carried out along the lines accepted in modern social work. The League has organized its activities as follows: Administration Department, Industrial Department, Research and Records Department, Children's Department, settlement work.

The work of the Administration Department involves, in addition to general management, co-operation with other agencies and co-ordination of their efforts for community improvement through interracial meetings, conferences, and joint undertakings.

The Industrial Department during 1920 placed more than 15,000 Negroes in positions, made industrial investigations in sixteen plants, provided lectures for workingmen in plants and for foremen over Negro workers. It also investigates complaints of workers, selects and fits men for positions, secures positions for Negroes where Negroes have never worked before, and assists in other ways the adjustment of Negroes in industry. More than 25,000 persons passed through the department during 1920.

The Department of Research and Records makes the investigations on the basis of which the programs of the League are carried out. Its information is a permanent and growing body of material useful to all agencies and persons interested in obtaining reliable information concerning Negroes in Chicago.

The Children's Department handles cases of boys and girls and co-operates with the schools, juvenile protective organizations, the juvenile court and probation department, and various other child-helping institutions. A total of 540 such cases were adjusted during 1920.

During 1919 a total of $28,659 was raised and used in the support of the Chicago Urban League.

The Wendell Phillips Settlement on the West Side is under the supervision of the League. The settlement has a day nursery and provides a center and leadership for twenty-five groups in the West Side community.

Wabash Avenue Y.M.C.A.—This organization is a branch of the local Young Men's Christian Association, but because of its location and the peculiar social problems of its membership and vicinity, it has become one of the strongest agencies of the community. Its work is among boys and young men, many of whom are industrial workers in various plants. Community work is vigorously promoted. In 1920 an enthusiastic group of 1,137 boys was enlisted in a neighborhood clean-up campaign, and 100 community gardens were put in operation. Moving pictures and community singing were provided during the summer months. The following list gives some statistics of activities for the first nine months of 1920.

SOCIAL ACTIVITIES

Attendance at building................................ 140,740
Attendance at reading-room........................... 19,402
Attendance at Bible classes........................... 1,514
Attendance at industrial clubs........................ 5,394
Attendance at entertainments......................... 6,542
Meals served.. 100,610
Dormitory attendance................................ 71,396
Persons directed to rooms............................ 614
Persons assisted..................................... 1,526
Persons reached through community work.............. 10,406
Personal religious interviews......................... 396
Men referred to churches............................. 196

PHYSICAL WORK

Men used swimming-pool............................. 3,604
Boys used swimming-pool............................. 14,096
Men and boys used shower baths...................... 24,332
Participated in leagues and tournament................ 3,906
Spectators.. 44,742
Men attended gymnasium classes...................... 5,622
Boys attended gymnasium classes..................... 17,106

In addition to the foregoing work this institution has promoted efficiency
and industrial clubs among Negro workers in industrial plants, three glee
clubs, noonday recreational programs, and nine baseball teams.

During 1919 the total contributions for support were $15,353, of which
$3,100 came from Negroes. The membership dues of the latter, however,
totaled $16,000 and receipts from operation amounted to $143,747.

*Chicago Branch of the National Association for the Advancement of Colored
People.*—This organization aims to carry out the general policies of the National
Association as far as they apply to Chicago. The national purpose is to
combat injustice against Negroes, stamp out race discriminations, prevent
lynchings, burnings, and torturings of Negroes, and, when they do occur, to
demand the prosecution of those responsible, to assure to every citizen of color
the common rights of an American citizen, and secure for colored children
equal opportunity in public-school education.

In Chicago, the principal efforts of this organization have been in the line
of securing justice for Negroes in the courts and opposing race discriminations
in public accommodations. Its most active period followed the riots of 1919.
With a number of competent attorneys, white and Negro, it gave legal support
to Negro riot victims and followed through the courts the cases of many Negroes
accused of participation in rioting.

Community service.—The South Side Community Service is a re-established
organization growing out of the Soldiers and Sailors' Club. It aims to provide
wholesome recreation and leisure-time activities for its neighborhood. At

SOCIAL AGENCIES
USED BY NEGROES

AGENCIES ESPECIALLY FOR NEGROES _ _ _ _ _ _ _ _ ■
GENERAL AGENCIES HAVING NEGRO BRANCHES _ _ _ _ _ ▲
GENERAL AGENCIES USED BY NEGROES AND WHITES _ _ _ ◀ C
NEGRO RESIDENTIAL AREA ▨▨▨▨▨

Oak St.

United Charities

Chicago Ave.

United Charities

Rush St.

Maxwell Phelps Settlement

Madison St.

Dependent Children, Department of the Juvenile Court.

Illinois Childrens Home & Aid Society.

Harrison St.

Roosevelt Road

16th St.

St. Lukes Hospital.

22nd St.

26th St.

Post Graduate Hospital.
Rosely Dental Clinic.
Mary Thompson Hospital for Women & Children.
South West Dental Dispensary.
Soldier's Bureau.
United Charities.
Chicago Urban League.
Frederick Douglas Center.
Day Nursery.
Olivet Baptist Church.
Unity Club.
Douglas Kimberly Home.

31st St.

South Side Soldiers & Sailors Club.
Day Nursery Equal Rights Protective Association.
Jane Dean's Home.
National Association for the Advancement of Colored People.
Illinois Free Employment Bureau.
American Red Cross.
Y.M.C.A.
Provident Hospital & Dispensary.

35th St.

Y.M.C.A.

39th St.

Abraham Lincoln Center.

43rd St.

United Charities Dental Clinic.
Elaine Home for Working Girls.

47th St.

Children's South Side Free Dispensary.
Julia Johnson Home for Working Girls.
Illinois Technical School for Colored Girls.

51st St.

55th St.

Home for Aged and Infirm Colored People.
Baptist Missionary Womens Home.

59th St.

Louise Training School for Colored Boys.

63rd St.

Woodlawn Community Association.

67th St.

71st St.

Robey St.
Ashland Ave.
Racine Ave.
Halsted St.
Stewart Ave.
State St.
So. Park Ave.
Cottage Grove Ave.
Woodlawn Ave.
Stony Island Ave.

Community House, 3201 South Wabash Avenue, it serves a number of organizations, arranges supervised dances, dramatics, programs, and other entertainment for the groups.

Wendell Phillips Settlement.—The Wendell Phillips Settlement is located on the West Side at 2009 Walnut Street and has been under the supervision of the Chicago Urban League since 1918. It has a day nursery, serves as a center for twenty-five different groups, and provides the only public meeting place for Negroes apart from the churches, on the West Side. There is a Boy Scout division and a division especially for women and girls.

Butler Community Center.—The Butler Community Center is located on the North Side in a neighborhood with about 2,000 Negroes. About 250 persons use the Center regularly. There are classes in citizenship, hygiene, Negro history, sewing, and china painting. There is an organization of Camp Fire Girls and a Boys' Group. Through courses of lectures instruction is given in hygiene, sanitation, and first aid.

Phyllis Wheatley Home.—The Phyllis Wheatley Home was established several years ago to provide wholesome home surroundings for colored girls and women who are strangers in the city and to house them until they find safe and comfortable quarters. The building at 3256 Rhodes Avenue, which has been purchased, accommodates about twenty girls.

Home for the Aged and Infirm.—The Home for Aged and Infirm Colored People on West Garfield Boulevard is supported almost entirely by contributions from Negroes.

Indiana Avenue Y.W.C.A.—The Indiana Avenue branch of the Y.W.C.A. on the South Side is under the general direction of the Central Y.W.C.A. of Chicago. Its directors are Negro women. Many girls are directed in their activities by volunteer group leaders from the community. The Industrial Department secures employment for Negro girls. A small number of girls live in the building at 3541 Indiana Avenue, and a room directory is maintained through which safe homes are secured for girls who are strangers in the city, or who have no family connections. Mrs. Martha G. McAdoo is the executive secretary.

Elaine Home Club and Johnson Home for Girls.—The Elaine Home Club and the Julia Johnson Home for Girls are small institutions which provide living accommodations under careful supervision for young working girls.

Hartzell Center.—Hartzell Center is a social institution under the direction of the South Park Methodist Episcopal Church. It has a commercial school, in which typewriting and stenography are taught, a cafeteria, and some social activities.

Illinois Technical School.—The Illinois Technical School for Colored Girls, a Catholic Institution, serves as a boarding and technical school for colored girls. It accommodates about 100 girls. Sister Augustina is the superintendent.

Woodlawn Community Association.—This is a neighborhood organization originally intended to interest the Negroes of the Woodlawn community in taking pride in their property and in making the neighborhood more desirable for residence purposes. It has extended its functions to include community activities and civic welfare program.

Louise Training School for Colored Boys.—This school is at Homewood, Illinois, about twenty-five miles from Chicago; until 1918 it was located at 6130 South Ada Street. It receives dependent boys between eight and fifteen years of age. Some of these boys are placed in the institution by the Cook County authorities. The institution can accommodate only a few. At present thirty-two boys are cared for in the dormitory. This is the only institution in the city for dependent colored boys.

B. AGENCIES CONVENIENT FOR NEGROES

American Red Cross.—The American Red Cross has a branch headquarters at 102 East Thirty-fifth Street. It gives emergency relief, general information and advice, and has been active in helping the families of Negro service men. During the riot of 1919 it provided food for thousands of Negroes who were cut off from work.

United Charities.—The United Charities, which provides relief and other help for needy families, has four branches convenient for use by Negroes: one at 2959 South Michigan Avenue, near the center of the main Negro residence area on the South Side; another at 1701 Grand Avenue, near the West Side Negro residence area; another at 102 East Oak Street, near the North Side area; and another at 6309 Yale Avenue, convenient for Negroes living in Woodlawn, in the vicinity of Ogden Park and in the southern part of the South Side residence area.

The Illinois Children's Home and Aid Society.—This society has two field representatives who find homes for dependent Negro children and supervise their placing. Since 1919 it has placed and supervised more than 168 Negro children.

Abraham Lincoln Center.—The Abraham Lincoln Center is at Langley Avenue and Oakwood Boulevard. Although originally not used by Negroes, the movement of the Negro population southward has added many of them to the group of people using its facilities. There is a boys' group, a branch library, and a neighborhood visitor. Negroes are welcomed in most of the activities of this center. Miss Susan Quackenbush is the resident.

C. MEDICAL INSTITUTIONS

Provident Hospital and Training School.—Provident Hospital and Training School is supported and controlled by whites and Negroes. It has a mixed board of directors. Practically all its physicians and all its internes and nurses are Negroes. For the year ended June, 1919, the hospital handled 1,421 patients, served 682 persons through its dispensary, and gave free medical

THE CHICAGO URBAN LEAGUE BUILDING
Located at 3032 South Wabash Avenue

THE SOUTH SIDE COMMUNITY SERVICE BUILDING
Located at 3201 South Wabash Avenue

care to 143. Of the total number of patients in the hospital during 1919, 1,248 were Negroes, and 173 were white. Support of the institution comes from patients and donations. During 1919 the receipts from patients totaled $36,445.81; from donations $5,782.07. Donations in drugs totaled $1,505.95, and from the dispensary $112.05. The expenses for the year were $42,002.35. The hospital has an endowment fund of $47,350, invested in securities. It has a training school for Negro nurses whose faculty is made up of prominent white and Negro physicians and surgeons.

Municipal Tuberculosis Sanitarium.—The two branches of this institution which are in Negro neighborhoods, at 2950 Calumet Avenue and 4746 South Wabash Avenue, and the Children's South Side Dispensary, 705 West Forty-seventh Street, are municipal agencies so located that they are convenient for Negroes.

South Side Dispensary.—This is at 2531 South Dearborn Street and is supported by the Northwestern University Medical School. It gives free care to those unable to pay for medical services.

D. SUPPORT OF INSTITUTIONS BY NEGROES

Social agencies, although their work is limited as respects the Negro group, have for many years taken second place to the churches in self-support. This is accounted for largely by the fact that social work in general has been regarded as a philanthropic rather than a co-operative matter. With Negro social and philanthropic agencies, especially during the period of general unsettlement following the migration, the number of possible beneficiaries greatly increased, while the group of Negroes educated in giving to such agencies grew more slowly. Recently, however, support from Negroes for their own institutions has gradually been increasing. An example is found in the Urban League. In 1917 Negroes contributed $1,000 and in 1919 $3,000. During 1920 six social agencies and twenty-seven churches raised among Negroes approximately $445,000. Although Negroes contribute in some measure to agencies like the United Charities and American Red Cross, there is no means of knowing or accurately estimating the amount.

CHAPTER V

THE NEGRO HOUSING PROBLEM

A. A STUDY OF NEGRO FAMILIES

Consideration of the housing problem as a continuing factor in the experience of Negro families led to an effort to study it from a new angle of approach—through histories of typical families in the Negro community.

The data thus gathered afford an opportunity to present an interpretative account of Negro family life, setting forth the intimate problems confronting Negroes in Chicago, their daily social difficulties, the reflection in their home life of their struggle for existence, just how they live, how they participate in the activities of the Negro community and the community at large, their own opinions concerning civic problems, their housing experience, how much they earn and how much they save, how much they spend and what value they receive from these expenditures, how they spend their spare time, and how they seek to improve their condition in the community.

A selection was made of 274 Negro families living in all sections of Chicago. Three Negro women, well equipped to deal intelligently and sympathetically with these families, gathered this information. These 274 families lived in 238 blocks, the distribution being such that no type of neighborhood or division of the Negro population was overlooked. The questionnaire employed contained five pages of questions and required an interview of about two hours. Special effort was made to secure purely social information without the aid of leading questions.

I. GENERAL LIVING CONDITIONS

For the most part the physical surroundings of the Negro family, as indicated by these family histories, are poor. The majority of these houses fall within the classifications noted as Types "C" and "D" in the discussion of the physical condition of housing.[1]

On the South Side, where most of the Negro population lives, the low quality of housing is widespread, although there are some houses of a better grade which are greatly in demand.

The ordinary conveniences, considered necessities by the average white citizen, are often lacking. Bathrooms are often missing. Gas lighting is common, and electric lighting is a rarity. Heating is commonly done by wood or coal stoves, and furnaces are rather exceptional; when furnaces are present, they are sometimes out of commission.

See p. 186.

Under the heading of "Housing Conditions" such notations as these are often found:

No gas, bath, or toilet. Plumbing very bad; toilet leaks; bowl broken; leak in kitchen sink; water stands in kitchen; leak in bath makes ceiling soggy and wet all the time. Plastering off in front room. General appearance very bad inside and out. Had to get city behind owner to put in windows, clean, and repair plumbing. Heat poor; house damp. Plumbing bad; leaks. Hot-water heater out of order. Needs repairing done to roof and floors. In bad repair; toilet in yard used by two families. Toilet off from dining-room; fixtures for gas; no gas; just turned off; no bath; doors out of order; won't fasten. Sanitary conditions poor; dilapidated condition; toilet won't flush; carries water to bathtub. Plumbing bad; roof leaks; plastering off; no bath or gas; general repairs needed; very dirty. Plumbing bad; plastering off in toilet; window panes broken and out; no bath or gas. Plastering off from water that leaks from flat above; toilet leaks; does not flush; washbowl and bath leak very badly; repairs needed on back porch; rooms need calcimining. No water in hydrant in hall; no toilet, bath, or gas; general repair needed. Water not turned on for sink in kitchen; water for drinking and cooking purposes must be carried in; toilet used by four families; asked landlord to turn on water in kitchen; told them to move; roof leaks; stairs and back porch in bad order. Sewer gas escapes from basement pipes; water stands in basement. House dirty; flues in bad condition; gas pipes leak; porch shaky. No heat and no hot water; no repairing done; no screens; gas leaks all over house; stationary tubs leak. Water pipes rotted out; gas pipes leak. Toilet leaks; plastering off; windowpanes out. Plastering off; large rat holes all over; paper hanging from ceiling.

This is the common situation of the dweller in the districts mentioned. The variations are in degree rather than kind. To dwellings a little better in sanitation and repair than those just described, the adjective "fair" was given.

Occasionally a Negro family manages to escape from this wretched type of dwelling in the "Black Belt." Some who were financially able purchased homes in Woodlawn, for example, where they live much as white residents do, supplied with the comforts and conveniences of life and in fairly clean, wholesome surroundings. There, as a rule, the physical equipment of their dwellings is good and is kept in repair. In some instances they have hot-water heating, electric lighting, and gas for cooking purposes. They ordinarily redecorate once a year, take proper care of their garbage, keep the lawns cut and the premises clean; and otherwise reveal a natural and normal pride of ownership.

In this respect the Negro residents of Woodlawn are far more fortunate than many of their race brothers who have purchased dwellings in the "Black Belt." Many of these purchases have been made by migrants on long-time payments, and large expenditure would be required to put the houses in repair and keep them so. Purchases made by Negroes in Woodlawn have been chiefly of substantial dwellings, not necessarily new but in good condition and needing only ordinary repairs from time to time.

II. WHY NEGROES MOVE

Except where the property is owned by Negroes there is frequent moving. The records obtained of these movements give a great variety of reasons. A strong desire to improve living conditions appears with sufficient frequency to indicate that it is the leading motive.   Buying a home is one of the ways of escape from intolerable living conditions, but removal to other houses or flats is more often tried.   For example, a man who now owns his home near Fifty-first Street and South Wabash Avenue—living there with his two brothers and five lodgers—has moved six times, "to live in a better house and a better neighborhood." A family now living near Thirty-first Street and Prairie Avenue, resident in Chicago since 1893, has moved four times, three times to obtain better houses in better neighborhoods and once to get nearer to work. A man and wife living near Fifty-third and South Dearborn streets have moved four times since coming to Chicago in 1908.   A family living on East Forty-fifth Street and paying $60 a month rent for six rooms has moved twice since 1900 to "better and cleaner houses."   Another family paying $65 a month for eight rooms on East Bowen Avenue has moved twice since 1905 into better houses and neighborhoods.   "Better house" and "better neighborhood" were the most frequently given reasons.

Of kindred nature are these: leaky roof; house cold; dirty; inconvenient; did not like living in rear flat; to better conditions; better houses away from questionable places; landlord would not clean; first floor not healthy; small and undesirable; not desirable flat; poor plumbing; didn't like neighborhood; moved to better quarters; landlord would not repair; house too damp; no windows; owner would not fix water pipes; more room wanted; better environment for children; better street; no yard for children; better people; house in bad condition; more conveniences for roomers.

III. THE FAMILY GROUPING

The normal family is generally recognized as consisting of five persons—two parents and three children.   Properly they should make up a single group and live by themselves.   The 274 families studied were chosen as follows: in the most populous district, from Thirty-first to Thirty-ninth streets and from Wentworth Avenue to Lake Michigan, ninety-nine family histories were taken; in the district north of Thirty-first Street to Twelfth Street and from Wentworth Avenue to the Lake, forty-six; in the narrow strip in Hyde Park known as the Lake Park district, thirty-seven; in the district from Thirty-ninth to Sixtieth streets and from Wentworth to Cottage Grove Avenue, thirty-six; on the West Side, sixteen; in the Ogden Park district, fifteen; on the North Side, fourteen; and in Woodlawn, eleven.   For convenience, as well as to show contrasts or like conditions, the material has been analyzed and interpreted by districts.

There was found a wide variation in the family groups, comprising six classifications, in three of which no lodgers appear.   A lodger here means an adult not a member of the immediate family. Thus relatives, unless infants or children, are classed as lodgers. The three groups without lodgers are: (1) man and wife; (2) two parents and children; (3) a parent and children. The other three groups with lodgers are: (1*a*) man and wife and lodgers; (2*a*) man, wife, children, and lodgers; (3*a*) man or woman, surviving head of the family, with lodgers.

Of the total 274 family groups there were 104 without lodgers and 170, or 62 per cent, with lodgers. For the most part the lodgers were found in "2*a*" classification—in families. There were ninety-two such groups and only sixty-one families with no lodgers. Forty-two couples had lodgers, and in thirty-six instances a man or woman living alone had lodgers. Thirty-nine couples were living alone, and in only four instances was there a parent alone with a child.

The Negro colony in Woodlawn approaches most nearly the normal family grouping. Home ownership in that district is fairly common, and the houses for the most part are substantial and well fitted and suited to the families. In the eleven Woodlawn families there was but one where the mother or father was dead or not living with the family. Lodgers were found in only four of the eleven families: two were couples, one a family, and the other a single woman. In the eleven families there were seventeen children.

A marked contrast with this section is found in the congested Negro district between Thirty-first and Thirty-ninth streets. Out of a total of ninety-nine families seventy-two had lodgers, or 72 per cent as contrasted with 36 per cent in Woodlawn and 62 per cent for the total 274 cases. In this district there were forty-two families with children, thirteen couples without children, and seventeen where a man or woman took lodgers. There were only fourteen families without lodgers, and thirteen couples living alone.

North of Thirty-first Street in this South Side area were similar conditions. Of forty-six households studied, twenty-seven, or 58.7 per cent, had lodgers: of these sixteen were families with children, nine were couples and two were man or woman with children. Of the households without lodgers, there were twelve families with children, five couples living alone, and two instances of parent and child.

The percentage of families with lodgers was highest in the Lake Park district, 75.6 per cent. On the West Side it was 68 per cent, a trifle higher than for the entire 274 families. On the North Side it was 57 per cent, on the South Side between Thirty-ninth and Sixtieth streets, 41.6 per cent, and in the Ogden Park district 40 per cent.

The Ogden Park district, with a relatively low percentage of families having lodgers, resembles the Woodlawn district in many respects. The houses are built for single families and are largely owned by Negroes who have lived in that locality for many years. Of the fifteen families there visited, nine had no lodgers; and of the seven with lodgers, four were families and two were couples without children.

Room crowding.—A study of Negro housing made in 1909 by the Chicago School of Civics and Philanthropy brought out the fact that, although Negro families find it extremely difficult to obtain a flat of three or four rooms, they do not crowd together as much as white immigrants; that Negroes take larger flats or houses and rent rooms to lodgers to help pay the rent, and thus lessen crowding among the members of the family. Among the 274 families studied by the Commission there was comparatively little overcrowding. One room to a person is a standard of room occupancy generally accepted by housing authorities as involving no overcrowding. Of these 274 Negro households, only sixty-seven exceeded the standard. There were, of course, wide divergences from the standard. For example, there were eight instances of six persons living in five rooms; six of eight persons living in six rooms; four of six persons living in four rooms; one of six persons living in three rooms; one of seven persons living in three rooms; two of seven persons living in four rooms; two of eight persons living in five rooms; one of nine persons living in five rooms; and one of eleven persons living in five rooms.

In the cases of unusually large families, either in the number of children or lodgers, there was a corresponding increase in the number of rooms. Thus in the case of fourteen persons making up one family, they were living in ten rooms.

The five-room dwelling was the most common, with fifty-nine families; six-room, forty-seven; seven-room, forty-two; four-room, forty-one.

In the Ogden Park district the standard of one person to one room was most closely adhered to. All the fifteen families studied in that district were housed in four-, five-, or six-room dwellings; ten of them in five-room dwellings. In Woodlawn the tendency was toward somewhat larger dwellings. There were no four- and five-room dwellings, but five of seven rooms and three of six rooms, one each of eight and three rooms. The four-room dwelling was most prevalent on the North Side. Of the fourteen families studied there, six were in such dwellings. There were two dwellings of six rooms, two of seven, one of five, two of three, and one of eleven rooms.

On the West Side, also, thirteen of the sixteen families were housed in four-, five-, six-, or seven-room dwellings, the five-room type predominating. In the Lake Park district the five-room type was most frequent, there being eleven of these out of a total of thirty-seven, six of six rooms and seven of seven rooms, the next largest group being five of eight rooms.

On the South Side in the district from Thirty-first to Thirty-ninth Street, out of a total of ninety-nine there were eighteen families in five-room dwellings, seventeen in four-room, nine in three-room, ten in six-room, fourteen in seven-room, and eight in ten-room dwellings. In the district north of Thirty-first Street the predominating size was six-room dwellings, of which there were eleven, and there were nine of four rooms, seven of five rooms, and seven of seven rooms, the rest scattering from one-room dwellings to one dwelling of thirteen rooms. From Thirty-ninth to Sixtieth streets, six-room dwellings were most frequent, there being eight of these out of a total of thirty-six, and there were seven of five rooms, six of six rooms, and six of seven rooms. The dwellings occupied by Negroes south of Thirty-ninth Street, it should be noticed, are larger than those north of that street.

The grouping of the 274 families according to number of persons is as follows:

Families	Persons to Family
48	4
40	2
35	3
37	5
30	7
29	6
22	8
17	9 or more
16	Not recorded
274	

Four persons to a "family" was the most common type, there being forty-eight of these out of the 274. In the Woodlawn and Ogden Park districts the group of three was predominant. The North Side district grouping of two persons to a family is partly due to the inclusion of nine "groups" of one person each who were interviewed mainly for data bearing upon industrial relationships. The tables show a total of sixteen such groups in the eight districts; but they are not deemed sufficient to vitiate the statistics.

Negroes have more space in their living quarters than do other Chicago people housed in similar grades of dwellings. They were usually found in dwellings of five rooms for each family, while the prevailing size among the foreign groups was four rooms, as disclosed by the Chicago School of Civics housing studies from 1909 to 1917. In the School's earliest study of the Negroes it was said:

The colored families do not as a rule live in the small and cramped apartments in which other nationalities are so often found. Even the families who apply to the United Charities for relief are frequently living in apartments which would be considered adequate, as far as the number of rooms is concerned, for families in comfortable circumstances.

Some marked exceptions, of course, were found.

The four-room dwelling was found to prevail among the Slovaks of the Twentieth Ward, the Lithuanians of the Fourth Ward, the Greeks and Italians in the neighborhood of Hull-House, the various central and southern European nationalities who work in the South Chicago steel mills and live near-by, and among the Jews, Bohemians, and Poles of the West Side.

The lodger problem.—The prevalence of lodgers is one of the most conspicuous problems in the Negro housing situation. It is largely a social question.
The difficulty of finding a home adequate for a family of four or five persons
at a reasonable rent has forced many Negroes to take over large buildings
in better localities and in better physical condition but with much higher rents.
To meet these rents they have taken lodgers. It was seldom possible to
investigate the character of the lodgers. The arrangement of these large
houses, originally intended for single-family use, prevents family privacy
when lodgers are added, making a difficult situation for families with children.
Again, the migration brought to the city many unattached men and women
who could find no other place to live except in families. Thus it happens that
in Negro families the lodger problem is probably more pressing than in any
other group of the community. Not only do lodgers constitute a social
problem for the family, but, having little or no interest in the appearance
and condition of the property, they are in many instances careless and irresponsible and contribute to the rapid deterioration of the buildings.

As previously explained, the term "lodgers," in this report, includes
relations as well as other adults unrelated to the family. It was apparent in
the study that there was a large number of relative-lodgers in Negro families.
The recent migration from the South had a distinct bearing on this situation.
Many Negroes came to Chicago at the solicitation of relatives and remained
in their households until they could secure homes for themselves. The migration further accounts for the accentuation of the lodger problem during the
period immediately following it. The 274 family histories include 1,319
persons, of whom 485, or 35 per cent, were lodgers, living in 62 per cent of the
households. The greatest number of households with lodgers were those
living in five-room dwellings. There were thirty-eight such households.
Living in six- and seven-room dwellings were thirty-four families with lodgers.
Families with only one lodger were most numerous. There were fifty-five
such families as compared with thirty-nine having two lodgers, twenty-five
with three lodgers, twenty-three with four lodgers, thirteen with six lodgers,
eight with five lodgers, and seven with more than six lodgers.

Naturally the lodger evil was found in its worst form in the congested
parts of the South Side. In the district from Thirty-first to Thirty-ninth
streets seventy-two of the ninety-nine families had lodgers. In twenty-two
families there was but one, however, as against twelve with three and four,
eleven with two, and six with five and six lodgers. Two families had ten each,
and one had thirteen. This last case was that of a widow who rented nine
sleeping-rooms in her ten-room house, in addition to catering at odd moments.
It was a typical rooming-house as distinguished from a family taking lodgers.
One family that had ten lodgers consisted of a man, his wife, and a son twenty-
five years old; they had eight bedrooms, seven opening into a hall. The other
family that had ten lodgers consisted of the parents and two children, a boy

of eight and a girl of seven, and had a ten-room house. The lodgers were two men and three women, with five children. Five of the ten rooms were used as sleeping-rooms.

In the district north of Thirty-first Street an increased number of lodgers appeared in only one family, that of a man and his wife, without children. They lived in a ten-room house, using eight of the rooms for sleeping purposes and accommodating seven male and five female lodgers.

In the district from Thirty-ninth to Sixtieth Street was one instance of seven male lodgers in a seven-room house with the man who owned the property. Two of the lodgers were his brothers. There was no heat and no bathroom. The house had been reported to the health department.

In the Lake Park district one, two, or three lodgers were the rule, only five of the twenty-eight families with lodgers in that district being outside of those three classes. Eight lodgers were found in an eight-room dwelling. The family consisted of man and wife, and the only female lodger was their niece. Five rooms were used for sleeping purposes.

In the other district no instances of excessive overcrowding due to lodgers were found.

Complaint has often been made of the numerical preponderance of lodgers over children among Chicago Negroes, and comment has been made on the economic significance. It has been suggested, for example, that economic pressure had lowered the birth-rate among Negroes and increased the infant-mortality rate. As indicated by the 274 family histories, the number of lodgers among the Negro population exceeds the number of children, that is, the number of boys less than twenty-one years and girls less than eighteen. The School of Civics and Philanthropy, in its housing studies, counted as children those less than twelve years of age. On this basis it found in its study of the Negroes of the South and West sides that there were less than half as many children as lodgers on the South Side, but a more normal situation in the West Side. Even extending the ages of children, as has been done in the present report, the situation does not appear in a much better light.

The proportion of lodgers and of children in the districts covered by the Commission is shown in Table IX.

By way of comparison similar figures from other housing studies of the Chicago School of Civics might be mentioned, the children in each instance being less than twelve years old.

Among the Slovaks of the Twentieth Ward, 13 per cent were lodgers and 32 per cent children; in South Chicago, 27.3 per cent lodgers and 25.7 per cent children; among the Greeks and Italians near Hull-House, 13 per cent lodgers and 30 per cent children; among the Lithuanians of the Fourth Ward, 28 per cent lodgers and 27 per cent children.

As far as the South Side is concerned, the situation with regard to the balance between lodgers and children has become aggravated since the earliest

School of Civics report was issued, whereas the situation on the West Side has improved somewhat.

Where there were children and lodgers together, a considerable number of instances were found which suggest probable injury to health or morals, and sometimes both. Even where lodgers are relatives, impairment of health and morals is threatened in certain circumstances, especially if the overcrowding is flagrant. For example, a household on South Dearborn Street near Thirty-fourth Street consisted of a father, mother, a son of nineteen years, and a baby girl of four months, with three lodgers, two men and one

TABLE IX

District	Percentage of Lodgers	Percentage of Children
South Side:		
Thirty-first to Thirty-ninth......	45.9	15.4
Twenty-second to Thirty-first....	37.8	20.4
Thirty-ninth to Sixtieth.........	30.1	21.4
West Side.......................	21.8	32.0
Lake Park......................	42.1	16.9
North Side....:	15.2	25.0
Woodlawn.......................	26.9	30.0
Ogden Park.....................	12.3	45.0
Total of 274 families..........	35.0	22.7

woman—seven persons living in seven rooms and sleeping in all parts of the house. One of the lodgers was a sister-in-law, another a nephew by marriage, and the third, a stranger, had a bedroom to himself. In a ten-room house in East Thirty-second Street parents having a boy of eight years and a girl of seven years were found to have taken in ten lodgers, two of whom were men. In another instance five children, four of them boys of eight, five, four, and two years and a girl of eleven, lived with their parents and two lodgers in a six-room house.

In Ogden Park, a district which shows a high percentage of children, lodgers sometimes are added to the family. In one house of five rooms, for example, there were found living twelve persons—father, mother, two sons, sixteen and seventeen years of age, four daughters, thirty-three, twenty-four, twenty-two, and thirteen years of age, and four lodgers—a daughter, her husband, and their two infants. There were only two bedrooms for the twelve persons. Another instance was that of a family of father, mother, four sons, nine; five, three, and two years, and two daughters, seven years and three weeks, with a sister of one of the parents for a lodger. The nine persons lived in five rooms. There were only two beds in the house, and one of the bedrooms was not in use.

On the South Side near Thirty-first Street there was a case where a man lodger occupied one bedroom, the other being used by the parents and their eight-year-old daughter—four persons in a four-room flat. On South Park

Avenue near Twenty-ninth Street two lodgers, a son-in-law and a nephew, occupied two of the six rooms, while the husband and wife, a son of twenty-three years, and a daughter of twenty-one years lived in the other four rooms, which included the kitchen and dining-room. A similar instance was found, on Indiana Avenue near Thirtieth Street, where two male lodgers lived with a family consisting of the parents, a son of twenty, and a daughter of eighteen, all in six rooms, two of which were not sleeping-rooms. On Lake Park Avenue near Fifty-sixth Street a family, including father, mother, and daughter of twenty, slept in the kitchen in order that three lodgers, one male and two female, might be accommodated in the five-room flat. In a five-room flat on Kenwood Avenue near Fifty-third Street the two male lodgers occupied both bedrooms, while the mother and her boy of nine and girl of seven years lived in the kitchen and dining-room. Seven persons were found living in a six-room house on East Fortieth Street; they were father, mother, a son of five years, a daughter of seven years, and an infant, with a male and a female lodger, friends of the parents. Virtually the whole house was used for sleeping purposes.

These are examples of the arrangements that sometimes occur when children and lodgers are found in the same dwelling. The fact that in the main Chicago Negroes live in more rooms per dwelling than immigrants, whose standard of living has not yet risen, does not necessarily mean that the Negroes have a greater appreciation of a house with more rooms. The explanation in many cases is that the Negroes take whatever living quarters happen to be available, which often are large residences abandoned by well-to-do whites, and then adapt their mode of living to the circumstances. Lodgers are one of the sources of revenue that aid in paying the rent. Negro families often expressed a desire to live by themselves if they could find a dwelling of suitable size for reasonable rent. They sometimes complained of lodgers and declared that they would prefer not to take them at all, especially women lodgers. The objection to married couples and unattached men was not so pronounced.

Smaller houses thus would seem to be a factor in the solution of the lodger problem. A Negro real estate dealer was asked if the Negro was as contented or as much disposed to live in a cottage as white people, or whether he wanted to live in spacious quarters where he could draw a revenue from roomers. The reply was that the Negro would rather live by himself. This is evidenced by the fact that many Negroes would rather live in an apartment and rent two or three rooms than take a large house and have it full of roomers.

Lodgers are often found in the smaller dwellings occupied by Negroes. Rent is often the determining factor in the selection of the smaller dwelling. When it is so high that it forms too large a proportion of income, economic necessity often drives the Negro family to admit one or more lodgers at the expense of overcrowding and its attendant harmfulness. This was noted in certain districts where the dwellings as a rule were small.

Rents and lodgers.—An effort was made to determine the economic necessity for lodgers as expressed by the relation of the wages of heads of families to the amounts of rent paid. It is assumed that in a normal family budget rent should not exceed one-fifth of the income of the head of the family. Wide variations from that proportion were revealed.

Facts as to both rent and wages were difficult to secure, owing to the variable earnings of various members of the family, variable sums received from lodgers, and other factors. For example, seventeen occupants owned their houses. In seventy-eight other cases information obtained by the investigators was not adequate or could not, for various reasons, be used in calculations.

The remaining 179 cases out of the 274 provided data from which the following facts are presented: In three instances the rent exceeded the income of the head of the family; in thirty-one instances the rent equaled one-half the income of the head of the family, and in an equal number it amounted to one-third. In one case the rent was equal to three-fourths of the income, and in twenty-three cases the rent equaled one-fourth. Thus eighty-nine instances were disclosed in which the rent was in excess of one-fifth of the income of the head of the family. In most of these cases, particularly the extreme ones, the income of the head of the family was greatly supplemented by money received from lodgers or from earnings of other members of the family.

The remaining ninety families in which the rent amounted to one-fifth or less of the income of the head of the family were divided as follows: Twenty-four fell in the one-fifth column, twenty-seven in the one-sixth column, fourteen in the one-seventh column, eleven in the one-eighth column, while fourteen were in the "low" column. The last named included those ranging from one-ninth to one-twenty-third.

On the South Side, in the district from Thirty-first to Thirty-ninth Street, rents exceeded the one-fifth proportion in one-half of the sixty-two families studied, two of them paying rent in excess of income, eight paying one-half of income for rent, fourteen paying one-third, and seven paying one-fourth. Of the remaining thirty-one families in that district, seven fell in the one-fifth column, twelve in the one-sixth column, six in the one-seventh column, four in the one-eighth column and two in the "low," being one-ninth and one-eleventh.

Rents were high also in the Lake Park district, where twenty-five families of a total of thirty-six were paying in excess of the one-fifth proportion. Fourteen of these paid one-half of the income for rent, five paid one-fourth, four paid one-third, one paid three-quarters, and in one instance rent exceeded income. In only five instances was the normal one-fifth paid, two paid one-sixth, two paid one-seventh, while two paid one-ninth and one-eleventh respectively.

In the district north of Thirty-first Street, eighteen out of a total of thirty-eight families paid in excess of the one-fifth proportion, four paid one-half, nine paid one-third, and five paid one-fourth. Six families paid the normal one-fifth, five paid one-sixth, two paid one-seventh, one one-eighth, and six less than that, running as low as one-twenty-third.

The Ogden Park area was found to be a district of low rents. None of the eight families studied paid as much as the normal one-fifth. Two paid one-sixth, one paid one-seventh, three one-eighth, one one-ninth, and one one-twelfth.

The other districts did not show much variation from the normal proportion.

Examination was made of all the factors in instances where the rent equaled one-half or more of the income of the head of the family or amounted to one-third. With regard to the former it was assumed, for the purpose of the study, that it compelled renting rooms to lodgers. With regard to the one-third column, lodgers were assumed to be an economic necessity when they offered the only source of income in addition to that of the head of the family. On these bases it was found that in forty-six families supplementary income afforded by lodgers was necessary, that in three instances they were the sole source of the income, while one instance was presented of a widow whose children partly supported her, but insufficiently for their common needs.

While in most instances of high rents and low income on the part of the head of the family good reason appeared for taking lodgers, in not a few instances further analysis revealed other sources of income which might indicate that there was no economic necessity for lodgers. There was one instance on Forest Avenue, for example, where the relation of the rent to the father's income was one-third, but where his sons earned more than double his income. In another family on South State Street near Thirtieth Street, the father earned $125 a month and paid $50 a month rent, but additional income was derived from the wife, son, and daughter, in addition to that obtained from lodgers. There was likewise the case of a waiter living on Lake Park Avenue whose rent was $30 a month as against wages of $10 a week. In addition to the tips he doubtless received in his work, his wife earned $18 a week, and $6 a week was derived from lodgers. In one instance a man living near Fifty-sixth Street and Wabash Avenue paid rent equal to one-third of his wages, but had considerable income from investments.

Such instances tend to explain why only forty-eight families were found in which lodgers seemed to be an economic necessity in aiding to pay rents, when eighty-nine cases were revealed in which the rent was in excess of one-fifth of the wages of the head of the family. The family histories also showed that various means besides lodgers supplemented the insufficient income of a family head. In some cases the wife or children worked, and not infrequently their incomes exceeded those of the father.

Lodgers were often found in families where the income from that source did not appear to be needed. This was the case in a number of families with unusually high wages and abnormally low rents. High wages and low rents explain most of the cases shown where the rent ranges from one-ninth to one-twenty-third of the income of the head of the family. In the one-twenty-third case the couple lived in two rooms on South State Street for which they paid $6 a month. The man earned $35 a week in an iron foundry, while the wife added $18 a week to the common fund. Another instance was that of a man who paid $16 a month rent and earned $48 weekly at the Stock Yards. His wife and a relative added $23.60 a week to the family income. A man in Ogden Park whose income as a contractor was $48 a week paid $16 a month rent. A man living on the West Side earned $48 a week and paid $15 a month rent. His children added $43.50 a week to the family income.

Even in circumstances such as these, lodgers were sometimes taken. In one case where the rent was one-tenth of the wages of the head of the family the man paid $15 a month rent for a five-room dwelling out of his $36 weekly wages earned in a coke plant at Gary. His son and lodgers increased the monthly income by $28. There was a teamster earning $30 a week who paid $15 a month rent for a six-room dwelling in which nine persons lived. The proportion of rent to his wages was as one to eight. His wife, one of his children, and lodgers added to the income. As in numerous instances where the income was high, a large amount was spent for food in this family.

An instance was found of a man earning $9.50 to $10.50 a day. His wife was a caterer. There was a daughter of fifteen years. They took three roomers. There was no need for the woman to work, but she said she wanted the money. She was a good cook, having served in that capacity in the South, and she said she earned $15 when she went out for a week-end of catering. In this instance there seemed to be little need for lodgers.

Another case was that of a man and his wife and two grown children living in a nine-room dwelling on Calumet Avenue and having nine lodgers. The man was earning $40 a week, and the lodgers paid $33.50 a week. The wife occasionally did day work, earning $3.65 a day. The monthly expenditure for food was $100, clothing $33, and rent $60.

Another instance was that of a widow with three children who lived on State Street near Thirty-seventh Street, in a three-room flat. Though the children's earnings amounted to $78 a week, the inevitable lodger was present, contributing $4 a week to the common fund. This little family spent $120 a month for food.

Large amounts spent for food were not uncommon in some families that took lodgers. A typical instance was that of the man and wife with three children and two lodgers who lived on Prairie Avenue. The man earned $25 a week, while $82 a month was derived from the lodgers. Food for the family alone cost $100 a month.

A man on North Wells Street earned $57 a week for the support of his wife and three adopted children. They lived in an eleven-room house which also accommodated the man's sister and brother. One of the sons earned $75 a week, and the lodgers paid $45 a month. This family spent $180 a month for food. Another earned $22 a week in the Stock Yards. Besides his wife and child they had in their nine-room house on East Thirtieth Street six lodgers paying $20 a week. This family spent $100 a month for food and $34 for clothing. Another man and wife on Forest Avenue paid $25 a month rent and spent $88 a month for food and $43 for clothing. They derived $3.75 a week from their two lodgers. A similar case was that of a family which lived on East Thirty-second Street. The man earned $30 a week in a foundry. He and his wife have one child, and they had ten lodgers, who paid $72 a week. In this family $80 was spent for food each month and $50 for clothing.

The heaviest expenditure for food in any one family was $330 a month. This was explained by the fact that there were twenty table boarders. The husband earned $22.50 a week, and there were three lodgers who paid $13 a week. The boarders collectively paid $13 a day. Rent was $55 a month, and $25 a month was spent for clothing.

Other reasons for the ready acceptance of lodgers in Negro dwellings were apparent, among them friendship and the desire to be obliging and to assist others in a new environment. Most Negroes would regard it as a breach of good faith to encourage friends and relatives to come to Chicago from the South and then fail to help them after their arrival. This accounts for the frequent designation of "relatives" and "friends" among the lodgers. Sometimes these lodgers seemed to be permanent, but often they were taken only until they could adjust themselves.

During the period of greatest migration, 1915–20, hundreds of unattached men and women could be seen on the streets as late as one or two o'clock in the morning, seeking rooms shortly after their arrival in Chicago. One instance was reported of a family to whose house four men came at midnight looking for rooms. Lack of lodging-houses or of hotels where accommodations could be had at reasonable prices was partly responsible for this swarm of migrants seeking shelter in private homes. The meager provision of such places for the accommodation of unattached Negroes has been a factor in the lodger problem.

IV. HOW NEGRO FAMILIES LIVE

How Negroes earn their living in Chicago, what occupational changes those from the South have undergone since arrival, how their present occupations differ from those in their former homes—information on all these points was gained from the family histories. Almost without exception, the Negroes interviewed declared that their economic situation had improved in Chicago.

In most instances they were able to earn more; some said they were obliged to work harder but felt well recompensed because of their improved economic condition.

From the occupations of persons included in the study it appears that there is a distinct departure from the domestic and personal service in which Negroes were commonly found a few years ago. Among the 274 families visited, the heads of 225 families were men. Of this number eighteen were idle at the time of the investigation, in the summer of 1920, nine were professional men, nineteen were in business, twenty-two were in some skilled trade or work, 110 were doing unskilled work, and only forty-seven were engaged in personal service. The latter term includes such occupations as doorman in a hotel or club, bellboy, bootblack, cook, waiter, porter, elevator operator, and chauffeurs who lack training as mechanics. These are chiefly functions which bring employees in contact with the public or with white employers in a more or less personal capacity.

Before coming to Chicago, forty-five of the 225 were farmers. Practically all of these entered the field of unskilled occupations here. Only sixty-four of the 225 had been doing unskilled work in their former home. Six more did skilled work in their former homes than were doing such work in Chicago; two more were in personal service; two less were in business; and one more was in a profession.

Of these 225 family heads, 122 migrated to Chicago, chiefly from the South, during the period from 1916 to 1920 inclusive. Three periods in the industrial history of the family head were taken: (1) occupation in the former home; (2) occupation on first arrival in Chicago; and (3) adjustment to new conditions in Chicago and occupation at the time of investigation, during the spring and early summer of 1920.

Many of these migrants had not yet made their adjustment to the new occupations at that time. However, certain tendencies were manifest. For example, in the former home thirty-one were farmers and forty-five were unskilled workers. In the period of adjustment seventy-seven were doing unskilled work. The unskilled occupations had apparently, in the shifting about, absorbed the farmers. The difficulty of continuing in skilled occupations in the North was evidenced. In the South fourteen of the 122 men were engaged in skilled occupations of some sort; in the period of adjustment there were fifteen; but at the time of the investigation there were but twelve.

In the South nineteen of the 122 were in personal-service occupations; during the transition period, eighteen; and at the time of the investigation, sixteen. In the South seven were in business; during the period of transition, three; and at the time of the investigation, five. In the South four were in practice as professional men; during the period of transition only three; while at the time of the investigation there were five, one just beginning to practice.

As to whether any previous occupational training was used or abandoned after coming to the North, it appeared that of the 225 only 91 utilized such training. In 134 cases previous training was not used, but these included many who were farmers in the South.

Of forty-nine who had been engaged in personal-service occupations before coming to Chicago, only twenty still continued in such work. Six were unemployed at the time of the investigation, nineteen were in unskilled work, one was doing skilled work, and three were in business.

Forty-nine women were heads of families as revealed by the 274 family histories. This does not include all the Negro women shown by the histories to be engaged in gainful occupations in Chicago. Often daughters were working. There were thirty instances in which man and wife both worked outside of the home. Before coming to Chicago 129 wives were employed, while in Chicago sixty-seven wives were gainfully employed, including the thirty who were working in addition to their husbands. During the period of transition, it appears, they helped out, since the records show that 132 were then at work. But the tendency plainly is to abandon the practice as soon as the family becomes settled in the new environment.

Of seventeen women who had worked as house servants in their former homes, seven were found in factories, three in offices, two in stores, and five in unskilled manual labor.

Some of the transitions in occupation are especially interesting. One oil-field worker in the South had become a shoemaker. A farmer had become a postal clerk. A former superintendent of a label factory attended high school during the adjustment period and became an undertaker. One who was a schoolboy in the South worked in a hotel on coming to Chicago but became a grocer. A barber in Kansas City became first a painter in Chicago, then a janitor. A bottler from Memphis, Tennessee, went to work in the Stock Yards but became a canvasser. A farmer from Alabama worked first in the Yards and later in woolen mills.

One man was a porter in a store in Mississippi. In Chicago he became a chauffeur. A farmer from Louisiana on arriving worked as a butcher and then secured employment in a tannery. A porter in a wholesale grocery in Memphis, Tennessee, who worked first in Chicago as a lard maker in a packing-house, later became a building laborer. A preacher from Tennessee worked at Swift's packing-house until he could become established in a church.

A Mississippi plumber who served as a butter maker for a time after reaching Chicago became a contractor within three years. A hotel porter from Alabama came to Chicago in 1918 and went to work in a steel foundry and later in a soap factory. A farmer who worked on shares in Georgia tried work in the Stock Yards in Chicago, but changed to a paint shop. An Alabama man who worked in a sawmill there found a job in a steel foundry in Chicago, and later went to the Stock Yards. A man who worked in an ice plant in Texas became a railroad porter after coming to Chicago and then found a job as a butcher at the Stock Yards.

A man who began life as a bootblack in Atlanta came to Chicago in 1893 and sold newspapers until he could enter business for himself. For many years he has been a jeweler. In the South his wife was a musician by profession. To aid her husband in his struggle she worked in a box factory for a time after arriving in Chicago.

Clergymen sometimes abandon their profession for more remunerative employment. One of these came to Chicago from Boston in 1904. For a time he worked as a fireman and later in a packing-house. One who served as a waiter on first coming to Chicago became an insurance agent, and another, who was a reporter on a Negro newspaper on arrival in Chicago, became the manager of a manufacturing company.

Few migrants continued in Chicago the employment in which they worked in the South.

The family histories show that the Stock Yards industry absorbed many of the migrants, and a large number went to work in the steel mills and iron foundries, as well as in lighter manufactures.

Many Negro women have become hairdressers and manicurists after a course in a school of "beauty culture" which also teaches the use of cosmetics. Considerable skill is often required in this work, and the earnings often supplement very substantially the husband's income and may be sufficient to make an individual self-sustaining in case of need. Hairdressing is most frequently done in the homes.

An occasional teacher, cateress, or seamstress was found among the Negro women. Some of them remained in personal-service occupations, but a decided tendency was noticeable toward office and factory employment.

In summary it is scarcely necessary to remark that wages in the North far exceed those in the South. The difference in some instances is so great that many foolish expenditures are indulged in before the relatively higher cost of living is appreciated, or other conditions are properly understood. High wages, supplemented by income from other sources, often proved a temptation to unnecessarily heavy expenditures for material comforts, such as food and clothing. With relation to food it did not appear that Negroes were deliberately taken advantage of in their buying, but that they frequently bought articles without considering prices that had been refused by others because they were deemed excessive.

Insurance of one kind or another was often carried in the families studied. In spite of high living costs, a considerable number of families were found to have bank accounts, Liberty bonds, War Savings stamps, and good interest-paying investments.

The testimony of Negroes who at some time had lived in the South was mainly that they were obliged to work harder for what they got North. They also declared that they were unable to save as much as they hoped or expected, because of high prices. But in the great majority of cases satisfaction was expressed over the improvement in their economic situation. While their movements in search of better housing in Chicago were extremely frequent, they still felt that they were better housed than in their former homes, where bathtubs, steam heat, and electric lighting were almost unknown. Being accustomed to a certain measure of dilapidation in their home surroundings in the South, the Negro is not necessarily dismayed by the extent of dilapidation in Chicago's Negro housing, though usually it is not long before he begins to think of more substantial dwellings in better surroundings than those he first obtains.

Also in Chicago he finds available and accessible to his home many churches, some with large memberships and adequately housed; the best schools he has ever known; fine hospitals and dispensaries at his command; some playgrounds, bathing-beaches, parks, and similar facilities for his recreation and that of his children; settlement houses; libraries; and many other civic and recreational societies that make a strong appeal to his interest and promote his ambition for physical and mental development. He finds many motion-picture theaters and other amusements for his leisure hours.

Where the habit has not already been established, he is learning to make liberal use of all these facilities through the guidance and direction of Negro newspapers and organizations working especially for the improvement of the Negro group. There are indications of improvement in moral standards, health, and civic consciousness through these contacts and the use of these up-building social agencies.

The opinions of migrants and their feeling toward the community were solicited. It appeared that above all they prized the social and political freedom of the North. Satisfaction was expressed over the escape from "Jim Crow" treatment in the South. They valued the independence possible in the North, and sometimes spoke of having come North "out of bondage." They recalled frequently the "shameful treatment received by the Negroes from the white people in the South," the "intimidation and discrimination," and they were surprised and sometimes amazed at the fact that they could go and come at will in Chicago, that they could ride in the front of a street car and sit in any seat. Satisfaction was also expressed over the fact that they could get a job at good wages and did not have to buy groceries at plantation stores where they felt they had been exploited.

Thus, while they may have to work harder and may find it difficult for a long time to adjust themselves to the environment, few indicated any intention of returning to the South. In some instances, where adjustments have not been made, some discouragement was evidenced, and they sometimes expressed the feeling that they were no better off in Chicago than in their former homes. The prevailing sentiment, however, was in favor of remaining in spite of some greater difficulties.

Often Negroes from the South said they missed the care-free social greetings and relationships that prevail in the rural South. They thought that people in the North were "colder," that they did not show sufficient hospitality.

Asked what conditions they would change if they could have their way, the most frequently expressed desire was for more and better housing. Improvement of social, moral, or political conditions followed. Some emphasized the necessity of improving the management of the migrants from the South, whose new-found freedom had led them to become offensive in their conduct. Interviews with migrants, however, indicated that instruction was being received without offense from many social agencies on how to act, dress, and speak in such a manner as not to create unfavorable impressions.

There were some complaints of political exploitation and of being obliged to live in proximity to gambling and vice that were encouraged by political bosses in their neighborhoods.

The inquiry showed that membership in clubs, lodges, and kindred organizations was almost as universal as church affiliation. There were only a few families in which no member had any association with a fraternity or club.

V. A GROUP OF FAMILY HISTORIES

The general statistical treatment of these 274 Negro families takes away many of their human qualities. For this reason a selection has been made of various types of Negro families in order that a rounded picture of the whole unit may be given. The family stories that follow include typical migrant Negroes from the South—common laborers, skilled laborers, salaried, business, and professional men. They illustrate the commonplace experiences of Negroes in adjusting themselves to the requirements of life in Chicago.

AN IRON WORKER

Mr. J—, forty-nine years old, his wife, thirty-eight years, and their daughter twenty-one years, were born in Henry County, Georgia. The husband never went to school, but reads a little. The wife finished the seventh grade and the daughter the fifth grade in the rural school near their home.

They worked on a farm for shares, the man earning one dollar and the women from fifty to seventy-five cents a day for ten hours' work. Their home was a four-room cottage with a garden, and rented for five dollars a month. They owned pigs, poultry, and a cow, which with their household furniture, were worth about $800. The food that they did not raise and their clothing had to be bought from the commissary at any price the owner cared to charge.

They were members of the Missionary Baptist Church and the wife belonged to the missionary society of the church and the Household of Ruth, a secret order. Their sole recreation was attending church, except for the occasional hunting expeditions made by the husband.

Motives for coming to Chicago.—Reading in the *Atlanta Journal*, a Negro newspaper, of the wonderful industrial opportunities offered Negroes, the husband came to Chicago in February, 1917. Finding conditions satisfactory, he had his wife sell the stock and household goods and join him here in April of the same year. He secured work at the Stock Yards, working eight hours at $3 a day. Later, he was employed by a casting company, working ten hours a day and earning $30 a week. This is his present employment and is about forty minutes' ride from his home. Both jobs were secured by his own efforts.

The family stayed in a rooming-house on East Thirtieth Street. This place catered to such an undesirable element that the wife remained in her room with their daughter all day. She thought the city too was cold, dirty, and noisy to live in. Having nothing to do and not knowing anyone, she was so lonely that she cried daily and begged her husband to put her in three rooms of their own or go back home. Because of the high cost of living, they were compelled to wait some time before they had saved enough to begin housekeeping.

Housing experience.—Their first home was on South Park Avenue. They bought about $500 worth of furniture, on which they are still paying. The wife then worked for a time at the Pullman Yards, cleaning cars at $1.50 a day for ten hours' work. Their house leaked and was damp and cold, so the family moved to another house on South Park Avenue, where they now live. The house is an old, three-story brick, containing three flats. This family occupies the first flat, which has six rooms and bath. Stoves are used for heating, and gas for light and cooking. The house is warm, but dark and poorly ventilated. Lights are used in two of the rooms during the day. The rooms open one into the other, and the interior, as well as the exterior, needs cleaning. There are a living-room, dining-room, and three bedrooms. The living-room is neatly and plainly furnished.

The daughter has married a man twenty-three years old, who migrated first to Pittsburgh, Pennsylvania, then to Chicago. He works at the Stock Yards. They occupy a room and use the other part of the house, paying half the rent and boarding themselves. A nephew, who was a glazier in Georgia, but who has been unable to secure work here, also boards with Mr. and Mrs. J—, paying $8 a week. He is now unemployed, but has been doing foundry work. Mrs. J— occasionally does laundry work at $4 a day.

How they live.—The cost of living includes rent $25; gas $5.40 a month; coal $18 a year; insurance $9.60 a month; clothing $500 a year; transportation $3.12 a month; church and club dues $3 a month; hairdresser $1.50 a month. Little is spent for recreation and the care of the health. The family carries insurance to the amount of $1,700, of which $1,200 is on the husband.

The meals are prepared by the wife, who also does the cleaning. Greens, potatoes, and cabbage are the chief articles of diet. Milk, eggs, cereals, and meat are also used. Meat is eaten about four times a week. Hot bread is made daily, and the dinners are usually boiled.

Relation to the community.—The whole family belongs to the Salem Baptist Church and attends twice a week. The wife is a member of the Pastor's Aid and the Willing Workers Club, also the Elk's Lodge. The husband is a member of the Knights of Pythias. He goes to the parks, bathing-beaches, and baseball games for amusement. The family spends much of its time in church and helped to establish the "Come and See" Baptist Mission at East Thirty-first Street and Cottage Grove Avenue. They have gone to a show only once or twice since they came to the city. During the summer they spend Sunday afternoons at the East Twenty-ninth Street Beach.

Heavier clothes were necessary because of the change of climate, and more fresh meat is used because of the lack of garden space and the high cost of green vegetables.

The wife thinks that northern Negroes have better manners, but are not as friendly as the colored people in the South. She says people do not visit each other, and one is never invited to dine at a friend's house. She thinks they cannot afford it with food so high. She thinks people were better in the South than they are here and says they had to be good there for they had nothing else to do but go to church.

She feels a greater freedom here because of the right to vote, the better treatment accorded by white people, the lack of "Jim Crow" laws. She likes the North because of the protection afforded by the law and the better working conditions. "You don't have an overseer always standing over you," she remarked.

Life here is harder, however, because one has to work all the time. "In the South you could rest occasionally, but here, where food is so high and one must pay cash, it is hard to come out even." The climate is colder, making it necessary to buy more clothes and coal. Rent also is very much higher here. They had to sell their two $50 Liberty bonds.

Economic sufficiency.—With all this, Mrs. J— gets more pleasure from her income because the necessities of life here were luxuries in Georgia, and though such things are dear here there is money to pay for them. Houses are more modern, but not good enough for the rent paid. They had to pay $2 more than the white family that moved out when they moved in.

Sentiments on the migration.—Mrs. J— says "some colored people have come up here and forgotten to stay close to God," hence they have "gone to destruction." She hopes that an equal chance in industry will be given to all; that more houses will be provided for the people and rent will be charged for the worth of the house; and the cost of living generally will be reduced. She does not expect to return to Georgia and is advising friends to come to Chicago.

A FACTORY HAND

In his home town in Kentucky, Mr. M— was a preacher with a small charge. Now, at the age of forty-nine, in Chicago, he works in a factory and is paid $130 a month. He has an adopted son, twenty-three years of age, who is an automobile mechanic in business for himself, drawing an income of $300 a month.

Mr. M— might still be a preacher on small salary but for the intervention of his wife. He came to Chicago about 1900. His wife came from Nashville, Tennessee, in 1902, and they were married in 1904. Mrs. M— felt that she was too independent to "live off the people" and persuaded her husband to give up the ministry. He got a job as foreman at a packing-house, where he earned $25 a week for a ten-hour day. Next he worked for the Chicago Telephone Company, and finally secured the position with a box-manufacturing company which he now holds.

Family life.—The M—s have adopted three children, having had none of their own—the adopted son already mentioned, an adopted daughter now twenty years of age, and another foster son of thirteen. The latter is in a North Side school. The girl is in a normal school in Alabama. Both Mr. and Mrs. M— completed high school. All speak good English.

Wife and husband have separate banking accounts. Living expenses for such a large family are, of course, heavy. For example, the bills for food aggregate from

$42 to $45 a week, and more than $200 a year is paid in insurance premiums. Frequently a woman is hired to come in and help with the housework. Food in good variety is used. Illness prevented adding to the bank accounts during the year of 1920. An operation performed on Mrs. M— cost $650 and the illness of Mr. M— and the daughter consumed between $900 and $1,000.

Housing experience.—The M—s' first home in Chicago was a cottage in the "Black Belt." They wanted a large house and found one on South State Street. The neighborhood, however, was displeasing to them, and they moved to the North Side to be near a brother's children. The house was too small, and they moved again to another North Side address. Again the neighborhood proved distasteful, so they bought the three-story dwelling on the North Side where they now live. It is in good sanitary condition and is supplied with gas. As lodgers they have the wife's sister and brother, who are actually members of the family.

Community participation.—They belong to the Baptist church. Affiliations of a secular nature include the Masons, the Household of Ruth, the Court of Calanthe, the Eastern Star, the Heroines of Jericho, the North Side Men's Progressive Club, the Twentieth Century and Golden Leaf clubs, and the Young Matrons and Volunteer Workers. Mrs. M— is president of a settlement club and a member of the Urban League. After coming to Chicago three years passed before she mingled much with people. She had always done community work in her southern home and feels that her reluctance here was due to the fact that she did not know what the northern people were like. She found them friendly enough when at last she did associate with them.

Sentiments on community problems.—They came to Chicago because they had visited here and liked it well enough to come back and settle. Conditions are not all that they would like. They would like to see Negroes allowed to live anywhere they choose without hindrance, they would suppress moving pictures that reveal murder, drinking, and similar acts that lead young people to commit crimes. They would also like to see newspapers abandon their habit of printing articles that are derogatory to the Negro, thus creating prejudice, and of printing items unfit for children. Also they would like to see better homes for Negroes.

For the Negroes, they feel, life in the North is considerably easier than in the South, since they can always get plenty of work and do not have to work so hard as in the South. The mixed schools in the North are especially appreciated because no discrimination can creep in. The general lack of segregation on street cars, in parks, and in similar public places also pleases them. Still they see difficulties for southern Negroes who come North to live and are easily led astray. Southern Negroes are not accustomed to the new kinds of work and are inclined to slight it. This is, of course, unsatisfactory to their employers and accounts in some measure for the frequency with which they change jobs. This may also account for the fact that white people are averse to paying migrants well.

A RAILWAY MAIL CLERK

Mr. L— was graduated from the Carbondale (Ill.) high school and the Southern Illinois State Normal School, while Mrs. L— was graduated from Hyde Park High School and the Chicago Normal School. The latter is a music teacher. Before coming to Chicago, Mr. L— was a school principal in Mounds, Illinois, and Mrs. L— also was a teacher. They are northern people, the husband having been born in

East St. Louis and the wife in Chicago. They have a daughter, three years of age, and have living with them a niece and nephew, six and five years old, as well as two adult women relatives.

Economic sufficiency.—As a railway mail clerk, Mr. L— earns $125 a month. He owns a house and lot in Carbondale and carries insurance on his life and property. They spend $37.50 a month for rent, about $10 for miscellaneous items, $15 a week for food, $4 a month for gas, $1 for barber's services, and always $10 a month is added to the family's bank account.

Housing and neighborhood expenses.—In April, 1919, a flat building south of Sixty-third Street, previously occupied by white people, was opened to Negroes. The L— family were the first of the Negroes to move in. A few white families wished to remain and lived in the same building with the Negroes. Mr. L— says: "We objected, as they were not the kind of people we wanted to live with. My sister-in-law acted as agent of the building, and the condition of some of the flats was terrible. The owner was arrogant when the Negroes first came in, but he soon found that we would not be pleased with just anything. He told us he saw that we were particular and wanted things nice, and, said he, 'Seeing that you are that way, I'll do the best I can for you, as I believe you will take care of the flat.' The Negroes insisted on the laundry being cleaned and it is now being used."

The L— family has had three stoves since moving in. After thoroughly renovating the building and making many of the repairs themselves, the sanitary conditions are good, and the owner makes no further objection to maintaining the good order of things.

The white people of the neighborhood objected to having the building occupied by Negroes. White boys of the neighborhood stoned the building, and its tenants were obliged to call upon the police for protection. This antagonism now seems to have disappeared. The white and Negro children play together amicably.

Community participation.—Mrs. L— attends the First Presbyterian Church regularly and Mr. L— is a member and secretary of the board of trustees of the A.M.E. Mission. He is a Mason and a member of the Woodlawn Community Organization, which has the betterment of the neighborhood as its aim. He plays tennis for recreation and goes to concerts and the movies for entertainment. The children in the family have made use of public playgrounds and libraries. Bathing-beaches have been sought occasionally, and contacts have been made with the St. Lawrence Mission, a neighborhood institution.

Opinions on race relations.—Mr. L— thinks that agitation is of no assistance to the problem and draws attention to the fact that lack of agitation on the part of newspapers averted a riot in connection with one recent racial disturbance. "Housing is the greatest difficulty confronted by the migrant from the South." It is his opinion, further, that the Negroes are not understood, that the white people fear them until they become really acquainted with the Negroes. "Contact," he says, "is the only thing that will help to make conditions better. It is just a question of understanding each other."

A MULATTO

Mr. A— was born in Chicago and his wife in Helena, Arkansas. He was educated in the Chicago public schools, and his wife attended Fisk University, Nashville, Tennessee, and afterward the Chicago Musical College.

Mr. A— is light in complexion and is frequently mistaken for a white man. Several years ago, without announcing his race, he obtained work in a label factory and remained for some time until it was discovered that he was not a white man, and therefore the only Negro in the establishment. The officials, being the first to learn his racial identity, decided to keep him as long as no objection came from the other white employees. In a few years he became superintendent of the factory, which position he held for eight years. He was treated as an equal by members of the firm, who visited him at his home and invited him to their club. He was also president of the company's outing club.

A short time ago he decided to enter business for himself, and both he and his wife took courses in an embalming school. He now has a business with stock and fixtures valued at $10,000.

Economic sufficiency.—His business income affords a comfortable livelihood and a surplus for investment. He has bought one house and built another. These two are valued at $8,000 and yield $90 monthly. He also owns stock in the Pennsylvania Railroad and a fire insurance company, has $300 invested in Liberty bonds and owns a $1,000 automobile.

Community participation.—Mr. and Mrs. A— attend Congregational church services every Sunday and get much pleasure from concerts, lectures, and shows in the "Loop." Their principal recreation is motoring. Mr. A— is president of an association of business men and of a charity organization. He is a member of several fraternal organizations, contributes to Provident Hospital, United Charities, and the Urban League. His wife is an active committee member of a charity organization.

Opinions on local race problems.—Mr. A— thinks there would be no housing problem if prejudice were not so marked. He mentioned a subdivision east of Stony Island Avenue where it is specifically stated that Negroes are not desired. Homes there are being sold for prices within the reach of Negroes, and he feels that at least 500 Negroes would be glad to pay cash for such homes anywhere in Chicago if they were given the opportunity. He feels that proper protection should be given Negroes against bombers.

A TRANSPLANTED HOUSEHOLD

Mr. B— is seventy-two years old and his wife sixty-four. They came to Chicago during the migration. They had difficulty in finding work suited to their advanced age and in accustoming themselves to the simplest changes in environment. Neither of them can read or write.

Home life in the South.—In Alabama they owned an eight-acre farm and a four-room house and raised hogs, chickens, and cows. They both had worked twelve hours a day for years and by denying themselves even a comfortable home had saved $2,000. They were members of a church, although they could not actively participate in church or other affairs of their rural community. When the migration fever struck them they sold their property, drew out their $2,000, and followed the crowd.

Home life in Chicago.—They first secured rooms and began the search for work. Mr. B— finally secured a job in a livery stable at $18 a week, but the work was uncertain and the wages insufficient. Mrs. B— went to work cleaning taxicabs. Illness and frequent lapses in work depleted their savings. They rented an eight-room house and took in lodgers, hoping to insure a steady income. They have nine lodgers in these eight rooms, in addition to themselves. There is no furnace heat; the bathroom is out of repair, the halls dark and dirty, and they are using their old furniture brought from the South. Three of the women lodgers came from the same Alabama community. The habits and customs of this household are unchanged. They go out seldom, and all of the women smoke pipes and use snuff.

Of the original $2,000 which Mr. B— brought with him, he has $250 left.

They make no use of civic and social agencies and do not go to church because they think Chicago Negroes are unsociable. They prize the fact, however, that work is plentiful for the lodgers, and they have no intention of returning South.

A BARBER FROM MISSISSIPPI

Mr. D— was a migrant and a member of a party of over a hundred Negroes who left Hattiesburg, Mississippi, in the autumn of 1916.

He was a barber at home and earned an average of $25 a week. Mrs. D— was a good housewife. They owned a house and lot valued at $1,000 and furniture valued at $500. They have two children.

Motive for coming to Chicago.—Mr. D— had always read the *Chicago Defender*, and usually got in a supply of these papers to sell to his customers and to supply topics for barber-shop discussion. His daughter, then a student at Straight College in New Orleans, was to be graduated that year, and he went to New Orleans to spend a week. While there he worked in a barber shop. He found that the migration was being much discussed. One day a man came into the shop and said he was a representative of a northern industry that was anxious to get Negroes to come North and work for it. He argued that the North had freed the Negroes, but had left them in the South where they had not received good treatment, so that at this late date the North was trying to right an old wrong and was now offering to Negroes a chance to work. On the other hand the Negroes were indebted to the North for their freedom.

When Mr. D— returned home he sold his barber shop and left for the North with his wife and children.

Life in Chicago.—Opening a place of business in Chicago, he called it the Hattiesburg Barber Shop. It is patronized largely by Hattiesburg people who came up in his party. His earnings are larger here, but at first his wife was forced to work in the Stock Yards at $10 a week to help meet the family budget. Occasionally now she works as a hairdresser. They pay $46.50 a month for rent. Their clothing bill amounts to $650 a year. Last year they spent $200 for medicine and an average of $18 a week for food. Their insurance premiums total $6 a month.

Community participation.—In the South the entire family was active in church affairs. In Chicago they have continued their church connections, and Mr. D— is one of the officials at the Olivet Baptist Church. They go to church four times a week.

Adjustments to Chicago.—They were quick to begin adjustment to their new surroundings, profiting by the advice and instructions of their present pastor. At the end of six months they felt themselves quite at home. They feel the need for using more careful English and are more formal in their greetings and relations with persons whom they meet. They enjoy the "freedom of speech and action" allowed in Chicago, the privilege of voting, the freedom from segregation, and the absence of Jim Crow laws. They think Chicago is fair to Negroes in so far as laws are concerned, but believe there should be better enforcement of the laws. They find life easier here, although there is more work to be done. They feel a great satisfaction in the more modern homes and other comforts and pleasures they are able to obtain. Each month they add a small amount to their bank account. They suggest that Negroes who have became adjusted to Chicago should take pains in a kindly spirit to inform newcomers concerning the proper deportment. They believe that if advice is offered in the right manner it will always be gladly received. They do not intend to return South.

A STOCK YARDS LABORER

A son-in-law of the B— family, also from Mississippi, is employed at the Stock Yards. His impressions throw light on the adjustment of migrants and on their views. He said:

"A friend met me when I first came to Chicago and took me to the Stock Yards and got me a job. I went to the front of the street car the first time I entered one here because my friend told me to; I would not sit beside a white person at first, but I finally got courage to do so.

"At Swift's the whites were friendly. There I was in the dry-salt department at $22\frac{1}{2}$ cents an hour. The foreman, a northerner, had been there thirty-five years. He was fair to all. I worked with Americans, Poles, and Irish. But the work was very hard, and I had to leave. I carried my lunch with me. Negroes and whites there eat together when they wish. I am now working at Wilson's. The Irish and Poles are a mean class. They try to get the Negroes to join the union. When the Negroes went to work Friday after the riot, most of the Irish and Poles quit and didn't come back to work until Monday. They came back jawing because the Negroes didn't join the union. White members of the union got paid when their houses had been burned—$50 if they had families and $25 if they were single. Colored members of the union got nothing when their houses had been burned. That's why I won't join. You pay money and get nothing. The whites worked during the riot; we had to lose that time. I lost two weeks. It seemed strange to me. It looked unfair. They are still mean and 'dig ditches' for us. They go to the foreman and knock us, just trying to get us out of jobs. The foreman so far hasn't paid any attention to it. I am working in the fresh-pork department, handling boxes.

"The Negroes stick together and tend to their business. Some of the Americans and Polish are very friendly. Everybody does his own work. We use the same showers and locker-rooms. They don't want us to work because we are not in the union. One asked me yesterday to join. The Poles said non-union men would not get a raise, but we got it."

Opinions on race relations.—"When I first came I thought the city was wide open— I mean friendly and free. It seems that there is more discrimination and unfriendly feeling than I thought. I notice it at work and in public places. Wages are not increasing like the high cost of living. As soon as one gets a raise, the cost of living goes up [May, 1920].

"The whites act just as disorderly on cars as the Negroes. Monday evening two white laborers sitting beside a white woman cursed so much that I had to look around. Nothing is ever said about such incidents.

"Rent goes up whenever people think of it. We have to pay $8 more since April. Things are getting worse for us and we need to think about it. Still it is better here than in the South."

AN OLD SETTLER

Mr. S— was born in Baltimore in 1851. At the time of the gold rush to California, his father took his family and started out to seek his fortune. They had got as far as Chicago when his father was robbed and the journey ended. Mr. S— has lived here since. He has seen many changes during his sixty-three years' residence in Chicago. When he came here the city limits were Twelfth Street on the South and Chicago Avenue on the North, and there were no street cars. The Negro population was 175. His parents took him on Sunday to the Railway Chapel Sunday School, started in 1857 in two passenger cars by a Presbyterian minister, Father Kent. The first building occupied by this congregation was on the site where the Board of Trade now stands, 141 West Jackson Boulevard. This was destroyed in the fire of 1871. The second church was at the corner of State and Thirteenth streets, where the Fair warehouse now stands. The next site of the church was that of the Institutional Church at Thirty-eighth and Dearborn streets.

Early housing experience.—Prejudice, Mr. S— says, was unknown in the early days. He has lived south of Thirty-first Street for thirty-five years. They were the first Negro family to enter the block in which they now live. He built his home there and has been living there twenty years.

A BASEBALL "MAGNATE"

Mr. G— was born in La Grange, Texas, the son of a minister. As a boy he worked on his father's farm, went to school, and progressed as far as the eighth grade. He was a good baseball player. He played first in Forth Worth, Texas, then in New York and Philadelphia, and finally came to Chicago in 1907. The highest amount he had been able to earn was $9 a week. His first job in Chicago netted him about $1,000 a year. In 1910 he had acquired ownership of the team, and now, at the age of forty, it nets him $15,000 a year. His team has traveled extensively, having covered the principal cities in the United States at least twenty-five times.

Home life.—Mrs. G— was born in Sherman, Texas. She completed the first-year high school at her home. She is a modest woman and a good housekeeper. They have two children, a son of nine and a daughter of three. Mr. G— has moved four times in Chicago, seeking desirable living quarters for his family. He owns a three-story brick building containing nine rooms, the house in which he now lives. In addition he owns $7,000 worth of Liberty bonds and values his baseball team and other personal property at about $35,000.

Community participation.—Both Mr. and Mrs. G— were church members in the South. This membership is continued in Chicago. Mrs. G— belongs to an A.M.E. church and is interested in and helps support Provident Hospital and Phyllis Wheatley Home for Girls, while Mr. G— is a member of several fraternal orders, City Federation of Clubs, and the Appomattox Club. Their recreation is baseball and dancing, and they find entertainment in attending theaters and orchestra concerts principally in the "Loop." Mr. G— is very much interested now in a playground which is being established near his home and a tennis and croquet club for young people in the same vicinity.

AN OLD RESIDENT

Before coming to Chicago in 1886 Mrs. L— had lived in Washington and Detroit. Mr. L— was successively a railroad porter, a night watchman, and a janitor. There are four children, three daughters and a son. Two of the daughters are married and have families. One is a dressmaker, another a stenographer, and another an accomplished musician. The son is a typist. Several years ago Mr. L— purchased a lot near Forty-seventh Street on Wells Street on which he built his home. In this neighborhood the family was reared. Mr. L— died several years ago.

Riot experience.—Although the L— family has been living at Forty-seventh and Wells streets for over thirty years, and relations between the family and the white neighbors in the block were cordial, gangs of hoodlums from other districts practically destroyed their property. The house was attacked, some of the furniture was stolen, and some was destroyed. The heavy pieces of furniture were broken up and burned in the street. The building was so badly damaged that they were forced to move into a boarding-house for a time.

Community participation.—The L— family lived in a section of the city in which there were few Negroes, but maintained an active relationship with organizations of the Negro community. They are members of the A.M.E. Church and Sunday school and of two fraternal organizations. Mrs. L— is a member of the Linen Club of the Provident Hospital and is actively interested in the Old Folks Home. Miss L—, one of the daughters, is well known in the community as a musician and composer.

A PHYSICIAN

Dr. W— and family came to Chicago in 1910. He had lived in Mexico City until the revolution made living there hazardous. He was in good circumstances, maintaining a comfortable household with servants. Since he has been in Chicago he has had considerable difficulty in finding a home in a neighborhood fit for rearing his children. He finally purchased a home on Grand Boulevard which is valued at more than $25,000. It is a three-story building with brown-stone front, ten rooms and two baths, and many works of art installed by the artist, Holslag, who formerly owned the house, and who himself painted some of the decorations. Dr. W— has spent several thousand dollars on the furnishings.

Home life.—Besides the doctor and his family there are two other relatives. The physician's income is adequate to maintain this establishment and in addition two high-class automobiles. Mrs. W— is a social leader and does much entertaining. She is a patron of community drama and attends grand opera and the leading theaters in the "Loop." They were formerly Catholics but now attend the Bahai Assembly. Dr. W— is a member of two fraternal orders and two social clubs. Their recreation is tennis, boating, motoring, and bathing. He is a director of the Chicago Health Society. He is an examining physician and a member of the board of directors in a life insurance company. Both are members of the Art Institute and are active in supporting the settlements and hospitals of the community.

In addition to her social duties Mrs. W— continues the study of music. She is chaperon at the regular dances of a post of the American Legion held in the South Side Community Center; a member of the Library Committee of the Y.W.C.A., and is interested in the entertainment of Negro students of the University of Chicago.

They are living in a neighborhood in which several bombings of homes of Negroes have occurred, but Mrs. W— says that their relations with the white neighbors are friendly.

A NATIVE OF CHICAGO

Mr. C— was born in Chicago in 1869. His grandmother was part Indian and his grandfather of Scotch extraction. The grandfather was born in Cincinnati, and was graduated from Oberlin College. His father's brother was a personal friend of Owen Lovejoy and Wendell Phillips. In Leavenworth, Kansas, a monument had been erected to him as the first Negro captain of a volunteer company. He fought with General Buckner in New Orleans, was active as an abolitionist, and his wife was one of the women sent to Kansas to establish schools among Negroes. She taught school for thirty-six years and was one of the first women in the country who were graduated as kindergarten teachers. His maternal grandfather bought a home in Chicago in 1854 and lived where the Federal Building now stands. At the time of Mr. C—'s birth his father lived on Plymouth Court, then called Diana Place. They lived for thirty-one years on South La Salle Street, where they owned their home.

Economic sufficiency.—Mr. C— is a graduate of the Chicago College of Dental Surgery and practiced his profession until ill health forced him into other fields. He has been a clerk in the county treasurer's office, assistant bookkeeper in a white bank in Memphis, which position he held for two years, and assistant electrician for a telephone company. Now, at fifty-one, he is superintendent of the Western Exposition Company's building. Twice he has lost his savings by bank failures. He lost $9,000 through the failure of the Day and Night Bank in Memphis, Tennessee. He owns a house and lot, oil and mining stocks valued at $4,600, Liberty bonds, Thrift stamps, and carries a small bank balance. His present home is a four-room flat in a building on South State Street, which contains forty apartments and two stores. With him lives the family of his younger brother, who has a twelve-year-old son. He is a member of the Baptist church and two fraternal orders. His chief recreation is swimming, and he finds his entertainment in the "Loop" theaters and the city library.

A MISSOURI FAMILY

Mr. and Mrs. T— came to Chicago in 1919, the wife arriving one month before her husband. They had been living in St. Louis, Missouri, where Mr. T— was employed as a roller in an aluminum works. Prior to that time he had been a houseman, and before that a teamster.

There are two children. One is fourteen years old and in the first-year high school, and the other is seven and in the first-grade grammar school.

Mrs. T— has always been a substantial aid to her husband, and, as she says, she "doesn't always wait for him to bring something to her, but goes out herself and helps to get it." Accordingly, when reports were being circulated that Chicago offered good jobs and a comfortable living, she came up to investigate while her husband held his job in St. Louis.

Home life in Chicago.—The family lives on State Street over a store. They have moved four times since coming to Chicago in 1919, once to be nearer work, once to get out of a neighborhood that suffered during the riot, and twice to find a more desirable neighborhood for their family. They are not satisfied with their present home and are planning to move again as soon as a more suitable place can be found. With them live a sister-in-law and her child, who are regarded as members of the family. The house is in poor sanitary condition. The toilet is in the yard and used by two families. There is no bath. The sister-in-law is a music teacher but does not earn much. She pays board when she can afford it.

Mr. T— is forty-seven and his wife forty-six years old. He is employed at the International Harvester Company and earns $35 a week for a nine-hour day. He consumes an hour and a half each day going to work.

Although Mr. T— lived on a farm and too far from school to attend, he taught himself to read and write. Mrs. T— went as far as the eighth grade in grammar school.

Community participation.—The entire family belongs to a Methodist church. Mr. T— is a member of the Knights of Pythias and Mrs. T— is a member of the Sisters of the Mysterious Ten. They have no active recreation. For amusement they attend motion-picture shows in the neighborhood. The children regularly use the playground near their home and the Twenty-sixth Street Beach.

Adjustment to Chicago.—Their most difficult adjustment has been in housing. They think landlords should be forced to provide better homes for the people in view of the high rents.

AN EMBALMER

Mr. B— was born in Texas, lived for a number of years in Tuskegee, Alabama, moved to Montgomery, and thence to Chicago in the summer of 1906. His first position here was that of coachman for $30 a month, room, and board. His next position was that of porter, working fifteen hours a day for $30 a week. He accumulated a small amount of money, and, wishing to enter business for himself, and not having sufficient funds to attend a specialized school, he secured a job with an embalmer and worked for him four years. In 1913 he entered the undertaking business for himself. He is now buying a two-story brick building on a five-year contract, to serve as a place of business and a home. The business is young and was begun on small capital. To establish himself he exhausted his little bank account and sold his Liberty bonds. His equipment is still incomplete, and he rents funeral cars and other equipment necessary for burials.

Community participation.—Both Mr. and Mrs. B— are members of several local improvement clubs; they attend Friendship Baptist Church, and each belongs to three fraternal orders.

Sentiments on local conditions.—Mrs. B— thinks the town too large for much friendliness. Mr. B— believes that there should be a segregated vice district. His principal objection to the present scattering of houses of prostitution is that his wife, who is frequently obliged to return home late at night, is subjected to insults from men in the neighborhood. He thinks there should be a law requiring that landlords clean flats at least once a year.

A YOUNG PHYSICIAN

Dr. C— is a good example of the numbers of young Negro professional men in Chicago. His office is on State Street near Thirty-fifth. He was born in Albany, New York, and his wife in Keokuk, Iowa. They have lived in Chicago since 1915.

Early experiences in profession.—Through a civil-service examination Dr. C— secured a place as junior physician at the Municipal Tuberculosis Sanitarium. At the same time he passed with high rating an examination for internship at the Oak Forest Infirmary. At the latter place he was promptly rejected because of his color, and at the former he was asked to leave nine hours after he reported for duty.

Economic status.—Dr. C— owns a house and lot in his former home, Albany, which he values at $14,000 and other property and stock holdings valued at $13,000.

Education.—Dr. C— was graduated from the Brooklyn Grammar School, the Boys' High School of Brooklyn, and Cornell University, where he obtained his A.B. and M.D. degrees. Mrs. C— is a graduate nurse. He is at present an associate surgeon and chief of the dispensary of a local hospital.

Community participation.—He has already assumed a position of leadership in the social activities of the community, is a trustee of the new Metropolitan Church, a thirty-second degree Mason, a member of the Knights of Pythias, Chicago Medical Society, American Medical Association, Urban League, and a director of the Community Service, and also an instructor at the Chicago Hospital College.

Opinions on race relations.—He believes that the recent migration of Negroes has been an advantage in teaching Chicago Negroes the value of property ownership and co-operation. He thinks the scarcity of homes for Negroes can be relieved by allowing Negroes "as much freedom as the American dollar." Definite suggestions for improving conditions within the race he gives as follows:

1. Establishment of a permanent medium for understanding between the two races—a permanent commission to act in the adjustment of difficulties of any kind. This body should be composed of Negroes and whites.

2. Rigid enforcement of existing laws.

3. A systematic campaign under the direction of the commission among Negroes to teach them personal hygiene.

4. Negroes should join labor unions and refuse to serve as strike breakers.

5. When Negroes do act as strike breakers, the doctor thinks, race friction is created and labor is cheapened. Negroes can obtain a square deal from the unions only when they have joined them in sufficient numbers to demand justice by becoming an important factor in the unions. If they are not permitted in certain unions they should form groups of their own for collective bargaining.

A YOUNG LAWYER

Numbers of young Negro lawyers are establishing themselves in Chicago, and their influence already is being felt in the community. A good example of this group is Mr. J—, who, although only twenty-eight years old, has been actively practicing law six years. He was born in Kentucky and has lived in Indiana, Kansas, Ohio, New York, and Oklahoma.

Education.—He completed high school in Kansas, graduated from Oberlin College, and then went to Columbia University, New York, and received the degrees of Master of Arts and Bachelor of Laws. His wife completed the junior year in college in New York, studied art in New York City, and is skilled in china painting.

Home life.—Mr. and Mrs. J— have one child of four years. They live in one of the 1,400 buildings owned by a real estate man of that district who "notoriously neglects his property." The struggle to establish himself during the first few years in Chicago was difficult. Now Mr. J— has the confidence of a large number of people, and a clientèle which provides a comfortable income.

Community participation.—Mr. J— is a trustee of the institutional A.M.E. Church, chairman of the United Political League, member of the Y.M.C.A., Knights of Pythias, a Greek-letter fraternity and the Urban League, and is a member of the Executive Committee of the Friends of Negro Freedom.

Civic consciousness.—He thinks that if working Negroes and working white men can be led to regard one another as workingmen interested in the same cause the color question will be forgotten. He believes that prejudice is based on the economic system. With respect to housing he thinks a Negro should, as an American citizen, be free to purchase real estate wherever he is able to make a purchase; that as long as artificial barriers are set up there can be no successful solution of the color question; that a man's respect for the rights of others increases in proportion to his intelligence, and that the press can be a great source of evil or good in educating the people. He believes that there should be clubs and educational meetings to instruct some of the less refined classes of Negroes in conduct.

A MIGRANT PROFESSIONAL MAN

Mr. and Mrs. F— lived in Jackson, Mississippi, until 1917, the year of the migration, when they moved to Chicago. He followed his clientèle and established an office on State Street near Thirty-first Street. Mr. F— received his commercial and legal training at Jackson College and Walden University. Mrs. F— is a graduate of Rust College and the University of Chicago.

Home life.—The F— home evidences their economic independence. It contains ten rooms and bath and is kept in excellent condition. They own six houses in the South, from which they receive an income. Mr. F— is the president of an insurance company incorporated in Illinois in 1918, which has a membership of 12,000. He has also organized a mercantile company, grocery and market on State Street, incorporated for $10,000, of which $7,000 has been paid.

They have two sons, nineteen and twelve years of age, and three adult nephews living with them. One nephew is a painter at the Stock Yards, another is a laborer, and the third a shipping-clerk.

Community participation.—They are members of the Baptist church and of the People's Movement, while Mr. F— is a member of the Appomattox Club, an organization of leading Negro business and professional men. In addition to membership in three fraternal organizations, they are interested in and contribute to the support of the Urban League and United Charities.

Opinions on race relations.—Concerning housing, Mr. F— feels that some corporation should build medium-sized cottages for workingmen. He thinks that the changes in labor conditions make it hard for Negroes to grasp immediately the northern industrial methods. Patience will help toward adjustment, he thinks.

He thinks that colored women receive better protection in Chicago than in the South. His experience in the courts leads him to believe that Negroes have a fairer chance here than in the South. Agitation by the press in his opinion can have no other effect than to make conditions worse.

B. PHYSICAL ASPECTS OF NEGRO HOUSING

The purpose of this section of the report is to describe by a selection of types the physical condition of houses occupied as residences by Negroes. This description includes the structure, age, repair, upkeep, and other factors directly affecting the appearance, sanitation, and comfort of dwellings available for Negro use.

In 1909 the Chicago School of Civics and Philanthropy included Negro housing in a series of general housing studies. This study was confined to the two largest areas of Negro residence, those on the South and West sides. Both of these were studied generally, and in each a selected area, of four blocks in one case and three blocks in the other, was studied intensively.

The South Side area included parts of the Second, Third, and Thirteenth wards between Fifteenth and Fifty-fifth streets, with State Street as the main thoroughfare. The four blocks bounded by Dearborn Street, Twenty-seventh Street, Armour Avenue, and Thirty-second Street were intensively studied. It was found that within these four blocks 94 per cent of the heads of families were Negroes. The buildings were one- and two-story, with a considerable amount of vacant space in the lots. Half the lots had less than 50 per cent of their space covered. The houses were for the most part intended for single families but had been converted into two-flat buildings. Rooms were poorly lighted and ventilated, the sanitation bad, and the alley and grounds about the houses covered with rubbish and refuse.

Comparisons with other districts studied showed the following: Of houses in a Polish district, 71 per cent were in good repair; in a Bohemian district, 57 per cent; Stock Yards district, 54 per cent; Jewish and South Chicago districts, 28 per cent; and in the Negro district, 26 per cent. A study made three years later by the School of Civics covering the same area showed a decrease of 16 per cent of buildings in good repair. Five buildings had been closed by the Department of Health as no longer fit for habitation. There were leaks in the roofs, sinks, and windows of five-sixths of the dwellings. In describing a typical house in this area, the report said:

There was no gutter and the roof leaked in two places, the sink drain in the basement leaked, keeping it continually damp, the opening of the chimney let the rain come down there, the windowpane in front rattled from lack of putty. The conditions in these houses are typical; almost every tenant tells of rain coming in through roof, chimney or windows, and cases of fallen plaster and windows without putty were too common to be noted. One aspect of the situation that should not be overlooked is the impossibility of putting these old houses in good condition. Leaks may be repaired, plaster may be replaced, windows may be made tight, and these things would certainly improve most of the houses, but when all were done it would not alter the fact that these are old houses, poorly built, through which the wind can blow at will.

Lack of repairs to the houses in the "Black Belt" is accounted for by the fact that owners do not regard the buildings as worth repairing, and that

TYPES OF NEGRO HOUSING

WOOD HOUSES
BRICK HOUSES
STONE FRONT HOUSES
OTHER BUILDING
NUMERALS INDICATE HOUSES MORE THAN ONE STORY HIGH
THE LETTER "B" INDICATES BASEMENT

DWELLINGS IN A BLOCK INTERSECTED BY A RAILROAD TRACK

DWELLINGS IN A BLOCK INTERSECTED BY AN ALLEY

tenants can always be found, even though it is necessary to reduce rents some-what. This reduction is indeed notable. The School of Civics found that while in 1909 50 per cent of the houses examined on the South Side rented for as much as $16 a month, in 1917 only 13 per cent could command as high a rental as that; that in 1909 the prevailing rents were $15 and $16 as against $10 and $12 in 1917.

On the West Side the area studied generally was that bounded by Lake Street, Ashland, Austin, and Western avenues. Here the situation was little better. One-third of the families visited in the three selected blocks bounded by Fulton and Paulina streets, Carroll Avenue and Robey Street were Negroes. The remaining two-thirds represented sixteen nationalities. It was reported that the white residents could get advantages and improvements for their houses that a Negro could not. While 35 per cent of the houses were reported in good repair, 31 per cent were described as "absolutely dilapidated" and in a worse state of repair than those in any other districts studied except the Jewish district. The report said:

Broken-down doors, unsteady flooring, and general dilapidation were met by the investigators at every side. Windowpanes were out, doors hanging on single hinges or entirely fallen off, and roofs rotting and leaking. Colored tenants reported that they found it impossible to persuade their landlords either to make the necessary repairs or to release them from their contracts; and that it was so hard to find better places in which to live that they were forced either to make the repairs themselves, which they could rarely afford to do, or to endure the conditions as best they might. Several tenants ascribed cases of severe and prolonged illness to the unhealthful condition of the houses in which they were living.

That there was a continuing demand even for the shacks and shanties of the "Black Belt" is evidenced in a report made by the Urban League of Chicago in 1917 that only one out of every thirteen Negro applicants for houses to rent could be supplied. At the height of the demand applications for houses were coming in at the rate of 460 to 600 a day, and only ninety-nine were available for renting purposes. This was due, of course, to the growing stream of Negroes arriving daily from the South.

Covering the same area on the South Side as that studied by the School of Civics in 1917 a canvass was also made in 1917 by Caswell W. Crews, a student at the University of Chicago. He found that tenants had remained in these dwellings in some instances as long as twenty years after their unfitness had become evident, because the rent was low and they could find nowhere else to go. He mentioned the mass of migrants from the South who, because of their ignorance of conditions in Chicago as to what was desirable and what was to be had for a given sum, fell an easy prey to unscrupulous owners and agents. Mr. Crew's description said:

With the exception of two or three the houses are frame, and paint with them is a dim reminiscence. There is one rather modern seven-room flat building of stone front, the flats renting at $22.50 a month and offering the best in the way of accommodations to be found there.   There is another makeshift flat building situated above a saloon and pool hall, consisting of six six-room flats, renting at $12 per month, but in a very poor condition of repair.   Toilets and baths were found to be in no condition for use and the plumbing in such a state as to constantly menace health.   Practically all of the houses have been so reconstructed as to serve as flats, accommodating two and sometimes three families.   As a rule there are four, five, and sometimes six rooms in each flat, there being but five instances when there were more than six.   It is often the case that of these rooms not all can be used because of dampness, leaking roofs, or defective toilets overhead.

The owners are in most instances scarcely better off than their tenants and can ill afford to make repairs.   One house in the rear of another on Federal Street near Twenty-seventh had every door off its hinges, water covering the floor from a defective sink, and windowpanes out.   A cleaning of the house had been attempted, and the cleaners had torn loose what paper yielded readily and proceeded to whitewash over the adhering portion which constituted the majority of the paper.   There were four such rooms and for them the family paid $7 a month.

In 1920 a cursory examination by investigators from the Commission showed that the only change in the situation was further deterioration in the physical state of the dwellings.

The movement of the Negro population across State Street eastward into the area once occupied by wealthy whites began as early as 1910.   Wabash Avenue was the first street into which they moved.   Gradually they scattered farther east toward Lake Michigan.   Following the migration from the South the Negro area east of State Street expanded to the lake and pushed southward.   The houses which they found in the new territory, although from twenty to forty years old, were a vast improvement over those they had left west of State Street.   These houses do not permit of any general classification, for some are very bad while others, though not new, are in a state of good repair, largely according to the care taken by previous occupants.   Along with descriptions of Negro homes must be considered the tendency among those Negroes who were able to move away from the congested areas of Negro residence.   Some of the best houses occupied by Negroes in 1920 were in districts until recently wholly white.

A rough classification of Negro housing according to types, ranging from the best, designated as "Type A," to the poorest, designated as "Type D," was made by the Commission on the basis of a block survey comprising 238 blocks, covering all the main areas of Negro residence, and data concerning 274 families, scattered through these 238 blocks, one or two to a block, whose histories and housing experiences were intensively studied by the Commission's investigators.   Approximately 5 per cent of Chicago's Negro population live in "Type A" houses, 10 per cent in "Type B," 40 per cent in "Type C," and 45 per cent in the poorest, "Type D."

I. "TYPE A" HOUSES

Type A houses, with those of the other types, were not concentrated wholly in any one section but were found widely scattered; there were none, however, in the areas which in 1910 held practically the whole Negro population. Examples of Type A were found on South Park Avenue between Thirty-third and Thirty-fifth streets, where some Negroes had lived for six years; on Grand Boulevard between Thirty-fifth and Thirty-eighth streets, where a few had lived for three years; on Champlain, Evans, Vincennes, and Langley avenues, between Forty-third and Forty-seventh streets, where some Negroes had lived four and five years; and on Wabash Avenue between Fifty-first and Fifty-third streets. In Woodlawn there are a few of recent occupancy, one of which was built by its Negro owner.

Most of the Type A dwellings are of substantial construction, principally of brick and stone. Some are old family residences in formerly high-class neighborhoods, built to withstand the test of years. Consequently, although they have been subject to the usual deterioration, they still afford a fairly high standard of comfort and convenience. Some are large and exceptionally well equipped with luxurious fittings and adornments installed by former owners. Most of these houses were built and owned by people of wealth who abandoned them. Many of them have since passed through several stages of occupancy. Somewhat less permanent in their physical aspects perhaps are the Type A houses in Woodlawn. Many of the houses in this district are of frame structure, and they are not as commodious as those in the formerly fashionable white districts. But they provide a desirable measure of comfort, with less waste space and superfluous rooms.

Comforts and conveniences.—Type A dwellings are fitted with all the conveniences required by well-to-do whites. Some of them have more than the customary one bathroom, have electricity and gas, and are well heated by steam or hot-air furnaces. One example of Type A housing is a three-story, stone-front, ten-room house on South Park Avenue owned and occupied by a lawyer and his family. There is a garage, and the place is kept in good condition. A twelve-room house, also on South Park Avenue, owned and occupied by a physician and his family, has two bathrooms, steam heat, and electricity, and is in excellent repair. Another physician on the same street owns a three-story brown-stone house, with a garage. It contains ten rooms and two bathrooms, has steam heat and electric lights, and is in good condition. For this property he paid $35,000. A three-story brick house on Vernon Avenue is owned and occupied by a business man. In addition to other modern conveniences there are lavatories in four of the bedrooms. The house is in excellent condition. A nine-room house on Langley Avenue, in good repair, owned by another business man, has gas, furnace heat, and a bathroom.

The occupants.—Although these buildings are occupied by the wealthier Negroes, business or professional men, it often happens that others secure and occupy such houses. High wages during the war and immediately afterward permitted some Negroes who arrived in Chicago during the migration to live in the best class of housing available for Negroes. For example, an undertaker owns such a house on Langley Avenue, with seven rooms, with gas, a bathroom, electricity, and hot-water heat. This building is ornate and in excellent repair. A postal clerk who has been in Chicago since 1897 owns a seven-room house on Champlain Avenue south of Sixty-sixth Street, where he lives with his wife and child. In the block south of Forty-third Street on Prairie Avenue is a nine-room house occupied by an employee of the American Express Company. In order to help pay the rent, four lodgers are taken, who together pay $20 a week. The house, which includes a bathroom, is furnace-heated and lighted by electricity. A transfer man pays $65 a month rent for an eight-room house of this class on Bowen Avenue. He earns $35 a week, and two lodgers pay $50 a month. The house has bath, electricity, and furnace. A railroad porter, who has been a doctor's assistant and has lived in Chicago since 1886, owns a house on Rhodes Avenue near Sixty-sixth Street. It has seven rooms and is provided with a furnace, gas, bathroom, and electricity.

Neighborhood conditions.—Surroundings of Type A houses are generally far more pleasant than those in areas where the majority of Negroes live. The streets and alleys are usually clean, except where Type A houses are in neighborhoods surrounded by poorer houses. The premises are generally well kept. This is especially true where the occupants are owners. When space permits, there is a lawn or a garden that shows signs of pride and attention. One block was noted, however, where the residents reported that the street was watered twice a day until Negroes moved in, after which it received no such attention.

II. "TYPE B" HOUSES

Type B designates a class of houses which have not the size, durability, permanence, architectural embellishments, or general standard of comfort and convenience of those classed as Type A. They are usually flat buildings, whether originally intended for that purpose or not. Frequently dwellings are rearranged by landlords, when Negroes are given occupancy, to accommodate two or more families in place of the one for which they were built. Type B houses have less floor space, the average number of rooms is fewer, and they have, as a rule, fewer modern conveniences. Still, they are good houses and much superior to the habitations in which Negroes are most often found.

Occupants of Type B houses are frequently found to be clerical workers, postal clerks, railway mail clerks, small tradesmen, artisans, and better-paid workers in steel mills and Stock Yards.

Most of the houses in the part of Woodlawn inhabited by Negroes are of Type B. Another district in which this type of house is found extends from Fortieth to Forty-seventh streets on Langley, Evans, Champlain, Vincennes, and St. Lawrence avenues. Although in this area a few dwellings are of

HOMES OWNED BY NEGROES ON SOUTH PARK AVENUE
Classified in text as "Type A"

AN ABANDONED RESIDENCE IN THE PRAIRIE AVENUE BLOCK
WITH A FACTORY IN THE REAR

Type A, the greater part of them fall under Type B. About 5 per cent of the dwellings occupied by Negroes on the West Side—for example, some of those on Oakley and Washington boulevards—might also be classed as Type B. Brick or stone dwellings predominate in the districts where this type is found. For example, the block survey made by the Commission covered twelve blocks in the Negro residence in Woodlawn on which there were 190 brick or stone and 119 frame houses. Practically all the Type B dwellings are one- and two-family houses, and the majority are two-family houses. The Commission's study shows that these dwellings are not overcrowded and house their families comfortably. Many of the occupants own their homes.

Comforts and conveniences.—Most of these houses have baths, electric lights, steam, hot-water or hot-air heating, and gas for cooking. Only a few are heated by stoves or lack electrical fixtures. They were found to be in good repair, well kept and clean. Special pride is taken by home owners of this class in keeping the property presentable and preventing rapid deterioration. Family histories reveal that most of the Woodlawn residents are long-time residents of Chicago.

Neighborhood conditions.—In the neighborhoods where Type B houses were found, no uniform standard of cleanliness was evident in streets and alleys or in adjoining properties. They were as frequently unkempt as tidy. Although the premises of Type B houses were generally kept neat, surrounding untidiness often detracted from their appearance. But a block containing a majority of this type usually had an appearance of being better kept, whether the surrounding property was occupied by whites or Negroes. In the Woodlawn area the surroundings of the houses were well cared for, and sanitary measures were commonly observed. In some blocks in the Langley Avenue neighborhood carelessness and neglect were evident. Vacant lots were no more littered with rubbish than in white areas of a similar grade.

III. "TYPE C" HOUSES

Type C houses are the most common in areas of Negro residence. In this classification are included about 50 per cent of the houses on the South Side east of State Street, most of those in the North Side area, about 60 per cent of those in the West Side area, practically all those in the Ogden Park area, and many dwellings in the little Lake Park district.

Heads of families occupying Type C houses were usually unskilled wage-earners, or in personal service. Their incomes were such that they could rarely afford more than $20 a month rent.

Types of houses.—Eleven blocks on the North Side were included in the Commission's block survey. In these blocks 146 of the buildings were of brick or stone, and 123 frame. Fifteen were single houses, four were double, and 167 housed three or more families, the largest proportion of such buildings in any district examined. There were also four rows of houses. They were in a fair state of repair.   Four-room houses or flats predominated among the fourteen families whose histories were taken.   In one instance seven persons were living in four rooms, in another nine persons were living in seven rooms, in another eleven persons were living in seven rooms.   The dwellings were mainly one- and two-story buildings, with a few three- and six-flat buildings.

A large proportion of buildings housing three or more families was found also in Ogden Park.   In eleven blocks there were 109 such buildings.   There were also sixty-eight single and no double houses.   The frame buildings numbered 189, and brick or stone forty-eight.   Most of the houses were one- and two-story frame buildings.   The majority were in good or fair repair, though one block showed gross neglect of repairs to exteriors, and practically all needed painting.   Five-room dwellings predominated· among the fifteen families whose histories were recorded.   Overcrowding was frequent.   In one instance eleven persons lived in five rooms; in another nine persons in five rooms.

In the part of the South Side area east of State Street and between Twenty-second and Thirty-first streets forty-two blocks were surveyed.   Michigan, Indiana, and Prairie avenues have excellent dwellings, practically all of which are still occupied by whites.   Until a few years ago these were fashionable residential streets, and the buildings are large, well built, and often ornate. Surrounding them, however, are hundreds of houses, old and difficult to keep in repair.   In these forty-two blocks there were 767 buildings of which 163 were frame and 604 brick.   About 37 per cent of these are of Type C.

The surroundings of these buildings appear in brief comments on some of these blocks, taken from investigator's notes, as follows:

Property has been allowed to run down.
Five vacant houses; yards full of rubbish; lodgers transient; families do not move.
Vacant lot dirty.
Two vacant lots; yards well kept.
Garbage piled up on vacant lot; Negroes moving in.
Roomers move often; one poolroom; empty church building.
Vacant lot used as dump; yards well kept.
Two vacant houses robbed of plumbing fixtures.
Yards poorly kept; whites moved out three years ago, except one family.
Vacant lot used as dump; one poolroom, two hotels; yards well kept; Negroes moving in.
Yards unkempt; mostly renters.
Formerly questionable houses for whites.
Mostly newcomers; property run down.
Yards well kept; boarding-houses.
People move in because they can't find anything better.

Between Thirty-first and Thirty-ninth streets east of State Street seventy-eight blocks were surveyed.   There were seventy-eight frame and 1,523 brick and stone buildings, 620 single houses, 559 double, 254 accommodating three

or more families, and nine apartment houses. Of this group 51 per cent were
of Type C. The property and general surroundings showed age and the
beginning of rapid deterioration everywhere; in some cases there had been
attempts to care for the premises and in some cases neglect was obvious.
The streets, except Michigan Avenue and South Park Boulevard, showed
much neglect, and the alleys generally were dirty. Many of these houses
were occupied by their Negro owners. Negroes were found to occupy about
40 per cent of these Type C houses.

Conveniences.—In these two parts of the South Side area conveniences
and ordinary sanitary facilities are often absent. Gas is the common form of
lighting, and often it is not used. Family-history data revealed that there
were about as many homes without as with bathrooms. In a large number of
buildings families were obliged to use common toilets located in halls or back
yards. The dwellings were out of repair in some respects in nearly every
instance. Defects of this kind were often in the plumbing. Leaky toilets
or water pipes were common complaints. Some toilets did not flush. Some
sinks were leaky, as were some of the roofs. In some houses windows or doors
were broken, loose, or sagging. Some houses were very dirty.

On the West Side a situation not essentially different was found among
the Type C dwellings. Possibly baths were a little more frequent. Occasionally there was a furnace, though stove heat was most common. Gas was the
usual means of lighting. The situation as to toilets was about the same, and
the buildings, being chiefly old, were usually out of repair in some respect.
The number of brick and frame dwellings was about equal. There were more
double houses in proportion to the single ones, and none that had three or
more families. Five-room dwellings were most numerous, and there was
little indication of overcrowding.

Neighborhood conditions.—Only two blocks in the West Side area were
rated as merely "fair," four in the North Side area were dirty, while only one
in the Ogden Park area was not cleaned. In the North Side and Ogden Park
areas distinct efforts were observed to keep yards clean. Premises showed
signs of care and attention, though an occasional vacant lot showed use for
dumping. Alleys in all three districts gave evidence of neglect. Some were
badly littered with garbage and rubbish.

IV. "TYPE D" HOUSES

Type D housing is the least habitable of all. The houses were usually
dilapidated, and in many cases extremely so. Most of the buildings are
among the oldest in the city. They were occupied only by Negroes at the foot
of the economic scale, many families living from hand to mouth, frequently in
extreme poverty.

This class of houses predominates in those parts of the South Side area
from Twelfth to Twenty-second Street along State Street and Wabash Avenue,

and from Twelfth to Thirty-ninth streets and Wentworth Avenue. Many Negro dwellings in the North Side area and about 35 or 40 per cent of those in the West Side area were of Type D. Even in the area of the South Side between State Street and Lake Michigan many of the older frame and brick buildings fall into this classification. It is safe to say that 43 per cent of the housing for Negroes is of this type.

Most of these dwellings were frail, flimsy, tottering, unkempt, and some of them literally falling apart. Little repairing is done from year to year. Consequently their state grows progressively worse, and they are now even less habitable than when the surveys quoted at the beginning of this section were made. The surroundings in these localities were in a condition of extreme neglect, with little apparent effort to observe the laws of sanitation. Streets, alleys, and vacant lots contained garbage, rubbish, and litter of all kinds. It is difficult to enforce health regulations.

Although there has been protest by Negroes against the necessity of living in places so uncomfortable and unhealthful, improvement comes slowly. Contentment with such insanitary conditions is usually due to ignorance of better living. For the poorest buildings low rents are offered to encourage continued occupancy and to forestall requests for repairs. Prompt vacating of many of these houses usually follows when a family can secure better accommodations in a better neighborhood.[1]

V. NEIGHBORHOOD IMPROVEMENT ASSOCIATIONS

Among the more intelligent Negroes neighborhood organizations were found similar to those of white people. Dissatisfaction with local conditions, failure of authorities to sweep and sprinkle streets or to provide adequate street lighting, corner signs, and similar equipment usually prompt these efforts. Three or four such societies have been instituted by Negroes in Chicago. One example is the Middlesex Improvement Club, organized following the riots of 1919 in a neighborhood including three blocks on Dearborn Street near Fiftieth. Among other things it seeks to promote a friendly spirit among the people of both races in a neighborhood which was turbulent during the riots. It has extended some financial aid to its members when required. It is financed by Negro business men with some help from white business men of the locality.

Woodlawn has a community organization which reflects the friendly attitude between the races in that district. Both whites and Negroes are members, with a common community interest. This organization goes somewhat beyond the usual neighborhood improvement association in scope and purpose. While it embodies the usual purposes, it also seeks to induce full use by all the people of the district of all public and semi-public institutions that contribute to good citizenship. One of the notices sent out by the associa-

[1] See "Family Histories," p. 170.

tion urged attendance at night sessions of public schools. It briefly set forth
the advantages for both young and older people, suggesting that their usefulness to the community might thus be enlarged, that they might be trained
for profitable employment, and incidentally that young people could be kept
off the streets and away from demoralizing places. Attention was drawn to
the fact that "business men of the city are seeking young people, both colored and white, for positions as stenographers, clerks, and trades people."
The notice closed thus:

We are desirous that you use your influence to maintain a spirit of friendliness
and good will among all citizens, white and black, and especially among the school
children, paying especial attention to the conduct of pupils to and from school. We
earnestly seek your co-operation in these matters.

In the neighborhood of Fifty-sixth Street and Wabash Avenue is another
of these neighborhood leagues; all the members are Negroes. Meetings
take place periodically at the houses of members, and special attention is
given to such matters as the condition of their premises, care of lawns, etc.

VI.   EFFORTS OF SOCIAL AGENCIES

Social agencies likewise have given considerable attention to the instruction
and encouragement of Negroes in better living. While this effort has been
directed mainly to the newer arrivals from the South, it has also had an effect
on many who have lived in the city for some time but have not yet adjusted
themselves to city life and more rigid standards of sanitation and deportment.

One of these agencies is the Urban League. Among other activities it
issued placards to be kept in sight in Negro homes, graphically contrasting good
and bad habits of living. Pictures showed the front porch of a Negro family
as it should and should not be used, with the pointed question, "Which?"
underneath. Then followed a sort of pledge of conduct:

I realize that our soldiers have learned *new habits of self-respect and cleanliness.*

I desire to help bring about a *new order of living* in this community.

I will attend to the neatness of my personal appearance on the street or when
sitting in front doorways.

I will refrain from wearing dust caps, bungalow aprons, house clothing, and
bedroom shoes out of doors.

I will arrange my toilet within doors and not on the front porch.

I will insist upon the use of rear entrances for coal dealers, hucksters, etc.

I will refrain from loud talking and objectionable deportment on street cars and
in public places.

I will do my best to prevent defacement of property either by children or adults.

The guidance and instruction given by the South Side Community Service,
pastors of churches and Negro newspapers have stimulated the Negro population to efforts at improvement of their property. One newspaper, for example,
conducted a column containing hints on cleanliness, sanitation, and deportment. It printed items concerning objectionable conditions at given addresses

and warned offenders that they were being watched by the neighborhood organization, which might take action against them if they did not improve their conduct.

Another way in which Negroes have been led to understand that habits of orderliness and cleanliness are expected of them in Chicago has been through a "Clean-up Week" in the spring of each year, when concerted efforts are made to collect and dispose of tin cans and other rubbish on vacant lots and yards. A "Tin Can Contest" was conducted by the Wabash Avenue Y.M.C.A., which offered prizes to the children collecting the greatest number of tin cans beyond 300. The 1,000 youngsters who participated in the Second Ward were divided into eight regiments. The eleven-year-old Negro girl who collected the greatest number of tin cans had a total of 6,840 to her credit. Next in order was Hyman Friedman, whose total was 5,347. More than 100,000 tin cans in all were obtained.

VII. EFFORTS OF INDIVIDUAL HOUSEHOLDERS

Individual householders, especially those owning their homes, were found to be trying to keep their premises presentable often in the face of discouraging odds. Throughout the family histories appear repeated protests by tenants at the failure of landlords to maintain a decent state of repairs and improvements.

None of the houses occupied by Negroes are of as high a standard, generally speaking, as those occupied by whites of a similar economic status.

Negroes rarely live in new houses. Virtually all live in neighborhoods where the housing is old. Negro houses, even of the best class, were built from twenty to forty years ago. Conditions in these old neighborhoods do not make for high standards of sanitation and cleanliness, nor the best habits of living generally; and Negroes labor under a handicap in striving to attain such standards.

Less attention is paid by public authorities to the condition of streets and alleys in such neighborhoods than in localities where the housing is of a higher grade. The streets are not cleaned and sprinkled as often and the alleys are more likely to be dirty, unpaved, and generally uncared for.

In most of the localities where Negroes live, buildings that have not already reached a state of great dilapidation are deteriorating rapidly because of the failure of owners to make repairs and improvements.

Escape from undesirable housing conditions is difficult for any Negroes, and for the vast majority it is practically impossible, particularly during a period of acute general housing shortage.

C. NEGROES AND PROPERTY DEPRECIATION

No single factor has complicated the relations of Negroes and whites in Chicago more than the widespread feeling of white people that the presence of Negroes in a neighborhood is a cause of serious depreciation of property

HOMES OCCUPIED AND IN PART OWNED BY NEGROES

Classified in the text as "Type B"

values. To the extent that people feel that their financial interests are affected, antagonisms are accentuated.

When a Negro family moves into a block in which all other families are white, the neighbors object. This objection may express itself in studied aloofness, in taunts, warnings, slurs, threats, or even the bombing of their homes.[1] White neighbors who can do so are likely to move away at the first opportunity. Assessors and appraisers in determining the value of the property take account of this general dislike of the presence or proximity of Negroes. It matters little what type of citizens the Negro family may represent, what their wealth or standing in the community is, or that their motive in moving into a predominant white neighborhood is to secure better living conditions—their appearance is a signal of depreciation. So it happens that when a Negro family moves into a block, most of the white neighbors show resentment toward both the Negro family and the owner or agent who rents or sells the property. Whites owning homes in the neighborhood become much exercised by fear of loss both of money and of neighborhood exclusiveness and desirability. The Negro suffers under the realization that, for reasons which he cannot control, he is considered undesirable and a menace to property values. Wherever Negroes have moved in Chicago this odium has attached to their presence. The belief that they destroy property values wherever they go is now commonly taken as a valid explanation of any unfriendliness toward the entire group. This feeling takes on the strength of a protective instinct among the whites.

So wide and menacing, indeed, has this feeling grown that the Commission deemed it necessary to make a thorough inquiry into its basis and to determine, if possible, to what degree the presence of Negroes is a factor in the depreciation of property values. Therefore it is essential to distinguish clearly between: (1) general factors in depreciation; and (2) presence of Negroes as an influence in these factors, and also as a direct factor.

What is meant by "depreciation"? Real estate men know it as "a loss in market value." Market value is "the price which a buyer who wishes to buy but is not forced to buy will pay to an owner who wishes to sell but is not forced to sell." Depreciation is reflected, not only in market values, but also in appraised or assessed valuations. Before purchasing property it is customary to take into account the surrounding conditions that affect its value, as well as its inherent value. Assessed valuations, fixed for taxing purposes by authorized public officials, fluctuate to some extent in harmony with appraised valuations. This analysis of the factors that tend to determine the value of real estate for one purpose or another gives a fairly dependable rule for finding whether it has risen or fallen in a given period. If property is thus shown to have decreased in value, it is said to have depreciated.

[1] See discussion of non-adjusted neighborhoods, p. 113, and of bombings, p. 122.

The value of real estate is determined largely by the human factors involved. This fact accounts for the striking differences in value of property, for example, on Sixteenth Street, on State Street, in the "Loop," on Chicago Avenue, and on Sheridan Road. Convenience, desirability, and other factors involving individuals who make up the public enter into the determination of realty values.

It is necessary to distinguish between land values and improved-property values. Usually buildings are erected that harmonize in cost with the value of the land on which they stand. But this harmonious relationship may not continue; developments in the neighborhood may increase materially the value of the land, while the value of the improvements decreases as time goes on. The values of the land and of the improvements do not necessarily rise and fall together, though improvements generally tend to add to the value of the land. Much, however, depends on the use to which the land is put, and even more on the use of adjacent land. That use may be such as seriously to impair the value of all the land within a given area or some particular tract in that area. Such impairment is a chief reason advanced for zoning, so that property values in various given districts may not be impaired through inharmonious uses, and that property values throughout a city may thus be stabilized,

It is also necessary to distinguish between "deterioration" and "depreciation." They are not interchangeable. Deterioration of improvements on land affects the value of the improvement, not necessarily the value of the land. The property as a whole may be depreciated by deterioration of improvements, but an increase in the land value might more than offset this loss. This would be accounted for by a possible change in the use of the land. For example, the buildings on the North Side in which Negroes now live are uniformly old and bad, yet the Negroes cannot buy them. The properties are in process, of change from residence to industrial use, and the values placed upon them for the latter use are far beyond the financial capacity of the Negro residents.

I. GENERAL FACTORS IN DEPRECIATION OF RESIDENCE PROPERTY

Apart from any racial influence there are many causes of depreciation in property values, the responsibility for all of which has often been thoughtlessly placed upon Negroes. Throughout the city may be observed blocks, streets, and neighborhoods running a declining course in desirability for residence purposes, losing value, changing in character and, in short, depreciating, but in or near which no Negroes live. The following are important factors of depreciation not due to race:

Physical deterioration.—The natural wear of time and the elements is a constant factor. Few houses are built to withstand these inroads over a long course of years, even though they have the utmost care. Neglect and lack of repairs and improvements hasten this deterioration sometimes greatly. Character of occupancy is often a factor. Some occupants are highly destructive, particularly in rented houses. Their careless or inept use of a house often adds vastly to the wear and tear and hastens deterioration. Over-crowding has a like effect.

Change in the character of a neighborhood.—Depreciation in property values in large cities is due in marked degree to factors not purely physical. There is always a continuing yet varying fluctuation in the character of neigh-borhoods; a restless shifting of population and conditions due to growth which rarely has been orderly or scientific. The psychological factor of residential property values is such that they may change very rapidly with the advent into a homogeneous neighborhood of a few families of a different nationality or social status. Between Twelfth and Thirty-first steeets in the South Side Negro residence area, once the most fashionable white residence section, property values based on residential uses slumped utterly, and then later began to increase because of industrial uses. Such a change is often due to an encroachment upon a residential district of commercial or industrial enterprises. Neighbors will move away rather than endure such disturbance of their peace and comfort. Their places may be taken by people less sensi-tive to such influences who may be drawn to the neighborhood by reduced rents resulting from the exodus of former residents. Then rapid deterioration usually sets in as the tone of the neighborhood falls. A like result follows a change from an exclusive residential district into one of rooming- and boarding-houses and large residences remodeled into flats.

The shifting of fashionable neighborhoods soon leads persons of means to abandon a high-grade residential section for some suburb or newer neighbor-hood which they think better suited to their social positions.

Use of buildings for immoral purposes.—Such use, though clandestine, eventually becomes known; and although the property yields high rents, it lowers the standing and value of the block or neighborhood and of adjacent areas. It not only deteriorates the buildings thus used, but also drives decent people from the locality; and the deserted houses either remain vacant or are taken by less desirable occupants. Depreciation inevitably results.

Public garages, theaters, and kindred nuisances.—People of a high-grade residential district do not wish to live too near a public garage, theater, bathing-beach, saloon, cabaret, dance hall, bowling-alley, or billiard room. If they are unable to keep such enterprises out of their neighborhood they will sell their property and find homes elsewhere.

Changes in transportation facilities.—These may depreciate property in two ways: (*a*) they may themselves introduce obnoxious dirt or noise-making features or bring in industries with such features; (*b*) new transportation facilities often open up more desirable localities to which people are drawn from the older localities. In both cases depreciation ensues.

Overbuilding.—Overbuilding is another and frequent cause of depreciation. Building booms are often followed by years of depression due to an oversupply of buildings.

II   DEPRECIATION ON THE SOUTH SIDE

The area from Thirty-first to Thirty-ninth Streets and State Street to the lake is now the center of the largest Negro residential area in the city, having approximately 20 per cent more Negroes than whites.

In the eighties and nineties this area was part of the most fashionable residential district in Chicago and included some of the city's most prominent families and business leaders. They lived in houses which they had built for their homes, and which were the first fine residences erected after the Chicago fire of 1871. Michigan, Prairie, and South Park avenues and Grand Boulevard were the most fashionable streets with the best houses.

The Negro population then lived immediately west, between Wentworth Avenue and State Street and north of Thirty-fifth Street.

The North Side and the North Shore had not yet developed as fashionable neighborhoods. Indeed, the most prominent residence on Lake Shore Drive and one of the earliest stood almost alone for many years before fashionable people settled around it.

As the North Side grew in fashionable favor the South Side began to lose its original exclusiveness, and its residences began to depreciate. These properties, while their original owners occupied them, were worth, many of them, from $30,000 to $100,000, including large grounds, elaborate interior decorations, and sometimes works of art. The usual range of the original costs of these houses was from $10,000 to $30,000. The change steadily continued, and these houses were rented and sold by the first owners at reduced prices to persons less prominent socially, until nearly all the original families had gone. A few refused to sell their houses and left them in charge of caretakers; and a very few still remain.

The gradual lowering of the market value of the property is pictured by prominent real estate men well acquainted with the neighborhood for many years:

It is a positive fact, an economic fact, that any time a poor class of people moves into a neighborhood formerly occupied by people who had an earning capacity greater than that of the people moving in, there is depreciation. That is true whether Italians move in, or Poles, Negroes, Greeks, etc. If the people moving into the neighborhood earn less and have less than the people formerly living in that neighborhood, there is depreciation.

Between 1900 and 1910 a few Negroes moved into Wabash Avenue. The houses were very old and built close together, with few single residences. Negroes did not progress farther eastward in any large numbers because the next street was Michigan Avenue, probably the most select of all the streets in the area. With the pressure of increasing numbers and ascending economic ability urging them out of the congested, uncomfortable, and unclean dwellings west of State Street, Negroes could and would pay higher rents than the class of white persons to which the oldest houses would next descend. In 1912,

in the area east of State Street, practically all of the original residents had
gone, and few Negroes had come in.   Real estate men estimate that generally
natural depreciation proceeds at the rate of 2 to $2\frac{1}{2}$ per cent a year.   When
Negroes first came into the area the buildings were at least twenty years old,
and many were much older, representing at the lowest figure a very substantial
depreciation.

There was another important factor in the depreciation of the area.   In
1912 the old vice district west of State Street and immediately northwest of
this area was broken up.   The inmates numbered approximately 2,000 and
were by no means confined strictly within the recognized limits.   They moved
into the nearest good houses available where they could continue to ply their
trade clandestinely.   They could afford to pay high rents, and numbers of real
estate owners profited greatly by dealing with them.   As many of these
houses stood, they again yielded rents almost as high as when they were new.
Cabarets, saloons, and amusement places packed the side streets, and buffet
flats opened up in the residence blocks.   Raids and prosecution, night visits
from men who did not live in the district, called attention to the changed
character of the neighborhood, and property values sank lower.   Pressure from
prosecuting agencies, as well as the attraction of better houses in less conspicuous neighborhoods, urged the vice element southward.   This southward
trend is indicated in the maps, facing pages 342 and 346, showing the environment of the South Side Negro.

While property in this area could be bought cheaply it was also possible
to obtain proportionately high rents by placing Negroes or prostitutes in houses
not rented to either class before.   Negroes were always charged higher rents
than were the whites who immediately preceded them.

The Juvenile Protective Association in 1913 made a study called *The
Colored People of Chicago* and published it in a small pamphlet.   Concerning
the disposition of real estate men to profit in this way, the reports say:

. . . . the dealer offers to the owner of an apartment house which is no longer
renting advantageously to white tenants cash payment for a year's lease on the
property, thus guaranteeing the owner against loss, and then he fills the building with
colored tenants.   It is said, however, that the agent does not put out the white
tenants unless he can get 10 per cent more from the colored people.

The fact that for like quarters Negroes pay much higher rents than any
other group in the city was discussed by the Chicago School of Civics and
Philanthropy in a special study of housing for Negroes in 1911-12.   The
report says:

The explanation for this condition of affairs among the colored people is comparatively simple; the results are far-reaching.   The strong prejudice among the
white people against having colored people living on white residence streets, colored
children attending schools with white children, or entering into other semi-social relation with them, confines the opportunities for residence open to colored people of all

positions in life to relatively small and well-defined areas. Consequently the demand for houses and apartments within these areas is strong and comparatively steady, and since the landlord is reasonably certain that the house or apartment can be filled at any time, as long as it is in any way tenantable, he takes advantage of his opportunities to raise rents and to postpone repairs.

It was during this period that buildings could be easily purchased by Negroes. One white real estate dealer whose interests are almost exclusively in the area under discussion has purchased more than 1,000 such houses which he rents to Negroes. These buildings were not purchased from Negroes but from first, second, and third owners, and at a price much below the original value.

With an opportunity for renting or purchasing the houses in this area, Negroes began to move in, first in small numbers and soon in larger numbers. They naturally sought to abandon the generally and often extremely dilapidated houses west of State Street.

III. DEPRECIATION AFTER THE COMING OF NEGROES

Buildings twenty to thirty years old deteriorate rapidly unless expensive repairs are made. As Negroes were often unable to make such repairs while paying for the property, the depreciation continued.

Widespread buying of property in this district by Negroes began during the period of the migration. Many home-owning Negroes, having sold their property in the South and brought the money to Chicago, found it easier to buy a house here on a first payment of $200 to $500, and on monthly instalments thereafter, than to pay the rents demanded. Few, however, knew anything of city property values; they were often exploited by agents or assumed larger obligations than they could easily handle.

Many Negroes purchased fairly substantial dwellings on the long-time instalment plan without providing for repairs and maintenance. Usually the monthly payment to cover interest, taxes, and instalment on principal was about all the Negro and his family could carry, even though his wife's wages supplemented his. Thus nothing was left for upkeep.

Real estate agents before the Commission agreed that Negroes meet these obligations with reasonable regularity. One white real-estate broker said: "Those of us who have dealings with Negroes find that they make very fair clients on the whole, pay their way, and ask no favors that any other human being would not ask."

Another referred to Negroes as "wonderful instalment buyers" who have a "tendency to invest in a home earlier than whites," and said that in fifteen years' experience his firm had never foreclosed on a Negro home buyer; and in only two cases, due to exceptional circumstances, had contracts been forfeited. Two Negro real estate dealers said:

A colored man usually feels that he will go without food rather than not meet his obligations. That is one reason why sometimes his home is run down, because he has spent every dollar he can get to meet the payments on that property.   He cannot spare the money sometimes to buy a lawn mower or sprinkling hose.

A colored man who buys a piece of property in a neighborhood has no financial connections.   He meets his obligations promptly for three reasons: first, he wants a home; second, he knows they may squeeze him; third, that mortgage is coming due and he doesn't know where to go to get it renewed.   We have no organization of our own to back him.   If the fence is to be fixed or the house is to be painted, and a year from that date the mortgage is due, and he has $500 in the bank, he will not paint his house for the simple reason that, if he did, when the mortgage is due he will not be able to meet it.   He saves, and when the mortgage comes due he has $500, $600, or $700 set aside to meet it.

Frequently Negroes overreach themselves in purchasing property.   Charles Duke, a Negro, in a pamphlet on Negro housing in Chicago remarked:

A very harmful result of present tendencies is manifested in the acquisition of homes by colored people beyond their social or economic advancement.   The economic waste in this particular has been especially great.   They represent in many cases a considerable outlay of capital.   The domestic facilities they afford are years beyond the needs of the people to whom they are allotted.   In many instances it costs a small fortune annually to maintain one of these establishments, and when this is not done the depreciation is both rapid and spectacular.

There is such lack of hotels and lodging-houses for Negroes, especially for single men, that many Negroes have bought or rented houses with the intention of paying for them, in part at least, with income from lodgers or boarders. Such use leads to overcrowding, with consequent rapid deterioration and depreciation.   This tendency is accentuated by the fact that the houses that Negroes can buy are usually old and deteriorated.

While new arrivals from the South soon learn that the poorest city tenement requires better care than plantation cabins, their carelessness meanwhile contributes to the property depreciation of their dwellings and neighborhood.

There are other factors of depreciation in this district which became active after the Negroes came, but for which they were not wholly responsible.   One was the remodeling of residences for business purposes.   While the remodeled property may bring larger returns, neighboring residence property declines in value.   Many fine old dwellings on Michigan Avenue and Grand Boulevard have been transformed in recent years into lamp-shade factories, second-hand fur shops, and small business houses; and these changes have depreciated neighboring property for residence purposes.

Another factor of depreciation is the city's tolerance of gambling and immorality in and near areas of Negro residence.   In most cities where Negroes are numerous a like tendency appears.   Little consideration is given to the desire of Negroes to live in untainted districts, and they have not been able to make effective protest.

In 1916 the *Chicago Daily News*, in a series of articles on the Negroes, described some of the disorderly saloons and cabarets in the South State and Thirty-fifth streets region, with their vile associations of disreputable whites and blacks:

Other resorts in the district are worse; some are better. These are typical of the roistering saloons, a kind which would not be tolerated in any other part of the city since the old Twenty-second Street levee was broken up. White proprietors have brought them into the district, and many of them are patronized largely by crowds from other parts of the city. The resorts are forced on the colored people. Those colored families in good circumstances and desiring respectable surroundings move away, only to find disorderly saloons trailing after them.

At 301 East Thirty-seventh Street, on the southeast corner of Forest Avenue, is the saloon of C—. With this exception the district is a quiet, respectable residence quarter. When it was known that this property was to be used for saloon purposes a petition of protest was signed by 300 representative colored men and presented to Mayor Harrison.

At night this saloon is an animated place. Reputable colored families object to it chiefly on account of the numbers of disorderly white women who meet colored men in its diminutive back room. In the barroom an automatic piano thumps through the night until closing hours. On the mirrors are pasted chromos of "September Morn" and other poses of nude women.

Buffet flats and disorderly hotels are adjuncts of the bad saloons. They make a better harvest for the police than the saloons. The borderland of a colored residential district is the haven for disorderly resorts. Protests of colored residents against the painted women in their neighborhood, the midnight honking of automobiles, the loud profanity and vulgarity are usually ignored by the police.

In one block between South State and South Dearborn streets which was canvassed by the *Daily News*, five places were found openly admitted to be disorderly houses. Some were in flat buildings, the other tenants of which apparently were respectable, some raising families of children.

Many white owners of real estate who speak in horrified whispers of vice dangers view such dangers with complacency when these are thrust among colored families. Two years ago a woman of the underworld and her gambler husband decided to open a "high-class" resort on the South Side. She got a location as a neighbor of reputable colored people by purchasing the home of a former alderman and leader in a church, the one of which the Rev. John P. Brushingham, secretary of Mayor Thompson's Morals Commission, is the pastor. The woman was one of the most notorious of the demimonde. An oil painting of her, as she was before her husband in a fit of jealousy bit off a part of her nose, for years hung in a saloon of international reputation.

These are some of the influences which the colored population is forced to combat in its fight for decency and good citizenship. A few secure political preferment and others profit by catering to the city's vices, while the rank and file are hedged around by demoralizing influences and the race is discredited unjustly.

Another chapter of this series dealt with gambling in the South Side district. Here are two excerpts:

HOMES OCCUPIED BY NEGROES ON FOREST AVENUE
(Note pavement and smoke)
Classified in text as "Type C"

REAR VIEW OF HOUSES OCCUPIED BY NEGROES ON FEDERAL STREET
Classified in text as "Type D"

Colored men are in active control of the gambling situation in the big part of their district in the second ward. Back of them are white police officials at one end of the line and white politicians who keep them in power at the other end of the line. When second ward, and even some adjacent ward, gambling is discussed by gamblers on the inside, certain colored men are always mentioned. They are called "the syndicate," and their approval is said to be necessary if the police are to let anybody run in the ward.

Whether gambling is a more dangerous cause of demoralization of a community than are disorderly saloons, buffet flats and dissolute women is an often discussed question. Gambling is a man's game, is more open, and the connection between it, the police, and politics easier to trace. In order to gamble the police must be evaded, which is difficult, or made blind by a peculiar remedy for itching palms or by orders from political powers that be. However, it usually is the same police and the same politicians who are protecting both classes of vice.

The contamination of these influences depreciates property and casts a blight upon all who live within their unrestricted range. The taint extends beyond the blocks in which they exist and serves to promote prejudice and ill feeling against the Negroes who are the unwilling sufferers from these vicious resorts.

There are many landlords who exact high rentals from Negroes for the use of run-down houses. All investigations of Negro housing on the South Side indicated that as a rule the rents are excessive, considering the inferior dwellings, their disrepair, and unsanitary conditions. This neglect by the landlords not only directly depreciates the property but encourages a careless use of it by tenants that leads to the same end. One can hardly expect tenants to respect property that is not respected by its owners.

Owners and agents of property occupied by Negroes differ in their opinions of Negroes as tenants and in their ways of handling them. Of course there are differences in character, standing, and responsibility among Negroes as among whites, and this fact partly explains the following differences of opinion expressed by experienced real estate men:

One real estate firm, on Indiana Avenue, that makes leases to both white and Negro clients, said that property occupied by Negroes was more likely to run down. Another firm on East Fifty-first Street reported that it rented to Negroes on regular leases and had no trouble about collections. A young Negro real estate agent on Indiana Avenue said that he had no difficulty with collections: about half of his tenants came to the office, and collectors called upon the other half. When a building supports a janitor, he said, there is no trouble about repairs, but if the responsibility is upon the tenants it is difficult to keep a building in repair. The office manager for a firm on Cottage Grove Avenue said that the majority of its Negro tenants are on leases; all pay the rent at the office; if they fall in arrears collectors are sent.

A firm which for many years has conducted a real estate business on the South Side reported that 75 per cent of its Negro tenants are on a month-to-month basis with thirty days' notice to terminate; and 95 per cent of them are north of Thirty-ninth Street. A firm on Indiana Avenue requires its tenants to sign leases; and in districts where there is much shifting about, or where the property is for sale, a sixty days' notice clause is inserted. It usually sends a collector, so that proper supervision may be kept of the property. Its head expressed the opinion that Negroes are just as good tenants as whites whose wages are on about the same scale.

The office manager of an owner with about 1,400 Negro tenants said that on the whole they compared very favorably with the white tenants who preceded them; while some Negroes are careless and ignorant, they all paid their rent promptly; his office did not average one eviction a month, and when Negroes are evicted they rarely cause trouble. Quite the contrary was the report of the office manager of a real estate firm on East Thirty-first Street, which does an extensive business with Negroes. Much depreciation, he said, can be attributed to Negro tenants; they are much harder on houses than white tenants of the same station in life; they do not take proper care of the furnaces or plumbing, and the higher rents paid by them merely cover the cost of the additional repairs; the recent comers pay their rent promptly when they have brought money with them or when they receive good wages, but later on become difficult to manage because they find it hard to adjust themselves to city life.

A firm on East Forty-seventh Street reported that it has a large number of Negro tenants, makes leases to them, has no difficulty in collecting rents, and considers them more desirable than the whites who preceded them; a firm on Indiana Avenue expressed the opinion that depreciation is very great in houses rented to Negroes. That Negro tenants pay their rent promptly was the experience of a real estate agent on Cottage Grove Avenue. He has many Negro tenants on leases and is well satisfied with them, although he does not think they take as good care of the property as do the whites; Negroes are usually occupants of old buildings, which are more difficult to take care of.

Another real estate dealer on Cottage Grove Avenue who leases to Negroes finds that usually they adhere to the terms of the lease, although they sometimes move without notice. A dealer on Wabash Avenue, who rents flats to Negroes, said that he looked up the housing record of Negroes carefully before letting them in, yet he sometimes had trouble with them. Once he rented a flat to a mother and daughter, and the next day he found another family living in it; but on the whole he was well satisfied to have Negroes as tenants.

A prominent official of the Grand Boulevard district of the Kenwood and Hyde Park Property Owners' Association, which seeks to keep Negroes out of Hyde Park, stated that a fundamental fault in connection with the strained relations between whites and Negroes was the failure of white owners to keep their property in good condition so that it might be occupied "efficiently," that is, by white persons. Another official of that organization said that Negro tenants could not be expected to repair white men's property; that there are a great many dwellings in the South Side Negro district that ought to be condemned by the city health department, and that Negroes are compelled to live in them because they can get nothing better.

In analyzing responsibility for depreciation, in the area from Thirty-first to Thirty-ninth Street and from State Street to the lake, it is difficult to determine to just what extent the Negroes are there because of prior depreciation, and to what extent present depreciation is due to their presence. It is certain, however, that a large part of the depreciation is not justly chargeable to them, and that their contribution is attributable partly to their economic status and partly to the deep-seated prejudice against them. There are many instances in which property occupied by them has appreciated in value. This will always be true when the use by Negroes, or the demand for such use, is higher or greater than any other use or demand. A symptom of the general prejudice is the very prevalent belief that if Negroes have once occupied property its value is thereby "destroyed" for white persons. This is true only until it has a value for use by whites greater than its value for use by Negroes. So long and only so long as Negroes as a class are, or are generally deemed to be, at the bottom of the economic scale will their presence in a neighborhood depreciate values. At present the fact stands out that Negro occupancy is an unmistakable symptom of depreciation—an indication that the value of property has fallen to their economic level, as well as an aid to depreciation in its last stages.

IV. DEPRECIATION IN HYDE PARK

The area bounded by Thirty-ninth and Fifty-fifth streets and Michigan and Cottage Grove avenues has several property owners' protective associations for the purpose of preserving property values. Their dominant interest has been the exclusion of Negroes because these associated property owners believe that Negroes always depreciate the values of real estate. Negroes have moved into the neighborhood and there has been depreciation. Therefore Negroes are the cause.

A complete understanding of the situation requires that it be determined to what extent property values decreased because Negroes moved in, and to what extent Negroes moved in because property values had decreased. There is no doubt that the thousands of protests against the "invasion" of Negroes were sincere. It is also true that scarcely ten Negroes now living there could have purchased their properties at the original prices.

A leading real estate dealer said that "when a Negro moves into a block the value of the properties on both sides of the street is depreciated all the way from $100,000 to $500,000, depending upon the value of the property in the block"; that it was a fact and that there was no escaping it.

It's a condition that is inherent in the human race. . . . . a man will not buy a piece of property or put his money in or invest in it where he knows that he is liable to be confronted the next day or the next year or even five years hence with the problem of having colored people living alongside of his investment. This depreciation runs all the way from 30 to 60 per cent. Some time ago a survey was made as a result of which it was estimated that the influx of Negroes into white neighborhoods during the last two years had depreciated property on the South Side about $100,000,000.

He cited as evidences of this the increased difficulty of negotiating loans on South Side realty on any terms, and the fact that some loan companies refused to write them at all, and loan values there had dropped enormously.

The Grand Boulevard district of the Kenwood and Hyde Park Property Owners' Association reported an even larger estimate of the depreciation caused by the coming of Negroes into property near that boulevard. A committee of the Association in a report made early in 1920 claimed that the coming of Negro owners and tenants into that territory had depreciated property values of $400,000,000 fully 50 per cent.

The advent of the first Negro families in a white district usually creates something like a panic. The white residents, in a great many instances, fearing contiguity with Negroes and property loss, hasten to offer their property for sale and move elsewhere. Even a threat that Negroes intend to occupy a certain block or neighborhood will cause an exodus of white people, and their property is customarily sold at a sacrifice. When many properties are thus thrown on the market low prices are the certain result.

When in recent years, Negroes moved into the Hyde Park district, animosity was aroused, and numerous bombings of property occupied by Negroes followed. One of the oldest South Side real estate dealers, quoted in the *Daily News'* series of articles in the summer of 1919, expressed the tense feeling of an association there that was seeking methods to drive out and keep out the Negroes:

We want to be fair. We want to do what is right, but these people will have to be more or less pacified. At a conference where their representatives were present I told them we might as well be frank about it, "You people are not admitted to our society," I said. Personally I have no prejudice against them. I have had experience of many years dealing with them, and I'll say this for them: I have never had to foreclose a mortgage on one of them. They have been clean in every way and always prompt in their payments. But, you know, improvements are coming along the lake shore, the Illinois Central, and all that; we can't have these people coming over here. Not one cent has been appropriated by our organization for bombing or anything like that.

They injure our investments. They hurt our values. I couldn't say how many have moved in, but there's at least a hundred blocks that are tainted. We are not making any threat, but we do say that something must be done. Of course, if they come in as tenants, we can handle the situation fairly easily, but when they get a deed, that's another matter.

This fear of Negro neighbors has been used by some real estate agents in promoting speculative schemes. By sending a Negro to inquire about property, they alarm the neighbors so that they will consider offers of purchase much below the normal prices. When the excitement has abated values rise again, and a profit is made.

In the actual depreciation of Hyde Park property there were several factors, usually overlooked, that were in no wise attributable to the presence of Negroes. Some of Chicago's finest residences were located on Michigan Avenue and Grand Boulevard south of Thirty-ninth Street. This was an extension of the early fashionable South Side district and had residences that cost $350,000. But as in the case of the earlier South Side the neighborhood long since had lost some of its first settlers and had begun to decline. The World's Columbian Exposition, held in Chicago in 1893, was near the Hyde Park neighborhood. To accommodate the millions of visitors at the Exposition hotels and apartment houses were built in that district far in excess of the normal need. The apartment houses, moreover, affected the exclusiveness of the residence streets. The buildings were speculations. Large sums were expended in the hope of immediate exceptional profits. Property on Sixty-third Street sold at the Exposition time for three times the price it could command today. This is typical of the speculative values that then prevailed there. After the Exposition the removal of the first residents to the North Side and to suburbs steadily increased.

The abnormal years just preceding the Exposition had brought in thousands of workmen, who were thrown out of work when the Exposition buildings were finished. This and the panic of 1893 made building costs very low and caused further construction of dwellings in that district. Mr. L. M. Smith, a prominent South Side real estate man, described this change at a meeting of the Kenwood and Hyde Park Property Owners' Association:

The condition that existed after the World's Fair, if you will remember, in the material yards and the labor market was this: Every yard was loaded up, and the carpenters and the mechanics that were stranded here after the World's Fair were glad to take jobs as janitors at $25 a month, in order that they could have good warm places for their families, and buildings that were put up three and four years after the Fair, along in 1894, 1895, and 1896, could be built at about 30 per cent cheaper than those that were put up during the World's Fair. The consequences were that you could rent a flat cheaper in a brand-new modern building than you could in a building that was put up during the World's Fair, and as the older buildings could not be rented, the owners finally had to come down in their rent more and more; they got in less and less desirable tenants until finally the whole territory became undesirable.

These first "undesirables" were not Negroes, for Negroes had not then moved across State Street. And there were other causes for the vacancies and removals that admitted Hyde Park's first undesirables beside the over-building. One was the proximity of the Stock Yards. Since the South Siders could not have the Stock Yards moved, many of them moved themselves. The railroads along the lake front, with their cinders, smoke, and noise, were also a factor. Another was the creeping in of industrial plants that located in and near the district, frequently in the face of protests. A striking instance of this is the large assembly plant of an automobile company at Thirty-ninth Street and Michigan Avenue. During recent years the automobile industry has practically taken control of Michigan Avenue, once the most beautiful street of the South Side.

The coming of apartment houses and boarding-houses was another signal of declining values. It was shown that for twenty-five years scarcely a new residence had been built on Grand Boulevard, once noted for its handsome residences—due principally to the extensive building of apartment houses there.

Racial prejudice other than that against Negroes has operated in many instances to depress property values. The presence of Jews, Germans, Irish, Italians, and Swedes has at times been objectionable to neighborhoods of Americans or of another race. A leader in the movement to remove Negroes from the Grand Boulevard area gave evidence of this, saying: "I know the Irish killed a certain boulevard. I know the Jews hurt another one, and I know the gambling element hurt another one."

On the South Side the Negroes were preceded by Irish. The original settlers in the area around Thirty-first and Dearborn streets were mainly Irish laborers who worked in the lumber yards and mills, the Stock Yards, and other South Side industries. When they moved westward among their own people, thirty-five years ago, the Negroes took their places.

Sometimes social or sentimental values are involved in the depreciation brought about when a new race or nationality breaks down the exclusiveness of a residence district. After the Exposition, for example, when wealthy residents of Michigan Avenue, and Grand and Drexel boulevards deserted their houses for more fashionable locations, many of them were bought by Jews. This operated to depreciate adjacent property in the opinion of those who disliked Jews as neighbors.

How the changes take place was well described by an experienced real estate man: The original families have divided up and moved away; sons and daughters have married; the servant problem has become acute, making it difficult to maintain large houses; thus apartment houses have become popular; houses are older and deteriorated, apartments are new and modern. In 1915 when the number of apartments for rent was in excess of the demand, a tenant would spend $25 or $30 in order to move into an apartment across the street merely because it happened to be fitted with glass door knobs; a high-class residence at Forrestville Avenue and Forty-fifth Street was sold twenty years ago for $12,000; yet he told the purchasers ten years ago that the property would not sell for more than $4,000 to $6,000; and that was before Negroes had moved into the neighborhood. Apartments in that vicinity still command a price approaching their original cost of building, because the demand for them is stronger than for houses.

This real estate man made the broad statement that the depreciation has taken effect, in the majority of cases, before a Negro family has moved into a neighborhood. There is depreciation, he thought, due to prejudice, when a Negro family moves into a good neighborhood that has been exclusively white, but that there are very few such instances for the reason that Negroes prefer to live where they are welcome, where there is no antagonism. With regard to the district between Thirty-ninth and Fifty-fifth streets, State Street and

Cottage Grove Avenue, he stated that the entrance of the Negro had not appreciably affected values.

Another real estate dealer, experienced in South Side property and in selling to Negroes, expressed similar opinions. The greatest depreciation, he felt, was in the expensive residences, and he doubted whether property as a whole in the square mile centered at State and Thirty-fifth streets had been depreciated much if at all.

There was agreement among the authorities consulted that in an exclusive neighborhood of wealthy residents marked depreciation in large residences has taken place, followed by the introduction of apartment buildings. One of the men who had earnestly opposed Negro entrance into the Grand Boulevard district recalled when valuations on Grand and Drexel boulevards were from $400 to $600 a front foot; then they fell to $125 or $150 a foot; and then gradually climbed back to $175 or $200 a foot on account of the introduction of apartment buildings.

Such variations in value are the usual accompaniment of unguided growth in a large city. This unguided development brought depreciation, which was manifest before Negroes began to make their appearance in the area.

The spread of clandestine prostitution, discussed in connection with the area north of Thirty-ninth Street, did not stop at Thirty-ninth Street. As the environment maps indicate,[1] there was a noticeable increase from 1916 to 1918 in the number of houses or flats used by prostitutes in the area south of Thirty-ninth Street. These changes occurred before the spread of the Negro population reached the neighborhood. Two houses, for example, at 4404 and 4406 Grand Boulevard, bought by a Negro woman and bombed four times after she moved in, had been occupied by prostitutes just prior to her purchase.

The coming of Negroes.—In 1916 hundreds of buildings in the Hyde Park area stood vacant and had been so for some time. Owners and real estate men were offering large concessions in the effort to get tenants. Values had fallen greatly. A prominent real estate man closely in touch with the neighborhood estimated that 25 per cent of the buildings there were vacant, and that there was little prospect of renting or selling them. Coincident with this oversupply in Hyde Park was an acute demand among Negroes for houses, intensified by the sudden addition of about 50,000 migrants. Many of them had sold their property in the South and brought the money with them. Hyde Park landlords were willing to sell or rent to them rather than lose their property entirely. Many Negroes, however, instead of renting, purchased the properties because of the exceptional terms offered.

This continued for about two years, when a demand for houses again arose among the white population. There was inactivity in building throughout the war period. Chicago was sharing in the housing shortage which affected the whole country, which was estimated in the early part of 1921 at 50,000 houses.

[1] See pp. 342 and 346.

As the demand of whites for housing became acute, Hyde Park owners began to feel that their property was at a disadvantage due to the presence of Negroes.

Plans for beautifying the lake front and improving Hyde Park were emphasized as a reason for holding on to property there. Alderman Schwartz, in addressing a meeting of the Grand Boulevard district of the Kenwood and Hyde Park Property Owners' Association, said:

The South Side, and Hyde Park and Kenwood in particular, in past years has been the choice residential section of Chicago, the show place of Chicago. Grand Boulevard is the most magnificent street in the world, the finest boulevard of our wonderful boulevard system. I know that for many, many years, in this town, it was the ambition of people living in other parts of the city to arrange matters so that they could have their homes on the South Side in the place where you now live.

We have seen the rapid deterioration. In the council and in the committees we have decided that we must do something. The law has some very definite limitations written into our constitution and statutes. It cannot afford any relief. You yourselves must resurrect the South Side.

As one instance of what we attempted to do in the way of assuring to the people who reside here that the South Side can and will continue to be the great place we live in, we passed the Lake Front Ordinance. You people probably never realized what a wonderful thing that will be for the South Side. It will take in the lake front from Twelfth Street south to Fifty-first; it will affect the very choicest residential district in Chicago, the territory between Thirty-ninth Street and Forty-seventh Street— in this portion of the ward where we now are, something like $125,000,000 will be expended in reclaiming the lake front for you people, you men and women who must stand together to save your homes, see that your homes are kept as fine places to live in, that your neighbors are kept the most desirable neighbors in the city of Chicago, so that you may enjoy the benefit of that wonderful improvement that is to come. Think of that tremendous stretch, from Thirty-ninth to Forty-seventh, of bathing facilities, the finest in the world. More than a year and a half ago an estimate was made of the loss in property values in the Oakland district, north of Forty-third Street, and that was estimated to be $100,000,000. Now it is not only the loss of money that interests us. It means not only that somebody has lost a certain amount of wealth, but it means that somebody has lost comfort in living; someone has lost joy in his home; someone has lost the opportunity to give his children the environment that he wanted to give.

A survey made by the Hyde Park Property Owners' Association in 1920 showed that there were then 3,300 property owners in the area bounded by Thirty-ninth and Fifty-fifth streets, Michigan Avenue and Cottage Grove Avenue, and that of this number 1,000 were Negroes. Then began the attempts to move Negroes[1] back into "their own neighborhood."

Many of the Negroes who moved into this area had substantial resources enabling them either to buy property outright or so to arrange for payments through instalments and mortgages as to render themselves secure against

[1] See "Contested Neighborhoods," p. 116.

efforts to remove them. But in so doing they further complicated the status of the neighborhood. Few white persons recognize the marked differences among Negroes, so that in purely commercial dealings they are not as careful in selecting Negro tenants as they would be among whites. As a result some Negroes who secured property there proved damaging to property values, just as would persons of a similar type from any other race.

Many of the houses for sale or rent were not suited to the incomes of ordinary wage-earners. White persons whose incomes were sufficient to pay the rental for such large houses preferred a different sort of house or neighborhood; and whites of smaller incomes could find more suitable houses elsewhere; while Negroes, hard pressed for houses, rented them, and took lodgers to fill them and help pay the rent.

The exclusive occupancy of a block by Negroes is usually followed by less care of streets and alleys. This neglect is general between Twenty-second and Thirty-ninth streets and is beginning to appear in the territory between Thirty-ninth and Forty-third streets where recently blocks have been "turned over" to Negroes. Community associations are being formed in some of these areas to protest against this laxity, and stimulate neighborhood interest in neat premises.

Appreciation of property.—When values fall extremely due to a selling panic among white owners, it is often followed by a decided recovery as the Negro demand grows. Such a new market among Negroes, however, seems never to have been strong enough to send prices for residence purposes back to original levels. But many instances have shown that prices rarely stay at the low "panic" level and frequently rebound to a level much above that at which panic sales were made. Mr. Gates, a prominent South Side real estate dealer, said: "If a Negro family locates in a street where the population is all white, values are cut in two, but this would not be likely to occur if a large number of Negroes were ready and willing to buy adjacent property at established prices. Supply and demand would rule in such a market." Other real estate dealers expressed the opinion that "if the white owners were not over-anxious to sell when the Negro 'invasion' begins, they might later on obtain as much or more for their property than they could have obtained before the advent of the Negroes."

In numerous cases Negroes created a market for property when there was none. A prominent white business man long resident on the South Side told of a row of houses on South Park Avenue and Grand Boulevard that were vacant for years until sold or rented to Negroes: they could not be sold at all until they took on a value because Negroes were ready to buy them.

A prominent Negro physician bought a piece of property in an exclusive white Hyde Park neighborhood. He lived there seven years and then sold the property at an advance, and, to his knowledge, there had been no depreciation in adjacent property.

A white real estate dealer bought a house in Grand Boulevard between Thirty-fifth and Thirty-sixth streets about five years ago. When Negro residents came some of the white people sold at a sacrifice. But he remained and four years later sold the property for $2,000 above its cost to him.

An interesting instance related to property on Langley Avenue into which a Negro family moved in 1919. The value of contiguous property remained the same as of property two and three blocks east where no Negroes lived. Six months later, across the street from this Negro family, a white man, aware of their occupancy, bought a house and paid $1,500 more than it had formerly been offered for.

Thus, notwithstanding the prejudice against Negro neighbors that usually obtains, a block or neighborhood into which Negroes move is not always and necessarily depreciated, so many and active are the other factors contributing to depreciation (or sometimes preventing); and so frequently has it occurred that these factors of depreciation have operated extensively prior to the arrival of Negroes.

The fluctuation of values in response to sentiment, both inherent and stimulated, manifested itself in a practice of certain real estate dealers on the South Side. Although it was stated and believed that values were irrevocably destroyed when a Negro family occupied a building, these agents boosted values by announcing that another building had been "saved" or "redeemed," *thoroughly renovated*, and restored to its "rightful occupants." The Kenwood and Hyde Park Property Owners' Association stated that this plan had succeeded in sixty-eight instances of buildings "reclaimed" by the Association.

A Prairie Avenue block.—To study the processes and factors of depreciation the Commission selected an obviously depreciated block on the once fashionable Prairie Avenue, between Twenty-ninth and Thirtieth streets, into which no Negroes had yet moved.

In 1885–90 Prairie Avenue was one of Chicago's most fashionable and exclusive residential streets. Imposing brown- and gray-stone residences, with balconies of stone and ornamental iron, broad bay-windows, and large well-kept lawns behind high iron fences, gave evidence of the wealth and social position of their owners.

The gradual decline of Prairie Avenue, as North Side and North Shore neighborhoods became more fashionable places of residence, and long before the approach of Negroes was even thought of, was exemplified in this block. *Chicago Blue Book*, a broadly inclusive social directory, published annually, shows that in 1890 the families living at forty-nine of the sixty-one addresses in the block were listed; in 1900 there were eighteen of the forty-nine left; in 1910 there were only ten, and in 1915 only two. Second and third occupants of the houses took the places of fifteen of the original forty-nine in 1900, of nine in 1910, and of four in 1915. The *Blue Book* listings at five-year intervals are shown in the table on the following page.

A CHANGING NEIGHBORHOOD

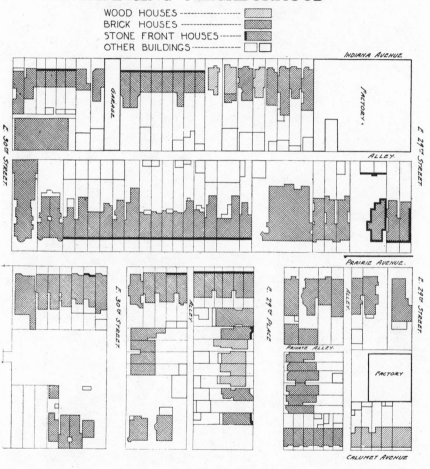

From 1895 on, those who moved away were to be found scattered all the way from Lake Shore Drive to Lake Forest. The newcomers who took their places appeared decreasingly in the *Blue Book* and more and more frequently they had Irish or Jewish names.

A closer examination of the changing occupancy of the sixty-one houses in the block shows strikingly the rapidity and extent of the decline and reveals some of its causes.

"BLUE BOOK" LISTINGS IN PRAIRIE AVENUE BLOCK

Year	Number of Houses Listed with no Change in Occupants	Number of Houses Not Listed	Number of Houses with Second and Third Occupants Listed
1890.	49	12	. . . .
1895.	26	25	10
1900.	18	28	15
1905.	12	36	13
1910.	10	41	9
1915.	2	54	4

The residents.—In a house with fifty feet frontage on Prairie Avenue lived a wealthy artist, son of a Chicago pioneer merchant and member of several exclusive clubs. He lived there until a large brick factory was erected at the rear of his residence which is now occupied by a medical fraternity. A prominent Chicago family lived in another house which they had built in 1885. In 1890, they moved to Cleveland and rented the property. For sentimental reasons they kept the property, although it was fast sinking in value. In 1919 a son living in Lake Forest proposed to remodel and improve the property, if by reasonable expenditures he could be assured by real estate men of "desirable" tenants. No real estate man felt able to do this, however, and the deterioration and depreciation were uninterrupted.

Another residence, formerly occupied by a capitalist and journalist since 1890, was a large two-story house with basement and attic and two-story brick barn. The family long since moved to the North Side, and the old mansion on Prairie Avenue is now a rooming-house of thirty-eight rooms, including the garage.

At another address lived the president of a large business corporation, in a two-story stone-front building. It is now cut up into flats; and in the window recently was a sign: "4th Flat for Rent, 6 Rooms, $20.00, *White Only.*"

Only one or two of the fine old residences in this block are still occupied by Chicago's "first families" or owned by their estates.

There are now two relatively modern three- and four-story brick apartment buildings in the block, and five old residences are rooming-houses. One is a club for railroad men, and another is a fraternity house. About a third of the places are in fairly good repair.

The altered character of the block is revealed also in the number of persons now at each address. The polling lists for March, 1920, disclose that fourteen persons are registered from one address, ten from another, seven from another, six each from three others, and so on, indicating more adults than are usually found in a single family. These are probably roomers.

The problem, however, is a complex one, for, although no Negroes moved into this block, they occupied parts of neighboring blocks during that period, and their occupancy contributed to the final stage of depreciation.

The picture in neighboring Calumet Avenue is not essentially different; perhaps the early occupants represented fewer of the "first families," and the deterioration is more obvious.

The evidences of the oncoming of commerce and industry from the north are numerous and inescapable. In this and adjoining blocks are now garages, an auto-repairing shop, the South Side Dispensary of the Municipal Tuberculosis Sanitarium, a factory for grinding bearings, and a carpentry and glazing shop. An auto-laundry occupies the old church building.

This area is a comparatively short distance from the "Loop." In real estate parlance it is known as "close-in" property. A former president of the Chicago Real Estate Board stated that a large part of this "close-in" property depreciated because of its change from residential to commercial property. He mentioned Prairie and Calumet avenues, north of Thirty-first Street—which includes the block studied. The depreciation, he asserted, was also due to the "departure of many owners of costly homes to other districts."

With the city's growth, transportation became an increasingly influential factor. The automobile made it easy to reach the business center from outlying and suburban regions. It thus became less desirable to live near the "Loop," particularly as such districts are susceptible to changes that may quickly destroy an exclusive residence district.

The rapidly developing automobile industry gravitated very largely to this part of the South Side. Its salesrooms, shops for the sale of accessories, and kindred business places spread along Michigan Avenue from Twelfth to Thirty-fifth street. Michigan Avenue is only two blocks west of Prairie Avenue and one block west of Indiana Avenue. Garages, repair shops, welding factories, and the like accompanied this invasion, and spread into adjoining streets. For instance, on an Indiana Avenue corner a large eight-story factory was built immediately adjoining the rear of a handsome Prairie Avenue residence, and a one and one-half story garage and repair shop was built in the rear of 2900 Prairie Avenue. Just northeast of the block are factories and breweries with their noise, smoke, and heavy traffic; and from the west and south Negroes have recently been approaching—long after these other factors were operating.

A peculiar fact about the property in this block and northward on Prairie Avenue is that the lots are long and narrow, and the houses are built to the side lines. These lots, when threatened with encroachment by factories and the automobile industry, lost their residence value but did not easily take on a new industrial value because they were individually owned and it required several lots to make a suitable industrial site. The owners, though not desiring to live there, were yet loath to sell as cheaply as the individual strip sales would make necessary. And no investor would buy a single lot for industrial purposes unless certain of getting two or three others adjoining.

In 1910 land values on Prairie Avenue between Twenty-sixth and Twenty-eighth streets were $250 a front foot; and from Twenty-ninth to Thirtieth streets, $200; on Indiana Avenue between Twenty-sixth and Twenty-eighth streets, $200, and between Twenty-ninth and Thirtieth streets $175. In 1920, however, values had dropped on Prairie Avenue to $60 a front foot while on Indiana Avenue, a semi-business street, they were $150 and $180.[1] Negroes first moved into the block on Prairie Avenue between Thirtieth and Thirty-first streets about 1917, though very few lived there at the time of the inquiry in 1920. In 1919 they purchased an abandoned church in this block which at one time was valued at $125,000.

To summarize the results of this investigation of depreciation: Negro occupancy depreciates the value of residence property in Chicago because of the prejudice of white people against Negroes, and because white people will not buy and Negroes are not financially able to buy, at fair market prices property thrown upon the market when a neighborhood commences to change from white to Negro occupancy; nevertheless a large part of the depreciation of residence property often charged to Negro occupancy comes from entirely different causes.

D. FINANCIAL ASPECTS OF NEGRO HOUSING

I. NEGRO PROPERTY CONSIDERED A POOR RISK

An important factor in the housing problem is the low security rating given by real estate loan concerns to property tenanted by Negroes. Because of this Negroes are charged more than white people for loans, find it more difficult to secure them, and thus are greatly handicapped in efforts to buy or improve property. The general opinion that condemns such property makes the risk poor, even for Negroes. A Chicago Trust Company representative said:

A Negro called to buy a mortgage. Our first thought was to submit to him one of the colored loans, which we did. We showed him a photograph; he liked the appearance of the building, and then he inquired, "Is this anywhere near the colored district?" He declined the loan on that account, showing that this uneasiness is not confined to the white investor.

When districts become exclusively Negro this reluctance to invest or to lend invariably appears. If there are sufficient Negroes with money to create

[1] Olcott's "Land Value Maps," 1910 and 1920.

a market the loss is somewhat relieved. Yet, deprived of the usual facilities for purchasing a home, they cannot relieve their housing shortage and are forced to seek houses in unfriendly neighborhoods.

The factors are similar to those in depreciation, often based on prejudices and erroneous beliefs concerning Negroes. Whatever depreciates real estate necessarily depresses its security value—whether the cause be fact or opinion. A South Side bank had difficulty in selling Negro loans to white people because "they say they don't keep up the property; they let it deteriorate; they don't improve it." The representative of another bank said:

I don't believe you could find enough colored people who could make a substantial first payment. There are a few that I have talked with recently who are on the police force, who wanted to know how we could help them out in buying places. One had in mind the purchase of a three-flat building; the price was around eight or nine thousand dollars. There was a first mortgage on it of about five. He had only $300 cash to buy it with.

A former president of the Chicago Real Estate Board said:

The percentage of Negro people in Chicago who will buy homes is comparatively small. The best evidence we have is that 85 per cent of the white people are tenants; 15 per cent of them are home owners. It follows, I think, that a smaller percentage of the colored race will buy homes, not more than from 3 to 5 per cent of the colored people at the present time.

A representative of a very large South Side realty business said: "There are ever so many mortgage men not familiar with the colored belt. That's one of their greatest reasons for refusing the loans—they are not familiar with the values."

Real estate men, white and Negro, were invited to present their views, and leading mortgage-loan houses and banks of the city were asked what they knew about Negroes as borrowers, investors, tenants, and clients, and their thrift and care of property. Their testimony, with the Commission's investitions, yielded a fairly accurate picture.

II. NEGROES AS HOME OWNERS

The first house in Chicago was a rude cabin built by a Negro in 1790. There were several Negro home owners when the city was incorporated in 1837. The first Negroes to settle near Thirtieth Street—long before the city had extended its limits that far—owned their homes. Although prior to 1916 most Negroes did not own homes, there were many, especially business and professional men, who had gradually acquired dwellings. The migration brought thousands of Negroes with ready cash who found it easy to buy dwellings on the South Side. The uncomfortable and inadequate dwellings of the "Black Belt" could be avoided only by the purchase of property elsewhere. Attention thus was directed, probably for the first time, to the question of home buying by Negroes. Indeed home owning is an essential feature of any solution of their housing difficulties.

Until the migration Chicago's Negroes had engaged chiefly in personal-service occupations that governed somewhat the location of their homes; when these were not in the "Black Belt" they were in shabby property in undesirable streets near their employment. Men who worked on dining- and sleeping-cars lived near the railroad stations—on State and Dearborn streets, Plymouth Place, and the surrounding neighborhood; they were generally renters and moved southward with the general trend.

Home buying stimulated by high wages and the migration.—The war brought wages to the Negroes that seemed fabulous to many; and the wages brought the migration. The first migrants were mostly drifters. Then came a great many who had acquired considerable substance in the South, and having sold out they came to Chicago with ready money, in some instances large amounts. This class of Negroes bought dwellings. Several of them bought apartment buildings, said a real estate dealer, and in one instance the buyer paid $10,000 in cash; and there were very many who were able and ready to pay from $1,000 to $3,000 on the purchase of a residence in a respectable neighborhood. Another dealer said that he was not able to supply the buying demand: "We have put renters on the side list; buyers are taking up the time. We used to think $500 a good-sized payment for them, but now they often have $3,000, $4,000, or $6,000. A Negro customer lately wanted a twelve-flat building and would pay cash."

"The average newcomer is a home-owner," said another realty dealer; "he has sold his home in the South to come here. Some say the high wages are not attracting them so much as better schools."

Another dealer said that the average amount per family brought from the South was from $300 to $500, and he knew of one family that brought $6,000.

It was the experience of another firm that three or four years ago Negro purchasers paid down about $500, but that now (1920) they frequently make first payments of $1,000 or more.

This sudden wave of home buying impressed Carl Sandburg, who wrote (1919) in the *Chicago Daily News:*

Twenty years ago fewer than fifty families of the colored race were home owners in Chicago. Today they number thousands, their purchases ranging from $200 to $20,000, from tar paper shacks in the still district to brownstone and greystone establishments with wealthy or well-to-do white neighbors. In most cases, where a colored man has investments of more than ordinary size, it is in large part in real estate. Realty investment and management seems to be an important field of operation among those colored people who acquire substance.

Several other factors contributed to this house-buying movement. One was that Hyde Park had many available houses in the early years of the war, while the Negro was excluded from the market west of Wentworth Avenue, with its smaller and less expensive houses, by the vigorous antagonism of the Irish and other people living there. The southern Negroes were glad to find that—at first, anyway—access was not denied them to districts having good schools, churches, recreation and amusements, and convenient transportation facilities. This feeling was reflected in their purchase of churches; two of these, one on Washington Boulevard and one on Prairie Avenue, are in districts of extensive home buying by Negroes.

The high war wages contributed to home buying. Though in many instances they induced extravagant expenditures, a surplus remained for many, and with the frugal the savings were large.

High rents were another primary contribution. Many of the ambitious newcomers figured that they could buy a house for about the same monthly amounts required for rent. In many instances they thriftily contrived to make the property pay for itself. Two- and three-flat buildings would furnish a family with a home while providing a considerable revenue from the rented flats. When old-fashioned houses too large for one family were bought, lodgers and boarders were often taken. Frequently wife and children added to the family income so that they might own a home.

A real estate dealer in Hyde Park said: "The Negro has purchased 90 per cent of the property where he lives, and 75 per cent of these are 'high-class colored men.'" This estimate is too high, but it shows the impression made by the large number of Negro home buyers.

An inquiry in two blocks on Prairie and Forest avenues disclosed that 40 per cent of the Negroes living on Prairie Avenue were property owners, in the intervening block on Thirty-seventh Street over 90 per cent were owners, while on Forest Avenue the Negro property owners were few.

In 1920 the School of Civics canvassed a small area occupied by Negroes in the district west of State Street, a district where, because of their low economic status, they would not be expected to buy. Of 331 families, thirty, or 10 per cent, were owners, and all but one had been owners for from four to twenty years, so that they had not been influenced by the migration.

Of the impression made by the home-buying migrants a very intelligent Negro real estate dealer said, referring to the Chicago Negroes:

I will dare say that 90 per cent or even a greater number did not own their property. They rented. It seems there has been a different spirit instilled into the northern colored man. We bow to the southern man because he is a home owner. The northern man was satisfied to rent. I was born in Chicago and felt the same as others do.

The present trend was indicated in these statements of two well-informed white real estate dealers on the South Side: "The colored people are demanding homes and the tendency is to buy"; and that Negroes were continuing to buy homes in the district between Thirty-ninth and Forty-seventh streets, Cottage Grove Avenue and State Street, more sales being made to Negroes in

that particular location than in any other.   And this has been during a period
of acute and general housing famine in every large city.

Methods of purchase.—When Negroes first began to buy dwellings during
the migration years, the average price was $4,000 to $5,000, and the
initial payment, usually $500, ranged from $300 to $1,000.   The time for
payment was ordinarily three years, though some contracts were for five
years.   Later on Negroes began to buy houses or apartment buildings running
as high as $8,000 or $10,000, and the payments were increased proportionately.

That the Negro assumed a heavy load, sometimes more than he could
reasonably be expected to carry, was the opinion of several careful observers.
While the surplus from his wages might be expected to cover the monthly
payments, money for taxes, repairs, and insurance would have to come from
the wages of wife or children, or from lodgers.

In April, 1920, when work at high wages was abundant, a well-informed
Negro real estate dealer said that any Negro family head could then assume
payments of from $40 to $55 a month on purchased property.   But many
Negroes made contracts calling for monthly payments of $65 to $75.

The opinions of experienced persons in close touch with the situation were
divided as to whether, in making such purchases, Negroes had assumed too
heavy obligations.   One said his long experience showed that Negroes carry
out what they undertake to do; that very few default on their payments, and
when Negroes buy on the instalment plan "they pay out better than the whites
do, as a rule."

Another said, though Negroes buy only old properties—and generally
pay more than white people—they are careful in assuming their obligations
and make their payments promptly.   They pay down to the mortgage, in
from three to five years, and sometimes within two years.

Another, who has been dealing with Negroes since 1907, gave his opinion
that they undertake their obligations seriously, and as instalment buyers of
property they are entirely satisfactory.

Still another South Side man who sells real estate to Negroes declared that
he had been getting better payments recently than he did three or four years
ago; in 1914, 1915, and 1916 he suffered considerable loss because of defaults
in payments on purchases or in rents.

A former president of the Chicago Real Estate Board remarked that
Negroes buy but do not build their houses, and are not yet sufficiently numerous to create a market for real estate; that white people will not buy back
property once occupied by Negroes; that, as the numbers of Negroes increase,
this situation might be changed, but that the Negro who tries to sell old property, on which he has put no improvements, will rarely find a buyer, because
there is so much old property available.

Certain banks and loan firms thought there would be a general foreclosure
of mortgages on recently purchased property as they fell due, that the Negroes

are carrying such heavy payments on their contracts that they cannot reduce their mortgages and consequently renewals will be denied; that the Negro has not yet acquired sufficient stability to carry on payments over a long term of years, and if wage reductions become general they will fall most heavily on unskilled workers and render difficult the meeting of payments by such Negroes, who constitute the great majority.

Most of the firms that had dealings with Negroes, whether as buyers, borrowers, or renters, expressed satisfaction with their transactions with them. Typical of their comments was that of John A. Schmidt, who found Negroes to be prompter than Jews in making payments, and of Milton Yondorf, who said that Negroes, like the Italians, finish paying for one house before undertaking to buy another, and are eager to make the final payment.

While the preponderance of opinion was that the Negroes do meet their payments, it may be that experience is still too limited in Chicago and conditions have thus far been too abnormal to afford the basis for final judgment and future policy.

The first wave of buying by Negroes was stimulated by both Negro and white real estate agents because many dwellings had been unremunerative for several years. With the tightening up of the real estate market that ensued, Negroes became home hunters, and they are continuing to search.

There has been a wide variation in the prices paid by Negroes for dwellings. For some houses Negroes have undoubtedly paid more than could have been obtained from a white purchaser. One dealer's opinion was that the Negroes have paid full value. Another said that the Negro never pays higher for property unless the price is measured by what has been paid for it by white persons of the "fourth class"—referring to property that has descended from the original owner through three classes of whites before coming into Negro hands. Many purchases during the last two or three years have been made direct from the owners. An attempt made by white real estate men to come to an agreement regarding sales in new districts—whereby they would turn over to Negro agents all inquiries as to blocks where Negroes already lived, and Negro agents would not place Negroes in exclusively white districts—was unsuccessful.

III. REAL ESTATE LOANS TO NEGROES

The most formidable stumbling-block in the way of home owning by Negroes is the unsalability of their mortgages. Except in a limited field these loans have no market. The Negro demand for home property has become so large in recent years that the search for it has extended beyond the fringes of the main existing districts on the South, West, and North sides into the outlying territory adjoining Negro settlements in Blue Island, Woodlawn, Morgan Park, and Robbins. How the Negro is to be financed in his effort to improve his citizenship and home life through home ownership thus becomes a matter of great concern.

The Commission sought to learn from banks, trust companies, brokerage firms, and similar institutions their experience with Negro clients and property and their purpose and plans as to future dealings. To thirty such institutions questionnaires were sent, and twenty-three gave careful replies.

Only a few real estate firms that have a large number of Negro clients have funds available for such loans. These meet but a small part of the demand. The three banks that have large Negro deposits, the Lincoln State, the Franklin State, and Jesse Binga's, make such loans when deemed desirable, but they seem not a large factor in relieving the loan situation. Many of the banks that are depositories for Negroes' funds do not make loans to them, giving as their reason that they do not lend on the class of property purchased by Negroes. Some of them have no real estate department. Only three of the downtown investment bankers make no restrictions regarding Negro borrowers that are not common to all; they have dealt with Negro clients for many years and have found them entirely satisfactory. Possibly one reason for this is that they educate their buyers of mortgages concerning the value of these loans; and thus have succeeded, they say, in overcoming many objections based upon race prejudice.

Most large real estate firms and loan companies decline to make loans on property owned or occupied by Negroes. With some of them this is a blanket provision that covers generally property in changing or depreciated districts. Difficulty of disposing of such mortgages is one of the commonest reasons given for refusing to handle them.

Even among the agencies that handle such loans opinion is not unanimous on fundamental points involved. The Commission asked several brokers representing large interests this question: "Does your experience indicate that loans up to 50 per cent of the valuation on property in the residence districts from Twenty-sixth to Sixtieth streets and from State Street to the lake have a safe-and-sound investment value?" Among those favorable to Negroes the answer of Yondorf & Company, a downtown firm, is perhaps typical: It is necessary to consider each house separately, as conditions vary widely; consideration must be given to future uses of the property, the present condition of the improvements, and especially the stability of the person asking for the loan. As a general rule, loans on old residence property are not as good as those on houses in new districts; on an old house about $1,000 would be loaned on a market value of $5,000, whereas in new districts the contractor can borrow up to two-thirds of the cost of the house; no conscious discrimination is made in the nature of higher rates because a borrower happens to be a Negro; careful consideration is given to the margin of safety, and safeguards are arranged in the way provided for payments.

Lionel Bell, another downtown loan broker, regarded this general type of mortgages on old residence property as fully secured, and does not hesitate to recommend mortgages in the district mentioned.

John A. Schmidt, who handles a large number of loans on Negro property in that district, considers them of high value, though the risks are both physical and moral; it is essential to know both the client and the property; the amount of the loan asked on Negro property usually is not high as compared with its value. No distinction is made as to the color of the borrower, the condition and value of the property being the only basis for the loan; loans to Negroes are less in amount than to whites, though clients thus far accepted are commonly found satisfactory; the period of payment is about the same, varying between three and five years, according to the amount paid monthly, the kind of property involved, and so on. The usual range of amounts requested was one-third to one-half of the value of the property.

R. M. O'Brien & Company, an active South Side real estate firm which also deals largely in Negro mortgages, found that the average amount loaned to Negroes was smaller, and that it is a smaller percentage of the value of the property than in the case of loans to whites, and that the average period for loans to Negroes was three years.

Mead & Coe, another real estate firm, found that the Negroes usually are allowed $1,000 to the white man's $1,500; that only 35 per cent of the value of the property is loaned to the Negro, whereas 50 per cent is granted to whites. Maximum time of loan was five years for the white and three years for the Negro.

The Chicago Trust Company answered that the same requirements were made of white and Negro; the range was from $2,000 to $6,000, limited to 50 per cent of conservative valuation, and five years.

In general it was found that property values in the districts where Negroes usually buy are affected by more factors than is the property in districts where whites usually buy. Where Negroes are buying the majority of white people are renting.

It was sought to find out whether Negroes ask for renewals more often than do white borrowers; whether there was any marked difference between Negroes and other racial groups in the promptness of making payments, in asking for additional time, in the difficulty of collections, and in compelling foreclosure. Comparison of Negroes and whites was found to be difficult because of differences between various nationalities as to repaying loans. The Poles pay promptly when dealing through loan companies or banks conducted by Poles. The Italians are eager to get their property cleared. Jews are likely to ask for renewals and to expect the property to pay the mortgage out of earnings. The Negroes pay if they can, but sometimes have difficulty because they have arranged heavy payments on their contracts; during the period of high wages there has been little trouble, but the feeling was that as yet there had been no real test. Speaking generally, a representative of Yondorf & Company said it was estimated that only about 25 per cent of working people are thrifty and save anything; 75 per cent save nothing; and that proportion holds true of the Negroes.

Firms that deal with Negroes ask for no larger reduction when a Negro renews his loan, they say, than when a white person renews if the character of the property is the same. The facts as to the reliability, character, and standing of the borrower are established when the loan is first made. Negroes buy old properties where deterioration is rapid, and when the renewal is asked the value of the property has fallen in proportion. White persons do not buy the same class of property. So it is necessary to ask the Negro to reduce his mortgage considerably, except when his property is in a location of newer houses, such as Morgan Park or Woodlawn.

Difficulty is experienced by mortgage bankers and brokers in selling Negro mortgages to white clients. Yondorf & Company declared that while their old clients would buy regardless of the color of the borrower, others had to be convinced of the value of the property and of the earning power and stability of the Negro borrower. The Negro mortgages are usually for smaller amounts and hence within the reach of small investors. When white investors find that Negroes' loans are promptly paid they continue to buy such securities.

Lionel Bell reported some difficulty in selling Negro mortgages to white clients, though he generally succeeded, by showing their value and by inspection, that the Negroes were keeping their houses in good condition as to both sanitation and repair.

E. A. Cummings & Company have difficulty in selling such mortgages because many of their clients are out-of-town buyers who are suspicious of Negro property.

E. and S. Lowenstein find no market for such loans; non-resident buyers and even local buyers fight shy of Negro property in particular, and property in general that is undesirable because of overcrowding and consequent hard usage

In general, the refusals to buy Negro loans are due to feeling against the Negro, a disbelief in the Negro's ability to pay them, and distrust of the old properties which Negroes commonly buy. The opinion was general that anything which would tend to stabilize values on the South Side, especially in the lower part of the district occupied by Negroes, would be desirable; that improvements such as the widening of South Park Avenue would aid materially.

Real estate men who have Negroes for clients are finding it advantageous to educate them in the meaning of mortgages, in the method of issuing and renewing them, and in what is expected of the mortgagor and what the mortgagor may expect. When the Negro is carefully informed of the processes involved in financing the purchase of a home, and the terms are thoroughly understood, there is much less likelihood of losing his property. Friendly real estate men are constantly helping Negroes to carry their mortgages and to find means of renewing when that contingency arises. It is helpful also to remind Negroes of the necessity of paying their taxes and meeting other obligations promptly, and of keeping their property in good condition. Some firms stated that the "natural honesty of the Negro and his love of home life" have been fostered by thoughtful friends and leaders, as well as by those who have business transactions with him. This pays dividends in better citizenship.

Widening the market for Negro loans.—The white people need to know the obstacles in the path of the Negro who wishes to establish a good home for his family and thus improve his citizenship and serve as a good example to others of his race. How to finance Negro home buyers is a large difficulty in solving the Negro housing problem. The Commission held a conference devoted almost entirely to this topic, at which various experts and authorities were consulted. It was sought to ascertain the fundamentals for meeting the needs of the future, assuming that the Negro population in Chicago is likely to continue in normal growth, and that the demand for adequate housing for the Negro population is not likely to lessen for several years. Particular attention was given to the question of how a market might be created for the Negro's loans.

An appraiser for the Fort Dearborn National Bank suggested that a system involving partial payments represented by $25 bonds paying semiannual interest might be helpful. Bonds of such low denominations might, he thought, be purchased by Negroes. By such a system Negroes would learn to invest their money wisely, and by putting money into substantial securities would encourage real estate investments. These securities could be sold by Negro bankers and real estate brokers. But he expressed confidence that not a few white people would buy bonds of that character. They would be based on about 60 per cent of the value of the property.

One real estate broker averred that success in financing Negro home buyers would be contingent upon creating definite districts in any portion of the city where the colored men may find it necessary to live in order to be able to reach their business or their place of employment, districts to be known as their exclusive territory. Then it would be possible to go to a mortgage loan house and present a definite case when a mortgage falls due. Knowing that the property was that of a Negro, and knowing the district, one would have a definite basis for estimating future increase or depreciation of value. It was his opinion that white people would support a market of that nature, because it would not only protect the colored man and the white man alike but all of the property interests of the city. He disclaimed any desire to promote segregation. , But he maintained that so long as the races mixed, clashes were inevitable, and that the problem of selling Negro loans, erecting houses, and renewing mortgages would solve itself under this plan, "because white men will be very glad to come to the assistance of colored."

It happens, however, that some subdivisions developed "especially for Negroes" present low standards as well as exploitation. One such subdivision is called Lilydale. An investigator reported on it as follows:

Lilydale is on a flat prairie and was laid out as a subdivision for Negro residents near the corner of Ninety-fifth and State streets several years ago. It is about five blocks square. The developer is a prominent white real estate dealer active in sub-division property generally. Another well-known real estate man, who is also a prominent local politician, is interested in establishing a Negro colony on this property. The latter is agent for a great deal of property on the South Side tenanted by Negroes.

Many Negroes purchased lots in Lilydale at fairly high prices, considering that virtually no improvements had been made to the property. Water has since been laid in some of the streets and some of them are supplied with sewers, but there is no paving and no lighting. Sidewalks are few, mud holes many. Yards, streets, and alleys are unkempt.

Those who promoted the subdivision set up the shells of a few houses, mainly of the bungalow type. Most of these were sold and the inside finish was supplied by the purchasers. Most of these sale houses, though, remain unfinished. The building of houses in Lilydale has been half-hearted, and most of the structures are so poorly constructed that they are conspicuously uncomfortable. Some of these were built by piecemeal with any kind of waste building material that could be gathered. The people in this isolated community apparently are making the best of a hopeless situation. They express a desire to recover the money they have invested. Provisions are obtained from two or three small stores. There is a church in the vicinity, but at the time of the investigation no services were being held in it. The children attend a branch of the Burnside School, which is conveniently located. The teacher is a Negro woman, a graduate of a southern normal school. She reported that there is apparently no prejudice between the white and Negro children; that their only differences are those to which all children fall heir. She regards the Negro colony of Lily-dale as a bad mistake and would discourage other Negroes from making purchases there. She regards the investment there as of doubtful value.

There is a car line on Ninety-fifth Street which connects with the industries of South Chicago, where a number of the men of Lilydale are employed.

Adding to the loneliness of the general aspect is the fact that most of the surrounding area is still what is termed "acreage."

Pertinent also is the statement of a man who for years has been interested in the housing difficulties of Negroes.

Some people have suggested taking a vacant piece of property and building it up for colored occupancy, but there is the biggest hubbub raised when any such attempt is made. People complain: "You will ruin this whole neighborhood! You will ruin the street car line! Everything out in that neighborhood will be ruined all along the street, because if you build up a colored neighborhood in any one particular location nobody else will want to go out that way." So that I have come to the point where I say there is no solution. I can't do anything. I'd have been willing to put in a million dollars in property anywhere where there would have been a chance to get 5 per cent return on my money. There isn't any use in doing a thing that isn't economically sound. I wanted to bring this up to show that I had given it some thought, and that I am very desirous of having somebody make a suggestion that is feasible so that something can be done.

The difficulty of disposing of loans in a district inhabited by Negroes was touched upon by a loan expert from the Chicago Trust Company, which handles such loans. The trouble, he thought, centers on the character of the property and of the district, rather than on the fact that the property happened to be owned or occupied by Negroes. He said that even Negro investors object to property in such a district for the reason that it is old, little in demand, and generally a poor risk. He suggested the possibility of small mortgage bond issues with separate notes. This would save the expense of printing the bonds, which is considerable at present prices, and the investor would be afforded the same security. He also suggested having "baby" bonds printed in standard form, so that they could be simply filled in, thus saving expense.

Another real estate broker who had dealt in mortgages of South Side Negroes for a number of years declared that the average mortgage buyer seems to prefer those on new bungalows where the margin of security is less than that on property in the Negro district. Since the bungalow's cost of construction was less, the chance of revenue under adverse circumstances would be less. He maintained that a ten- or twelve-room apartment house in the Second Ward (South Side) affords a better margin of security than the ordinary cheap bungalow, and that it was therefore a question of educating mortgage buyers on the question of security. The best evidence on this, he maintained, would be the number of foreclosures. He had never had to foreclose with Negroes in the fifteen years of his experience. In that time only two contracts had been forfeited, both because of disputes between the heirs and the buyers. His firm had, however, made new contracts when illness or other adverse circumstances had halted payments, thus allowing the buyers to start over again. Means had also been taken to see that buyers paid their taxes, in which process they had required education. White people must be depended upon to buy the Negro's loans. Very few Negroes buy loans. Their tendency, he said, is to invest in a home earlier in their career than the white people, and they buy as soon as they have accumulated enough to make the initial payment.

According to a bank appraiser's opinion Negroes do not understand values, and they are often led to purchase a building at much more than its worth. In consequence the amount of loans they need is much greater than it ought to be. He had not found, however, that the Negroes allow their property to deteriorate unduly. A different situation had been found where white people lease to Negroes.

According to some real estate dealers, there are cases where houses are allowed to deteriorate, where the payment has been larger than the purchaser could carry conveniently. But "after he has taken care of the payment and has his deed, he will give attention to the improvement of the house." Others agreed that the Negro mortgage debtor is quite as reliable as a white debtor of the same class.

The president of the Cook County Real Estate Board suggested that one means of creating a market for Negro loans would be the passage of the "Home

Loan Bank Bill." Its provisions are that no loan would be made in excess of $5,000, but loans would be made up to 80 per cent of the fair value of the property. Many of the loan houses, he declared, do not consider small loans, a fact confirmed by the Commission. He cited one house that will not consider a loan of less than $500,000. For this reason he suggested that this business should be handled by the building and loan associations, since they do business on a smaller margin of operating cost and he regarded them as the proper media for finding suitable markets for Negro mortgages.

Involved in the plan for funding the Negro's loans was the question of segregation. It has been maintained that not much financing could be expected from white people unless boundaries were allotted to the Negroes, so that investors in loans would know definitely what to expect. Opinions, of course, differed on segregation. It was admitted that a spreading out of the Negro population in Chicago is to be expected, that Negroes can hardly be expected to remain in the districts in which they have hitherto virtually segregated themselves. But the opinion was also given that their tendency is to remain among and near their own people.

IV. FINANCIAL RESOURCES OF NEGROES

The chief concern of investors, brokers, and real estate dealers is as to the ability of Negroes to meet obligations. There is a common belief, not shaken even by the satisfactory experiences of those who have dealt with them, that Negroes have no financial resources, and are thriftless and improvident. Inasmuch as a large part of the present housing difficulty hinges upon this point, the Commission made inquiries as to the thrift of Negroes. A group of large banks in the "Loop" and in neighborhoods of Negro residents were asked to give their experiences with Negroes as depositors and investors. In spite of contrary opinion it appears that the resources of Negroes in Chicago are astonishingly large. In the summer of 1920 in one of the South Side banks operated by white men Negroes had deposits of $750,000. One banker told of a Negro banker who sold among the Negroes a bond issue of $150,000 on an old building on Wabash Avenue, paying solicitors 10 per cent commission to make sales. The savings deposits in his bank recently had grown very materially. It was his experience that only a few Negroes buy bonds. They only inquire casually about them.

The sales manager for bonds at a large savings bank, however, told of the sale of $3,000 worth of bonds to a Negro woman who paid for them from a roll of bills of $10 to $50. Another "downtown" broker told of a Negro porter in a "Loop" hotel, who recently loaned $6,000 through his firm.

The information as to Negro deposits, sought by the Commission, was provided by seven trust and savings banks, three state banks, two national banks, and one trust company. These were able to isolate and check up their Negro deposits. One of the banks had $1,500,000 on deposit for Negroes;

another $1,000,000.   Still another had 4,000 Negro depositors.   A state bank
had $650,000 on deposit for Negroes, another $150,000 and one of the national
banks had $47,000.

The average deposits of the Negroes are not so large as those of all the
depositors.   The comparison, however, reveals a fair porportion when it is
considered that there are many very large individual depositors and business
houses among the whites.   This is how the amounts run, by institutions:

Average Individual Savings Balance (White and Negro Combined)	Average Individual Balance (Negroes Only)
$125.00	$ 50.00
108.88	66.76
545.00	332.00
400.00	200.00
120.00	60.00
235.00	100.00
125.00	10.00
196.00	105.00
186.82	300.00
230.00	186.00

It was the almost unanimous report that Negroes are more likely to withdraw their accounts than are white people, that their accounts are less permanent.   In two instances only was the opinion expressed that they were about
the same with both races.

Accompanying the questionnaire to banks was a list of questions concerning
real estate loans.   One of these was: "Does your bank make loans to Negroes
on real estate, collateral, commercial paper, or personal notes?"   All except one
of the trust and savings banks replied in the affirmative.   One of the state
banks buys commercial paper on proper security, but not real estate loans
because of the difficulty in selling them.   One of the national banks buys
commercial or collateral paper on its merits, without regard to color.   Indeed,
it appears that no color line is drawn in this line of business except by the
few institutions that decline all loans to Negroes.

In general it was found that the Negroes are showing strong tendencies to
open bank accounts, that they are steadily improving in the amount of deposits
made, in the steadiness of their accounts, and in thrift in general.   However,
it appears that in only a few of the banks are they welcomed and in most of
them they are only tolerated.   In banks located in neighborhoods in which
Negroes live there is an amazing number of Negro depositors, who receive,
as a rule, friendly advice and help in their financial transactions.   Thus
Negroes are taught banking formalities, while thrift is encouraged, and a
good spirit is developed among the white employees toward Negro depositors.
In some instances, however, Negroes, like their white brothers, show suspicion
of banking institutions when they have suffered losses.

It appears also that, in addition to the growing desire to invest in homes of their own, Negroes are showing a strong tendency to engage in business ventures. They are developing insurance companies, co-operative stores, retail stores of various kinds, and kindred enterprises.

Negroes' lack of opportunities for banking experience.—In order to carry forward successfully their business undertakings Negroes need practical personal experience and training in banking and financial methods. Yet there is a strong tendency to bar Negroes from employment in banks, except as porters or in some unskilled capacity, and they are thus denied the experience needed in solving financial problems among their own race.

Bankers were asked: "If Negroes competent to learn practical banking were available, could you employ them?" Here are some of the condensed replies:

1. Other employees would refuse to co-operate with them and associate with them.

2. They are not reliable as a rule.

3. Do not think so.

4. Yes.

5. No.

6. We have no objections beyond the fact that 95 per cent of our depositors are white; consequently we would not care to employ colored tellers or clerks in handling their business.

7. We could not have them in clerical positions.

8. In a general way we feel that the employment of Negroes by banking institutions would cause trouble with certain classes of our depositors.

9. Very difficult to work white and colored in same office or cages. White customers prefer to have white clerks wait upon them.

10. Clerks who were antagonistic to Negroes would bring about constant difficulties through the misplacing of papers, mistakes, etc., which would seem to be the fault of the Negroes.

11. Have found that a Negro will appear to be strictly honest for a period of years and then turn around and prove not to be.

12. Our section of the city is entirely white, but with a fear of colored invasion. There is, therefore, a strong prejudice against them. We have only about half a dozen accounts with colored people. Two of these are in the savings department and are maintained with large balances. These two customers are thrifty and careful with their money. The others are not.

13. In former years a bank position was eagerly sought and considered exceptionally good. At present, because of higher salaries which can be offered by concerns which make greater earnings than banks and can therefore pay more, the banks are not getting the same high grade of employees. With the former class it would have been possible to appeal to their sense of duty to help educate the Negroes and to overcome prejudice. With present conditions it is not likely that this appeal would have the same effect, and prejudice against Negroes would make trouble in our routine.

14. Social factors enter. For instance, banks often have dinners or other events for or among their employees. No "Loop" hotel would put on an affair for whites

and Negroes. There is also the difficulty of washrooms, and lockers, etc., where prejudiced employees could make a great deal of trouble.

It would seem, then, that there is not much chance for the hundreds of intelligent Negro high-school and college graduates in Chicago to obtain a practical education in banking methods through direct experience. Banks owned by Negroes are few and small, and there is scarcely any opportunity to obtain similar experience in Negro building and loan, insurance, and other companies, which are also limited in number.

CHAPTER VI

RACIAL CONTACTS

INTRODUCTION

Contacts of whites and Negroes in the North and South differ according to the institutions and traditions of the sections in which they have been reared. In the South relations are fixed and generally understood, although Negroes consider the institutions on which these relations are based oppressive and consistently oppose them. There the "color line" is drawn rigidly without reference to the desires or comfort of Negroes or the free expression of their citizenship privileges. Because it is nearer than the North to the institution of slavery, the South still maintains an almost patriarchal relationship with its Negro population. Small communities, the plantation system, and the great numbers of Negroes in domestic service hold the two races steadily in contacts so close that class as well as race lines are maintained with deliberateness and persistence. Even where there are no laws specifically regulating association of the races, the sentiment of the community is enforced, frequently in disregard of existing general laws. Thus Negroes may not eat in a restaurant with whites, sit in adjoining seats in a theater, live in the same neighborhoods, work together on the same jobs, or attend the same schools.

In northern communities the institutions are more liberal and with few exceptions there are no restrictive laws applying specifically to racial association. In fact, the trend of legislation and of court decisions is strongly toward adopting and enforcing general regulations without regard to race or color. Relations are less personal, contacts are wider and more frequent.

From a very simple organization of relations in the South, Negroes are transported to more complex relations based on more elaborate urban distribution of responsibilities. Thus it happens that whites and Negroes in Chicago may be found working together in industry, riding together on street cars, attending the same schools, sharing political activities, with an increasing number of Negroes holding public office, transacting business in banks, stores, and real estate, competing in athletics in public schools, colleges, and the Y.M.C.A., and conferring on social problems in civic and reform clubs.

The increasing number of these contacts cannot fail to influence the necessary adjustments. The general public seems to accept necessary contacts with a minimum of outward friction, as is shown by thousands of daily contacts. Each contact, however, where there is friction, is a focus of comment, antagonism, resentment, prejudice, or fear. But association in such places as hotels, restaurants, barber shops, dance halls, and theaters is often limited by tradition and custom in the North as strictly as by regulation in the South.

A. LEGAL STATUS OF NEGROES IN ILLINOIS

The legal status of Negroes in Illinois differs in no respect from that of white persons. The limitations which affect Negroes are established through rules imposed by persons who offer public services and accommodations. When these rules are unfair, evasive, or even illegal, they can be enforced only because of non-enforcement of existing laws. Federal and state courts are in accord in holding Negro men and women in Illinois to be citizens of the United States and of the commonwealth, protected by the laws against discrimination or oppression on account of their race or color.

There are two lines of decisions in Illinois relating to discriminations on account of color. One line of cases prohibits discrimination in certain public places and the other prohibits discrimination against school children. All but two of these cases were tried since the passage of the School Act and the Civil Rights Act, prohibiting such discrimination, enacted in 1874 and 1885, respectively. The civil-rights cases[1] are briefly reviewed below by a consideration of the school cases.

I. CIVIL RIGHTS IN PUBLIC PLACES

The Civil Rights Act, originally passed in 1885, was amended in 1903, and again in 1911. Section 1 of this act now provides:

That all persons within the jurisdiction of said State of Illinois shall be entitled to the full and equal enjoyment of the accommodation, advantages, facilities and privileges of inns, restaurants, eating houses, hotels, soda-fountains, saloons, barber shops, bathrooms, theaters, skating rinks, concerts, cafés, bicycle rinks, elevators, ice-cream parlors or rooms, railroads, omnibuses, stages, street cars, boats, funeral hearses, and public conveyances on land and water, and all other places of public accommodation and amusement, subject only to the conditions and limitations established by law and applicable alike to all citizens; nor shall there be any discrimination on account of race or color in the price to be charged and paid for lots or graves in any cemetery or place for burying the dead, but the price to be charged and paid for lots in any cemetery or place for burying the dead shall be applicable alike to all citizens of every race and color.

Section 2 provides:

That any person who shall violate any of the provisions of the foregoing section by denying to any citizen, except for reasons applicable alike to all citizens of every race and color and regardless of color or race, the full enjoyment of any accommodations, advantages, facilities or privileges in said section enumerated or by aiding or inciting such denial, shall for every such offense forfeit and pay a sum not less than $25 nor more than $500 to the person aggrieved thereby, to be recovered in any court

---

[1] Civil-rights cases are: *Williams* v. *Chicago & Northwestern Railroad Co.*, 55 Ill. 185; *Baylies* v. *Curry*, 128 Ill. 287; *Cecil* v. *Green*, 161 Ill. 265; *People* v. *Forest Home Cemetery Co.*, 258 Ill. 36; *Grace* v. *Moseley*, 112 Ill. App. 100; *Dean* v. *Chicago & N.W. R.R. Co.*, 183 Ill. App. 317; *Thorne* v. *Alcazar Amusement Co.*, 210 Ill. App. 173; *White* v. *Pasfield*, 212 Ill. App. 73.

of competent jurisdiction in the county where said offense was committed, and shall also for every such offense be deemed guilty of a misdemeanor, and upon conviction thereof, shall be fined not to exceed $500 or shall be imprisoned not more than one year or both; and *provided* further, that a judgment in favor of the party aggrieved, or punishment upon an indictment, shall be a bar to either prosecution respectively.

Anna William v. *Chicago & Northwestern Railway Company* (55 Ill. 185)—the first case of color discrimination which reached the supreme court of Illinois—was heard in 1870, before the passage of the Civil Rights Act. The court decided that a railroad company could not exclude a Negro woman on account of her color from a certain car reserved for the use of ladies. The evidence showed that the brakeman had refused to permit the Negro woman to enter the "ladies' car" and pushed her away. The jury awarded her $200 damages, which the court upheld as reasonable.

Before the Amendment of 1903, the Civil Rights Act of 1885 provided that all persons should be entitled

to the full and equal enjoyment of the accommodation, advantages, facilities and privileges of inns, restaurants, eating houses, barber shops, public conveyances on land or water, theaters, and all other places of public accommodation and amusement, subject only to the conditions and limitations established by law and applicable alike to all citizens.

In 1896, in *Cecil* v. *Green* (60 Ill. App., 61; affirmed, 161 Ill. 265), the court decided that the expression "all other places of public accommodation" embraced only places of the same general character as those enumerated, and therefore that soda fountains were not included within the general term.

The amendment of 1903 included soda fountains, saloons, bathrooms, skating rinks, concerts, bicycle rinks, elevators, and ice-cream parlors.

In *Baylies* v. *Curry* (30 Ill. App. 105; affirmed, 128 Ill. 36), decided in 1889, a Negro woman, after being refused tickets at the box-office of Curry's Theater, had a white woman purchase two tickets for her in the balcony. Upon attempting to use them, the Negro woman and her husband were referred back to the box-office and their money returned. The proprietor introduced evidence to show that his theater was in a bad neighborhood, and he had, therefore, adopted the rule of reserving certain rows for Negroes in each section of the house. The supreme court, in affirming judgment for $100 damages, said: "Beyond all question, the Civil Rights Act prohibits the denial of access to the theater and to the several circles or grades of seats therein, because of race or color."

In 1903, in *Grace* v. *Moseley* (112 Ill. App. 100), it was held that the statute imposes liability only where the defendant denies or incites a denial of service, not where he merely fails to provide service.

The amendment of 1911 provided that there should not be any discrimination on account of race or color in the price charged for lots or graves in any cemetery.

Relying upon this provision, Gaskill, a Negro, applied for a writ of mandamus to compel the Forest Home Cemetery Company to receive the body of his wife for burial (*People ex rel. Gaskill* v. *Forest Home Cemetery Company*, 258 Ill. 36, 1913). The cemetery company had passed a resolution in 1907 that thereafter the cemetery would be maintained for the burial of white persons only—except that colored persons owning lots in the cemetery, and their direct heirs, should be admitted for burial. Gaskill did not own a lot in the cemetery, but four of his children had been buried there fifteen to twenty years before in single graves separated from each other; and when he applied in 1912 for space for the burial of his wife, the company refused permission solely on account of her color.

The court held that the 1911 amendment did not prohibit a cemetery corporation, which did not have the power of eminent domain under its charter and which had no monopoly of the burial places in its vicinity, from making and enforcing a rule excluding colored persons from burial in its cemetery. The case was taken on writ of error to the Supreme Court of the United States (238 U.S. 606), but the writ was dismissed for want of jurisdiction without further comment.

In *Dean* v. *Chicago & Northwestern Railway Company* (183 Ill. App. 317; 1913), Dean, a Negro, recovered damages of $300 from the railway company for its refusal to allow him to ride in a station elevator because of his color.[1]

II. DISCRIMINATION IN PUBLIC SCHOOLS

The first school case was decided in 1874, before there was any statute forbidding discrimination against Negro children in the public schools.[2] In *Chase* v. *Stephenson* (71 Ill. 383; 1874) a taxpayer filed a bill to enjoin the directors of a school district from maintaining a separate school for Negro children; and the court held that the directors had no authority to discriminate on account of color, and the separate school was enjoined.

[1] *White* v. *Pasfield*, 212 Ill. App. 73; 1918. A Negro filed a bill in equity to enjoin the lessees of a public pavilion and swimming-pool from excluding him therefrom. It was held that a court of equity had no jurisdiction to enjoin such a violation of the Civil Rights Act, but left the party to his statutory remedies of either an action for damages or criminal prosecution.

Thorne v. *Alcazar Amusement Company*, 210 Ill. App. 173, 1918, was an action to recover the penalty provided by the Civil Rights Act for refusing to permit a Negro woman to occupy a theater seat for which she had purchased a ticket. Judgment in favor of the plaintiff in the municipal court was reversed in the appellate court on the ground that the municipal court had no jurisdiction to impose penalties for criminal acts occurring outside the city limits.

[2] School cases in Illinois are as follows: *Chase* v. *Stephenson*, 71 Ill. 383; *People* v. *Board of Education of Quincy*, 101 Ill. 308; *People* v. *McFall and Board of Education of Quincy*, 26 Ill. App. 319, affirmed, 124 Ill. 642; *People* v. *Board of Education of Upper Alton School District*, 127 Ill. 613; *Bibb* v. *Mayor of Alton*, 179 Ill. 615; 193 Ill. 309; 209 Ill. 461; 221 Ill. 275; 233 Ill. 542.

In March, 1874, "An Act to Protect Colored Children in Their Rights to Attend Public Schools" was passed which provided:

That all directors of schools, boards of education, or other school officers, whose duty it now is or may be hereafter to provide in their respective jurisdictions schools for the education of all children between the ages of six and twenty-one years, are prohibited from excluding directly or indirectly any such child from such school on account of the color of such child.

Two school cases have since arisen at Quincy, Illinois. The first, decided in 1882 (*People ex rel. Longress* v. *Board of Education of Quincy*, 101 Ill. 308), was a *quo warranto* proceeding, attacking a regulation of the school board, requiring all Negro children to attend one school, and excluding them from all others. The court held that the laws of Illinois prohibited such discrimination and the board was without authority to make the regulation.

In the second Quincy case, decided in 1888 (*People* v. *McFall and Board of Education of Quincy* 26 Ill. App. 319; affirmed, 124 Ill. 642), the petition for *quo warranto* charged that the Board of Education had continued the illegal discrimination against Negro children ever since the decision in the first case. The petition was supported by a number of affidavits of Negroes. After a full hearing on affidavits and counter-affidavits the trial court denied the petition. The appellate court affirmed the judgment, characterizing the affidavits in support of the petition as "vague and unsatisfactory"; and the supreme court affirmed the judgment.

Quincy has fourteen schools, and the School Board has divided the city into four school districts. The Lincoln School is exclusively a Negro school and is the only school in the district in which most of the Negroes live. All white children in that district are transferred to other schools, and the few Negro children outside the Lincoln district are urged to attend the Lincoln School. The Negro teachers and Negro principal of the Lincoln School are paid higher salaries than other teachers in Quincy, and are told that if they wish to maintain themselves in the Quincy schools, they must persuade Negro children in other districts to attend the Lincoln School. In this way the board has succeeded in confining Negro children with few exceptions to the Lincoln School. Yet some Negroes are attending five other schools, including the high school.

There have also been two school cases from Alton, Illinois. The first case was *People* v. *Board of Education of Upper Alton* (127 Ill. 613), decided in 1889. This was a proceeding by mandamus, begun in the supreme court by John Peair, to compel the Board of Education to admit his two children to the high school of Upper Alton. Certain issues of fact were certified to the circuit court for trial by jury. The jury returned a general verdict in favor of the Board of Education, notwithstanding the following special findings in answer to questions asked by the relator, John Peair:

Q.: When application was made . . . . to the principal in charge of the said building on behalf of relator's two children for permission to attend school in said building, was such permission refused by said principal because said children were colored ?

A.: Yes.

Q.: Have not the children of relator, John Peair, been excluded from attending school in said high school building by the defendants on account of the color of said children ?

A.: Yes.

The supreme court held that the general verdict in favor of the Board of Education was "so manifestly the result of misdirection by the court as to be entitled to no consideration," and a writ of mandamus was ordered.

The second school case from Alton, though begun in 1899, was not finally decided until 1908. This was a petition for mandamus filed in the supreme court by Scott Bibb to compel the mayor and city council of Alton to admit his children to the Washington School which they had been attending, and from which he alleged they were excluded on account of color and were transferred to a school attended only by Negro children. The supreme court certified the case to the circuit court of Madison County for the trial of certain issues of facts. Before the supreme court finally ordered the mandamus to issue in 1908 the case had been tried by a jury seven times, had been before the supreme court five times, and the Bibb children were grown up. It is interesting as a flagrant example of race prejudice in the trial judge and jury.

In this case (*People ex rel. Scott Bibb* v. *Mayor and Common Council of Alton*, 233 Ill. 542) the supreme court said:

The issues in this case have been tried seven times by juries in the circuit court, and in two of them the jury disagreed. Upon the first trial where there was a verdict it was in favor of the respondents, and it was certified to this court. That verdict was set aside for manifest error prejudicial to the relator in rulings of the court in the admission of evidence. (*People ex rel.* v. *Mayor and Common Council of Alton*, 179 Ill. 615.) There was another trial resulting in a verdict in favor of the respondents, which was set aside on account of a misdirection of the court in submitting to the jury a question of law. (*People ex rel.* v. *Mayor and Common Council of Alton*, 193 Ill. 309.) Upon another trial there was a third verdict in favor of the respondents, which this court set aside because clearly contrary to the facts proved and without any support in the evidence. It was proved at that trial, beyond dispute or controversy, that the respondents were guilty of the charge contained in the petition, and the evidence introduced by them had no tendency to prove that the intention clearly manifested by their acts did not exist. The verdict could only be accounted for as a product of passion, prejudice or hostility to the law. (*People ex rel.* v. *Mayor and Common Council of Alton*, 209 Ill. 461.) The attorney for relator then urged that a peremptory writ should be awarded on the ground that the evidence in the record clearly showed the relator to be entitled to it. The relator, however, had not requested the circuit court to direct a verdict in his favor, and it was said that if such a motion had been made the court would doubtless have granted it. The court said that the issues were sent to the circuit court for trial in conformity with the practice governing the trial of issues of fact in actions at law before a jury, and it was not deemed advisable, in the existing condition of the record, to set aside that order. The case was sent back for another trial, and upon the next trial the attorney for relator moved the court to direct a verdict in his favor, and this the court refused to do, assigning as a reason that this court had directed that the issues be submitted to another jury. The excuse was so shallow and baseless as to justify a conclusion that it was a mere pretext to evade a compliance with the law as declared by this court, and the verdict was set aside and the circuit court directed, in the trial of the questions of fact, to proceed in accordance with the opinion then filed and the earlier opinions in the case. (*People ex rel.* v. *Mayor and Common Council of Alton*, 221 Ill. 275.) The case has been again tried, and a verdict in favor of the respondents, unsupported by any evidence, has been returned to this court. The evidence was to all intents and purposes the same as upon the former trials, and demonstrated, beyond the possibility of a doubt, that the children of relator were excluded from the Washington School, which was the most convenient of the public schools of the city to which they had the right to be admitted, and that the exclusion was solely on account of their race and color, and for no other reason whatever. The evidence for the respondents that nothing was said about schools or colored children by the mayor and council in changing the ordinances for the purpose of excluding colored children from schools attended by white children; that the intention to exclude them was not declared, or that orders were never issued to the police, or that the mayor never intended the police force under his control to do what they did and what he knew they were doing, had no tendency whatever to prove that the children of the relator were not excluded by the respondents on account of their race or color. At the conclusion of the evidence the attorney for the relator moved the court to direct a verdict finding the issues in favor of the relator and presented to the court a written instruction for that purpose, but the court denied the motion and refused to give the instruction. In so doing the court erred, and the error was in a matter of law, and contrary to the law in this case as declared by this court in previous opinions filed in the case.

The attorney for respondents says that we ought to approve this verdict for the reason that the questions of fact have been tried seven times in the circuit court; that the juries have twice disagreed and five juries have decided in favor of the respondents, and all the trials have been presided over by learned judges. Great weight is justly given to the conclusion of a jury upon controverted questions of fact where the verdict appears to be the result of an honest exercise of judgment and the weighing, with fair deliberation, of the credibility of witnesses, but it is beyond dispute that this verdict, when viewed in the most favorable light for the respondents, does not represent any conclusion of the jury from the evidence, and that all of the verdicts represent nothing but a refusal by juries to enforce a law which they do not personally approve or which is distasteful to them. In the first opinion filed in this case it was said that it might be that the wisest of both races believe that the best interests of each would be promoted by voluntary separation in the public schools, but that it is no less the duty of courts to enforce the law as it stands, without respect to race or persons. We would be remiss in our duty to enforce the law and would forfeit the respect of all law-abiding citizens if we should approve this verdict for no other reason than because it is one of a series which represent, not the enforcement of law or the discharge of duty, but a deplorable disregard for the law and for the rights of citizens. The verdicts have all been more offensive and dangerous assaults upon the law, the government, and organized societies, than utterances of individuals or societies who are opposed to all law, and which are regarded only as the sentiments of the ignorant, depraved and vicious who are the enemies of a government of laws. These verdicts were pronounced, not by those who were avowed enemies of law and government, but by those who constituted a part of the governmental machinery for the enforcement of the law and who had been sworn to discharge their duty in that regard. Such verdicts not only denote opposition to the enforcement of the law, but they also jeopardize the highest interests of society and individuals. When the law, through the refusal of jurors to regard their oaths, becomes impotent to protect the rights of the humblest, the rights of no person are secure; and jurors may take heed that they obey and enforce the law, lest their refusal to enforce the law for the protection of others becomes effective to deprive them of their legal rights and substitute the beliefs of jurors and courts as to the the wisdom of laws enacted for their protection. The error of the court in refusing to direct a verdict is not obviated by the fact that there have been so many verdicts contrary to the law and the evidence. The verdict must be set aside, and the next question is whether the issues shall be again sent to the circuit court for trial.

In this case the effort to obtain a fair trial of the issues of fact before a jury has proved utterly futile, and upon the trial now under review the court refused to direct a verdict in passing upon a question of law raised by the motion of the relator for such a direction. It is clear that after so many trials there can be no further evidence produced by either party but that all the evidence relating to the issues is before us. We are of the opinion that it would be a wrong to the relator to further delay him in establishing his rights and to compel him to add to the trouble and expense already incurred in an effort to compel obedience to the law. The verdict of the jury is set aside and the issues will not be again certified to the circuit court for trial but will now be finally disposed of. The averments of the petition have been fully proved upon repeated trials and the evidence is preserved in the record. The evidence produced by the respondents affords no support to their answer.

We therefore find that all the material facts alleged in the petition are true as therein stated and that the relator is entitled to a writ of *mandamus* as therein prayed, and it is therefore ordered that a peremptory writ of *mandamus* issue according to the prayer of the petition, that the respondents pay the costs, and that execution issue therefor.

B. CONTACTS IN CHICAGO PUBLIC SCHOOLS

The public schools furnish one of the most important points of contact between the white and Negro races, because of the actual number of contacts in the daily school life of thousands of Negro and white children, and also because the reactions of young children should indicate whether or not there is instinctive race prejudice.

The Chicago Board of Education makes no distinction between Negro and white children. There are no separate schools for Negroes. None of the records of any teacher or principal shows which children are Negroes and which white. The board does not know how many Negro children there are in any school or in the city at large, nor how many of the teachers are Negroes. It was impossible to obtain from the board, for example, a list of the schools having a large Negro enrolment with which to begin the investigation. An unfortunate but unavoidable incidental effect of the investigation was the focusing of attention of principals and teachers on the Negroes in their schools.

Frequently white teachers in charge of classes with Negro pupils are race conscious and accept the conduct of white children as normal and pay disproportionate attention to the conduct of Negro children as exceptional and distinctive. As a result of the focusing of attention on Negro children, the inquiry, which was intended to get balanced information, developed a disproportionate amount of information concerning their conduct as compared with that of whites. Teachers who considered both races were inclined to believe that Negro children as a group had no special weaknesses that white children as a group did not also exhibit; that some Negro children, like any other children, were good, some were bad, and some indifferent, and that no generalizations about the race could be made from the characteristics or attitude of a few.

It became evident as soon as the investigation started that it was necessary to distinguish between the northern and the southern Negro. The southern Negro is conspicuous the moment one enters the elementary schools. Over-age or retarded children are found in all the lower grades, special classes, and ungraded rooms, and are noticeable all the way to the eighth grade, where seventeen- and nineteen-year-old children are sometimes found. In some schools these children are found in the regular classes; in others there are special rooms for retarded children, and as these groups are often composed almost entirely of Negro children, there is an appearance of segregation which made necessary a study of these retarded children from the South.

The southern child is hampered first of all by lack of educational opportunity in the South. He is usually retarded by two or more years when he enters the northern school because he has never been able to attend school regularly, due to the short term in southern rural schools, distance from school, and inadequacy of teaching force and school equipment. According to a report by the United States Bureau of Education on *Negro Education*[1] 90 per cent of the Negro children between fifteen and twenty years of age attending school in the South are over-age. Says this report:

The inadequacy of the elementary school system for colored children is indicated both by the comparisons of public appropriations and by the fact that the attendance in both public and private schools is only 58.1 per cent of the children six to fourteen years of age. The average length of the public school term is less than five months

[1] *Negro Education*, I, 33. Bulletin No. 38, 1916. Department of the Interior, Bureau of Education. 2 vols.

in practically all of the states. Most of the school buildings, especially those in the rural districts, are in wretched condition. There is little supervision and little effort to improve the schools or adapt their efforts to the needs of the community. The reports of the state departments of Georgia and Alabama indicate that 70 per cent of the colored teachers have third grade or temporary certificates, representing a preparation less than that usually given in the first eight elementary grades. Investigations made by supervisors of colored schools in other states indicate that the percentage of poorly prepared colored teachers is almost as high in the other southern states.[1]

The inadequacy of Negro teachers' salaries is shown by the per capita expenditure in six southern states for each white and Negro child between six and fourteen years of age. The salary of the teacher, expressed in per capita for each child, ranges from $5.27 to $13.79 for white pupils and from $1.44 to $8.53 for Negro pupils. South Carolina pays its white teachers ten times as much as its Negro teachers. Alabama pays its white teachers about nine times as much. In Kentucky the per capita for white and colored is about the same.[2]

Distribution of school funds by counties indicated a decreasing per capita expenditure for the Negro as the proportion of Negroes in the county increased. A table from the Bulletin shows:[3]

County Groups, Percentage of Negroes in the Population	White School Population	Negro School Population	Per Capita Expenditure, White	Per Capita Expenditure, Negro
Counties under 10 per cent..............	974,289	45,039	$ 7.96	$7.23
Counties 10 to 25 per cent..............	1,008,372	215,774	9.55	5.55
Counties 25 to 50 per cent..............	1,132,999	709,259	11.11	3.19
Counties 50 to 75 per cent..............	364,990	661,329	12.53	1.77
Counties 75 to 100 per cent.............	40,003	207,900	22.22	1.78

A southern state superintendent of education is quoted in the report, as follows:

There has never been any serious attempt in this state to offer adequate educational facilities for the colored race. The average length of the term for the state is only four months; practically all of the schools are taught in dilapidated churches, which, of course, are not equipped with suitable desks, blackboards, and the other essentials of a school; practically all of the teachers are incompetent, possessing little or no education and having had no professional training whatever, except a few weeks obtained in the summer schools; the schools are generally overcrowded, some of them having as many as 100 students to the teacher; no attempt is made to do more than teach the children to read, write, and figure, and these subjects are learned very imperfectly.[4]

[1] Negro Education, II, 14.   [3] Ibid., I, 28.
[2] Ibid., I, 23.   [4] Ibid. II, 15.

Another difficulty was suggested by the principal of a Chicago school (Webster) where 30 per cent of the children are Negroes, who said: "We base our educational ideas on certain backgrounds. The curriculum in Chicago was planned for children who come from families who are educated. It doesn't take children coming from uneducated families into consideration. That isn't fair either to the white or colored children."

The problem of readjustment to life in a northern city also affects the child's school life, and he is self-conscious and inclined to be either too timid or too self-assertive. A Negro teacher in speaking of the difficulties confronting the southern Negro, as well as the whole Negro group, said:

The southern Negro has pushed the Chicago Negro out of his home, and the Chicago Negro in seeking a new home is opposed by the whites. What is to happen? The whites are prejudiced against the whole Negro group. The Chicago Negro is prejudiced against the southern Negro. Surely it makes a difficult situation for the southern Negro. No wonder he meets a word with a blow. And all this comes into the school more or less.

Another Negro teacher thus analyzes further the adjustment problems which tend to make the Negro newly come from the South unpopular with the Chicago Negro, as well as with the whites:

These families from the South usually come from the country where there are no close neighbors. . . . . Then the family is transplanted to Chicago to an apartment house, and even in with another family. The whole environment is changed and the trouble begins. No sense of property rights, no idea of how to use conveniences, no idea of how to live in the new home, to keep it up, to live with everybody else so near. On top of that, the father does not fit into his work, and therefore cannot support the family; the mother goes out to work, and what is the result? Poorly kept houses and poorly kept children. . . . . A normal home shows itself in the school, and poor home conditions show up still more.

The Negro child born in the North is not found to an unusual extent among the retarded children. He has been able to enter school on time and to attend the full term of nine months; his teachers compare favorably with those in white American and foreign neighborhoods, and his parents as a rule have a better background. Many teachers say that the progress of northern-born Negroes compares very favorably with that of whites.

I. PHYSICAL EQUIPMENT OF SCHOOLS

Since the Board of Education keeps no record of Negro children as such, it could not furnish a list of the schools having a percentage of Negro children. Therefore a list was made up of all the schools in the Negro residential areas, the boundaries of these schools were obtained from the Board of Education, and the percentage of Negroes in each school district was worked out from the 1920 census figures. The schools listed in Table X were found to be situated in districts where the Negro population was 10 per cent or more. The figures at the right show the approximate percentage of Negro children in the school, as given by the principal of the school.

Fuller School is a branch of Felsenthal and has the same principal; it is in a neighborhood where the percentage of Negroes is practically the same as in the neighborhoods around Felsenthal, but there is a very great difference

TABLE X

SCHOOLS IN DISTRICTS HAVING AN AVERAGE NEGRO POPULATION
OF 10 PER CENT OR MORE

School	Percentage of Negroes in District	Percentage of Negro Children in School
Colman..........................	81	92
Copernicus.......................	18	23
Doolittle.........................	65	85
Douglas..........................	72	93
Drake...........................	28	24
Emerson (branch of Hayes)........	70	75
Farren...........................	69	92
Felsenthal.......................	38	20
Forrestville......................	20	38
Fuller (branch of Felsenthal).......	42	90
Haven...........................	24	20
Hayes...........................	70	80
Keith............................	89	90
McCosh..........................	13	15
Mann (branch of Raymond)........	39	25
Moseley..........................	46	70
Oakland..........................	17	26
Raymond.........................	85	93
Sherwood.........................	20	25
Tennyson.........................	14	28
Webster..........................	50	30
Willard..........................	15	13

in the percentage of Negro children in the two schools, according to figures given by the principal. It appears from this that the principal, who is a believer in separate schools, places the large majority of the Negro children in Fuller School. Negroes in the vicinity say that Fuller School is run down and neglected, that the staff of teachers is below the average, that the school has no playground of its own but must use the one at Felsenthal, and that all the unmanageable children are sent there from Felsenthal. It is also believed by these Negroes that Fuller is used as a feeder for the other schools in the neighborhoods where there are fewer Negro children.

The points in regard to physical equipment stressed by a district superintendent in the area containing the largest number of schools attended mainly by Negroes were: date of erection, an assembly hall located on the main floor, gymnasium, and, in the congested districts, bathroom and lunchroom. Table XI shows such facts concerning these schools.

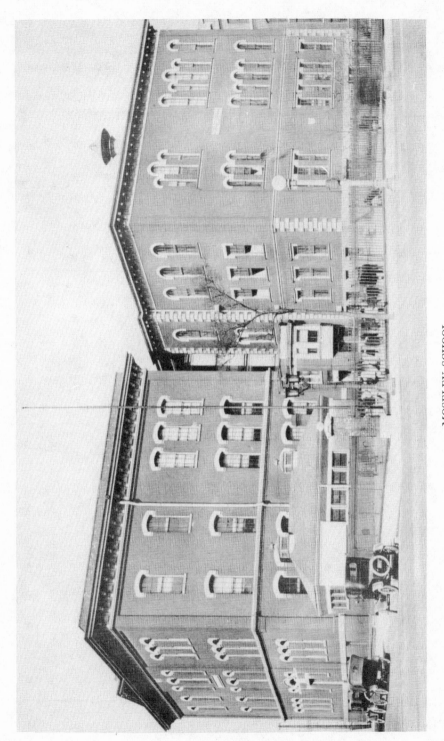

MOSELEY SCHOOL

Located at Twenty-fourth Street and Wabash Avenue, 70 per cent Negro attendance

It will be noted that only five of these schools, or 23 per cent, were built since 1900, and four of these five are in sections where the Negro population is less than 25 per cent. The ten schools serving the largest percentage of Negroes were built, one in 1856, one in 1867, seven between 1880 and 1889, and one between 1890 and 1899. Of the 235 white schools 133, or 56 per cent, were built after 1899.

TABLE XI

PHYSICAL EQUIPMENT OF TWENTY-TWO SCHOOLS ATTENDED LARGELY BY NEGROES*

School	Date of Erection	Location of Assembly Hall	Separate Gymnasium	Bathroom	Lunchroom
Colman.................	1887	None	None	Yes	Yes
Copernicus..............	1907	First floor	Yes	None	None
Doolittle...............	1885	Third floor	Combined	None	None
Douglas.................	1889	Third floor	Combined	None	None
Drake..................	1900	None	None	None	None
Emerson................	1884	None	None	None	None
Farren.................	1898	Third floor	Combined	Yes	Yes
Felsenthal..............	1901	Third floor	Combined	None	None
Forrestville.............	1896	First floor	Yes	None	None
Fuller..................	1890	None	None	None	None
Haven..................	1885	Fourth floor	Combined	Yes	None
Hayes..................	1867	Fourth floor	Combined	Yes	Yes
Keith..................	1883	None	None	Yes	Yes
McCosh................	1895	None	None	None	None
Mann..................	1890	Third floor	Combined	None	None
Moseley................	1856	None	None	Yes	None
Oakland................	1903	First floor	Combined	None	None
Raymond...............	1886	Third floor	Combined	Yes	None
Sherwood...............	1892	Third floor	Combined	None	None
Tennyson...............	1895	First floor	Combined	None	None
Webster................	1883	None	None	None	None
Willard................	1915	Basement	Yes	None	None

* Data obtained from *Directory of the Public Schools of the City of Chicago*, 1919–20, published by the Board of Education.

Assembly halls and gymnasiums were totally lacking in seven of the twenty-two schools, and in the remaining fifteen the assembly hall was on the third or fourth floor, where, according to the district superintendent, it cannot have maximum use for community purposes. A really useful assembly hall, he stated, should be on the ground floor, opening directly on the school yard, and capable of being shut off entirely from the rest of the building so that it could be lighted and heated separately for evening gatherings. Only three of these fifteen schools had separate gymnasiums. In the others the gymnasium was combined with the assembly hall. There was little in the way of apparatus; what there was consisted mainly of hand apparatus, including clubs, dumbbells and basket-balls, that could be used in the assembly hall or the corridors. The district superintendent emphasized the need for gymnasiums in Negro residential areas because the children were weak physically and needed special exercises.

Playground space for schools attended largely by Negroes compares favorably with that for schools attended largely by whites, though Douglas School (92 per cent Negro), with 1,513 pupils, has only one playground 96×125 feet. Most schools have two playgrounds, one for boys and one for girls. The only other school having such limited play space as Douglas is a foreign school, Von Humboldt, where there are 2,500 pupils and the playground is 50×100 feet. Like Douglas, this is a double school with inadequate space for the children inside the school and outside. Sometimes there is a public playground near by which relieves the congestion on the school playground except in the case of Keith School (90 per cent Negro), the principal of which emphasized the need for a playground near her school.

In a group of twenty-four schools, six of which are attended mainly by Negroes, six mainly by white Americans, and twelve mainly by children of immigrants, it was found that there was no unusual crowding of classrooms in those attended mainly by Negroes except in the case of Douglas School. Conditions were practically the same in the three groups of schools.

Indications of overcrowding are the average number of seats in a classroom, the average number of pupils per teacher, and the double-school or shift system. There is little variation among the three groups of schools in the number of seats in the classroom and the number of pupils to each teacher, except that the school having the largest number of pupils to each teacher (57) is Colman, 92 per cent Negro. Although there are no double schools in the group attended mainly by white Americans, one of the six schools attended mainly by Negroes and five of the schools attended mainly by children of immigrants are double schools. Under this system, which is a makeshift in a neighborhood where another school is needed to take care of the children, the children go to school in two shifts, one shift an hour later than the other, and leave correspondingly later in the afternoon. Under this arrangement more children are at the school during the major part of the day than can be seated in the classroom and the full school curriculum can be carried on only under pressure, as one group of children must always be hurried on before the next group appears.

II. SCHOOL CONTACT PROBLEMS

Information as to problems of contact in the schools was gathered from conferences to which the principals of high and elementary schools were invited, and by personal visits to the schools. Thirteen elementary schools were visited, seven of which had an enrolment of less than 50 per cent Negro, and six of which had an enrolment of more than 50 per cent Negro. The schools with the smaller percentage were: Drake (30),[1] Felsenthal (20), Forrestville (38),

---

[1] The figures after the name of the school throughout this section refer to the percentage of Negro children in the school in 1919–20.

Haven (20), Oakland (26), Webster) (30), and Kenwood (a very small number of Negroes). The schools having a majority Negro were Colman (92), Doolittle (85), Douglas (93), Farren (92), Keith (90), and Moseley (70).

The high schools visited were Englewood, Hyde Park, and Wendell Phillips. In Englewood and Hyde Park the percentage of Negroes was very small, while in Wendell Phillips the Negro children were about 56 per cent of the enrolment.

The opinions of principals and teachers about Negro children are a cross-section of public opinion on the race question with all its contradictions and irritations. It must therefore be borne in mind in reading this section on school contacts that whether Negro children are reported good or bad, bright or dull, quarrelsome or amiable, whether antagonism and voluntary grouping or their lack are reported, there is an inevitable tendency for the teacher to see the facts in the light of any prejudice or general views she may have on race relations.

It was thought, for example, that for the purposes of this discussion the schools could be put in two general groups: those with less than 50 per cent Negroes and those with more than 50 per cent Negroes. But it was immediately apparent that no generalizations could be made on the basis of the percentage of Negro children in the schools, because sometimes two principals of schools having the same proportion of Negro pupils reported widely different experience with reference to friction; and in some cases principals of schools with a small percentage of Negroes reported friction, while other principals of schools with a larger percentage reported harmonious relations. The most important factor determining the attitude of the teachers in a school was invariably the attitude of the principal. Though there were many cases where individual teachers held views entirely different from those of the principal, yet the attitude of the principal was usually reflected in the expressed opinion of the teachers and in the atmosphere of the school.

But there is no explanation for total disagreement between two teachers in the same school as to whether or not there is race friction in the school except difference in points of view on the race problem. This factor is to be taken into consideration in weighing the testimony of teachers regarding school contacts of the races.

The attitude of some of the principals and teachers was revealed in their fear that their schools, with 20 per cent or 30 per cent Negro children, would be regarded as largely Negro schools. The principal of a school with 30 per cent Negro children considered it an insult to be asked to have his school take part in a song festival with schools largely attended by Negroes. A teacher in a school 26 per cent Negro was much incensed because the Board of Education had sent Negroes to the school to talk to the children on cleaning up the neighborhood. She said that the white children did not seem to mind and listened interestedly; it was the teachers who considered it an outrage that Negroes should come to "tell a community seven-eighths white to clean up."

Since the elementary schools and high schools present rather different problems, due to the greater number of social activities in the latter, it was decided to consider the two groups separately.

The contacts in the elementary schools fall naturally under three heads: classroom contacts, building and playground contacts, and social contacts.

Classroom contacts.—There was much less variety of opinion in regard to classroom contacts than the other two. Most teachers agreed that there was little friction so far as school work was concerned, even when it meant sitting next to one another or in the same seats. Most kindergarten teachers found the most natural relationship existing between the young Negro and white children. "Neither colored nor whites have any feeling in our kindergarten," said one principal in a school 30 per cent Negro (Webster); "they don't understand the difference between colored and white children." In visiting one school the investigator noticed that the white children who objected to holding hands with the Negro children in the kindergarten and first and second grades were the better-dressed children who undoubtedly reflected the economic class and race consciousness of their parents. The Armour Mission near the school had excluded Negroes from its kindergarten, thereby fostering this spirit among the whites. A teacher in Doolittle (85 per cent) told of a little white girl in another school who cried because she was afraid the color from the Negro children's hands would rub off on hers; in her present school she has known no such instances in the kindergarten. This conduct is paralleled in instances in which Negro children who have never had any contact with white children in the South are afraid of them when they first come North.

Most of the teachers in the higher grades reported that there were no signs of race prejudice in the room. A teacher at Oakland (26 per cent) said that white girls sometimes asked to be moved to another seat when near a very dirty Negro child, but that this often happened when the dirty child was white. This teacher said it was the white mothers from the South, not the children, who wanted their children to be kept away from the Negroes. "The white children don't seem to mind the colored," she said. "I have had three or four mothers come in and ask that their children be kept away from the colored, but they were women from the South and felt race prejudice strongly. But they are the only ones who have complained."

A teacher in a school 90 per cent Negro said that when doubling up in the seats was necessary whites and Negroes frequently chose each other. A teacher at Moseley (70 per cent), when the investigator was present, called upon a white girl to act as hostess to a Negro girl who had just come from the South, and the request was met with pride and pleasure by the white girl. On the same occasion a white boy was asked to help a Negro boy with his arithmetic, and the two doubled up and worked together quite naturally.

"Race makes no difference," declared the principal of a school 92 per cent Negro (Colman). "The other day I had them all digging in the garden, and when they were all ready to go in I kept out one colored boy to help me plant seeds. We could use another boy, so I told Henry to choose anyone out of two rooms and he returned with an Italian. The color makes no difference."

A few instances of jealousy are cited. In one of them resentment ran high because when a loving cup was presented in McKinley (70 per cent) for the best composition, it was awarded by a neutral outside jury to a white girl. The principal of this 70 per cent Negro school, in addition to finding the Negro children jealous, considered their parents insolent and resentful. On the investigator's first visit she said that military discipline was the only kind for children, and that absolute segregation was necessary. At the next interview she said she preferred her school to any other; that there was never any disciplinary difficulty, and that white children who had moved from the district were paying car fare to finish their course at her school.

Discipline.—There was considerable variety of opinion among the teachers as to whether Negro children presented any special problems of discipline. The principal of a school 20 per cent Negro (Felsenthal), for example, said that discipline was more difficult in this school than in the branch where 90 per cent were Negroes (Fuller). This principal is an advocate of separate schools. She was contradicted by a teacher in her school who said she had never used different discipline for the Negroes. In schools where the principals were sympathetic and the interracial spirit good the teachers reported that Negro children were much like other children and could be disciplined in the same way. One or two teachers reported that Negro children could not be scolded but must be "jollied along" and the work presented as play. This is interesting in view of the frequent complaint of the children from the South that the teachers in Chicago played with them all the time and did not teach them anything.

Attitude toward Negro teachers.—Few Negro teachers were found in the schools investigated.

At Doolittle (85 per cent) there were thirty-three teachers, of whom two were Negroes. There was also a Negro cadet. At Raymond (93 per cent) there were six Negro teachers and a Negro cadet in a staff of forty. At Keith (90 per cent) there were six Negro teachers in a staff of twelve. Two of these principals said that their Negro teachers compared favorably with their white teachers and that some of them were excellent. Asked whether there was much antagonism if a Negro teacher was assigned where all the children were white, the principal of a 93 per cent school (Raymond) said there had been one or two such cases. "They are most successful in the foreign districts on the West Side. The European people do not seem to resent the presence of a colored teacher."

Another principal said that this was especially true where the foreign element was Jewish. A Negro teacher in a West Side school, largely Italian, is considered one of the ablest teachers in the school and proved herself highly competent during the war, when she assisted with the work of the draft board in the district.

One or two principals said that they would not have Negro teachers in their schools because the white teachers "could not be intimate with colored teachers," or because Negro teachers were "cocky," or because "the *Defender* preaches propaganda for colored teachers to seek positions in white schools." Sometimes an effort was made to explain the principal's objection to Negro teachers by saying that Negro children had no respect for Negro teachers. One principal whose white teachers were rather below the accepted standard said that the one colored teacher who had been there was obliged to leave because of the children's protest against her. A Negro teacher in a 20 per cent school (Haven) was valued highly by the principal, who advised with her as to what measures could be taken to prevent the appearance of race feeling. This teacher formerly taught in a school where there were no Negro children and had experienced no difficulty in either type of school. "The children just seem to forget I am colored," she said.

In Farren School (92 per cent) a teacher of a special room for children recently arrived from the South expressed the belief that these children "have a distinct and decided fear of the white teacher and it's up to the teacher to change this fear into respect." They were very timid at first, she said, due to the new environment and the contact with so many more people, especially white. This timidity lasted for about a year and then these children became more like Chicago children.

Building and playground contacts.—At six out of the thirteen elementary schools some friction about the buildings and on the playgrounds was reported, and none at the other seven schools. On further analysis it appeared that the friction reported was general at only two of the six schools. At the other four the instances cited seemed either to involve a few troublesome individuals or to be quarrels among Negro children rather than between Negroes and whites. The two schools reporting general antagonism between Negro and white children had about 30 per cent Negro children. The principals of these schools said that the white children were dominated by the Negroes and did not dare stand up for their rights. The testimony of the principal of one of these schools showed a disposition to regard many acts as characteristically racial. For example, she needed no further evidence that a Negro boy had

FARREN SCHOOL

Located at Forty-eighth Street and Wabash Avenue, 92 per cent Negro attendance

cut up a white boy's cap than the fact that it was cut with a safety-razor blade. Although both white and Negro boys commonly carry safety-razor blades to sharpen their pencils, she thought of razors only in connection with Negroes. She also believed that "Negro children of kindergarten age are unusually cruel," and that "Negroes need a curriculum especially adapted to their emotional natures." Again she said that a Negro boy who asked to be put back from the third to the first grade, because the third-grade work was too hard for him, was typical of Negro children, who "shut down on their intellectual processes when they are about twelve or fourteen years of age." In view of the numbers of Negro children in the higher grades who are advancing normally, this is obviously an unwarranted generalization.

There were some signs of friction at a school 20 per cent Negro (Haven) when a school largely Italian was combined with it, but the situation was handled tactfully by the principal and there had been no trouble. At a school 85 per cent Negro (Doolittle), where the white element was Jewish, all the teachers reported that there was no antagonism between the races.

Voluntary grouping.—The only school where the investigator noticed Negro and white children playing in separate groups was Webster (30 per cent), whose principal reported antagonism between Negroes and whites. At the other schools natural mingling was reported by some teachers or observed by the investigator. At a school 26 per cent Negro (Oakland) three teachers said that Negro and white children did not mingle on the playgrounds, while another teacher said they all played together regardless of color. The principal and twelve teachers at a school 85 per cent Negro (Doolittle) agreed, with the exception of one teacher who was a southerner, that there was never anything but the most natural mingling in the classrooms, about the building and on the playground. At a school 30 per cent Negro (Drake), the principal of which stated that the relations between the races were not harmonious, the investigator observed a free and natural grouping of Negroes and whites of all ages on the playground. The principal explained that this was "a forced rather than a natural grouping because of lack of apparatus for all." The white children at a school 20 per cent Negro (Haven) were Italians, Jews, and Greeks, and all the races played so naturally together that passersby frequently stopped to watch them.

Social contacts.—There are few social organizations and gatherings in the elementary schools. The principal of a school 93 per cent Negro (Raymond) said that there were clubs through all the grammar grades and that the friendliness between the two races was marked, but added:

We have not more than fifty or sixty white children in this particular building. One white child was elected vice-president, the first white child elected in eight years. It shows the friendly relationship when a white child could be elected to office with a large preponderance of colored children. A Jewish boy was elected to a smaller office of clerk. The white children are not foreign. In their meetings the question of color never arises at all.

In a few instances principals had found that graduation presented some difficulties, as white mothers would appear at the school a few days before and request that their children do not march with Negro children. "About the only time I see a white mother is near graduation," said the principal of a school 38 per cent Negro (Forrestville). "They always say they wouldn't care for themselves, but a friend might see and they would feel ashamed." "White children prefer not to march with colored at graduation," said a teacher at Oakland School (26 per cent), "and mothers sometimes come to ask that it be so arranged that their girls can march with white girls. They usually say that for themselves they don't mind, but friends might see and wonder why that should be."

A number of the schools have orchestras or occasional musical programs. The investigator heard one orchestra of eleven pieces in Doolittle School (85 per cent), which played remarkably well. All but one of the children were Negroes. A teacher in Webster School (30 per cent), where there was reported to be constant friction between Negro and white children, gave an incident of a Negro boy in the school playing the violin with a white accompanist and being enthusiastically applauded by the children.

The principal of a 92 per cent Negro school (Colman) reported an unpleasant experience when pupils from her school were invited to take part in a musical program at a West Side Park.

A group of sixty went with two white teachers in charge. On the way over a group of foreign women called out insulting remarks to the teachers, but no one paid any attention. After the program the group started marching out of the park and were met at the gate with a shower of stones. The teacher told the children to run for their lives, and they all had to scatter and hide in the bushes in the park or run toward home if they could. A rough set of boys had got together and were waiting for those children, stones all ready to throw. Since that time we have never accepted an invitation to sing outside our own neighborhood. Invitations have come from time to time, but the children all come with excuses. All of them, children and parents throughout the neighborhood, are afraid but you can't get anyone to come out and say it.

Attitude of parents.—Principals and teachers were questioned about their relations with the parents of both Negro and white children—whether they received co-operation from the parents in matters of discipline; what was the attitude of the parents toward Negro teachers; and whether many requests were received from Negro or white parents for transfers to schools where there were fewer Negroes.

In general it may be said that the principals who found Negro parents unco-operative, unambitious, and antagonistic were those who believed in separate schools, found Negro children difficult to discipline, and would have no Negro teachers in their schools. Such principals declared that Negro parents were "10 to 1 in the complaints brought into the office,"[1] and that "they fuss over everything and tell their children not to take anything from a white child." They also cited cases of insolence and threats which appeared to be exceptional rather than typical.

Some teachers said the reason they did not receive any co-operation from Negro mothers was because a large proportion of them were working. Tardiness and absence were due mainly to this cause, according to one principal, though a teacher of a room for retarded children in another school said there was little tardiness and practically no absence in her group. This teacher expressed the conviction, as did many others, that Negro parents were appreciative of school advantages and eager to have their children learn. Principals who came in contact with both Negro and foreign parents found the Negro parents much more interested and ambitious than the foreigners. Even the principal of a school 30 per cent Negro (Webster), who was somewhat prejudiced in her attitude toward Negroes in the school, said she had more Negro than white boys able to go to work whose parents wished them to remain in school.

Negro teachers were apparently acceptable to Negro parents, only one of the principals or teachers interviewed reporting objections by Negro parents. One teacher in a school 30 per cent Negro (Webster) said that Negro parents had their children transferred there from schools with more Negroes, so that they would have white teachers. The district superintendent said he had had some difficulty in placing Negro teachers in Negro schools, which he attributed to the fact that Negro parents felt that Negro teachers had not had the same opportunity for thorough training as white teachers. Some Negro parents, however, had indicated that their attitude was not due to belief that Negro teachers were inadequately trained, but to fear that too general placing of Negro teachers over Negro pupils was a step toward segregation.

The principal of a school 90 per cent Negro (Keith) thought Negro mothers preferred Negro teachers because several had said to her that the "colored teachers understand our children better."

The district superintendent in the area including most of the schools largely attended by Negroes said that few requests for transfers were made during the year, but he believed more were made at the request of Negro than of white parents. A number of these Negro children transferred not to go to a school largely white but to a school 70 per cent Negro, because they said they were afraid to go to the school in their own district which was across Wentworth Avenue. The race feeling between certain groups in this district was very intense, according to the superintendent. It was especially violent

---

[1] A preponderance of complaints from Negro parents could easily be accounted for by a high proportion of Negro pupils.

between the Negro children and the Italians and between the Jews and the Bohemians. The principal of a school 93 per cent Negro (Raymond) also testified to the spirit of antagonism along Wentworth Avenue:

Wentworth Avenue is the gang line. They seem to feel that trespass on either side of that line is ground for trouble. While they will admit colored members to the school without any trouble for manual training, they have to be escorted over the line, because of trouble, not from members of the school, but groups of boys outside the school. To illustrate: We took a kindergarten group over to the park. One little six-year-old girl was struck in the face by a man. The condition is a tradition. There does not seem to be any malice in it. "He is from the east side," or "Hit him, he is from the West Side," are remarks frequently heard.

Transfers from schools with a predominant Negro membership were reported by one or two principals and teachers in schools with a Negro minority, who said that the Negro mothers objected to having their children in schools "where there are so many common niggers." One of the principals said she had many requests from Negro mothers for transfers from the branch of the school with 90 per cent Negroes to the main school with 20 per cent. The Commission did not find in its inquiry among Negro mothers that such an objection was prevalent, but that most of the transfers requested were due to the reputation of the school for being overcrowded, poorly taught, and generally run down.

2. HIGH SCHOOLS

Classroom and building contacts.—In the high schools the ordinary contacts in classes and about the building become subordinate to the more difficult problems created by the increased number of social activities—athletics, gymnasium exhibitions, clubs, and parties.

The dean of Englewood High School, which has only about 6 per cent Negro children, said that the white and Negro children mingled freely with no sign of trouble or prejudice but thought that if more Negro children came to the school the spirit would change. A teacher in this same school who had formerly been at Wendell Phillips, where the majority are Negro, said that a spirit of friendliness had grown up there between the two races, and race distinction had disappeared.

There was only one Negro teacher in the high schools of Chicago at the time of this investigation, the teacher of manual training at Wendell Phillips. He is a graduate of the University of Illinois and had substituted around Chicago for several years. Although they spoke very highly of him, none of the principals of three high schools with small Negro percentages and in which there were vacancies could use him. The principal of Wendell Phillips, with a large proportion of Negroes, told, however, of a different experience when this teacher was at that school. "In answer to complaints by pupils I told

WENDELL PHILLIPS HIGH SCHOOL

Located at Thirty-ninth Street and Prairie Avenue, 52 per cent Negro attendance

them that this man was a graduate of the University of Illinois, a high-school graduate in the city, and a cultured man. 'Go in there and forget the color, and see if you can get the subject matter.' In the majority of cases it worked."

Racial friction about the buildings and grounds was not reported by any of the high-school principals. "I have not known of a fight between a colored and a white boy in fifteen years," said the principal of Hyde Park.

Two principals said that the Negro children voluntarily grouped themselves at noon, either eating at tables by themselves in the lunchroom or bringing their own lunches and eating in the back part of the assembly hall. The gymnasium instructor at Wendell Phillips said that she had no difficulty in her work if she let the children arrange themselves. The gymnasium instructor at a school with a small proportion of Negroes said that the white girls had objected to going into the swimming-pool with Negro girls, but that she had gone in with the Negro girls, which had helped to remove the prejudice.

Athletic teams.—In the field of athletics there seems to be no feeling between the white and Negro members of a school team, but the Negro members are sometimes roughly handled when the team plays other schools. "The basketball team is half and half," said the principal of Wendell Phillips. He reported some friction in previous years but said that "this year it is not shown at all." "They played a strenuous game with Englewood last week. A colored boy was roughly treated by the other team. Our white boys were ready to fight the whole Englewood team."

The principal of Hyde Park High School also said that there was no feeling in his school against Negro members of athletic teams, and that he did not know of a single instance in which a Negro boy was kept off an athletic team if he was the best for the place.

Two Seniors in a high school mainly white (Tilden) thus described the way they handled the Negro members of a visiting basket-ball team:

On the way over here fellows on the outside bawled them out, but our fellows sure got them on the way home. There were three black fellows on the team and those three got just about laid out. Our team wouldn't play them, so there was a great old row. Then, when they went home some of our boys were waiting for them to come out of the building to give them a chase. The coons were afraid to come out, so policemen had to be called to take them to the car line. The white fellows weren't hurt any, but the coons got some bricks.

Transfers between high schools.—Requests for transfers from Wendell Phillips to Englewood and Hyde Park schools had been made by both white and Negro children, according to the principals of the latter schools. The permits of the Negro children had frequently been revoked after they had been admitted to classes, and the children returned to Wendell Phillips. A teacher at Wendell Phillips pointed out the injustice of transferring a child in the middle of a term. After a child has been admitted to classes he should be permitted to remain through the semester, she believed, for otherwise a full term's work was lost because the courses in the schools were different. "All this transferring is nonsense, anyway," she said. "Children should be made to go to school in the district where they live and that would end the trouble."

This teacher told of an incident at Tilden School when a group of Negro boys registered for entrance:

About sixty colored boys entered Tilden High School either for the regular high-school course or prevocational work and were thrown out by the Tilden boys. They made it so hot for the colored boys that the sixty had to withdraw. Some came back here; others dropped out of school entirely. It's pretty bad when one set of boys can put out another set and nothing is done to punish one and call back the other group.

Two boys at Tilden who took part in this affair gave this version of the incident:

About thirty colored boys registered at Tilden last fall, but we cleaned up on them the first couple of days and they never showed up again. We didn't give them any peace in the locker room, basement, at noon hours, or between classes—told them to keep out of our way or we'd see they got out. The fellows who were in school before we didn't tackle—they know where they belong. There's one colored fellow in our class everybody likes. He's a smart nice fellow to talk to, and he doesn't stick around when you don't want him. He didn't say anything when we made the new coons step around, but I guess he didn't like it very well.

It was this same group of boys who objected to playing a visiting basket-ball team with three Negroes on it and "just about laid them out."

Social activities in high schools.—In high schools, with their older pupils, there is an increased race consciousness, and in the purely social activities such as clubs and dances, which are part of high-school life, there is none of the general mingling often found in semi-social activities such as singing and literary societies. Although Negro pupils do not share in the purely social activities, they do not organize such activities among themselves.

"The colored never come to social affairs," said the dean of one school. "They are so much in the minority here that they leave all organizations to the whites." The principal of this school told of having seen two colored girls at a class party who danced together for a while and left. "It is the only time I've seen the two races at the same social gathering."

The dean of Englewood said: "We have colored children in singing clubs, in the orchestra, in literary societies, in class organizations, and on athletic teams. Always when there is a class party there will be five or six colored children. They will always dance together, but they are present and welcomed by the white. Between dances it is not uncommon to see white and colored talking."

An incident showing lack of feeling against individuals of special achievement was given by the principal of this last school:

Several years ago we organized a voluntary orchestra which met after school. The director accepted all applications, among them a number of colored boys. The white boys balked; it should be white membership or they would leave. As it was near the end of the year the orchestra was dissolved. The next year I suggested to the teacher that he fill the orchestra places by a general tryout, so understood, but really with the policy of excluding the colored. This was done and a white orchestra organized. Shortly, the father of H. F., a colored boy who had been excluded, protested in my office, saying that his boy had been excluded because of race prejudice and that he was going to carry his protest to the Board of Education, for he knew his boy played better than any boy in school. I admitted that it was a choice in the school of white orchestra or no orchestra, but that if his boy was the fine musician he said he was I would gladly see what could be done. Soon after that H. appeared on a school program and played with remarkable skill and technique. He was applauded enthusiastically and recalled three times. Straightway the orchestra members asked him to play with them. He became unusually popular throughout the school. His standing was the highest and he was awarded a scholarship of $100 allowed by the Board of Education for the best student. He was also chosen to represent the school on the Northwestern University scholarship, and in his Freshman year he won another scholarship for the next year. The death of his parents made it necessary for him to leave college to support his brothers and sisters. At this time he was stricken with infantile paralysis. The interest on Liberty bonds taken out by the high school is paid in to H., and when the colored people gave a benefit for him the pupils sold 500 tickets. He is improving and teaching violin to thirty pupils at present. His sister is in the school now on a scholarship and is doing remarkably well also.

At Wendell Phillips the situation was quite different, for there were no school or class social affairs which were general. There were invitational affairs to which the Negroes were not invited. All the clubs in the school were white, Negroes being excluded. The principal said he would not insist on mixed clubs until he saw the parents of the children mixing socially. The glee club was an especially difficult problem because of its semi-public as well as social character. The Negro children maintained that a glee club composed entirely of whites was not representative of a school in which the majority were Negroes. The Negroes had not responded to the suggestion of the principal that they form a glee club of their own, and as the white children would not be in a glee club with Negro children, there was constant friction over this club.

Other principals expressed the conviction that the racial problem of school social affairs could not be solved until the prejudice and antagonism of adults had disappeared. One principal said he had had to call off an arrangement for a class affair because the hotel would not accommodate the Negroes. Another principal thought that the schools would not wait to follow the lead of the parents in forgetting the race prejudice but would themselves be the greatest factor in destroying it.

Relations with parents.—In most cases the high schools were receiving splendid support from Negro parents in matters of discipline. "I have never had a case where the parent did not back up the teacher in the treatment given to a colored child," said one principal, speaking of cases where children had got into difficulty when they complained that the teacher had "picked on them" because they were Negroes. The parents always made the child withdraw the statement and admit that the trouble was not due to color at all.

3. TECHNICAL HIGH SCHOOLS

Reports were received from three technical high schools, Lane, Tilden, and Lucy H. Flower. Lane and Tilden had few Negro students, while in Lucy H. Flower the Negroes were about 20 per cent. The principals of Lane and Tilden said they were not conscious of any racial difference in their pupils, that no special methods of instruction were necessary for the Negro children, that there were no quarrels with a racial background in the schools, and no voluntary or compulsory groupings of white and Negro. The principal of Lucy H. Flower found racial differences between the Negroes and whites which she believed created special problems of education and discipline. The children got along together very well in school, and whatever quarrels there were, the principal thought were due to personal dislikes rather than to race prejudice. The colored girls grouped themselves voluntarily at noon and at dismissal time, and the white girls did the same.

III. RETARDATION

1. RETARDATION IN ELEMENTARY SCHOOLS

With the assistance of the Board of Education a selection was made of three groups of schools to be studied for comparative retardation. The group comprised six schools having the largest percentage of Negro children, six attended mainly by whites in neighborhoods where the family income might be comparable, and twelve attended mainly by children of immigrants. Table XII gives the number and percentage of accelerated, normal, and retarded children for each school, for each group, and for the whole group of twenty-four schools.

This table shows the much greater amount of retardation among schools attended by Negroes than in schools attended by white Americans or by children of immigrants. The percentage for the group attended by Negroes is 74, while for the different schools in the group it varies from 67 to 81. For the two groups of schools attended by white Americans the percentage of retardation is the same, 49, though there is greater variation among these schools than among the schools attended by Negroes. In the group attended by children of immigrants, for instance, only 32 per cent are retarded in the Jungman (Bohemian) School, while 71 per cent are retarded in the Holden (Polish) School. A similar discrepancy appears in the group attended by white Americans, where the figure is 40 per cent for the Armstrong School and 62 per cent for the Byford School.

TABLE XII

NUMBER AND PERCENTAGE OF CHILDREN IN ACCELERATED, NORMAL, AND RETARDED GROUPS IN SCHOOLS ATTENDED MAINLY BY WHITE AMERICANS, BY NEGROES, AND BY CHILDREN OF IMMIGRANTS

School	Accel.	Percentage	Normal	Percentage	Retarded	Retarded Ungrad.*	Percentage	Total
Attended mainly by white Americans:								
Armstrong..................	202	21	365	39	355	19	40	941
Byford.....................	118	9	361	29	783	......	62	1,262
Harper.....................	291	17	609	35	829	......	48	1,729
Howe......................	220	17	421	35	577	......	48	1,218
Key.......................	173	25	205	29	314	......	46	692
Morse.....................	169	14	450	37	581	......	49	1,200
Total..................	1,173	17	2,411	34	3,439	19	49	7,042
Attended mainly by Negroes:								
Coleman...................	54	8	124	17	561	2	75	743
Doolittle..................	267	16	261	16	1,099	24	68	1,651
Douglas...................	136	9.3	197	13.7	1,126	......	77	1,463
Keith.....................	77	11	93	14	497	......	75	667
Moseley...................	62	7.5	95	11.5	551	122	81	830
Raymond..................	112	13	179	20	578	......	67	869
Total..................	708	11	949	15	4,412	148	74	6,217
Attended mainly by children of immigrants:								
Bohemian:								
Bryant..................	385	21	735	37	809	15	42	1,944
Hammond................	161	12	503	34	795	......	54	1,459
Jungman................	375	35	350	33	357	......	32	1,082
Polish:								
Chopin..................	298	17	631	36	818	1	47	1,748
Hibbard.................	392	29	445	32	535	......	39	1,372
Holden..................	122	11	208	18	759	......	71	1,089
Italian:								
Goodrich................	157	14	240	22	693	......	64	1,090
Jackson.................	360	15	731	32	1,174	......	53	2,265
Jenner..................	176	11	524	33	875	......	56	1,575
Jewish:								
Herzel..................	609	25	731	30	1,085	......	45	2,425
Lawson..................	466	16	944	32	1,407	20	52	2,837
Von Humboldt...........	528	22	848	34	1,072	......	44	2,448
Totals.................	4,029	19	6,890	32	10,379	36	49	21,334
Totals for three groups...	5,910	17	10,250	30	18,230	203	53	34,593

* The figures in this column represent children who were listed as being in "ungraded classes" in the Board of Education records. They are not included with the column of "Retarded" children because the grades of the "Retarded" children were given in the board of Education records and were used in determining the amount these children were retarded (see Table XIV). The "Retarded Ungraded" children are included with the "Retarded" children in determining the percentage of retarded children.

The retardation figures for the group of twenty-four schools studied are close to those for the city at large, 53 per cent retarded in the special group and 51 per cent for the city at large.   In the accelerated group the percentage of accelerated Negro children, 11, is smaller than the percentage of accelerated white children, 17, or the percentage of accelerated foreign children, 19.   This variation is not so striking as that in the normal group where only 15 per cent of the Negro children appear to make normal progress as compared with 34 per cent of the white children and 32 per cent of the foreign children.   From this it would appear that there are factors in the lives of many Negro children which prevent them from making normal progress.

The degree of retardation, as shown in Table XIII is again quite different for the white and Negro groups.

The largest single groups of backward white American and foreign children are retarded less than one year (42 per cent of the white American and 39 per cent of the foreign group), and the numbers decrease rapidly as the degree of retardation increases.   In the case of the Negroes 19 per cent are retarded less than one year.   The decrease as the degree of retardation increases is slower than in the white groups, and many more children are retarded two, three, four, five years and more.   In the white American group only one child out of 3,439 retarded children is retarded five and one-half to six years, while there are forty-one in the corresponding Negro group out of a total of 4,412. One white child is retarded six and one-half to seven years, while seventeen Negro children are retarded this amount;   twelve foreign children out of 10,379 retarded children are retarded six to ten years, and thirty-seven Negro children are found in these groups.

Though the main reasons for the high degree of retardation among Negro children are set forth in the next section under "Causes of Retardation," a partial explanation is to be found in the fact that Negro parents are frequently more interested in keeping their over-age children in school than white parents, especially foreign parents, whose anxiety to have their children leave school as soon as they are old enough to get work-permits is well known.

Causes of retardation.—It is generally understood of course that comparisons of Negro with white children are hardly fair, since Negro children have not had the same opportunities as whites to make normal progress.

A study was made of the reasons why children were retarded in the groups of schools attended mainly by Negroes, by white Americans, and by children of immigrants.   Records were obtained at the schools for 1,469 Negro children and 1,560 white children who were listed according to the Board of Education's classification for retarded children.

Table XIV shows clearly that the predominating cause of retardation among Negroes is late entrance, which, according to the board's classification, means that they did not enter school until more than six years of age.   This is generally explained by the fact that the family came from the South, where there was no school near enough for the child to attend, or the school was overcrowded, or the family was uneducated and indifferent.   In some cases

TABLE XIII

NUMBER OF CHILDREN IN TABLE XII WHO ARE RETARDED ONE-HALF TO ONE YEAR, ONE YEAR TO ONE AND ONE-HALF YEARS, ETC.

SCHOOL										YEARS										
	½ to 1	1 to 1½	1½ to 2	2 to 2½	2½ to 3	3 to 3½	3½ to 4	4 to 4½	4½ to 5	5 to 5½	5½ to 6	6 to 6½	6½ to 7	7 to 7½	7½ to 8	8 to 8½	8½ to 9	9 to 9½	9½ to 10	10 to 10½
Attended mainly by white Americans:																				
Armstrong	143	84	62	31	15	13	3		4											
Byford	317	175	105	64	54	20	11	32	2	2		1	1	1						
Harper	364	234	106	67	28	12	6	4	3	1										
Howe	275	128	93	57	20	9	2		4		1									
Key	141	106	33	19	20	2	2	1												
Morse	229	160	81	56	27	14	8	3	1	1	1									
Total	1,470	887	480	294	143	70	32	40	14	4	1	1	1	1						
Attended mainly by Negroes:																				
Colman	109	114	109	66	50	46	27	18	7	8	4	2								
Doolittle	229	175	146	152	117	86	69	44	37	16	8	4	4		1		1		2	
Douglas	190	198	191	142	126	83	71	45	26	21	14	10	7		4	4		1		2
Keith	94	66	71	78	54	34	30	32	17	8	16	4	3			1				
Moseley	95	104	96	54	59	31	34	26	20	15	7	4	2							
Raymond	135	115	111	69	50	39	27	12	10	6	2		1	3	1					
Total	852	772	724	561	456	319	258	177	117	74	41	24	17	3	6	5	1	1	2	2
Attended mainly by children of immigrants:																				
Bohemian:																				
Bryant	369	224	107	51	36	15	3	1	2	1										
Hammond	306	225	114	69	47	13	10	8	2	1			1							
Jungman	173	87	49	27	12	6	2	1				2	2	1						
Polish:																				
Chopin	323	216	125	57	43	23	16	9	2	1		2								
Hibbard	252	158	68	28	18	5	4		2			2								
Holden	216	190	112	91	60	36	18	13	9	8	4						1			
Italian:																				
Goodrich	236	185	104	68	42	28	10	9	2	3	4	2								
Jackson	369	284	202	141	84	53	16	13	4	4	4		1							
Jenner	281	253	135	86	42	20	20	10	3	4	4	2	2							
Jewish:																				
Herzel	521	294	124	71	38	19	9	4	4	2	1									1
Lawson	574	370	233	109	65	24	19	7	2	1							1	1		
Von Humboldt	498	145	145	76	37	17	6	6	1								1		2	
Totals	4,118	2,710	1,518	874	524	271	133	81	36	25	17	6	3	1			1	1		1
Totals for three groups	6,440	4,290	2,722	1,720	1,123	660	423	298	167	103	59	31	21	5	6	5	3	1	2	3

TABLE XIV

Reasons Why 1,469 Negro Children and 1,560 White Children Were Retarded in Group of Twenty-four Schools

Schools	Total N.	Total W.	Late Entering N.	Late Entering W.	Foreign N.	Foreign W.	Physical Defect N.	Physical Defect W.	Ill Health N.	Ill Health W.	Family Difficulties N.	Family Difficulties W.	Defective Vision N.	Defective Vision W.	Defective Hearing N.	Defective Hearing W.	Variant Mentality N.	Variant Mentality W.	Backward N.	Backward W.	Low Mentality N.	Low Mentality W.	Feeble-Minded N.	Feeble-Minded W.	Irregular Attendance N.	Irregular Attendance W.	Temp. in Grade N.	Temp. in Grade W.	Demoted for Conduct N.	Demoted for Conduct W.
Attended mainly by Negroes:																														
Colman, 92 per cent Negro attendance	29	1	20						1		1								4				1			1			2	
Doolittle, 85 per cent	603	20	282	11					68		141		7				35		73		10				68	6	8			
Drake, 24 per cent	72	58	7	11		6	1		4	15	21	3		2			12	7	7	12		1			19	5				
Farren, 92 per cent	171	7	49	13			3		34	1	56	15	2		1		7	2	18		11	1			21		1			
Felsenthal, 20 per cent	173	69	58	13		3			6	12	10			2			4	1	33	10	3	3			13	1				
Forrestville, 38 per cent	93	5	34			2	1		4										30		4	4	1		6	3				
Haven, 20 per cent	71	59	56			6			5	9	18		4		1	1	3	3	7	19	4	6			4	5				
McCosh, 15 per cent	18	31	7				1		5	8	6							6	1	5	6	3			3	9				
Oakland, 26 per cent	50	44	18			2	1		4	5				2					3		9	6			12	1				
Raymond, 93 per cent	133	31	6			2	1		7	7		18	1				1	1	5						19					
Webster, 30 per cent	52	31	27			2	1		5	9		6							4			1			1					
Attended mainly by white Americans:																														
Fiske	2	88		3		6		2		11		34	1	3				9		21		10		1		6		1		
Howland		101		13		7		2		17		3		8				2		28		3		1		7				
Kenwood		25				5				4		4								5		8				3				
Attended mainly by children of immigrants:																														
Farragut		107		12		10		2		11		6		3				5		23		32				3				
Goodrich		92		32		28		3		8		7		8				3		23						8		2		
Jackson		255		11		48		12		38		38				1		12		45		23		2		19		9	1	
Jungman		21		23		2				9												4				7				
Kosciuszke		144		7		17		4		19		18		2		1		25		4		18		2		39				
Lawson	1	155				15		1		7		20				1		2		39		9		5		5				
McCormick		21		19		2		1		14		10				1						13				1		5	1	
Seward		131		3		29		1		9		4		2		1		2		13		14				20		2	1	
Smyth		157		9		14		1		7		4		2						14		6		1		5				
Swing		46				2				4								1								1		4	1	
Totals by races	1,469	1,560	564	187	3	217	9	33	140	204	253	175	12	38	2	5	62	81	192	271	49	146	9	12	167	161	9	24	3	
Totals of both races	3,029		751		220		42		344		428		50		7		143		463		195		21		328		33		3	

the parents have come North, leaving the child with grandparents who made no effort to see that it went to school.

The next most important cause of retardation among the Negroes is family difficulties. The fathers are often kept away from home weeks at a time by their work. A large number of the mothers are working, and the parents' lack of education is frequently the cause of a home life that is below standard, physically and morally.

Among the whites, late entrance, inability to speak the language, ill health, backwardness, and low mentality are the main causes of retardation. While it is often maintained that the Negro is the mental inferior of the white, these figures do not bear out that contention. Also the retardation figures do not show the home life of the Negroes to be productive of as much ill health as is the case with the whites.

Approximately the same number of Negro and white children were retarded because of irregular attendance.

In addition there were forty-two Negro children and 155 white children who were classified under two, three, or four different causes for retardation. Children who were late entering also had some physical difficulty, or children who were retarded because of family difficulties were also of poor mental endowment. In some cases such double classification represented a realization by the teacher that retardation is a complicated and delicate thing which cannot be explained by one hard-and-fast reason. Others, finding it difficult to decide whether children were backward, of low mentality, or feeble-minded, classified them under all three causes. In two instances Negroes were found to be retarded because they were late entering and "foreign"—that is, they were handicapped by an "initial lack of the English language."

Intensive study of 116 retarded Negro children.—The presence of retarded Negro children in the Chicago public schools within recent years has been regarded by many teachers and principals as a problem of Negro education. Some assume that this retardation is due to an inherent incapacity for normal grade work. Inquiries of the Commission early disclosed the fact that although the retardation rate of Negro children was higher than that of white, the great majority of the retarded Negroes were from southern states, and that Negro children born in the North had, as a rule, no higher rate of retardation than the whites. In the belief that the causes of retardation among Negro children could be found in the same factors of social background and environment which operates to retard white children, an intensive study was made of 116 Negro children taken at random from among all the retarded Negro children in several schools to learn what elements in their former life and present home environment might explain their retardation.

Out of the 116 children 101 had been in school before coming to Chicago. Of these eighty-six had lived in the South and attended southern schools. Since this group was chosen at random, the large proportion from the South tends to bear out the statements of school principals and teachers that Negro children from the South constitute the bulk of retarded children. Previous school records were obtained for eighty-four of these eighty-six southern children, and in sixty-four cases the children were retarded when they came to Chicago. Many of them were retarded two and three years, and some three, four, five, and even six years. Forty-seven of the sixty-four were retarded more than one year. In a number of cases children who were in the normal grade for their age in the South were put back one or two grades when they entered Chicago schools because they were not equipped to do the work of this grade in the North.

The states from which these children came are Alabama, Arkansas, Florida, Georgia, Kentucky, Louisiana, Mississippi, North Carolina, South Carolina, Tennessee, Texas, and Virginia. Twenty-three of the eighty-six children who had lived in the South were from Mississippi—the largest group from any one state—and of these three were up with their normal grade, eleven were retarded three or four years, one was retarded six years, and one who was in the normal grade in the South was demoted two years. One reason for the poor record of these Mississippi children is undoubtedly to be found in that state's inadequate compulsory-education law which provides a school term of eighty days in districts which do not reject the law. Eight of the Mississippi children lived on plantations which were so far from school that regular attendance was impossible.

Information gathered concerning the parents of these 116 retarded children showed that in eighty-six cases the father was living with his family. In six cases the father was dead, in one case he was insane, in fifteen cases he had separated from or deserted the mother, and in eight cases there was no report on the father.

The mother was found to be living with her family in 112 cases. In two cases the mother was dead, and in two cases she had deserted father and child.

All of the eighty-six fathers who lived at home were working, though one was reported as working irregularly, and two as having deserted their wives occasionally for periods of several weeks. In two of the cases where the father had separated from the mother he was reported as contributing to the support of the child.

In forty out of the eighty-six cases where the father was living at home and working, the mother was also working, and in the fifteen separation cases where the mother was supporting the child, she was working. The fact that a total of fifty-five out of 112 mothers, or 49 per cent, were working is undoubtedly a large factor in the retardation of the children. The statement was frequently made by teachers that 40 or 50 per cent of the Negro mothers worked, and that the child was therefore neglected, and the teacher could get no co-operation from the mother, as she was never free to come to school to talk over matters affecting the child.

Some teachers felt that many mothers worked where there was no economic necessity, as the father was earning enough to support the family. It should be noted in this connection that at the time this material was gathered there were more opportunities for work than there were men to fill them. Under ordinary conditions there would doubtless be a certain amount of unemployment in these Negro families which would cause more mothers to work from economic necessity. Many of the families investigated, where both parents were working, were reported as getting on very well, though there were some cases of real poverty. In a number of instances the families could not seem to make ends meet on a good income because they were ignorant and did not know how to spend their money, or because they had not been able to adjust themselves to city life.

Of the eighty-six fathers who were working, few were in skilled occupations which would command a substantial wage. Most of the mothers were engaged in work that took them away from home. A few did sewing, hairdressing, and laundry work in their homes, but the large majority went out to work. Work carried on in the home frequently has as bad an effect on the child's school attendance as the mother's absence, for the child is sometimes kept at home to help and often finds the work more interesting than school.

The following occupations of mothers of retarded children were noted:

Day work	22	Car cleaner	1
Stock Yards	12	Cleaning (hospital)	1
Hairdresser	4	Dishwasher	1
Laundry	4	Elevator	1
Maid	4	Foundry	1
Barrel factory	3	Housekeeper	1
Seamstress	3	Lamp-shade factory	1
Domestic service	2	Waist factory	1
Box factory	1		

Education of parents.—Of the eighty-six fathers, thirty-one were illiterate, and forty-eight had gone to elementary school but had completed only the second, fourth, or sixth grade. Five of the fathers had gone to high school, and two were college graduates.

The figures are slightly better for the mothers. Out of 112, twenty-one were totally illiterate, seventy-six had gone to elementary school, ten had been in high school or college, and five were not reported on. Eighty-eight per cent of the mothers, therefore, and 91 per cent of the fathers had less than a high-school education. Though there were many illiterate or poorly educated parents who were eager for their children to have advantages which they never had themselves, others, as in any illiterate group, no matter what the color, failed to appreciate the importance of school.

Home discipline.—A number of teachers reported that they were unable to discipline the children in school because they were undisciplined at home.

In seventy-three of the 116 homes there was found to be discipline, in twenty-two a lack of discipline, and twenty were not reported on. Discipline seemed to be the responsibility of the mother in the large majority of cases, and many of the twenty-two undisciplined children were boys who were beyond the control of the mother. In every case but four where there was no discipline the mother was working, so that the child did not receive much care during the daytime and the mother was too tired to bother about discipline at night. Lack of discipline can also be traced to the fact that the child has not always lived with the parents but with relatives who have been lax in the matter of discipline.

Home care.—The physical condition of the home, the preparation and substance of the meals, may be expected to affect a child's health and therefore his attendance at school. The homes of eighty-four children were reported to be clean and twenty-five not clean, while seven were not reported on. In twenty-one cases out of the twenty-five reported not clean, the mother was working. In forty-seven cases out of the eighty-four reported clean the mother was working. In many of the forty-seven cases there was an aunt or grand-mother who took care of the house.

In many homes the ignorance of the parents was obviously responsible for failure to provide the kind of food adapted to the needs of the children. A great deal of fresh meat, usually pork and bacon, potatoes, rice, and coffee were the staples, while green vegetable, fruits, cereals, and milk were noticeably lacking. Also, when the mother is away all day the food is hastily prepared, which usually means that it is fried. The girl who gets home from school before her mother has finished her day's work usually starts the dinner, or brings something from the delicatessen. Many children are given twenty-five cents with which to buy lunch, and in three extreme cases the children were given money to buy all their meals, with no supervision over what they ate.

Difficulty of adjustment.—When all the causes contributing to retardation were taken into consideration in the histories of the 116 retarded children studied, it was still obvious that the greatest stumbling-block to normal progress was previous residence in the South. The retardation of children from the South is explained in a variety of ways.

Some of the children from the South did not get along well because they had not been able to adjust themselves to city life. They had been accustomed to the freedom and outdoor life of the farm and did not like the confined life of the city. They felt timid and shy in the midst of so many people, as they did not come much in contact with people when they lived on southern farms four or five miles from the nearest town. Most of these children had never gone to school for more than a few months at a time, either because the school term was short or they lived too far from the school to attend regularly. Consequently some of them found the nine months' term irksome.

Demotion.—A number of children were found to be over-aged for their grades because they had been demoted one or two years when they came to Chicago. Some of these had gone to school regularly in the South and were of normal age for their grades, but the school term was so short that it was impossible for them to complete the same amount of work in the same number of years as children in northern schools. Children who were in the fifth or fourth grade in the South had been put back to the third or second grade on entering Chicago schools. This sometimes discouraged them so much that they dropped out of school on reaching fourteen, the age limit of the compulsory-education law.

Inadequate schools.—Overcrowded and poorly taught schools also are responsible for the retardation of southern Negro children. One girl attended a school which was in session only three months a year and where there were 100 to 125 children under one teacher. Consequently this girl was retarded four years. A boy who, when he came to Chicago, was fifteen years old and six years behind his grade had always lived in small country towns in the South. In one of these his teacher was the iceman. "He didn't come to school until he was through totin' ice around," said the boy. "Then if anyone wanted ice they comed after him. He wasn't learning me anything so I quit." This boy was found to be ambitious and was attending school regularly in Chicago in spite of the fact that he was conspicuously over-age for his grade.

Other causes of retardation.—Some over-age children are extremely sensitive about their size and are irregular at school on this account. A fifteen-year-old boy who was 5 feet 8 inches tall was in the fifth grade. He refused to go to school because he was larger than anyone in his class. At one time he was so ashamed of being seen in the room with smaller children that he would go out of the classroom every time a girl passed the door.

As in many white families where the importance of regular school attendance is not fully understood, work at home or work after school hours is sometimes permitted to interfere materially with school attendance. Older children are kept at home to look after young children while the parents are away at work and sometimes when the mother is home. A fourteen-year-old girl who was three years retarded had always been kept out of school to do housework. The five younger children were all in the normal grades for their ages but the fourteen-year-old girl had been out of school so much she had lost interest. Other children were working after school hours selling papers and delivering packages and wanted to leave school as soon as possible so that they could work all the time.

The attitude of the teacher seemed in a few instances to be responsible for the child's lack of interest. In one case the teacher threw a paper at a boy instead of handing it to him, and the boy had refused to recite to her ever since. He went to school but recited to his mother at home. Another boy had been kept back in school by a misunderstanding between his mother and the principal. The principal took the boy home with her to do some work around her house and kept him until nine o'clock. The mother became so worried she had the police out looking for him. When she found out the cause of his lateness coming home, she went to the school and threatened the principal. The principal afterward refused either to promote the boy or transfer him to another school.

Recreation.—A study of the favorite forms of recreation among 116 children, aside from the few who reported that they had no time to play, showed the movies to be in the lead. Children economized on lunch, buying potato salad and pickles, in order to have enough left from their lunch money to go to the movies. One boy who worked outside of school hours made $3 to $5 a week and spent most of it on the movies; he went three or four times a day if he had the money. A few children played truant in order to go to the movies.

TABLE XV

FAVORITE RECREATION OF 116 RETARDED NEGRO CHILDREN

Movies	85
Baseball	32
Reading	31
Marbles	29
Skating	20
Jumping rope	11
Music	6
Jacks	6
Vaudeville	5
Running games	4
Singing games	4
Sewing	3
Basket-ball	2
Target practice	1
Pool	1
Mechanical toys	1
Drawing	1
Dolls	1
Bicycle	1
Typewriting	1
Swinging	1
Rolling hoop	1
Card games, checkers, etc.	1
Total	248

Most of these children had two and even three forms of recreation, and the second was usually some form of outdoor recreation—baseball, marbles, or jumping rope. Most of the younger ones went to the playgrounds, except those who had housework to do or the few who did not care to associate with other children.

A reference to the section on "Recreation" will show that Negro children are limited in their recreational activities by lack of recreation centers where they are welcome. There are playgrounds for the younger children in the areas of Negro residence, but no recreation centers with their varied indoor facilities for the older children.

2. OPINIONS ON SCHOLARSHIP OF NEGRO CHILDREN

Progress of the southern Negro.—The retarded Negro child, usually from the South, who is conspicuous in the elementary schools, has been referred to in the section on "Retardation in Elementary Schools." In some schools such children are put in the regular grades, where they receive no special attention and can progress only one year at a time, though most teachers agree that retardation is due to lack of educational opportunity rather than to inability to learn. In other schools there are special rooms for these children where they are advanced through several grades as rapidly as possible.

Doolittle School (85 per cent) had six first-grade rooms for such children. In one of these rooms there were about twenty-five children from twelve to seventeen years of age doing all the lower-grade work up to the sixth. The teacher said that many of these children who were unable to read or write when they came from the South showed remarkable progress in a few months, and in less than a year were able to do fourth-, fifth-, and sixth-grade work.

"One big girl of thirteen, when she arrived from the South," this teacher said, "pretended to read with her book upside down, but in a little more than a year she was doing sixth-grade work. One twelve-year-old boy from the South, unable to read the primer or write his name, after about nine months of applied work just ate up everything I gave him and during the following year read sixty library books."

A thirteen-year-old girl, just five days in the school, had come from Alabama, where she had never attended school. "There wasn't room for me," she explained. She read for the investigator on the tenth page of the primer, haltingly but with understanding. The teacher was confident that she could put her through several grades next year. She said further:

These children who have been deprived in the South of their rights educationally are very eager. At first they are timid, but they learn very quickly. They're as smart as whips if they'd just get down to business. Without question this is the kind of attention all the colored children from the South need when they enter school in the North. The plan has been successful and should be adopted throughout the school system. One appreciates by comparison the injustice of putting the fifteen-year-old newcomer from the South into second grade, requiring of him only second-grade work over the nine months' period.

Another school, 92 per cent Negro (Farren), has a special room for children from the South. "Our dull children are almost without exception those from the South who have never been to school," said the teacher. "Those children should not be classed as dull, either, for they learn remarkably fast and often catch up to grade."

A teacher of the ungraded room in a school 38 per cent Negro (Forrestville) said:

Practically all of the colored children are from the South, where they have not been in school. Once they get started they learn very rapidly and often catch up to the proper grade if they are not too old when they start school. The older children in this room have good power of concentration and consequently learn much in a short time. Take, for example, a boy twelve years old who came here not two months ago from the South. When he came he had no idea how to write his name. A few days ago he wrote for me a fourth-grade eight-line memory passage with but three mistakes in spelling. Now I call that remarkable. I have taught in this school all my teaching years, and they have been many, and have never seen any child equal this, either white or black.

Capacity for advanced work.—Teachers in the seventh and eighth grades usually found Negro children equal to the work, though in some cases they felt that these children had been pushed out of the lower grade because of crowded conditions before they were ready for the more advanced work. An eighth-grade teacher gave the following statement:

When children get this far they have a good foundation and do their work very well. One of my colored girls is the brightest child in school—arithmetic is hard for her but she works at it. One of my colored boys is seventeen years old. He came here from the South last fall to live with an uncle and to get to a better school. His father wants him to be a doctor and thought he wasn't getting along as well in the South as he would in the North. When the boy came to me he said he had been going to a college[1] in the South. I took him into the eighth grade but saw he didn't have the fundamentals. On close questioning he told me he had been in the seventh grade in that college. Now he is doing excellent work for me. He has much broader interests than the other children. He reads, reads, reads, all the time and is well informed.

Other teachers believed that there was nothing to keep the Negro children from making equal progress with the white, given similar opportunities. "The progress of the colored children in Drake school (30 per cent) cannot be compared with that of the white," said an upper-grade teacher, "because the colored are all from the South and have had the poorest opportunities. But comparing a Negro child and a white child who have had the same advantages in school and equal opportunities for observation and example in the home, the Negro makes the same progress."

"I say that under the same conditions a Negro child will do as well every time as a white," said the teacher of an ungraded room in a school 38 per cent Negro (Forrestville). Many do as well as the white and live in very poor

[1] Many so-called southern "colleges" include elementary and high school, as well as college work. The term is general and does not mean necessarily an institution of the same academic standing as a northern college.

neglected homes. I think every person who is not prejudiced must admit that the colored do fully as well in school as the white."

An upper-grade teacher in the Felsenthal School (20 per cent) held a similar point of view: "The colored are making wonderful strides. They advance just as rapidly as the white, given equal opportunities. But their background is so slight and so short in years that one cannot fairly compare them. The southern colored child must be studied individually to get his point of view in the school or he gets nowhere in his work."

High-school work.—The principal of Wendell Phillips High School prepared tables showing the numbers of white and Negro children dropping out at the end of each school year. They show that the largest number of Negro children dropped out during the first year, and the largest number of white children during the first and second years, the number of drop-outs being the same for both years. Some children repeat the work so that all of them do not leave school.

One or two teachers in other schools stated concerning Negro children that a "very limited number go beyond the first year." "They cannot grasp the subject," said an English teacher; "they do not understand as the white child does. They lack the mentality."

In the same school the Latin teacher held quite the opposite opinion. "The colored children are in every way equal to the white children. They are just as well equipped mentally and make similar progress. My best student at present is a colored girl. Her choice of English and her vocabulary and construction are far ahead of that of any white student."

Several teachers and principals testified to the brilliancy of individual Negro students who not infrequently had the highest standing in the school. The principal of an elementary school (Crerar) who had formerly had experience in a school largely Negro felt that the junior high school would meet the needs of the Negro children to a large degree:

More of them than the immigrant enter high school but do not stay to finish. I suppose the parents insist upon some high-school training, but it is necessary for the child to go to work before he finishes. Another reason for the dropping out might be the teachers' lack of interest in the child. In the high school you don't find the teachers taking a keen interest in every individual child as you do in the grades, and just what colored children need is a keen interest in them. They do better work.

Academic v. other courses.—A preference of Negro children for academic work was reported by principals and teachers at two high schools. This may be due in part to the fact, testified to by many teachers, that Negro children excel in languages and music and find mathematics and sciences difficult. The usual implication was, however, that Negro children took academic work because they thought it gave them better social standing. A principal who said that "Negroes want to know nothing about industrial training" and that "the girls don't care for sewing and cooking," said on another occasion that the majority of children in auto-mechanics, printing, and household arts were Negroes. He also reported more Negro than white children in the normal course preparing themselves to be teachers, though this was the first year that this had been the case.

Comparative scholarship in elementary schools.—Negro children are reported to be slower than the Jews, less responsive than the Bohemians, and more ambitious than the Italians. A manual-training and domestic-arts teacher thought Negroes did as good work as the Jews, Bohemians, and white Americans whom he taught. A Latin teacher said that the Negroes were studious and ambitious, and that in every way she preferred them to the Jews.

Several teachers thought the Negroes were slow and lacked logic and "sticking qualities." An upper-grade teacher explained the slowness as partly due to the fact that they had been pushed out of the crowded lower grades before they were ready for more advanced work. A physics teacher who was convinced that Negro children had no ambition said it was his policy to promote a Negro child if the child had made the effort, because he appreciated that the child had come "to the limit of his mental ability."

The principal who said that Negroes had no "sticking qualities" gave a single instance of a boy who wanted to become a mechanical engineer but gave up the course after five months, because he said he did not care enough about the course to work at it for several years. In endeavoring to prove that Negro children are not successful in completing high-school work, this principal emphasized the fact that in the 3-B class 20 per cent of the Negroes dropped out as compared with 6 per cent of the whites. In actual numbers three Negroes and two whites dropped out. He did not mention that in the 2-A class 12 per cent of the whites (sixteen children) as compared with 3 per cent of the Negroes (three children) dropped out. In the 4-B grade 21 per cent of the whites (three children) and none of the Negroes dropped out. The fact that 21 per cent of the whites dropped out was explained by the principal to be due to the fact that the white children wished to graduate from a high school wholly white. However, only three children were involved.

Attendance and failures.—Table XVI shows the record for attendance and failures in three groups of schools attended mainly by Negroes, by children of immigrants and by white Americans. It will be noticed that the best attendance records are found in Douglas and Farren schools, both mainly attended by Negroes. The other schools, attended mainly by Negroes, compare favorably with those attended by whites.

The smallest percentage of failures is at Colman (92 per cent), while the next to the largest percentage is also at a school attended mainly by Negroes (Raymond, 93 per cent). This may be explained to a certain extent by the fact that there is a higher economic class of Negroes in the neighborhood of the Colman School. In the other schools the percentage of failures compares very favorably with that of whites.

TABLE XVI

ENROLMENT, AVERAGE ATTENDANCE, AND NUMBER OF FAILURES IN TWENTY SCHOOLS

School	Enrolment	Average Attendance	Percentage of Attendance	Number of Failures	Percentage of Failures
Attended mainly by Negroes:					
Colman, 92 per cent..................	964	709	73	13	1.8
Doolittle, 85 per cent.................	1,784	1,282	72	77	6.0
Douglas, 93 per cent..................	1,443	1,341	93	....	....
Farren, 92 per cent...................	986	924	93	83	8.9
Forrestville, 38 per cent..............	1,493	1,085	73	130	12.0
Haven, 20 per cent...................	1,165	700	60	24	3.4
McCosh, 15 per cent..................	1,280	1,017	79	....	....
Moseley, 70 per cent..................	923	605	66	81	13.3
Raymond, 93 per cent.................	1,532	1,299	85	200	15.4
Webster, 30 per cent..................	805	654	81	....	....
Attended mainly by children of immigrants:					
Farragut............................	1,729	1,502	86	107	7.0
Goodrich............................	1,305	1,039	78	121	11.6
Kosciusko...........................	1,134	775	68	33	4.2
Lawson.............................	3,069	2,545	83	292	11.5
McCormick..........................	1,432	1,266	88	204	16.1
Seward.............................	1,058	708	67	43	5.9
Smyth..............................	1,106	860	77	69	8.0
Swing..............................	810	629	77	99	15.8
Attended mainly by white Americans:					
Fiske...............................	1,535	1,272	83	45	3.5
Howland............................	2,161	1,809	84	100	5.0

C. CONTACTS IN RECREATION

In studying contacts between the races at places of recreation a survey was made of the various recreational facilities maintained by the Municipal Bureau of Parks, Playgrounds, and Bathing Beaches, the South Park Commission, the West Chicago Park Commission, and the Lincoln Park Commission. Recreational facilities maintained by twelve park boards which control smaller areas in outlying parts of the city were not included in the survey unless they were in or near Negro areas. Visits were made by the Commission's investigator to places in or bordering on the Negro areas at a time of day when the use of the park would be greatest; the director or one of his assistants was interviewed and observations were made as to the relations between Negroes and whites.

The information thus gathered was supplemented by a conference held by the Commission, at which representatives of the various park boards discussed policies and experiences with reference to race relations in the various recreation places under their charge.

I. CLASSIFICATION OF FACILITIES

Although there is no definite city-wide classification, the publicly maintained recreation facilities of the city may, for the purpose of this study, be grouped by types and defined as follows:

1. *Playground.*—A small tract of land, usually adjacent to public schools, providing space for ball games, gymnastic and play apparatus, and in most cases a small building used as an office and storage place for apparatus.

2. *Recreation center.*—Including outdoor and indoor gymnasiums for men, women, and children, a swimming-pool, and a little children's playground out doors, and a field house providing an assembly room and dance hall, club-rooms, shower baths, and often an infant-welfare station and branch library.

3. *Large park.*—A large area with lawns, shrubbery, and general recreation facilities, such as tennis, golf, baseball, and boating.

4. *Bathing-beach.*—Intended primarily for swimmers and usually including no other recreation equipment. A dressing-house, showers, and towel supply are provided with life guard and attendants on duty.

5. *Swimming-pool.*—In some instances a swimming-pool or natatorium is maintained separately from a recreation center.

II. DISTRIBUTION OF FACILITIES IN RELATION TO NEGRO AREAS

Of a total of 127 public places of recreation excluding the large parks, thirty-seven are in or near Negro areas. Of the eighty-two playgrounds, fourteen are in the Negro areas and nine are adjacent. Of the twenty-nine recreation centers, none is located within the Negro areas, but seven are adjacent.

Though these figures seem to indicate that the Negro areas are fairly well supplied with recreation facilities, it should be borne in mind that their use by the Negroes in their vicinity is by no means free and undisputed. The reasons for this are shown in the next section on "Use of Facilities," but the following summary of use will aid in considering the distribution of recreation facilities in relation to the Negro areas:

	Total for City	In Negro Areas	Near Negro Areas	Number Used 10 Per Cent or More by Negroes
Playgrounds	82	14	9	13
Recreation centers	29	None	7	1
Bathing-beaches	8	3	2	1

The type of recreation facility most commonly found in the Negro areas is the playground. The lack of recreation centers within the Negro areas is conspicuous, as is also the fact that six of the seven recreation centers accessible to Negroes are not used as much as 10 per cent by them. The playground is intended for the use of young children and has practically nothing to attract older children and adults, except sometimes a baseball or athletic field. Indoor facilities are not a part of the equipment of a playground, so that the average maintenance cost of a playground is not more than $2,000 to $5,000 a year.[1]

[1] See illustration facing this page.

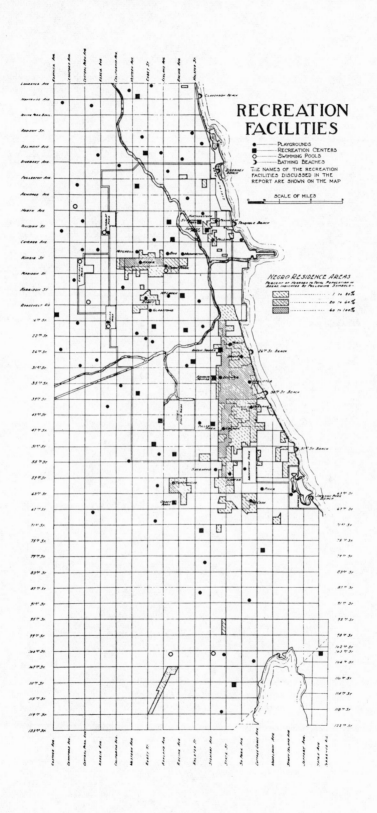

RECREATION
FACILITIES

- Playgrounds
- Recreation Centers
- Swimming Pools
- Bathing Beaches

THE NAMES OF THE RECREATION
FACILITIES DISCUSSED IN THE
REPORT ARE SHOWN ON THE MAP

SCALE OF MILES

NEGRO RESIDENCE AREAS

Percent of Negroes in Total Population in
Areas Indicated by Following Symbols:

- 1 to 20%
- 20 to 60%
- 60 to 100%

The recreation center is the most unusual and notable feature of Chicago's recreation system but one from which the Negro gets little benefit. It is a complete community center, with both indoor and outdoor facilities. It represents an investment of from $200,000 to $800,000, according to the amount of ground, the location, and the extent of its facilities. The yearly expenditure necessary to maintain such a recreation center where older children and adults can hold meetings, dances, and entertainments, and where there are concerts, indoor games, swimming-pools, showers, etc., is shown by the reports of the park boards to be from $30,000 to $50,000. Though the argument that wholesome recreation makes for better citizenship applies to Negroes as well as to whites, no recreation center has been located within the Negro areas and only seven near them.[1]

The director of Armour Square, a recreation center which is just beyond the edge of the main Negro area, but which the Negroes do not feel free to use for reasons discussed later, was asked what places of recreation for adult Negroes existed in that neighborhood. She instanced a social settlement that had been out of existence for more than six years, an infant-welfare station and a commercial amusement park known to be in bad repute.

Although in recent years the Negro population has been increasing in density in the neighborhood directly east of Wentworth Avenue along which Hardin, Armour, and Fuller recreation centers are located, this has not increased the use of these centers by Negroes. It has tended, rather, to increase the antagonism of the whites in the vicinity to the use of the centers by Negroes. In this neighborhood the hostility toward Negroes of whites, especially gangs of hoodlums, is shown by the many attacks upon Negroes in this area as discussed in the sections on the "Riot of 1919" and "Antecedent Clashes."

Several representatives of the park boards strongly deprecated the lack of recreation centers within the Negro area and said that such facilities should be provided. The South Park representative recommended the area east of Wentworth Avenue between Thirtieth and Forty-seventh streets as one needing additional facilities. The West Park representative said: "A complete all-year-round recreation center for the colored people should be established at Ashland and Lake streets. We need greater facilities, or equal facilities, for the colored people. There isn't any place on the West Side that I know of, but yet we have many of these complete recreation centers there for the whites." Although the Negroes on the West Side had never asked for additional facilities, the white people in that neighborhood had frequently asked the West Park Commission to provide greater facilities for the Negroes. The Negroes in the district were not organized, according to the West Park official, but the white people realized that something ought to be done for the Negroes and made the request.

The director of Seward Park said the maintenance cost was the chief obstacle to additional recreational facilities. "The law permits acquisition of property for small parks by request of citizens and bond issues for the purchase of the property and its development," he said. "When it comes to maintenance the question of taxes comes in, and unless people are willing to be taxed in excess of what they are taxed now, there won't be any possibility of maintaining more parks."

Though there are three public bathing-beaches near the main Negro area, the whites seem to expect Negroes to confine themselves to the Twenty-sixth Street Beach. It is quite limited and unattractive in approach and surroundings. The approach is over a rough road through a much-neglected neighborhood, and then up a long flight of stairs to a four-foot viaduct over the railroad tracks, and a roundhouse and switch yards are near by. The beach is a strip of sand about fifty feet wide and a short block in length; it narrows at one end to the tracks and at the other end is walled by a high embankment. While it offers a chance to get into the lake, the atmosphere of wholesome, recreative outdoor life is entirely lacking.

In the Morgan Park region there is a large Negro population but no park or playground within its Negro area. Barnard Playground and Ridge Park are the nearest facilities, a mile or more distant. Negro children said they did not go there because "those are in Beverley Hills and only rich folks go there—no colored people." The directors of these parks said there was no discrimination against Negroes but that they did not come because they felt that these parks were "for white folks only."

III. USE OF FACILITIES

Table XVII gives estimates by the officers in charge of the Negro attendance at the places of recreation in or near the Negro areas.

Factors influencing attendance.—Out of the thirty-five playgrounds, recreation centers, and bathing-beaches in or near the Negro areas for which attendance figures were secured, at fifteen Negro attendance never amounted to more than 10 per cent, and usually was less. In several cases distance or such barriers as railroad tracks seemed to explain the small percentage of Negro patrons. In other cases it seemed due to the existence of other facilities nearer the center of the Negro area which were more largely patronized by the Negroes; an example is Stanton, which though not far from the Negro area is farther than Seward Park. The small number of Negroes at other places often could not be explained by the director. At Gladstone Playground, for example, in a neighborhood where the Negro population was increasing rapidly, practically no Negro children were found, though the white children said there were plenty of Negro children in the school. "They don't stick around after school hours or in the summer," said the children, but no one appeared to know why this was the case, as there had never been any difficulty at this playground. Negro children used Drake and Sherwood playgrounds much

TABLE XVII

Number of Negroes Attending Parks and Playgrounds in or near Negro Areas and Their Percentage of the Total Attendance

NAME	AVERAGE DAILY ATTENDANCE			PERCENTAGE OF TOTAL DAILY ATTENDANCE		
	School Time	Through Year	Vacation Time	School Time	Through Year	Vacation Time
South Side District:						
Twenty-sixth St. Beach	......	200	......	......	95	......
Thirty-eighth St. Beach	......	500	......	......	Less than 1	......
Fifty-first St. Beach	......	500	......	......	Less than 1	......
Moseley Playground, Twenty-fourth St. and Wabash Ave	900	......	150	......	80	
Colman Playground, Forty-sixth and Dearborn Sts	350	......	700	......	90	......
Doolittle Playground, Thirty-fifth St. near Rhodes Ave	800	......	500	......	90	......
Oakland Playground, Fortieth St. and Langley Ave	600	......	400	......	75	......
Beutner Playground, Thirty-third St. and LaSalle St	1,400	......	1,000	......	67	
Sherwood Playground, Fifty-seventh St. and Princeton Ave	1,500	......	900	50	....	None
Drake Playground, Twenty-seventh St. and Calumet Ave	1,100	......	600	......	25	
McCosh Playground, Sixty-sixth St. and Champlain Ave	1,200	......	450	25	....	15
Carter Playground, Fifty-eighth St. and Michigan Ave	1,200	......	500	......	25	
Fiske Playground, Sixty-second St. and Ingleside Ave	1,500	......	1,000	......	2	......
Fuller Park Recreation Center, Forty-fifth St. and Princeton Ave	......	1,500	......	......	3	......
Armour Square Recreation Center Thirty-third St. and Shields Ave	......	1,500	......	......	1	
Hardin Square Recreation Center, Twenty-sixth St. and Wentworth Ave	......	800	......	......	1	......
Washington Park	......	27,000	......	......	10	......
Jackson Park	......	47,000	......	......	2	......
Ogden Park District:						
Copernicus Playground, Sixtieth and Throop Sts	1,400	......	800	7	....	16
Ogden Park Recreation Center, Sixty-fourth St. and Racine Ave	......	3,000	......	......	Less than 1	......
South Chicago District:						
Thorp Playground, Eighty-ninth St. and Buffalo Ave	500	......	350	......	5	......
West Side District:						
Robey Playground, Birch and Robey Sts	500	......	800	......	20	......
Mitchell Playground, Oakley Ave. and Ohio St	1,200	......	200	......	5	......
Washington Playground, Grand Ave. and Carpenter St	......	200	......	......	1	......

TABLE XVII—*Continued*

NAME	AVERAGE DAILY ATTENDANCE			PERCENTAGE OF TOTAL DAILY ATTENDANCE		
	School Time	Through Year	Vacation Time	School Time	Through Year	Vacation Time
West Side District—*Cont.*:						
Otis Playground, Grand Ave. and Armour St.	......	200	......		1	
McLaren Playground, Polk and Laflin Sts.	300	......	400	......	....	
Gladstone Playground, Robey St. and Washburne Ave.	1,300	......	400	......	1	......
Hayes Playground, Levitt and Fulton Sts.	......	......	Closed	......	....	
Union Park Playground, Washington St. and Ashland Blvd.	......	1,500		......	40	......
North Side District:						
Northwestern Playground, Larrabee and Alaska Sts.	......	300	......	......	None	......
Orleans Playground, Orleans St. and Institute Pl.	150	......	400	......	5	......
Franklin Playground, Sigel St. near Wells St.	1,500	......	300	5	....	25
Seward Park Recreation Center, Elm and Sedgwick Sts.	......	1,500	......	......	15	......
Stanton Park Recreation Center, Vine and Rees Sts.	......	2,000	......	......	1	......
Lincoln Park	......	60,000	......	......	15	......

Maximum attendance, 100,400. Negroes approximately, 19,000.*

* Of these 19,000 about 200 use the beaches, 4,100 the playgrounds, 700 the recreation centers, and 14,000 the large parks.

less, or not at all, after school hours and in summer. At Drake, though the two races mingled in games in the daytime and no disorders had occurred, the Negro boys took no part in the games in the evening when the older white boys were home. This, the director said, was due not to timidity or fear of aggression, but rather to "lack of ambition." At Sherwood Playground, west of Wentworth Avenue, where 50 per cent of the children using the playground during school hours were Negroes, there were no Negroes on the playground in the afternoon and evening and all summer. This was said to be due to the fact that the Negro children in the school, especially the girls, were larger than the white children and during the school session were the dominating group. After school, however, the older white children got home from other schools or from work and assumed control, allowing no Negroes in the playground. The Negroes then went to Carter Playground, which is east of Wentworth Avenue, in the main Negro settlement. This separation, the attendant stated, was due entirely to action on the part of the children, as the officials did not discriminate in any way. This neighborhood has been much disturbed and is discussed in more detail under "Contacts."

A TYPICAL SCHOOL YARD PLAYGROUND IN A WHITE NEIGHBORHOOD

Representatives of each park commission said that they had no rules or regulations of any kind discriminating against Negroes, and that all races were treated in exactly the same way. The only case in which this rule appeared to be violated was in connection with Negro golf players at Jackson Park. Two Negroes participated in the Amateur Golf Tournament at Jackson Park in the summer of 1918 and made good records. The only requirement for entrance into the tournament at that time was residence in the city for one year. In 1919 the requirements were increased, entries being limited to the lowest sixty-four scores, and membership in a "regularly organized golf club" being required. Since Negroes are not accepted in established golf clubs, the Negro golf players met this qualification by organizing a new club, "The Windy City Golf Association." In 1920 the restriction was added that contestants must belong to a regularly organized golf club affiliated with the Western Golf Association. As it was impossible for Negro clubs to secure such affiliation, it is impossible for Negroes to compete in the tournament.

Unofficial discrimination, however, frequently creeps in. According to the representative of the Municipal Bureau, "the person in charge of the park is largely influenced by the attitude of the people outside the park. We had trouble at Beutner Playground because of the tendency on the part of the director, who was a white man, to be influenced by the attitude of the white people in the neighborhood, and either consciously or unconsciously showed by his actions to the colored people that they were not fully accepted." Beutner Playground later became an example of unofficial discrimination in favor of the Negroes, for the Municipal Bureau decided to "turn over the playground particularly to Negroes" and instructed the director "to give them more use of the facilities than the whites." But this was found to be impossible as long as a white director was employed, because he was influenced by the feeling of the whites in the neighborhood who did not want the playground turned over to the Negroes. The desired result was finally obtained by employing a Negro director. "Then the switch suddenly came," said the park representative, "and the playground was turned over to the Negroes almost exclusively."

A similar method was employed with reference to the Twenty-sixth Street Beach, according to the head of the Municipal Bureau, who said: "As the colored population gradually got heavier and more demand came for the use of that beach it gradually developed into a beach that was used almost exclusively by Negroes. And we did as we did in the Beutner case: we employed a Negro director when the preponderance was Negro."

This beach has since been transferred to the South Park Commission, and there is no longer a Negro director there, though most of the attendants are Negroes.

Park policemen will not let Negroes go in swimming at the Thirty-eighth Street Beach, according to a Negro playground director. "The park policemen

tell you, 'You can't go in, you better not go in, I'd advise you not to go in,'"
said the director. "If you try to go in he keeps you out."

The Negro director of Beutner Playground reported an unpleasant personal
encounter with the policeman of Armour Square. "Last summer I had occasion
to go over there with my assistant who is colored. We went to the library
and the park police officer we met said, 'niggers ought to stay in Beutner
Park.'" Policemen in Armour Square also had helped to drive out Negro
boys who had gone over there to use the showers, according to this director.
In addition he said that Negro boys had been refused permits to play baseball
at Armour Square. The director of the park said, in answer to these statements, that there was no discrimination on the part of the management and
if such things had occurred it was without the knowledge of the management
and due to the fact that the applicants did not see anyone in authority. "The
only applicants I have had for a colored baseball team this year was for an
outside industrial team, and they were given permission," said the director.
"Whether the police officer followed them up and told them they shouldn't
come back, I don't know, but they didn't come back. I gave them the permit
to come."

At one or two parks definite efforts had been made to encourage larger
numbers of Negroes to make use of the facilities, but at Armour Square the
director did not believe this to be advisable. "I have never gone out to do
any promotional work to bring them in," she said, "because I would not choose
personally to be responsible for the things that would happen outside my
gates if I were responsible for bringing large groups into Armour Square.
If such groups come to me for reservations I give them, but they don't come."
This director also said that she would feel it necessary to warn any Negro
group that might come to her park that she could not be responsible for their
protection outside the park.

At Union Park, which has a playground and swimming-pool and is situated
on the edge of the densest Negro residential area on the West Side, every effort
has been made to encourage the Negroes of the neighborhood to make use of
the limited facilities, according to the representative of the West Chicago
Park Commission, who said:

We have advertised among the colored people and done everything we could
to get them to use the swimming-pool, shower baths, and reading-room, and send their
children to the playground. The result to some extent is satisfactory but of course
they are not using it in proportion to the population of the Negroes in that neighborhood. That, I think, is partly due to the fact that we ought to have some other
facilities there. We ought to have some equipment for boys over sixteen years of
age, and we ought to have an assembly hall, a regular library, clubrooms, and other
facilities for the recreation of older boys and girls.

The director of Fuller Park told of a special effort he had made, with the
assistance of a Y.M.C.A. physical instructor, a Negro, to increase the use of

the park by Negroes living east of Wentworth Avenue. The Y.M.C.A. instructor guaranteed to get the people, and 400 application blanks were distributed among Negro children in the Sunday schools of the neighborhood. All the blanks were signed with the names of Negro children between eight and sixteen and returned to the office. When the classes started a few weeks later, no Negro children appeared. The distributor of the blanks tried for three or four weeks to find out why the Negro children did not come but failed to discover any reason. Then the director sent a notice to the *Defender*, a widely circulated Negro newspaper, saying that the children who had signed application blanks for classes at Fuller Park were requested to come at any time and were just as welcome as white children. Thereupon a few children came—two or three out of a class of thirty. Additional notices were put in the *Defender*, and an effort was made to interest the Negro pastors, but the attendance did not increase, and finally the attempt was given up for that year. The next year a similar effort was made but with only slightly better results. At the band concerts and moving pictures the Negro attendance is fairly good, and a large number of Negroes use the library, but the gymnasium and the children's playground are used very little by the Negroes, and the swimming-pool practically not at all.

The reasons advanced by the park officials for the non-use of convenient recreation facilities are that the Negro is timid and reluctant to go where he feels he is not wanted, or that he fears attack in the park or near it. At a conference the West Park representative said:

When we first opened the doors of Union Park we thought, owing to the large colored population in the district, that the colored people would come there most willingly and avail themselves of the facilities just as freely as any person would. But we found that it was not so, that the greater number of persons who came there were the whites, and they as usual availed themselves of the facilities freely. The colored were timid, came in gradually, and as soon as they found they were welcome, that there was no line of discrimination drawn, the attendance of the colored increased.

At Sherwood Playground, Armour Square, and Fuller Square, all west of Wentworth Avenue, which is considered the dividing line between the white and Negro areas, fear is probably a large factor in the small Negro attendance, as the feeling in the neighborhood is bitter and fights have been frequent. At Sherwood Negro children use the playground during school hours when they feel that they have the protection of the school, but not after school when they feel that protection is lacking. Webster School at Wentworth Avenue and Thirty-third Street, which is 30 per cent Negro, has its graduation exercises in Armour Square, but the Negro children do not go to Armour Square at any other time, and they did not go over at night for an entertainment which the principal of Webster School arranged at Armour Square. Negro children use the Armour Square library freely, according to the director, but there has never been an application for the use of a clubroom, and no Negroes come to the outdoor moving pictures which are given one night a week. "There's absolutely nothing to prevent them coming," said the director. "Why don't they come? There is nothing within the park they need to be afraid of. There has been absolutely no distinction made in the handling of colored children or colored men or colored women coming to Armour Square, but they do not come." The director was positive that the failure to come to the park was due to the attitude toward Negroes outside the park. She explained that although she could guarantee safety and police protection inside the park, she could do nothing to protect Negroes outside the park gates. The park policemen are employees of the park boards and not of the city and have no jurisdiction outside the parks. This is true of the police at all parks and beaches maintained by the park boards, but the police at the playgrounds and beaches maintained by the Municipal Bureau of Parks, Playgrounds, and Bathing Beaches are members of the regular city police force.

Continuing, the Armour Square director said:

Personally I know of no disturbances that have started within Armour Square, and yet we have had outside of Armour Square every year at least two riots, not counting the general race riot—riots that started largely in school clashes. There have been some very serious riots between the children of the Webster School and the Keith School just east of it, and there have also been some very serious clashes between the black and white children going to and from the parochial school—actual fights in which they have had to call large detachments of the police. Armour Square is not used by the colored people in proportion to their numbers in the neighborhood, but it has absolutely nothing to do with our management. It is because they are afraid to come to the park. They know absolutely that within the four walls of the park nothing is going to happen to them.

The testimony of the Negro director of the Beutner Playground seemed to indicate that Negroes were kept out of Armour Square in ways that its director did not know about.

IV. CONTACTS

Behavior.—The behavior of Negroes at the parks apparently has not been the major cause of the difficulties that have arisen in the past. Such complaints as were made by park officials in regard to the behavior of Negroes at the parks concerned groups of rough or domineering children at the playgrounds rather than adults.

The playgrounds where the attitude of Negro children was criticized were Sherwood and Moseley, both in neighborhoods where unusually bitter racial feeling was reported by the playground directors. The older Negro girls were particularly rough and hard to control, these officials said, abusing small children both white and Negro, monopolizing apparatus, and refusing to leave the playground when asked to do so.

BEUTNER PLAYGROUND
The largest in the Negro residence area

FIELD HOUSE EQUIPMENT AT BEUTNER PLAYGROUND

NEGRO ATHLETIC TEAM REPRESENTING DOOLITTLE PLAYGROUND IN
CITY-WIDE MEET

FRIENDLY RIVALRY

White and Negro boys at a playground near the Negro residence area

Testimony in regard to adults indicated that the park directors found them quiet and desirable patrons of the parks. Said the director of Seward Park:

One of the most interesting and best-conducted and best-behaved groups I have ever seen is a group of colored people known as the "Jolly Twenty," a dancing organization. They started coming eight years ago and had a system of couple dancing which was marvelous. I have never seen it equaled anywhere. They have been coming every year, once a year, for a dance at Seward, and the "Jolly Twenty" has grown to be about the "Jolly Four Hundred," but the larger the group the better they seem to behave and the better they dance.

The director of Ogden Park told of a Negro club which holds frequent dances at Ogden Park. He said: "About 300 attended the last one. They are the best-behaved group that come. I never have to object to improper dancing or boisterousness, and they always leave on time. I have had to object several times to conduct at white dancing parties."

This testimony in regard to Negroes at dances is interesting in view of the situation regarding the recreation facilities at the Municipal Pier. Negro attendance there is about 8 per cent of the total attendance of four million or five million a year, according to the director of the Pier. They are well dressed and well behaved and inclined to segregate themselves. There had never been a single instance of an intoxicated Negro or of one who had made himself in the least objectionable, the director said. The only people whom the pier authorities have had to reprimand for violation of pier rules in regard to cleanliness, monopolizing of furniture, etc., have been whites. Many of the attendants are Negroes, and the band which plays for the dance concessionaire is composed of Negroes. Negroes are welcome everywhere on the Pier, as are all races, according to the director, except in the dance hall, where their appearance is discouraged by the concessionaire. The following method is followed to discourage the appearance of Negroes on the dance floor, according to a white man who had observed it:

Admission to the dance floor is at the rate of five cents per couple, per dance. Each dance lasts about three minutes. If a Negro couple buys a ticket and dances one dance nothing is said. If the couple comes in for another dance, one of the floor managers—employed by the concessionaire—speaks courteously to the couple. He expresses regret that he must mention the matter of their dancing to them, but that they are not dancing properly, and he invites them to come to a corner of the dance floor where he will instruct them in the proper way to dance. This usually occupies the remainder of the particular dance, and results in the Negroes not coming on the floor again. If the couple does reappear, the floor manager again speaks to them saying he is very sorry he has to tell them again that they still are not dancing quite properly and again he invites them to a corner of the dance floor for further instruction. This is the procedure by which the Negroes are embarrassed and discouraged from using the dance floor.

Relations between the children.—Lack of antagonism was reported at a large number of playgrounds. Apparatus was used by both groups without friction, Negro and white children mingled freely in their games and in the swimming-pools, and both Negroes and whites played on baseball and athletic teams. Occasional playground fights had taken place, but usually without any element of racial antipathy. "There might be personal misunderstandings and disagreements between a white and a black just the same as between two whites," said the director of Union Park, "but I wouldn't lay it to race prejudice. They work together and play together and seem to harmonize in most instances." When this director came to Union Park a year before he found a tendency among Negroes and whites to group by themselves, but steps were taken to bring them together in games of various kinds, and toward the end of the season the director felt that they "harmonized better and worked together more cordially than they did before." When the investigator from the Commission visited Union Park Playground, he saw the small children playing together on the same pieces of apparatus—a Negro child on one end of a teeter ladder and a white child on the other.

These children were ten years or under. The director felt that it was not until children reached the age of eleven years or older that they began to feel racial antipathy. In the swimming-pool at this park, which is used by the older children and adults, the Negroes and whites kept separate. There was no trouble between them, but they stayed in separate groups. The director felt that there was little likelihood of trouble ever starting in this park, because "where such nicknames as 'Smoke' are applied to colored boys by white boys, and is given and accepted in a friendly spirit, there is little chance for serious disturbance."

As this playground in Union Park is intended for children under ten, the occasional difficulties between older children might be alleviated if the Hayes Playground, one of those in the system maintained by the Municipal Bureau, were kept open in the summer. The playground at the Hayes School, 80 per cent Negro, was closed and the apparatus dismantled in the summer of 1920 when the investigator visited it. Though it is not a large playground it is the one the older Negro children are accustomed to use during the school year, and they are doubtless reluctant to go in the summer to other school playgrounds which they do not ordinarily use.

At Seward Park the Negroes use the facilities freely and play with the white children on the apparatus and in the ball field. The only difficulty reported here was in connection with a wrestling tournament. The director described it as follows:

Last season we had a wrestling championship tournament. There were some colored groups who had wrestled at Seward who were eligible for entrance into this tournament, and when the night came for weighing in, the director for one of the other parks said, "What are these colored people doing here?" "They are weighing in." I said. "They will not wrestle with my group," he said. "Very well, then, I guess your groups will not be in it," I said.

It looked as though we were up against a problem, but the night when the wrestling came the colored contestants didn't show up, so that the problem was solved for that time. Of course we couldn't say that any white man must wrestle with a colored man. It presented a problem that had to be settled in some way. I think the reason they didn't show up was because I told my investigator to say to these colored men, "Next season if you have a sufficiently large group you can have a contest of your own. We'll award the same prizes to colored wrestlers as we do to the white."

The representative of the Municipal Bureau also spoke of occasional difficulty in wrestling, though there may be no objection to Negro participation in other events. He said:

We have athletic meets in which a Negro team has competed and for five years has won the championship in athletics. In baseball there is no trouble. The difficulty comes in some of the activities, particularly wrestling, because of the nature of the activity. It is a closer contact. We make no distinction, however, and when a Negro boy gets up to face a white boy and the white boy doesn't face him, the bout is forfeited to the Negro. I think more meet than fail to.

At Fiske Playground, where there are few Negroes, as they do not live near, the investigator witnessed a baseball game with a team from Colman Playground composed entirely of Negro boys except the pitcher. They played as any teams would, with no evidence of racial antipathy. The Negro team seemed to be the better, and according to the director had won every game so far that season.

At McCosh, Robey, Carter, Oakland, Colman, Doolittle, and Beutner playgrounds the children mingled without friction, according to the directors. Negroes were in a minority at the first three and in a majority at the last four. At Carter Playground the investigator witnessed the presentation of a medal for athletics to one of the white boys while the Negro boys looked on in admiration and, after it was over, invited the white boys to "come on out and play ball." The only trouble that has been experienced at this playground was a few days before the 1919 riot, when a fight between a white boy and a Negro started on the playground and the spectators divided along racial lines, especially after the fight was transferred to the street. A riot call was sent in, and the police put a stop to the fight. No trouble has occurred since and the director believed it could not happen again. "The boys have learned better," he said.

Free mingling of Negro and white children was observed at Oakland and Robey playgrounds and was encouraged by the directors. Italian and Negro boys were playing ball together when the investigator visited Robey Playground, and Negro and white girls were playing on the same slides. The director said that in the evening the ball games were watched by both Negroes and whites, and that frequently the Negroes had a game themselves, which white onlookers enjoyed watching. The only incident of importance at Robey Playground had occurred a few day before, when a dispute over a baseball game arose between a white boy of fourteen and two Negro boys of eleven, resulting in a fight in which the director had to interfere. The director said there was not the slightest chance that such a fight would divide the playground along racial lines, as there had never been any disorders there, and that animosity between the Negro and white groups was entirely lacking.

At Oakland Playground, where neither race predominated strongly, the assistant director said there had never been any difficulty. The investigator witnessed a ball game in which Negro and white girls participated and saw groups of Negro and white boys talking outside the playground in a friendly manner.

At Colman, Beutner, and Doolittle playgrounds, where the Negroes come in the majority, no difficulties were reported. The Negro director of Doolittle Playground encourages comradeship between Negro and white children and allows no discrimination against white children. "If a white boy can make a team, he makes it," this director says to a Negro team which objects to a white boy being allowed to play on it. When this director was assigned to Doolittle Playground he was told that 60 per cent of those who made use of the playground were Negro and 40 per cent white. When he got there he found that 70 per cent were white and 30 per cent were Negroes. He said:

I had to look around to find a colored child, but I never had any trouble. Of course the white people gradually moved out and the colored people moved in. We never had any trouble with colored boys or white boys—they played on the same teams. In fact, I think we won the district championship for four years. Then they moved me over to the Beutner and the majority of the white children got up a petition to bring me back to Doolittle Playground. That shows there was no distinction there. They wanted me because we carried on activities.

White ball teams often use the field at Beutner Playground in spite of the fact that Armour Square is only two blocks away. "Last year [1919] there were several games between white and colored teams," said the assistant director, "but there have been none so far in 1920."

No difficulties between Negroes and whites were reported at Palmer Park, Bessemer Park, or Thorpe, Otis, and Orleans playgrounds, which are patronized by a few Negroes, though they are too far away from the Negro areas to be generally used.

The supervisor of girls' work in the Municipal Bureau made the following statement in regard to the relations between the Negro and white children visiting the municipal playgrounds:

From my observation and supervision of the girls' work in the municipal playgrounds I can only say that in all our activities colored and white children mingle without restriction. In indoor gymnasium and dancing-classes as well as in games, athletics, and general informal use of the playground, they take part together. Ability and sportsmanship are the only qualifications considered in candidates for any playground team. In the field of adult recreation, since we have no community centers conducting indoor activities in connection with any of our playgrounds within the colored area, my observations refer only to outdoor gatherings. On such occasions adults of both races mingle without friction. It is my experience that the most harmonious relations are established in connection with band concerts, field days, festivals, pageants, etc., including all forms of community art, which tend to unify rather than to split those taking part. In the Illinois Centennial Pageant, presented by groups from thirty-eight neighborhoods in 1918, girls from Doolittle Playground represented "Dances of the New Freedom," bringing "Liberty and New Strength to Illinois." In preparation of this episode several rehearsals were held at Doolittle Playground, white dancers from other playgrounds taking part; and the interest and co-operation shown by the neighbors made each evening memorable.

Voluntary racial grouping.—Voluntary racial grouping appears to be a characteristic of the large parks and beaches, which adults frequent, rather than of the playgrounds which are used mainly by children. One instance of voluntary grouping among children was found at Copernicus Playground. The percentage of Negroes using this playground is much larger in summer than in winter. The playing space is in the shape of an "L," one end intended for boys and the other for girls, but by common consent the children divide along race lines rather than sex. The investigator saw small white children playing at one end of the playground, while Negro boys were playing ball in the larger end. Later, after the Negro boys left, some of the white children used the larger space while some Negro children collected around the apparatus in the smaller end. No instance of mixed play was observed, but there seemed to be no antagonism between the groups, and no disorders were reported.

The director of Union Park in speaking of boys who play games in the recreation rooms, said that there seemed to be a tacit understanding between the blacks and whites that they had certain nights. On certain nights all the attendance would be black and on other nights it would all be white. Asked whether Negro and white boys who were school friends played separately at the park, the director said that blacks and whites often came in together, but that for every case where they came in together and played a sociable game, there were probably three instances where groups were either of one race or the óther. However, the director said that this grouping was casual, and that there was no prevailing community sentiment that the Negroes should use the park on separate nights. He believed that additional recreation facilities would help greatly in doing away with this tendency to voluntary segregation. He also said that the Negroes had a tendency to separate from the whites, not because they wished to avoid them, but because they preferred to associate with their own race.

In the general use of Lincoln and Washington parks the Negroes and whites stay in separate groups. There has never been any difficulty, according to the Lincoln Park representative, arising from the fact that Negroes have taken possession of a spot desired by whites for a picnic or other amusement.   No part of either park is especially set aside for the use of one race, and groups of both Negroes and whites are seen everywhere in the parks, but they do not mingle.   While there was no outward evidence of antagonism toward Negroes at the time of the investigator's visit to Washington Park, white visitors who were questioned showed an antipathy to the Negro which seemed to have its basis in the influx of Negroes into the residence districts. One man, originally from the South, was bitter against Negroes.   He said he had left the Socialist party because it accepted Negroes as equals.   At an open-air "free-speech" meeting speakers representing various radical doctrines were addressing a crowd composed almost entirely of whites.   The chairman of the meeting, however, was a Negro, whose humorous remarks made him popular with the white crowd.

The only place in Washington Park where there seemed to be a general mingling of Negroes and whites was on the ball field.   There were games in which the two teams were composed entirely of Negroes, and games in which the teams were composed entirely of whites; there were also games in which both Negroes and whites were engaged.   The investigator watched one game in which vacancies on two teams from American Legion posts had been filled by Negroes.   There was the best of spirit between the players and among the spectators.   The white spectators were lined up along the first base line and the Negro spectators along the third base line, but rooters and players joked with each other with no sign of racial antagonism.

The South Park representative testified to the good feeling between Negroes and whites at a baseball game, and said the whites often preferred to watch the Negro games.   At other points in the park, however, particularly the tennis courts and the boathouse, difficulties between the races were reported. These will be discussed in the next section on "Clashes."

Separate racial grouping is the general rule at the beaches, though it is not always voluntary.   At the Thirty-eighth Street Beach, for example, Negroes are prevented by white boys and the park policeman from going into the water, according to a Negro playground director.   "Boys who live around there from Thirty-ninth to Thirty-first Street have to swim at the street end between Thirty-third and Thirty-second.   They rock you if you go in."   This director was invited by white boys of the Vincennes Club to swim at Thirty-eighth Street, but when he suggested bringing some Negro boys along the white boys said, "Oh no, they can't come."

At the Diversey Beach in Lincoln Park both races go in the water, but a Lincoln Park representative said that the few Negroes who used this beach kept by themselves on one part of the beach, though there was no official rule compelling them to do this.   There have never been any racial disturbances at this beach.

ARMOUR SQUARE RECREATION CENTER
Located at Thirty-third Street and Shields Avenue

BEUTNER PLAYGROUND
Located at Thirty-third Street and La Salle Avenue

From the Twenty-sixth Street Beach, which is patronized almost entirely by Negroes, down to Thirty-sixth Street, Negroes and whites go into the water in separate groups, except at Twenty-sixth Street, where the few whites who go in mingle amicably with the Negroes. The investigator saw a white couple who had gone out to a raft and could not get back rescued by a Negro life guard. The other bathing-places along the shore for those ten blocks have been allotted by custom exclusively to one race or the other. At Twenty-ninth Street, where the 1919 riot started, a policeman is now stationed, and no trouble has occurred since the riot, though many fights have started which the police have stopped. Gangs of young men come from as far as Halsted Street, according to the policemen, ready to fight at the slightest opportunity. Fights usually occur because of some remark made by one group about a girl in another group. On the whole, however, few Negroes come to Twenty-ninth Street, the policeman said, going instead to Twenty-sixth Street.

At the beaches outside the main Negro area, such as Fifty-first Street and Triangle Park, and Clarendon and Rogers Park beaches to the north, the only Negro patrons are a few young children. The attendants at these beaches believe there would be trouble if adult Negroes started to use them. Negro children have been objected to at Clarendon Beach, where a man asked the director to put a little girl out because "she was a nigger."

Several directors reported that the Negroes did not use the swimming-pools much and segregated themselves when they did go in. The director at Union Park said the Negroes did not use the swimming-pool in proportion to their numbers, and that when they did use it, they came in small groups and confined themselves to a certain part of the pool instead of mingling with the whites. He said that there was nothing in the attitude of the white boys to make them do this, but that it was the "natural impulse of the colored people to do that in the swimming-pool." He thought that many Negroes did not use the pool more because "they are afraid of the water." A Negro playground director testified that he had frequently seen a white boy dive off one side of the pool at Union Park when a Negro boy dived off the other side and hold the Negro boy down until, when he came up, he was gasping for air.

The director of Ogden Park gave an incident that had occurred recently at that park:

One day I noticed three small colored girls sitting among the others in the "swimming line" waiting for the doors to open. A few minutes afterward they were at the end of the line. I tried to find out the reason but could discover nothing either from the colored girls or the others. I saw that they went back to the place in the line they had before and went to my office. Some minutes later I looked out and saw that while the swimming had begun, these three had not gone in but were sitting there watching the rest. I was unable to discover why they didn't go in—they said merely that they "didn't want to." Whether there was some threat or whether the girls were naturally timid about going into the pool I do not know.

The representative of the South Park Commission said that in the South Park district the parents were opposed to race contacts in swimming- and wading-pools. "Not 10 per cent of the families will allow contact with Negroes in the pools," he said.

None of the three natatoriums maintained by the Municipal Bureau is patronized by Negroes, with the exception of the Washington Heights pool which is used by a few Negro children in the summer. This pool is near a Negro district, but the other two are remote from the Negro areas.

A distinction was made by several directors between formal and informal activities at playgrounds and recreation centers. It was their theory that Negroes and whites mingled successfully in informal activities, but not in formal ones. "There is a difference in the informal use by children of a playground and the use of a recreation building where there are clubs and dances and classes and things of that sort," said the director of Armour Square. "Children and adults come in individually to use the library and other facilities, but there are no applications from organized groups of Negroes for any of the facilities at Armour Square." The real distinction in most cases is probably not between formal and informal use but between use by children and use by adults, as the formal activites are those in which older children and adults engage, as was pointed out by the representative of the West Chicago Commission.

Clashes.—Clashes between Negroes and whites at various places of recreation are reported as far back as 1913. These clashes in the main have been initiated by gangs of white boys. In 1913, for example, the secretary of boys' work at the Wabash Avenue Y.M.C.A. (for Negroes) conducted a party of nineteen Negro boys from the Douglass Center Boys' Club to Armour Square. They had no difficulty in entering the park and carrying out their program of athletics. The party then took shower baths in the field house. The Y.M.C.A. secretary had noticed the increasing crowds of white boys near-by but had no misgivings until the party left the park. Then they were assailed with sandbags, tripped, walked over, and some of them badly bruised. They were obliged to take refuge in neighboring saloons and houses in Thirty-third Street west of Shields Avenue. For fully half an hour their way home was blocked, until a detachment of city police, called by the park police, scattered the white gang.

That same year the Y.M.C.A. secretary had found it impossible to proceed east through Thirty-first Street to the lake with groups of Negro boys. When this was tried they inevitably met gangs of white boys, and fights ensued with any missiles procurable. Attempts to overcome this antagonism by continuing to demonstrate that the Negro boys had a right to use these streets were unavailing for the next two years.

In 1915 similar conflicts occurred. That winter Father Bishop, of St. Thomas Episcopal Church, took a group of the Negro Y.M.C.A. boys to Armour

Square to play basket-ball. The party, including Father Bishop, was beaten up by white boys, their sweaters were taken from them, and they were otherwise maltreated. The Y.M.C.A. staff then decided not to attempt to use the park or field house during the evenings.

The same year an attempt was made to take seventy-five of these boys through the Stock Yards. They had received tickets of admission to the annual stock show, in the pavilion at "the Yards." In spite of the four adult leaders, several of the boys were struck by sticks and other missiles while passing from one section of the show to another. The gang of white boys continually increased in numbers, and the situation by three o'clock, two hours after the Negroes had entered, began to look desperate. Police assistance was required to get the Negro boys safely out of the building and into street cars. No effort was made to restrain the white gangsters, who were allowed to range through the building at will.

An altercation between white and Negro boys in Washington Park is on record as early as the summer of 1913. These boys were sixteen or seventeen years of age. During the spring and summer of 1919, numerous outbreaks occurred because of the use of the baseball diamonds in Washington Park by Negro players. White gangs from the neighborhood of Fifty-ninth Street and Wentworth Avenue, not far from the park, also came there to play baseball, among them some of "Ragen's Colts."[1] Gang fights frequently followed the games. Park policemen usually succeeded in scattering the combatants. The same season gangs of white boys from sixteen to twenty years of age frequently annoyed Negro couples on the benches of this park. When the Negroes showed fight, minor clashes often resulted.

In Ogden Park, as far back as 1914, there were similar instances of race antipathy, expressed by hoodlums who were more or less organized. A Negro playground director said that if Negro boys attended band concerts in that park, white gangs would wait for them outside the park, and the Negroes were slugged. The white gangs also tried to keep Negro boys from using the shower baths at the park. This director told how a party of Negroes whom he had taken there was surrounded by white gangsters when they emerged from the shower house. "A boy reached around and caught me and pulled me up close to the other fellow," he said. "I dug down and got out. Of course they rushed for me. In the rush the other colored lads got out. Brass knuckles were used on me. When I looked up they said, 'My God, you have hit L—; you have hit the wrong fellow.'" The director declares that the man who hit him with the brass knuckles was discharged by the court with a reprimand.

This condition in the parks continued up to the early summer of 1920. George R. Arthur, secretary of the Negro Y.M.C.A. branch, expressed the fear at that time that a riot might occur in Washington Park any Sunday afternoon.

[1] See p. 12

He described the condition in the vicinity of the boathouse in that park as "fierce." There were fights there every Sunday. Five white men had beaten a Negro there one night the previous week. That sort of thing had been going on for years, he said. The Y.M.C.A. had long been dealing with the situation but he had noticed this trouble especially in the last two years. He attributed it to the gang spirit and to racial antipathy, which ordinarily would not amount to much, but which because of the tense situation in Chicago might lead to serious riots.

The director of the Negro branch of Community Service of Chicago ascribed the trouble to the same source. He said that most of the white boys came to Washington Park from the "Ragen's Colts" Club, that some of them went to poolrooms where the mischief was hatched. There was but one policeman in charge of about fifteen baseball games in the park, he said.

The racial difficulties at the baseball fields in Washington Park had doubtless never been brought to the attention of the representative of the South Park Commission, because he cited these games as an example of good feeling between the two races. He believed that there was never any difficulty at the baseball fields, and that the white people who enjoyed the Negro games would be the first to object if the Negroes were not permitted to play in the park. This opinion coincides with the situation at the ball fields observed by the investigator for the Commission, but apparently there are occasional clashes here as in other parts of the park.

The representative of the South Park Commission did not think Negroes hesitated to use any of the facilities of the park because of fear of mistreatment in the park, though they might have some fear of being mistreated outside the park. He did not know that any difficulties have ever occurred at the boathouse. though a Negro doctor testified that he had treated many Negro boys who had been assaulted there. The South Park representative said:

I have never known of any actual abuse of a colored patron in any park to which I was personally assigned. I have known people coming and going who were abused, mistreated, and actually assaulted, outside the park reservations, but I don't believe our records would show very many cases—probably no more than occur where the Poles and the Irish get together, or the Bohemians and the Germans.

Fights of a racial character were reported at one or two playgrounds. At Franklin Playground, where fights among boys between ten and fourteen are frequent, the director said he was always especially careful to stop a fight between a white and Negro boy because "a race riot would be easy to start."

At Sherwood Playground Negro children do not use the playground after school hours or during the summer. The attendant declared that "things used to be mighty rough but are better now." The change may have been due to a younger group of children replacing the former pupils, among whom were many children fourteen to seventeen years of age. There was much fighting between Negroes and whites in the neighborhood of Sherwood Playground, according to the attendant. Street fights were frequent, often ending in the use of knives or stones, and numerous arrests had been made. The fight usually started between two boys over some trivial dispute, a mixed crowd gathered, and the fight became general. Fights were also frequent within the playground, the attendant said; sometimes as many as three were going on at once. But a policeman had been stationed near-by, and conditions were improving. The playground had no director at the time it was visited.

An example of objection to the first Negroes appearing in a park was given by an official of the Municipal Bureau:

I remember a particular instance at the Beutner Playground in about 1903. Prior to that time we had very few colored people in that vicinity. One evening a young colored boy, probably seventeen or eighteen years of age, came in there. I happened to be on the athletic field at that time. He came in the rear gate, and the first thing I noticed there was quite a crowd of white fellows chasing this fellow all over the field. He ran down to where the Armory now stands, doubled, and came back and got out of the gates.

This official said that after that incident there was little trouble between the races at the playground until about 1910, when the balance of the patronage became almost equal. He continued:

That was when the trouble started. There wasn't any preference shown on the part of the park management to any particular race, but it was the people outside. They absolutely took the stand that as long as they could keep the colored people away they were going to do it. They used every means they could to keep the colored people away from Beutner Playground and Armour Square.

Another instance of whites objecting to the use of recreation facilities for the first time by Negroes was given by the representative of the West Chicago Commission:

Not long ago, two colored men, for the first time in the history of Garfield Park, came out there to play tennis. Immediately somebody in the neighborhood called up the Park Board and complained about Negroes breaking into Garfield Park. We frankly told the people who were complaining that they had equal rights to the use of the facilities at Garfield Park. But it seemed that while we said nothing, the colored gentlemen never appeared again to use the tennis facilities.

The representative of the South Park Commission in commenting on this same point said:

There is a history of development in amicable race relations. Most of the troublous conditions are where there is injected for the first time the question of racial intermingling. Where it is established, where it has gradually grown up, in time there comes an adjustment.

At Armour Square individual Negroes have been accepted as "part of the scheme," according to the representative of the South Park Commission, practically ever since the park was opened. But the director says that it is group action which stirs up trouble:

I think the trouble will adjust itself as the colored people continue to come into the neighborhood, but we are in the situation of having colored people come into the neighborhood where there haven't been any before. I think it will adjust itself in a year or so, and that possibly at that time colored people will begin coming.

The head of the Municipal Bureau thought the difficulties arose, not when Negroes first entered a white neighborhood, but when a balance between the two races was struck, and it was a question which race was going to predominate. "That has been my experience with the municipal playgrounds," he said, citing the case of the Beutner Playground which the Municipal Board decided to turn over to the Negroes.

Where Negroes are accepted and live amicably near white people, or where there has not been enough influx of Negroes to arouse feeling against them the contacts in the playground are usually peaceful. On the other hand, in communities where Negroes are looked on as intruders and objectionable neighbors, and where the white people are antagonistic, a contact between a Negro and white child, which would normally be peaceful, will result in a disturbance and tend to increase existing antagonism. This is the situation at Moseley and Sherwood playgrounds.

At Thirty-eighth Street Beach the prejudice is such as to prevent any Negro from bathing there, although it is as near the center of the main Negro area as the Twenty-sixth Street Beach, to which Negroes are expected to confine themselves. At Armour Square neighborhood sentiment permits a few Negroes to use the park, but trouble starts if new groups come. At Ogden Park a Negro playground director was assaulted by white boys and hit with brass knuckles in 1914, but now, according to a prominent Negro familiar with the situation at the center, there is order and fair treatment both within the park and on the way to it, and the Negroes prefer to travel out there than to go to Washington Park, which is closer at hand, but where they may be attacked if they try to use a boat or may be obliged to wait indefinitely for a tennis court.

The use of the parks by Negroes is determined almost entirely by the degree of antagonism in the neighborhood, and Negroes are afraid to make use of the parks where the neighborhood sentiment is hostile. "The neighborhood condition pretty much governs the feeling of security, on the basis of which the Negro will come in and use our park facilities," said the representative of the South Park Commission. "Without feeling secure in his neighborhood and in his access to the park, I don't think anything we could do would pull the Negro in."

A NEGRO AMATEUR BASEBALL TEAM

At Mitchell Playground, in a district with a reputation for lawlessness, and at Seward Park, two blocks from a region known as "Little Hell," no racial difficulty is reported.

The two causes of neighborhood antagonism most commonly cited were the real estate and the sex problems. Among visitors to Washington Park the real estate problem in the residence districts near the park seemed to be the primary cause of ill feeling. One of the property owners in that region showed his feeling by complaining that the park ought to be rechristened "Booker T. Washington Park." The figures in Table I indicate that only about 10 per cent of the patrons of the park are Negroes.

An important point in considering neighborhood sentiment is whether the white hoodlum who appears to be mainly responsible for the clashes which have taken place is a cause of neighborhood antagonism or whether he merely reflects the attitude of the community. The fact that the hoodlum is permitted to terrorize and mistreat Negroes without serious protest from whites is an indication that the hoodlum expresses what the white community feels. The hoodlum does not always live, however, in the immediate neighborhood of the place of recreation where he makes trouble. The gangs of white boys who come down to Twenty-ninth Street Beach and start trouble, for example, do not live near the beach, the policeman in charge says, but over at Halsted Street. The director of Armour Square, though she stated that the feeling in the immediate neighborhood of the park was responsible for keeping Negroes away from Armour Square, said that the boys who were active in starting trouble at the time of the 1919 riot came from west of the park, and that the boys in her vicinity tried to stop the others.

The head of the girls' work in the Municipal Bureau said:

It [hoodlumism] is a symptom, the reflection and logical carrying out of an attitude widely accepted by the community as a whole. Although a serious and troublesome symptom, I believe it should be faced and welcomed as evidence of the potential brutality of this attitude. Men and women of good standing in white society condone much that they would hesitate to do in person; and by their failure to protest prove themselves equally responsible for results.

The director of Fuller Park believed that the groups of hoodlums mainly responsible for keeping Negroes out of the parks were the athletic clubs "composed usually of a bunch of young sports that are not athletes at all." "These clubs, which have only about one athlete on the roster," he said, "are so situated that the Negroes have to pass them going to and from the park. Those are the boys, numerous in every park neighborhood, who are keeping the colored people out of the parks."

The director of Ogden Park took the part of a Negro boy set upon by a white gang during the 1919 riot and rescued by the police, though they did not keep the mob from killing the Negro. He advocated the formation of "square-deal" clubs to defend innocent people from hoodlums. "Members would be bound to fight for the square deal—whites against white hoodlums and blacks against black hoodlums," he said. "Until both races will act, the lawless elements will continue to cause trouble."

It is possible in some cases, such as those in which the "athletic clubs" are involved, to find out the identity of boys who molest Negroes, but, according to the testimony of several park directors, it is absolutely impossible to control these boys because the courts will not convict them. The director of Armour Square stated:

I have had boys taken down to the courts time after time, and now my policeman refuses to take them down to the court any more, because he is reprimanded when he brings them in. . . . . One of our attendants was shot through the lung and is now absolutely incapacitated for work, and the policeman was reprimanded because he had kept the boy in jail two nights. When it came to trial, they had already seen somebody and the policeman got the reprimand.

There was a general feeling among park representatives that the presence of a director with a proper attitude toward the problem was the greatest factor in bringing about amicable relations within the park, but there was considerable difference of opinion as to whether the park management could or should attempt to influence the surrounding neighborhood. The West Chicago Commission representative said that there was no instructor at Union Park the first year it was open, and that considerable segregation and undesirable conduct on the part of both whites and Negroes resulted. Since then, there had always been a director in charge, and a very harmonious mingling of the two races had been brought about on the playground. He believed that a similar relationship could be brought about within the recreation building by a director with the right personality, if adequate facilities were provided.

The Seward Park director did not consider it a proper function of a recreation center to try to direct the community life outside it.

The director of Armour Square felt that she could do nothing to promote Negro activities there. She did not approve of the suggestion of turning over Armour Square to the Negroes as the best way of solving the problem. She thought this would result in ill feeling and trouble, since there was a well-established tradition that the whites should use Armour Square to the fullest extent. But since the Negroes had no such recreation center as Armour Square available to them, she believed that a new center with full equipment should be started in a neighborhood part white and part Negro with the understanding that it should be a Negro recreation center where the whites were welcome if they wished to come. She thought that white people would patronize such a recreation center and, with careful leadership, would mingle with the Negroes on friendly and peaceable terms.

Two recreation-center directors favored entirely separate recreational facilities for Negroes with whites excluded. One of these was the director of Fuller Park, who told the Commission that he had made every effort to get Negroes to come to the park, and that he considered it part of his duty to go out into the neighborhood and try to get Negroes to use the park. "Separate parks and playgrounds for colored people are advisable," he said, "not because one group is any better than the other, but because they are different. Human nature will have to be remodeled before racial antipathy is overcome."

The director of Hardin Square, another recreation center little used by Negroes, though it is near the main Negro area, believed that separate facilities for each race would be the best solution of the problem. He did not encourage Negroes to come to Hardin Square. The policeman at the park also believed that "you can't make the two colors mix." This policeman said he knows a group of young men in the district, mostly ex-service men, who would "procure arms and fight shoulder to shoulder with me if a Negro should say one word back to me or should say a word to a white woman." He thought it would not take much to start another riot, and that the white people of the district would resolve to make a "complete clean-up this time." This policeman is the one whose failure to arrest a white man accused of stoning the Negro boy, Williams, at the Twenty-sixth Street Beach was an important factor in precipitating the riot in 1919.

The director of Moseley Playground, who was born and raised in that vicinity, said there had been antagonism between the two races in that neighborhood for thirty years. He believed that separate recreation facilities would be impracticable because the taxpayers could not be divided in such a way that they would not be paying for fields their children could not use.

The director of Seward Park thought that it might be arranged in the small parks to give special hours to Negro groups. This would meet what he believed to be the desire of the Negroes to be by themselves and also the objection of the white girls who had protested against having Negro girls in the same gymnasium classes with them.

V. TRAINING FOR RECREATION DIRECTORS

The importance of the personality of the park director in determining the conditions in the park, which was often emphasized, led to a consideration of the training for the work—whether training was required that would develop the understanding and vision necessary to handle the problems involved in racial contacts. The representative of the Municipal Bureau said that every effort had been made to get trained men, but that there was no school or curriculum of training that determined the efficiency of a person in charge. Some of his best directors had had no specific training, while some of the poorest came from the best recreational training schools.

Few Negro instructors were found at the places of recreation and these were employed by the Municipal Bureau. The representative of the West Side Commission said that he had been trying for a long time without success to get a Negro to take the civil-service examination for playground instructors, as he was anxious to get a Negro for Union Park. The representatives of the Lincoln and South Park commissions said that they used Negroes only as life guards, attendants, janitors, etc. The South Park Commission representative said the question of the desirability of having Negro instructors and play leaders had never come up, because no Negro had ever become a candidate for a position as a result of the competitive examinations.

Training opportunities for Negroes.—It was found that the Y.M.C.A. has a four-year recreational training-course in which no distinction is made between Negroes and whites. As the courses are not open to women, the Y.M.C.A. has no such race problem as arises in recreation courses where women are admitted. The president of the graduating class at the Y.M.C.A. College the year previous was a Negro, though the rest of the class was composed entirely of whites. The number of Negroes taking the Y.M.C.A. recreation course is relatively small, usually about two in a class of 150.

The American College of Physical Education and the Chicago Normal School of Physical Education reported that they did not admit Negroes to any courses, saying that their students would object to physical contact with Negroes.

The Recreation Training School of Chicago, successor to the Recreation Department of the Chicago School of Civics and Philanthropy, admits Negroes to the recreation course on the same terms as all other students and has trained several, both in the short courses and in the full year's course. This school admits both men and women.

VI. SUMMARY

Though the Negro areas are as well supplied with ordinary playgrounds as the rest of the city, they are noticeably lacking in more complete recreation centers with indoor facilities for the use of older children and adults. Several of these recreation centers, such as Hardin, Armour, and Fuller squares, Stanton and Ogden parks, border on Negro areas but are not used to any great extent by Negroes because the Negroes feel that the whites object to their presence. Though there are three publicly maintained beaches within the main Negro area the Negroes feel free to use only the Twenty-sixth Street Beach, though many of them live as far south as Sixty-sixth Street. Where Negroes do not use nearby facilities to any great extent they have usually either been given to understand, through unofficial discrimination, that they are not desired, or they have been terrorized by gangs of white boys. Few attempts to encourage Negro attendance have been made, and with the exception of Union Park these attempts have failed.

In the main there seem to be no difficulties arising from contacts between young white and Negro children at the playgrounds, no matter whether the playground is predominantly white or predominantly Negro, with the exception of one or two playgrounds, such as Sherwood and Moseley, which seem to share in traditional neighborhood antagonism between the two races. Voluntary racial grouping at the playground was found only in rare instances and usually involved the older rather than the younger children. The swimming-pools, for example, are patronized more by older children, and voluntary racial grouping at swimming-pools was reported in several instances. In the ordinary playground sports and athletic contests the two races mingle with the best of feeling.

Voluntary racial groupings and serious clashes are found mainly at the places of recreation patronized by older children and adults—the large parks, beaches, and recreation centers. Trouble is usually started by gangs of white boys, organized and unorganized. The members of so-called "athletic clubs," whose rooms usually border on the park, are the worst offenders in this respect. If they do not reflect the community feeling they are at least tolerated by it, as nothing is done to suppress them. Some park authorities that have made sincere efforts to have these hoodlums punished are discouraged because they get no co-operation from the courts, and the policeman who takes the boy to court gets a reprimand, while the boy is dismissed.

Another source of racial disorder is the lack of co-ordination between park and city police. The park police stop a fight between a white child and a Negro child and send them from the park. Outside the park gates the children start fighting again, and the park police have no power to interfere. The spectators may then get into the fight, dividing along racial lines, and before the city police can be summoned a race riot may be well under way. Either city police should be stationed directly outside every park, ready to co-operate with the park police, or else the jurisdiction of the park police should be extended to include the area immediately surrounding the park.

The most important remedies suggested to the Commission for the betterment of relations between Negroes and whites at the various places of recreation were: (1) additional facilities in Negro areas, particularly recreation centers which can be used by adults; (2) an awakened public opinion which will refuse longer to tolerate the hoodlum and will insist that the courts properly punish such offenders; (3) selection of directors for parks in neighborhoods where there is a critical situation who will have a sympathetic understanding of the problem and will not tolerate actions by park police officers and other subordinate officials tending to discourage Negro attendance; and (4) efforts by such directors to repress and remove any racial antagonism that may arise in the neighborhood about the park.

D. CONTACTS IN TRANSPORTATION

I. INTRODUCTION

Volume of traffic.—The number of passengers carried in 1916 in a twenty-four-hour day by the Chicago surface lines was 3,500,000 and by the elevated railway lines 560,000, according to a tabulation made by the Chicago Traction and Subway Commission in 1916. With the city's growth in population the traffic in 1920 doubtless showed an even larger volume. This traffic is distributed over approximately 1,050 miles of surface and 142 miles of elevated track. It is most congested in the "Loop" area of the downtown business section, which is a transfer center for the three sides of the city, North, South, and West; and of course it is heaviest at the hours when people go to and from work.

Concentration of Negro traffic.—Negroes constitute 4 per cent of the city's population, according to the federal census for 1920, and presumably about that percentage of the city's street-car traffic. The Negro traffic, however, instead of being scattered all over the city, is mainly concentrated upon twelve lines which traverse the Negro residence areas and connect them with the manufacturing districts where Negroes are largely employed. These twelve lines, which are shown on the two transportation diagrams facing page 300, cover 11 per cent of the total mileage of the surface and elevated lines. Because of this concentration, however, the proportion of Negroes to whites on these twelve lines is much higher than 4 per cent, and on such lines as that on State Street, which runs along the principal business street of the main South Side Negro residence area, it often happens that the majority of the passengers are Negroes. In addition to these twelve lines of heaviest Negro traffic, there are others traversing less densely populated parts of Negro residence areas. In varying degrees contacts of Negroes and whites may be found on other lines which serve the small proportion of the Negro population scattered throughout the city.

The main area of Negro residence, on the South Side, where about 90 per cent of the Negroes in Chicago live, is traversed by the State Street, Indiana Avenue, Cottage Grove Avenue, Stony Island Avenue, and the South Side elevated lines, running north and south, and by eleven cross-town lines, running east and west, beginning with the Twenty-second Street line at the north and ending with the Seventy-first Street line at the south. From six to nine o'clock in the morning, and from four to six o'clock in the afternoon, there is a heavy Negro traffic on the lines going north to the "Loop," on the Cottage Grove Avenue line going south to the South Chicago manufacturing district, and on the Thirty-fifth Street and Forty-seventh Street lines and the elevated branch line at Fortieth Street going west to the Stock Yards. To reach the Stock Yards, Negro laborers must ride through a territory between Wentworth Avenue and Halsted Street in which, as shown in the sections of the report dealing with housing and with racial clashes, hostility toward Negroes has often been displayed. This Negro traffic west of Wentworth Avenue is, therefore, chiefly confined to a few hours in the morning and the afternoon.

The West Side Negro residence area is connected with the "Loop" by the Madison Street and Lake Street surface lines, and the elevated line on Lake Street, and with the Stock Yards by the Halsted Street and Ashland Avenue lines.

The North Side Negro residence area is connected with the "Loop" by the lines on State and Clark streets and by the Northwestern elevated lines. Contacts on these lines, however, are not as important as on the lines serving the South and West Side areas, because the number of Negroes involved is only about 1,500, or less than 2 per cent of the Negro population.

Contacts and racial attitudes.—As in other northern cities, there is no "Jim Crow" separation of the races on street cars in Chicago. The contacts of Negroes and whites on the street cars never provoked any considerable discussion until the period of Negro migration from the South, when occasional stories of clashes began to be circulated, but only one such incident was reported in the newspapers. Even since the migration began there have been few complaints based upon racial friction in transportation contacts.

In response to inquiries, the South Side Elevated Company, which has the largest Negro traffic of any elevated line, replied that except during the riot in 1919, when a few cases of racial disorder were reported, there had been no complaints from motormen or trainmen since 1918, when a trainman was cut by a Negro but not seriously injured. No complaints from white passengers had been received since the spring of 1917, when white office workers objected to riding with Stock Yards laborers, mainly Negroes, on the Stock Yards spur of the elevated. White laborers in the Stock Yards mostly lived within walking distance of their work, but Negroes found it necessary to use car lines running east to the main Negro-residence area. The Chicago Surface Lines replied that complaints due to racial friction were negligible.

Information obtained by investigators for the Commission showed that the attitude of Negroes and whites toward each other was being affected by contacts on the cars. A white woman in the Hyde Park district, an officer of the Illinois Federation of Woman's Clubs, when interviewed upon race relations, made special reference to transportation contacts. She said:

While Negroes are coming into this neighborhood, especially on Lake Park, I see little of them, except on the street car. There I must say I have a decided opinion. Just last evening around five o'clock, I took a Lake Park car at Fortieth Street and Cottage Grove Avenue, and several colored men saw to it that they were first to board the car. I had to sit near the front and a great big Negro man sat next to me, smoking a cigar right in the car. I told my husband when I got home, I was for moving them all out of the city, and I never felt like that toward them until just of late. There's a feeling of resentment among us white people toward the colored people on the cars, and they feel that, and they feel the same resentment toward us. I think I see that very plainly. Last night, on this same car, a colored man was hanging over me, and I know he didn't want me there near him, any more than I wanted him.

As a factor in attitudes on race relations, transportation contacts, while impersonal and temporary, are significant for several reasons. In the first place, many whites have no contact with Negroes except on the cars, and their personal impressions of the entire Negro group may be determined by one or two observations of Negro passengers. Secondly, transportation contacts are not supervised, as are contacts in the school, the playground, and the workshop. If there is a dispute between passengers over a seat it usually rests with the passengers themselves to come to an understanding. Any feeling of suspicion or prejudice on either side because of the difference in race accentuates any such misunderstanding. In the third place, transportation contacts, at least on crowded cars, involve a degree of physical contact between Negroes and whites which rarely occurs under other circumstances, and which sometimes leads to a display of racial feeling.

Scope and method of investigation.—In obtaining information as to transportation contacts the Commission's investigators, both white and Negro, men and women, made many observation trips on the twelve lines carrying the heaviest volume of Negro traffic and therefore involving the greatest amount of contact. Counts of passengers, Negro and white, were made, behavior and habits were noted, passengers and car crews were questioned, and officials of the surface and elevated lines, starters, and station men were interviewed.

Superintendents of 123 industrial plants were interviewed to ascertain the numbers of whites and Negroes employed in offices and in plants, transportation lines used by workers, nature of work and its effect upon cleanliness of person and clothing, provision of baths, etc. A further source of information was a report made for the officers of the Central Manufacturing District, setting forth the transportation facilities for the 12,000 employees of the district and providing data drawn from questionnaires filled out by these employees. The district includes the area from Thirty-fifth to Forty-third streets and from Morgan to Robey streets.

II. DISTRIBUTION OF NEGRO TRAFFIC

Negro traffic is fairly continuous throughout the day in the Negro residence areas, and the proportion of Negroes and whites is about the same at different hours of the day. Except during the times of going to and from work the cars are not overcrowded, and the danger of friction is therefore small. On the routes connecting the Negro residence areas with the Stock Yards and with South Chicago, where many Negroes are employed in steel plants, the Negro traffic is confined to a few hours in the morning and late afternoon, but at these hours the cars are very crowded. There is much rushing to board cars and get seats, and white office workers and other non-laborers are thrown into contact with Negro laborers still in their working clothes. It is under such circumstances that irritation and actual clashes are most likely to arise. It should be noted that similar contacts with white laborers in their working clothes are disagreeable in the same ways, though in such cases the odors and grime are not associated with race and color.

The hours of greatest general travel and car crowding were found to be from six to nine o'clock in the morning and from four to six o'clock in the afternoon.

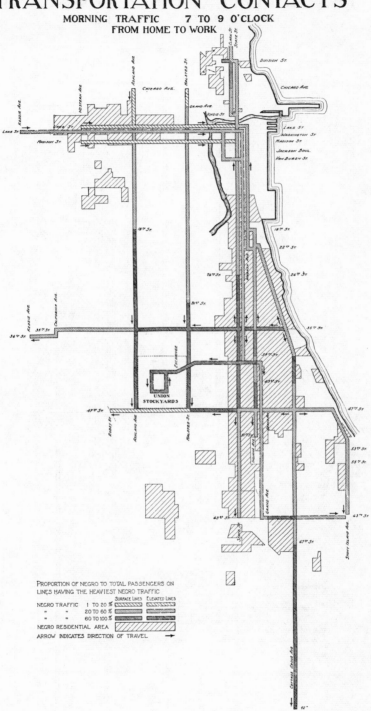

TRANSPORTATION CONTACTS
MORNING TRAFFIC   7 TO 9 O'CLOCK
FROM HOME TO WORK

PROPORTION OF NEGRO TO TOTAL PASSENGERS ON
LINES HAVING THE HEAVIEST NEGRO TRAFFIC

		SURFACE LINES	ELEVATED LINES
NEGRO TRAFFIC	1 TO 20 %		
" "	20 TO 60 %		
" "	60 TO 100 %		
NEGRO RESIDENTIAL AREA			
ARROW INDICATES DIRECTION OF TRAVEL			

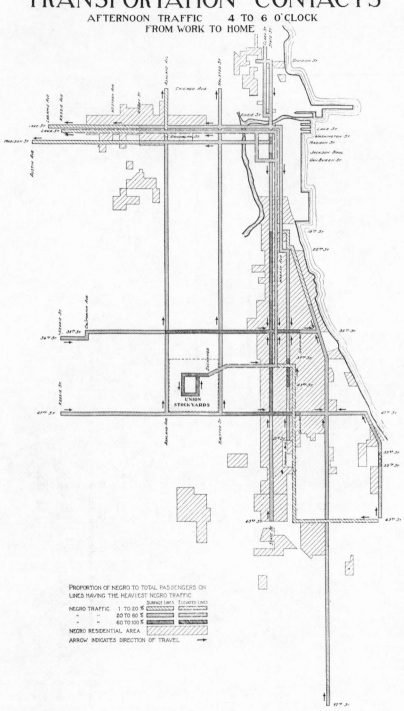

TRANSPORTATION CONTACTS
AFTERNOON TRAFFIC   4 TO 6 O'CLOCK
FROM WORK TO HOME

PROPORTION OF NEGRO TO TOTAL PASSENGERS ON
LINES HAVING THE HEAVIEST NEGRO TRAFFIC

		SURFACE LINES	ELEVATED LINES
NEGRO TRAFFIC	1 TO 20 %		
" "	20 TO 60 %		
" "	60 TO 100 %		
NEGRO RESIDENTIAL AREA			
ARROW INDICATES DIRECTION OF TRAVEL		→	

The proportions of whites and Negroes on lines carrying the largest numbers of Negroes to and from work are shown in two diagrams. These are based on counts of white and Negro passengers, several trips being averaged to show typical car loads during the heavy travel of early morning and late afternoon. The first diagram shows the proportions in travel from the Negro residence areas of the South and West sides toward the Stock Yards, the other large industries employing Negroes, and the "Loop" district during the period from six to nine A.M. The second diagram shows the proportions in travel from the Stock Yards, the other industries, and the "Loop" toward the Negro residence areas of the South and West sides during the period from four to six P.M.

III. CONDUCT RESULTING FROM CONTACTS

As already noted, contacts of Negroes and whites on street cars provoked little discussion until the migration of Negroes from the South began to be felt. The great majority of the migrants are laborers. Many of them are ignorant and rough mannered, entirely unfamiliar with standards of conduct in northern cities. It is this type which is meant in references hereinafter to the "migration" or "southern" Negro.

Coming to a city like Chicago, with no "Jim Crow" racial segregation, was a new experience to many southern Negroes. They felt strange and uncertain as to how they should act. Many whites and Negroes long resident in Chicago have said that they could tell a migration Negro by his ill-at-ease manner and often by his clothes.

The conspicuous points in the behavior of the migration Negro before he became urbanized were his "loud laughing and talking," his "ill-smelling clothes," his "roughness," and his tendency to "sit all over the car." These are easier to understand when one considers the background of the southern Negro.

Few white people realized how uncertain the southern Negro felt about making use of his new privilege of sitting anywhere in the car, instead of being "Jim Crowed." One Negro woman who came to the city during the migration said, when she was asked about her first impression of Chicago: "When I got here and got on the street cars and saw colored people sitting by white people, I just held my breath, for I thought any minute they would start something. Then I saw nobody noticed it, and I just thought this is a real place for Negroes." There were exceptional cases in which southern Negroes walked miles, rather than take a car.

It may seem strange in view of such uncertainty of mind and timidity that the most noticeable point of behavior of the southern Negro was loud talking, joking, and laughter. The South Side Elevated Company, replying to the Commission's inquiries, said: "These colored people are of a happy-go-lucky type and are often noisy, especially when two or more acquaintances meet on the trains or station platforms or crossing from one side of the station to the other.   They laugh and talk a good deal and seem to be happy and care free."

Although some of this boisterousness was no doubt due to a care-free spirit and a broad good humor, some of it had quite a different source.   Many a southern Negro thinks that the whites like him to be "typical," and that they will tolerate him as long as his dialect, his wit, and his manner are amusing enough.   A Negro newspaper of Chicago took the southern Negroes to task for using this safety device in Chicago.

Many whites, clerical workers, shoppers, and others of a non-laboring type, have expressed objections to what they term a tendency of Negroes to "sit all over the cars," meaning to sit anywhere in the car.   This was most conspicuous when whites had to ride in the morning on a car which had come from one of the Negro residence areas and was already filled with Negroes, or when Negroes and whites were boarding a comparatively empty car near one of the big industrial plants in the afternoon.   The employment manager of the Corn Products Company plant at Argo reported a complaint about this tendency made to him by one of the girls in the office:

An office girl told me she had trouble getting a seat on the cars.   She was not able to get a seat by herself and did not want to sit next to a Negro.   She said that Negroes would rush in and get all the seats by the windows.   She thought they did it more to tease the office help than anything else.   This girl was undoubtedly prejudiced.   That was one of her arguments to explain why she had difficulty in getting to work in the morning.   She is a St. Louis girl of Flemish extraction.

Many of the southern Negroes were found to be very hesitant about taking seats next to whites.   The southern tradition was so ingrained in them that they tried to be as inconspicuous as possible.   On the other hand, some, with the sudden removal of the restraints of the South, used their new freedom without thought of the effect of their behavior on Chicago whites and Negroes.

The attitude of migration Negroes was sometimes expressed to the Commission's investigators.   For example:

You can spend your money as you please, live better and get more enjoyment out of it—I mean go where you please, without being Jim-Crowed.

There's no lynching or Jim Crow.   You can vote, you receive better treatment and more money for your work.

The freedom of speech and action.   You can live without fear and there's no Jim Crow.

Some southern Negroes apparently came to Chicago with a real grudge against all whites and ready at slight provocation to display their resentment. The minister of one of the Negro churches in Chicago said:

After years of restriction and proscription to which they were subjected in the South, they suddenly find themselves freed in a large measure of these conditions. Their mind harks back to that which they endured at the hands of members of the

Aryan race in the South, and they grow resentful, and in the midst of their new environment they vent their spleen. One has but to ride on any of the surface lines running into the section of Chicago largely occupied by my race group to be convinced of the facts mentioned above.

The southern Negro who got into trouble with whites by insisting on his right to a seat sometimes belonged to the class of suspicious and sensitive Negroes, and sometimes he was simply a "greenhorn." The following cases show how "green" the migration Negro could be, and how easy it was for him to make himself disliked and ridiculous. The first case was observed by a Negro man, the second by a Negro woman, both long resident in Chicago:

I boarded a crowded car in the "Loop" going south and was forced to stand near the rear door. There are two lengthwise seats at the rear of the car, one of which will hold three people and one of which will hold two. Two colored women, carelessly dressed and holding greasy paper bundles in their hands, got on the car at Twelfth Street and stood in the back of the car hanging on to straps. They rode this way until Eighteenth Street, when one of them, a large woman, noticing that there were three white people on one of the seats and only two on the other said to her companion, "If three folks can sit on that seat, I ain't going to stand over these white folks, who are just like they are down South, and don't want you to sit down. I'm going to sit down myself." She then inserted herself between the two white women, one of whom was pushed to the floor. The Negro woman was much embarrassed, but I don't think she has yet realized that the seats were of different lengths.

I was on a State Street car when two southern Negro women got on, talking loud, and throwing themselves around loose and careless like. I was sitting on one of the end seats, just big enough for three, and one of the women says to the other, "Here's a seat, here's a seat." "You move over," she said to me. There was fire in their eyes, and I don't like fighting, so I made up my mind that if they started anything I'd get up and give them my seat. Most people would have understood how you felt if you did that, but I am not sure they would have understood. I said to one of them, "There really isn't room on this seat." She gave me a shove, so I said, "But I'll get up and give you my seat." You wouldn't believe what happened then. The conductor came in and said, "You just keep your seat." And a white man, who was sitting in one of the cross-seats, turned around and said, "I'll see that she does."

Soiled and ill-smelling clothes were a large factor in making Negro working-men objectionable to many whites even of the same working class.

At the time of the migration, in the fall of 1916 and the spring of 1917, the Stock Yards were taking on hundreds of Negro laborers to increase their war-time production, and these new hands, most of them migration Negroes, rode to and from work with white office workers. How the white office workers felt about it is shown by a statement of a white woman clerk in the Stock Yards:

Some of the Negroes on the Thirty-fifth Street car are very rough. Most of them work out at the Stock Yards and the smell of the Yards is very bad. They seem to try to clean up, but the smell is there, especially in cold weather when the cars are closed. I would suggest that they run special cars from the Stock Yards for those people, and that would leave enough cars for us and we wouldn't get the odor either.

This situation was somewhat remedied by the fact that most of the Negro laborers at least changed their clothes before going home, even if they could not entirely rid themselves of the Stock Yards odor; also the hours for Stock Yards employees were so arranged that the office workers came to work later and left later than the white and Negro laborers.

The Negro press of Chicago tried to make the migration Negro realize how the odor attaching to his clothes was affecting public opinion. The *Chicago Searchlight* of May 22, 1920, had this exhortation by the editor:

Did you ever get on the elevated train at Indiana Avenue about 5:30 o'clock in the afternoon, and meet the "gang" from the Stock Yards? It would make you ashamed to see men and women getting on the cars with greasy overalls on and dirty dresses in this enlightened age. There is really no excuse for such a condition to exist. There is plenty of soap and water in the Stock Yards and you have better clothes in your homes. Why not take a suit to the yards and wash up and change your clothing, before attempting to mingle with men and women, many of them being dressed for theaters and club parties, etc.? Don't you know that you are forcing on us here in Chicago a condition similar to the one down South?

In order to find out whether Negroes working in other plants than the Stock Yards do work which leaves the worker soiled and smelling, superintendents or foremen were questioned. It was learned that much other work done by Negro laborers leaves oil, grease, and acid stains, that many of the plants have no baths or adequate facilities for washing, and that sometimes where there are such facilities they are not kept in order. Three-fourths of the superintendents and foremen interviewed had the impression that Negroes were more careful about bathing and changing their clothes than whites. They said the difference was probably due either to the fact that the white laborer who was doing the same class of work as the Negro, was an immigrant, or to the fact that the white laborer often lived near the plant where he works, and preferred to wash up at home.

The Negro laborer meets little objection when he is riding with white laborers; it is when he comes in contact with whites of a non-laboring class that there is the most likelihood of trouble. Such whites often find white laborers quite as objectionable. A lawyer in Indiana Harbor who was questioned about the transportation contacts in the Calumet industrial district, said:

So far as transportation is concerned, little trouble need be expected. Most of the people here are working people, and they know what to expect when a dirty workman comes and sits down next to them. The fact of it is that if there is any complaint to be made, it would be against the foreigners. In the winter, when the doors are closed, the smell of garlic is almost unbearable.

Another complaint from whites is that Negroes on the street cars are "rough." It is significant, however, that all the incidents related to the Commission in regard to "roughness" occurred on crowded cars. The rush to get on a car before or after working hours is often heavy. The Commission's investigator, describing the loading of cars at an important transfer point near the Stock Yards at the evening rush hour, said:

I observed the loading and transfers at Ashland and Forty-seventh from three to four o'clock in the afternoon. With the possible exception of six to seven in the morning the traffic is heaviest at this time. The transfers from the Ashland to the Forty-seventh Street car are mostly Negroes from the government plants at Thirty-ninth and Robey. About 40 per cent of them are women. Cars going east on Forty-seventh Street leave every five minutes. There is a supervisor on this corner, whose duty it apparently is to supervise the arrival and departure of cars. He pays no attention, however, to the matter of loading. Usually the men meet the car in the middle of the block and climb on while it is moving. By the time the car reaches the corner the seats are all taken and the doorway is congested. The women, like the men, get on as they can. No deference is shown them. Most of those who get on this car are colored, and most of them, colored and white alike, are workmen.

Some friction between whites and Negroes has occurred during the boarding of cars. It may be caused by general racial attitude as well as by the circumstances of the particular case. The following cases were both related by white men, one an assistant superintendent in a foundry, and the other a barber:

One of our employees (Negro) in running to catch a car accidentally knocked over a white man. The white man became particularly abusive, and the crowd joined in with him. The crowd attempted to beat the Negro up, but he ran back to the plant here for protection and we quieted them down.

I remember one time about three years ago, I was coming home on the Forty-seventh Street car and two Negroes were standing on the back. It was pretty crowded. A man swung his wife on board, and two more white men jumped on too. He got her through into the car, and one of the Negroes said to her: "I'm going to get that husband of yours." I went up and stood in back of the white man and told him I'd stand by him, if anything happened. There were lots of whites on the car but about half Negroes, I guess. I think the Negroes have too much freedom. They don't know how to act. Some of those Negroes on the street car are real uncivilized.

The South Side Elevated Company, in answer to a questionnaire said: "It requires constant watching to prevent Negroes from entering and leaving cars through the windows." The following incident, reported by the Commission's investigator, who traveled over all the lines used by Negroes, shows that both whites and Negroes may climb through the windows under the same conditions of crowding:

I was transferring from the Argo car to the Sixty-third Street car with a number of white and Negro workmen from the Corn Products Refining Company. The crowd rushed for the door, and the doorway soon became congested. Two white men climbed in the car through the back window, followed immediately by a Negro. When the conductor came up, a white woman, who was standing next to me and had seen the whole performance, said to the conductor, indicating the Negro, who had climbed in through the window: "I wouldn't take his fare, if I were you. He came in through the window."

Selection of seats by white and Negro passengers often provides instances of conduct which is based on racial prejudices. These seem to be most frequent on lines with comparatively light travel by Negroes and where there is thus less opportunity for the races to become accustomed to contact. Sometimes whites show plainly their avoidance of Negroes.

Some Negroes have timidly offered their seats to women standing, and have been chagrined by the refusal of the white women to accept the courtesy. The superintendent of one of the plants where Negroes work made the following comment:

Negroes seemingly refrain from showing courtesy to white women, such as offering them their seats, because of two facts. Either the woman to whom the courtesy was extended, or outsiders, seem to the Negro to place a wrong construction upon his courtesy. They think him either fresh or servile, and in the majority of cases where a Negro would extend such courtesies, he refrains from doing so.

A few Negroes justified themselves by pointing out that white men did not give up their seats for Negro women, and so they did not intend to give up their seats for white women. The editor of a Negro newspaper took Negro men to task for their disregard of white women and also women of their own race, as follows:

Do you know that there is a growing tendency among the young men of our race to show disrespect for our womanhood? If you don't think so, just get on a street car or visit public amusement places, or even notice their actions as they walk along the street. It is nothing to see hundreds of big strong young men sitting on our cars, while women stand until they become almost exhausted, while those "fellows" sit and read their papers or gaze out of the car windows.

There is one trait, and I might say only one, that I take off my hat to the southern "Cracker" for, and that is his respect and high regard for women. While he hasn't any for the other fellow's [the Negro's] wives and daughters, yet he respects his own. We must set a good example for him and respect all women, regardless of race, color, or creed. Then you will win the admiration of all civilized people. Men who do not respect and honor their women are not worthy of citizenship. Do you get me, brother?

White men have become much incensed when they have given seats to white women, and Negro men, not realizing what had happened, took the seats. The timekeeper at a large industrial plant said:

I was on an East Chicago Whiting car. Six Negro workmen were standing. The car was full about one-third with Negroes. A man got up to let a white woman sit down. A Negro, seeing the seat vacated, sat down before the woman had a chance to get to it. The man who had proffered the seat became indignant, cursed the Negro, yanked him out of his seat, and proceeded to beat him up. The Negro drew out a knife. About this time, it became a general race clash. One of the Negro workmen had a gun: he pulled it out of his pocket and cleaned out the car.

The following incidents were reported by two white investigators:

I was on a Cottage Grove Avenue car at 5:30 P.M. The car was crowded, about one-third colored people. A young, well-dressed colored boy of about twenty was standing in the aisle beside a white man and a white woman. The seat directly in front of this colored boy was vacated, and the white man made a move to seize it, but the boy by holding his arm on the back of the seat barred the white man's way and stepped aside to allow the woman to sit down. The woman nodded her thanks to the boy, and the white man went on reading his paper.

I was on an eastbound Oak Park elevated train at about 10:30 A.M. Several Pullman porters got on at Campbell Avenue and had to stand, as did several white women and men. As the crowd began to thin out, I noticed that the white men were apt to drop into a vacant seat themselves, while the Negro porters were careful to wait until the women sat down before they took advantage of any vacant seats.

A white woman in the Hyde Park district said to one of the investigators:

On the street cars I would rather ride with Negro gentlemen than with many of our so-called white gentlemen. A Negro man who has the slightest training is courteous and genuinely so. My children use the street car every day to go to the Hyde Park High School, and it's not the Negro men on the street cars I hate to think of; it's the cheap white men. A very rough element of whites congregate every night on Lake Park near Fifty-first Street—hoodlums that the colored people living there must fear.

No case of attempted familiarity by a Negro man toward a white woman on the street cars was reported to the Commission. Cases were reported, however, of accidental contacts between Negro men and white women which might easily have been misunderstood, but which seemed to the investigator, a white woman, to be due to the clumsiness of southern rural Negroes in crowded cars. Two such cases follow:

I was on a Madison car going west. A number of Negroes got on at the North-western Station. The car was crowded, and I felt someone in the aisle leaning heavily against my shoulder. I was very much annoyed and glanced up. I saw that the man was a Negro about twenty years old. He was with a girl, obviously his sister, who was also standing in the aisle. They both had childlike faces, and I could see that he was quite unaware that he was leaning against me. I didn't say anything, as the car was really crowded.

I was in the aisle seat of an Illinois Central suburban car about 5:00 P.M., waiting for the train to start. A Negro man standing in the aisle next to me suddenly leaned against my shoulder so hard that it hurt. I looked up at him resentfully but he didn't notice me. He looked as though he had been picked up in a little western town and dumped down in a city for the first time. He had a wide western hat on,

and his face was lean and weatherbeaten. I take it he was about fifty years old.
He was in animated conversation with a woman in a seat behind me. This woman
had many bundles. Apparently they wanted to find seats together. Soon another
man joined them who had been scouting for seats in the car ahead, and they all set
out together for another car. They were so concentrated on this problem of getting
a seat that they didn't know there was anyone else in the car. They lunged down
the aisle knocking against people as they went along, but no one paid any particular
attention to them.

Another case of accidental contact, showing an attitude of suspicion on
the part of a white woman, was reported by a Negro Y.M.C.A. secretary:

I was on a street car going west through the "Loop" on Madison Street. A
colored man, apparently a workman, was sitting across the aisle from me, looking
out of the window, with his left arm stretched along the back of the seat. A white
woman came in, glanced at the vacant seat beside me, and sat down beside the
colored man across the aisle. He looked around and saw the woman sitting in the
seat, and apparently was confused. He attempted to remove his arm, and in doing
so his arm brushed across the woman's shoulder. She got right up and exclaimed:
"How dare you put your arm around me?" The man looked at her dumbly, his
face the picture of excitement and wonder. I said to the lady, "I was watching this
man and he was honestly trying to remove his arm from the back of the seat. I
think he was more surprised to find you there than anything else, and the whole thing
was sheer accident." She wanted to know what I had to do with it, and I simply said
I wouldn't like to see a matter of that kind misunderstood. She resumed her seat
beside the colored man and nothing further happened.

Many cases of improper advances by white men toward Negro women
were reported to the Commission by Negro women, well known to the Commission, whose character is beyond question. The following are typical:

Going south on a State Street car to Fifty-third Street, I noticed a man in the
aisle staring at me. He kept moving down nearer and nearer to my seat and sat
down in front of me. He handed me a note written on a scrap of newspaper. I
opened it because I was curious to know what his motive was. He was a young man,
in his twenties, and well dressed. He had written down his name and telephone
number and the words: "Call me for a date."

I remember one man especially, because I used to ride downtown on the same car
he took every morning. The first time I ever saw him, he stared at me a great deal
and when I got off the car, he got off too. As he got off he said to me, "Don't take
that car, wait for the other one." I noticed then that he went over to the corner and
took a car going in the opposite direction from mine. I saw him lots of times after
that, and he always got just as close as he could and stared. I always arranged it so
that he could not sit next to me.

I was on the elevated with a friend the other day. We were sitting on end seats.
A man got up to give a white woman his seat and then came over and stood close
to us. He stood with his legs against my friend's knees, until she jerked around

and sat facing me. Then he tried standing close to me. He had me so hedged in I could hardly move, and I had to make a very abrupt movement to get away. He moved on after a while.

What may be done to prevent misunderstanding and check in its incipiency trouble which might easily and suddenly become serious, is illustrated in the action of a white woman, a resident of the Chicago Commons Social Settlement:

One evening, soon after the race riot in July, 1919, I was riding on a State Street car, going south from Grand Avenue. I had only ridden a block, when there was a general stir in the car, a young woman fainted, and I learned that the conductor had been struck and his cap knocked off. Word went around the car that a "nigger" did it. Ugly remarks were being made and I feared there would be trouble. I stepped to the back of the car and asked two colored women if they knew who struck the conductor. One said, "He looked like a colored man," the other said, "I don't know." Then I asked the conductor, in a voice loud enough so that the rest of the car could hear me, whether it was a white or a black man that struck him and why. He said: "It was a white man. I wouldn't let him bring his big drum on the platform, it was too crowded." Having learned this, I turned to two young couples who were still showing much feeling and said, "A white man struck the conductor." The whole car then quieted down, and there was no more feeling.

Most of the difficulties in transportation contacts reported and generally complained of seem to have centered around the first blundering efforts of migrants to adjust themselves to northern city life. The efforts of agencies interested in assisting this adjustment, together with the Negro press, and the intimate criticisms and suggestion for proper conduct of Chicago Negroes, have smoothed down many of the roughnesses of the migrants, and as a result friction from contact in transportation seems to have lessened materially.

E. CONTACTS IN OTHER RELATIONS

Here are included:

I. Contacts in public places, such as restaurants, department stores, theaters, and personal-service places.

II. "Black and tan" resorts, which present a much-criticized association because of the vicious elements of whites and Negroes in contact there.

III. Cultural contacts which indicate associations on a purely intellectual basis.

IV. Contacts in co-operative efforts for race betterment, which includes most of the social organizations working among Negroes.

I. CONTACTS IN PUBLIC PLACES

On the street, in public conveyances, stores, restaurants, and commercial places of amusement, contacts of races and nationalities are unavoidable and have not the supervision that is common in schools or even public amusement places.

Where large numbers of Negroes live there are theaters, restaurants, stores, barber shops, and personal-service places, which are used by Negroes in the proportion in which they predominate in the population of the area. In any or all of these places, however, white persons are served.

The business district along State Street between Twenty-sixth and Forty-seventh, and on the car-line cross-streets, is maintained partly by, and largely for, the Negro residents in the general neighborhood. Since, however, about 50 per cent of the population is white, there are personal-service places which are used almost exclusively by whites. Barber shops are wholly exclusive, and several restaurants attempt to make themselves so. For example:

At Thirty-first Street and Indiana Avenue, in the heart of the Negro residence area, a restaurant proprietor maintains an L-shaped establishment. Fronting on Thirty-first Street is a neatly arranged and well-kept dining-room, with tables for ladies, and a lunch counter with white waiters. Fronting on Indiana Avenue is a narrow, dark dining-room, with a counter served by colored waitresses. It is not kept neatly, and is not so well supplied. Both dining-rooms are served from the kitchen in the corner of the L, and patrons in either dining-room would never suspect that there were two dining-rooms with connection through this kitchen. At the time of the investigation, the dining-rooms had different names.

Negroes entering the Indiana Avenue dining-room are given prompt service. If they enter the Thirty-first Street room they are given indifferent service, are required to wait long and the service given them is reluctant and discourteous.

At another restaurant in the same neighborhood, similar means are used to discourage Negro patronage. Sometimes in addition to long waiting and discourtesy, food is spoiled. For example, egg shells are placed in egg orders, and salt is poured into the food.

In the districts where whites predominate, the measures taken to exclude Negroes are very definite. In a lunchroom near Forty-third Street and Vincennes Avenue, a well-educated, well-appearing young Negro had the following experience:

I went into the restaurant about two o'clock June 13, and sat about four seats from the front at a counter. After about ten minutes the waiter came and asked me to move to a seat at the rear of the counter. I asked him why and he told me he could not serve me where I was sitting. He said the management reserved the right to seat its guests, and pointed to a sign on the wall bearing that notice. I asked him if he could not serve me just as well where I was sitting as on the rear counter. He said maybe he could, but it was a rule of the house not to, and he would not. I left without being served.

Another Negro experience in a lunchroom on Forty-third Street near the Elevated is thus described: "Service given was very poor. When protest was made, the police were called and the young man was arrested for disorderly conduct. The case was dismissed."

Fifty-ninth and Halsted streets: "Service refused in a Swedish café. No witnesses."

Near Berwyn and Broadway (North Side): "Service refused, and investigator ordered out."

In the "Loop," experiences are widely varied. In all of the following cases, carefully selected investigators were sent and asked to report in detail what happened. It is possible to gather large numbers of personal experiences, from any group of Negroes, but as the facts cannot be verified they have not been used. These instances usually go unnoticed by all but the participants, except where the parties offended may secure witnesses among the guests present, which is difficult.

At a large, popular, general restaurant on Randolph Street, two women investigators had this typical experience showing how a manager can refuse service, and still attempt to keep within the law:

Entered about 7:30 P.M. The restaurant was well filled; I counted only six vacant tables. A woman head waitress took us through the main dining-room to the annex, where another head waitress preceded us down the length of the room to a corner table in the rear. There was a vacant table on either side of us. We waited almost a half hour, with no attention, until a couple was seated at the next table. When the waitress brought water to them she also brought water to us. She took the orders for both tables. Mrs. H— ordered steak, salad and tea. I ordered chicken salad and tea. Steak and potatoes were served to the next table in about ten minutes. The waitress came to me and said the chef said he was out of chicken. I ordered steak. After another long period of waiting, she came back and said, "The chef says he is out of small steaks." I asked, "What have you?" She said she would go and see. She did not return, but after about fifteen minutes a man came to our table, put his hands on it, leaned down and said, "Do you want to see me?" Although I suspected he was the manager, he had not said so, and I replied, "Who are you? I don't know anything about you. No, we don't want to see you." He then said, "I am the manager. What do you want?" "I came to be served with dinner." He replied, "We have nothing to serve you." I asked, "Why, what is the reason?" He replied "There is no reason; we haven't anything to serve you." He was evidently cautious to keep within the letter of the law, but was determined that we should not be served. He would give no reason, simply repeating his former statement. We left without further discussion, and without being served.

Mrs. T— says the waitress was courteous, and evidently regretful of the embarrassment of repeated refusal to serve. None of the patrons sitting near made any protest at their presence. It has been her experience that patrons, waitresses, ushers in theaters rarely show any hesitancy in accepting the presence of colored people who are orderly and self-respecting. Almost invariably the disagreeable incidents happen through the management, or through the carrying out of orders.

An interview with the manager of this restaurant was willingly given to a white investigator who later visited the place, and questions were answered freely and carefully. He said he had a number of Negro friends and appreciated the differences in them, as he did in whites. The main points in a long discussion of restaurant management in general, and the particular problem with reference to serving Negroes, he summed up as follows:

In the past five years, only one Negro has been served in this restaurant. She came in with a southern family as maid to a small child. The family was told that she could be served at a table with them, or in a side room, but could not be served at an adjoining table, even with the child. After some discussion, the maid ate at one end of a long table with the child, while the family sat at the other end.

At the time of the recent instance, when the two Negro women came in, the manager was not in the restaurant. From what he was told of the incident, he thinks he should have asked them to come to the office, and explained the situation to them. He had no doubt they would have understood, as he has always found intelligent Negroes readily responsive to the things which might be injurious to their relations with whites.

Before he was manager, a man brought in two Negroes, seemingly to get a basis for a suit and damages. The manager offered to serve them in a side room, but refused service in the main dining-room. They left without being served, and nothing further was heard from them.

In former years he had seen dishes broken in the presence of Negroes after being used in high-grade restaurants where their patronage was not wanted.

Barring Negroes was not personal, he said. A successful restaurant must watch closely the desires of its patrons, and not allow anything to interfere with smooth running. Complaints are made after each appearance of Negroes. He did not know what he would do if Negroes insisted on being served, but was firm that no Negro could be served in the main dining-rooms. He would vary procedure to suit the circumstances.

The following case, illustrative of the witnesses and testimony necessary to a court decision, was tried before Judge Adams, and damages of $100 with costs were awarded:

In August, 1920, Miss Lillian Beale, Negro secretary to Miss Amelia Sears, white, superintendent of the United Charities, went as the guest of her employer to a candy shop and lunch room on Michigan Avenue. They seated themselves and remained for two hours without service. During this time several friends of Miss Sears came in, were served and left, all of them commenting on the apparently deliberate oversight of the party. They remained for some time and left. Suit was brought against the company, supported by Miss Sears and her friends. At the first hearing it was stated that the waitress was ill at a hospital in Cincinnati. The judge, however, was insistent, and she was produced. When placed on the stand she admitted, contrary to the expectations of the management, that she had been ordered by the management not to serve any colored persons at any time. Miss Beale was awarded and collected damages of $100 and costs.

Eight months later, in July, 1921, a test was made of the same restaurant. Two Negro women went together to the restaurant, and a white woman observer went along to watch what might happen. Their reports agree and are as follows:

Time, one o'clock. Restaurant 50 per cent filled. Mrs. L— and Mrs. S— came in and seated themselves at a table for two near the center of the room. Waitress followed usual routine of bringing water, taking order, etc. Service of a table d' hôte luncheon was prompt and courteous. No inattention was observed, nor any disturbance on part of neighbors. Two white women came in and seated themselves at the next table, though there were several others vacant.

Two other Negro women and a white observer were sent to another restaurant operating under the same firm name. It was reported by the white observer as follows:

Restaurant two thirds filled—12 o'clock. Mostly women patrons, though a fair number of men alone, and of couples use this restaurant. Mrs. T— and her friend came in through the long passage by the candy counter, and crossed to a table for two in the middle of the room. The manager, who is a young women of considerable poise and ability, came at once and gave them water, took their order, and later served them. Two young white women at an adjoining table moved, but it may have been because they were sitting with strangers and preferred a table for two. After finishing my lunch, I joined Mrs. T— and her friend, and the manager kept us under observation, but nothing was said.

In a subsequent interview with the manager at the general office of this chain of tea rooms cautiously worded replies were made to questions, with constant reiteration of the statement, "But you know we must serve them." In general it was said:

Negro patrons are infrequent, and there has been no noticeable increase. After many cases, complaint is made by white patrons, either in person or by letter, to the effect that if the tea room caters to Negroes, the white patrons will no longer use it. They had never known of a case of objectionable conduct but whites simply objected to their presence.

No instructions were given waitresses, but each case was handled by the head waitress as it occurred. Some girls made no objections to waiting on Negroes, and some refused to do it, but each attitude is individual, and not from instructions. No question that Negro patronage would hurt any high-grade place, as white patrons would be likely to leave. Rights did not enter into the problem—simply a matter of profitable business.

Interviews with managers of tea rooms in department stores brought out uniformity of attitude and of practice, as is shown in the following reports:

The manager of one tea room is a young woman of considerable experience. She was emphatic in saying that Negroes were not wanted, and that every effort would be made to discourage their coming. Considerable personal feeling was manifested in her statements.

Not enough Negroes can afford to pay the prices in high-grade restaurants to make them a real problem, and stray cases are handled as they appear. The effort was made to make them feel uncomfortable so they would not return. Slow service, indifferent attention were given, but there was no overcharging, and no spoiling of food.

Had never observed any objectionable conduct. Objections of white patrons was only reason. Especially difficult in summer, when many southern white people come to Chicago as a summer resort.

Waitresses are largely young married women with spare time. Manager finds them more unwilling than regular waitresses to give service to Negroes.

At another tea room practically the same statements were made, and the following instance was given: "Last winter a telephone reservation was made for a large luncheon party—about forty. When the group arrived, it was a club of colored women. Screens were placed around the tables, and luncheon served. A rule was then made and enforced that no telephone reservations would be made."

Following are reports from investigators seeking to learn at which restaurants, tea rooms, and lunch counters, service would be given to Negroes:

We had been shopping down town, and went into ——'s on State Street to get a light lunch. There were vacant tables and we sat down. No one came to wait on us. After waiting until several persons who had come in after us had been served, I went to one of the men who appeared to be the manager, and asked him why we were not served. He did not respond very cordially, but sent a girl. We ordered several dishes from the card, and were told that they were "just out." Although orders were being served, the girl stated that they were "just out" of everything we ordered. To cover our embarrassment, we practically begged her to serve us cups of chocolate. She gave us the chocolate and our check; we paid it and left.

Mrs. T— and Mrs. — were served promptly and without incident in a well-known candy store in the shopping district on State Street. Mrs. T— says that for many years this place has been known for its courtesy to colored people. Soon after it was opened, about World's Fair year, Mrs. —, a Negro woman, was refused service by a waitress. She reported the fact to the owner, who investigated, and finding her statement correct, discharged the waitress. He made the rule that every patron was entitled to prompt, courteous service, and that discharge would follow any justified complaint. Although the store has been under other management for many years, later adding light luncheons to candy and soft drinks, the tradition has continued. Mrs. T— says neither waitress nor patrons paid any attention to the serving of two colored women.

This case, involving three races, was reported from one of the Chinese restaurants on South Wabash Avenue:

About 7:00 P.M. we entered a Chinese restaurant. There were three or four white couples eating in the main dining-room, and two in booths. A Japanese waiter ushered us toward the furthest booth at the rear of the room. "I prefer sitting in the main dining-room," I said. He replied, "I can't serve you here." "Why?" "These seats are reserved. I will serve you in there [pointing to the booth] but not out here." We left.

One of the largest chains of cafeterias in Chicago is noted for the fairness of its treatment of Negroes, but even here there are exceptions. One of the Commission's staff observed two incidents within a short time in the same cafeteria of this system and reported them as follows:

Just in line before me was a small, quiet, well-dressed colored woman. She passed the checker, carried her tray to an unoccupied table, and then counted her check. She took her tray back to the checker, and made complaint of overcharge. The checker did not recount, or explain, simply saying, "That is our price." The woman went back to her table, ate, paid, and went out without further protest.

A few nights later, I noticed two young, well-mannered colored girls at a nearby table. As I went out I met the manager and said to him, "Do many Negroes come here to eat?" He said, "No, occasionally they come in, but they don't come back more than once, or at most twice." "How do you manage it?" "Well, under the law, we can't refuse to let them eat, but we can charge them any price we like. The first time we charge them enough to keep them from coming back. Then if they persist and come again, as soon as they go down the line, I see to it that something is put in their food which makes it taste bad—salt or Epsom salts. They never come back after that." After a pause he added, "You know we are within the law. We can't have them coming here—it would ruin our trade."

In the inexpensive restaurants on the edge of the "Loop," various practices are followed, as indicated by the following reports:

Miss B. S. met a friend and went into the —— Cafeteria on Lake Street, near State, upstairs. They were served, but the waiter put screens around their table while they were eating.

In May, 1921, I went to a lunchroom on Van Buren Street to get a lunch at noon. Six or seven men were at the counter, and were served as fast as they came in. Finally all seats were filled and three waiters were doing nothing, so I asked to be served. The waiter pretended not to hear me, then said roughly, "What do you want?" I said, "I do not know until I get a bill of fare." He pitched it at me and I asked for some baked beans. He stuck his head through the chef's window and gave my order. He brought me a plate on which were fourteen beans, and one small roll. I asked for a glass of water and he brought me a half-glass. I asked for butter (which had been served with two rolls to white patrons) and he said it would cost me a nickel. He said with emphasis, "It will cost *you* a nickel." I said, "You give me the butter, and then watch me and see if I pay for it." I asked for some pie and he gave me a piece about half the size he was serving the others. Then he said again, "Remember that butter will cost you a nickel extra." I said, "I won't pay it." He said, "You will pay for that dinner before you eat a bite of it." I said, "No chance, because I am not going to pay you at all, either before or after I eat. After I have finished I will pay the cashier at the desk." He looked at me hard and I kept on eating. Then he threw me down a check for 25 cents. I said, "Brother, you are wrong. My bill is only 20 cents. Your menu says beans are 15 cents and pie is 5 cents, and you gave me only one roll when to all of the others you served two." He said again, "I told you your butter would cost you a nickel." I said, "Now, you watch me right close when I go out and see if I pay for it." I told the cashier that my check called for 25 cents when it should be 20, "beans 15, pie 5, and if you can make 25 out of that all right." She said, "You know I have to collect what the check calls for, or else make good myself." I told her I appreciated her position but would not pay 25 cents for a 20-cent lunch. Then my waiter stepped up with an iron tap in his hand,

and said, "I told you that butter would cost you a nickel, and now you pay it or else ——." I said, I will "else," and laid down twenty cents and walked out. At the door he gave me a push but did not strike me.

The white proprietor of a drug-store in a residence neighborhood volunteered this story to a member of the Commission's staff:

Several years ago, there was a fine old colored man who used to come in frequently to buy drugs, supplies, etc. One day he came in with his wife, sat down at one of the little tables, and asked for soda water. My clerk refused to serve them, and the idea occurred to me that I would serve them myself in such a way that there would be no possibility that they would ever come back. I compounded a vile concoction and served it to them. They tasted it, paid for it, thanked me, and went out without making any complaint. I have never got over feeling mean about it. I not only humiliated them, and insulted them, but I cheated them out of their money.

An instance of unusual absence of friction in contacts under conditions which might be expected to produce it was given by a white woman who visited a restaurant patronized by many whites and Negroes:

In talking with Mr. O— he asked me, "Would you consider it possible that you would voluntarily go into a restaurant and eat your lunch where you might have a Negro sitting on the next stool, or perhaps one on either side of you at a table?" I answered promptly, "No, I can't imagine it." He said, "A year ago I wouldn't have imagined such a thing possible myself, but now I do it quite frequently. There is a restaurant across the street from my office, right here in the heart of the Negro district, which a few years ago was a very good one, with regular table service, excellent food, and all the rest. Last year it was changed into a sort of a cafeteria, with a lunch counter down one side, and some tables. You get your knife and fork, go to the serving counter, and a man gives you on a plate whatever you order. The other day I found myself between two colored men, and took a good look at the restaurant. There is absolutely no disturbance, or even consciousness of any reason for disturbance."

Today I decided I would try it myself. The restaurant has no frills; it is simply an eating-place. I chose a corner seat at a table, because I could see all over the room. As I sat down, a courteous arm reached across the table to shove back the used dishes. I looked up to say "thank you," and found a good-looking young colored man opposite. No further attention was paid to me, nor was there any consciousness in his face, other than courtesy. In a few minutes, two young white truck drivers took the other places at my table. They were in working jeans, and except that the color was blue instead of khaki, looked just like the young soldiers in transport service who used to come into my canteen in France. At the next table was a quietly dressed young colored girl eating her lunch in a business-like way. A young white father brought in his little daughter. At the long lunch counter were neighborhood business men, white and colored, some professional men, each taking whatever stool happened to be vacant. Occasionally a truck driver or roughly dressed working man came in. Even the white dandy, immaculate in linen and with a cane hooked over his arm, took his cup of coffee to the counter and sat between a laborer and a business man.

In theaters, as in restaurants, there are petty evasions of the law, disagreeable encounters, and small but insistent snobberies. A colored investigator reported the result of a test of the purchase of tickets for a play which had had a long run, as follows:

On July 5 I went down to the —— theater and asked the ticket seller if I could get two seats for Thursday or Friday night between the third and ninth rows, center. She hunted out two seats in the ninth row for Thursday. I said, "If you have them I would prefer them for Friday." I asked the price, paid her, and she thanked me.

Friday, I went to the theater, and handed the doorman my tickets. He tore off the coupons, and directed me to the main-floor door. The lady usher seated us three rows from the back on the aisle. I counted and found that I was in the seventeenth row. I went to the usher and said, "I beg your pardon, but you seated me in the wrong place." She took the coupons, said, "Wait a second," and started out with them. I followed to see that she did not exchange my coupons. She went to the lobby and talked with the manager. He looked at me and said, "Well, seat them; there is nothing else to do now." She went back, gave my coupons to another usher, who asked her if I was to be seated in the seats the coupons called for. She answered, "I guess so." Then we were shown to the correct seats. There was no protest from those around us.

The manager of this theater was later interviewed. He had been in Chicago only a few months and was not at all interested in the general question of race relations, but was decided in his opinion that the attendance of Negroes in any high-class theater was not desirable. His views were about as follows:

Not many Negroes buy seats down stairs. Usually the ticket seller gives them tickets in the balcony or gallery and on the side aisles. Usually had complaints from white patrons if they found a Negro seated near them, especially if there were ladies in the party. It was not that the conduct of the Negroes was objectionable, but their mere presence was objectionable. If Negroes present tickets for the best main-floor seats, ushers try to put them in less conspicuous places. If they insist on taking their seats as shown on tickets, nothing can be done. If white patrons object, every effort is made to change their seats. Usual objection is offensive odor and proximity.

In making the study of theaters, certain tests were established. A Negro would ask at the box-office for seats on the main floor within certain rows and on the aisle. In the preceding report it will be noted that seats were sold readily, but some difficulty was found in using them. In the next report, conditions were reversed:

Mr. J—, Negro, asked for tickets, and was told that there was nothing on the main floor further in front than the twenty-third row. Miss H—, white, who was standing by him as he made the request, and heard the answer, moved up to the window and was immediately and without any remark, sold tickets in the seventeenth row on the aisle.

These tickets were presented by Mr. and Mrs. S—, Negroes. They report:

We arrived at 8:15, five minutes before the opening of the performance. The ticket taker tore off our stubs and returned them to us without any hesitancy. The ushers, who were women, glanced at the seat numbers and directed us to our seats, which were in a very conspicuous location on the first floor. They were in the seventeenth row, on the aisle. The people around us, even the ones immediately next to us, were not in the least concerned at our presence. The treatment accorded us in general could not have been surpassed.

A different report comes from another "Loop" theater, which has always been rather conservative in the standard of plays which it presents:

My husband and I wished to see a play at —— Theater, and bought seats several days in advance that we might have a choice. When we were shown to our seats, however, we were surprised to find that our tickets called for seats in the gallery, and in a corner which did not afford a view, and made them more than undesirable. We noticed that there were several vacant seats in the balcony, also on the first floor. My husband went to the box office and tried to exchange the seats. The ticket seller refused to make the exchange and also became insulting in his remarks to us. Afterwards we made the attempt to secure seats on the first floor of this same theater several days in advance of the performance which we wished to attend. We were told there were no seats on the first floor which we could get.

A contrasting experience follows:

On Tuesday I went to the ——Theater, and applied for two tickets on the main floor, center aisle, between the third and eleventh rows. The ticket seller stated politely that he had two tickets in the ninth row on the left. When we attended the performance, nothing unusual occurred. Other patrons made no comment, and in no way could we observe any objection made to our presence. There were no other Negroes at the performance.

Reports of investigators indicate that the managers of movies are convinced that their main floors, at least, should be guarded against Negroes. In most of the commercial amusement places, Negroes seldom have difficulty if they are willing to sit in the balcony, though attempts are frequently made to seat them on the aisles next to the walls, even when there are center seats empty. It is rare that any report is obtained of objections by white patrons to the actual presence of Negroes when they are well-mannered, well-dressed, and appreciative auditors.

As a rule movie theaters do not sell reserved seats, general admission entitling any patron to any seat in the house. But the following detailed report of the experience of two intelligent, well-dressed, quiet-mannered Negro women at a new movie theater on State Street is typical:

Purchased tickets, and entered the large lobby which extends across the front of the house. From this lobby there are closed doors at the entrance of several aisles, so that patrons are directed by ushers to different aisles, supposedly wherever there are vacant seats. We followed directions, and went to the extreme left of the lobby.

We opened the door, and the usher in charge of this aisle started down toward the front to show us seats. We saw at once that the narrow section of seats next to the wall was empty except for one colored woman sitting about the middle of the section. Instead of following the usher down the aisle, and taking seats indicated to the right of this section, we turned through a row of empty seats on the left-hand section, and sat next to a woman in the aisle seat. This put us two rows from the rear in a side middle section, instead of in the section which seemed to be reserved for colored patrons, next to the wall. As the usher returned to his station he said, "We have some lovely seats in the balcony; wouldn't you prefer sitting there?" He was courteous, and I thanked him, telling him that we were quite satisfied with the seats we had taken.

Later, seeing two vacant seats further front in the center section which gave us a much better view we decided to take them and see what would happen. As we rose, the usher tried to block us by putting his hands on the back of the seat in front, and saying, "I am sorry that you can't take those seats." I brushed by him and took one of the seats. He tried the same thing with Mrs. H—, and she also brushed by and joined me. There were scattered vacant seats both in the section we left and the one to which we moved. We remained until the end of the show without embarrassment.

The manager of this theater has had many years of experience in Chicago, and was quite willing to discuss race contacts. Nothing in his words would indicate any strong prejudice against Negroes, even when expressing his conviction that they should keep to places intended especially for them. He said, in substance:

Not many Negroes buy tickets—perhaps ten or a dozen a day. An effort is made to seat them in one section of the house, preferably the balcony, to which they are directed by ushers. Reason is the complaint by white patrons who object to sitting next to them for an hour, or hour and a half. Offensive odor reason usually given. White patrons often complain to manager as they go out if Negro has been sitting near them.

Conduct of Negroes is not often objectionable—runs about the same as all patrons. Occasionally one tries to "start something." Recently two Negroes came to manager in crowded lobby after they had attended the show and objected to their seats on the balcony to which they had been sent by ushers, saying there were vacant seats on the main floor. Wanted to know why they were discriminated against. Manager did not want an argument in the presence of other patrons, and told them that as they had seen the show, heard the music, and shared everything with other patrons, he did not see they had any real cause for complaint. Called attention to the notice printed on almost every theater ticket in some form or other to the effect that the management reserves the right to revoke the license granted in the sale of the ticket, by refunding the money paid.

The same two women bought tickets the next day and attended a movie in an older and very popular "Loop" theater. They reported that they had no difficulty of any kind.

On a test made of a new and popular movie theater in an outlying section the investigator reported:

There were four of us in the party on June 5. We were told by the usher that there were no seats on the first floor, and that we would find seats in the first balcony. I think he was right, for there were white people also sent to the balcony. We were ushered in promptly, but another usher met us and said, "Right on up to the second balcony." We said we preferred seats in the first balcony, and walked by him. He went and got two more ushers and stood in front of us to prevent us from going into the first balcony, insisting that there were no seats there. One of the young ladies stepped around the usher, and saw three vacant seats. She called them to the attention of the usher, and he then said he meant there were no seats for four. Two of our party took those seats, and the other two waited about twenty minutes till they could get the seats they wanted. After getting into the first balcony, we saw vacant seats in at least four rows, two, three, and four seats together into which we might quietly have gone had the usher been courteous.

On June 18, 1920, a well-known Negro employed in the City Hall was denied admission to a movie theater at Halsted and Sixty-third streets. There is a small but long-established Negro colony about a mile west of this location.

In business places of various kinds, contacts are determined largely by the kind of service offered. Department-store managers questioned by investigators concerning their Negro patronage and the use of Negro girls as clerks, stated that the public had definite preferences, and probably would not willingly tolerate Negroes either as patrons or as clerks. In stores selling general merchandise, courteous treatment is, as a rule, accorded to Negro patrons, although there are occasional annoying incidents. The attitude then taken is determined by the standing and influence of the Negroes discriminated against. For instance:

At one of the largest department stores, two Negro women, both school teachers, were refused service in the basement shoe department. The clerks refused to fit shoes for them. A Negro alderman became interested in this case, and because of refusal of service, canceled his account.

The wife of a prominent Negro attorney went into a State Street candy store and was flatly refused service. Her husband brought suit and got damages.

Miss V— was refused service at a large State Street department store by one of the clerks. The manager was interviewed and the clerk reprimanded and transferred. On the second visit, Miss V— received attention.

In residence areas which are largely white, certain stores practice a peculiar subversion of the law in the effort to regulate contacts. A Negro resident of Woodlawn stated that his seven-year-old daughter had gone to the store to purchase goods for a costume to wear at a school entertainment. She was given material for which she had not asked, which she did not want, and for which she was overcharged. Frightened at the manners of the clerk, she took it. When it was returned, the clerk was extremely abusive, and told her that colored people were not wanted in the store. The little girl had, according to her parents, made a mistake in entering the store. Her parents were acquainted with the attitude of the management and avoided the place. In the following reports, there is evident the sense of injustice felt by both whites and Negroes concerned in the contacts:

Miss S. T— wrote a prominent musical college and made arrangements for taking the summer normal-training courses. Her tuition fee was accepted, and the classes arranged. On her arrival, the manager received the balance of her money for the entire course, but told her the classes she wanted were full, and she would have to take private lessons with another teacher. The teacher of the desired classes told her the manager had not been frank, and that he feared the objection of southern white girls in the classes. Miss T— made repeated attempts to get into the classes, but each time was told to apply again. This she did until it was too late to catch up with her back work. Other pupils were given prompt admission to the classes.

Two investigators were instructed to go to a public restroom in a large office building on State Street where there are many small shops selling women's wearing apparel. Their experience follows:

On July 6, at one P.M. with Mrs. H—, I visited the public restroom in the —— building. It is on the eleventh floor, on the main hall, and the door to the suite of rooms stood open. On one side of the entrance hall there is a small room used for a shoe-shining, with a Negro in attendance. Next on the same side is a large lavatory. Facing the outside door is the entrance to the restroom proper, which is large enough for ten or fifteen women, and is fitted up with wicker chairs, lounge, table, etc.

As we were about to enter the restroom, the woman in charge stood with her arm across the door, and said, "You are not to go in there; you may go into the lavatory." We asked why, and she said, "Those are the orders of the office." We went into the restroom, and she did not offer any opposition, but a little later came to us and said, "You are not allowed in here. You will have to see the manager."

I asked the attendant for the manager's name and room number, which she gave me. I related the incident to him. He told me that the attendant had informed me correctly, that the eleventh-floor restroom was reserved for "white folks" and that "colored folks" were not allowed to use it. They could use a restroom on the nineteenth floor set aside for colored employees of the building, and for any "colored folks" who might come into the building. He said it was one of the "iron-clad rules of the man who owned the building," and that "the attendant had it down in black and white."

Difficulties of this sort which confront Negroes and the efforts by Negroes to share equal treatment in public accommodations as well as the experiences met with when cases reach the courts were commented upon by Judge Cook, of the municipal court, in testimony before the Commission. He said:

During the earlier part of 1918 I sat in what was known as the criminal jury branch. That is the branch to which were assigned all criminal cases in the municipal court where the defendants demanded a trial by jury and were not tried at the police station. Among them were cases involving violations of what is known as the civil-rights law, where a colored man had a druggist or the proprietor of a moving picture or legitimate theater arrested for refusing to serve him soda water or refreshments at the drug store or to furnish him admission by ticket at a movie or legitimate theater, or if he did furnish him admission by selling him a ticket, limiting the ticket which he would sell to some undesirable portion of the house or to the gallery and not to the main floor, claiming that the theater was crowded downstairs and that there were no seats.

I suppose I tried during the early part of 1918 and the summer of 1919 probably a half-dozen of those civil-rights cases. In every one of them that I tried, there was virtually a clear case against the defendant. The jury in every instance was practically a white jury, or may have had one or two colored men. Notwithstanding that I gave very positive and clear instructions as to what the law was—to wit, that they were entitled to equal rights and privileges in public places and that if the jury believed from the evidence that the plaintiff was not accorded such right, there was a violation of the law and the defendant should be punished, and after elaborate argument by counsel for both the prosecution and the defendant (and by parenthesis I may say in all of these cases the state's attorney prosecuted vigorously), the jury, notwithstanding the plain evidence and the instructions of the court, went out and in about such time as it would take them to sign the verdict and return to court, would bring in a verdict of "Not Guilty."

Of course in the criminal court in a case of that kind, the jury is the judge of both the law and the fact. Therefore, I was not in a position to grant a new trial. The white jury simply say that law was not the law in Illinois or they would not convict under such circumstances, and having once acquitted the man the court and the state were without any remedy. Now I have always thought that was unjust.

It was his opinion that those Negroes who did bring cases into court made a mistake in prosecuting them from a criminal standpoint. It seemed to be, in his opinion, hopeless for Negroes to assert their rights through the criminal courts.

Another judge of long experience in the Chicago courts expressed the view that few Negroes brought in cases involving discrimination. He thought that especially the better class of Negroes would not bring them because of the unpleasantness involved and because the damages obtained in most cases would not pay the attorney's charges. "Most Negroes," he said, "have found out by experience what the actual feeling is and act accordingly, trying to avoid unpleasant experiences as much as possible. Although there would be no trouble in getting a verdict in any clear case, the amount obtained would not compensate for the trouble involved." He did not believe that any jury would convict a white defendant on a criminal charge of discrimination. A prominent Negro attorney, who formerly held a responsible state office, in giving his general experience said:

In cases involving only Negroes on each side, both judges and juries will act squarely between them; in cases involving white defendants and Negro plaintiffs, the tendency is to give considerably less credibility or weight to Negro testimony; in cases involving Negro defendants and white plaintiffs, the tendency is to give more weight to white testimony.

He stated further that in discrimination cases, where the law had been clearly violated, there was usually no difficulty in getting a verdict and damages for $25 and up, but that he did not care much about handling such cases and Negroes did not care to push them, because they were unpleasant and expensive.

II. "BLACK AND TAN" RESORTS

The intimate association of Negroes and whites in the cabarets of the South Side has occasioned frequent and heated protests. Negro men are there seen with white women and white men with Negro women. Although mixed couples constitute somewhat less than 10 per cent of the patronage, this mingling is used to characterize all of the association there. These resorts, with their liquor selling and coarse and vulgar dancing, are highly dangerous to morals and established law and order, and a nuisance to the neighborhoods in which they are located. They are used as amusement places, both by white couples living in other sections of the city and by Negro couples who live near them. In fact, although many of the resorts are patronized by an equal number of whites and Negroes, the actual mixed couples are few. The habitués of these resorts are usually of an irresponsible type of pleasure seekers, and frequently they are vicious and immoral. Newspapers and several of the civic agencies have violently criticized these places as a menace, but in their attacks the emphasis has usually been shifted from the menace to morals to that of arousing sentiment against the mingling of races. The police on numbers of occasions have been urged to close the places in which this form of association took place. In most cases they have not done so, stating as their reason that, although mingling was undesirable, there was no law prohibiting such contacts, and that evidence of violations of such laws as those concerning liquor selling or decency would be necessary to warrant their closing.

During 1920 the Negro press began a series of attacks on violations of law and against the immoral resorts in the Negro residence areas, including the so-called "black and tan" cabarets, some of which were the most notorious violators. This was followed by similar attacks from the white local newspapers. The emphasis in the white papers, however, was on the race mingling. An extract from one of the articles in a white paper is given:

"LID" A JOKE AS PEKIN SHIMMIES DEFIANCE OF LAW

LIQUOR, SIRENS, JAZZ, RACE RAINBOW RIOT IN CAFÉ

"Lawless liquor," sensuous "shimmy," solicitous sirens, wrangling waiters, all the tints of the racial rainbow, black and tan and white, dancing, drinking, singing, early Sunday morning at the Pekin café, 2700 South State Street. . . . .

"BLACK AND TAN AND WHITE"

The crowd began to arrive. In came a mighty black man with two white girls. A scarred white man entered with three girls, two young and painted, the other merely painted.

Two well dressed youths hopped up the stairs with two timid girls. Seven young men—they looked like back o' the Yards—came with two women, one heavy footed, the other laughing hysterically.

Two fur-coated "high yaller" girls romped up with a slender white man. An attorney gazed happily on the party through horn rimmed glasses. The waiters called, shouted, whistled when each party arrived—a full table meant big tips.

At one o'clock the place was crowded. Meanwhile a syncopating colored man had been vamping cotton field blues on the piano. A brown girl sang. . . . . All the tables were filled at two o'clock, black men with white girls, white men with yellow girls, old, young, all filled with the abandon brought about by illicit whisky and liquor music. . . . . The Pekin is again the Pekin of years ago. Only more so.

The reply of a Negro newspaper to the series of articles in the white press on these resorts expresses the reactions of Negroes to this view:

BLACK AND TANS AND RACE RIOTS

It is an established conviction that the so-called "intermingling of races" in the cabarets of the South Side is a fruitful source of riots. To those whose minds are bent in this belief, the fact that no riot has ever yet started in one of them is of little importance. Men believe, as a rule, most readily what they earnestly wish to believe. It matters little how absurd the proposition, if it expresses a desire they will make of it an everlasting verity even though it costs them the kingdom of heaven. And so it happens that we are told that the Abyssinians burned a flag and almost precipitated a race riot because they happened be to standing in front of the Entertainers' Café where Negroes and white persons dance on the same floor and occasionally together.

To carry further these deductions the United Cigar Store also should be closed because one of the fanatics shot into it and killed a white man. The connection of both of these places with the incident is just about the same, if not a little worse for the cigar store.

The fury back of complaints like that, for instance, of one Mr. Farwell of the Law and Order League invites suspicion. In all seriousness what is this crime of association for which Mr. Farwell would have these places closed? If demoralization of character is more certain in mixed places or liquor sold more openly can it be urged that race contact is responsible? It cannot. The sore point is the contact. These places are located in the most densely populated Negro neighborhoods. Attendance is voluntary and so is whatever amount of association that follows. There is no manhandling of white innocents to force them into the society of Negroes. Neither do Negroes go snooping around the high lights of the West or North sides seeking white companionship. But that is not the point. When this antipathy is analyzed it becomes apparent that there is a well defined intention to prove that any relationship varying too sharply from the master and servant type is wrong. It is the yelp of tribal jealousy. It is the gaunt denial of a fallacious orthodoxy which proclaims that certain instincts will keep certain persons eternally apart. It is that complex of emotion into which all discussions of race relations resolve themselves.

The resentment of Negroes at the poorly veiled thrusts is perfectly justifiable. However unwholesome to morals these places may be they refuse to join in the chorus of hate against amusement places just because they put no restraints upon their associations. They feel that they are human and at liberty to seek pleasure if they so desire where contacts are mutually agreeable. Those who do not care for this contact will stay away. Because a white woman will dance with a colored man or a white man with a colored woman there is no argument that a riot will follow. Persons who dance together are not so likely to fight as persons who stand at a distance and call each other bad names

Rationally considered there is no ground for these contentions. They are insulting. If danger is ahead for the city when the Irish and Italians visit the same places of amusement or the Swedes and Lithuanians, then some thought will be given by Negroes to eliminating their dangers. There is no point to calling the patrol because Mr. Farwell and the *News* think it complicates the race question.

This paper condemned all of these places because they were nuisances to the neighborhood—the blacks, the black and tans and the whites—it did not by this condemnation imply that color affects morals.

III. CULTURAL CONTACTS

Contacts of whites and Negroes in institutions of learning, general cultural agencies, and meetings ordinarily involve no friction and are frequently directly beneficial to race relations. Many Negroes visit and use the public libraries. In fact, instances of objections on the part of the public in this institution appear to be extremely few. In the reading-rooms Negroes sit where they wish, and no objections to their presence are noted. At a branch library on Oakwood Boulevard over 70 per cent of the patronage is of Negroes, and, the director says, very cordial relations exist. The civil-service system has made a number of Negroes eligible for positions in the direct public-service branches of the city government. No apparent difficulties or objections have resulted.

The University of Chicago and Northwestern University have for many years had Negro students. There were in 1921 more than sixty at the University of Chicago, and, although many southern white students attend, there have been no conspicuous difficulties resulting from the associations. On the contrary, certain individual Negroes have been very popular with the student body. During the 1920 football season two Negroes were members of the football squad, and for several years the favorite of the "track" was Binga Dismond, a Negro runner.

There is no Negro member of the City Club or of the Woman's City Club, although the question of admitting Negroes has occasionally been discussed. The Chicago Woman's Club has two Negro members, one for more than fifteen years. Negroes, however, have been welcomed to meetings and in some instances have themselves held meetings there.

A few white churches have several Negro members, usually of long standing. There are instances of white churches accepting particular Negro members, with some apprehension that they might bring friends. The Catholic and Christian Science churches welcome the presence of Negroes at their services.

There is no Christian Science church exclusively for Negroes, and several hundred Negroes attend the various services of this church.

Many of the more definitely intellectual agencies like the Chicago Ethical Society, the Chicago Rational Society, and the Sunday Evening Club have regular Negro attendance. At the Chicago Rational Society one of the young hostesses is a Negro.

In these forms of contact it is seldom, if ever, that Negroes are discourteously received. This may be due to the relatively high class of whites and Negroes who share these associations.

IV.   CONTACTS IN CO-OPERATIVE EFFORTS FOR RACE BETTERMENT

Most of the important social organizations and agencies of the city which aim definitely at the improvement of the Negro group have mixed boards of control and supervision. The philanthropy, business ability, and influence of white members is combined with the influence of Negro members and their intelligent understanding of their own group problems.

The Young Men's Christian Association, the Young Women's Christian Association, the Chicago Urban League, Community Service, the National Association for the Advancement of Colored People, and the Inter-racial Committee organized by the Chicago Woman's Club are examples of this form of joint effort. The sentiments of both groups in contact may be discussed and, on the basis of represented group conditions and sentiments, programs are formulated and carried out. This association and exchange of sentiment provide a means of breaking down the isolation between the groups and at the same time offer a means of extending the representative thought of Negroes through their white associates to circles in which contacts are either prohibited or restricted by custom and tradition.

CHAPTER VII

CRIME AND VICIOUS ENVIRONMENT

The crime rate of Negroes is so largely controlled by a tangle of predisposing circumstances that it is hardly possible to isolate and measure its factors. The most important element is the general lawlessness, crime, and vice in the whole population, irrespective of race.

I. GENERAL CRIME SITUATION

During 1919 there were 330 homicides in Chicago. In 1920, in addition to 162 murders, 559 persons were slain by automobiles, largely through carelessness. According to the Chicago Crime Commission's report for 1920 there are 10,000 professional criminals in Chicago, and the annual loss from larcenies, robberies, and burglaries aggregates $12,000,000. Chicago pays a higher rate for burglary insurance than any other American city.

Crime conditions in Chicago are even worse than is indicated by these figures, which are based on incomplete police records. In 1919 the police records showed 1,731 burglaries or persons arrested for burglaries, while *Bulletin No. 9* of the Chicago Crime Commission reported 5,509 burglaries during the first eleven months. During the same period the police records showed 1,975 robberies or persons arrested for robbery, while the Crime Commission bulletin listed 2,470 robberies. This bulletin says:

An investigation in August, 1919, to determine whether all crimes were being reported from the Eleventh Precinct and the Englewood precinct showed that in forty instances burglaries and robberies committed during the ninety days preceding had not been reported. A detailed statement of these offenses was prepared giving the victim's names, addresses, date and amount of loss, and presented to the general superintendent of police. The list was checked by the departmental inspector and found correct.

Another investigation by the Crime Commission showed that in one month a certain police captain reported only thirty-seven of the 141 criminal complaints made to him for his district.

In his book, *Crime in America and the Police*, Raymond B. Fosdick wrote (1920):

London in 1916, with a population of seven and a quarter million, had nine premeditated murders. Chicago, one-third the size of London, in the same period had 105, *nearly twelve times London's total*. In 1916 Chicago with its 2,500,000 people had twenty more murders than the whole of England and Wales with their 38,000,000. The Chicago murders during the year totalled one more than London during the five-year period, 1910–14 inclusive.

In 1917 Chicago had ten more murders than the whole of England and Wales, and four more murders than all England, Wales, and Scotland. In 1918 Chicago had fourteen more murders than England and Wales, and in 1919 the number of murders in Chicago was almost exactly six times the number committed in London.

Chicago in 1916 had 532 more burglaries than London; in 1917, 3,459 more; in 1918, 866 more, and in 1919, 2,146 more. In 1918, for example, Chicago had twenty-two robberies for every robbery in London, and fourteen robberies for every robbery in England and Wales.

Chicago's arrests for 1917 exceeded London's by 61,874.

Thefts of automobiles reported in 1919: New York, 5,527, Chicago 4,316. . . . . London, 290, Liverpool, 10. Comparative statistics as to the number of automobiles in English and American cities are impossible to obtain.

It is apparent that this reign of violence and lawlessness must have a potent effect upon the crime rate of Negroes in Chicago.

II. PREVALENT IMPRESSIONS REGARDING NEGRO CRIME

In its inquiry the Commission met the following current beliefs among whites in regard to the Negro criminal:

That the Negro is more prone than the white to commit sex crimes, particularly rape; that he commits a disproportionate number of crimes involving felonious cuttings and slashings; that the recent migrant from the South is more likely to offend than the Negro who has resided longer in the North; and that Negroes willingly tolerate vice and vicious conditions in the midst of their residence districts. These and similar impressions are compared with the facts as found by the Commission.

III. CRIMINAL STATISTICS

In its effort to secure information regarding Negro crime the Commission sought the only available records kept of all crimes—the police records, especially the annual report of the Department of Police. On examination these records were found to be of questionable value for any accurate presentation of Negro crime, or, in fact, of general crime. In 1913 the City Council Committee on Crime made a study of crimes in Chicago and encountered the same difficulty. Says the report of this Committee: "The police and criminal judicial statistics in Chicago are wholly incomplete and are not even assembled or published by any authority." Further commenting on this inadequacy, it says:

Unfortunately, there is in Illinois no central bureau of criminal statistics through which statistics from the police department, the courts, the jails, prisons, and the probation department are collected and correlated. A state bureau of criminal statistics does exist on our statute books, for, by a law approved June 11, 1912, the State Charities Commission was directed to establish such a bureau with the secretary of the Commisson as director in charge. This proposed bureau was charged with the duty of collecting and publishing annually the statistics of Illinois relating to crime, and all courts of Illinois, police magistrates, justices of the peace, clerks of all courts of record, sheriffs, keepers of all places of detention for crime or misdemeanors or violations of the criminal statutes are to "furnish said bureau annually such information on request as it may require in compiling such statistics." Up to the present time, however, owing chiefly to the fact that no appropriation has been made to cover the expenses of this work, no steps have been taken by the executive secretary of the Commission towards putting this law into effect. Moreover, there has never been in Chicago any attempt at an annual "stock-taking" in which the statistics furnished by the various departments and agencies dealing with the problem of crime might be brought together and examined with the hope of determining how far the problem is being adequately met.

Because there has been no systematic handling of criminal statistics, no method has been developed for accurately measuring the prevalence of crime. The Crime Commission expressed its difficulty here in this manner:

It is very important to note that the number of arrests is not synonymous with number of crimes, among others reasons because (1) a large number of persons may be arrested for complicity in a single crime; (2) many innocent persons are arrested through misapprehension and later discharged; and (3) the vast majority of arrests are for petty offenses that are not serious enough to be called "crimes" at all. Some consideration should be given to the question of "new crime." When laws are passed creating new offenses, there may be an increase in arrests without any corresponding increase in criminality. As a matter of fact, however, the new offenses are chiefly those involving misdemeanors and violations of ordinances. New felonies are rarely created. In Chicago the police classification does, however, include two new offenses improperly classed as felonies, "contributing to delinquency" and "pandering."

To the difficulties experienced by the City Council Crime Committee in determining the extent of general crime may be added the even greater difficulty of comparing the crime record of Negroes with that of other racial groups. The sources of the police statistics are the bookings by the desk sergeant in the police station. These are taken from arrest slip notations made by police-station desk sergeants, before whom persons arrested are brought. The ability of these desk sergeants correctly to ascertain the prisoner's race or nationality is open to question. Reports from the Immigrants' Protective League show that the foreigners arrested are often given wrong racial designations. On the other hand the classification of Negroes, even of half blood, is never in doubt. This fact should be remembered in interpreting the figures, for the Negro will be debited with all the crimes he commits, while figures for other groups will probably not indicate the full extent of their criminality. Added to this is the disposition, conscious or unconscious, to arrest Negroes more freely than whites, to book them on more serious charges, to convict them more readily, and to give them longer sentences.

This bias does not appear in the bare figures, which thus seem to substantiate the already existing belief that Negroes are more criminal than other racial groups. An example of this is found in the bookings in murder cases. For the six-year period 1914–19 inclusive, 1,121 whites and 193 Negroes were booked for murder, while 501 whites and only twenty-one Negroes were booked for manslaughter. While Negroes were charged with 17.1 per cent of the murders, they were charged with only 4.1 per cent of the cases of manslaughter. This, of course, takes into account bookings before trial. On the other hand, according to the testimony, they are more easily convicted on the charges on which they are booked. This fact introduces another element in the figures, which, although not representing the actual criminality of Negroes, yet gives plausibility to records. These situations presented such obvious dangers that the Commission considered it best to avoid giving currency to figures which carried such clear evidence of their own inaccuracy and misrepresentation. Since it is necessary to employ some of these figures despite their inaccuracies, the effort has been made to use them only where clear comparisons are possible.

The Commission is aware that statistics have been prepared giving the relative crime rates of different national groups, and has inquired into the sources of such statistics. In one case, for example, population estimates were based on 1910 census figures, arbitrarily increased by one-third. But when the abnormal situation with respect to immigration caused by the war, to mention only one important disturbing factor, is taken into consideration, it will be appreciated that any estimate is of doubtful value for careful calculation.

After much study and experimentation, and particularly after the counsel of statistical authorities had been obtained, the Commission's plan to work out comparative racial crime tables was abandoned.

Aside from the striking discrepancies between the crime figures of the Police Department and those of the Chicago Crime Commission, it is doubtful whether a reliable index to Negro crime as a separate item could be obtained even if the police figures showed the whole, instead of one-fifth or one-half, of the crimes committed.[1]

It was brought out in the testimony of judges and other authorities that Negroes are more easily identified and more likely to be arrested, and it is reasonably certain that a smaller proportion of Negroes who commit crimes escape than whites. But there is absolutely no means of determining what proportion of crime unrecorded by the police or other authorities is committed by whites or Negroes.

Adequate comparison of criminal statistics requires at least comparable units. This is rarely taken into account in comparing Negro and white crime. For example: a true comparison of relative crime rates between the two groups would require that the age distribution in each should be the same. For, although the population figures include children, women, and old persons,

[1] See *Report of Chicago Crime Commission*, p. 8.

the greatest proportion of crimes is committed by persons within what is known to criminologists as the "violent ages," or between eighteen and thirty. If the population is overbalanced in these ages the crime rate will be exaggerated. Such an overbalance exists in the Negro population because of the migration to Chicago of more than 50,000 Negroes, mainly adults. Besides, a greater proportion of these adults were men without families, another factor known to overweight crime figures. It is a curious fact, however, that, although the Negro population of Chicago increased from 2.1 per cent of the total in 1914 to 4.5 per cent in 1919, an increase of more than 100 per cent, the Negro crime rate during the same period increased 50 per cent, or less than half as rapidly as the Negro population.

The court cases studied intensively by the Commission show that the majority of Negro criminals are recruited from the lowest economic class of the Negro group. The frequency with which these persons are taken to the Bureau of Identification; their inability to provide bonds; their lack of means to employ attorneys, and their commitment on account of inability to pay fines, all tend to emphasize the relation between poverty and crime. The economic factors, as well as the actual commission of crime, determine largely the size of groups eligible for arrest and conviction. For example, laborers are likely to contribute more crimes proportionate to the total than salaried men, and salaried men more than professional men. The proportion of white laboring men to the total white population is considerably smaller than the proportion of Negro laboring men to the total Negro population. As a consequence, the "eligibles" for arrest and conviction are fewer in the white group than in the Negro group.

The reports of the City Council Committee on Crime, known as the "Merriam Report," and of the Chicago Vice Commission, both indicate that the economic factor is an important cause of both vice and crime. The following is from the Vice Commission report:

Among the reasons why women or girls enter the life of prostitution, the economic question plays a more or less conspicuous part. The low wages paid, the long hours of standing, insanitary conditions under which girls work in factories—all these have a powerful effect on a woman's or girl's nerves or physical force.

First among these causes [for prostitution] should be named unfavorable home conditions. . . . . Often when the home is not entirely degraded there are conditions of crowding and poverty which lead to misfortune. Working all day, the girls are often obliged to work at home in the evening, and if they live in a crowded house they must go on the street to receive their friends. They are thus practically forced on the streets for social life.

Among the economic conditions contributing to the social evil are the following: low wages, insanitary conditions, too long hours and high pressure of work; the over-crowding of houses upon lots; of families in the house, and of persons in single rooms.

The Merriam report similarly said:

The pressure of economic conditions has an enormous influence in producing certain types of crime. Unsanitary housing and working conditions, unemployment, wages inadequate to maintain a human standard of living, inevitably produce the crushed or distorted bodies and minds from which the army of crime is recruited. The crime problem is not merely a question of police and courts; it leads to the broader problem of public sanitation, education, home care, living wages and industrial democracy.

The greater liability of Negroes to unemployment introduces another factor. A plant official told the Commission that his plant had dismissed more than 500 Negro girls for business reasons. These girls, it was stated, could not easily find re-employment and were therefore probably exposed to certain necessities and temptations from which white girls of comparable status are exempt.

Ratio of convictions to arrest.—Police statistics of the relation of convictions to arrests do not involve the question of faulty source and bias and can therefore be used. They show that Negro defendants are more frequently convicted than whites, and this difference is even more pronounced in the more serious crimes. This excess ranged from 3 to 8 per cent during the period 1914–19.

The Negro and sex crimes.—Examination of the records of sex offenders brought into the criminal court in the two-year period 1917–18 showed a total of 253, of whom thirty-two, or 12.6 per cent, were Negroes. This was lower than the Negro rate, according to police statistics, for felonies in general. The sex offenses of Negroes were committed for the most part only against Negroes, and the specific charges were rape, attempted rape, accessory to rape, crimes against children, indecent liberties, contributing to delinquency, incest, adultery, murder by abortion, bigamy, crimes against nature, seduction, and bastardy. Of crimes against children two out of forty-six were committed by Negroes, or about 5 per cent, substantially the proportion of Negroes to the total population. The figures, however, are not a reliable index either for white or Negro crime because they include only cases passing through the social-service department of the criminal court.

IV. THE NEGRO IN THE COURTS

During the Commission's inquiry an effort was made to ascertain conditions in some of the various courts into which Negroes are brought; to learn the comparative attitudes of judges, prosecutors, and policemen toward Negro and white offenders, and to learn some of the pertinent facts in the social history of Negroes brought into these courts.

In all, 703 cases were studied, 538 white and 165 Negro. The social histories showed a conspicuous lack of schooling in the Negroes arrested, more than half of whom had left school before reaching the age of twelve. This is two years below the minimum age for children in Illinois. Only eight had gone beyond the fifth grade.   More than 76 per cent were engaged in unskilled work, and more than 70 per cent had incomes of less than $25 a week.   Few were property owners.   More than 50 per cent were locked up because of inability to furnish bonds.

Compared with white prisoners there was little difference in economic class, ability to provide bonds, or legal representation.   There was some noticeable difference in the character of offenders, varying with the type of neighborhood, but no general comparisons were possible because the courts were selected in a manner to get the greatest number of Negro cases.

While judges in most courts treated Negro defendants as considerately as they did whites, conditions in other courts were quite different.   One judge frequently assumed an attitude of facetiousness while hearing Negro cases. The hearings were characterized by levity and lack of dignity.   In one instance the judge was shaking dice during the hearing of the case.

1. JUVENILE COURT

Between 1913 and 1919, inclusive, the number of Negro boys brought into the juvenile court increased from 123 to 288, and the number of Negro girls from 71 to 112.   The proportion of Negro boys to the total during this six-year period decreased from 9 to 6.8 per cent; and the proportion of Negro girls increased from 5.6 to 14.8 per cent.   The proportion for Negro boys represents a little over twice the proportion of the Negroes to total population, and for Negro girls about three and one-half times.   Although the proportion for both Negro boys and girls increased from 7.9 per cent in 1913 to 9.9 per cent in 1919, the Negro population for the same period increased over 100 per cent.   The constant disproportion in the number of Negro boys and girls coming into the juvenile court points again to infective environment and to other circumstances heretofore mentioned involved in the crime rate for Negroes.

Northern and southern Negro delinquents.—Miss Mary Bartelme, assistant to Judge Arnold, before whom all cases of delinquent girls are tried, said: "In recent years we have had a large number of colored girls who have come up from the South to Chicago because their fathers sent for them.   Their education has not been equal to the education of white girls and their mental development has not been the same."

Joseph L. Moss, chief probation officer in the juvenile court, believed that Negro girls might be more affected by the war situation, the abnormal excitement, the lure of the uniform, than white girls.

Mr. Moss further said:

My impression is that southern Negroes contribute just about their portion to the total number of delinquents.   If any difference could be noted I might say that the delinquencies of the southern Negro might be more often classed as misdemeanors than as the more serious offenses.   One noted at times a sort of irresponsibility on the part of southern Negro delinquents which seemed to me to be traceable to the difference in standards between former environment and the present one.

Differences in delinquency of Negro and white children.—No information could be secured to show that the conduct for which Negro children are brought into court is in any way different from the conduct of all delinquent children. On this point Miss Bartelme testified: "I get all offenses committed by girls under eighteen years of age. I want to say that the offenses of white and colored are very much the same as far as those offenses come before me." Mr. Moss testified before the Commission: "From my experience I would say that there is no significant difference between acts for which colored delinquent boys are brought into court, and the acts for which white delinquent boys are brought into court, with this exception: that larceny, as an offense, seems to have a considerable lead over other offenses."

Comparative environment.—Since many of the delinquent children who come into the juvenile court, particularly first offenders, are placed on probation, comparative environment of white and Negro children is important. This subject does not lend itself to statistical presentation, but Miss Bartelme said:

Negro girls have not the same supervision that many of the white girls of their same class have, because in so many instances both parents are working, and the girls are left alone. They come home from school to a house that is closed. There is no one to receive them, and that, with a child, is always a very serious matter. The environment in which they live is not equal to the environment of the white girls. In these homes lack of privacy is greater than in the homes of the same class of white girls, therefore making life much more difficult and temptations more numerous. These conditions are much worse on account of the recent congestion, but they have existed right along. Negro children have been allowed to live in worse quarters, more crowded quarters, than the other children. . . . . We feel that in placing the children on probation, especially colored girls, they are placed in a home which often is not a home because the mother is away at work.

Mr. O. J. Milliken, for many years a public-school principal in Chicago, and now superintendent of the Chicago and Cook County School for Boys, to which the milder delinquent cases are committed, testified:

I should not like to be recorded as giving a criticism of the Board of Education, because I know that the present Board of Education believes in what I have to say now, but this is true: the colored boys are in the district that has practically been abandoned by the white people and the schools are only boxes for them to go to school in. You don't find any of the $900,000 school buildings in the colored population district, and I think that the time is approaching when the old system will be changed and we will have the vocational work, etc., thoroughly organized in the schools in these districts where most needed.[1] In dealing with boys I think more complaints come along that line than in any other, and I have made a report to the superintendent of schools on that at different times.

Boys who are "trusties" in the above school are allowed to secure jobs in Chicago. Their difficulties were outlined by Mr. Milliken as follows: "After a boy has been committed by the Juvenile Court, he is known by the

---

[1] See "Racial Contacts"—"Physical Equipment of Schools," p. 241.

police, and I have four or five colored boys today who are carrying letters from me asking the police to please allow these boys to go to work, and if the boys are in trouble to notify our institution."

Mr. Milliken told how, when the boys are seen on the streets, they are picked up by the police. He referred to "one of the finest lads we have had" and said, "I think probably within the last three months I have had to get him out of the hands of the police by calling up the police department twenty times, to get him to work." This difficulty, in Mr. Milliken's opinion, was more common in regard to Negro than white delinquents.

2. BUREAU OF IDENTIFICATION

While only 11.5 per cent of all persons arrested in Chicago in 1919 were Negroes, more than 21 per cent of all persons held on criminal charges in 1919 and taken to the Detective Division Identification Section were Negroes. In proportion to total arrests about twice as many Negroes as whites were taken to the Identification Bureau. Explanations of this disproportion by officials indirectly connected with this branch of the department and familiar with its methods are illuminating.

Judges of the criminal court have stated that "Negroes look alike," and that it is "more difficult offhand to place them than it is to identify a white criminal"; that Negroes are frequently taken to the Bureau for identification when white men would not be arrested or would be at once recognized, picked up, and booked.

Again, it is explained that it is unquestionably safer "to pick up and mug" a Negro than a white person, because there is less fear of an unpleasant "comeback." Negroes have fewer resources and less influence with which to insure their fair treatment, and so are more likely to be subjected to annoyance.

The fundamental reason, however, is perhaps more economic than racial. The *City Council Crime Committee Report*, or "Merriam Report," says:

The department of police maintains a bureau of identification with a system of photographs and finger prints, but it is largely a matter of chance as to who is photographed, and as to whether the record of criminality is asked for before he is sentenced, the judge relying largely on the statement of the prisoner and the memory of the officer. In general, all prisoners who are held to the Grand Jury and are not released on bail are taken to the bureau, photographed, and their finger prints are taken. This seems a very unfair and illogical arrangement. If there is a reason for photographing a man before he is tried and while he is still only a suspect, the reason should apply equally to those in jail and those on bail. The practice of taking the finger prints and photographs of only the men and women who cannot afford bail, seems hard to justify.[1]

3. PROBATION AND PAROLE

It appears from the testimony of officials and others interested in the care of offenders that the Negro on probation or parole is handicapped by his color.

[1] *City Council Crime Committee Report*, pp. 40–41.

He is more likely to be interrogated as a suspect; is more frequently arrested, and perhaps "mugged," and is in more danger of being molested even while on legitimate business. The principal sources of information on this subject were:

1. Statistics from the Municipal Department of Adult Probation.

2. Statistics from state institutions.

3. Testimony of John L. Whitman, state superintendent of prisons; John M. Houston, head of the Municipal Department of Adult Probation; and Dr. F. Emory Lyon, superintendent of the Central Howard Association.

The figures provided from institutions are probably accurate, since they are based on actual count, and do not involve any of the factors overweighting crime statistics.

Number admitted to probation.—From 1911 to January 1, 1920, 27,252 whites and 1,917 Negroes were admitted to probation after conviction in the municipal and criminal courts. Negroes were thus slightly less than 7 per cent of the total. For the six-year period ended January 1, 1920, Negro arrests for misdemeanors, according to police records, averaged 8.20 per cent and for felonies 11.13 per cent. On convictions for misdemeanors, Negroes average about 8.5 per cent of the total, and for felonies, over 13 per cent. The percentage of Negroes among all offenders placed on probation is thus less than the percentage of Negroes among those convicted in either group. In other words, the convicted white man seems more likely to be put on probation than the convicted Negro.

Probation depends largely upon the attitude of the judges. The total number of persons placed on probation has remained virtually the same from year to year. In fact, 164 fewer persons were put on probation in 1920 than in 1919; so that the migration of southern Negroes does not seem to have affected this situation.

Extent to which probationers "make good."—There are no exact figures showing the relative degree to which white and Negro probationers justify the leniency shown them, but Judge Houston testified before the Commission: "I do not think there is any difference. I am satisfied that the results are equally as good in the colored cases as in the white. I don't see any material difference between a colored man and a white man, so far as their truthfulness and reliability are concerned."

Institutional figures.—Official reports were submitted by the following state correctional and penal institutions: Chester State Hospital for the Criminal Insane, Pontiac Reformatory, Southern Illinois Penitentiary at Menard, and Joliet Penitentiary. No prisoners are paroled from Chester State Hospital.

Pontiac reported that last year 45 Negroes and 294 whites had been paroled. Of the Negroes 88 per cent, and of the whites 80 per cent, had "made good.

Menard reported that 50 Negroes and 168 whites had been paroled. Of the Negroes 76 per cent, and of the whites 81 per cent, had "made good."

Joliet reported that 61 Negroes and 223 whites had been paroled. Of the Negroes 69 per cent, and of the whites 74 per cent, "made good."

Totals for all the above institutions show that the percentages of Negro and white paroled who "make good" are nearly the same, the Negro rate being 76.9 per cent and the white 78.2 per cent.

John L. Whitman, state superintendent of prisons, who has had a continuous experience covering more than twenty-six years in correctional and penal institutions, testified before the Commission:

If there is a consistent effort being made to prepare inmates of prisons for good citizenship when they are released, the colored man responds as readily as the white, but it is a question in my mind whether the colored man can profit as much by it when he gets out as the white man can. That, however, is not due to a natural inclination; perhaps his opportunities on the outside are not as good. . . . . I think if the reports of those on parole from the state institutions now are closely studied, it will be found that they have more difficulties to surmount on the outside than the whites. If you assumed the white and colored ex-convicts on a par when they get out, the colored ex-convict would find it more difficult to lead the "straight and narrow"—on account of the forces set against him he is more greatly handicapped.

Dr. F. Emory Lyon, superintendent of the Central Howard Association, an organization which for twenty years has been dealing with ex-convicts, testified:

We have found this greater difficulty in dealing with colored men—in finding suitable rooming places within their means. Of course we could always find rooms recommended by the colored Y.M.C.A., or some such source as that, but generally for desirable places charges were beyond their means.

My experience in dealing with the colored and white, and in getting them employment, and in observing their satisfactory fulfilment of their paroles, is that possibly a little larger percentage of colored men make good on their paroles. They take any kind of employment by which they can make an honest living. I notice in our report of this year that out of 972 assisted, discharged and paroled men, ninety-two were colored men. This would be just about 10 per cent. I think that is probably a fair proportion each year in the history of the Association.

Colonel C. B. Adams, managing officer of St. Charles School for boys, said: "We have seven farm cottages . . . . but we rarely send a Negro boy to the farm cottage for the reason that it is almost impossible for him to secure employment on the farms. The farmers in northern Illinois . . . . are prejudiced against colored help, and it is almost impossible for us to secure employment on the farm for a colored boy."

Dr. Clara Hayes, managing officer of the State Training School for Girls at Geneva, said: "I think the proportion of the colored girls who are returned for one cause or another is practically the same as the proportion of white girls. . . . . I think the proportion of those recurring from misconduct is practically the same."

Mr. O. J. Milliken, of the Chicago and Cook County School for boys, said that Negro boys equaled white boys in fulfilling satisfactorily the requirements for those paroled.

4. INSTITUTIONAL INQUIRY

Through the co-operation of John L. Whitman, state superintendent of prisons, information was secured regarding comparative treatment and conduct of white and Negro inmates of Illinois. The data covered the State Penitentiary at Joliet, Southern Illinois Penitentiary at Menard, State Reformatory at Pontiac, and State Hospital for the Criminal Insane at Chester.

Total number of prisoners.—In the total number of inmates in those institutions, the percentage of Negroes is much larger than the percentage convicted of felonies in Chicago. The percentage of Negroes among all persons convicted of felonies in Chicago for a six-year period averaged 13.1 per cent, whereas their proportion among all inmates of these prisons is about 23 per cent. Omitting the Southern Illinois Penitentiary, the proportion is about 20 per cent. This disproportion is in part explained by facts brought out elsewhere showing that Negroes receive much longer sentences and fewer paroles (see p. 330).

All these institutions reported that in no cases were Negro and white prisoners kept in the same cells. Mr. Whitman stated that this arrangement was preferred by both whites and Negroes. Negro and white prisoners are not segregated in separate cell sections but occupy adjoining cells in the same block. "They are all in the same cell house; they are together in the shops; in cottages; in the farm where there are dormitories."

Negro and white prisoners eat in the same dining-room at the same time and at the same table. "The tables are for six or eight and there will be colored and white at the same table." They also attend public meetings together. Mr. Whitman also stated that in all the institutions Negroes and whites mingled without distinction, and that the result had been satisfactory. There was no difference in food, clothing, employment, cells, or discipline for Negro prisoners as a group from that of white prisoners because of the Negro's character or deportment. In no case was racial discrimination in such matters used as a means of discipline or punishment.

Conduct in prison.—There is no exact system for appraising conduct within the prison, but at Mr. Whitman's request persons were appointed in each institution to examine the record of each inmate as to conduct and tabulate the results. These and other data secured by Superintendent Whitman indicate that Negroes are less amenable to prison discipline than whites, but that their violations of rules are not so grave.

The percentage of Negro inmates whose conduct was marked "satisfactory" was smaller in all institutions than the percentage of whites. At Pontiac the difference in conduct was negligible. The greatest disparity was in Menard (in the southern part of the state), where the difference amounted to more than 20 per cent.

5. OTHER CORRECTIONAL INSTITUTIONS

St. Charles School for Boys receives delinquent boys between ten and seventeen years of age from the whole state. Negro and white boys are accepted up to the capacity limit. Negro boys are 12.5 per cent of the total, or slightly above the proportion which the Cook County Juvenile Court report shows Negro boys bear to the total of delinquent boys. Since 1915, the Negro population at St. Charles has increased from 8 per cent to 12.5 per cent of the total, or approximately half as rapidly as the Negro population in Chicago. St. Charles is conducted on the cottage plan, there being twenty-two cottages. Negro and white boys live in the same cottages, eat in the same dining-room, and use the same playground.

Four out of the twelve cadet companies have Negro captains, and these have more white than Negro boys under them. There are no racial difficulties in regard to employment or discipline, and the general conduct of Negro and white boys was reported to be the same. Colonel C. B. Adams, managing officer, said: "I really think mentally, and I am sure physically, the colored boys, such as come into the institution today, are superior to the white boys. We make much of athletics in the school and the best athletes we have are colored boys."

Geneva State Training School for Girls had 417 girls in 1917, 475 in 1918, and 445 in 1920. The increase over 1917 is proportionately the same for white and Negro girls. In 1920, out of 445 girls, eighty-three, or about 18.5 per cent, were Negro. Conditions at Geneva are substantially similar to those at St. Charles, with the exception that in one cottage, Negro and white girls eat at different tables. This, the managing officer, Dr. Clara B. Hayes, says is mutually agreeable. No difficulties exist with regard to employment or discipline. As to conduct on probation and parole, Dr. Hayes thought there was no material difference between Negro and white girls.

Chicago and Cook County School for Boys. This school is located in Riverside, just west of Chicago, on a farm belonging to the City of Chicago. The county feeds and clothes the boys; the city erects the buildings, and the Board of Education manages the school and pays all salaries. There are three buildings holding forty boys each. About 600 boys go through the institution in a year. It is a "testing out" school and working boys' institution to which first offenders between the ages of ten and eighteen are committed through the juvenile court. In 1919 the Negro boys were 15 per cent of the total; in 1920, less than 7 per cent. This decline Mr. Milliken, the managing officer, thought to be due to the cessation of Negro migration.

The treatment accorded Negro boys in cottages and at meals, play, and work is identical with that given white boys. There is no difference in discipline. Race prejudice is not prominent, and the boys are said to be most democratic with each other regardless of color. The director says: "They work together, beautifully; the idea [of prejudice] never enters into their heads. I think it is the outside influence that brings about these conditions [of prejudice]."

Chicago Parental School. To this school, situated on the North Side of the city, truants from the public schools of Chicago are committed by the juvenile court. The total number of pupils last year included 993 boys and eighteen girls. The Negro boys numbered eighty and the Negro girls five.

The treatment accorded white and Negro children is the same. No difference in regard to discipline or punishment exists. Race prejudice is not apparent, and the children's attitude toward each other seems not to be influenced by color. The deportment of Negro and white children is reported to be the same.

House of Correction. To this institution adult misdemeanants are committed. Information concerning conditions was furnished by Joseph Siman, superintendent.

The total number of inmates in 1919 was 5,723, and 1,151, or more than 20 per cent, were Negroes. This percentage is larger than the percentages of Negroes among persons arrested on misdemeanor charges and among those convicted.

Negro inmates are not put in the same cells with whites, but are frequently lodged in the same tier of cells. There are separate blocks of cells, but no separate tiers for whites and Negroes.

The prisoners eat together in the same dining-room. They march from their cells or work to meals, meetings, and church services and usually sit in the same order as that in which they march.

No race prejudice is noticeable among prisoners, and no racial clashes or unpleasant experiences have occurred in the institution.

Cook County Jail. The greatest discrimination noted in the course of the institution inquiry was at the Cook County Jail, where segregation has been carried out in nearly every department. The statements below are based on interviews with Chief Deputy Sheriff Laubenheimer and with Mr. King of the sheriff's office, who was chief clerk at the jail at the time of this study.

Negroes are completely segregated in cells on the first two floors in the new jail. Sometimes, when the jail is crowded, a few Negroes are put in among the whites, but whites are not often put in the part of the jail where Negroes are segregated. A condemned Negro murderer is placed with white condemned murderers in the section set apart for condemned murderers. Similarly Negro boys are placed with white boys in the boys' section of the jail.

Meals are served to all prisoners in their cells. The Negroes have a separate "bull pen" for exercise but are given the same facilities as the whites. They have separate church services. Negro guards have charge of the Negro prisoners. The conduct of Negroes, according to the observation of Mr. King, is practically the same as that of the whites.

Out of a total of 8,616 inmates in the county jail in 1919 there were 1,655 Negroes, or about 19 per cent. This is larger than the proportion of Negroes among all arrested or convicted. The report of the City Council Crime Committee showed that inmates of the county jail were confined there to a large extent on account of poverty.

V. NEGRO CRIME AND ENVIRONMENT

Housing.—Housing must be considered as an important element in the environmental causes of crime. Elsewhere this report presents a more detailed study of housing and it will suffice here to call attention to the prevalence of taking lodgers which is economically necessary in many Negro homes, and the consequent danger to the integrity of the family; to the laxity of law enforcement in certain sections; to the condition of streets and alleys; and to frequent instances of defective housing which have the effect of driving the children into the streets or to questionable places of amusement.

Recreation.—A comprehensive inquiry into the relations between recreation and delinquency, made by the Cleveland Foundation in 1917, showed that the use of leisure time had a relation to delinquency in 75 per cent of the cases observed, and that 51 per cent of the leisure time of the delinquent child was spent in ways that were aimless and undirected; while in the case of the "wholesome" child, only seven-tenths of 1 per cent of the spare time was thus spent. Local studies made by T. J. Szmergalski, of the West Chicago Park Commission, show that the establishment of a supervised park or playground tends to decrease complaints of delinquency from 30 to 40 per cent within the range of its usefulness—a radius of about three-quarters of a mile. With these facts as a background it is significant that there is no recreation center and only a few small playgrounds freely available for Negro children within the congested Negro district. In many of the crowded areas inhabited by foreign colonies are well-equipped recreation centers with model field houses, used by thousands of persons from these districts. The facilities available to Negro children and young people in this respect are much less adequate.[1]

Bathing-beaches, which are a summer-time boon to Chicago residents, foreign and native, are not freely accessible to Negroes. The tragic incidents in which the riot of 1919 began, illustrate the discriminatory attitude frequently observed when Negroes attempt to enjoy some of these recreational facilities.

The importance of these recreation opportunities is further emphasized in the *Annual Report of the Crime Commission* in its section on recreation.

The answer to the lack of a sufficient number of well-ordered places of recreation and amusement is to be found in the thriving condition of Chicago's cheap dance halls, underworld cabarets, unsupervised movie theatres of the cheaper class and the large number of pool-rooms scattered throughout the city. These establish-

[1] See "Recreation," p. 272.

ments are the worst breeders of crime with which this community has to contend and they should be subjected to rigid police regulations on the part of the municipal authorities.

The chief counteracting influences of such places of amusement are the parks, playgrounds and other municipal recreation centers, and there is a great need for the establishment of more of these, particularly in the congested districts.

Psychological.—It is the opinion of criminologists that a "warped" mind is responsible for many crimes. This general condition is true of Negroes as well as whites. But another factor appears in many crimes of Negroes. The traditional ostracism, exploitation and petty daily insults to which they are continually exposed have doubtless provoked, even in normal-minded Negroes, a pathological attitude toward society which sometimes expresses itself defensively in acts of violence and other lawlessness. A desire for social revenge might well be expected to result from the facetious and insulting manner in which Negroes are often treated by officers of the law.

"Infective" environment.—Much of what is said in the *Annual Report of the Crime Commission* for 1920 regarding the relation of infective environment to crime, can be fairly applied to the congested South Side areas of Negro residence:

Infective environment as a cause of crime is classified separately from problems of home environment because where the latter may be conducive to the proper rearing of children into manhood and womanhood, the influence immediately outside the home may be exactly the opposite. There are, in a great city like Chicago, certain neighborhoods in which influences are at work continuously to produce criminals. While the production of criminals is by no means confined to any one section of the city but is widespread throughout the community, still there are sections in which conditions are such that the growing child is indeed fortunate if he can attain manhood without being led to commit some offense against society.

In Chicago our chief district of this character is, or was until recently at least, "Canaryville" and much of the other territory immediately adjacent to the Stock Yards. It was this section which produced "Moss" Enright, "Sonny" Dunn, Eugene Geary, the Gentlemen brothers and many others of Chicago's worst type of criminals. It is in this district that "athletic clubs" and other organizations of young toughs and gangsters flourish, and where disreputable poolrooms, hoodlum-infested saloons and other criminal hangouts are plentiful.

Often it has been the case that public officials having such constituencies have utilized these conditions to further their own political advantages without making the slightest effort to bring about improvements, in some instances, actually assisting their constituents to violate the law in order to aid the building up of their political machines. . . . . Improvement of districts of this character and the elimination of such conditions within them is highly essential if organized crime is to be reduced.

Vice.—Vice districts and Negro residence districts are now and have long been close together. As late as 1905 a segregated vice district was tolerated on the West Side, on Green, Peoria, Sangamon, Morgan, Curtis, Carpenter,

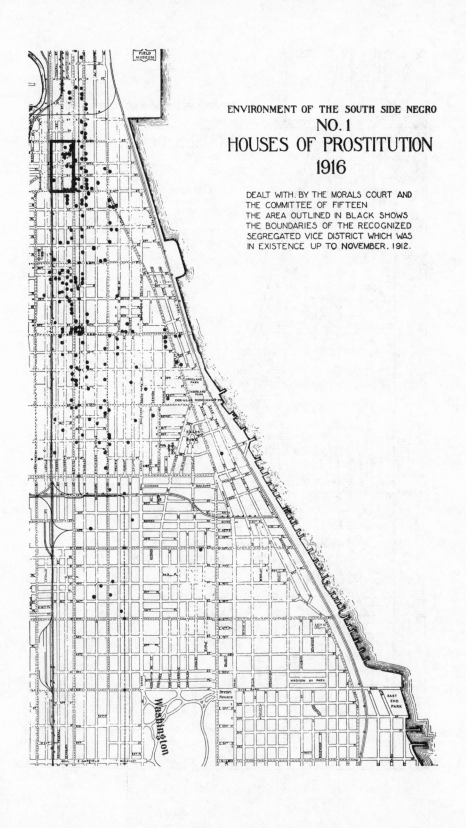

ENVIRONMENT OF THE SOUTH SIDE NEGRO

NO. 1
HOUSES OF PROSTITUTION
1916

DEALT WITH. BY THE MORALS COURT AND
THE COMMITTEE OF FIFTEEN
THE AREA OUTLINED IN BLACK SHOWS
THE BOUNDARIES OF THE RECOGNIZED
SEGREGATED VICE DISTRICT WHICH WAS
IN EXISTENCE UP TO NOVEMBER. 1912.

ENVIRONMENT OF THE SOUTH SIDE NEGRO
NO. 2
HOUSES OF PROSTITUTION
1918

DEALT WITH, BY THE MORALS COURT AND
THE COMMITTEE OF FIFTEEN
THE AREA OUTLINED IN BLACK. SHOWS
THE BOUNDARIES OF THE RECOGNIZED
SEGREGATED VICE DISTRICT WHICH WAS
IN EXISTENCE UP TO NOVEMBER, 1912.

and Randolph streets, and Washington Boulevard. Just north of this district, on Lake, Walnut, and Fulton streets, lived Negroes, segregated by public sentiment. Another vice district was along Custom House Place, now Federal Street, near which Negroes lived, similarly segregated by public sentiment. When this vice district was moved southward to Twenty-second Street it had a fringe of Negro residence. Later this district was abolished, and now vice of this kind is scattered and more clandestine and is to be found farther south, largely between Thirty-first and Fifty-fifth streets. More than 75 per cent of the Negro population of the city lives in this area.

Concerning the proximity of Negro residence areas to vice areas, the Chicago Vice Commission report in 1911 said:

The history of the social evil in Chicago is intimately connected with the colored population. Invariably the large vice districts have been created within or near the settlements of colored people. In the past history of the city every time a new vice district was created downtown or on the South Side, the colored families were in the district, moving in just ahead of the prostitutes. The situation along State Street from Sixteenth Street south is an illustration.

So whenever prostitutes, cadets and thugs were located among white people and had to be moved for commercial or other reasons, they were driven to undesirable parts of the city; the so-called colored residential sections.

The chief of police in 1912 warned prostitutes that so long as they confined their residence to districts west of Wabash Avenue and east of Wentworth Avenue, they would not be disturbed. This area contained at that time the largest group of Negroes in the city, with most of their churches, Sunday schools, and societies.

The Vice Commission report further said:

In addition to this proximity to immoral conditions young colored girls are often forced into idleness because of prejudice against them and they are eventually forced to accept positions as maids in houses of prostitution.

Employment agents do not hesitate to send colored girls as servants to these houses. They make the astounding statement that the law does not allow them to send white girls, but they will furnish colored help.

In summing up, it is an appalling fact that practically all of the male and female servants connected with houses of prostitution in vice districts and in disorderly flats in residence sections are colored. . . . .

The apparent discrimination against colored citizens of the city in permitting vice to be set down in their very midst is unjust and abhorrent to all fair-minded people. Colored children should receive the same moral protection that white children receive.

The prejudice against colored girls who are ambitious to earn an honest living is unjust. Such an attitude eventually drives them into immoral surroundings. They need special care and protection on the maxim that it is the duty of the strong to help the weak. Any effort, therefore, to improve conditions in Chicago should provide more wholesome surroundings for the families of its colored citizens who now live in communities of colored people.

oes live near vice districts is not due to their choice nor
ds, but to three causes: (1) Negroes are unwelcome in
ice localities; (2) small incomes compel them to live in
ices regardless of surroundings; while premises rented
ring notoriously high rentals, they make the neighbor-
and the rent of other living quarters there abnormally
ow; and (3) Negroes lack sufficient influence and power to protest effectively
against the encroachments of vice.

The records of convictions in the morals court and the evidence of the
Committee of Fifteen show the gradual drift of prostitution southward coinci-
dentally with the expansions of the main area of Negro residence.

Between 1916 and 1918 houses of prostitution decreased from forty-eight
to twenty-five in number in the territory between Twelfth and Twenty-second
streets, and from 130 to 107 between Twelfth and Thirty-first streets. Between
Thirty-first and Thirty-fifth streets, the number had slightly increased,
while there was an increase of nearly 80 per cent between Thirty-fifth and
Thirty-ninth streets. In the combined districts between Thirty-first and
Thirty-ninth streets the number increased from sixty-two to eighty-four;
and between Thirty-ninth and Fifty-fifth streets the increase was from eleven
to fifty-four.

These are probably only a fraction of the number that really exist there,
and while they are too few to be conclusive, they are significant when considered in relation to the movement of the Negro population. The accompanying maps show that the figures coincide substantially with the expansion of
Negro residence areas southward and eastward.

Further evidence of this movement of vicious resorts, and an abnormally
large number of them, into the Negro areas was obtained from the state's
attorney's office, the Commission's investigations, and from confidential
reports submitted by other organizations. Most of these places are maintained
by white persons, because in this district there is less likelihood of effective
interference, either from citizens or public authorities.

Cabarets and gambling.—In close relation to the disorderly houses are the
vicious cabarets in the Negro areas on the South Side. Their reputation and
the conditions existing in them have been given much publicity by the local
press.

Gambling was found to be prevalent at many places in this section, and
only slight effort was made to conceal violations of the law. Under the guise
of "clubs" some places were being operated as gambling houses with dice and
card games predominating. Other places, apparently with little fear of the
police, both conducted and permitted gambling with cards and on pool games.
Baseball pools and "policy," as well as betting on horse-race returns, were
prevalent.

VI. VIEWS OF AUTHORITIES ON CRIME AMONG NEGROES

Much information was secured from conferences with numerous authorities on crime. judges of the juvenile, municipal, circuit, superior and criminal courts; the general superintendent of police and police captains, former high police officials; heads of correctional and penal institutions; the state's attorney; experts on probation and parole, representatives from the sheriff's office; and social workers having intimate knowledge of crime conditions.

The views of those authorities are an important aid in giving proper interpretation to the factors which cause crime among Negroes, and to the circumstances connected with crime prejudicial to Negroes as compared with whites. For example, the testimony is practically unanimous that Negroes are much more liable to arrest than whites, since police officers share in the general public opinion that Negroes "are more criminal than whites," and also feel that there is little risk of trouble in arresting Negroes, while greater care must be exercised in arresting whites.

The Negro crime rate is exaggerated quite as much by the fewer arrests of whites than Negroes, in comparison with the number of crimes committed, as by the ease with which many Negroes may be arrested for one crime. We have already noted the remarkable discrepancy between the police reports of crimes committed and the actual crimes listed by the Crime Commission. Fewer Negroes than whites escape arrest and prosecution. When comparisons are made on the basis of statistics for arrests and convictions, there is presented, unless proper explanations of the statistics are made, an exaggerated picture of Negro crime.

The views of many of these authorities on various branches of this inquiry are here given:

1. FEWER PROFESSIONAL AND BANDED CRIMINALS AMONG NEGROES

Judge Edmund Jarecki, municipal court:

I know of no built-up organization of Negroes that would have any particular control over criminals.

Judge Daniel P. Trude, municipal court:

I think Negro criminals are more isolated. My experience in the boys' court was with the colored boys who would go out and steal clothes, a new shirt or some socks, or something of that sort that they could pick off the back porch. I found that there was considerable of that, but they are very partial and take from their own people.

Judge Charles M. Thomson, criminal court:

Negro crime is not organized, but individual, I should say, almost without exception.

Judge Kickham Scanlan, criminal court:

In May, 1920, I was assigned to the North Side to try some unbailable murder cases. It was found that there were over 500 homicide cases . . . . these were nearly all cases in which gangs of young white men confederated together to go out and hold up places, and they made a business of it, and some of these gangs have committed any number of hold-ups, and one member of the gang explained that he had killed as many as twenty victims.   The evidence showed that they killed when they didn't have to kill, just recklessly and wantonly.   In none of the cases of the character I have talked about were there any colored defendants.   They were all white men . . . . there were some of the most vicious cases I know anything about in my thirty-four years of experience.

I just want to make that one point to this Commission, that never in the history of this community has the white race stood so low from the standpoint of crime as it does at the present time.   White young men are banding together in gangs and deliberately going out and holding people up, right and left, and shooting them down. I notice that there are a few colored imitators of the white men, but the bad man of the city of Chicago at the present time is the young white man.

General Leroy T. Steward, former chief of police:

I think generally speaking that the Negro criminals work as individuals.   I only recall one instance where there was a gang of colored men that came to my attention, but I know of many white gangs.

Dr. Herman Adler, state criminologist:

You asked a question in regard to gangs—whether there is a combination among Negroes.   There are not many.   They are more individual, but on the other hand the lower grade of Negroes are likely to be the tools of the others at times; they have been used that way.   Where you are dealing with murder, with sex crimes, with certain forms of burglary, larceny, you are usually dealing with individual criminals. . . . .

Now there is here, in Chicago, professional organized crime.   The colored people as a whole are less engaged in professional crime and they are more the accidental, casual criminal or the low-grade person with a strong temper and a strong physique etc., who slips into crime by following the line of least resistance.

Major L. M. C. Funkhouser:

Negro criminals are not organized.

Professor Charles E. Merriam:

My belief is that the Negro criminals are not so well organized as the white. They don't go much in bands; furthermore, they are not so much in the class of professional criminals as they are in the class of occasional criminals.   It seems to me that the colored offender is the individual offender; his crimes are more of haste or passion.   He is in the occasional offender class.

2. SEX CRIME AMONG NEGROES AS COMPARED WITH WHITES

Judge Edmund Jarecki:

So far as sex crimes are concerned, during the time I have been there [in the boys' court] I have not noticed anything that would indicate any difference between colored and white boys.

Judge Charles M. Thomson:

In my work with the criminal court, I was astonished at the large number of criminals involving the sexual abuse of children, but I remember no case in which a colored defendant was charged with that crime. Almost all races were represented, but I don't remember one colored man charged with the abuse of a child. There were many, however, accused of adultery.

Judge Hugo Pam, criminal court:

I have had more serious rape cases against white than against colored people. The most serious case I had was about ten days ago, and I sentenced the man to life imprisonment. I never had such a case involving a Negro.

Judge Kickham Scanlan, criminal court:

I do not think Negroes are more liable to sex crimes than whites. I tried a colored man six or eight years ago for rape. He founded an alleged orphan asylum. The evidence showed that he had held a number of young children in that place. He got life in the penitentiary. He was the only colored man ever tried before me with any offense of that character. The children in that case were colored children. But I have tried a number of white men for rape, and while I have had ten or a dozen cases of crimes against children, in my twelve years' experience on the bench, I have never had a case of a colored man charged with crime against children.

3. OFFENSES AGAINST MORALS

Judge Arnold Heap:

The number of colored cases in the morals court is largely disproportionate to the number of Negroes in the total Chicago population. There are more colored cases now in the morals court than formerly because in the past the houses kept by white people with colored inmates were alone held responsible. Since colored people are now doing business on their own responsibility, they are at present brought in the same as white people. At first the Negro newcomers were strangers to our surroundings and were not such frequent offenders, but as that strangeness wore off they became familiar with vice as it exists among us today. The offenses of these new comers are about the same as those of the northern Negroes. Some persons think that the immorality of the colored is more gross than that of the whites, but I have my doubts about it. One factor in the problem is that colored people of the poorer class crowd together in smaller quarters than whites, and this tends to a lesser type of morality because they are so crowded.

Judge Wells M. Cook, municipal court:

Prostitution among the white people in Chicago in 1918 was more or less clandestine, in flats and cheap hotels and in private homes, and more or less under cover. The colored people, living largely in one section of the city, and being naturally of a social, emotional temperament, are apt to congregate in places and in resorts where the police could more easily raid them, and are much more easily apprehended. That is about the only reason I can see for the disproportionate number of colored defendants brought into the morals court. It is not that there is any greater percentage of immorality, but prostitution among whites was more clandestine.

O. J. Milliken, superintendent, Chicago and Cook County School for Delinquent Boys:

I don't think that homosexual relations are a racial matter with the boys. The sex problem, I think, doesn't manifest itself between races as much as it does in the lower classes of whites that come in.

4. LYING AND STEALING

Judge Daniel P. Trude:

"I think the colored man, if he is not a desirable citizen, is undesirable because he has not been given a chance; he has not been given the advantages that a white fellow has from birth." Judge Trude agreed with the view expressed in a question that if the Negro were found careless as to the truth and as to his promises, it was due to his heredity and lack of training rather than anything inherently bad in him.

Judge Wells M. Cook:

I think there is a great deal of nonsense in the talk about the colored man being more apt to lie or steal than the white man. I think that is largely a question of environment and training. He is not more inclined, in my judgment, to tell a lie or steal than a white man.

Judge Charles M. Thomson:

I would say there is a far larger number of larceny cases involving the white than the colored man, even in proportion to the population. The larger proportion of cases involving the colored is in having to do with fights, involving murder in some instances.

Judge Edmund Jarecki:

No, I don't think Negroes are more likely to be guilty of theft than whites; that is not usually the case.

5. TYPES OF NEGRO CRIMES

Judge Hugo Pam:

The colored man is frequently charged with robbery with a gun, and a great many have guns. Relatively speaking, more colored men have guns than white men.

Judge Kickham Scanlan:

The most prevalent crimes or types of crimes amongst Negroes, according to my observation, are gambling, assault cases, caused by drinking or women, petty theft.

F. Emory Lyon, superintendent, Central Howard Association:

My experience in dealing with colored offenders would indicate a slightly larger proportion of crimes of violence than in the case of white men.

Dr. Clara Hayes, Geneva School for Delinquent Girls:

I think there is a little more tendency on the part of colored inmates toward violence than there is among white girls. I mean such misconduct as attacks on other girls, etc.

6. MENTAL

Judge Daniel P. Trude:

I today received a letter from a young colored man who has been in the boys' court several times. His father is a mental defective, and he is a mental defective. That is the reason he keeps committing these crimes. He is in the Dixon Home for Feeble Minded. There are a number of colored boys that come up from the South that way, and it is my judgment that southern institutions are turning them loose. I think Illinois does as well as other states. They all discharge mental defectives as cured, and they wander all over the face of the earth, in and out of other institutions.

Judge Charles M. Thomson:

As a rule the mentality of colored offenders was not high. I had a few cases where the reverse was true, and one which involved a man who was as smart a man as I ever tried.

Mary Bartelme, associate judge of the juvenile court:

As to mentality, I would say that in recent years we have had a large number of girls who have come up to Chicago from the South and their educations have not been equal to the educations of the white girls and their mental development has not been the same.

Dr. Herman Adler:

At Pontiac we find in general that the average of intelligence in the colored people is rather less than in the whites. Take the white people separately and you will find about the same proportion of low grades as in the colored race. In actual group comparison, the colored race is somewhat below that of the whites. That is, in general the distribution is about the same, but there is always a slight lag of the colored below the white. The lower the intelligence, on the whole, the more likely it is that the individual is in the institution for a crime of violence or a sex crime or incendiarism; the higher the intelligence, the more likely that the crime is forgery or some crime involving fraud.

7. CHANGE IN CHARACTER OF CRIME OR INCREASE IN CRIME DUE TO MIGRATION

Judge Hugh Stewart:

I am of the impression that the colored men from the South are in the courts in larger numbers than are those who have lived here a long time. . . . . A great many of the colored people from the South are very dark skinned, and there is a larger proportion, in my estimation, of offenses among dark-skinned colored people than among those of the light color. I sometimes try to trace out where they come from. I find a great many of these cases come from the South.

I think there is a difference between offenses committed by colored persons from the South and colored persons who have resided for a long time in the North. I think there are more hold-ups and burglaries committed by men who come from the South than by the colored population before the influx.

I am of the opinion that Negroes who have recently come from the South and find their way into the police courts do not typify or reflect the general character of the southern Negroes as a class, any more than the white people who find their way into the police courts typify other whites who manage to keep out of them.

Judge Daniel P. Trude:

It was frequently true that the boys would jump freights from down South and come up here and be picked up and brought into court and be left in jail for a while with nobody to keep after them, or furnish bail. The South has never given the Negro adequate educational advantages, so they come up here more or less uneducated, many of them, and they are not given a helping hand as they should be.

In the boys' court the number of southern boys recently arrived in Chicago was startling. While I was in the boys' court, I made it a practice to give every one of them a card to the Urban League, so that they would know where to go to get advice on any difficulty.

Judge Wells M. Cook:

I would say that of the colored men and women brought into court in the summer of 1918, the greater percentage were colored people who had recently come to Chicago. In most instances the colored man brought in had money; he was receiving more wages than in the South; the city was "wet"; he had come from districts in the South where he could not get whiskey; in a great many instances he had not brought his wife and family with him, so he was easy prey for those engaged in commercial sexual vice. In consequence he would be arrested in these raids, made usually by the police on the night when the underworld was supposed to be the busiest, usually Saturday and Sunday nights. I do not think there are any more vicious colored men than there are vicious white men, but the colored man who was brought in largely was a newcomer. There had been no particular increase in vice that I observed among the native-born colored people or the man who had come to Chicago a reasonable number of years back. As to the women, they were almost entirely typical southern prostitutes, who had come here from New Orleans, Memphis, Nashville, Atlanta, Galveston, and other large cities in the South, attracted to Chicago by reason of the fact there were a lot of colored men up here who were making good money. I would say that so far as the colored women of Chicago were concerned, there was no noticeable increase in immorality among them.

Mr. O. J. Milliken:

In 1919, we ran up to 15 per cent colored. This year, 1920, it is less than 7 per cent. The reason is found in the boys from the South. They have stopped coming now and we are getting back to normal. The boys from the South have been very illiterate. We have received a number who could not write their own names and would almost be counted subnormal on first examination but are often found to be very bright. A great many asked to come back or asked to remain in the institution until they could get some education. I never noticed any difference as to color in the handling of the boys in any department.

8. LIABILITY OF THE NEGRO TO ARREST

Judge Daniel P. Trude:

I think that at the time of the riot there was more disposition on the part of the officers to make arrests of colored offenders, frequently for protection. I think it was due to what Dr. Shepardson used to call, out at the University, "the mind of the mob"—a disturbed view of things which makes one likely to go too far one way or the other. These people were that way. They had to arrest a certain number and try to check the riot, and they went too far in many cases.

Judge Charles M. Thomson:

I have seen cases where Negroes were arrested on suspicion; I would not say there was any large proportion. I remember one case was a young colored fellow arrested purely on suspicion. The jury disagreed the first time. The next time he was tried before me, and the jury found him guilty. Because it was a second trial, and because of the disagreement, I watched it very carefully as the evidence went in, and I became convinced that it was a pure case of the officers having had some trouble with this fellow before. A crime occurred in their district, and they pounced on this chap. I felt pretty sure he was not guilty. The state's attorney called the trial off. He became convinced himself.

Mr. O. J. Milliken:

After a boy has been committed by the juvenile court, he is known to the police, and I have four or five colored boys today who are carrying letters from me asking that the police will please allow these boys to go to work. Prejudice on the part of the police in picking up alleged offenders is more apt to occur against Negroes than whites.

Judge Kickham Scanlan:

Negroes are more likely to be arrested on suspicion than white persons. If you will tell me why race prejudice exists in this world, I will tell you why this is so. I don't think the police are quite as careful with reference to the rights of the colored man as with the white man. I think they hesitate a little longer when a white man is involved; I am certain that it is so.

State's Attorney Maclay Hoyne:

In the race riots, the police arrested almost exclusively Negroes, and practically no white men.

General Leroy T. Steward:

Recently there have come to Chicago from the.South large numbers of colored men who have formerly lived in the country and are not accustomed to city environments. These men have largely been employed at the Stock Yards and, being unknown to the police, there is concerning them naturally a greater suspicion than would attach to the white man who had lived for a greater length of time in the same district, and who also would be more easily identified and traced, if need be, and he would not, therefore, perhaps, be arrested but simply be observed, while the police would, no doubt, feel if they permitted the colored man to pass on at the time, they would lose him completely. This would seem to me to be the real basis of the feeling that has maintained on the part of these men, that they are discriminated against as compared with the whites.

Another matter in this same connection that no doubt has a bearing on the subject is that these same men who have been accustomed to rather close surveillance in the South, seem to feel that when they come to the North they must conduct themselves in a manner to evidence to all concerned that they have equal rights of every kind and character, with the result that they sometimes are guilty of unnecessarily accentuating these matters, and thus bringing on disputes which occasion bad feeling and perhaps lead to disturbances resulting in arrest.

Dr. Herman C. Adler:

Repeatedly colored men have been convicted on evidence which I know perfectly well would not have been satisfactory in white cases. I know that was so in the case of the East St. Louis riot where a colored man was sent down to the Southern Illinois Penitentiary for participating in the riots on the charge of murder. Even the prosecuting office, on reviewing the facts, a year later, admitted he did not believe the evidence sufficient. If that had been a white man the chances are that he would not have been convicted upon that evidence.

We had the same thing here in Chicago: a colored man sent to the penitentiary on a charge of attempted rape where the identification was made by a child of six or eight years who picked him out of a crowd under suspicion. No such evidence ought to be accepted. We know there is prejudice, and when there is prejudice we know the person against whom the prejudice is directed has a hard time.

9. DISCRIMINATION IN THE COURTS

Judge Daniel P. Trude:

I think in the main the Negro gets as good a show as the white man when he gets before the judge. Whether the other forces before he gets up to that point treat him right or not, I cannot say. . . . . A certain number of policemen have "got it in" for him and are going to "take a crack" at him because he is a colored man.

Judge Hugo Pam:

In a murder case lawyers will challenge a Negro; if there were a colored man in the box he would soon be put out.

Judge Charles M. Thomson:

Take for example a gun case, with twelve men in the box, and one a colored man, and suppose that the lawyer challenged the Negro. If you went to the lawyer and said, "Give me your reason," I don't think he would give you any reason. . . . . If you had a case where the defendant was colored that juror would stay in the box so far as the defendant was concerned.

Judge Kickham Scanlan:

Of course there is another thing about the colored man in the criminal court that must be kept in mind. It is a peculiar thing about human nature, that no man wants to admit that he has prejudices. He will talk loosely on the outside that he doesn't like the Negro, or doesn't like the Jew, or doesn't like this person or that person, but you get him under oath in the jury box and in my twelve years on the bench I never knew a juror to admit that he was prejudiced against anybody. It goes without saying that in such a state of affairs you will probably get men on the juries that try colored men who have some prejudice against Negroes. I would say that when there is a colored defendant and white prosecuting witness there would be grave danger that the jury might unconsciously favor the white side of the case. Juries will convict a colored man with less hesitation than they will convict a white man on the same kind of evidence. For that reason, in the many cases in which the colored man is involved, I watch the evidence like a hawk. The verdict has got to pass me.

10. EASE WITH WHICH NEGROES ARE CONVICTED

Judge George Kersten, criminal court:

There is unfortunately a difference in the ease or difficulty with which white and colored persons brought into court are convicted, and the misfortune operates adversely towards colored people. In many cases jurors have been excused from service because upon examination under oath to test their qualifications to act as jurors they said they could not give a colored person a fair trial. In my experience I have known verdicts to be set aside by the presiding judge, because he was convinced that the jury was influenced by color prejudice. As to the prosecution of colored offenders by white plaintiffs and white offenders by colored plaintiffs, I believe that the influence of color prejudice is sometimes felt in our courts. I think it is easier under similar facts and circumstances in evidence to convict a colored defendant than a white one. And for the same reason, a white person on trial is less liable to conviction if the prosecuting witnesses are all colored. Perhaps an enlightening phase of the whole situation is to be found in the fact that colored offenders, on being brought in for trial, usually ask to be tried by the judge instead of a jury.

Judge Hugo Pam:

In light cases involving pocket-picking, larceny, stealing a bag of sugar, a barrel of flour, clothing, etc., I think the races stand on an equality, but in a serious offense I think the colored man has the less chance. I feel that the colored man starts with a handicap. I haven't any question about it in my mind. In the more serious crimes, where a hold-up is committed or guns are used, I think there is great prejudice. I think very few white or colored men are convicted that shouldn't be; no judge would allow such a case to stand if he thinks there has been unfair trial, but, for instance, where a white man will be found guilty of manslaughter, a colored man will be found guilty of murder. A white man might escape with three to twenty years in the penitentiary, while the colored man would get ten years to life.

I think the colored man would not be convicted if he is not guilty, but I am not certain that the white man would be convicted if he is guilty.

I see colored men, very resigned men, very often feeling that most people are not interested in them. They come and take their medicine, and go away. I feel that they are being disposed of without the interest being shown that should be.

11. LEGAL REPRESENTATION FOR NEGRO DEFENDANTS

Judge Daniel P. Trude:

My experience in court work is that Negro lawyers in the main lack education such as is necessary, but there are among the members of the bar some very good colored attorneys. Many Negroes cannot afford to pay the attorney's fees necessary to obtain these, so that they are handicapped in court by lack of competent counsel, and it becomes necessary for the judge to give them more careful hearings and more careful consideration to protect their interests.

Judge Wells M. Cook:

The handicap that the colored man seems to be under in the severe cases is that he frequently does not get a good lawyer. As a rule he is not represented by as good a lawyer as the white. Of course there are capable Negro lawyers in Chicago, but there were few such retained in the cases tried before me.

Judge Hugo Pam:

I do not think that Negroes have as able lawyers as whites. I had a case of a colored man who I felt was misrepresented instead of represented. He was convicted of murder and sentenced to life imprisonement. I felt that the sentence was too severe. I set it aside and granted a new trial and it resulted in a verdict of man-slaughter which was the thing that should have been done.

Judge Kickham Scanlan:

The Negro hasn't the money to employ proper attorneys, competent attorneys. In two out of three cases tried before me in which there were colored defendants, I have appointed attorneys to defend them. I appointed white attorneys. I asked the defendants whom they wanted. They told me and I appointed the white lawyers mentioned and made them serve.

12. IDENTIFICATION

Judge Daniel P. Trude:

I did find where certain of the police were going into Negro clubs and arresting Negroes they found there, bringing them into court without a bit of evidence of any offense. Somebody would tip off the police that there was gambling going on so they would raid the place, locking up all the men they found there for the night and send them to the Bureau of Identification, but that was all. Some policemen take many people to the Bureau of Identification who absolutely should not be taken there, but the judge only knows about it after they have been taken there, when they are brought into court after the damage has been done.

13. PROBATION ON PAROLE

Dr. F. Emory Lyon, superintendent, Central Howard Association:

In dealing with colored men on parole, our experience has been that fully as large a proportion have completed their parole with credit as in the case of white men under parole. I should say that the task of securing employment has been less difficult because colored men as a rule have been less critical as to the kind of employment they would accept. They have been willing to make an honest living at any work that is offered.

John L. Whitman, superintendent of state prisons:

I have seen many colored men, young men or boys, who gave every evidence of a sincere desire to do well on the outside. They meet with disappointment that they did not expect, hardships, difficulty in securing work as well as homes, and they fall. The desire was there just the same. The opportunities were not. But when the employer gives him a chance, the Negro appreciates it and he sticks—and we have had employers say during the last year many times, "If you have got such colored men as you have sent before, give them to us in preference to the whites, because there is a lack of appreciation on the part of white men."

14. ENVIRONMENT: VICE IN NEGRO RESIDENCE AREAS

General Leroy T. Steward:

Where Negroes have come in and as a result white people have moved out and the neighborhood has, plainly speaking, deteriorated, there is a great tendency to permit infractions of the law, as in any neighborhoods which are regarded as not as important as high-class residence neighborhoods. For instance, Calumet Avenue from Thirty-first to Thirty-ninth streets is entirely colored. Fifteen years ago it was entirely white. Now it would be much easier to establish vice there than it would have been fifteen years ago when a lot of well-known people lived in the neighborhood.

Major L. M. C. Funkhouser:

Most of the Negroes found in disorderly houses are employees. There was one notorious place down there that we closed where they were all colored. That was the most notorious one we had.

Professor Charles E. Merriam:

I think there is this to be said about the colored side of it there [on the South Side]: I am asked whether the colored protest against disorderly resorts would be as effective as a protest made by an equal number of white men. Making allowance for the fluctuating conditions in a long period, I don't believe it would be quite as effective. Not only that, but I don't think the colored people are so well organized to fight these evils as a class of men . . . . they have not the wealth. In the territory upon the North Side or in any territory where there are many lawyers and people of some means, if they found a place like that they would never rest until they got it out. They would just keep at it with time and money until they forced it out.

Dr. F. Emory Lyon, superintendent, Central Howard Association:

Our observation would indicate that the Negro delinquent has suffered under the handicap of unsatisfactory home conditions, Owing to the general public discrimination, fewer opportunities have been offered him. In addition to adverse conditions in the home, some opportunities in public places have been denied him. Some of the discrimination and ostracism on the part of his associates has been unconscious in many instances. The colored boy has especially few recreational facilities.

Mr. O. J. Milliken:

It is up to us to give them the best that there is, and we can clean up those districts. I don't believe the question of color is going to enter into the matter at all if we once clean up the districts where they are obliged to live.

Myron Adams, former pastor of the First Baptist Church:

North of my church for a block or two along Thirty-first Street at the time I went there was almost exclusively a white residence district. The moral conditions could not have been worse. I had a list in my church study of the houses of prostitution and other lawless agencies gathered by the police and the Committee of Fifteen. I don't know of a district in Chicago where there were more gunmen, more high-class criminals, more high-class prostitutes than there were within three blocks of the First Baptist Church when I came there as pastor.

Speaking from my observation I think that any colored community is liable to be imposed upon by white men who are vicious, and the colored people get no encouragement when they themselves endeavor to rout out that vice. White prostitutes and white gamblers and vicious resorts come into the "Black Belt" because it is black; they operate with more safety than they do in the white belt. That is true of every American city that I know of personally.

15. ECONOMIC AND INDUSTRIAL ASPECTS OF NEGRO CRIME

Judge Charles M. Thomson:

Colored people who were up before me in the criminal court were mostly men who did not have steady employment. . . . . My experience was that the environmental conditions out of which the colored defendant arose were an environment of idleness, very largely. I would say, as to the economic factors, that I don't remember a case that I had involving a colored defendant whom I would call prosperous, whereas there were many white defendants who were very prosperous. Most of the colored people tried were in stringent circumstances and poverty.

Judge Kickham Scanlan:

My experience in the criminal court is that the colored defendant, even in bailable cases, is unable to give bail. He has to stay in jail, and therefore his case is very quickly disposed of by the prosecutor. Defendants locked up are usually tried first. The colored man is more apt to be out of work than the white man, and that is a possible reason for the large number of arrests of Negroes. His sphere is very limited, and if there is any let up in the industry that is involved in that sphere, he is a victim. I have often wondered if you could change the skins of a thousand white men in the city of Chicago and handicap them the way the colored man is handicapped today, how many of those white men in ten years' time would be law-abiding citizens.

Professor Charles E. Merriam:

This problem as I see it is very complicated. We have to deal first with the matter of economic class which is at the bottom of a good deal of it, then with the matter of race, which is at the bottom of a good deal more of it, although perhaps not as much as class; then there is the matter of politics or a system which has grown up for thirty or forty years back, which makes the class and race relations a good deal more difficult to deal with.

If every man had good housing conditions and a steady job, at a living wage, a good opportunity for education, there would not be very much crime. . . . . Particularly in the case of the colored people, the crime is on the part of the community, on the part of the city that allows bad conditions to exist. Negroes ought to be protected. They don't get protection for the same reason that it is always hard to protect the economically weak against the strong. There is not any use of making a lot of fine phrases about it—that is largely where the trouble lies.

CHAPTER VIII

THE NEGRO IN INDUSTRY

A. EMPLOYMENT OPPORTUNITIES AND CONDITIONS

I. INTRODUCTION

1. NEGRO WORKING POPULATION IN 1920

Between 1910 and 1920 the Negro population of Chicago increased from 44,103 to 109,594. Of this number it is estimated that about 70,000 were engaged in industries in 1920 as compared with about 27,000 in 1910.[1]

Questions which naturally suggest themselves for answer in connection with this great increase in the Negro working population in Chicago are: How did this large number of Negroes fit into the industrial life of the city? What were and are the opportunities open to them? Have they given satisfaction to employers? Are they discriminated against by employers or fellow-workers? Has racial friction developed because of competition between white and Negro workers? Were the riots of 1919 in any sense the result of labor troubles? What part have the Negroes taken in strikes? What is the relation of the Negro to organized labor? What is the outlook for the Negro in industry? These and other questions guided the inquiries and investigations of the Commission in the industrial field.

2. OPPORTUNITIES CREATED BY THE WAR

The Negro's position in the industrial life of Chicago is so intimately connected with the changes due to the war that a brief reference to certain facts of common knowledge in connection with the war will be helpful. With the beginning of the war in 1914 came an abnormally large demand by the belligerent countries for American munitions, food products, clothing, leather, iron and steel products, and other manufactured goods. Existing establishments were enlarged and new ones were erected in response to the demand for increased production. It was not uncommon for a plant to double or treble its labor force. A typical case was one of the large packing-plants in the Chicago "Yards" which increased its workers during the war from 8,000 to 17,000.

The war stimulated the demand for goods, and therefore for labor, and at the same time decreased the available labor supply. Immigration from the belligerent nations immediately ceased, and there was a marked decrease in

---

[1] In 1910 the number of Negroes gainfully occupied was 27,317, or 61.94 per cent of the total Negro population. The percentage gainfully occupied in 1920 would be higher because of the large number of men without families who migrated from the South.

357

immigration from other countries; aliens in large numbers departed to join the fighting forces of their native lands.

The labor shortage became acute soon after the United States entered the war in 1917, and enlistments withdrew hundreds of thousands of men from northern industries. An unprecedented demand for Negro workers was the result. The migration from the South was mainly a response to the call of larger opportunity and higher wages in the North.

3. INDUSTRIAL BACKGROUND OF NEGRO WORKERS

For the United States as a whole in 1910 the industrial condition of the gainfully occupied Negro population is shown in Table XVIII:

TABLE XVIII

GAINFULLY OCCUPIED NEGRO POPULATION TEN YEARS OF AGE AND OVER
IN THE UNITED STATES IN 1910

Industry	Both Sexes	Percentage	Male	Female
Agriculture....................	2,893,674	55.7	1,842,537	1,051,137
Domestic and personal service.....	1,074,543	20.7	234,063	840,480
Manufacturing and hand trades....	657,130	12.6	575,845	81,285
Transportation..................	276,648	5.3	274,565	2,083
Trade.........................	132,019	2.5	123,635	8,384
Professional service.............	69,471	1.3	39,400	30,071
Public service..................	26,295	0.5	25,838	457
Others	62,755	1.4	62,671	84
Total United States*........	5,192,535	100.0	3,178,554	2,013,981

* Census Bureau, *Negro Population in the United States, 1790 to 1915*, p. 503.

In 1910, more than three-fourths of the gainfully occupied Negroes in the United States were engaged in two forms of industry—agriculture and domestic and personal service. In the South at that time 78.8 per cent of the Negro population lived in rural communities[1] and 62 per cent of those employed were engaged in agriculture.[2] It is evident, therefore, that the northward migration involved a sudden transition of the southern Negro from farms or small towns to the highly specialized industries of northern cities, with marked changes in modes of living.

On many southern plantations the Negroes were required to buy food and clothing on credit at such high prices that their shares of the return were usually spent before the crops were harvested.[3] This system encouraged careless spending and did nothing to induce habits of thrift. Even the hardest-working Negroes frequently found themselves in debt to their landlords at the

[1] *Negro Population in the United States, 1790 to 1915*, p. 90.

[2] *Ibid.*, p. 503. Negroes gainfully occupied in the South, 4,592,353; in agriculture, 2,845,163.

[3] Emmett J. Scott, *Negro Migration during the War*, p. 92. "Carnegie Economic Studies," No. 16.

end of the year.[1] Incentive to sustained effort and regular work was lacking in the hand-to-mouth existence under this prevailing system of share rent and credit. It naturally produced habits such as drawing against wages and working irregularly under the spur of temporary need. Men handicapped by such habits joined the migration in great numbers. Though ill-fitted for the keen competition, business-like precision, and six-day-week routine of northern industry, the southern Negro, in spite of these handicaps, has succeeded in Chicago.

II. THE NEGRO IN CHICAGO INDUSTRIES IN 1910 AND 1920

Of the Negro population of 44,103 in Chicago in 1910 the gainfully occupied numbered 27,317. The distribution of this number, according to industrial classification, is given in Table XIX, which shows that 60 per cent of all such Negroes were engaged in domestic and personal service, as compared with 15 per cent in manufacturing and 3 per cent in clerical occupations.

TABLE XIX

NEGROES GAINFULLY OCCUPIED IN CHICAGO IN 1910*

Industries	Both Sexes	Percentage	Male	Female
Manufacturing and mechanical....	4,071	15	3,073	998
Transportation..................	1,852	7	1,849	3
Trade..........................	1,241	5	1,148	93
Public service..................	224 }	4	{ 224	0
Professional....................	963 }		{ 640	323
Clerical occupations.............	934	3	771	163
Domestic and personal service.....	16,389	60	9,426	6,963
Agriculture, mining, and unclassified	1,643	6	1,306	337
Totals.....................	27,317	100	18,437	8,880

* Thirteenth Census, 1910, Vol. IV, Table VIII, pp. 544–47.

I. METHOD AND SCOPE OF INVESTIGATION

To discover the industries in Chicago which were employing Negroes in appreciable numbers in 1920, preliminary questionnaires were sent to 850 employers compiled from lists furnished by: (1) the Chicago Association of Commerce (covering 591 establishments, with a total of 350,000 employees); (2) the Employment Department of the Chicago Urban League; (3) the Illinois Free Employment Bureau; (4) the Federal Employment Bureau; and (5) the classified telephone directory.

Questionnaires were returned by 460 establishments of 850 to which they were mailed. We are satisfied that the replies received cover the field of Negro

[1] "In many cases the Negro does not dare ask for a settlement. Planters often regard it as an insult to be required even by the courts 'to go to their books.' A lawyer and planter cited to me the planter's typical excuse: 'It is unnecessary to make a settlement when the tenant is in debt.' As to the facts in the case, the landlord's word must suffice." From report by W. T. B. Williams in *Negro Migration in 1916–17*, p. 104. Bulletin of the U.S. Department of Labor, Division of Negro Economics.

labor, and that no establishments of importance in this field have been over-looked. Table XX shows the results:

TABLE XX

Negroes Employed	Number of Establishments	Total Negroes Employed
No Negroes....................	264	0
Less than five Negroes.............	59	111
Five Negroes or more (manufacturing)	69	12,854
Five Negroes or more (non-manu-facturing)......................	68	9,483
Totals....................	460	22,448

Answers came from 156 manufacturing establishments employing fifty-one or more wage-earners. The representative character of this group is indicated by the fact that over three-fourths of the total wage-earners in Chicago engaged in manufacturing in 1914 were employed in factories of this class. The United States Census of Manufactures for 1914 reported the total number of wage-earners employed in manufacturing in Chicago in that year as 313,710; of this number, 244,827, or 78 per cent, were employed in 1,032 establishments employing fifty-one or more wage-earners. The 156 question-naires therefore represented 15 per cent of the 1,032 establishments in this class (in 1914) and included 107,403 wage-earners, or almost 44 per cent of the total wage-earners in this class and 30 per cent of the total wage-earners engaged in manufacturing in 1914.

Questionnaires reporting Negro employees were returned by 104 manufactur-ing establishments of all classes. Of these, sixteen employed one to fifty wage-earners, representing a total of 435 wage-earners; and eighty-eight employed fifty-one or more wage-earners, representing a total of 78,919 wage-earners.

Since thirty-five of the manufacturing establishments reporting Negro labor (or 33 per cent of the 104 so reporting) employed less than five Negroes each, or a total of seventy Negroes in all, while sixty-nine employed 12,854 Negroes, or 99.4 per cent of the total Negroes reported by manufacturing establishments, it seemed advisable in this report to consider only those employing five Negroes or more, in order not to give undue weight to condi-tions where only a relatively few Negroes were concerned. A similar situation was disclosed by the returns furnished by non-manufacturing establishments, and the returns from twenty-four employing a total of forty-one Negroes have been disregarded in this report in order to give proper weight to conditions in the sixty-eight employing five or more Negroes which reported a total of 9,483 Negroes.[1] The combined number of establishments, both manufacturing (69) and non-manufacturing (68), employing five or more Negroes each was 137.

[1] The total number of establishments (manufacturing and non-manufacturing) reported but not considered is fifty-nine, employing a total of 111 Negroes, or less than $\frac{1}{2}$ per cent of the total number reported.

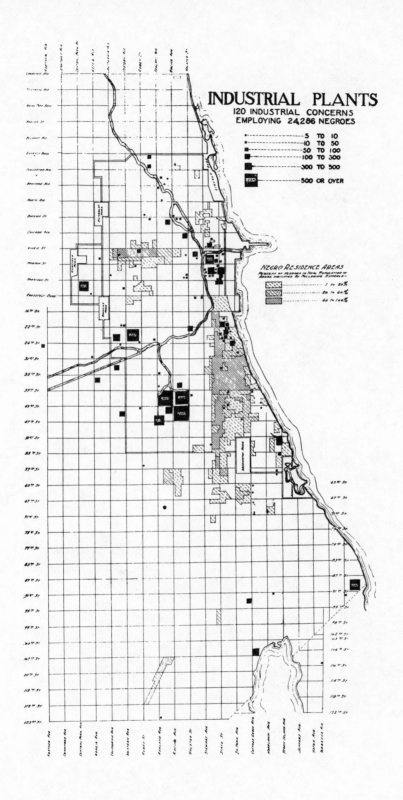

INDUSTRIAL PLANTS
120 INDUSTRIAL CONCERNS
EMPLOYING 24,286 NEGROES

5 TO 10
10 TO 50
50 TO 100
100 TO 300
300 TO 500
500 OR OVER

NEGRO RESIDENCE AREAS
PERCENT OF NEGROES TO TOTAL POPULATION IN
AREAS INDICATED BY FOLLOWING SYMBOLS

1 TO 30%
30 TO 60%
60 TO 100%

On the basis of the returns reported in the preliminary questionnaires certain establishments and industries were selected for more intensive study through personal interviews with employers, conferences participated in by employers and members of the Commission, and interviews with employees. The basis on which the selection was made was either the number of Negroes employed or the length of time during which Negroes had been employed, special attention being given to those industries and establishments which had employed Negro labor for the first time since the war. The industries employing large numbers of Negro workers which were selected for further study were: slaughtering, meat packing, and other food products; iron foundries and iron and steel products; laundries; needle trades; hotels; railroads; Pullman and dining-car services; tanneries; taxicab upkeep and repair; mail order.

An investigator for the Commission visited 101 establishments of the 137 reporting five or more Negro employees (ten establishments employing less than five Negroes each were also visited). Four industrial conferences or informal hearings were held by the Commission, large employers of Negro labor being invited to co-operate with the Commission by giving it the benefit of their experience with Negro labor. Among those who reported were general superintendents, assistant superintendents, employment managers, and other representatives of the large employers of Negro labor in Chicago as shown in Table XXI:

TABLE XXI

	No. of Negroes Employed in 1920
Pullman Car Shops	450
Armour & Co., Stock Yards	2,084
Morris & Co., Stock Yards	1,400
Swift & Co., Stock Yards	2,278
Wilson & Co., Stock Yards	818
Corn Products Refining Co., food products	500
International Harvester Co., agricultural machinery	1,551
Yellow Cab Co., taxicab	250
American Car and Foundry Co.*	20
American Brake Shoe and Foundry Co.	265
Brady Foundry Co.	125
National Malleable Castings Co.	427
Western Foundry Co	200
Sears, Roebuck & Co., mail order	1,423
Montgomery Ward & Co., mail order.	350
Gage Bros. Wholesale Millinery	73
Spring-filled Products Co., automobile cushions	250
Total	12,464

* This company formerly employed 200 Negroes.

2. NUMBER AND PERCENTAGE OF NEGRO EMPLOYEES

The number and percentage of Negro employees to the total employees in 136 establishments reporting five or more Negroes are shown in Table XXII.

TABLE XXII
NUMBER AND PERCENTAGE OF NEGRO EMPLOYEES IN ESTABLISHMENTS REPORTING FIVE OR MORE NEGROES

Industry	Number of Establishments	Total Employees	Negro Employees	Negro Percentage of Total
Manufacturing:				
Box manufacturing (paper)............	3	995	143	14
Clothing.............................	9	1,405	203	14
Cooperage...........................	2	327	106	32
Food products.......................	8	35,278	7,597	22
Iron and steel products (iron foundries)...	27	37,773	3,879	10
Tanneries............................	7	2,230	462	21
Miscellaneous:				
Lamp-shade manufacturing..........	1	275	75	27
Auto-cushion manufacturing..........	2	500	250	50
Other industries (manufacturing)......	10	2,571	139	5
Totals...........................	69	79,354	12,854	16
Non-manufacturing:				
Hotels..............................	9	1,714	923	53
Laundries...........................	20	1,736	764	44
Mail order*.........................	1	17,450	1,423	8
Railroads, dining- and Pullman-car service	16	7,816	5,408	68
Miscellaneous industries†..............	21	10,028	615	6
Totals...........................	67	38,744	9,133	23

* One mail-order establishment employing 350 Negroes is omitted from this table owing to incomplete return of total employees.

† This includes the following: public service, warehouse storage, taxicab up-keep, telegraph, etc.

3. INCREASE IN NEGRO LABOR SINCE 1915

The data obtained from questionnaires, interviews, and conferences with employers disclosed the fact that there has been a remarkable increase since 1915 in the number of Negro workers employed in manufacturing, in clerical occupations, and in laundries. As was to be expected, the number of Negroes in personal service (hotels, dining-cars, and parlor-cars) also increased, but the increase was negligible in comparison with the gain in the other fields mentioned.

Inability to obtain competent white workers was the reason given in practically every instance for the large increase in the number of Negroes employed since 1914. All of the large employers of Negro labor attending the conferences assigned shortage of labor as the principal reason for the increased number of Negroes reported. A few establishments (not represented in the conferences) reported that Negroes had first been employed to take the place of strikers, and increasing numbers had been employed thereafter. The establishments so reporting were hotels, a small clothing factory, and a warehouse company. Because of the labor shortage in the North, large numbers of Negroes left the southern states.

TABLE XXIII

NEGROES EMPLOYED FROM 1915 TO 1920 IN SIXTY-TWO MANUFACTURING
ESTABLISHMENTS CLASSIFIED ACCORDING TO INDUSTRIES*

Industries	Number of Establishments	1915	1916	1917	1918	1919	1920
Box making...........	3	3	3	116	116	145	143
Clothing..............	9	75	110	140	108	161	203
Other needlework.......	3	0	0	0	25	325	325
Cooperage.............	2	29	34	95	110	155	106
Food products†........	16	1,103	2,529	4,765	6,518	5,789	5,379
Iron and steel‡........	22	121	672	1,115	1,580	3,002	3,829
Tanneries.............	7	0	17	36	87	229	462
Miscellaneous manufacturing..............	10	15	15	24	48	75	140
Totals...........	62	1,346	3,380	6,291	8,592	9,881	10,587

* Seven manufacturing establishments omitted on account of insufficient returns.

† Two packing establishments employing 2,218 Negroes in 1920 have been omitted. They reported a large increase since 1914 but gave no definite figures.

‡ Five foundries employing a total of fifty men in 1920 have been omitted owing to failure to report figures for preceding years.

TABLE XXIV

NEGROES EMPLOYED FROM 1915 TO 1920 IN FORTY-SEVEN ESTABLISHMENTS
(NON-MANUFACTURING) CLASSIFIED ACCORDING TO INDUSTRIES*

Industries	Number of Establishments	1915	1916	1917	1918	1919	1920
Hotels...............	9	544	559	615	684	693	956
Laundries............	20	118	180	220	350	520	764
Mail order (clerical occupations)..............	2	0	0	0	664	1,650	1,400
Railroads (dining- and parlor-car service)....	16	3,939	3,940	4,274	4,493	4,506	5,363
Totals...........	47	4,601	4,679	5,109	6,191	7,369	8,483

* Establishments omitted owing to insufficient returns.

4. CHICAGO EMPLOYERS AND SOUTHERN NEGRO LABOR

During the course of its inquiry the statement was frequently made to members of the Commission or to its investigators that large employers of labor in Chicago, and particularly the packers, had imported many Negroes from the South. Although the Commission made a thorough investigation of such statements, no evidence of any value was discovered to support them.

The general superintendents of the Armour, Morris, Swift, and Wilson plants who attended conferences declared emphatically that their companies had not engaged in any encouragement of migration.

Mr. Samuel Gompers, president of the American Federation of Labor, being asked through correspondence from the Commission if he could furnish any evidence tending to prove the importation of Negroes into the Chicago district by employers, replied, "There is a plentitude of such evidence," but when Mr. Gompers was urged to cite the evidence, his reply was: "It cannot be unknown to you that some 30,000 Negroes were imported into the Chicago district during the steel strike. They did not go there of their own volition, but through inducements which were held out to them by the agents of employers who visited southern and western cities."

As, however, the Chicago race riot occurred a year prior to the steel strike, importation of Negroes at the latter time could not have affected the situation out of which the riot came. But the fact remains that labor leaders insist that employers in the Chicago district imported Negroes from the South, notwithstanding their inability to cite facts in support of this belief.

5. CLASSIFICATION OF NEGRO WORKERS

An accurate classification of Negro laborers into skilled, semi-skilled, and unskilled would help to an understanding of the position of the Negro in industry. In manufacturing, such a classification was attempted, but the results were unsatisfactory. These classes cannot be strictly defined, and different employers give them different meanings. In a number of important cases employers reported the total number of skilled and unskilled, and that figures for each class could not be compiled without great labor. In all such cases the total is listed as "unskilled." This class is thus unduly enlarged at the expense of the semi-skilled and the skilled. So the number of semi-skilled workers appears to be less than the skilled. These facts show that accuracy cannot be claimed for the classification in Table XXV.

TABLE XXV

NEGRO EMPLOYEES IN SIXTY-SIX MANUFACTURING ESTABLISHMENTS
CLASSIFIED AS SKILLED, SEMI-SKILLED, AND UNSKILLED

Industry	Number of Establishments	Total Negroes	Skilled	Semi-skilled	Unskilled
Box manufacturing............	3	143	....	....	143
Clothing....................	9	203	57	29	117
Cooperage....................	2	106	8	45	53
Food products*..............	8	7,597	229	12	7,356
Iron and steel.............	27	3,879	434	180	3,265
Tanneries...................	7	462	175	....	287
Miscellaneous................	10	139	24	1	114
Total†..................	66	12,529	927	267	11,335

* These figures include skilled and semi-skilled in three packing establishments reporting that Negroes were employed under each classification but giving no separate figures.

† Three establishments (lamp-shade, auto-cushion manufacturing) not included. Failed to classify the employees but reported that they had hand sewers and machine operators, including skilled, semi-skilled, and unskilled.

The attempt to classify Negro workers according to occupation failed because the necessary information was not obtainable, especially from large employers. Nevertheless the number of workers in certain occupations reported by a few establishments is suggestive of the fields recently opened to Negroes in Chicago. In 1910[1] there were only thirty-one Negro molders in Chicago, while in 1920 there were 304 reported by ten establishments. In 1910 there were but twenty-eight factory sewers or machine operators, while in 1920 there were 382 in twelve factories. In 1910 there were 934 Negroes employed in clerical occupations as compared with 1,400 in two concerns in 1920. In 1910 there were but 287 Negro laundry operatives in Chicago, while there were 764 reported by twenty laundries in 1920.

6. WAGES OF NEGRO WORKERS

The period of this industrial investigation—the spring and summer of 1920—was one of exceptional demand for labor and of high wages. Employers were glad to get workers of any sort at high pay.[2] In branches of employment where Negroes were permitted to work, their wages were generally the same as those of the white workers. In interviewing many Negro workers the Commission's investigators found practically no complaints of discrimination in wages on the same tasks. And the Chicago Urban League which, through its industrial department, places more Negroes in employment than any other agency in Chicago reported that it had very few complaints of such discrimination.

Some discrimination was practiced by foremen in placing or keeping Negroes at work on processes that yielded smaller returns than those to which white workers were assigned. In the field of common labor, where the largest number of Negroes are employed, some kinds of piecework yield greater returns than others. The tendency of foremen in some plants was to place Negroes on those processes yielding the smallest returns. The following are instances of such discrimination in favor of the white workers in the same plants.

In two large foundries white molders were given standard patterns, which remain the same throughout the year and permit the working up of speed; while patterns that were changed frequently, and made production slower were given to the Negroes. As speed determined the piecework earnings, the Negroes could not earn as much as the white molders in the same foundry.

In the several plants the white workers were favored in the distribution of overtime work; or Negroes were not permitted to work at all on overtime

[1] Figures quoted for 1910 are taken from the Thirteenth Census, 1910, Vol. IV, Table VIII, pp. 544-47.

[2] The contrast between these high wages and the wages which Negroes coming from the South had previously earned is shown in the study of family histories of migrant Negroes.

at "time and a half" rates or on Sundays at "double pay" as long as white workers were available.

While in the larger industries there was seldom any complaint about inequality in the basic rate of pay for common labor, restrictions upon the promotion and advancement of Negroes frequently prevented them from earning higher wages. In one department of a large food-products plant Negroes reached the maximum rate of 61 cents per hour after a few months' employment. No further advancement could be had because the superintendent was not willing to place Negro foremen over white workers. A Negro in the starch-mixing department held a skilled position as starch tester. It became apparent that in carrying out his duties many of the starch mixers would be subject to his immediate direction. The foreman apparently did not approve of this and ordered him to teach his duties to a Polish workman. The Negro declined to do this, and the matter was referred to the general superintendent. After an investigation it was decided to permit the Negro to retain his position as tester, but he was given no authority over the men.

In view of the fluctuations in wages, the impracticability of getting actual records of wages from all plants, and the discrepancies which in some instances did appear between reported and actual wages, it seemed desirable to supplement the information of the Commission's investigators. The records of the industrial department of the Chicago Urban League afforded the most complete data on wages received by Negroes that could be found in Chicago. During the year 1919 it placed more than 14,000 Negroes in plants in the Chicago District. In each case, when securing Negro employment, it kept a record of the wages actually offered and of conditions of work. If the Negro made complaint that the wage or work conditions did not prove to be as stated, it investigated the complaint.

Included in these records are the Pullman Company, Wilson & Company (packers), Armour & Company, Morris Company, Swift & Company, Illinois Malleable Iron Company, National Malleable and Castings Company, International Harvester Company, the General Can Company, the Republic Box Company, Chicago Fire Brick Company, Sears, Roebuck & Company, Superior Process Company, Consumers Coal Company, Corn Products Refining Company at Argo, United States Quartermasters' Department, Adams & Westlake Company, Griess Pfleger Tanning Company, and Inland Steel Company.

In the industries listed above, the minimum wage rate per hour is 42.5 cents, which is the minimum rate for the packing industries. The maximum rate is sixty-one cents per hour paid by the Corn Products Refining Company at Argo and the International Harvester Company. Neither of the latter, however, represents a basic wage. The average wage for the thirty-six companies is 48.7 cents. These wage rates cover the most arduous tasks found in the list of common labor. Three items for track laborers are included. Others include freight handlers, yardmen, truckers, sweepers, foundry laborers, etc. Six companies work ten hours per day, twelve companies nine hours, one company nine and one-half hours, seventeen companies eight hours. Four pay bonuses, not including packers, who also pay a bonus in compliance with the award of a judge acting as mediator between the packers and the union.

The building trades are not included, but of the three independent contractors listed the wage paid common laborers is 50 cents per hour, 60 cents per hour, and 70 cents per hour, respectively, for eight hours, while the union rate of pay for common labor is $1.00 per hour for eight hours, time and one-half for overtime, and double time for Sunday.

7. WOMEN EMPLOYEES IN INDUSTRIAL ESTABLISHMENTS

Negro women employed in thirty-one industrial establishments worked, in five of them forty-four hours a week, in fifteen of them forty-eight hours, in seven of them forty-nine hours, and in four of them fifty-one hours. The weekly pay ranged from $9.00 to $15.00 a week as clothing folders, to as high as $20.00 to $35.00 a week as clothing drapers or finishers. Map mounting paid $15.00 a week, book binding $15.00, paper-box making $13.00, tobacco stripping $16.40, core making (foundry work)$16.40, twine weaving $17.40, silk-shade making $10.00 to $18.00, food packing $12.00 to $15.00, mattress making $12.00 to $22.00, riveters (canvas) $15.00, paper sorters $12.00, steam laundry workers (unskilled) $13.00 to $16.00, steam laundry hand workers $18.00 to $29.00, power-machine operators on men's caps $15.00 to $18.00, on aprons $14.00 to $18.00, on dresses $15.00 to $18.00, on overalls (union shop) $18.00 to $25.00, and on overalls (non-union shop) $15.00 to $18.00.

Of fourteen companies employing colored girls as operators, five paid on a piecework basis only. Two paid from $12.00 to $18.00 per week, depending on the skill of the operator, two companies paid $14.00 per week to beginners, one paid $15.00 per week to beginners, three paid $12.00 per week to beginners, one paid $18.00 per week to beginners, the latter being a union shop.

Considerable unrest has been traceable to delay on the part of the managers in promoting beginners above the beginning wage. Girls have been retained at a beginning wage for an unreasonable time after acquiring satisfactory skill and production. This condition is known to the Women's Trade Union League, but no well-directed effort has ever been made to unionize colored workers in the garment trades, except when they have been called in as strike breakers to replace white workers. An instance of this was the strike at the C. B. Shane Company, manufacturers of raincoats, where colored girls were employed to replace striking white union workers. At that time very few colored girls were members of the local union. According to an official of the Women's Garment Workers' Union not more than 125 colored workers have become members.

8. HOTEL AND RESTAURANT EMPLOYEES

Men.—In about twenty-five hotels and restaurants in which colored men are employed, wages are as follows:

Chief cooks	$25.00 to $50.00 per week
Waiters.........................	25.00 to 40.00 per week
Bus boys........................	14.00 to 20.00 per week
Hotel porters....................	45.00 tб 65.00 per month
Dishwashers.....................	15.00 to 20.00 per week
Second cooks....................	20.00 to 35.00 per week
Bell-boys.......................	40.00 to 45.00 per month
Shoe shiners and washroom porters..	15.00 to 17.00 per week

In all of the above-listed occupations the wages are augmented by tips. It is difficult to form an accurate estimate of the amount earned in tips for the reason that it is conditioned upon the character of service rendered and the inclination of the person served to pay for personal service. It would be fair to estimate that in hotels and restaurants known to employees as "good houses" the tips range from $2.00 to $5.00 per day. In a colored restaurant in the neighborhood of Thirty-first and State streets a wage of $5.00 per week is paid to waitresses, while the tips have been known to total five times that amount.

Women.—The twenty-five hotels and restaurants concerning which the Chicago Urban League's Industrial Department has records, employ women in the occupations and at the wages listed as follows:

Waitresses.........	$ 8.00 to $15.00 per week and tips (board)
Chambermaids.....	25.00 to 45.00 per month and tips (board)
Pantry girls........	15.00 to 18.00 per week and board
Kitchen help.......	9.00 to 16.00 per week and board

Allowing an average of 35 cents per meal for three meals, $1.05 per day or $7.35 per week should be added where board is included. This would make the following schedule of wages:

Waitresses...............	$15.35 to $22.35 per week
Chambermaids...........	54.40 to 74.40 per month
Pantry girls..............	22.35 to 25.35 per week
Kitchen help.............	16.35 to 23.35 per week

In clerical positions colored men have had very little opportunity, except in the post-office. There are exceptions, however, such as shipping clerks, storekeepers, and bookkeepers.

The girls employed as long-hand entry clerks, typists, checkers, routers, and Elliott-Fisher and adding-machine operators received during 1920 from $15.00 to $16.00 as a beginning wage. The chief supervisor (colored) in charge of 600 girls in one of the large mail-order houses received $23.00 per week, and the assistant superintendent, a white man, received $50.00 per week while studying the mail-order business under the chief supervisor. When the management's attention was called to the inequality, two additional supervisors were added and the work lessened without increase of pay.

Another firm employing several hundred colored girls paid a welfare worker $20.00 per week, while another with half that number of girls paid $25.00 per week.

There was a deep-seated suspicion existing among the clerical force of a firm employing a large number of colored girls that the white girls employed by the same company received a higher wage than that paid the colored girls. The suspicion grew out of the mistake of an employment manager in mistaking a colored girl for a white one.

9. RAILROAD WORKERS

Dining-car men.—According to the records of the Railway Men's International Industrial Benevolent Association, wages of dining-car waiters prior to 1916 were universally $25.00 per month, with the exception of the Santa Fe, which paid from $35.00 to $40.00 per month for "preferred" runs. The Chicago, Burlington & Quincy allowed an additional $3.00 to the $25.00 standard for men in service ten years or more.

In 1918, after the roads had been federalized, the minimum wage became $48.00 per month. In May, 1919, a further increase to $55.00 per month and overtime on a mileage basis was granted. This gave an average of $62.00 per month for so called "transcontinental" runs, that is, service between Chicago and the Pacific Coast.

Effective February 1, 1920, wages were adjusted to an hourly basis, which gave payment for overtime in excess of 240 hours per month. On July 20, 1920, most roads allowed a general increase to dining-car men which brought the average to $65.00 per month.

An official of the Railway Men's International Industrial Benevolent Association estimated that the tips and salary of the average waiter were $105.00 per month, including three meals valued at 35 cents per day. This estimate was accepted by the Federal Railway Labor Board. This low estimate is arrived at because it is generally the custom to feed waiters and kitchen crews on leftovers which would otherwise become waste.

Porters.—The wages of porters, including tips, is estimated at $105.00 per month. The present salary paid to porters is $65.00 per month. In May, 1919, the minimum basis was $60.00 per month on a mileage basis of $.0055 per mile in excess of 11,000 miles per month. In December of the same year a final adjustment of the wage scale was made in which length of service was taken as a basis. For three years or less the pay was $63.00 per month; for from three to ten years the pay was $66.00 per month; for ten years or more the pay was $69.00 per month. The Railway Men's International Industrial Benevolent Association furnished the above information.

According to the same authority, on January 1, 1921, most roads reduced the hourly overtime for waiters, cooks, and stewards and placed it on a straight time service, with pay ranging between $60.00 and $65.00 per month. A twenty-four-day month was also established. This was equal to a reduction of wages for the class of labor referred to.

In the case of thirty-one orders for porters in stores, restaurants, cafés, and drugstores, office buildings, etc., the wages ran from $12.00 per week to $25.00. Some difficulty was experienced in determining a minimum wage, for the reason that in many instances full time is not required, porters being allowed to do odd jobs on their own account. Of these thirty-one, three received $12 a week, one $13, four $15, two $16, one $17, four $18, two $19, six $20, three $21, one $21.25, one $22, and two $25.

Apartment-house janitors usually are affiliated with the labor unions. An instance of financial benefit is as follows: F—, who is engineer for an apartment in Evanston, before joining the union received $45.00 per month for his services, with quarters in a basement apartment. He now receives $125.00 per month with the same quarters.

Firemen with licenses were offered from $125.00 to $150.00 per month in ten different positions filled by the League.

10. DOMESTIC WORKERS

Eighty-one orders for maids for service in private families were listed with the following results: maximum, $18.00 per week with room and board; minimum, $6.00 per week with room and board; average, $12.84 per week with room and board. Of these, twenty-six were paid $15, eight $14, twelve $12, fifteen $10. Three received $18, and one $20.

Children's nurses.—Fifteen were listed, of whom five were paid $15.00 per week with room and board, six were paid $12.00, one was paid $7.00, two were paid $5.00, and one was paid $3.00.

Cooks.—Sixteen were listed as follows: one was paid $25.00 per week with room and board, four were paid $18.00, three were paid $16.00, six were paid $15.00, and two were paid $14.00.

The minimum wage for cooks indicated is $14.00 per week with room and board. The maximum wage is $25.00 per week with room and board, while in the case of children's nurses the maximum wage is $15.00 per week and the minimum $3.00 per week for part time.

Housemen.—Out of a list of twenty-five orders, a minimum of $40.00 per month with room and board, a maximum of $100.00 per month with room and board, and an average of $65.00 per month with room and board.

Chauffeurs.—Minimum of $100.00 per month with room and board and maximum of $150.00 per month with room and board. It is difficult to outline the duties of chauffeurs for the reason that they often perform the duties of butler, houseman, yardman, etc., in addition to that of chauffeur.

Couples.—(Man and wife.) Out of twenty-five orders listed, the following wages were offered: minimum of $85.00 per month with room and board. A maximum of $165.00 per month with room and board.

Laundresses.—Usually employed by the day. The prevailing rate per day over the past year was $4.00 and car fare, with one meal. This wage was asked by common understanding and without any visible form of organization. Since November 1, 1920, when the unemployment situation became manifest, $3.60 per day, car fare, and one meal has been accepted.

From 1918 to November 1, 1920, a serious shortage of domestic help was noted. Colored girls and women deserted this grade of work for the factories, where shorter hours and free Sundays were secured. The larger pay of domestic employment did not attract the average worker, for the reason that free evenings for recreation and amusement were apparently more desirable than the isolation and long hours of domestic service.

Recently housekeepers secured Negro girls from the southern states and imported Negro girls from the British West India Islands[1] in an attempted solution of the domestic-help problem. Transportation and clothes were furnished by employers and some sort of verbal agreement entered into by which the girls were expected to work out this indebtedness. Instances have come to the attention of the Chicago Urban League which seem to indicate that these agreements have not worked out satisfactorily. For example: One colored woman was brought from a small town in Florida to a Chicago suburb by a white family on such an agreement. After a few weeks' service the employer complained that the work performed by the woman as a general maid was unsatisfactory. Abuse followed. The woman sought to go to a Negro family under the pretence that she wished to return a pair of borrowed shoes. Her employer, fearing that she wished to escape, drove her to the home of the Negro family in his automobile. Once inside the home, she told a story of how her employer had kicked, beaten, and threatened her with a revolver if she attempted to leave. The Negro family gave asked-for shelter and informed the employer that she would not return. After threatening to take her away by force, the employer went away and the woman remained. A suit followed on a charge of assault and battery and the employer was discharged for lack of evidence.

A few weeks ago a white resident of another Chicago suburb applied to the juvenile court for the guardianship of a colored girl. The court, being unable to handle the case, requested the advice of the Chicago Urban League. The details of the case were substantially as follows:

A Roman Catholic organization in Jamaica, British West Indies, sent ten or twelve Jamaican girls to the United States, upon applications of housekeepers, to serve as domestics. Some verbal agreement had been entered into whereby the girls were to accept service as domestics and work out the cost of transportation and clothing at a stipulated rate per week. The arrangement seems to have progressed fairly until the girls became acquainted with

[1] The importation of these girls from the British West Indies was noticed by the Commission after its period of investigation had ended.

other colored people residing in the neighborhood. It was then discovered that they were working at a wage considerably lower than the usual wage. The girl in question, who was a minor but seems to have misrepresented her age when applying for a passport, was receiving $6.00 per week, one dollar of which was paid in cash and the balance deducted to cover the expense of clothing and transportation. After becoming dissatisfied with these wages, the girl left the home of her white employer, who sought to be appointed her guardian so that he could restrain her. A guardian has not thus far been appointed, for the reason that the legal status of the girl and the legality of the contract entered into are doubtful.

III. EMPLOYERS' EXPERIENCE WITH NEGRO LABOR

The entrance of Negroes in large numbers into manufacturing industries and clerical occupations is one of the striking facts shown by this investigation. Shortage of labor due to war conditions created many openings for the Negro. Whether he will remain in these fields and become an increasingly important factor in them will depend in a large degree upon his efficiency and reliability, as well as upon absence of racial friction, satisfactory wages, etc. It was therefore deemed important to learn how the Negro improved his industrial opportunities.

The Commission made some investigation of this subject, seeking the opinion of as many employers as possible who had had experience with Negro workers. The inquiry covered two points: (1) a general question in the preliminary questionnaire, to learn whether Negro labor had proved satisfactory; and (2) a comparison of the Negro with the white worker in efficiency, reliability, regularity, and labor turnover. The facts under each head are considered separately below, following a brief consideration of the difference between the southern and northern Negro.

I. SOUTHERN AND NORTHERN NEGROES COMPARED

Many employers drew a distinction between the recent southern migrants and northern Negroes, and commented upon certain shortcomings of the former, although they expressed themselves as satisfied on the whole with Negro labor.

For instance, the representative of a foundry company with 200 Negroes out of a total of 950 employees said:

It appears to me that the men coming from the South get here and for a limited length of time seem to have a different view of things. They do things that probably the Chicago Negro wouldn't do. They don't seem to know exactly how to control themselves. They are unsettled and to a great degree unsteady. The northern-born Negro is more active. He is brighter in a way and a little more ambitious. The southern Negroes are inclined to work today, lay off tomorrow, and be back the next day on the job again.

A representative of a large machinery-manufacturing establishment employing 1,500 Negroes out of a total of 23,000 employees in Chicago expressed the same opinion in these words:

Our experience with Negroes has a tendency to show that these people do not realize that there is such a thing as steady work. They work for possibly a week or two, then say they are obliged to lay off for some imaginary cause and will probably return within a week or four weeks. We believe they are improving and will be better as time goes on and they become more used to the way work and business are done in the North.

The superintendent of a foundry which increased its Negro employees in five years from six to 125 out of a total of 466 employees was of the following opinion:

The Negro up here from the South never heard of working six days a week and being on time every morning and staying until the job was done. It is entirely foreign to his idea of things, but with a little persistent effort and showing him that it is necessary he soon learns the system the same as the others, and I do not believe he is any worse than the white man after he has been here a year or two.

The superintendent of a company employing more that 2,000 Negroes out of a total of 10,000 employees in Chicago declared:

The southern Negroes have not yet become thoroughly reconciled to working six days a week. Down South they are accustomed to taking off Saturdays, and they are quite frequently absent on Saturday. That is not true of the colored man who has been with us a long time. He is accustomed to the regularity of six days a week, but the men from the South have the weakness of being away on Saturdays.

In general it was the employers of large numbers of Negroes who differentiated between the southern and the northern Negro. Employers of Negroes in small numbers were more inclined to judge all Negroes by those recently arrived from the South.

2. NEGRO LABOR SATISFACTORY

One of the questions contained in the preliminary questionnaire was: "Has your Negro labor proved satisfactory?" Of 137 questionnaires returned by establishments employing five or more Negro workers, 118 reported that Negro labor had proved satisfactory and nineteen that it had not proved satisfactory.

The significance of these returns is disclosed by Table XXVI, in which the establishments are classified by industries, and the number of Negro employees in establishments reporting Negro labor satisfactory is shown to be 21,640 as contrasted with 697 Negro employees in the nineteen establishments reporting Negro labor unsatisfactory.

TABLE XXVI

NEGRO LABOR SATISFACTORY OR UNSATISFACTORY IN ESTABLISHMENTS
CLASSIFIED BY INDUSTRIES

INDUSTRY	TOTAL NUMBER ESTABLISH-MENTS	TOTAL NEGROES EMPLOYED	ESTABLISHMENTS REPORT-ING NEGRO LABOR SATISFACTORY		ESTABLISHMENTS REPORT-ING NEGRO LABOR UN-SATISFACTORY	
			Number	Number of Negroes Employed in These Estab-lishments	Number	Number of Negroes Employed in These Estab-lishments
Manufacturing:						
Clothing.........	9	203	8	191	1	12
Food products....	8	7,597	7	7,547	1	50
Iron and steel....	27	3,879	22	3,750	5	129
Tanneries........	7	462	6	421	1	41
Miscellaneous*...	18	713	13	464	5†	249
Totals.......	69	12,854	56	12,373	13	481
Non-manufacturing:						
Railroads........	16	5,408	16	5,408	....	....
Hotels..........	9	923	8	911	1	12
Laundries.......	20	764	16	587	4	177
Mail order.......	2	1,773	2	1,773	....	....
Public service....	4	42	4	42	....	....
Taxicab upkeep...	1	250	1	250	....	....
Miscellaneous†...	16	323	15	296	1	27
Totals.......	68	9,483	62	9,267	6	216
Totals, all in-dustries...	137	22,337	118	21,640	19	697

* Includes a scattering list of industries represented by one to three establishments—Negro labor not important factor in these industries.

† Includes three paper-box manufacturing plants with ten, twenty, and 113 Negro employees, largely women; and cooperage plant with ninety-six Negro employees and one sausage-casing plant with ten Negro employees. These plants reported Negro labor "slow," "lazy," or "unreliable."

3. NEGRO AND WHITE LABOR COMPARED

At a conference at which Negro and white workers were under discussion a large foundry representative suggested that such a comparison was unfair to the Negro because he was still a newcomer in manufacturing industries and could not be expected to be as efficient, reliable, and regular as the white worker who had been thus engaged much longer. Other employers felt that this point should be borne in mind.

Efficiency.—Comparing the efficiency of the Negro worker and the white worker, seventy-one employers interviewed (thirty-four manufacturing and thirty-seven non-manufacturing establishments) considered the Negro equally efficient, and twenty-two employers (thirteen manufacturing and nine non-manufacturing) considered the Negro less efficient.[1]

[1] Representatives of a number of the 101 establishments visited did not feel able to make a comparison between the Negro and white workers.

The seventy-one establishments which reported Negro labor as equally efficient as white labor included all of the large employers of Negro labor, with very few exceptions. Ability shown by Negro workers in widely dissimilar occupations and industries was commented upon. The following instances are of interest:

Foundries: "Our star molder in the foundry is a Negro who has been with us twenty years. Our best truck driver is a Negro who has been with us about eighteen years." "About the best grinder we have in one department is a colored man." The superintendent of a large foundry employing 125 Negroes said:

I covered thirty foundries, members of the National Association when I was serving on a certain Committee, and I know that in their departments Negroes have made very good. Out of the thirty foundries, there are half or more which have colored men in now which did not have colored men two years ago. One of the instances, a little foundry I know of, had four men in the grinding department; one colored man and his partner wanted to take the job of running the grinding room. The partner wanted to do it all himself, and is now doing what four men were doing formerly.

That the Negro is apt in learning new work is illustrated by an instance cited by the same superintendent:

I know of a Pullman porter who has been with the Pullman Company twenty years who turned out to be as good a helper as we had in the foundry. Take a man who has made beds for twenty years, put him to carrying melted iron in a ladle, which is a real man's job, and make good at it, and I think he's going some! We had one man who did that and did it well. He was a helper that the different foremen tried to get hold of, wanted to have him with them.

Public service: The probation department of the juvenile court reported six Negro employees. "The colored employees are intelligent, efficient persons. With one exception they are probation officers. One employee is in charge of the probation clerk's office and not only works with white clerks but directs the work of nine white persons."

The office of the recorder of deeds reports seventeen Negro employees in the folio or record-writing department. "The employees are marked on their efficiency. Percentages of efficiency run from 94.5 to 98 per cent among the colored clerks, and several of them averaged 97.9 per cent and 98 per cent for the past three years."

Stock Yards: "Negroes make skilled workmen. They are among the best of what are known as 'knife-men' we have."

Whether Negro labor shows greater efficiency in a working unit composed entirely of colored workers or in a mixed unit of Negro and white workers is an unsettled question. Only a few employers expressed an opinion on this point (not affording a sufficient basis for generalization), but it is interesting to note that of four foundries, one favored the separate unit and three the mixed unit, while a large food-products company had found both satisfactory.

Several employers mentioned the fact that, because of his knowledge of English, the Negro is frequently more efficient than the foreign-speaking worker. One wool warehouse company, for example, reported that Poles were satisfactory under the old method of shipping wool in carloads from a single shipper, but the new system, with shipments of hundreds of sacks tagged with the names of as many shippers, required laborers unloading the cars to separate the shipments into sections. This the Poles were unable to do, while the Negroes did the work very efficiently.

Reliability.—Does the Negro require more supervision than the white worker in order to secure equally good results? An opinion was expressed on this point by ninety-two employers; sixty-three (thirty manufacturing and thirty-three non-manufacturing establishments) considered that the Negro did not require more supervision while twenty-eight (sixteen manufacturing and thirteen non-manufacturing establishments) considered that he did. The general superintendents of two of the large packing companies expressed contrary views on this point during one of the conferences. One said:

Negroes do not require as much supervision as some of those racial groups who do not understand the language. We can talk to a man and tell him what to do, where to go to do the work and how to do it, we can accomplish a whole lot more than if we had to send an individual with him constantly from place to place to show him how to do it. To that extent the Negro has the advantage over the man who cannot talk the English language.

The superintendent of the other company expressed the opinion that Negroes require more supervision than white workers:

For example, when they are working together in groups, especially after pay-day, they are inclined to wander into isolated spots and shoot craps. We've a good deal of trouble of that kind. They spend their money when they get it more recklessly than white people.

The representative of a food-products company with 500 Negro employees in the working force of 3,000 stated that the company had found no need of greater supervision of Negro workers than of white.

A representative of a taxicab company employing 250 colored workers stated:

We have some colored employees we trust absolutely and as far as any white employees. We have some colored men in the garage, and they take more supervision not because they are colored but because they lack education and are shiftless, but this you would find in the same grade of white workers.

A preliminary questionnaire returned by the president of a laundry company employing eighty-two Negroes out of a total of 110 employees reported:

We have a number of exceptionally good and reliable Negro employees. These men and women need very little supervision. We get some, who have never worked in industries, who require more supervision and are not very steady. On the whole we are pleased with our Negro employees.

Regularity.—Of the employers interviewed, fifty-seven (twenty-three manufacturing and thirty-four non-manufacturing establishments) expressed an opinion that "absenteeism" among colored workers was no greater than among white workers, while thirty-six employers (twenty-four manufacturing and twelve non-manufacturing establishments) reported that it was greater. In this connection the habits of the southern Negro, commented upon above, would naturally exercise great influence. The superintendent of one of the packing companies employing 2,084 Negroes reported:

Previous to the war and up to the war the Negro was the poorest in attendance in the plant. Since the war his attendance compares favorably with any other class of employees in the Yards. It is pretty hard to explain excepting this, as they lived here longer they acquired better habits, I mean more ambition, and ambition brought about the necessity for better methods of living, better clothing, and they required more money and I guess they found out in a short time that work brought its compensations.

The tendency to work and accumulate a little and then take a vacation is no more pronounced among the colored workers than among the white workers, according to the representative of a food-products company employing 500 Negroes out of a total of 3,000 employees.

Labor turnover and "hope on the job."—Of the fifty-two employers expressing an opinion on the comparative labor turnover of Negro and white workers, twenty-four (eleven manufacturing and thirteen non-manufacturing establishments) considered the labor turnover about equal, and twenty-eight (eighteen manufacturing and ten non-manufacturing establishments) considered the turnover greater among the Negro workers.

Closely connected with the question of labor turnover among Negroes is the question of "hope on the job," as one alert Negro expressed it. The desire to secure improved conditions of work and higher wages is shared by all workers irrespective of race. If Negro workers are not allowed to advance to better positions in a given plant, or if they are discriminated against by having their efficiency underrated by foremen, the turnover of Negro labor will naturally be high. The attitude of foremen largely determines whether Negro workers will succeed or fail. Superintendents of large plants realizing this fact have taken special care to educate foremen in the treatment of Negro labor.

For example, the superintendent of a tannery with 175 Negroes out of a total of 600 employees notified his foremen that he intended to use Negro labor, and that any foreman who felt that he could not teach colored workers would have to yield his place to someone who could. Frequent lectures to foremen were necessary to make them realize that fairness to Negro labor meant tolerance of a beginner's awkwardness and shortcomings and refraining from the use of insulting terms such as "nigger," etc.

Another company reported that when it attempted to fill skilled positions with Negroes the foremen said they would never be able to teach them as long as they lived. "It couldn't be done." The foremen were told they had to do it, and they now agree that it can be done and are "quite won over to the point of employing Negroes." The experience of this plant led the superintendent to the conclusion that no particular race is especially fitted for any given kind of work.

The superintendent of a foundry employing 2,500 men, of whom 427 are Negroes, said:

The foremen told me one time that they never could get a colored man to grind because he was afraid of the wheel. I thought we'd better try out a few of them. We found that was not the fact at all. One of the best grinders we now have is a colored man.

In discussing the attitude of foremen toward colored labor, the superintendent of another large foundry made this significant statement:

I think 50 per cent of what trouble we who employ Negro labor have is due to inefficient foremen, and the failure is in the foreman directly over the man to understand the Negro. As I see it, the Negro must be handled differently from the Pole whom we have usually had in the common labor capacity. We cannot handle the Negro the same as we could the Pole. Our foremen have not been accustomed here in Chicago in our shops to handling Negroes, and at times I have a real fight to see a Negro get an absolutely square deal.

The industrial secretary of the Chicago Urban League, referring to a large firm engaged in the manufacture of machinery, remarked:

I find the attitude of the company liberal. Negroes are advanced to high-grade positions, although some foremen need education in order to have them take the proper attitude toward the employment of Negroes. One foreman set their efficiency down to 75 per cent; the matter was taken to the efficiency department and his statement was found to be untrue. This bears out the point that Negroes will not succeed where foremen do not intend them to succeed.

Despite occasional statements that the Negro is slow or shiftless, the volume of evidence before the Commission shows that Negroes are satisfactory employees and compare favorably with other racial groups.

4. NEGRO WOMEN IN INDUSTRY

Before the war created openings in industry for Negro women, they were even more definitely restricted in their choice of occupations than were Negro men. Restricted opportunity is evident from the fact that, in 1910, almost two-thirds of the gainfully occupied Negro women in Chicago were engaged in two occupational groups, "servants" and "laundresses not in laundries," these being included among those in domestic and personal service who numbered more than three-fourths. The enumeration of Negro women gainfully employed in Chicago in 1910 classified in the census according to industries is given in Table XXVII.

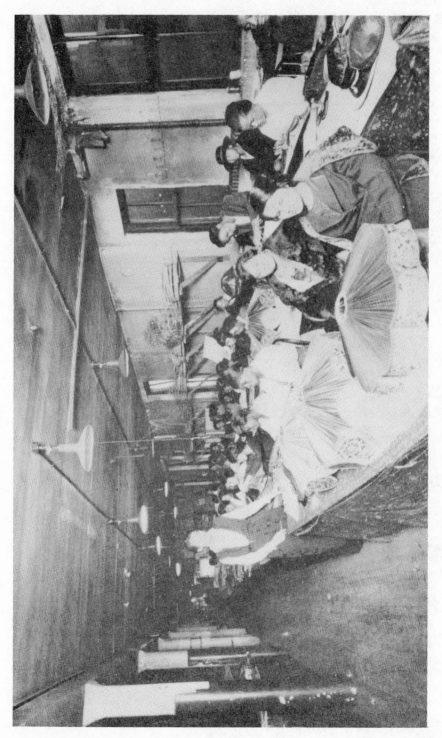

NEGRO WOMEN AND GIRLS EMPLOYED IN A LAMP-SHADE FACTORY

Work room is poorly lighted and generally unattractive

To learn the special problems concerning Negro women in industry, one conference was devoted to the industries recently opened to them. Representatives of four establishments employing a total of 1,713 Negro women

TABLE XXVII

NEGRO WOMEN GAINFULLY OCCUPIED IN CHICAGO IN 1910,
CLASSIFIED BY INDUSTRIES

Industry	Number	Percentage of Total
Manufacturing and mechanical industries....	998	11
Trade and transportation.................	96	1
Professional service......................	323	4
Clerical occupations......................	163	2
Domestic and personal service:		
Laundresses not in laundries.............	2,115	
Servants...............................	3,512	78
Other domestic and personal service.......	1,336	
General and unclassified occupations........	337	4
Total gainfully occupied.............	8,880	100

TABLE XXVIII

NEGRO WOMEN IN FIFTY ESTABLISHMENTS CLASSIFIED BY INDUSTRIES IN 1920*

Industry	Number of Establishments Reporting	Total Employees	Total Negro Employees	Total Negro Women Employees
Manufacturing:				
Tanneries.....................	1	600	175	50
Iron and steel.................	3	10,435	1,729	74
Slaughtering and packing.......	3	20,990	4,818	437
Cooperage....................	2	327	106	30
Clothing......................	9	1,405	203	202
Other needle trades...........	3	775	325	325
Box making (paper)	3	995	143	104
Miscellaneous.................	3	1,543	95	73
Totals....................	27	37,070	7,594	1,295
Non-manufacturing:*				
Hotels.......................	4	550	250	69
Taxicab upkeep...............	1	1,600	250	100
Laundries....................	16	1,511	664	543
Mail order (clerical occupations)†	2	....	1,773	1,400
Totals....................	23	....	2,937	2,112

* Of the eighty-seven establishments (employing five or more Negroes) covered by the investigation but omitted from this table, forty-two had no Negro women employees and forty-five failed to classify Negro workers by sex.

† One establishment failed to report total employees.

attended the conference. The investigation of the 101 establishments (employing five or more Negroes) disclosed the presence of women in a large majority of cases, but in a number of instances the management was unable to tell the sex of workers from the records kept and gave the investigator the total number of Negroes employed without classification by sex. Of the 137 establishments reporting, forty-two had no Negro women employees; forty-five kept no separate sex records; fifty reported separately the number of Negro women workers.

Comparing the industries in which Negro women were employed in 1910 with the figures quoted for 1920, a striking increase is seen in the total engaged in manufacturing, 998 being the total Negro women reported for all manufacturing establishments in Chicago in 1910, as compared with 1,295 Negro women reported by twenty-seven establishments in 1920.

Comparisons for special industries and occupations show the contrasts between 1910 and 1920 in Table XXIX.

TABLE XXIX

Industry	1910	1920	Number of Establishments
Sewers and sewing-machine operators in factories..............	25	527	12
Slaughtering and packing-house operatives....................	8	437	3
Box making (paper)..............	3	104	3
Tanneries......................	0	50	1
Clerical occupations.............	163	1,400	2
Laundry operatives.............	184	543	16
Taxicab cleaning................	0	100	1

Labor shortage was given as the reason for employing Negro women and girls by all of the firms employing them in large numbers. The outlook for Negro women in industry when there is a labor surplus is uncertain. Employers employing 1,713 Negro women represented at a conference, May 18, 1920, agreed that there were no indications of a reduction of employment. This question is considered at length hereafter in "Future of the Negro in Chicago Industries."

EXPERIMENTS WITH NEGRO WOMEN WORKERS

Employers' opinions regarding the character of Negro labor without reference to sex were considered above. Particular comments concerning male workers were quoted there, comments upon women workers are now given. Four employers of Negro women in large numbers within the past two years gave the Commission the benefit of their experience. They were two mail-order concerns, a manufacturer of automobile spring cushions, and a wholesale millinery shop.

The mail-order house which established a large office for Negro entry clerks in September, 1918, was the first to try the experiment. It had no precedent to guide it and "did not know how the colored girl would act in business." The unit was opened with ninety girls, and increased in the fall

NEGRO WOMEN EMPLOYED ON POWER MACHINES IN A LARGE APRON FACTORY

This concern when it increased its number of Negro women combined its four shops and moved into this modern daylight factory building

of 1919 to 650 girls, who were given the promise of advancement and Negro supervision. In the early summer of 1920, when the investigator visited this office, there were 311 girls at work, as follows:

Operators on Elliott-Fisher machines..... 30
Mail-order workers.................... 76
Instructing new girls.................... 9
Checkers...........................138
Supervisors.......................... 5
Mail opening, sorting, etc.............. 27
Posting.............................. 26

They were above the average in education, 75 per cent being high-school graduates and 12 per cent having had two or more years in college.

The employment manager said that misunderstandings had arisen occasionally, due to the colored girl being oversensitive and suspicious. "The colored girl seems to suspect that her employer is going to put something over on her. She is suspicious of any whites that come in her vicinity and is ready to believe that any white person is prejudiced against her on account of race."

The Negro welfare worker for this unit suggested that what might seem supersensitiveness was often overzealousness on the part of girls who have not had experience enough to judge their limitations or qualifications. Being eager to succeed, they are very much disappointed when advancement does not reward their efforts: "I think the best type of colored girl we have in business is very ambitious. This is her first opportunity, and she feels that she is really a pioneer making history for her race. She is possibly a little overzealous, but can be made to get the right attitude and accept it all very gracefully."

Another characteristic of Negro girls, in the opinion of the employment manager, was an "excitable nature" which made it possible for a good leader to influence them readily:

They complain of a change of supervisors, for instance. You attempt to shift supervisors from one point of the office to another and you immediately receive a petition signed by all the girls, saying, "We love So-and-So, and please don't change her." This is not to be criticized too harshly, but it does represent something that does go on. It shows inexperience. The white girl would expect that those things would take place. The colored girl, not having been in the office very long, would feel that the fact that the supervisor was changed was something derogatory to the supervisor.

The whites didn't want to act as instructors, and the colored girls didn't want to receive instructions from the whites. By being very careful in the girls that were selected, and showing the white girls where they were wrong, and then attempting to show the colored people that these girls were not to exercise supervision, but were merely to be instructors, both sides came to an understanding on it, and we had pretty good results. The white girls that we had over there became very used to it and usually hated to leave, but we have always insisted that they leave as soon as the girls learned the work.

During the conference on Negro women in industry the representative of this mail-order establishment was asked why the Negro workers were put into a separate unit instead of being intermingled with white girls. He answered:

The first reason is that we haven't any room. The second is, I imagine, because the officials who started the office and who have carried it on since felt that it wouldn't be policy. We haven't discussed the question because we've never had occasion to consider such a move seriously. Our main office is not large enough to accommodate any more employees than we have white employees in the house. We keep that office constantly recruited up to its present strength, and there has never been any necessity or any reason to seriously consider bringing colored girls in with the white girls. . . . .

Another thing to consider there would be the type of girl that we employ. They are all young girls, mostly under twenty-five years, and they don't think for themselves; they are influenced very easily by what other girls say. You take one girl in an office of that size who was very anti-colored, and it wouldn't be very long until her sentiment would spread and pretty soon you'd have a strong sentiment against the colored girls.

If a colored girl should want to obtain employment in that part of our concern where we now employ all white girls, even if she were very competent she would undoubtedly have some trouble in securing employment in that department.

The result of the experiment with the colored unit, he said, was highly satisfactory: "We have been very favorably impressed. . . . . The girls have made very rapid progress, in fact they surprised all of us. Their progress along lines of leadership, as supervisors, etc., has been remarkable."

About six weeks after this conference the colored unit was closed. The reasons given were lack of business, trouble with the lessor of the office, and failure to find another convenient location. A letter of recommendation was given to each employee showing that her service had been satisfactory, and a letter was also sent to the Urban League, through which the women had been employed, explaining why it had been necessary to close the office and emphasizing the fact that this action should not be considered in any sense a reflection upon the Negro workers employed.

The other mail-order house opened a unit for Negro women in the fall of 1918, with 650 women who worked until the end of the "fall rush" in January, 1919. In the following fall the unit was again opened, with 1,050 Negro women; and the office was still in operation in 1920. This office was just outside the "Loop" district. The sudden influx of Negro girls there caused complaints by the local restaurants, fearing the loss of old patrons in handling this new business. The company then installed an "at cost" cafeteria service. The work of these girls was clerical, billing, labeling, addressing, etc. Considering their inexperience, their service has been highly satisfactory. The employment manager said: "It's not a defect in their minds, it's a defect in the country. They haven't had the opportunity to gain the education and experience needed for responsibility; the Negro girl is equal to the Italian or Bohemian in working ability and superior for executive work, such as instructing or supervising." Among 143 girls interviewed in the entry offices of these two mail-order houses only three expressed dissatisfaction with the conditions of work. The girls seemed to take pride in the fact that they had succeeded in "making good" in a new and attractive field of work.

The experiment of the establishment manufacturing automobile spring cushions had a very modest beginning. A factory was rented in the Negro residential area on the South Side, and twenty machines were installed to test out Negro women as sewing-machine operators. Gradually the number increased to 120 in this plant, and a second plant was opened in the same vicinity with about the same number of operators. During the year 1919–20 there were 250 Negro women employed as machine operators in these two plants. The superintendent considered that they required less supervision than the white workers in the company's other shops and rated them equal to white workers in efficiency. "We could take our best white girl and our best colored girl, and they earn about the same amount of money on piecework rates, in the same number of hours."

The superintendent of the wholesale millinery establishment represented in conference considered that the employment of Negro women in that industry had outgrown the experimental stage. Although a long period of training is necessary in order to become a skilled milliner (four years for hand sewers, eight years for machine operators), Negro women were keen to learn the trade and willing to accept the low wages paid to beginners. Of the forty-seven Negro women employed on the day of the investigator's visit, thirty-three received less than $12.00 a week and forty-two received less than $15.00 a week. These women were all employed as hand sewers, and in the opinion of the superintendent they had done "just as well as the white. They learn as quickly and are as persevering, and in every respect equal to the whites as far as their work is concerned. We are absolutely satisfied with their work."

Other industries in which Negro women are engaged in considerable numbers include laundering, the manufacture of clothing, lamp shades, gas mantles, paper boxes, barrels, and cheese making. An investigator from the Commission visited establishments employing Negro women in each of these industries.

Laundry operatives.—The fact that 543 Negro women laundry operatives were reported by sixteen laundries, as contrasted with 184 in all Chicago laundries in 1910, gives evidence of an increase in the number of Negro women in this field proportionately much greater than the increase in Negro population in Chicago in the same decade. The opportunity to work in a laundry was practically denied to Negro women until labor shortage forced laundry owners to tap this reserve labor supply. Negro women were eager to desert work as domestic servants and "family washer-women," with the social stigma and restricted human contact involved, to enter laundries where more independence was possible, hours were better standardized, and association with fellow-workers enlivened the work day. The employment department of the Urban League experienced great difficulty in supplying the demand for domestic servants and laundresses in the home, but had no difficulty in filling openings in laundries.

The work of Negro women in this field has proved satisfactory except in a few establishments. Of the twenty laundries which reported Negro labor satisfactory or unsatisfactory (included in Table XXVI), four failed to report separate figures covering male and female employees. Of the remaining sixteen establishments, twelve, with a total of 409 Negro women, reported Negro labor satisfactory, and four with a total of 134 Negro women, reported Negro labor unsatisfactory. The complaint in two instances was unwillingness to work overtime and on Sundays. In both these instances the employees interviewed complained that hours were long (nine-hour day) and the treatment by the management harsh and inconsiderate.

Laundries which did not make a practice of requiring overtime and Sunday work found Negro women workers cheerful, loyal, and industrious. The employees interviewed in these establishments expressed satisfaction with working conditions and with hours.

One efficiently managed laundry, employing seventy-six Negro women and six Negro men, out of a total of 110 employees, reported: "We have a number of exceptionally good and loyal Negro employees. These men and women need very little supervision. We got some who have never worked in industries. They require more supervision and are not very steady. On the whole, we are well pleased with our Negro employees."

Sewing-machine operators and sewers.—Denial of opportunity to enter the sewing trades is evidenced by the small number of Negro women listed in the 1910 census as sewers and sewing-machine operators in factories, the number being twenty-five. That this exclusion was not because of any natural inaptitude for sewing is indicated by the fact that the 1910 census listed 867 Negro women as seamstresses not in factories. Negro women have entered millinery work and proved apt hand workers; they have also proved efficient sewing-machine operators in the manufacture of automobile cushions. The lampshade manufacturers employed Negro women as hand sewers and found them to be efficient workers. The clothing establishments which reported Negro women workers found them satisfactory machine and hand workers, with the exception of one apron factory which complained that they are shiftless, often unreasonable, and do not stick to the job. An investigation of this establishment by the Urban League disclosed the following facts: The shop was located in a shabby-looking, unclean store, inadequately heated by a coal stove. The work day was nine and one-half hours, and piece rates on several operations were so low that it was impossible to earn a decent wage. In this

NEGRO WOMEN AND GIRLS IN A LARGE HAT-MAKING CONCERN

This shop has been partitioned for the accommodation of Negro women workers. The workshop is unattractive and the lighting extremely poor for the character of work required.

case the large labor turnover was evidently a healthy protest against poor working conditions.

Other industries.—Three paper-box-making plants employing Negro women were investigated. They reported that Negro women had proved unsatisfactory, either slow or lazy. The experience of a cheese factory is worth noting in this connection. Because Negro women appeared to be slow at their work it was decided to measure their tasks. It was then found that many were doing as well as and some better than the white girls in whose places they were working.

Whether such tests had ever been made in the box-making plants does not appear. The employees interviewed in one box factory complained of low wages and no chance for advancement. Negro women in this plant were averaging only $2.40 a day. A cooperage company reported fifteen women stave carriers and fifteen machine operators. Negro labor in this plant was reported satisfactory. Negro women in the garage of a taxicab company, cleaning automobiles, have shown themselves not afraid of hard work; 100 Negro women were reported working in this capacity. Negro women as Pullman-car cleaners have also proved satisfactory.

Before the war Negro women were popularly thought of as a class of servants unfitted by nature for work calling for higher qualifications. It is difficult to say how long this popular misconception might have survived had it not been for the labor shortage which forced employers to experiment with Negro women workers and to learn with surprise that they were as teachable as white women and became as efficient workers after receiving the necessary training.

IV. INDUSTRY AS THE NEGRO SEES IT

1. ATTITUDE TOWARD INDUSTRIAL OPPORTUNITIES

In order to learn the attitude of the Negro toward his work, and his special problems, including the treatment accorded him by foremen and by fellow-workers, 865 Negro employees were interviewed by a Negro investigator at their work or at home. Less than 1 per cent of those interviewed complained of disagreeable treatment by white workers. Approximately one-half had no complaints to make about conditions of work. On the contrary, they expressed themselves as being glad of the opportunity to work and earn good wages.

The attitude of a large number of the workers interviewed is illustrated by the following:

C— W— was referred to in one of the industrial conferences before the Commission. The superintendent of the foundry said he was the "star molder" in the plant. When interviewed C— W— said he had come to Chicago in 1910 from Kentucky because he was tired of being a flunkey. He had been in the high school for two years, but could only get work as janitor in a public building in his home town. After coming here he worked in a foundry as a molder's helper until he learned the trade. "I was getting 38 cents an hour then, but I got on piecework and my wages have steadily gone up. I'm an expert now and make as much as any man in the place. I can quit any time I want to, but the longer I work the more money it is for me, so I usually work eight or nine hours a day. I am planning to educate my girl with the best of them, buy a home before I'm too old, and make life comfortable for my family. There is more chance here to learn a trade than in the South. I live better, can save more, and I feel more like a man."

R— N—, who is working as a helper in the same foundry, says he has just gone from one job to another. In the South he worked on a section gang on the railroad most of the time. "Didn't have to know much to get a job on the section gang— just able to lift." Friends here wrote him of the chances to make money, so he came because he was just drifting anyway. When he got here he thought Chicago was "full of life." Every night for a month he went to cabarets. He likes his work and his wages. "My wife can have her clothes fitted here; she can try on a hat and if she don't want it she don't have to buy it. I can go anywhere I please on the cars after I pay my fare, and I can do any sort of work I know how to do."

When M— G— came to Chicago in 1900 he thought it "the biggest place in the world and the world didn't reach much further. Life is easier here because you can make more money. Working conditions are better than in the South, but they could be better still." He worked as a butler in the South, but when he came to Chicago he got out of personal service and became a laborer in the Stock Yards. Later he went to Gary, Indiana, to the steel works, where he is earning about $40.00 a week. His wife is doing clerical work in a mail-order house and is going to night school three nights a week to learn typing.

H— B— with his family left Mississippi in 1916 and came to Chicago, where he found work as a coal heaver at $3.20 a day. His wife sorted paper in a junk house at $10.00 a week, and his daughter entered a canning department at the Stock Yards at $18.00 a week. When Mr. B— was interviewed in June, 1920, he was working in the Stock Yards and earning $27.00 a week for an eight-hour day. He said he didn't have to work nearly as hard here as in the South and was earning enough money so his wife could stay at home. "In the South you had to work whether you wanted to or not unless you were very sick. White people did not work there as they do here. They made the Negro do the work. Men and women had to work in the fields. A woman was not permitted to remain at home if she felt like it. If she was found at home some of the white people would come to ask why she was not in the field and tell her she had better get to the field or else abide by the consequences. After the summer crops were all in, any of the white people could send for any Negro woman to come and do the family washing at 75 cents to $1.00 a day. If she sent word she could not come she had to send an excuse why she could not come. They were never allowed to stay at home as long as they were able to go. Had to take whatever they paid you for your work."

M— H— "likes the air of doing things here." He is able to earn enough to keep the family without having his wife go out to work. There are four "youngsters," the oldest being eight years old. Mr. H— came to Chicago in 1918 from Tennessee. He complained that there was not much work for a man in his home town. He did whatever odd jobs turned up. People there were talking about the chances in Chicago, so he came here and went to work as a monument setter on the West Side.

Later he found a better-paying job in a mattress factory and was able to send for his family. He is now working in a foundry and makes $35.00 a week but finds it hard to live on this. If he can go to night school he feels he will be able to earn more money.

Mrs. L— works as an entry clerk in a mail-order house and likes everything connected with the place. She used to be a maid in a private family but says she wouldn't work in service again "for any money. I can save more when I'm in service, for of course you get room and board, but the other things you have to take—no place to entertain your friends but the kitchen, and going in and out the back doors. I hated all that. Then, no matter how early you got through work you could only go out one night a week—they almost make you a slave. You can do other work in Chicago and you don't have to work in such places."

Mrs. L— had taught school in Atlanta, Georgia. After her husband died she had tried to get back in the school but could not. Friends here advised her to move to Chicago, so she sold her property in 1915 and came here. She got work in the Stock Yards but gave music lessons on the side to help keep up expenses. "I hated the surroundings at the Yards and the class of people who worked there, so when I had a chance to work in a mail-order house I changed. The first work here was filing. I learned it very quickly and tried so hard to make good that they made me a supervisor." She likes the freedom of the North and the opportunities to advance in work. Her ambition is to get into the public schools as a teacher.

Miss T— S—, twenty-two years old, started to work when she was fourteen, helping her mother cook for a large family in Lexington, Georgia. Her mother died when she was about seventeen, and she continued to work in the same family about three years. Then some relatives persuaded her to come north with them in 1919. She worked as a waitress in Chicago until her cousin got her a job in a box factory. "I'll never work in nobody's kitchen but my own any more. No, indeed! That's the one thing that makes me stick to this job. You do have some time to call your own, but when you're working in anybody's kitchen, well, you're out of luck. You almost have to eat on the run; you never get any time off, and you have to work half the night, usually. I make more money here than I did down South, but I can't save anything out of it—there are so many places to go here, but down South you work, work, work, and you have to save your money because you haven't any place to spend it."

Many of those interviewed were grateful for the opportunity to work overtime at overtime rates. A number complained that they were able to spend but little time with their families, or in recreation, because they were compelled to live in districts far from the plants in which they worked, so that two, and often three, hours a day were wasted on the cars. The Negroes who had come to Chicago within the past two or three years as a rule were satisfied with conditions of work, including hours, wages, and treatment.

2. COMPLAINTS ABOUT CONDITIONS OF WORK

Among the Negroes who had lived in Chicago for a longer period the most insistent complaint was lack of opportunity for advancement or promotion. This was occasionally coupled with the complaint that foremen discriminated in favor of the white workers. In certain industries no complaint of treatment by foremen was made, while approximately 10 per cent of those interviewed in three industries (mentioned below) complained of discrimination in favor of white workers, in the distribution of work, in recognition of efficiency, or in permitting the earning of overtime rates. The industries registering the greatest percentage of complaints were: (1) foundry and iron and steel mills, (2) Stock Yards, and (3) railroad dining-car and Pullman service. The common complaints in each of these fields are considered briefly below.

Foundries and iron and steel manufacturing.—The ninety-three Negro employees interviewed in fourteen establishments in this field were of different grades of skill: fifty-nine unskilled, twelve semi-skilled, nineteen skilled, and three apprentices to skilled trades. The length of time in the plant varied from a week to twenty years (forty-one employees less than one year, and eighty less than five years). To the inquiry, "Is anything wrong with your conditions of work?" fifty answered, "No"; sixteen complained that hours were too long (in these cases the men were working a twelve-hour day and a seven-day week); ten complained of low wages; six that foremen or straw bosses were not fair in the distribution of work or of "heats"; four complained that straight-time pay only was allowed for overtime, three that working gangs were reduced without decreasing the work demanded or increasing the pay of the men who remained; one thought that Negroes were paid lower wages than white workers; one said the work in his plant was much dirtier than it need be; and two were dissatisfied because shower or locker accommodations were insufficient.

A foundry company employing twenty Negroes out of a total of eighty employees was one of the establishments reporting Negro labor unsatisfactory. Negroes interviewed there complained of harsh and unfair treatment by bosses and said that Negroes usually did not stay longer than thirty days. The employment manager of a large foundry employing 427 Negroes out of a total of 2,488 employees told the investigator that the foremen in the plant would refuse to use Negroes if white labor could be obtained, and if such a time should come the foremen would have their way, because it took years to make a foreman, but a laborer could be picked up any day. The investigator was not permitted to interview any of the employees at this plant, but he visited some of them at their homes. They complained of harsh treatment by foremen, reduction in piece rates without notice, and discrimination in favor of white workers. The labor turnover reported by this plant was 70 per cent for Negro as compared with 14 per cent for white workers. This contrast is readily accounted for when the attitude of foremen toward Negroes is known.

Negroes interviewed at one of the plants of another foundry company employing seventy-five Negroes out of a total of 300 employees complained that the foreman in one department established conditions discouraging to Negro workers. He had an even number of Negro and white workers employed as partners on a certain process of piecework rates, each doing one-half of a joint task. When a man was absent, partners would be shifted about so that a Negro worker would be left without a partner instead of a white man. This handicapped the single worker by slowing down the process so he could not earn a full day's pay. Complaint was also made that the same foreman allowed white workers to accumulate a supply of material for their work, although he ordered Negro workers to stop this practice, thus forcing them to lose time in making frequent trips for material.

In a large iron and steel plant a few of the workers interviewed complained of unfair and abusive treatment by foremen. Numerous complaints had likewise come to the attention of the industrial secretary of the Urban League, who took the matter up with the chief of the industrial-relations department of the company. An investigation was ordered, and it was found that a certain foreman had made a threat to drive all the "niggers" from the department. This foreman, who had been employed by the company for more than sixteen years, was discharged as a result of the investigation. The company states that considerable pressure has been brought to bear for the foreman's reinstatement, but that it will not reinstate him because it wants his case to be a warning to others in the plant who may be prejudiced against Negro workers. The discharged foreman has been told that he may seek employment with the company in some other capacity, with the loss of his seniority rights.

In contrast with conditions in the preceding cases, the investigator found no complaints of mistreatment by foremen or other causes for dissatisfaction among Negro workers at another foundry which employs 125 Negroes out of a total force of 466 employees. Negro labor in this foundry was reported "satisfactory" and as efficient as white labor. The attitude of foremen evidently contributed to the contentment and success of Negroes in this plant.

Stock Yards.—Interviews with seventy-four Negroes employed in the Stock Yards disclosed much dissatisfaction with treatment by foremen. Specific instances of discrimination were cited in great detail, leaving no doubt in the mind of the investigator that these workers felt that they did not have an equal chance with white workers in many departments in the Yards. Some of those interviewed were well pleased with the treatment of present foremen, but had worked in other departments in the same plants where they said foremen had been unfair and insulting to Negroes. The Negroes interviewed, with one exception, considered their treatment by white fellow-workers good or "O.K." The following are typical of the complaints made by the men interviewed in three of the large establishments in the Yards:

G— R— had worked in one plant in the Yards for four years. He said that he was not given a chance to make overtime, while Poles who had not been with the company as long as he had were given this privilege.

Another worker had been dismissed by a foreman when a white worker in the boiler room had shut off the supply of water for washing hogs. No blame was attached to the real offender, but the Negro worker was discharged. He wrote a letter to the general superintendent, who investigated and ordered his reinstatement. The foreman then tried to reinstate him as a new hand, which would deprive him of his seniority rights.

Another worker interviewed said that one assistant foreman had openly made the statement that he would not work with "niggers."

The foreman over pipe fitters was accused of placing new Negroes on the hardest work, with no one to give assistance. He permitted white men to work as helpers for two or three months, and then to quit for a month or two and return as pipe fitters, advancing them over Negroes who had more training for the work.

The foreman in the sheep-killing department of one of the plants was said by one worker to make advancement difficult, if not impossible, for Negroes. Another worker complained that this foreman had recently taken one man off the jaw-trimming machine but ran the chain just as fast, with the evident intention of overtaxing the remaining Negroes and reporting that they were not equal to the job.

The foreman in the hog-killing department was charged with showing preference to the Poles in shoulder sawing. If a Negro made complaint to the superintendent and was sent back with instructions to the foreman, the latter would try to "burn" the Negro out with work.

It would seem from the discussion of the representatives of the packing companies before the Commission that the Negro in reality has little opportunity for promotion in the Yards. There are no Negro foremen over mixed gangs. The highest position a Negro is able to reach is that of subforeman over a group of Negro workmen. The general superintendent of one of the packing companies admitted that he had never tried out a Negro as foreman over a mixed gang because he wouldn't want to work under a Negro himself. Such an attitude on the part of a general superintendent closes the door to experimentation and limits the opportunities of even the most capable Negroes. It was this same official who said, as previously noted, that Negro labor required more supervision than white labor, and that the turnover of Negro labor was greater. Lack of "hope on the job" would seem an adequate explanation of both conditions.

Railroad dining-car and Pullman service.—Negroes are used as dining-car waiters on all roads running out of Chicago which carry such accommodations. Certain of the roads also use Negro cooks and kitchen help. The dining-cars on all roads are in charge of white stewards. The source of greatest complaint among the 204 Negro waiters interviewed was the arbitrary use of authority by the stewards and the fact that color bars Negro waiters from becoming stewards. They say that when stewards are needed, intelligent and experienced Negroes are passed over and white men, often entirely ignorant of the work, are taught their duties by these Negroes and are then placed in authority over them. One road carrying seven dining-cars uses white stewards on two cars and the remaining five cars are in charge of Negroes called "waiters in charge." Negroes complained that these men get little more than the wages of a waiter, and in many cases do all that is required of steward and waiter.

The outstanding complaint concerned the drawing of the color line in promotion. In view of the fact that many college graduates are serving as waiters, it would seem absurd to say that Negro waiters are incapable of performing a steward's duties, which consist of receiving and checking supplies for the car, seating dining patrons and issuing checks to them, having general supervision of the other employees on the dining-car, and making daily reports to the car superintendent of business transacted. Race prejudice on the part of administrative officials of railroads seems to be the only explanation for barring Negroes from becoming stewards, in view of the fact that Negro waiters have been used in dining-cars for over forty years and have been accepted by the white traveling public as a matter of course, though some contend that some patrons who accept Negroes as waiters would object to seeing them in positions of stewards, particularly if that brought white employees under them.

Negroes are employed in large numbers in Pullman cars as porters, cleaners, cooks, and mechanics. The main complaint made by the sixty porters interviewed was poor wages and necessity of dependency on tips to make a decent living. The wages of porters, as stated by a representative of the Pullman Company before the Commission, are:

The minimum rate for a porter on a standard sleeping or parlor car is $60.00 per month; when running in charge of one car the rate is $70.00 per month; when running in charge of a private car the rate is $75.00 per month; but when operating in charge of two or more cars the rate is $155.00 per month.

In 1914 the minimum was either $27.50 or $30.00 per month. Asked whether the Government Railroad Administration had anything to do with the increase granted by the Pullman Company, he indicated that the Pullman Company was under the direction of the Railroad Administration.

Another complaint by Pullman porters was that no promotion was possible for them, since only white men are used as Pullman-car conductors. The explanation of the company, given by one of its representatives at a conference with the Commission, was: "It is merely carrying out an ancient and honorable custom—we started out with white conductors and colored porters and have always continued that way."

Interviews with Negro workers revealed individual differences in attitude and temperament, but the more ambitious and thoughtful Negroes expressed the conviction that they were barred by color from positions for which they were better qualified than the white men who held them. Their complaints were largely variations of the same theme—race discrimination.

V. INDUSTRIES EXCLUDING THE NEGRO

Several important industries in Chicago have not yet employed Negroes. The traction companies (both elevated and surface) do not employ them as conductors, motormen, guards, or ticket agents. The large State Street department stores have no Negro clerks, and taxicab companies do not employ

colored drivers.   In these industries, which depend directly upon the public
for patronage, it is to be expected that the employing of Negro help will be
determined by the employer's views of the wishes of his patrons.   If there is
any fear that they are unfavorable, any individual employer in a competitive
industry will hesitate to try the experiment alone.   The employment managers
of five State Street department stores made the following statements:

1. Our customers would object to colored salespeople, I am sure.
2. We have never employed any Negroes in our Chicago establishments.   I don't
care to go into the matter.   It will not do you any good and will not do us any good.
3. Customers and white employees would object if they were used as clerks.
4. No Negroes are ever employed because we have sufficient white applicants.
5. If we ever tried using Negroes as clerks the white workers would make trouble,
I am sure of that.   Our customers would object.   A good many are from the South
and would make trouble even if Chicago people did not.

One large taxicab company, employing 250 Negroes for repair work and
upkeep of automobiles, does not employ Negroes as drivers.   A representative
of this company stated that the company had gone as far as many employers,
and often farther, in the employment of Negro labor; that it had done this in
a progressive way, one step after another, but had "not yet got as far as employing Negro chauffeurs," although this might come in time.   When asked
whether he thought such action would affect the company's business unfavor-
ably he said, "I do not know.   It is a matter that I have never thought about."

The Chicago Telephone Company does not employ Negro telephone operators.   Its only Negro employees are porters, window washers, and maids.
A representative stated that it has always had sufficient white applicants for
positions as telephone operators and has not considered taking on Negro girls,
although the suggestion has often been made that Negro operators be used at
the Douglas Exchange (located in the Negro area of the South Side).   This
official thought there was very little possibility that they would employ Negro
operators in the future.   He feared objection from white employees.

In connection with the foregoing it may be borne in mind that the company
has answered complaints of poor telephone service within the past few years
with the statement that it is difficult to secure capable girls, and that the
Telephone Company is continually advertising for girls as operators.

Social waste involved.—The industrial secretary of the Urban League has
called attention to the large number of educated Negro girls who are unable
to secure industrial openings where education is required.   It is impossible to
estimate how great a social waste is involved in relegating trained and educated
Negroes to inferior positions, and there is evidence that such waste is considerable.   Negroes with college training are found working as waiters; young
women college graduates are frequently forced to serve as ladies' maids,
theater ushers, or in some other capacity where they are unable to use their
educational training.   The fact that it was not difficult to find over 1,500

Negro women of more than average education for clerical positions in two Chicago mail-order houses when the opportunity offered is some indication of the extent of the social waste when Negroes are not used in other positions which require training.

VI. RELATIONS OF WHITE AND COLORED WORKERS

The entrance of Negroes into new industries and occupations means that the workers already in these fields will meet increased competition. The self-interest of white workers in a given shop may therefore cause them to resent the presence of Negro workers. On the other hand, through contact and association with Negroes during working hours, white workers may come to look upon Negroes, not as members of a strange group with colored skin, but as individuals with the same feelings, hopes, and disappointments as other people. Whether the hostile attitude prompted by self-interest or the friendly attitude born of understanding, acquaintance, and daily association will prevail in any given shop depends on many factors, over some of which the workers involved have no control. Some of these are:

1. The attitude of the management when Negro labor is first introduced.

2. Circumstances under which Negroes are hired, whether because of recognized labor shortage, or as strike breakers, or to reduce labor costs.

3. The attitude and characteristics of the particular Negroes employed.

4. The attitude of the white workers toward Negroes as a result of previous contacts with Negroes.

The spirit displayed in the shop is likely to spread beyond it and affect relations between the races on the streets and in cars and other public places. It is therefore important to know what the relations between white and Negro workers are, both because of their importance to the Negro in industry and their bearing on the broader social aspect of race problems.

1. RACE FRICTION AMONG WORKERS

Information concerning race relations in industry was received from employers through questionnaires returned by 137 establishments employing a total of 22,337 Negroes, through interviews at places of business with representatives of 101 employers, through industrial conferences held by the Commission, and through interviews with 865 Negro workers. Since the best judges of the existence of race friction would be the Negro workers themselves, who would bear the brunt of any ill-treatment resulting from such friction, it was considered that any extended canvass of opinion among white workers beyond the inquiries made in connection with the trade-union investigation was unnecessary.

Race friction between white and Negro workers sufficient to interfere with output would militate against the use of Negro labor. The fact that Negro labor has proved satisfactory in the great majority of cases where it has been used is therefore indirect evidence that race friction is not pronounced in

Chicago industries. Direct evidence from employers on this subject was also secured in answer to a specific question on the point. Out of 137 establishments employing Negroes, which returned questionnaires, only two reported that race friction was a disturbing factor in their plants. The facts in these two cases were as follows:

In a steel-manufacturing plant there was a total of 1,300 employees, of whom seventeen were Negroes, eleven men and six women. During the steel strike of 1919 Negroes were employed in this plant in large numbers. Feeling was antagonistic on the part of the whites, "particularly Austrians and Slavonians." The total number of Negroes employed during the strike and the turnover were reported as "an average force of 175."

Friction in the foregoing case was probably due to the heritage of bitterness over the use of Negroes as strike breakers and to irritation caused by the low grade of workers employed more than to difference in color. They were described by the manager as "irresponsible and shiftless."

In the other case fear of Negroes' competition rather than race prejudice was apparently the cause of friction. The manager of a wholesale millinery house employing forty-three girls in one department, out of a total of 700 employees, said:

We decided to take on colored help in June, 1919. Our white people resented very much the fact of employing colored people in our business, and I believe the blame, if there is any, lies as much with the whites as with the blacks in the difficulties we have had. I find a great resentment among all our white people. I couldn't overcome the prejudice enough to bring the people in the same building, and had to engage outside quarters for the blacks. We had a meeting of our colored operators after employing the hand workers. We thought it would be nice if we would start a school for machine operators. It was, of course, rumored that we were going to do this, and I received a delegation from our sewing hall who said they resented the idea. They wouldn't listen to it at all, and I had to abandon the project. Their argument was: "If you let them in it won't be long until we are out entirely." The attitude against the colored is only the same as it was against the Slavs or the foreign races when they first intruded in the field. There was no prejudice, particularly against the color. In millinery establishments in New York City colored girls and white girls work together and do not seem to have any trouble, but, we can't do it here.

The resentment felt by the white girls in this shop may be accounted for in part by a fact to which the manager apparently attached no importance. In speaking of the loyalty and good spirit of the Negro girls, he said casually:

In a few instances, where we have had difficulty in getting work done by the whites, we have been able to use the colored workroom as a level. We have sent it over to them and gotten it out. The white girls have refused either through stubbornness or some condition to get the work out.

Friction was also reported between women employees in a plant where relations between the men of both races were reported harmonious. This plant which manufactures machinery, has a total of 6,647 employees, including 1,225 Negro men and sixty Negro women. A representative of the company said:

Among the girls we had quite a lot of trouble in some departments against our hiring colored girls. To every colored girl employed we lost five white girls. There was friction in the washrooms due probably to race, though it may have been personal.

The report from a foundry employing 950 men, of whom 200 were colored, said:

As a rule if any objection is made to working together it comes from the white men (Polish) on the grounds that the colored man is being given the preference.

A laundry company employing ten Negroes out of a total of thirty-five employees, reported that when the first Negro girl was employed the white girls threatened to quit. The manager asked them to wait a week and, if they still objected, he would let her go. There was no further objection; they grew to like her.

The reports of employers regarding the absence of friction between white and Negro workers is borne out by the testimony of Negro workers themselves. Among 865 Negroes interviewed in all the industries covered, the number who complained of disagreeable treatment by white workers was practically negligible. It is possible that some Negro workers among those interviewed at their work places, sometimes with white fellow-workers and foreman near by, felt hesitancy in voicing such complaints. But the fact that the information was sought by an investigator of their own race, and confidentially for the Commission, may be considered as a factor likely to encourage the expression of any grievance, especially if felt at all deeply.

Conditions of work in large foundries would seem to offer plenty of opportunity for friction even where workers are all of the same race. This is particularly true of foundries where the piecework system prevails. The work is done in the confusion of smoke, heat, dust, and noise, with men shouting at each other, each striving to be first to receive this pouring of molten iron from the vats. Notwithstanding the fact that the work is carried on under great tension, the ninety-three Negroes interviewed in fourteen foundries, when asked how they got along with the white men with whom they worked, said: "Good," "Fine," or used other words to indicate friendly relations. Not a single complaint was made against treatment by white workers in any of the foundries or iron and steel establishments investigated.

One interesting instance of happy working relations in which several nationalities of whites were involved was found at Hull-House. A Negro has been in charge of the Coffee House there for six years. He had nine employees working under him: three Negro girls, one German boy, one Greek man, two Polish girls, and two Italian women. The Greek man and the two Polish girls were in the employ of the Coffee House when he took charge. The others have all been employed for a considerable period. In commenting upon the amicable relations of people representing so many different races and under a Negro manager, he said, "We are all working for a living, and there will be no discrimination. It is very simple. The thing to do is to get acquainted."

2. WORKERS REFLECT ATTITUDE OF MANAGEMENT

When the employment of Negroes is decided upon, there is an effort to make the change with as little disturbance as possible to white workers. Frequently the manager tries to imagine himself in the place of his white workers in order to discover what their reaction will be. In so doing, he considers, not what they will think or feel, but what a man with his own social background would feel in their position. The attitude of the management therefore determines whether Negro workers shall be segregated or treated like other workers in the plant without regard to color. Separation once decided upon and partitions erected, white workers may insist upon the distinction being maintained where they would not have raised the point in the first instance. Establishments following both courses gave the Commission the result of their experiences. Of 101 establishments employing five or more Negroes each, eighteen maintained separate lavatory and toilet accommodations for Negro workers. This condition was accepted without complaint in some establishments, while in others it was a source of dissatisfaction among the Negro workers, who resented this manifestation of "Jim Crowism" in the North. The fact is worthy of note that the eighteen establishments reporting separate accommodations or separate departments for colored workers employed but 2,623 Negroes out of a total of 22,337 covered by the investigation, or slightly more than 11 per cent. The remaining 89 per cent, or 19,714, were using all accommodations in common with white workers.

One large foundry company employing 427 Negroes out of a total of 2,488 employees tried a different method in each of its three plants. In one a partition in the locker and shower rooms was erected, to which the Negro workers objected. The general superintendent said he would not have consented to the erection of the partition in the first place, but he was afraid to take it down. In the second plant separate lavatory accommodations were provided in connection with separate departments for Negro and white workers on different floors, and there was no trouble. In the third plant, where no color distinctions were made, all workers using the same lavatory accommodations, the manager never heard of any complaint from white or Negro workers.

In another foundry employing 125 Negroes out of a total of 466 employees the representative said that the Polish workers had objected "that the colored people used the showers and basins all the time and they did not get a chance to. We checked up on this and limited some of our showers to colored only, and we only had two men use the white showers in something like two weeks,

time, and in the colored there was something like 200 baths taken." The use
of the same accommodations in this plant caused no further complaint after
this incident. Another foundry reported that the white and Negro workmen
ate lunch and smoked together. There were no separate accommodations and
there was no ill-feeling whatever. Another firm employing 500 Negroes out
of a total of 3,000 employees reported: "The relationship between our Negro
and white employees is very friendly. During the past year we have not had
a single encounter of any kind between the white and colored workers. They
work together in most of our departments, use the same locker rooms and washrooms, and eat in the same restaurant in the plant." In one foundry the
superintendent was nearly compelled to install separate accommodations
because of stealing in the locker rooms. Suspicion was aroused against the
Negro workers, and the white workers had a shop meeting to demand separate
accommodations. The manager said: "The same day the janitor caught a
red-headed Irish boy red-handed. We paraded him through the shop and
made quite a grandstand operation out of it, and it ended my troubles from
that time on, but if I hadn't caught him I might have had to maintain separate
locker rooms."

There were only six establishments which maintained separate departments
for Negro workers. In some cases segregation was effected by a partition;
in others by maintaining a complete Negro unit in a different part of the city.
The second plan has worked satisfactorily, but segregation by partition in the
same plant is resented by Negro workers. Representatives of the largest
employers of Negro labor expressed the opinion that erecting a partition, by
drawing the "color line," causes friction which in all probability would not
otherwise appear.

The industrial secretary of the Urban League, who has been actively interested in extending the range of opportunity for the Negro in industry, firmly
believes that the attitude of the management on racial matters is reflected by
the employees, that wherever an uncompromising stand is made for fair play
for all employees, racial differences do not cause annoyance. He cites the
following incident as one of several tending to support his view:

During the fall of 1919 the general manager of the S— F— P— Company was
approached on the subject of employing colored girls. To our surprise, it was discovered that colored girls were already employed by him in all branches of the industry,
and mixed freely with white employees. There was no discrimination in the character or kind of work or the use of plant facilities. Mr. N— explained that he had
never thought of segregating white and colored workmen, and the wisdom of his plan
had been proved by the experience of his father, who employs both white and colored
girls, but keeps the groups separated by a partition. According to Mr. N— the partition had been a source of trouble for the reason that the placing of the partition
itself indicated that the company intended to make a difference between white and
colored workers. This put each group in a frame of mind which caused them to
resent the presence of any worker on the side of the partition on which she was not

employed. The elder Mr. N— realized his mistake but did not dare to take the partition down, fearing that by so doing he would precipitate further trouble which would result in the most desirable girls in each group quitting the plant.

Foremen, because they personify the management in the mind of the workmen, play a large part in shaping the attitude white workers adopt toward Negroes. If the foremen are antagonistic or insulting in their treatment of the Negro, white workers find favor with the foremen by adopting the same attitude. A construction company employing sixty Negroes reported:

There were always difficulties with this gang when the Italian foreman was here, as he constantly endeavored to place Italians at work displacing some very good Negro workers. When I was sent here I dug under the difficulties and found the Italians were very clannish and were using the foreman to carry out the plan of giving every Italian who came along a job, at the expense of some Negro's job. I am a French Canadian and have worked with colored men before. After failure in trying to get Italians to see how bad the old system was, I was forced to let all the Italians go. I have an excellent gang of Negroes now.

The representative of a large foundry said:

I believe I have a harder time to get the Polish foremen to handle Negro help than any other. Our foremen are accustomed to handling the Polish workers pretty rough. While employers don't want that, it goes on that way. A Pole is "cussed" around and does not care what he is called. It's all the same to him, but a colored man is a pretty thin-skinned individual. You call a colored man something, and he will grab his hat and is gone. He thinks that when the foreman uses those words he means it. He will not stand for the same kind of language that the Polak will.

3. USE OF NEGRO LABOR TO UNDERMINE WAGES

If Negroes are introduced into a plant during a strike and retained afterward, a period of strained relations between white and Negro workers is almost certain to ensue. They are given a similarly unfavorable start when they are introduced to reduce labor costs. In the smaller establishments, where wages and conditions of work were not well standardized, white workers were suspicious that Negroes were working for lower wages, and the Negroes suspected that they were being paid lower wages than white workers. It is obvious that where mutual distrust and suspicion are present, friction readily develops which may lead to serious social consequences.

To what extent Negroes are being paid lower wages than white workers it is impossible to say. In this connection the Chicago Urban League made the following statement:

The charge of inequality in the wages of white and colored workers is frequently made, but the League is not always permitted to inquire into wage scales, and therefore verification of some of these rumors has been impossible.

The League has taken up this matter with such companies as ——, ——, ——, and numerous others, with the result that in each instance the statement has been made that white and colored workers receive the same pay for the same work. There is a deep-seated suspicion, however, that this is not true. In some cases this suspicion seemed to be justified. Complaints have come to our attention where colored people have been mistaken for white in the offices of the ——— Company and employed at a higher rate of pay than that given colored girls for similar work. This, however, has never been verified. Pay inequalities have been explained away by larger experience, seniority, superior production, etc., in favor of whites.

The employment manager of one company has told representatives of the Chicago Urban League that the colored girls employed in their South Side Branch Office started at a wage in excess of that given white girls for similar work in their main office.

The statement can be correctly made, however, that many employers of colored girls, particularly in the needle trades, have refused to pay colored workers a wage equal to that of white. There are well-known instances of sweatshop tactics used on colored girls because of their inexperience in industry and lack of organization.

An official of the Women's Garment Workers' Union reported that ——— Company, upon finding that they had to pay the union scale of wages, requested the local to supply white girls instead of the colored girls who were already in his employ. The colored girls were employed to replace the striking whites.

No complaint has come to our attention of inequality of wages in union shops employing white and colored workers, or in any of the larger industries. Colored workers are usually exploited in the smaller shops. White workers have been known to refuse to work in shops paying white and colored workers the same wage.

All of the representatives of employers appearing in conferences and all but one of the representatives interviewed stated that Negro and white workers were being paid equal wages in their establishments. The exception was a wholesale hardware company where the employment manager admitted paying Negroes "a dollar or two less per week" because they could not be shifted from one department to another as readily as white workers on account of prejudice of workers or foremen in certain departments.

It was learned that employers occasionally refuse to hire Negro unionists when they learn they must pay them "white men's wages." Unionists allege that even Negro employers object to paying Negroes the same union scale as white workers. To the extent that Negro labor is being used to undermine wage standards, misunderstanding and race friction develop.

4. RELATIONS OF WHITE AND NEGRO WORKERS DURING THE RIOT

In contrast with the violence that characterized street encounters during the riots it is significant that no unfriendly demonstrations occurred between workers in any of the establishments covered by the investigation, according to statements made by representatives of employers. On the contrary, white workers are said by employers to have expressed sympathy in many ways with their Negro fellow-workers. The general superintendent of one of the largest packing companies in the "Yards" emphasized the good feeling that existed between the workers at this critical time:

I think this Commission ought to know that there wasn't a single case of violence in what we call Packingtown during the race riot, and the morning that the Negroes were brought back to work in this packing-house there was not a single argument—

there wasn't a single indication in this plant of any racial feeling. In fact the two classes of common labor we have are the Slavs and the Negroes, and they met as old friends. In many instances they put their arms around one another's necks. In one particular instance a Negro and a Pole got on an elevated truck and rode all around this plant simply to signify to the rest of the workers that there was a good spirit existing between the two. There was nothing in the contact between the Negro and the Pole or the Slav that would indicate that there had ever been a race riot in Chicago, and there was nothing from the beginning of the race riot to the end that would indicate that there was any feeling started in the Stock Yards or in this industry that led up to the race riot.

That there was at least one case of mob violence is shown by the report of the coroner's jury which investigated the riots. William H. Dozier, a colored man, was killed in the Stock Yards, according to this report. The jury's finding in this case was:

We find that during the race riots at a point about Cook Street and Exchange Avenue in the Union Stock Yards, and at about 7:15 A.M., July 31, 1919, deceased, a colored man, was struck by a hammer held and wielded by one Joseph Carka, that the deceased ran east on Exchange Avenue toward the sheep pens at Morgan Street, that he was followed and chased by a mob of white men, and that while so running the deceased was struck by a street broom, held and wielded by one Joe Scovak, and that he was also struck by a shovel in the hands of an unknown white man, and by one or more stones or missiles thrown by one or more unknown white men; injuries sustained causing death.

This was the only serious case of violence in the Stock Yards discovered, although a number of rumors were investigated, which could not be substantiated by facts.

Because of the nature of the work in the "Yards" and the presence of knives and other dangerous implements which could be turned to ready use, it is significant that more rioting, with deaths and injuries resulting, did not take place. But it is also true that the riot, which started on Sunday afternoon, became so serious by Monday morning that few Negroes made an effort to reach their work at the Stock Yards.

VII. FUTURE OF THE NEGRO IN CHICAGO INDUSTRIES

The investigation of the Negro in industry points to the conclusion that Negro labor has made a satisfactory record, and that there is little race friction in evidence between white and Negro workers. What the future will hold for him depends upon many complicating factors, some of which are: renewal of immigration in large volume, depressed business conditions, attempted reductions in labor costs, increasing unemployment, falling wages, the announced determination of many employers' associations throughout the country to undermine the strength of unions by establishing the "open shop" which might involve the use of Negro labor, and the admitted prejudice of foremen against Negro labor in many plants. It was labor shortage which forced employers to experiment with Negro workers in new fields. Whether Negro employees will be retained when a surplus of white labor is available is an open question.

Employers' representatives, in April and May, 1920, stated (with one exception) that no reduction in labor force was contemplated; that when such reduction became necessary, efficiency and seniority rights would determine which workers would be retained; that the question of color would not enter into the decision in any way. The employment manager of a firm employing a very large number of Negroes expressed the general opinion of the employers' representatives when he said:

I feel that our house will continue to run a colored office as long as they can run it as efficiently and economically as they could a white office; while, on the other hand, if they could not run it as efficiently and economically of course they wouldn't run it, because it's just a matter of dollars and cents, and as far as charity and good will goes, all good business men have it, but they are not going to run their business according to that entirely.

On the other hand, the employment manager of an establishment which had experienced friction between white and Negro workers was of the opinion that white workers resented the intrusion of Negroes. He thought that this feeling would be a factor if a time came when there was an oversupply of labor; that Negroes would then have to give way because no employer would be strong enough to resist the resentment of white workers; and Negro workers would thus be thrown out of work and would be a standing menace to the community.

The investigations and inquiries of the Commission in industry took place almost entirely in the period from March to September, 1920, and the statistics concerning Negroes employed were gathered in the earlier part of this period. During these months the general industrial situation was such as to demand all the labor, both white and Negro, that could be secured. In the autumn of 1920, however, a period of decline began, with increasing unemployment. This affected both white and Negro workers. Its own investigational staff no longer available for additional service, the Commission sought information concerning these changed conditions, so far as they affected Negro workers, from the industrial secretary of the Chicago Urban League. Through its industrial department the League places more Negroes in employment than any other agency in Chicago. The industrial secretary made the following statement on November 20:

At the present time the unemployment among colored people has reached what seems serious proportions. While there is no indication that colored people are suffering more in this respect than any other group, the constantly swelling number is a cause for grave concern. For three weeks our employment office has been crowded with job seekers. At first it appeared that those who failed to take their work seriously suddenly found themselves unable to get employment, but now hundreds of men with good records have been forced out by temporary "shut downs" and reduced forces of various plants.

During the working days included between November 15 and 20, our attendance record is 1,073 job seekers with only 131 openings. One month ago the attendance figure was 571 persons for the equal period (259 men and 312 women).

Our labor reports for May, 1920, indicated an attendance of 941 males and 739 females; about 1,000 orders for male help and about 500 for female help; there were 722 placements for males and 371 for females. The total attendance was 1,680; orders, 1,500; placements, 1,093.

A casual survey including most of the leading industries . . . . shows a general decline and a letting off of workers. Some few report difficulty in keeping their present forces.

There have been some complaints of discrimination against colored workers, but few comparatively. . . . . Most industries are keeping their proportionate share of Negroes. In some instances the proportion has been slightly increased. . . . .

During the week, workers have registered from cities in states from Mississippi to Michigan. Detroit predominates, where the automobile industries show a marked depression.

Women's work presents a very discouraging outlook. Hundreds of needle workers are out of employment by the closing of many of the smaller shops which employed colored girls. The Women's Trade Union League reports many workers unemployed, due to the slowness of the trade. Immigrant white girls are said to be consuming much of the work offered to domestics. . . . . Colored women seem in most cases as reluctant as ever to accept domestic employment.

The present unemployment problem is probably as serious as any the League has known. What shall become of the army of jobless men is a problem serious and perplexing.

As a result of the necessity of reducing costs in response to depressed business conditions, managers of establishments employing both white and Negro workers may be tempted to pit Negro and white workers against each other, paying Negro labor less than white labor as a means of forcing down wages or undermining labor-union organizations. Such attempts would certainly be conducive to increased racial animosity. On the other hand, managers who are hostile to Negro labor may take advantage of the change in the labor situation by discharging Negroes indiscriminately, replacing them with white workers.

During the period of business depression which had already begun, both white and Negro workers seemed certain to lose some of the advantages which they had gained as a result of the labor shortage caused by the war. After the industrial depression has passed, discrimination against the Negro, to whatever extent it may exist, will make the recovery of lost ground more difficult for Negro workers than for white workers. In considering the question of race discrimination, it is evident that the Negro who has lived in the North for a number of years feels keenly the fact that color bars even the most capable members of his race from the hope of promotion to executive or administrative positions, while prejudice on the part of persons in authority prevents the rank and file of Negroes from developing the degree of efficiency which they could develop if they knew their efforts would be judged on merit alone. Where advancement is precluded by color, the incentive supplied by recognition of effort is lacking.

One door of escape from the discouraging prospects held out in industries managed by white men, where there is no chance for promotion to executive positions, is the opportunity for an increasing number of the more ambitious Negroes to enter business among members of their own race. According to Black's *Blue Book* (1919–20) there were over 1,200 Negro business houses and professional offices in Chicago in 1920. Among others, the list included five banks, forty dentists, fifteen druggists, twenty-four employment agencies, six hotels, three insurance offices, forty-eight real estate offices, eleven newspapers and magazines, 106 physicians, seventy lawyers, 161 barber shops and billiard rooms, and 120 hairdressing parlors. Although the list of Negro business men in Chicago is growing rapidly, it must necessarily remain but a small percentage of the total Negro population. The great majority of Negroes gainfully occupied will continue to be employees in industry. Therefore the fact that a large number of Negroes feel that discrimination is practiced and that, no matter what abilities they show, they can "go so far and no farther" in industries managed by white men is of great importance in any consideration of race problems. These men are the more thoughtful, aspiring members of their race, and their opinion accordingly carries more weight than the opinion of an equal number of care-free Negroes who may consider that the high wages of the present are an offset for all handicaps. Negroes who feel keenly the injustice of unequal opportunities are the ones to seek expression in Negro newspapers and magazines with the aim of arousing widespread resentment against race discrimination. Men who frequently would not resent discrimination directed against themselves are stirred to resentment by well-told recitals of injustice to others. Specific instances may seem to be of trifling importance, but in being retold they reach an ever-widening audience, which is constantly growing more race conscious.

B. ORGANIZED LABOR AND THE NEGRO WORKER

I. INTRODUCTION

Industry involves the continuous contact of more whites and Negroes than any other field. It therefore affords wide opportunity for the operation of racial misunderstanding and friction. It is also a field in which the lines of economic interest are so tightly drawn and so closely watched that any misunderstanding or friction is thereby greatly accentuated.

Irritation and clashes of interest have been conspicuous in the relations between labor unions and Negro workers. This friction has extended to the relations between whites and Negroes generally. The efforts of union labor to promote its cause and gain adherents have built up a body of sentiment that cannot easily be opposed by non-union workers. The strike breaker is intolerable to the union man. Circumstances have frequently made Negroes strike breakers, thus centering upon them as a racial group all the bitterness which the unionist feels toward strike breakers as a class. This tends to increase any existing racial antipathy or to serve as concrete justification for it.

On the other hand, Negroes have often expressed themselves as distrustful of the unions because prejudice in the unions has denied them equal benefits of membership. They often find that their first opportunity in a new industry comes through the eagerness of a strike-bound employer to utilize their labor at wages more than they have previously earned, even if less than the union scale. This often tends to make them feel that they have more to gain through affiliation with such employers than by taking chances on what the unions offer them.

There is a gradually increasing sympathetic understanding by unionists of the struggle of Negroes to overcome their handicaps, and an increasing realization of the importance to the unions of organizing them. Negroes are themselves showing more interest in efforts toward organizations, but there is still much mutual suspicion and resentment in their relations.

To understand these relations it is necessary to know (1) the policy and attitude of organized labor toward the Negro and how its expressed policy is carried out in practice; and (2) what the Negro believes the facts to be and what his attitude is toward organized labor. In its investigation the Commission used the following methods of inquiry: Questionnaires were sent to all labor organizations; interviews were held with union officials and members, both white and Negro, with officers and members of Negro "protest" unions, with non-union Negroes, and with persons who were not connected with unions but had certain special information. Ninety-one persons, of whom twenty-five were Negroes, were interviewed. Trade-union meetings were attended by the Commission's investigator. Union constitutions, magazines, convention reports, etc., were collected and studied. Conferences were held by the Commission at which the following labor leaders and organizers presented their information and views:

George W. Perkins, president of the International Cigarmakers' Union, and prominent in the affairs of the American Federation of Labor since its organization.

Victor Olander, secretary-treasurer, Illinois State Federation of Labor, and vice-president of International Seaman's Union.

John Fitzpatrick, president, Chicago Federation of Labor.

W. Z. Foster, organizer of the American Federation of Labor in the steel and packing industries.

A. K. Foote, Negro, vice-president of Stock Yards Labor Council and secretary-treasurer, Local 651, Amalgamated Meat Cutters and Butcher Workmen of America.

I. H. Bratton, Negro organizer for Amalgamated Meat Cutters and Butcher Workmen of America.

John Riley, Negro organizer for the American Federation of Labor in the Stock Yards district.

Max Brodsky, secretary-treasurer, Local 100, International Ladies' Garment Workers' Union.

Agnes Nestor, president, Women's Trade Union League.

Elizabeth Maloney, treasurer and organizer, Chicago Waitresses' Union.

Robert L. Mays, Negro, president of an independent Negro union, the Railway Men's International Benevolent and Industrial Association.

II. POLICY OF THE AMERICAN FEDERATION OF LABOR AND OTHER FEDERATIONS

From its beginning the American Federation of Labor has declared a uniform policy of no racial discrimination, although this policy has not been carried out in practice by all the constituent autonomous bodies. At its fortieth annual convention, held at Montreal, Canada, in June, 1920, a plan was presented to "use every means in its power to have the words 'only white' members stricken out of the constitution" of the Brotherhood of Railway Clerks, an organization which exercises jurisdiction over 100,000 colored employees, although barring them from membership, and "admit the colored workers to full membership in their Brotherhood or have them relinquish jurisdiction" over these Negro employees and allow them to establish a brotherhood of their own.

This failed to receive favorable action, but a resolution was passed reaffirming the position taken at the Atlantic City convention in 1919 that "where international unions refuse to admit colored workers to membership, the American Federation of Labor will be authorized to organize them under charters from the American Federation of Labor." This means that in such cases the American Federation of Labor itself becomes the national or international union of such locals. According to the information given to the Commission by George W. Perkins, "the American Federation of Labor has organized hundreds of local unions and thereby directly attached to the American Federation of Labor colored workers." President Gompers states: "Of the 900 unions affiliated directly with the American Federation of Labor there are 169 composed exclusively of Negroes."

A brief reference to the history of the national federations which preceded the American Federation of Labor shows that the foregoing policy has been followed since shortly after the Civil War.

The National Labor Union (1866–72), at its first convention in 1866, was the first national federation of labor unions to deal with the problem of meeting Negro competition after the Civil War. The formation of trades unions among colored people was favored. In 1869 Negro delegates were admitted to the annual convention. A separate national Negro Labor Union, formed in 1869, was short-lived. The unfriendly attitude of the unions toward the Negroes was the subject of bitter comment at the various sessions of the latter organization. The Knights of Labor, which rose to prominence after the decline of the National Labor Union, admitted all workers without regard to color. Many Negroes in the South joined the organization. When the leadership of organized labor shifted from the Knights of Labor to the American Federation of Labor in the late eighties, the Federation continued to express the policy of no racial discrimination and has stood for that policy to the present time.[1] At the convention of the American Federation of Labor in Atlantic City, 1919, there were present about fifty Negro delegates, men and women. A large number of Negro delegates also attended the last convention of the Federation at Montreal.

The policy of the Illinois State Federation of Labor was outlined to the Commission by Victor Olander, secretary-treasurer, as follows:

The State Federation of Labor is under the jurisdiction of the American Federation of Labor, and the laws governing the national would necessarily govern the state federation, so that in respect to law they are the same. I might add that they are carrying out the law in much the same manner with respect to the Negro. There hasn't been a convention of the Illinois State Federation of Labor held in many years that hasn't had in attendance Negro delegates. That is the usual thing at every convention. There is no discrimination.

The Chicago Federation of Labor is the city central body of the various local unions in Chicago which are connected with the American Federation of Labor. Each of these local unions elects delegates to represent it at the semi-monthly meetings of the Chicago Federation. Negro delegates take an active part in these meetings, and are cordially received. The Federation and its president have been very active in all efforts to organize Negroes, especially in the Stock Yards, the steel industry, and the culinary trades.

III. POLICY OF NATIONAL AND INTERNATIONAL UNIONS

In considering the policy of national and international unions, that of the unions affiliated with the American Federation of Labor will be discussed first, and following this the policy of six of the most important of the independent internationals.

I. UNIONS AFFILIATED WITH THE AMERICAN FEDERATION OF LABOR

The American Federation of Labor has consistently followed a policy of no racial discrimination. It has, however, no power to compel its constituent national and international unions to follow this policy. The question of race discrimination by an autonomous national or international union has been frequently the subject of spirited discussion at American Federation of Labor conventions, but the outcome has been merely a recommendation to the offending union that the discrimination be discontinued. Since strict auton-

[1] F. E. Wolfe, *Admission to American Trade Unions*, pp. 113-17.

omy of national and international unions is recognized in the constitution of the American Federation of Labor, no more effective action can be taken.

In order to learn the racial policy of the 110 nationals and internationals affiliated with the American Federation of Labor inquiries were sent to each, and direct responses were received from sixty-nine. The policy of twenty-five additional unions was learned through their district councils or locals in Chicago. Thus all but sixteen of the 110 national and international unions in the American Federation of Labor were covered. Of these, two were suspended from the American Federation of Labor in 1919–20. Only three have locals in Chicago, and all have little significance for Chicago. Information concerning the racial policy of the sixteen unions not heard from was supplied by labor leaders in touch with the whole union situation and able to speak with authority on this subject.

Of the 110 national and international unions affiliated with the American Federation of Labor, eight expressly bar the Negro by their constitutions or rituals. These unions are: Brotherhood of Railway Carmen of America, International Association of Machinists, American Association of Masters, Mates, and Pilots, Railway Mail Association, Order of Railroad Telegraphers, the Commercial Telegraphers' Union of America, American Wire Weavers' Protective Association, and Brotherhood of Railway Mail Clerks.

Thus 102 of the 110 national and international unions affiliated with the American Federation of Labor admit Negroes. Not all of these unions, however, have Negro members, notwithstanding the fact that Negroes are eligible to membership. In accounting for the absence of Negro members, twenty-eight national and international unions reported "no Negroes in the trade," or "no applications ever received." Certain of the 102 nationals and internationals reported a small Negro membership with the following explanations:

Eleven stated that employers discriminated against Negro members of the union—wanted white men if they had to pay the union scale of wages.

Seven internationals and five delegate bodies reported that special efforts were now being made to organize Negro workers.

Twelve internationals called attention to long periods of apprenticeship—four had a three-year period, six a four-year period, and two a five-year period—as a factor which accounted for the failure of Negroes to join.

In their comments, some of these union officials unconsciously express their prejudice, sometimes attributing traits to the Negro which they seem to take for granted as being characteristic. The following are some examples:

No Negroes have applied for membership in our union or did not have nerve enough as it requires lots of climbing.

We do not have any Negroes in our organization, but there is nothing in the constitution which prevents them from becoming members after they have learned the trade. No one has ever made application for a Negro. I judge this is because they have to blow in the same pipe [in glass blowing].

I find nothing in our laws which bars Negroes from becoming members of this union, but in my thirteen years in this office I have never known one to make application for membership. This may be due to the hazardous nature of our work.

Ours is usually very hard work. Negroes as a whole do not like hard work. They instead very often prefer employment where they can get along at their own gait or in their own way, especially working in gangs.

National and international unions which had Negro members in appreciable numbers reported the following facts:

Sixteen had Negro officers or organizers.

Twenty-three reported that relations between the races in the unions were undisturbed by race prejudice.

Thirty-three stated that Negroes had belonged to the union for the following periods:

	Number of Unions		Number of Unions
2 years or less	12	8 to 15 years	4
2 to 4 years	8	20 years	4
4 to 6 years	1	25 years	1
6 to 8 years	2	35 years	1

2. UNIONS NOT AFFILIATED WITH THE AMERICAN FEDERATION OF LABOR

There are a number of unions[1] not affiliated with the American Federation of Labor, of which the most important are: the four railway brotherhoods—Brotherhood of Railway Clerks, Brotherhood of Locomotive Firemen and Enginemen, Brotherhood of Railroad Trainmen, Order of Railway Conductors of America—Amalgamated Clothing Workers of America; Industrial Workers of the World (I.W.W.). The four railway brotherhoods exclude the Negro by constitutional provision. The Amalgamated Clothing Workers of America and the Industrial Workers of the World admit the Negro and make special efforts to organize Negro workers. The I.W.W. has its main foothold in the lumber, mine, and textile industries and does not have any strong unions in Chicago.

Disregarding the classification of nationals and internationals based upon affiliation with the American Federation of Labor, a review of the figures presented above shows that 104 national and international unions admit the Negro, and that twelve exclude the Negro by written provision.

The outstanding fact with reference to these twelve organizations is that, with the exception of the Wire Weavers, they are all connected with the transportation industry: seven are members of the American Federation of Labor Railway Department and the other four constitute the big "railway brotherhoods." The latter are sometimes referred to by members of the unions as the "aristocrats in the labor movement." All of these unions, except the Masters, Mates, and Pilots, have been organized more than twenty years. None of the unions formed within the last twenty years, except the Masters, Mates, and Pilots, excludes the Negro.

[1] It was impossible to get in communication with others of the smaller scattered independent internationals besides those mentioned. No directory is yet published.

In these crafts, excepting such trades as carmen, machinists, clerks, and firemen, it may be that in general the Negro would not be much of a factor at present, because these trades demand an amount of education and skill not yet possessed by a large percentage of Negroes.   But this by no means proves that the Negro would not acquire the necessary skill and education if opportunities in these trades were actually open to him.

The Railway Department of the American Federation of Labor is composed of fourteen craft unions, all but two of which exclude the Negro worker.   The Stationary Firemen and Oil Men of the American Federation of Labor Railway Department are openly soliciting Negro members.   The only other craft organization which admits Negroes is the Maintenance of Way Craft, which really means the common labor group.   Negroes can get into this craft through an auxiliary charter to a Negro local.   Regardless of how skilled or how intelligent the applicant may be, or how logically he falls into some other craft, he can only come in through one or the other of these two craft unions.

The attitude of the railway brotherhoods is typified in remarks made to an investigator for the Commission by a member of the Brotherhood of Railway Clerks who is now serving on an important public commission.   He was emphatic in upholding the brotherhood's policy of excluding Negroes. "As long as the engineers have anything to say about it, they certainly will not get in."   He said that the modern locomotive was a highly complicated and scientific mechanism, and that the Negroes "did not have brains enough to run one."

As showing the contrasting view of another trade-union man, an employee of the public commission mentioned said that he had been a member of the United Mine Workers since 1901, and in that organization no color line is drawn; that he had worked beside Negro miners and feels no prejudice.   He pointed out that the national conventions of the miners always have a large representation of Negro delegates, and some of the ablest and best speakers come from the Negro race.   He expressed the feeling that the policy of the railway brotherhoods is a mistake, and is a case of "swell-headedness."

The general exclusion policy of the railway brotherhoods and certain of the unions in the Railway Department of the American Federation of Labor has created a feeling of bitterness among Negroes which spreads beyond these crafts and is directed against unions in general, notwithstanding the constructive and progressive policy of the many unions which admit Negroes.   In the transportation crafts it has led to the formation of a "protest" Negro railway union.

The Railway Men's International Benevolent Industrial Association.—This organization is a labor union open to Negro railway employees.   It is a protest organization which has grown up because of the exclusion of Negroes by the railway brotherhoods and certain unions in the Railway Department of the American Federation of Labor.

The Association was organized May 12, 1915, and has seventeen locals in Chicago and a membership of about 1,200, all railway employees.   The leaders of this group disclaimed any intention of building up "a rival American Federation of Labor among Negroes," but stated that, as far as they were personally concerned, they would be willing to affiliate with the American Federation of Labor in its proper department, *providing* all forms of discrimination in national and international unions, both in constitution and practice, were done away with, and the Negro worker was assured of equal treatment and opportunity with the white worker. They realize that the highest welfare of both groups depends upon co-operation. But, as to what the membership would want to do when that time comes, they of course do not know.

Mr. Mays, the president of the organization, was asked by the Commission's investigator what he would do in a situation where both Negroes and whites were organized separately, and the whites were going out on a strike and had requested the Negroes to come out also. He stated that several such local strike situations had arisen in the South, and that he had advised the Negro union in each of these cases to use its own judgment, but that if it decided to support the white unions, it should, before doing so, have a joint committee of both groups meet and make it understood absolutely that any agreement finally reached with the employers must include both groups on equal terms. In one case, after such an agreement had been reached and the men had gone back to work, the employer tried to keep out certain Negroes, but the white unionists insisted that the agreement must be lived up to.

The officials of this organization are exceptionally capable Negroes; its advisers are professional men, well educated and thoroughly familiar with the history and tactics of white labor unions.

A more definite statement of the purpose and policies of this protest organization was made before the Commission by R. L. Mays:

The Railway Men's International Benevolent Industrial Association really protests as an organization against unfair and bad working conditions of the employer and against unfair practices on the part of the American Federation of Labor and the railway brotherhoods.

This is the crux of the problem as we see it. We agree with the policies and principles of the American Federation of Labor so long as they are American and in the interests of the workmen, but if their practices are against Negroes, then we are against the American Federation of Labor unflinchingly.

Question: To what extent have you found their practices unfair to the colored people?

Mr. Mays: There are fourteen unions in railway employment in the American Federation of Labor. The United Brotherhood of Railway Employees has been accepting Negroes in full membership, but the other thirteen organizations do not accept Negroes in membership. As a matter of fact, they are secured on contract, which is the greatest holdback for the Negroes and breeds more distrust on the part of the Negro in these places, so far as the American Federation of Labor is concerned.

Before the roads were under government control certain discriminatory practices were found in the South, but now you will find colored men in certain skilled positions. In the Brotherhood of Carmen, if a colored man is not organized into the local union,

OFFICERS OF THE RAILWAY MEN'S INTERNATIONAL BENEVOLENT INDUSTRIAL ASSOCIATION

he cannot advance automatically from repair to car building. He might be a member of one of these local unions chartered by and affiliated with the American Federation of Labor. But under contract they say their members must be white, and they use only white men. In the South our men have enjoyed these jobs; under war conditions they were brought here, but under this contract no Negro can be employed as a carman, although he has all the experience in the world. They refuse to take the colored man but take the white man. No colored boy can go in as an apprentice and work up to a skilled mechanic's position. Consequently they are reducing the Negro railway worker to a position of common laborer and automatically are keeping him down. If this is the condition in the railways in the North, I say it will prevail everywhere. I have said that it is a northern prejudice coming South.

IV. ATTITUDE AND POLICY OF LOCAL UNIONS IN CHICAGO

I. WHITE AND NEGRO MEMBERSHIP IN CHICAGO LOCAL UNIONS

Much effort was made to obtain statistics of white and Negro membership in local trade unions in Chicago. Information was sought through requests addressed to the national headquarters of all national and international unions affiliated with the American Federation of Labor for data as to any local unions they might have in Chicago. Requests were also addressed directly to these local unions as listed in a directory published by the Chicago Trade Union Label League. Further requests were addressed to local unions in Chicago directly affiliated with the American Federation of Labor as listed in a directory of all such unions published by that organization.

It was difficult to ascertain the exact number of local unions in Chicago. Those covered embraced, however, as full a list as could be supplied by trade-union offices in Chicago. But the president of the Chicago Federation of Labor said that the number of local unions was changing so continually by reason of the organization of new ones and the consolidation of two or more into one, that no accurate list was available.

Data for the Amalgamated Clothing Workers of America and for the Railway Men's International Industrial Benevolent Association were obtained directly from those organizations.

Reports were received from the railway brotherhoods saying that they exclude Negroes, but giving no data as to the number of white members.

The information which was obtained may be summarized as follows:

	Members
371 local unions affiliated with the American Federation of Labor, comprising locals of national and international unions so affiliated, and also federal and local unions directly affiliated with the American Federation of Labor	253,237
11 local unions of the Amalgamated Clothing Workers of America	40,000
17 local unions of the Railway Men's International Industrial Benevolent Association	1,200
	294,437

The total Negro membership reported for Chicago by the foregoing organizations was 12,106. The number of locals through which this Negro membership was distributed cannot be stated with any approach to accuracy, due to the fact that in a number of cases the district council or the national body reported the membership for its Chicago locals jointly. In such cases it could not safely be assumed that each of the locals in question had Negro members. Disregarding all such cases, however, there still remains a total of at least eighty-five Chicago locals for which, individually, Negro members were reported.

It is interesting to note that, judging by the figures here shown as to white and Negro membership in local unions in Chicago, the proportion of Negro union members to the Negro population in Chicago is almost exactly the same as the proportion of white members to the white population in Chicago.

2. METHODS OF DEALING WITH NEGRO APPLICANTS

If the unions which bar the Negro are chosen as examples, organized labor might appear to be very unfair to Negro workers. On the other hand, if unions which admit them into the same locals and have Negro organizers and officers are chosen as examples, it might appear that there was no prejudice whatever against Negroes on the part of trade unions. Neither extreme would represent the facts. On the basis of policy toward the Negro, unions in Chicago may be divided into four classes or types. These classes are:

A. Unions admitting Negroes to white locals.

B. Unions admitting Negroes to separate co-ordinate locals.

C. Unions admitting Negroes to subordinate or auxiliary locals.

D. Unions excluding Negroes from membership.

The existence of these classes indicates the fact that the union attitude and policy toward the Negro cannot be summed up by any simple generalization. Each class or type has its own policy, and even within the class there are minor variations of attitude and policy.

A. UNIONS ADMITTING NEGROES TO WHITE LOCALS

Wherever and whenever Negroes are admitted on an equal basis and given a square deal, the feeling inside the union is nearly always harmonious. This is true in such unions as the Butcher Workmen's, Hodcarriers', Flat Janitors', and Ladies' Garment Workers', which include important fields of Negro labor in Chicago.

Stock Yards' unions.—The Stock Yards' strike of 1904 was broken by the use of Negroes. This was the opening wedge for the admittance to the union of the large number of Negroes which followed. No organization thereafter could hope to amount to anything in the Yards unless it took in Negroes. From 1917 until the riot of 1919 Negroes in large numbers were joining the Amalgamated Meat Cutters and Butcher Workmen's Union of North America. Forty locals were formed. The Negro was welcome to join any local he desired, whether it was prodominantly Polish or Irish or Negro. However, the majority gravitated to Local 651, which was composed mainly of Negroes and had Negro officers and organizers and headquarters near the "Black Belt."

This was not unnatural, since the headquarters of the various local unions are distributed over the city with a view to their convenience for the members. Most of the Negro members live within the "Black Belt." The most active Negro organizer in the city is connected with this local. Negroes living outside this area belong to the locals nearest their homes.

Efforts to organize Negro workers in the Yards are commented upon in the *Negro Year Book* of 1918–19 in the following paragraph:

That the unions are doing much to organize Negro labor is indicated by the fact that of the more than ten thousand Negro workers in the Chicago packing houses, over 60 per cent are reported in the unions. The International Union of Butchers' Workmen, which has jurisdiction over 90 per cent of the employees in the packing houses of the country, has three paid Negro organizers. In other lines of work there is equal activity in organizing Negro labor.

The unions succeeded in securing an agreement under which Judge Samuel Alschuler was mutually accepted by the packing companies and the unions as an arbitrator on matters affecting working conditions in the Yards, especially hours and wages. This agreement applies to all who work in the Yards, whether in or out of the union, but, according to labor leaders, union action and union money "put it across." Consequently there was the feeling that all who benefited should join and help share in the expense, and a feeling of hostility toward such Negroes, and whites as well for that matter, who did not join because they found that they could get all the benefits of the arrangement without paying dues.

While the Commission's investigator was interviewing the officials of one of the unions of the packing industry at their headquarters, a number of the white members dropped in to pay their dues. In conversation they showed, quite unsolicited, that considerable feeling existed because the Negro workers were not coming into the union. They felt that the Negroes were receiving all the benefits secured for the workers by the unions without paying their proportion of the expense of the organization. In fact, several used rather strong terms with the words "fink" and "scabs."

The sentiment of the men present seemed to be that, while mistakes had been made on both sides in the 1904 strike and since, the antagonistic feeling had been pretty largely eliminated, as was shown by the large Negro membership prior to the riot, and they said that every effort was being made at that time and since to bring the Negro into the union. Conferences had been held with Negro ministers and other organizations explaining the position of the unions, literature had been distributed, and a great deal of money had been spent through Negro organizers, and yet the results were disappointingly small. These white union men contended that they were opposed by an effective combination of "packers'" influence hard to beat and intensively interested in keeping the races apart for its own purposes in opposing union organization.

The Hod Carriers have sixteen locals in Chicago with a large total membership. No racial record is kept, but Negroes are admitted without discrimination into all of the unions. A few years ago the Negro membership was between 1,200 and 1,400; at present with an increase of 300 to 500 from the South, the secretary of the executive council estimates the total Negro membership to be at least 1,700, most of whom have joined two locals. The president of the Evanston union and the vice-president of the Chicago Heights union are colored. No feeling of discrimination exists, all being treated alike as long as they pay their dues and live up to the rules. The Hod Carriers have joint arbitration agreements with the employing contractors' associations in this industry, and no strikes have been called since 1900.

The International Ladies' Garment Workers' Union is another illustration of a union which accords Negroes the same treatment as white members, and where the relationship is entirely harmonious. This union has never drawn the race, creed, or color line and is trying to leave out the word "white" and "colored" from its minutes and reports. The Negro girls came into this industry as strike breakers within the last three years.

The officials of this union, in interviews and in testimony before the Commission, claimed that whenever any friction did arise it was due to the fact that the employers in this industry discriminated against Negro girls and paid them less than white girls. The agreement between the ladies' garment manufacturers and the union provided a weekly wage of $37.40 for skirt and dress operators—85 cents per hour for a forty-four-hour week. Negro operators in non-union factories for the same work were being paid from $18.00 to $25.00 per week. Union skirt and dress finishers were being paid $26.40 per week—60 cents per hour for forty-four hours. Negro operators in non-union factories averaged $15.00 per week for the same work and frequently worked longer than forty-four hours.

The relations of whites and Negroes in the union were discussed before the Commission by Max Brodsky, a representative of the union, who said:

As a result of the 1917 strike we have now about 450 colored women workers in our industry. We lost the strike, and this is how the colored women got into our industry. Now the union knew the object of the colored women coming into our industry, and we decided to have them organized just like the white women and girls, so we established this particular union. They are at present conscientious union girls and women. It was the policy of the union not to discriminate against the colored women who broke the strike in 1917. This helped us.

At the same conference, Agnes Nestor, president of the Women's Trade Union League, testified as follows:

Miss Nestor: In the ladies' garments work, the unions have taken in colored girls on the same basis as the white girls. They made a colored girl a chairman of their shop meeting. There is no feeling there with them as far as I know.

Miss McDowell: Didn't they elect a colored girl as shop steward where they had both white and colored girls?

Miss Nestor: Yes.

As an illustration of employers' discrimination against Negro workers, and of the efforts of the union to protect Negroes when they become members of the union, the case of a manufacturer was cited whose shop had only Negro workers. Shortly after the union had organized them they were locked out. Later the employer was willing to settle "providing you sent us a set of white workers." The union refused to do this and called a strike.

The union claimed that in many recent cases where Negro girls were sent out on jobs the employers would refuse them when they found out that they had to pay them the same scale as white workers. During 1917–18, owing to the war, the manufacturers worked in harmony with the unions because they had to; since the war, and largely within the first few months of 1920, the manufacturers have opened many shops on the South Side employing only non-union colored girls. In the various strikes in which this union has been engaged for this same period, the strike breakers have been Negro girls secured for the employers through a Negro minister acting as a labor agent or solicitor.

The Flat Janitors' Union has a membership of approximately 5,000, of whom 1,000 are Negroes. It includes many nationalities with strong racial feelings, yet, as stated by Mr. Fitzpatrick, president of the Chicago Federation of Labor, rarely is any complaint made against this union by Negroes.

Interviews with the president and other officials, attendance at a session of the Executive Board, and attendance at a crowded meeting of the union, where transaction of general business, nomination of candidates for the coming election, and initiation of new members occurred, gave the Commission's investigator ample opportunity for observation of the attitude toward Negroes.

This union, organized in 1904, started out with a Negro as recording secretary and business agent. At the time of the interviews, the vice-president and three members of the Executive Board were Negroes. These had been elected for a three-year term. At the general meeting attended, the Negro officers were renominated unanimously to hold office for a period of five years. In addition, several more Negroes were nominated as stewards and as delegates to the Chicago Federation of Labor.

According to the members, discrimination in this craft is practiced by the flat and apartment owners. The experience of the union is that as soon as a Negro is taken into the union and demands the union scale the owner calls up the union and says, "If I have to pay these wages I'm going to get a good white man."

The position taken by the union is that if a Negro has had the job he must be allowed to stay there and get the scale, and the union will back him up in the fight for it. The threat of a strike against a building is usually effective.

Inquiry among Negro janitors in the residence districts brought up a case in which one Negro claimed that Negroes were forced into the union and then usually found themselves discriminated against by the white members, especially by Belgians, and soon or later, were squeezed out of the good jobs. However, this Negro admitted that he had not attended a union meeting since his initiation, except to stop in to pay his dues, and that he had never made a complaint to the Negro officer of the union. The officers of the union admitted that there was, in the many racial groups in this craft, strong racial feeling, especially among Austrians and Belgians, who seemed to feel that whenever a janitor died or left the job, or an assistant or helper was needed, such job should always be filled with members of their own nationality. However, the Negro officials claimed that with three Negroes on the Executive Board and a Negro vice-president, any complaint coming from a Negro would surely be fairly dealt with; but that unless their attention was called to unsatisfactory conditions the union could not be expected to know of them, and in such cases it was not the union that was to blame, but the member himself.

Frequently, in those unions in which the Negroes are not admitted into the same locals with the whites, the reasons given for putting them into separate locals or auxiliaries is that the white members object to the close physical contact or association in meetings, especially where there is some element of ritual in connection with the meetings. At the meeting of the Janitors' Union attended by the investigator, new pass words were given out, and all members, white and Negro, had to come before the Negro vice-president, who whispered the words to each and they in turn repeated them to him. Not the slightest hesitancy was noted on the part of the white members, but rather a hearty handshake or a slap on the back seemed to be the rule. Again, in taking in nineteen new members, four of whom were Negroes, the major part of the ceremony was performed by the Negro vice-president. At this meeting, packed to standing-room and attended by well over a thousand members, Negroes were a large percentage of those present. These were not confined to a group by themselves, but were scattered in all parts of the hall and seemed to be in cordial conversation with the white members.

A number of interesting comments by members and officers of unions admitting Negroes on equal terms with whites were volunteered, either in interviews or in correspondence. In one union of 700 highly skilled workers receiving $1.50 an hour, or $12.00 a day, no Negroes were found to be members, although they are not barred by the constitution. It was suggested that the five-year apprenticeship period discouraged Negroes. It was further noted that admittance was by a two-thirds vote, a provision which could easily result in the exclusion of any race which two-thirds of the members did not like. The investigator's report of his interview says:

The business representative of this union was strongly of the personal opinion that unions had made a mistake in ever admitting the Negro into any of the unions. He claimed that the employers' only interest in them was as a lever to keep wages down for the workers.

Two other members of the League took a contrary position and held that Negro labor was in the field, and that while the employer's interest in the Negro was simply to play one group against another to keep expense down as low as possible, it was really up to labor itself to solve the question and that the Negroes must be taken into unions. They admitted that undoubtedly prejudice existed, but that it was gradually being overcome.

Other comments are as follows:

From an officer of the Teamsters and Chauffeurs: "We have had one Negro holding office as trustee for several years. So feeling is brotherly."

From an officer of a specialized mechanics' union: "There has been no sign of race feeling or hatred since we have been organized. We have six officers (one colored). I myself, being colored, have no complaints whatever against my white brothers."

From a Negro officer of the Mattress Makers: "Discrimination and race prejudice does not exist in this union. We are one happy family. It seems impossible to organize the other Negro mattress makers. Would appreciate some assistance."

B. UNIONS ADMITTING NEGROES TO SEPARATE CO-ORDINATE LOCALS

Certain unions organize Negroes into separate locals which are in all respects co-ordinate with the white locals belonging to the same unions. The reason for maintaining separate Negro locals is either (1) preference of the Negro workers for locals of their own, or (2) unwillingness of white workers to admit Negroes to white locals. It often seemed that the second indicated the real situation, the first reason being given as an excuse for it.

The important factor is the reason for the existence of separate Negro locals rather than the fact of separation. This is illustrated by the experience of the Painters' and Musicians' unions on the one hand, and that of the Waiters' Union on the other.

During July, 1920, twenty Negro painters applied to the Painters' District Council for membership in the Painters' Union. They passed the required examination but, instead of being placed in the existing Painters' Union, were given temporary working permits which identified them as members of "South Side Colored Local." They immediately suspected that some effort was being made to place them in a separate Negro local in which they could not get the full benefits of union membership. They then went to discuss the matter with the editor of a Negro paper which had expressed the point of view of many Negroes concerning labor unions in its editorial columns. This editor told them his belief that the Painters' District Council was merely duplicating the practices of several other unions in the city, and was attempting to limit these men to a "Jim Crow" union. They returned to the president of the District Council, who explained that he had to keep track of all temporary permits issued, and inasmuch as the charter for their local was not yet issued he could not know the number until issued. He had to put the description on the cards to identify the men temporarily.

A charter for the local was given from national headquarters, and the new cards were issued, designating them simply as members of Local No.—. The membership of this local, exclusively Negro, grew from twenty to seventy-five in two months. One of the Negro officials of the local stated that its members had been working in all parts of the Chicago District, including the North Side and Evanston, and that they had a representative on the District Council. The attitude of the white workers, he stated, was a little cool on the first day, but there is now no evidence of friction. He thought that the members of this local were well pleased and happy.

The Negro Musicians are organized into a strong separate local, chartered in 1902. It has a membership of approximately 325. It has held the Municipal Pier dance-hall contract for three years, and besides many other contracts in the city. It furnishes players for various occasions for a considerable territory outside of Chicago. This group much prefers its own union, but works jointly with the large white union, the Chicago Federation of Musicians, whenever matters come up affecting both organizations Both unions have the same wage scale.

Where Negro workers are permitted to join white locals but prefer to have their own colored local there is no feeling that they are discriminated against, occasional joint meetings with white locals being characterized by friendly interest and good fellowship. Where, however, a union closes the door of its white locals to Negroes and organizes them into separate locals because the white members object to contact with Negroes, a very difficult situation exists. This condition is illustrated by the methods of the Waiters' Union in Chicago.

Negro waiters are not admitted into the white Waiters' Union, but are placed in the Pullman Porters and Dining-Car Waiters' Union, which is a local affiliated with the same international as the white Waiters' Union. The makeshift of putting Negro waiters, although employed in city hotels, restaurants, and cafés, into this local is pointed to by Negroes as unmistakable evidence of discrimination.

The culinary strike in Chicago, which started May 1, 1920, resulted in failure for the unions concerned largely because Negroes acted as strike breakers. This is easily accounted for by the fact that seventeen years ago Negro waiters lost their positions in many of the first-class hotels and restaurants in the business district through circumstances in which they felt that they had been "double-crossed" by the unions, of which they then were members.

The Negro strike breakers in 1920, however, found themselves again displaced, this time through the action of employers. A typical instance was found in the restaurant of a hotel patronized largely by people of German descent, the managers as well as many of the former waiters being of German extraction. These waiters, some of whom had been employed for many years in this restaurant, were members of the union and went out when the strike was called. The managers replaced them with Negroes. The latter filled the positions with apparent satisfaction for nearly a year, when suddenly they were all discharged and the old waiters taken back.

A regular patron of the restaurant, a man of German descent, expressed vigorous views upon the "injustice" with which the Negroes had been treated by the management, which should have appreciated their service through the period when the former waiters caused trouble. He said he had always found the Negroes efficient and willing, and many of them "very intelligent fellows." Although of the same nationality as the managers and the former waiters, many of whom he had known for years, he did not let this national feeling blind him to what he considered most unfair treatment of the Negroes. He said that he had discussed the matter with one of the managers and had been told that the reason why the Negroes had been discharged and the old waiters taken back was because of complaints against the Negroes by patrons of the restaurant. He added, "I think that's bunk."

A change in the officers of the Waiters' Union at the recent election has placed in power a group which recognizes that the entire policy of the culinary unions must be co-ordinated and proper provision made for the large Negro element in the field. If this is not done, it is felt that a rival Negro union may be organized, similar to that organized by the Negro railway workers. In fact, even now a beginning has been made toward such an organization by a few high-grade Negro waiters who have been in active charge of the waiters of several of the large hotel dining-rooms during the recent strike.

C. UNIONS ADMITTING NEGROES TO SUBORDINATE OR AUXILIARY LOCALS

The practice of admitting Negroes to subordinate locals appears to be very unusual in Chicago. The investigation disclosed only one instance where the policy of the union was to admit Negroes only to subordinate locals. The Commission is not at liberty to publish the name of this union, which makes the following provision for Negro locals in its constitution:

Where there are a sufficient number of colored helpers they may be organized as an auxiliary local and shall be under the jurisdiction of the white local union having jurisdiction over that locality; and minutes of said auxiliary local must be submitted to duly authorized officers of said white local for their approval.

In shops where there is a grievance committee of the white local, grievances of members of said auxiliary local will be handled by that committee.

Members of auxiliary locals composed of colored helpers shall not transfer except to another auxiliary local composed of colored members, and colored helpers will not be promoted to . . . . or helper apprentice; and will not be admitted to shops where white helpers are now employed.

Auxiliary locals will be represented in all conventions by the delegates elected from the white local in that locality.

The officials of this union stoutly maintain that the provisions above quoted are not discriminatory, and they are at a loss to explain why attempts to organize Negro workers in Chicago into auxiliary locals have not met with success.

D. UNIONS EXCLUDING NEGROES FROM MEMBERSHIP

Chicago locals which exclude the Negro do so either in conformity with the laws of their national unions or in the exercise of "local option." Locals belonging to the national and international unions which bar the Negro by written provision in their constitutions or rituals are obliged to follow the same racial policy as their parent bodies. This number includes the Chicago locals belonging to the eight American Federation of Labor national unions which exclude the Negro, and the locals of the four railway brotherhoods which likewise exclude the Negro by constitutional provision.

In addition to the locals which are bound to follow the policy of their nationals, there are certain other locals which are known to reject Negro applicants. By allowing their locals to practice "local option" or to require a majority or two-thirds vote for election to membership, the progressive policy of certain American Federation of Labor national and international unions which admit the Negro is nullified.

The Machinists' Union has frequently been referred to as a union which, although complying in its constitution with the American Federation of Labor policy of no racial discrimination, still effectually bars the Negro by a provision in its secret ritual. In effect, however, there is no real difference between such a policy on the part of the Machinists' Union and that of the unions which apparently practice exclusion as an unwritten law. With the Machinists' Union must then be grouped such unions as the Amalgamated Sheet Metal Workers' International Alliance, International Brotherhood of Electrical Workers of America, and United Association of Plumbers and Steam Fitters of United States and Canada. The Electricians' Union has only one Negro member out of a total membership of 11,000 in Chicago.

V. ATTITUDE OF NEGROES TOWARD UNION ORGANIZATION

From its attitude toward labor unions the Negro population of Chicago may be considered in four groups: (1) racial leaders outside the labor movement—ministers, editors, politicians, etc.; (2) Negroes with a special interest in opposing unions; (3) Negro workers outside of the unions; (4) Negro workers within the ranks of the unions.

I. RACIAL LEADERS OUTSIDE OF THE LABOR MOVEMENT

Within this group are found many sincere workers for the welfare of the race. Their attitude is determined by the apparent practicability of courses of action for Negroes in relation to the unions. These attitudes again depend upon their familiarity with the principles and purposes of unionism. They recognize that the entrance of large numbers of Negroes in industry has been recent. The belief is that the employers rather than the labor unions provided this first opportunity, and since, under most frequent circumstances, the holding of these positions has been due to the kindly attitude of employers, they felt that first loyalty was due to them.

They have also been affected by experiences with labor unions which in the past have not been disposed to accept Negroes freely into membership with them.

Although the interest of employers in securing Negroes has not always been merely the granting of an opportunity for work, where Negroes have entered as strike breakers they have usually remained. This recent entrance into industry has made them, for the first time, a considerable factor, and they feel that the unions, recognizing their importance to the accomplishment of union aims, are making appeals to them for membership, not out of a spirit of brotherhood, but merely to advance their purposes.

These considerations have largely determined the attitude of many Negro leaders, especially the ministers, some of whom have been requested by employers to recommend members of their congregations for jobs in various fields of industry. At a recent industrial convention of Negro organizations controlling the employment of thousands of Negro workers, it was decided that Negroes would not be sent as strike breakers to plants where the strikers' unions accepted Negroes, and that they would advise Negroes to join the unions wherever possible, but that where Negroes are offered positions by employers in trades where Negroes are excluded from the unions, they would not be advised to forego the opportunity.

An intelligent Negro woman, who has been active in trying to acquaint ministers with union aims and methods, commented upon the fact that until recently Negro ministers knew very little about unionism, except that employers were opposed to it. This was enough to influence many ministers to urge Negro workers to stay out of labor unions and thus demonstrate their loyalty to employers who had given them a chance in industry.

A prominent Negro leader, a member of the Illinois legislature, stated his position respecting unions, at one of the industrial conferences held by the Commission, as follows:

I want to confess that I have never felt that I could intelligently advise the colored people who ask me whether laboring people should join the unions. It has been the opinion of the leaders of our race for years that employers of labor felt more kindly toward colored labor and were less concerned about the color of the workmen—were only concerned about the character of the service. We felt as leaders of the race that the labor employer was given a square deal much more than the employee himself. . . . . We had a strike here of waiters several years ago when the Kohlsaat lunchroom waiters were involved. I was the president of a men's Sunday club, and some labor agitators got the colored boys to join the white Waiters' Union, and I remember when the matter came before the club I told them, "They raised your wages to the white man's scale, and the white men are raising you out in the street," and that is what they did too. . . . . I have been somewhat influenced by that experience.

2. NEGROES WITH A SPECIAL INTEREST IN OPPOSING UNIONS

The rift between employers and labor unions has provided a field of exploitation for certain less responsible Negroes. Their operations have occasioned bitter feeling between Negroes and labor unions and have accomplished little or nothing for the Negro workers. A Negro editor of a small and irresponsible paper advises Negro workers not to join the white man's union, but instead to join a union which he has formed and of which he is president. He is looked upon with suspicion by representative Negroes of Chicago, who believe that he is willing to sacrifice the best interests of the race to serve his own purposes. A well-informed Negro outlined the method employed by the editor in question to represent himself to employers of labor as one who controls large numbers of Negro laborers. In furtherance of this plan, which appears to have prospered, he organized a group which he called the "American Unity Labor Union." The appeal on the one hand to Negroes was that white unions would not admit them on an equal basis and that white employers preferred Negro non-unionists to white unionists and would pay them the same wages while according them better treatment. To white employers he represented the Negroes as being opposed to unions because they were white men's unions, and as such discriminated against Negroes, and that they belonged in large numbers to his organization, which was designed to improve the quality of Negro labor by increasing Negro pride in special and unmixed endeavors.

That certain employers did give money for this kind of service is apparent in several instances. A Negro ex-clergyman secured for a long period something like $2.00 per capita for every Negro supplied by him to any one of ten iron foundries in the Calumet district.

The following are typical of advertisements which appear regularly in the paper of the Negro editor referred to above:

WANTED

100 Building Laborers to work in the city of Chicago at Building Scale Wages. Union Job. If you are not a Union man you can get a permit to work as a Union Man at —— Indiana Avenue.

Do not pay $33.00 to join a white man's union, when you can join the black man's union for $5.00 and work on any building in Chicago.

WAGE EARNERS CLUB

American Unity Labor Union was organized March 10th, 1917, Chicago, Illinois.

GET A SQUARE DEAL WITH YOUR OWN RACE

Time has come for Negroes to do now or never. Get together and stick together is the call of the Negro. Like all other races, make your own way; other races have made their unions for themselves. They are not going to give it to you just because you join his union. Make a union of your own race; union is strength. Join the American Unity Packers Union of the Stock Yards, this will give you a card to work at any trade or a common laborer, as a steam fitter, electrician, fireman, merchants, engineers, carpenters, butchers, helpers, and chauffeurs to drive trucks down town, delivering meat as white chauffeurs do for Armour's and Swift's, or other Packers. A card from this Union will let you work in Kansas City, Omaha and St. Louis, or any other city where the five Packers have packing houses.

This Union does not *believe in strikes*. We believe all differences between laborers and capitalists can be arbitrated. Strike is our last motive if any at all.

Get in line for a good job. *You are next. Office, —— Indiana Ave.*

THE WORKING MEN'S CLUB

Join the American Unity Steel and Metal Union, a Union of your own race with officers of your own race with a President. A card from this Union will entitle you to work any place in the United States as a steel and iron worker, craneman, engineer, molders, rail straighteners, and any job that it takes brains and skill to do and common laborer. *Join one big union and demand a square deal with your own strength.* 8 hour day's work.

Get in line for a good job. You are next. Office, —— Indiana Ave.

All classes and kinds of work waiting for good people in our Association.

During the latter part of December, 1920, the editor in question visited the large daily newspapers in Chicago and presented an article which purported to tell of a large mass meeting of his union at which this group decided that they would work at the Stock Yards, steel mills, and all other plants in Chicago and the Calumet region and at all foundries and factories at a 15 per cent discount on wages previously paid for skilled labor, and 10 per cent on common-labor wages. Although only one paper gave any attention to this statement, the opinion of some of the more responsible Negroes was expressed in a Negro newspaper in Chicago, which characterized the man as "a public nuisance" and his story as "bunk."

3. NEGRO WORKERS OUTSIDE OF UNIONS

Negro workers outside of the union ranks often do not see any necessity for unonism or do not understand its aims and methods; many are frankly suspicious of the good intentions of white unionists toward Negroes; others condemn unions generally because of some bitter experience with a particular union, while still others are enthusiastic believers in unionism and expect to join a union at some time. Several shades of opinion are illustrated by the following quotations taken at random from interviews with a large number of Negro workers.

H— G—, thirty-four years old, left a farm in Georgia to come to Chicago in October, 1919. Employed as a laborer in a paper-box manufacturing plant. He said he didn't know much about unions but couldn't see what good they were doing. They made prices go up, but wages didn't go up with prices. If unions did any good he would join, but he can't see that they do.

W— W— had spent nearly all of his life hauling logs to be made into ties for railroads. When he came here from the South he worked as a trucker in the Quartermaster's Department of the army until the department closed. After loafing half a month, he got his present job trucking at a box factory. Unions would be all right, in his opinion, if they let all of the men in who would do right, but when they don't, they do more harm than good. He used to belong to the Butchers' Union at the Stock Yards and "got along fine," but he quit butchering. He intends to get back in a union if possible. Strikes are too hard on the man that "ain't in the union; strike out here recently and now we can't make overtime and we hardly make enough in regular time to live on. Unions are secret—I can't remember all the bunk about them now, but you pay dues and go to meetings, something like a lodge I guess. If anything goes wrong on your job you tell it in meeting, and your branch of the union takes it up with the people. You don't have any of that worry on yourself. They are all right if you are on the inside, but mighty hard if you ain't."

J— McN—, forty-two years old, had been a farmer in the South all of his life until he came to Chicago in January, 1920, and went to work in the Yards as a meat trimmer. He has been asked to join the unions but hasn't done it as yet—he isn't quite sure they mean a square deal by the colored man, although he can't see why they would ask him to join if they didn't. Don't know much about the "workings of 'em" but they pull together, sort of "lodge like." He thinks everybody who belongs is mighty "close mouthed" about what they do at the meetings. He knows that they pay dues and have assessments, that they look after sick members and have some sort of initiation.

J— L—, fifty-two years old, is foreman over the truckers in a box factory. He said: "Unions ain't no good for a colored man, I've seen too much of what they don't do for him. I wouldn't join for nothing—wanted me to join one at the Yards but I wouldn't; no protection; if they had been, the colored men who belonged might have worked while the riot was going on; only thing allowed out there then was foreigners. If a thing can't help you when you need help, why have it? That's the way I feel about unions. I tell you they don't mean nothing for me."

H— S—, twenty-four years old, had lived in Chicago only two months. He said: "Well I don't know, you see these other folks been here longer than me; they ain't joined, and I reckon they know more about it than me. No, they didn't have no unions where I comed from—ain't nothing there anyway but farmers. I reckon, though, if I had a chance I might join. They can't do much harm here to a fellow."

J— H—, thirty-eight years old, came up from Alabama in 1916 with about thirty other men during the big rush from the South. They went to work almost immediately at the Stock Yards, where he worked as a laborer, stripping bacon. After he quit this he was out of work for nearly a month. He heard about the wool mills. They put him on the very first day and he has been there ever since.

He does not belong to a union. He "would join one if I had a chance and it meant anything to me materially." He does not understand them, "can't understand why they strike and keep men out of work."

M— L—, forty-two years old, came to Chicago from Tennessee in 1894. He said: "I tried every job under the sun since I came. My first job was porter in the Palmer House; made good tips here but not very much salary. Changed to bellboy; was finally made head bellboy; stayed there four years; boss made me mad and I quit. Along about this time I met my wife. I wanted to make her think I was a regular man, so got a job as a laborer in a foundry. Since then I've gone from one foundry to the other. Work got so hard I quit one time; went on the road; stayed there for about four years, then went back to the foundry work; worked for Illinois Malleable for three years first time; had trouble with straw boss; he fired me; went to McCormick's but they didn't pay so well, so I got back on my old job. Yes, unions are the best thing in the world for a working man. If I'd been in a union my boss couldn't have fired me that time. I wish it was so you could join a union regardless of your color. We need protection on our jobs as well as the white man. I guess though that time is coming. I don't know much about the workings of a union, but I do know it's a protection to the man who belongs."

F— D—, twenty-eight years old, does not belong to a union because there are no unions in the car shops where he works. He says unions are the best things in the world if the right kind of people are at the head, and if all the fellows will join, but when half of them won't join, unionism won't do because it just means loss of your job.

R— R—, thirty-four years old, has been working in Chicago three months at his regular trade as a stove joiner. He learned to join stoves at a mill in Helena. He has never had a chance to join a union, but all the white men in the mill at Helena belonged, and they fared lots better than the Negro men. He wants to join one here the very first chance he gets. He is a skilled laborer, knows he can put out as much work as any man doing his line of work, feels he should be paid as much as anyone else, and knows the only way this can happen to him is to get in a union where he has some protection and backers. There is a union where he is, but he hasn't been asked to join it yet. He says he has found out that the colored man, if he wants the same thing as a white man gets, has to get in things with them.

Mrs. N— M— found work as a maid in a Chicago hospital after she was deserted by her husband. She wants to save money enough to run her while she takes "nurse training." She did not know anything about unions until she went to the hospital. The nurses there had a union, and she saw just how much they can mean to people. "They usually make the employers do the right thing by the people; unless the nurses asked too much they got what they wanted." That was what made her decide she wanted to be a nurse; she saw how square they were with each other, and how the union made them pull together regardless of whether or not they liked each other. That is what she liked about the unions: "They make you treat the other fellow right regardless how you feel toward him."

Nellie W—, age thirty, doing clerical work in a large mail-order establishment, said that "unions don't mean anything to colored people. The only reason they let them in when they do is so they can't become strike breakers." She didn't know how her husband felt about unions, as they had never talked about the matter, but she knew that she wouldn't join one.

O— L—, thirty-eight years old, had migrated from Georgia in the summer of 1917. To him unions are "the best thing that ever came the colored man's way. Out here [in a box factory] it doesn't make quite so much difference whether I'm in one or not, but if I ever go back to my trade as plasterer, that's the first thing I intend to try and do. You get protection, you get more money, and then too the white man gets a chance to see that you are not all for yourself, for when you are in a union you work for everybody's good."

H— has been a head waiter in a hotel. He believes the big reason why Negroes are not strongly enthusiastic for unions is because they feel they will not get square treatment. This he based upon continual references to the 1903 waiters' strike.

The attitude of indifference or suspicion so frequently encountered among Negro workers outside of the unions is attributed by white and Negro labor leaders and union men to the following reasons: (a) traditional treatment of Negroes by white men; (b) influence of racial leaders who oppose unionism; and (c) influence of employers' propaganda against unionism.

The traditional treatment of Negroes in the South, increasingly reflected in the North, has made the Negro suspicious of the white man's sincerity. Negroes, therefore, naturally feel that they will not get a "square deal" in white unions. In support of this attitude the waiters' strike of 1903 is still cited as an instance of "double-crossing" by white unions.

This strike was so often referred to by Negroes as a justification for their attitude toward labor-union policies that it seemed worth while to attempt to learn the facts, even though seventeen years had elapsed since the strike occurred.

Two organizers for the American Federation of Labor, a newspaper editor, an officer of the Negro local during the strike, the head waiter of one of the large hotels (all Negroes), and John Fitzpatrick, president of the Chicago Federation of Labor, were asked to tell the facts.

Reports are conflicting in many instances. However, the explanations of circumstances as presented to the Commission are as follows:

The union of cooks and waiters involved in the strike of 1903, affiliated with the American Federation of Labor, had a membership of 20,000, of whom over 2,000 were Negroes. The Negroes had only recently been taken into the union as a separate local under their own officers. The strike first centered on Kohlsaat's chain of restaurants. This lasted seven weeks, during which time all of the union members were out. The strike terminated in circumstances on which there is general disagreement. Negroes state that the white unionists "double-crossed" them, and when Kohlsaat refused to take back the Negro waiters who had walked out with the whites the latter went back to work and left the Negroes without jobs. It is known that during the general excitement the charter of the Negro local was revoked, although no one appears to know how or by whom this was done. The white union leaders have frequently attempted to absolve the union of responsibility for this situation and place the blame on the Kohlsaat restaurants and the *Chicago Herald*, controlled by Kohlsaat. John Fitzpatrick, before the Commission, referred to the incident thus:

Commissioner: Concerning the waiters' strike several years ago, the Kohlsaat strike, were they unionized under your direction in order to raise the scale of dinner men [they were known as dinner men] to the union scale? What was the success of it as far as the colored waiters were concerned?

Mr. Fitzpatrick: They weren't organized for financial purposes. They were organized as workers. We felt they ought to have our co-operation, so we went out to organize them. The Kohlsaat newspaper was one of the instruments by which they perpetrated the conspiracy, and some other papers went into a scheme and tried to bring about an atmosphere of fear and suspicion between the colored and white workers.

It was Sunday, and the charter of the colored workers was in my possession. That night they met, and I was installing officers at Twenty-third Street and Washington Avenue. That morning the *Herald* ran a front-page story, first column, teeming with a set-up against organized labor and warning the colored workers to beware.

When I got up on the platform I read the story to them and said, "That sets up one side of the story, and there is a conspiracy to destroy your rights. What do you want to do about it?"

They said, "We will go ahead. We know what the employers want and you go ahead and instal us." They went ahead and got into that strike. The employers said: "We are going to supplant colored men with white union girls." We told them we wouldn't permit union girls to go on the job. The Kohlsaats begged of us to give them white union women, and we refused to do so.

Now then, while this was going on, the newspapers had different reports out, and they went out and had the charter of this local revoked. How they did it, I don't know. But I have my own notions how a newspaper operates. I think that a newspaper has influence and money and other things, and that is the only way I can account for that thing happening. They went to the international organization to revoke the charter of this organization.

This whole situation was obscured by a mass of charges and counter-charges, but the fact that the strike failed was evident enough. Regardless of what the facts actually were, there is a widespread belief among Negro workers that the colored waiters were "double-crossed" by white unions in this strike. Since it is men's belief about facts which determines behavior, it is not surprising to find that Negro strike breakers could be found in large numbers to take the place of waiters who went on strike in May, 1920.

The influence of some employers is also a factor in the attitude of Negroes toward labor unions. In many open shops the employers and unions are engaged in a continuous struggle. In such cases, if persuasion and argument fail, there is an effective instrument in strike breakers. For this purpose Negroes have frequently been used. Instances in Chicago are found in the strikes in the steel industry, the Stock Yards, and the culinary industry. Many labor leaders and union members believe that welfare clubs, company Y.M.C.A.'s, glee clubs, and athletic clubs are encouraged and supported by employers as a substitute for a form of organization which they cannot control. The subsidizing of social movements and churches is regarded as one of the means employed by large employers to insure this reserve of strike breakers. The union organizer in the steel strike, W. Z. Foster, stated at one of the conferences held by the Commission that, after an address to the Negro steel workers at a church in Pittsburgh, the Negro preacher had said to him: "It nearly broke up the congregation, but we decided you were going to speak here in this church." The organizer continued:

Then I got the underneath of all this thing and found that this church had lost a donation of $2,500.00 from the Steel Corporation for allowing me to speak. They had tried to block my speech to these colored workers in Pittsburgh. Whenever it's a question of a donation to a poor, struggling church like that, we know what usually happens.

The statement made by George W. Perkins, president of the Cigarmakers' International Union, was typical of the view of labor leaders:

If you go to the root, you will find that economic reason; the employers, not all of them but many of them, in our industry as well as others, will divide the workers if they can. That is the history all along. They will divide them, not because they are black and white, but to keep them divided so they won't unite in the organization.

Another labor leader, acting as an organizer in large industries in various cities, stated at another conference:

I want to tell you that a strike breaker is a very precious animal for the employer, and if he thinks he has a great body of colored workers in this country who are apt to learn trades with very little practice, as an inexhaustible well of strike breakers, he is not going to stop at a little thing like propaganda. He will find plenty of excuses to keep men out of the union. In the Stock Yards, in the steel industry, he will find arguments and he will carry on propaganda.

The difficulties inherent in the whole question of organizing Negroes were probably best brought out before the Commission by W. Z. Foster, who took a leading part in organizing Negroes in the Stock Yards, the most important industry in Chicago so far as Negroes are concerned:

We found in the steel industry that the colored worker was very unresponsive to organization. The same was true in the packing industry. Let me give you first what steps we took in the packing industry in Chicago in 1917, the big campaign which resulted in the organization of men. The first meeting we had we sat around a table and talked it over, and we realized that there were two big problems, the organization of the foreign worker and the organization of the colored worker. We shortly dismissed the problem of organizing the foreign worker, but we realized that to accomplish the organization of the colored worker was the real problem. When we went into the packing-house situation we were determined to organize the colored worker if it was humanly possible to do so, and I think I can safely say that the men who carried on that campaign realized fully the necessity for the organization of the colored worker, not wholly, or at least not only, from the white man's point of view, but from his own point of view to a certain extent. In other words, we were not altogether materialistic. We like to think that we were a little bit altruistic in the situation. There was a total employment of twelve or fourteen thousand. We found that we had tremendous opposition to encounter.

First of all it took this attitude, that the colored man would not be allowed to join the unions at all. We met that broadcast with such circulars as those already shown. I wrote some of them up myself as secretary of the council, inviting these men in such a way that these colored men could not help but realize that there was nothing to this argument that they would not be allowed to join the union. . . . . The next argument that developed was, "Sure, the white man will take you into his union because you are in the minority." But we fought all of these arguments, and we organized a local union on State Street.

Then the argument was raised that it was a "Jim Crow" proposition. It was quite general along State Street that it was a "Jim Crow" proposition. It seemed to make no difference what move we made, there was always an argument against it, so we overcame the "Jim Crow" argument by combining the white locals and the black. We said to the boys: "This is not a colored local. This is a neighborhood local of miscellaneous locals. Any colored man can belong to this local." We told the white men: "You are free to come in here and join this union."

Well, we punctured that argument that there was discrimination in the Stock Yards, and I would challenge anyone to show where the unions in the Stock Yards campaign have discriminated against the colored man. There may have been isolated cases of an individual here and there, but I will say this, and I was on the organizing committee and probably in closer touch with the situation than anyone else here in the city with those four or five thousand colored workers that we organized, I dare say that 40 per cent of the total amount of grievances that were presented by all the workers in the Stock Yards came from these colored workers, and the standing instructions were to look after them very carefully. . . . .

But the more we tried to help the colored worker the more intense the opposition was, because there was a force working against us, and we could not help but feel it. We got it from the colored people themselves, and it is a fact that some of the organizers were actually afraid to go around to some of these saloons and poolrooms where they congregated because of the agents of the packers, or whoever was responsible for that propaganda, and they felt that their lives were in danger. . . . . Out in the Stock Yards we could not win their support. It could not be done. They were constitutionally opposed to unions, and all our forces could not break down that opposition. . . . . We tried to make our appeal quite general in scope. We got the best organizers. A good colored organizer is very rare—a man who is thoroughly qualified to represent the trade-union point of view. We tried to find one and picked out a colored member of the Engineers' Union, a man highly honored in all the trade unions of Chicago. . . . . The reason the colored man gave for not joining you will find in the circular "Beware of the White Man's Union," and that the only way that they can ever make any headway in the industry is to stick in with the boss and then when there is a strike to step in and take the jobs that are left there. . . . .

Race prejudice has everything to do with it. It lies at the bottom. The colored man as a blood race has been oppressed for hundreds of years. The white man has enslaved him, and they don't feel confidence in the trade unions. But there is more real fraternal feeling among the black and white workers than in any other grade of society. . . . . As soon as the colored man becomes a factor in industry, he is going to be organized, providing he does not become a victim to the line of tactics that are laid out by the employer. In the steel strike he lined up with the bosses.

4. NEGRO WORKERS WITHIN THE UNIONS

Negro workers inside the ranks of such unions as the Stock Yards', Janitors', and Hodcarriers', types of the unions which accept Negroes with complete equality, feel, with very few exceptions, that they are being given a "square

deal" by the unions.   By coming into the unions they say they have been able
to secure better working conditions and higher wages.   They express satisfaction with the treatment accorded them by white unionists on the job and at
meetings, where the grievances of Negro members are given the same attention
as the complaints of white members.   The situation in the unions mentioned
has been so fully described already in this report that there is no need for further
details on the friendly relationship which exists between white and colored
members of these unions.   Many Negro unionists look to labor organization
as one of the most promising solutions of race problems.

VI.   THE NEGRO AND STRIKES

The attitude of Negro workers during strikes is closely connected with
the attitude of Negroes toward union organization.   As stated before, there
are many cross-currents at work, some tending to keep Negroes out of unions
and others impelling them toward the unions.   All the forces at work to
prejudice the Negro against union organization are factors which help to explain
his willingness to take the place of striking white workers.   The loyalty of the
Negro during strikes by white employees was referred to by a number of the
representatives of large employers attending the industrial conferences held
by the Commission.

Some of the most conspicuous cases coming to the attention of the Commisson in which Negroes have taken the place of white strikers or have
remained at work during strikes are the following:

The Stock Yards strike of 1904 lasted from July 4 to the middle of September.
The general superintendent of one of the plants in the Yards, appearing before the
Commission, said: "The strike was called at 12:00 o'clock.   Every employee practically that we had went out.   Within two or three days we had any number of colored
employees return to work. . . . . I'd say Negroes helped us to break the strike by
coming to work.   A number of Negroes that we understand belonged to the union did
not remain out more than two or three days.   Practically all the Negroes came back
before the strike was called off."

The strike in the Corn Products Refining Company plant at Argo, where, in the
summer of 1919, before the strike, 300 Negroes were employed, during the strike 900,
and when it was over about 500.

The steel strike of 1919.   Representatives of several of the iron and steel plants
stated that Negroes had helped to break this strike.   The *Inter-Church World Movement Report on the Steel Strike of 1919* (p. 177) lists the "successful use of strike-
breakers, principally Negroes, by the steel companies" as the second cause of the
failure of the steel strike.   "'Niggers did it' was a not uncommon remark among
company officials."

The waiters' strike in 1920.

Less important cases were the following:

A clothing shop where Negro women broke a strike in 1916 and continued in the
employ thereafter.   A wool warehouse and storage company which used Negroes

at slightly higher wages to replace striking Polish laborers in 1916, and have since continued to employ Negroes.

The strike of Pullman-car cleaners about 1916. Negroes were used as strike breakers and have since been employed in large numbers, men cleaning the windows and outside of cars and Negro women doing most of the inside cleaning.

Many other instances where Negroes have been used as strike breakers could be cited.

During a strike, feeling runs high and the word "strike breaker" or "scab" carries with it a decided stigma among the strikers. White workers ordinarily do not try to understand why the Negro acts as he does. They do not reason that the Negro is often loyal to the employer because he feels that the employer, sometimes at considerable risk, has opened to him industrial opportunities which, translated into wages, mean better living conditions for himself and his family. If the white worker took into account the struggle of the Negro to gain entrance into the fields outside of personals ervice, the latter's eagerness to take advantage of any opening, however created, might be better understood and regarded with more tolerant spirit.

What bearing this use of Negro labor has on the attitude of white workers toward Negroes depends upon whether the subject is approached from the point of view of the employer or of the trade unionist. Representatives of the packing companies emphasized the employers' appreciation of the Negro's loyalty and discounted the antagonism caused by Negroes serving as strike breakers, while trade-union leaders and others having the workers' point of view emphasized the seeds of dissension that were sown by such action and contended that the good will of the employer gained at such a cost was in reality a handicap to the Negro. White workers feel that Negroes who serve as strike breakers are helping to earn for their race the stigma of being a "scab" race. This is especially serious in the case of Negroes, because color identification makes it easy to focus hatred for the "scab."

Union leaders and social workers who participated in the conferences held by the Commission condemned the practice of some private employment agencies in sending Negroes to plants as strike breakers without informing them that a strike was in progress. Investigations in several states have disclosed such practices of some private employment agencies, "misrepresentation of terms and conditions of employment" being the most frequent abuse, according to the report of the Federal Commission on Industrial Relations: "Men are not informed about strikes that may be on at places to which they are sent, nor about other important facts which they ought to know."[1]

Private employment agencies following such practices try to do so against colored as well as white workers, although with probably less success because of the ability of the Negro to speak English. However, the part played by private employment agencies in supplying Negro strike breakers in Chicago

[1] U.S. Commission on Industrial Relations, *Final Report and Testimony* (1916), p. 111.

appears to be of relatively little importance. Ordinarily agents of employers find Negro strike breakers directly by going into the Negro residence section with autos or trucks and recruiting the number of men desired. The industrial secretary of the Urban League made the following statement regarding Negro strike breakers:

According to all information available to the Chicago Urban League, it does not appear that any of the private employment agencies except the one conducted by R. G. Parker, editor of the *Chicago Advocate*, who advertised for cooks and waiters to break the strike of the Cooks and Waiters' Alliance during the National Republican Convention in June, 1920, have been instrumental in strike breaking.

The method used in the organization of strike breakers among colored people is not well defined. Generally labor scouts work directly for companies affected by strikes. These scouts have frequently applied to our office for workers, but we have refused assistance. The men are usually gathered from the streets, poolrooms, or wherever they can be found. It is the policy of the Chicago Urban League not to interfere in strikes unless the striking unions have refused to admit colored workers to their membership. The League is not opposed to unionism, but is interested primarily in the welfare of colored workers.

VII. ATTITUDE AND OPINIONS OF LABOR LEADERS

From the eleven representative labor leaders attending the trade-union conferences held by the Commission, from the various interviews by the investigators with these and other union officials and members, and from letters received from labor officials from various parts of the United States, it was apparent that there were certain definite views held by most of these leaders as to the relationship of organized labor to the Negro. These views are summarized and set forth in the following pages:

1. GENERAL PUBLIC HAS RACE PREJUDICE

Race prejudice exists generally in all groups of the white race and only changes slowly. The worker is just as much subject to it in the beginning as are the members of all other groups.

2. UNIONS FAIRER TO NEGRO THAN ARE OTHER GROUPS

The unions have given the Negro a fairer deal than other social institutions or groups, such as department stores, clubs, churches, theaters, fraternal organizations, hotels, and railways.

3. UNIONS BLAMED FOR CONDITIONS THEY CANNOT CONTROL

Unions are many times blamed for situations in which Negroes are not admitted to an occupation or industry over which the unions have no control, the exclusion existing because the attitude of either the public or the employer prevents the entrance of Negroes into the industry. For example, Negroes are not employed in Chicago as motormen or conductors on surface or elevated transportation lines, as telephone operators by the telephone company, as sales clerks in department stores, as chauffeurs by taxicab companies, nor as upholsterers and drapers by firms sending such employees to work in private homes.

The position taken by the unions is that they cannot organize a miscellaneous public, but that they can only organize those that have the jobs, that as long as street and elevated lines do not employ Negroes as motormen and conductors the unions cannot take them in. True, there might be objection on the part of the members in these unions, but the question has never come up. Also the traction companies are not in business to reform public opinion and so, because the public might object, do not engage Negroes in these jobs. In this their position is similar to that of the large taxicab companies, which, however, employ non-union workers. They have Negroes in the garages but not as chauffeurs, probably because they believe that the general public would object if Negroes were employed as chauffeurs. In such cases the unions feel that they are not responsible, any more than they are accountable for the policy of the telephone company which engages no Negro operators. Among other large businesses must be listed the department stores, which have no Negroes as sales clerks.

Exclusion of Negroes from a trade or industry results in inability to join the unions in such trades. This fact is well illustrated by the Upholsterers' Union, which has three branches—furniture upholsterers, drapers, and mattress makers. Upholsterers and drapers are frequently sent out by the large stores to residences of customers, and the stores will not risk offending customers by sending a Negro into their homes. Consequently there are no Negroes in these branches of the union. The mattress makers' local, on the other hand, has more Negro than white members, and the secretary of the union is a Negro. This situation would not be possible if Negroes were excluded from employment in mattress factories. In view of the fact that the Upholsterers' Union freely admits Negroes into the mattress makers' local, Negroes would also, no doubt, be admitted into the locals of the upholsterers and the drapers if employers hired Negroes for such work.

4. EXCLUSION POLICY CONDEMNED

The policy, wherever it exists, of excluding Negroes from unions, whether by direct or indirect means, is considered wrong and shortsighted by the great majority of labor leaders. They believe that the small group of "aristocratic and conservative" unions cannot long withstand the American Federation of Labor policy of organizing Negroes in local and federal unions, nor the policy of the more progessive national and international unions. As the number of Negroes increases in the unions now admitting them, as the number of Negro delegates to city centrals, like the Chicago Federation of Labor, increases, and as the number of delegates to conventions of the State Federation of Labor and to the American Federation of Labor increases each year, more and more

pressure is being brought to bear on these unons from without and also by
the progressive leaders from within, so that gradually all barriers will be swept
aside.   That a gradual change is taking place in the policy of many unions is
evidenced by the following instances:

International Brotherhood of Firemen and Oilers.—"In 1902 a local union of
Negro stationary firemen in Chicago could not be chartered because the white
local union would not give its consent."[1]   In 1920 the president of Local 7,
Chicago, reported as follows:

> The symbol of our organization is, "We shall not discriminate against creed, color
> or nationality."   The membership of our organization is open to the Negro as much
> as to any other man who earns his living by the sweat of his brow.   I should say,
> offhand, that we have approximately about 100 Negroes who are members of our
> Chicago local and who take an active part in all of our deliberations.   So far as has
> come under my observation the feeling towards these men has always been of the
> most cordial nature.
>
> I am, however, free to say that we have found that a great many of the employers,
> who do not desire to play fair, use the Negro to offset any high standard of wages
> which the organization may deem proper and just, and I have found, in my experience,
> an endeavor on the part of some of the employers to only use the Negro when he would
> want to maintain a lower standard of wages, but when compelled by force of
> circumstances to pay a living rate of wages, immediately a request would be made
> on the organization that the Negro be removed and a white man furnished.   This we
> emphatically refuse to do.   If the Negro was efficient and competent to perform his
> duties prior to the establishment of a living wage he certainly should be competent
> enough to perform the same duties afterwards.

Metal Polishers' International Union.—The general secretary informed the
Commission:

> At the last international convention held, the question of Negroes entering our
> trade was taken up, and the delegates anticipated that, at some future time, Negroes
> would be employed, and we felt that, if the manufacturers were left under the impres-
> sion that we would refuse to accept them into the organization, it would be an incentive
> to the Manufacturers' Association to import Negroes or hire them, so a resolution was
> passed that any skilled polisher, buffer, or plater, even though a Negro, should be
> admitted to our organization.

International Association of Machinists.—Although at its convention at
Rochester, New York, in 1920, this union again voted down the proposition to
strike out the word "white" from its ritual, there was significance in the fact
that seven resolutions were introduced at the convention to remove the excluding provision.   These resolutions came from unions in the following cities:
two from different locals in Chicago; one from Columbia, South Carolina;
one from Akron, Ohio; one from New Haven, Connecticut; one from Tucson,
Arizona.   Resolutions opposing came from Bakersfield, California;   Pine

---

[1] F. E. Wolfe, *op. cit.*, p. 128, n. 3.

Bluff, Arkansas; Whistler, Alabama; and Savannah, Georgia. As an instance of enthusiastic appreciation of the mutual advantage to whites and Negroes of joint effort in union organization with no discrimination the following comment from an office of the Hotel and Restaurant Employees' National Alliance was received by the Commission:

We have one local union composed of white and colored workers—that union is located in the city of Boston, Massachusetts; roughly speaking, there are approximately 400 in a total membership of about 2,000; at our convention held at Providence, Rhode Island, last August, one of the delegates from that union was a colored man. Six years ago Boston colored waiters woke up, and so did the whites, to the fact that for decades they had been used one against the other by their employers; they got together, and they affirm with considerable emphasis that amalgamation has proved beneficial.

5. UNIONS INSTRUMENTAL IN REMOVING RACE PREJUDICE

Labor leaders emphasize the influence of contact in union meetings in promoting a friendly understanding between white and colored members. They point out the fact that the Negro ceases to be a stranger or an object of prejudice when once he has identified himself with the union. A common interest in common problems binds the members together, and a spirit of loyalty to the union develops in the effort to realize the aims of the group. White members come to have a more kindly feeling for a Negro within the union group than they have toward a white man who remains outside the union ranks. Said one union leader:

Some day the white worker is going to coax the black man to line up with him; all that he needs is a crusader's heart and a genuine desire to make the black man and himself free, and when he succeeds there won't be, in the economic field at least, the differences which now exist, due to this pitting of one race against the other and both being walloped by the action.

CHAPTER IX

PUBLIC OPINION IN RACE RELATIONS

The Negro in the United States: "A person of African blood (much or little) about whom men of English descent tell only half the truth, and because of whom they do not act with frankness and sanity either toward the Negro or to one another—in a word, about whom they easily lose their common sense, their usual good judgment, and even their powers of accurate observation. The Negro-in-America, therefore, is a form of insanity that overtakes white men."—*The Southerner* by Walter Hines Page.

The Stoic proverb, that "men are tormented by the opinions they have of things rather than by the things themselves,"[1] applies as aptly to the relations between the white and Negro populations as to other of our problems. Because the "race problem" has been so vaguely stated, so variously explained, and so little understood, discussions of it and the conduct of whites and Negroes toward each other usually express feeling rather than intelligence.

The public is guided by patterns of behavior and traditions generally accepted, whether sound or unsound. False notions, if believed, may control conduct as effectively as true ones. And pre-established notions lose their subtle influence when it appears that their basis is in error.

White persons are generally uninformed on matters affecting Negroes and race relations. They are forced to rely on partial and frequently inaccurate information and upon traditional sentiments. This same ignorance applies to Negroes, though not to the same degree; for they know white people in their intimate personal and home relations and in connection with their work in factories and stores. They read their books and papers and often hear their discussions. Negroes are perhaps more race conscious than whites because every day they must face situations which remind them of their race. They are sensitive to moods and antagonisms expressed in words and shown in manners. Their impressions from the white group are subject to distortion as are those received by the whites from them. Negroes manifest characteristics which, though the natural result of their circumstances and experiences, are yet misunderstood and often resented by the white group. For Negroes live and think in a state of isolation which is almost complete; and no white group understands it, or can fully understand it.

The riot of 1919 is an example of the effects of this isolation and misunderstanding. The accumulated resentments, unchallenged mutual beliefs and resultant friction, culminated in a surprising calamity and wholesale bloodshed.

[1] James Harvey Robinson, *Mind in the Making.*

This chapter, therefore, has a thesis and a purpose. If these beliefs, prejudices and faulty deductions can be made accessible for examination and analysis, many of them will be corrected. If a self-critical attitude toward these prejudices can be stimulated by typical examples, a considerable step will have been taken toward understanding and harmony.

The study of public opinion in race relations attempted by the Commission does not presume to set down definite laws of its working, or to tell all about how it works. The aim is merely to make apparent and objective its place and importance in race relations, to indicate some of the ways in which it has developed; how it expresses itself, how it affects both the white and Negro groups; how, in its present state, it is strengthened, weakened, polluted, or purified by deliberate agencies or even by its own action, and finally how it may be used to reduce, if not to prevent, racial unfriendliness and misunderstanding.

The following plan is employed in presenting this branch of the subject:

1. Beliefs regarding Negroes, which greatly influence the conduct of white persons toward them, are described as they apply in the local environment, and their origin and background are traced suggestively to their responsible literature and circumstances.

2. Types of sentiment which are variants of these basic beliefs are presented with a view to making them intelligible, and to classifying them according to resolvable factors of misunderstanding.

3. Since personal attitudes and beliefs are molded by traditions and heritages apart from the exclusive influence of literature, material collected through intimate inquiry is presented objectively to describe the processes by which they appear to be created and to grow. Replies to a searching questionnaire on attitudes and opinions express the result of painstaking self-analysis.

4. Negro opinion on these same issues is described and illustrated with a view to making it intelligible. Their views are listed and their interpretations of current white sentiment are explained as far as possible.

5. From the subjective aspect the study then turns to the instruments by which these opinions are formed and perpetuated and the individual attitudes created. The following are deemed the chief agencies: (a) the press, (b) rumors, (c) myths, (d) propaganda. Conscious and unconscious abuse of these instruments of opinion-making is pointed out and explained.

6. Finally, means are suggested by which public opinion may, where it is faulty, correct itself, and employ its own instruments in the creation of wholesome sentiments among Negroes with respect to whites, and among whites with respect to Negroes.

A. OPINIONS OF WHITES AND NEGROES

I. BELIEFS CONCERNING NEGROES

Literature concerning Negroes has been written chiefly by southern students facing the problem in its most intense form and usually meeting the most backward of Negroes. Negro habits have been objectively explained and standards of judgment upon the entire group have usually been deduced therefrom. This constitutes the bulk of serious literature on the subject of the Negro; it is generally used in research into the problem.

In the North as in the South the assumptions regarding the Negro have their basis in similar sources. The beliefs, in general, are the same, though held by individuals in varying degrees. Though northerners do not believe so firmly and with such emotional intensity all that southerners believe about Negroes, yet they share these beliefs in proportion as they have been influenced or informed by southerners. It may happen, for example, that in a small northern town with but a handful of Negroes there is no discernible distinction in the treatment accorded them. The growth of the colony, however, can bring to the surface at first almost undiscernible shades of the usual beliefs, and finally the identical beliefs entertained by other communities.

There is, for example, no section of the country in which it is not generally believed by whites that Negroes are instinctively criminal in inclination. Some believe that they are criminal by nature and explain it as a result of heredity; some feel that it is a combination of heredity and environment; while others may feel that this inclination is due to environment alone. How, indeed, may the belief be avoided? Crime figures on Negroes are consistently unfavorable to any other conclusion. Students have gone so far as to accept without question these figures and proceed to explain that criminal tendency scientifically. This is also true as to low mentality, sexual immorality, and a long list of other supposed racial defects.

Below are presented some of the more important beliefs among whites about Negroes that have become crystallized by years of unchallenged assumption. They divide themselves into two general classes: (1) Primary beliefs, or fundamental and firmly established convictions which have, all around, the deepest effect on the attitude of whites toward Negroes. These are usually presented as revealed by statistics, authorities, and research. (2) Secondary beliefs, or the lighter modifications and variants of the supposed attributes of Negroes included in the more important assumptions.

I. PRIMARY BELIEFS

Mentality.—The chief of these is that the mind of the Negro is distinctly and distinctively inferior to that of the white race, and so are all resulting functionings of his mind.

This view is held by some to be due to a difference in species, by others to more recent emergence from primitive life, and by others to be due to backwardness in ascending the scale of civilization. For this reason it is variously assumed as a corollary that the mind of the Negro cannot be improved above a given level or beyond a given age; that his education should be adapted to his capacities, that is, he should mainly be taught to use his hands. Thus a teacher in one of the elementary schools of Chicago finds that "colored children are restive and incapable of abstract thought; they must be constantly fed with novel interests and given things to do with their hands." Accordingly they are given handicraft instead of arithmetic, and singing instead of grammar.

In seeking the opinion of white trades unionists on the admission of Negroes to unions in Chicago, the Commission encountered in perhaps the harshest form the conviction that Negroes were inherently unable to perform tasks that white men did as a matter of course. A member of the Brotherhood of Locomotive Engineers felt that no Negro had, or could ever acquire, intelligence enough to run an engine. Employers frequently expressed the belief that Negroes are incapable of performing tasks which require sustained mental application. This view of their mental weakness appeared in the following statement made before the Commission by a school principal concerning her experience with Negro children:

So far as books are concerned there are set types of learning which they take with great difficulty. Last Friday a colored boy came to me and said, "I want to go back to the first grade." We have gotten him in the third grade. He came to me and cried—a great big boy—because he said the work was much too hard for him, and he didn't want to study. His teacher was cross with him and insisted he must get to work. It is an exception to have a boy so frank. But I don't think the instance is far from the truth. I have never had a white child complain that he was graded too high and wanted to be put down. Sometimes when they come in, they say to me: "I went to school in the South, and I am in high fifth grade." "How long were you in school in the South?" "Three sessions." Two months, and they are in high fifth grade! I put them into the first or second grade. Sometimes I can't fit them into the smaller grades, and sometimes they resent it, but when they get into the actual school work and find they can't do it, they can't complain. I should say therefore that there is a certain amount of mental backwardness found in colored children not found in whites.

A teacher in a Chicago public school said: "I believe like Dr. Bruner [director of Special School, Board of Education] that when a Negro boy grows a mustache his brain stops working."

A teacher in Moseley School said: "The great physical development of the colored person takes away from the mental, while with the whites the reverse is true. There is proof for this in the last chapter of Ecclesiastes."

Morality.—Another of these primary beliefs is that Negroes are not yet capable of exercising the social restraints which are common to the more civilized white persons. Sometimes it is said that they are unmoral rather than immoral. This view, while charitably explaining supposed innate defects of character, places them outside the circle of normal members of society. Thus the assistant principal of a Chicago high school attended by Negroes said:

When it comes to morality, I say colored children are unmoral. They have no more moral sense than a very young white child. Along sex lines they don't know that this is wrong and that is wrong—that wrong sense isn't a part of them. Of course we say they are immoral and a white child doing the same thing under the same circumstances would be. The colored and white children here don't get mixed up in immorality; they are too well segregated. Not that we segregate them: the whites keep away from the colored.

This belief appears in statements that there is no family life among Negroes and but little respect, even in Chicago, for the ordinary decencies; when serious students of society speak of the promiscuity of colored women and men in sexual as well as social relations; and when social institutions assume the impossibility of locating the real father of children in a Negro family. Much public emphasis is given to the subject of venereal disease among Negroes, and certain deductions regarding this incidence of disease have resulted from comparative statistics.

Criminality.—The assumption back of most discussions of Negro crime is that there is a constitutional character weakness in Negroes and a consequent predisposition to sexual crimes, petty stealing, and crimes of violence. Sexual crimes are alleged and frequently urged in justification of lynching. Popular judgment takes stealing lightly, because Negroes evidence a marked immaturity and childishness in it. It is supposed that they appropriate little things and do not commit larger thefts. Crimes of violence are thought to be characteristic of Negroes because crimes involving deliberation and planning require more brains than Negroes possess.

The president of a branch of the Illinois Federation of Women's Clubs thus explained the decision of that organization not to discuss the Negro question in its meetings:

Most of the presidents expressed themselves as against discussion of the Negro question because as women's names come out as being against the Negroes these women and others of the club would have to live in fear of Negro men. A woman must be careful not to put herself in a position of causing them to have a grudge against her, as you know a white woman has to fear a colored man.

A resident in an exclusively white residential district said:

Mother, sister, and I lived here alone and we had a car which we kept in a garage in the back yard. Whenever we came in at night we never used the back door, but always went around front. Several times in walking up the back steps to the porch we had been frightened by colored men sitting on the steps or lying on the porch, and so we couldn't use that way into the house.

Another white woman, in the course of a discussion of housing indicated this fear of Negro men:

When we came here this was a nice neighborhood. After some years a colored family moved in, then two or three more, and more and more, until you see what we have here now. I tell you the white people right on this street have to be afraid for their lives.

Another, living on Langley Avenue, near Forty-third Street, said:

I don't hold any conversations with Negroes. It's better to be on the safe side when you've got grown-up daughters. I worry a good deal about my two daughters as they go and come from work, but they've never had anything happen.

The principal of a Chicago public school was questioned by a visitor concerning the attitude of white parents toward the association of their children with Negro pupils in that school. "The white parents are cautious about stirring up trouble," he said, "for they know the emotional tendency of the colored to knife and kill."

Petty thefts by Negroes, especially of food, are regarded as annoying evils most easily dealt with by a sort of half-serious firmness. A white resident of a district largely inhabited by Negroes said:

A white neighbor keeps chickens in her back yard. She gets the burglar alarm from the hen house sometimes twice in a week, and the running thief is always colored. . . . . The colored buy whatever they want; they'll spend their last cent and not worry about the next day. If they want a chicken for dinner and it's $1 a pound, they buy it or steal it.

Physical unattractiveness.—Objections to contact are often attributed to physical laws which, it is said, make the sight or other sensory impression of the Negro unbearably repulsive. This attitude is found in protests against indiscriminate seating arrangements in street cars. The word "black" has long been associated with evil and ugliness, and it is not always a simple task to disassociate the idea from impressions given by a black man. Not merely is the color regarded as repulsive, but it is the further belief that Negroes have a peculiar and disagreeable body odor. A Christian Science practitioner in Chicago, giving her opinion of Negroes, had an idea that they carried a "musky odor," and were therefore to be avoided. A student at the University of Chicago and a resident of Hyde Park, talking with an investigator, said: "It is conceded that the Negro in Chicago must have some place to live, but to permit promiscuous distribution through scattered sections of the city would tend to increase the difficulties rather than mitigate them, partly because a white man would shrink from having a Negro live near him."

In the spring of 1919 there appeared in one of the Chicago daily papers a series of articles on the Negro question. In describing the relations between Negroes and whites in Chicago, the writer said:

A second phase of the situation, and the one that causes more inutile railing than any other, is the crowding into the street cars of colored people. Well, they must ride on street cars, if only for the reason that most of them live remote from their work. Even the North State Street line, that used to be considered the special conveyance for "the quality," has come to be known as the "African Central." If you can't stomach it, you'll have to walk. They won't.

Living in neighborhoods infrequently visited by Negroes and where, as a general rule, their occupancy is effectively discouraged, some white residents occasionally express objections as based on a "natural physical opposition." Following is a typical statement:

I came here six years ago and there was a very noisy set of white people living in the apartment house back of mine. Four years ago the landlord put them all out and rented to colored families. We were all up in arms then; but say, I never had nicer, more quiet, and respectable neighbors. Their children all behave well, and we can't kick. But at the same time, black people aren't what one would pick out to have around—I guess it's just because they are black.

Emotionality.—This is commonly regarded as explaining features of conduct in Negroes, some of which are beautiful in their expression while others are ugly and dangerous. The supposed Negro gift of song is thus an accepted attribute of his emotional nature. So with his religious inclination. This same emotionalism is believed to lead him to drink and is frequently made to account for "his quick, uncalculated crimes of violence." The natural expression of Negro religious fervor is supposed to be noisy and frenzied. This view of the *Chicago Tribune's* special writer is, roughly speaking, the view of thousands of Chicagoans:

I passed grand old stone churches, once the pride of rich and powerful white congregations, whither I used to be sent as a reporter not so many years ago, to hear some of the premier pulpiteers of this town. They are colored people's churches now, and beneath the arches, where a sedate gospel once was expounded you hear today the jubilant yell of the dusky brother who has found grace. . . . .

The service was, indeed, an incident in a three weeks' series of revival meetings they have been holding at Olivet. The principal performer was the Rev. S. E. J. Watson, a revivalist from Topeka, a big man—mulatto, I should say, or perhaps quadroon—with a powerful voice, a masterly platform style, and enormous ardor. He spoke fluently, used no notes, and demonstrated a free, wide skill in homely imagery, which, however, included no slang nor vulgarities, but was racy of the plantation and the cabin kitchen. His picture of God "opening the front door of this good old world every morning to let in the sun" was one of the most gorgeous flights in primitive poetry I ever heard, and his narrative, accompanied by the most vivid pantomime, of the Roman soldiers lifting up the cross after they had nailed Jesus to it was hardly less than terrifying—it certainly was terrific—in its sweep of passion and its reality of detail.

And so he wrought them to a high emotional state. Many were crying. Then came the direct personal appeal to "the unsaved," the threat of the everlasting fire, and the "lifting up" again and again of the thought of the all-forgiving, all-saving Jesus. The soft crying became heavy, convulsive sobbing. One by one the unsaved who made the surrender to whatever it was that had been holding them back, were led to the seats near the pulpit. Those who did not surrender promptly were evidently in terrible stress, or thought they were. They emitted shrieks that, truly, made my heart stand still, and I would have trembled for the sanity of the poor creatures except that I observed from the corner of my eye that the "saved" in the assemblage took the shrieks with perfect equanimity.

In addition to the primary beliefs there are others supposedly not so serious or significant in their effects.   These are usually modifications of primary beliefs, and are accepted as a consequence of frequent and almost unvaried repetition.   In this manner these secondary beliefs have edged their way into the popular mind.

George Jean Nathan and H. L. Mencken in a recent volume, *The American Credo*, point out fairly striking instances of this tendency of the American mind. They have compiled a series of 435 commonly accepted beliefs covering a wide range.   Among these 435 listed American beliefs there are some very real ones which involve and include the following popular notions about Negroes:

1. That a Negro's vote may always be readily bought for a dollar.

2. That every colored cook has a lover who never works and that she feeds him by stealing the best part of every dish she cooks.

3. That every Negro who went to France with the army has a liaison with a white woman and won't look at a colored woman any more.

4. That all male Negroes can sing.

5. That if one hits a Negro on the head with a cobblestone the cobblestone will break.

6. That all Negroes born south of the Potomac can play the banjo and are excellent dancers.

7. That whenever a Negro is educated he refuses to work and becomes a criminal.

8. That every Negro servant girl spends at least half of her wages on preparations for taking the kink out of her hair.

9. That all Negro prize fighters marry white women and then afterwards beat them.

10. That all Negroes who show any intelligence are two-thirds white and the sons of U.S. Senators.

11. That the minute a Negro gets eight dollars he goes to a dentist and has one of his front teeth filled with gold.

12. That a Negro ball always ends up in a grand free-for-all fight in which several Negroes are mortally slashed with razors.

The most usual of these secondary beliefs which figure in the experience of Negroes and whites in Chicago are apparently of southern origin.   This is due, not so much to any deliberate effort of southerners to infiltrate them into northern race relations, as that northerners largely regard as authoritative the experience of the South which holds almost nine-tenths of the total Negro population.

Some of the secondary beliefs are:

1. That Negroes are lazy; that they are indisposed to, though not incapable of, sustained physical exertion.

2. That they are happy-go-lucky; that their improvidence is demonstrated in their extravagance, and that their reckless disregard for their welfare is shown

in a lack of foresight for the essentials of well-being. It is asserted that they do not purchase homes and do not save their money; that they spend lavishly for clothes to the neglect of home comforts and the demands even of their health; that they work by the day, and before the week is ended confuse book-keeping by demanding their pay.

3. That they are boisterous. Hilarity in public places and especially in their own gatherings is thought to be common. They are considered as rude and coarse in public conveyances and are believed to jostle white passengers sometimes without thought and sometimes out of pure maliciousness.

4. That they are bumptious; that when a Negro is placed in a position of unaccustomed authority relative to his group he has an unduly exaggerated sense of his own importance and makes himself unbearable.

5. That they are overassertive; that constant harping on constitutional rights is a habit of Negroes, especially of the newer generation; that in their demands for equal rights and privileges they are egged on by agitators of their own race and are overinsistent in their demands; that they resent imaginary insults and are generally supersensitive.

6. That they are lacking in civic consciousness. Absence of community pride and disregard for community welfare are alleged to be the common failing of Negroes. It is pointed out that the "Black Belt" has been allowed to run down and become the most unattractive spot in the city. To this fact is attributed the tolerance of vice within this region. Negroes generally, it is still believed, can be bought in elections with money and whiskey. They are charged with having no pride in the beauty of the city, and with making it unbeautiful by personal and group habits.

7. That they usually carry razors. Whenever a newspaper reporter is in doubt he gives a razor as the weapon used. Some time ago a woman was found murdered in a town near Chicago. She had been slashed with a razor, and the broken blade was left beside her body. The murder was particularly atrocious, and the murderer left no other clew. Several Negroes were arrested on suspicion but were released when a white youth confessed the crime.

A Negro lawyer said:

During the riot a Negro was arrested for having a razor in his pocket. I was his attorney, and the evidence showed that he always shaved at work. After having shaved at this particular time, he put his razor in his pocket and forgot it. He started home and was accosted by two officers, who searched him and found the razor. The judge heard the evidence and then whispered to me that he was going to give the fellow ten days because "you know your people do carry razors." He asked me if I thought it all right and I said that I did not.

8. That they habitually "shoot craps." The Negro's supposed fondness for gambling is a phase of the belief concerning his improvidence. It is not unusual for whites, in conversation with any Negro whom they do not know well, when they wish merely to be friendly, to refer to dice. Employers fre-

quently say that Negroes never keep money because as soon as it is earned it is thrown away on gambling with dice. The state's attorney believed that the riot of July, 1919, began over a beach craps game.

Negroes are believed to be flashy in dress, loving brilliant and gaudy colors, especially vivid red. Again, they are believed by white unionists to be natural strike breakers with deliberate intentions to undermine white living standards. Similarly they are believed to be fond of gin. Pauperism among them is believed to be unduly high, and they are thought to have no home life.

II. BACKGROUND OF PREVAILING BELIEFS CONCERNING NEGROES

Lying back of the current opinions about Negroes is a chain of circumstances involving the history of divers racial groups over hundreds of years. Slavery placed a stamp upon Negroes which it will require many more years to erase. Probably there would have been no doubt at all in the minds of Americans that essential inequalities existed between white and Negro had not their emancipation developed numerous unsuspected qualities. Thomas Jefferson is responsible for the observation that "a Negro could scarcely be found who was capable of tracing and comprehending the investigations of Euclid." John C. Calhoun asserted that if a Negro could be found capable of giving the syntax of a Greek verb he would be disposed to call him human. The Fourteenth and Fifteenth Amendments to the Constitution fixed the Negro's status by law, and as soon afterward as his broader contacts with American institutions provided an outlet for more human participation, serious questions concerning his fitness for citizenship were put. The first studies that followed have been accepted for many years as the standard of judgment.

Mentality.—Regarding Negro mentality, Dr. Jeffries Wyman, anatomist of Harvard University, about 1870, said: "It cannot be denied that the Negro and ourang do afford the point where man and the brute, when the totality of their organization is considered, most nearly approach each other."

As a corollary he adds:

The Negro may be a man and a worker in some secondary sense; he is not a man and a brother in the same full sense in which every Western Aryan is a man and a brother. To me the Negro is repulsive.

The Negro is not yet a man and he is not yet a brother to the white. It will take generations, no man can say how many, to bring him to the level of supreme Caucasian man. He will have to reduce the facial angle and he will have to have a more spacious cranium before he can come into brotherhood with the more advanced species of mankind.

Professor A. H. Keane, author of *Man Past and Present*, at least gave some sanction to the disposition to regard the Negro and Caucasian races as having nothing in common. To quote from his book, published in 1890:

No historic or scientific reason can be alleged why these races, black or white, should be grouped together under one appellation if by such name it is meant to convey the idea that the human type can have any sanguinary affiliation. In the Negro groups it is absolutely shown that certain African races, whether born in Africa or America, give an internal capacity almost identical of 83 cubic inches. It is demonstrated through monumental, cranial and other testimonials, that the various types of mankind have ever been permanent; have been independent of all physical influences for thousands of years.

Dr. J. C. Nott, scientist and author of *Types of Mankind* said:

It is mind and mind alone which constitutes the proudest prerogative of man, whose excellence should be measured by his intelligence and virtue. The Negro and other unintellectual types have been shown in another chapter to possess heads much smaller, by actual measurement in cubic inches, than the white races; and although metaphysicians may dispute about causes which have debased their intellects and precluded their expansion, it cannot be denied that these dark races are, in this particular, greatly inferior to the others of fairer complexion.

This school of anthropology very clearly belongs to the period of slavery when it was necessary to rationalize the wishes of persons who, in order to treat Negroes as if they were mentally different, had first to convince, then justify, themselves in so doing.

Following them was another type of scientific writers who, while assuming that Negroes possessed brains, denied that they were like those of white persons or ever could be.

G. Stanley Hall thought that the Negro's development came to at least partial standstill at puberty. E. B. Tylor, author of *Anthropology*, assumed, from the accounts of European teachers who had taught children of the "lower" races, that after the age of twelve the colored children fell off and were left behind by the white children. Odum thought that the Negro child's mental development ended at the age of thirteen. None of these opinions, however, was the result of experimentation. A. T. Smith, author of *A Study of Race Psychology*, is responsible for the association and memory study of what he called a "typical" Negro boy of sixteen years. He discovered that "the Negro child is psychologically different from the white child, superior in automatic power but decidedly inferior in the power of abstraction, judgment and analysis." A. McDonald, author of *Colored Children—A Psycho-physical Study*, gave physical and mental tests in 1899 to ninety-one Negro children and concluded that dulness in colored children sets in between thirteen and sixteen. M. J. Mayo, author of *The Mental Capacity of the American Negro*, in 1913 studied 150 white and 150 colored high-school pupils in the schools of New York, and found the efficiency of colored pupils 76 per cent of that of the white. His selection included a large number of emigrants from the South, which, he explained, would increase the quality of the colored group, since only the more ambitious Negroes would seek to better their conditions by moving North. No account was taken of the defective school system of the South. Phillips made a study of retardation in the schools of Philadelphia and concluded that the course of study was not suited to Negroes, since colored children showed a greater degree of retardation than the whites.

Charles Carroll's book on the Negro points out by texts drawn from the Bible that the Negro is a beast created with an articulate tongue and hands in order that he may serve his white master. To bear out this theory Carroll's book says that man has been created in the image of God, but since, as everyone knows, God is not a Negro, it follows that the Negro is not in the image of God; therefore he is not a man.

There is a plain explanation of the origin of these beliefs. The science of anthropology itself has remarkably advanced during the past fifty years. When Negroes emerged from slavery, illiterate and unaccustomed to freedom, it was natural that their condition should be accepted as evidence that they could neither learn nor absorb the standards of the civilization around them. But although their illiteracy, for example, has decreased from 98 to 27 per cent, the original beliefs persist.

Morality.—The reputation of Negroes for immorality is based largely on southern authority and is historically explained by reference to slavery, in which state immorality is asserted to have been common between the master and the woman slave. There are many authorities on this character trait. Perhaps the most pretentious study on this subject is by Howard O. Odum in "Studies in History, Economics and Public Law," Columbia University, 1910. It is called *A Study in Race Traits, Tendencies and Prospects.* Writing of immorality among Negroes, Odum says:

It has generally been assumed that the Negro is differentiated by a distinct sexual development. It is affirmed that the sex development crowds out the mental growth. It is affirmed that the period of puberty in boys and girls is marked by special manifestations of wildness and uncontrol. It is true, too, that the practices of the Negroes leave little energy for moral and mental regeneration. Their lives are filled with that which is carnal; their thoughts are most filthy and their morals are generally beyond description. Again, physical developments from childhood are precocious and the sex life begins at a ridiculously early period. But granting these truths, it is doubtful if there is sufficient evidence to warrant such a conclusion. The Negro reveals a strong physical nature; the sex impulse is naturally predominant. But its manifestations are probably no more violent and powerful than are the expressions of other feelings already suggested. The Negro's sensuous enjoyment of eating and drinking and sleeping, relatively speaking, are no less marked than his sexual propensities. Likewise lack of control and extreme manifestations characterize the discharge of other impulses. It is true, again, that the part played by sexual life among the Negroes is large for a people; but to state that the Negro is inherently differentiated and hindered by a sexual development out of proportion to other physical qualities is quite a different proposition. But whether the question here raised is answered in the affirmative or not, it still remains that in the practical life of the Negro his better impulses are warped and hindered by his unreasonable abuse of sexual license. And it is safe to suggest that the Negro need hope for little development of his best qualities until he has learned to regulate and control his animal impulses.

Statistics on illegitimate births and abortions are frequently quoted as evidence of Negro immorality. It is further asserted, with rarely an attempt at correction, that these immoral tendencies are responsible for rape and attempted rape of white women.

Tradition maintains that it is a part of Negro nature to desire a white woman and similarly a part of his nature to be lacking in those restraints and inhibitions which might control this desire. C. H. McCord, author of *The American Negro as a Dependent, Defective, and Delinquent*, said: "The average Negro is a child in every essential element of character, exhibiting those characteristics that indicate a tendency to lawless impulse and weak inhibition."

Numerous magazine articles and written studies in the South on this subject have given weight to this belief through sheer repetition. It is now not necessary to prove assertions or present an array of instances; they are taken for granted. Allusions to the "well-known immoral character" of the Negro or his instinctive tendency to commit sex crimes appear to carry as strong an impress of certainty as proved conclusions.

Other supposed social characteristics.—Discussions of each of the characteristics mentioned and many others are found in the literature on the subject. It will suffice here to give selections typical of the trend of descriptions to indicate the manner in which the picture of the Negro in practically every phase of his life has been set. Of his industrial habits Odum, in the social study of the Negro, says:

In any discussion of the economic situation this (the question of the efficiency of Negro labor) is an important consideration. A portion of the Negroes wander about and seek to get a living as best they can without working for it; they must necessarily live at the expense of the other Negroes and the whites. The number of vagrants in every community is surprisingly large. They are naturally divided into several groups; those who never work but wander from place to place, never fixed and without a home, stealing, begging, and obtaining a living from any source possible. Such men never work except when forced to do so in little jobs or on the streets or in the chain gang.

Of the Negro's social affairs he says:

The description of one of these [Negro] dances would be repulsive. The Negroes have "good times" on such occasions and will go a long distance to attend. The whole trend of the dance is toward physical excitation; they are without order and the influence is totally bad.

Of the condition of the Negro's home:

It will be seen that there is little orderly home life among the Negroes. Health conditions and daily habits are no better than the arrangement of the house. Sometimes an entire family consisting of father, mother, large and small children occupy the same rooms. Nor do they ventilate, and especially when any of the inmates are sick they are loath to let in the fresh air. Physicians testify that three or four often sleep in a bed together; they do not change clothing before going to bed in many cases, and often go for many days without a change of garments. It has been suggested that the personal habits of the Negroes are filthy; such is the case. Filth and uncleanness are everywhere predominant.

Of his religion:

In spite of pretentions and superficiality, there is nothing so real to the Negro as his religion, although it is a different "reality" from what we commonly expect in religion. The Negro is more excitable in his nature, and yields more readily to excitement than does the white man. The more a thing excites him, the more reality it has for him. . . . .

The criminal instinct appears to overbalance any consciousness which makes for righteousness, and the Negro has little serene consciousness of a clean record; he is ready to rush at any surprising or suspicious turn of affairs. The Negro does not value his word of honor; he apparently cannot always tell the truth. Only about one in every ten will keep an important engagement made in seriousness.

The Negro's conception of heaven and hell, God and the devil are very distinct. Heaven is an eternal resting-place where he shall occupy the best place. He sings of his heavenly home in striking contrast to his earthly abode. Perhaps for the reason that the Negroes have little satisfactory home life, they expect to have a perfect home in the next life.

Of his finer emotions:

While it is doubtful if there is enough evidence to warrant a full statement concerning the affections of the Negroes, it is apparently based on the gregarious impulse and upon a passive sympathy rather than upon individual emotions intellectually developed. The emotion is rarely of long duration. . . . . The Negro mother rarely mourns for her wandering child, or sits up at night waiting for his return or thinking of him. The father shows little care except that of losing a laborer from his work. . . . . The Negro has no loved ones. Numbers were asked for the names of those whom they considered friends or whom they loved or those who loved them. The question was put in various ways with different subjects, but the returns were the same. . . . . But as a rule the Negro is without friendship among his own people.

It may help to comprehend the range of conclusions found in the literature on the subject of Negro traits of character to note the array of descriptive adjectives employed, thus: sensual, lazy, unobservant, shiftless, unresentful, emotional, shallow, patient, amiable, gregarious, expressive, appropriative, childish, religious, unmoral, immoral, ignorant, mentally inferior, criminal, excitable, imitative, repulsive, poetic, irresponsible, filthy, unintellectual, bumptious, overassertive, superficial, indecent, dependent, untruthful, musical, ungrateful, loyal, sporty, provincial, anthropomorphic, savage, brutish, happy-go-lucky, careless, plastic, docile, apish, inferior, cheerful.

Much might be said of influences which have operated to counteract the opinion-making literature as to the utterly hopeless condition of Negroes. The object of this study, however, is not to attack these conclusions, but merely to cite them as indicating how certain attitudes detrimental to racial friendliness and understanding have had their rise.

In academic circles the more balanced opinions of anthropologists are gaining some headway. Franz Boaz, probably the foremost anthropologist in the United States, in *The Mind of Primitive Man,* maintains:

Our considerations make it probable that the wide differences between the manifestations of the human mind in various stages of culture may be due almost entirely to the form of individual experience, which is determined by the geographical and social environment of the individual. It would seem that, in different races, the organization of the mind is on the whole alike, and that the variations of mind found in different races do not exceed, perhaps not even reach, the amount of normal individual variation in each race. It has been indicated that, notwithstanding this similarity in the form of individual mental processes, the expression of mental activity of a community tends to show a characteristic historical development.

This author in an article in the *Nation* for December, 1920, comments thus on Lothrop Stoddard's book, *The Rising Tide of Color:*

Mr. Stoddard's book is one of the long series of publications devoted to the self-admiration of the white race, which begins with Gobineau and comes down to us through Chamberlain and, with increasingly passionate appeal, through Madison Grant to Mr. Stoddard. The newer books of this type try to bolster up their unscientific theories by an amateurish appeal to misunderstood discoveries relating to heredity and give in this manner a scientific guise to their dogmatic statements which misleads the public. For this reason the books must be characterized as vicious propaganda, and gain an attention not warranted by an intrinsic merit in their learning or their logic.

Each race is exceedingly variable in all of its features, and we find in the white race, as well as in all other races, all grades of intellectual capacity, from the imbecile to the man of high intellectual power. It is true that intellectual power is hereditary in the individual, and that the healthy, the physically and mentally developed individuals of a race, if they marry among themselves, are liable to have offspring of a similar excellence; but it is equally true that the inferior individuals in a race will also have inferior offspring. If, therefore, it were entirely a question of eugenic development of humanity, then the aid of the eugenist would be to suppress not the gifted strains of other races, but rather the inferior strains of our own race. A selection of the intelligent, energetic and highly endowed individuals from all over the world would not by any means leave the white race as the only survivors, but would leave an assembly of individuals who would probably represent all the different races of man now in existence.

Jean Finot, in *Race Prejudice*, says:

When we go through the list of external differences which appear to divide men, we find literally nothing which can authorize their division into superior and inferior beings, into masters and pariahs. If this division exists in our thought, it only came there as the result of inexact observations and false opinions drawn from them.

The science of inequality is emphatically a science of white people. It is they who have invented it and set it going, who have maintained, cherished, and propagated it, thanks to their observations and their deductions. Deeming themselves greater than men of other colours, they have elevated into superior qualities all the traits which are peculiar to themselves, commencing with the whitness of the skin and the pliancy of the hair. But nothing proves that these vaunted traits are traits of real superiority.

W. I. Thomas, in *Sex and Society*, concludes his discussion of relative mentality with this statement:

The real variable is the individual, not the race. In the beginning—perhaps as the result of a mutation or series of mutations—a type of brain developed which has remained relatively fixed in all times and among all races. This brain will never have any faculty in addition to what it now possesses, because as a type of structure it is as fixed as the species itself, and is indeed a mark of species. It is not apparent that we are greatly in need of another faculty, or that we could make use of it even if by a chance mutation it should emerge, since with the power of abstraction we are able to do any class of work we know anything about.

III. TYPES OF SENTIMENTS AND ATTITUDES

In the South the relations between the white and Negro races are determined by custom as well as law, which, however, permit the close personal relationships of family servants. In the North, when these relations become more impersonal and contacts are widened through change of occupation from domestic service to industry, these close personal ties are weakened. There is no established rule of conduct binding on whites and Negroes in their relations with each other; and although traditional beliefs may influence present relations in the North, they do not always dominate them. So it happens that there are to be found shades of opinion concerning Negroes varying from deliberate indifference to vituperative abuse of Negroes, whatever the subject, depending on one's beliefs about them. The selections of sentiment which follow are examples collected at random over the city— through interviews and discussions, from group publications, speeches and reports. They illustrate the real sentiments that white persons express when brought into contact with Negroes, or when their opinions are solicited.

I. THE EMOTIONAL BACKGROUND

Hostile sentiment.—The refusal of Policeman Callahan to arrest Stauber, a white youth accused of throwing stones which resulted in the drowning of Eugene Williams, is regarded as the significant incident precipitating the riot of 1919 (see p. 4) Callahan was dismissed from the force, but reinstated. One year later, when questioned by an investigator for the Commission, he gave his racial philosophy freely in the following remarks:

So far as I can learn the black people have since history began despised the white people and have always fought them. . . . . It wouldn't take much to start another riot, and most of the white people of this district are resolved to make a clean-up this time. . . . . If a Negro should say one word back to me or should say a word to a white woman in the park, there is a crowd of young men of the district, mostly ex-service men, who would procure arms and fight shoulder to shoulder with me if trouble should come from the incident.

The following is from a letter written by a white employee of Albert Pick & Company:

Negroes in street cars refuse to double up with others of their race, but seem to delight in sitting beside some dainty white girl.

The Thirty-fifth Street cars are crowded by low-grade "plantation niggers" who crowd on at Ashland Avenue via windows and doors, then awkwardly step and fall over passengers; it is maddening.   About this time girls from Albert Pick & Company, the Magnus Company, and the tailoring establishments are crowded together breast to breast with Negroes.   Often he falls asleep and leans on his white seat-mate's shoulder.

Laws should be urged preventing intermarriage.

Assaults upon white women are frequent, but hushed up by fear of newspaper publicity, and the Negro is thus encouraged in his felony.

In cases where a white girl is involved in an assault case by a colored man, the white woman should be shielded, and her name withheld from the newspapers and public, before and after the trial.   This will prevent race riots.

A movement is now afoot to declare a silent boycott against employers of colored help.

A physician living on Oakwood Boulevard said: "The increasing amount generally of sex immorality is being contributed to by mixing Negroes and whites in schools and parks."

A teacher in the Felsenthal School said:

The colored people are coming from the South all the time, for political purposes. It's propaganda for the colored man to sit down by the white woman, and not to double up to make room for the whites.   Their papers tell them to do it.   I was the only white person in an empty car one day and a colored man came in and took the seat beside me.

Fear.—From *White Americans* circulated in Chicago:

In the United States Negroes not only vote and hold office, but the Negro vote is the deciding factor in the national elections, and also in many of the northern cities, and they trade their vote for jobs and offices and other privileges.   The Negroes control the great city of Philadelphia, and the press said the Negro delegates at the Republican Convention in Chicago openly offered to sell their support to the presidential candidate who would pay the most money.   Just think this thing over, you sovereign United States citizens: the Negroes control the elections, and thus your law-makers, judges, and officials; and the Negroes have so much pull and confidence, that they not only defend their political rights, but they start riots and race wars, and openly threaten that they are going to make the white folks stand around.

Fear and pity.—A resident in the 6600 block on Langley Avenue said:

A colored family lives next door north of me, and you'll be surprised when I tell you that I haven't been able to open my bedroom window on that side to air that room for three years.   I couldn't think of unlocking the windows because their window is so near somebody could easily step across into this house.   It's awful to have to live in such fear of your life.

When asked if she considered her neighbors so dangerous as that, she said:

Well, no, the woman seems pretty nice. I see her out in the back yard occasionally and bid her the time of day out of charity. You can't help but pity them, so I am charitable and speak. Where the danger really is, is that you never know who's in their house; they bring such trash to the neighborhood, even if they are good and decent. How do I know what kind of people this woman next door associates with? There's awful-looking people sit on the front porch sometimes. Why, I couldn't sit on my porch on the hottest day because I'd be afraid they would come out any minute. And what white person will sit on a porch next door to a porch with black ones on it? Not me, anyhow, nor you either I hope.

Hostile but resigned.—A resident near Dorchester Avenue and Sixtieth Street said:

I have nothing against the black man as a black man. He comes into my place of business (drug-store) and I sell him. Not many come in, as there aren't a lot of colored people around Sixty-third and Woodlawn or Dorchester. But I don't want to live with niggers any more than you or any other white person does. People who say, "I like the colored people and don't see why others can't get along with them" don't talk practical common sense. Theoretically all this talk is all right, but you get a white man of this sort to come right down and live with a nigger and he won't do it.

Niggers are different from whites and always will be, and that is why white people don't want them around. But the only thing we can do, it seems to me, is make the best of it and live peaceably with them. The North can never do what the South does—down there it is pure autocracy. I might say like Russia. That might have worked here in the North from the start, but can't be started now, and we wouldn't want such autocracy anyway. They are citizens, and it is up to us to teach them to be good ones. How it can be done I don't know—it will have to come slow, and no one can give a solution offhand. Everybody says, "We don't want the niggers with us." Well, here they are, and we can't do anything. Must let them live where they want to and go to school where they want to, and we don't want to force their right away.

It is not uncommon to find in some circles and with many individuals a resolute indisposition to discuss any phase of the Negro problem. Convictions regarding the race are so firmly set and hostile that no argument or appeal to fair-mindedness can alter their position.

"Eye Witness," a special writer for the *Chicago Tribune*, encountered this state of mind in interviewing whites and Negroes for a series of articles on the Negro question which appeared in the *Tribune* in May, 1919. He characterized it as insensate and dangerous. His own statement, published May 4, 1919, said:

Among men like publicists and administrators of large affairs, who, when they discuss the problems and troubles of their race, are wont to speak in a rational, or at least mannerly way, there was often an unfeeling kind of don't-give-a-damn cry when they talked on this subject that made one wonder how they had managed so well in maintaining a human and successful relationship with their white associates in business and with their employees.

I heard more, far more, insensate language from the lips of white men than of black men throughout the series of interviews. The horrible part of that, to me, was that when a white employer more or less accountable for the well-being of colored workmen, or a publicist entrusted with a pen that forms and directs opinions, had railed about "these damn niggers" they appeared to think they had said something rather gallant and decisive, for they would smile fatuously and expect acquiescence.

And more terrible than the language was the insensate state of mind such language betrayed. The only way one could avoid the suspicion that one was listening to a potential lunatic or a desperately stupid person without a human or a community sense, was to allow much for the vehemence of the American tongue and to concede that these men don't mean one-tenth of what they say. If they did they would be fomenters of race wars.

2. SENTIMENTAL RELATIONSHIPS

Sentiment for the "old family servants."—A white physician born in the South said:

My father owned slaves. He looked out for them; told them what to do. He loved them and they loved him. I was brought up during and after the war. I had a "black mammy" and she was devoted to me and I to her; and I played with Negro children. In a way I'm fond of the Negro; I understand him and he understands me; but the bond between us is not as close as it was between my father and his slaves. On the other hand, my children have grown up without black playmates and without a "black mammy." The attitude of my children is less sympathetic toward the Negroes than my own. They don't know each other.

Paternal relationship.—In testimony before the Commission a witness said:

The prejudice against the colored people in the South isn't as strong in some instances as it is in the North. It's a queer thing, but the white man in the South, and the white woman, too, has a sort of paternal feeling that he must look after him and that the colored man's interests are better in his hands than if he is left to drift for himself. I don't state that as an actual fact, but I believe it is true. That is their point of view. They don't hate the colored man. They don't dislike him, but I should say this, that they won't take him into their homes. They don't dislike him, provided he keeps his place. I believe the white people of the South think more of the Negro than the white people of the North.

3. ABSTRACT JUSTICE

A trained nurse of Woodlawn said:

I meet colored people only on the cars. There are none anywhere around here, I believe. I don't know how I would feel if they came to Woodlawn to live. But they must live, and I hear their quarters are getting too small. It seems that Chicago ought to let them live somewhere. Some people treat Negroes terrible and I think that is all wrong. Why can't we act respectably toward colored people on the cars and treat them nice on the street? We surely don't want to be like the people in the South who make colored persons get off the walk when they come along. But I see white people here almost that bad—can't see a black man live.

The pastor of a church in Woodlawn said:

I have come to no final conclusion as to the best policy to pursue in the adjustment of the race problem. I am thinking about it a great deal and am deeply concerned over the whole matter. In the present state of popular mind, there is no doubt but property values are depreciated by the presence of Negro tenants or property owners in residential sections. However, if everyone felt as I do, it would not be so. I mean, provided that the same general social standards were observed by all nationalities in the city. It would be very fine, it seems to me, to maintain certain standards in each neighborhood. Why not bring pressure to bear on white landlords and make them keep their property up to a given average standard in the community, that only such a class of people will rent or buy as are already there? I am very anxious that the Negro shall be treated fairly. I do not want him to feel that I have stood in the way of his opportunities and his rights.

A professor at the University of Chicago said:

The final solution, it seems to me, must come as a result of honest and successful efforts for mutual understanding between the races. There must be apparent on the part of the white race an attempt to treat the Negro with justice, and I feel sure that he will respond. I do not think the black race, as a race, desires intermarriage more than the white race, yet the assertion to the contrary is much overworked by the white opposition in these neighborhoods.

A minister said:

All I want for the Negro is justice—then I think the economic laws will settle this problem. Let the people interested try justice; they will find it will solve the race problem faster than any other course, just as it will solve any other problem. Treat the bad Negro just as rough as you treat the bad white man, but acclaim the good Negro after the same manner of your acclamation of the good white man.

4. SENTIMENTS STRONGER THAN RACE PREJUDICE

Class kinship stronger than race.—A Swedish employee in a department store said:

We have quite a number of Negro neighbors where I live, and several black men work with me, and I want to say I think they are just as good as anybody. There are classes of people in every race, and of course there is a rough element among the blacks. Some highbrows try to make out that they are representative, but I think opposition to the Negro in Chicago comes from the "swell" class. I do not have any different feeling for them than for the same kind of people in any other race. I think race relations will get better in Chicago. The workingman has learned that the Negro will treat him right when he is treated right, and as soon as the other folks find that out, things will be all right.

The secretary of the Cook County Labor Party said:

I have thought about this problem a good deal, and I think you will find it is the so-called middle class that is making all the trouble. The laboring-man does not care who his neighbor is, so long as he is a good neighbor. I think you can trace most of the racial activities to jealousy on the part of a certain class of American citizens who are not any too wealthy and feel constrained to maintain a sort of fictitious position in life at the expense of anybody, in this case the Negroes. You will find that the very well-to-do are not nearly so much aroused over the problem.

A Japanese said:

I think it is simply a matter of race prejudice, which of course means first of all that the color is not acceptable, while, in the second place, they were imported to the United States as slaves, and thus it always occurs in the American mind that they are a lower class of people. Furthermore, as they were slaves and the American does not like them, they don't have equal opportunities to educate themselves up to such a degree which means no more than environment. In the last place, they want to keep away from them. I think it might be said that they are willing to receive lower wages, which tends to lower the wage system; thus the American worker suffers a good deal. In the whole process the Negroes have been kept out of social and political activities that would have given them a chance to develop. Allow them to have these activities in the future and they will make more rapid progress than they have even in the past.

General historical comparisons.—A Jewish resident of the West Side said:

I believe that the segregation movement is wrong because it is unjust and because it is devoid of any principle whatever. It has not risen out of the consideration of the needs of the colored people, nor out of consideration of real advantages that the whites might thereby gain. What is back of race prejudice? Nothing more than the spirit of superiority and selfishness which moves the aristocrats to move out of a neighborhood as soon as a few common people move in. This is here too prevalent. The segregation movement has its parallel in history. Who does not remember the old Jewish Ghetto of Amsterdam, Frankfort, etc., or the Pale of Russia? What has this segregation done for the Jews? It curtailed their rise, depriving them of an opportunity to develop, and I foresee the same result in the new segregation movement, and therefore deem it a great public evil and moral issue.

5. TRADITIONAL SOUTHERN BACKGROUND

A window dresser said:

I am from the South, and I am used to seeing the Negro kept in his place. I would colonize them, every one of them, and make them stay where they are put. I would colonize them in Africa if I had to do it. There's where they came from and there's where they belong. Of course, some few northern folks say that they were taken away against their own wills, but I say they ought to go back against their own wills.

The woman manager of a tailor shop, Fifty-fifth Street, said: "I am a southerner, and I feel the way they all do about it. I guess you know what I mean. I think the nigger should stay in his place."

6. GROUP SENTIMENTS

Fear of social censure.—A property owner at Langley Avenue and Fifty-fifth Street said:

"I am not proud to be living on the same street with Negroes, so I never tell my friends—they would say: 'You must move out.'"

George L. Giles Post of the American Legion is a Negro post with head-quarters at the South Side Branch of the Community Service. Invitations to a musicale and dramatic entertainment for the benefit of ex-service men were sent to all the local posts by the Community Service. It was responded to by the adjutant of George L. Giles Post, who received a reply from the executive secretary saying:

I am quite sure you will understand that our sending one to the George L. Giles Post was a slip. Will you kindly let me know if there are other Posts of colored men in the city?

Similar recognition of the force of public opinion may be found in industry. The manager of a large industrial plant, speaking of Negro workmen, said: "I have a feeling that white workers would object to Negroes in any position but that of common laborers, although I have no basis for this opinion." Another said: "I have heard whites remark that they wouldn't want to work here if many colored were employed but none left on that account."

7. ATTITUDES DETERMINED BY CONTACTS

No contacts but a hostile attitude.—A resident at Drexel Avenue and Sixty-fifth Street said:

I don't see many niggers around here; most of them are west of Cottage Grove Avenue. I never had any dealings with them, so can't tell you anything much. I know I don't want niggers living next door to me, but I can't tell you why. Do you want them next-door neighbors to you? There are some living down in the next block—two families of them—between Sixty-fourth and Sixty-fifth, and I guess they are pretty wild, but I have never seen them. It's just what people tell me. I never had any dealings with them.

Generalization from a particular experience.—A teacher in the Wendell Phillips High School said:

You can't trust the best of them. The minute you have your back turned something disappears. They are the worst bunch of little thieves I ever struck. A few weeks ago I had a colored girl helping me fix costumes in my little office. During the hour she was in there I was absent about five minutes. She had hardly got out of the building before I discovered that a dollar had disappeared out of my purse. I questioned her for thirty minutes next morning, but not a word of confession. Another time I had small change in the top drawer of my desk. While I was teaching a class, two girls slipped into the office and helped themselves to half of it. I surprised them when I unexpectedly entered the office to get something. Everything here that isn't tied or watched walks off. It didn't used to be this way before the colored came in so thick; then I never locked my office, and now I have everything under lock.

The proprietor of a woman's dress shop on Sixty-third Street said:

Little of my trade is colored, possibly 2 per cent. We do not cater to colored trade. We do not want it. If colored people come in, we will sell them if they buy quick and get out. Our trade does not care to deal where colored people are also accommodated. . . . . You will find it pretty hard to be neutral in Chicago. The more I know of niggers, the more I am convinced that there is no good nigger but a dead one.   I had a colored helper who wanted tips every time he was asked to render services outside of his recognized regular duties.   I gave him a good salary, $18 per week, and yet he was never satisfied, and one day he got hold of the keys to the cash drawer and ran away with $300.

Exaggerated notion of prosperity.—A physician said:

I think that the solution of the race problem can come only by recognition by white men of the Negroes' potential equality.   They are only fifty years out of slavery, and in that fifty years they have progressed faster than the white race has done in a hundred years.   The Negro man of forty today is less advanced than the white man of forty, but I expect his son to be almost on a par with our sons, and his grandson will be every whit as good.   The husband of the colored woman who has been getting our dinners for us for a number of years is making more killing steers for Armour than I am.   He makes $16 a day.   They have $12,000 worth of Liberty bonds.   They are sending all of their relatives through high school and declare they will put them through the University of Chicago.   In fact we are compelling the Negro to get an education, and he cannot help but progress.   Colonizing the Negro is merely making him bitter and postponing the day of settlement.   Presently we shall have with us under such a régime a race of comparative equals very much disgruntled by the unfair treatment accorded them.   I think you will find that practically all the professional men in this building, at least a very large percentage of them, think as I do on this subject.

Contact with servants.—A resident of Woodlawn said:

Practically my only contact with Negroes is with servants and laundresses. I have had colored women working for me for many years, and the majority of them I could not trust outside my sight.   By that I don't mean they would steal—they just weren't dependable.   It is all wrong for colored children and white children to be in school together.   There should be separate schools, because the two races of children are as different in everything as in their color.

The interviewing of hundreds of white persons, members of practically every social class, reveals little information regarding the sources of their beliefs about Negroes.   Some think them instinctive; some hold that their opinions are a result of observation; some, who make discernible effort to stem the current of prejudiced views and remain fair, have read the books of Negroes. But by far the greater number either admit or otherwise give evidence of having absorbed their views from tradition.

Information by word of mouth, unquestioned statements, uncorrected accounts, all continue to add credence to any current interpretation of an act involving Negroes.   The fault lies for the most part at the information source. Fairly to judge the Negro group, or any member thereof, there should be some unquestioned basis of fact, yet the assumption is common that almost any Negro can be judged by what has been observed in the conduct of the family cook or chauffeur, who no more represents the whole or the majority of Negroes than a white cook or chauffeur can be said to represent the whole or the majority of the white race.

IV. SELF-ANALYSIS BY FIFTEEN WHITE CITIZENS

To secure definite information upon this background twenty representative white persons were selected at random, and eighteen carefully prepared suggestive questions were put to each of them. The purpose was to draw out the raw material of their unqualified opinions on the question of the Negro, and to ascertain as far as possible the background in their early experiences. The questions were suggestive in order to compel a disclosure of mental attitudes. The only qualification in the selection of persons was their probable capacity for self-analysis and a willingness to answer. The length and difficulty of the questions put made it necessary to limit the selection of persons to a few, who in appreciation of the inquiry, could and would give it a careful study. Fifteen of these persons entered into the spirit of the inquiry and submitted the results of their self-scrutiny.

These fifteen include business and professional men and women, none of whom, however, is actively associated with racial movements. They represent probably a fair sample of sentiment and at the same time ability to analyze accurately their own feelings and opinions.

The questions put were as follows:

1. Have you formed definite opinions about Negroes? Briefly, what are they?
2. Do Negroes in your opinion possess distinguishing traits of mentality or character?
3. As well as you can remember, on what facts, authorities, information, sources, do you base your opinions?
4. What incidents or experiences involving Negroes either in Chicago or elsewhere stand out in your memory?
5. As a child, did you have contacts of any kind with Negroes?
6. Can you recall any early prohibitions of association by word or printed warnings of any sort, implied prohibitions in institutional or social arrangements?
7. When were you first conscious of a racial difference?
8. Whom of your friends, acquaintances, favorite authors, scholars, etc., do you regard as best fitted to speak with authority on the question?
9. Do you ever inquire for information on this subject? Whom do you ask? What Negroes do you know whom you would consider leaders among colored people in Chicago? in the United States?
10. Did you ever read a Negro periodical? What did you think of it?
11. What subjects of discussion most frequently lead to the Negro?
12. In what circles is this subject most frequently discussed?
13. If it were in your power to make whatever social adjustment you deemed wise, what disposition would you make of the Negro population?
14. If Negroes obstinately objected to your plan and you still had power, what would you do?
15. What do you think of the following propositions:
    a) When you educate Negroes you increase their demands. Either their education should be curtailed or modified or their demands granted.
    b) Prejudice has its principal basis in fear.

c) Isolating groups favors the unhampered development of special group prejudices. Do prejudices form a background of conflicts? The greater the
isolation, the greater the prejudices and, as would naturally follow, the greater
the chances of conflict.

d) A minority of the population should not expect complete justice at the hands of
an overwhelming majority.

Their answers are given separately. The letters used to designate the
different persons are arbitrary.

A—

I have rather definite opinions of Negroes. As a class they cannot be depended
upon. They are shiftless and really must be treated like children. I make allowance
for the fact that they have not the years of education back of them.

My opinions are based on visits made to the South and on information obtained
from relatives who live in the South as well as from the colored help we have had. As a
child my contact with Negroes began with our Negro house servants, and my first
consciousness of a racial difference came while visiting relatives in the South. I know
but two persons who might speak with authority on the race question. They are
Edgar A. Bancroft and Miss Mary McDowell. It is very seldom that I inquire for
information on this subject. People whom I know are not interested in the problem.

The only Negroes whom I know are my present colored help and those who have
worked for me. I don't know whom to consider leaders among the colored people
either in Chicago or in the United States. Concerning the Negro periodicals, I
have occasionally read copies of one of their newspapers which bore out my opinion
of their simple minds. Discussion of domestic help and of newspaper articles about
Negroes and sociological conditions most frequently lead to the discussion of the Negro
in my circle. If it were in my power to do so, I would segregate Negroes as to living
quarters and do all possible to help them educate and help themselves.

Concerning proposition (*a*) I agree that if you educate Negroes, you increase their
demands, but I also believe that as they become educated, greater demands will arise
in their own groups.

In my opinion prejudice has its principal basis in the fact that one can't depend
upon Negroes.

I do not believe that it is necessarily true that a minority of the population should
not expect complete justice at the hands of the majority if the proper appeal is made.

B—

I have more or less definite opinions about Negroes. I believe that as a race they
are entitled to more leniency and consideration than we would give to adult whites
because as a race they are not as mature as whites. I think it is unfortunate that we
have such a race question to deal with, but we ought to meet it squarely and insist
that under the law Negroes are entitled to equal protection and equal consideration.
I do not believe in any attempt at social equality because the antipathy between
whites and Negroes is so acute that such attempt would not only break down itself
but it would lead to serious race difficulties. I think the Negro race has as much right
to protect its race purity as the white race. I believe Negro women are entitled to the
same protection from white men that we demand on behalf of white women against

black men. I believe Negroes should have decent housing conditions, proper social outlets and opportunities to earn a living at the same wages paid white men for the same class and character of work. They should share equally in the benefits of government, with particular reference to schools, bathing-beaches playgrounds, parks, etc. They should be protected against exploitation by employers, property owners, merchants, etc.

I do think Negroes possess distinguishing traits of both mentality and character. For many years now I have come into more or less personal contact with Negroes. I have been in contact with them in public schools, in colleges, in politics and in civic work. I cannot say that any particular incidents or experiences stand out in my memory.

My opinions are based upon my personal observation, personal contacts with Negroes and discussions with other white persons having independent contacts. As a child I had practically no real contact of any kind with Negroes. I don't recall now any Negro children in any of my primary grades, and while there were Negroes in my native city, they were few and in a neighborhood far removed from my own home. I imagine that I was first conscious of a racial difference when I first saw a Negro.

I don't recall any early prohibition against association with Negroes although I do recall clearly that the attitude of my family and associates, generally, was not one of approval. Negroes were regarded as an inferior race, and I think as a child I gathered the impression that contact with them was to be avoided. My feeling is that if in normal circumstances I had been thrown into more or less contact with Negroes, prohibition against association, except where absolutely necessary, would have been forthcoming.

I have never formally asked for information on the subject, but I have discussed the matter with a good many people and have given thought to it. I know a good many Negroes, not only in Chicago but outside, but I don't know many of them intimately. Among the leaders of the Negroes in Chicago are Dr. Bentley, Dr. George C. Hall, Edward H. Morris, Edward H. Wright, Louis B. Anderson, Oscar De Priest. In the United States, since the death of Booker T. Washington, I imagine that two of the outstanding men are Mr. Moton and Professor Du Bois.

I am a subscriber to the *Crisis*. In general my feeling is that the tendency of this periodical is to stimulate and foster race feeling among the Negroes. I don't say this critically. It may be the best thing to do, considering all the circumstances, and anything that will make for growth in self-respect, character and initiative on the part of the Negroes is to be commended even if, at the same time, race spirit is fostered and developed.

Generally speaking, I find that discussion most frequently leads to the Negroes when there are questions of lynching, race riots, crimes or disturbances in which Negroes are involved. It also comes up in connection with public schools, churches, parks and public transportation systems. I had it arise recently in connection with the Naval Academy at Annapolis. My experience is that this subject is most frequently discussed among those interested in social problems.

I used to think that the Negro question might be best solved if the Negroes would be colonized in some favorable spot in Africa under an American protectorate until they were capable of self-government. I realize, however, that no such scheme ought to be attempted if the Negroes obstinately objected, and in that event I would see to it, if I had the power, that they were protected from exploitation, were given a square deal and had the equal protection of the laws. They should have schools adequate to their needs and average living conditions.

I believe the Negro race should be educated, but I believe at the same time that the most solid foundation for the race is education in accordance with the ideas of the late Booker T. Washington as I understand those ideas. While I think this type of education will mean more for the race in the long run I believe at the same time that individual Negroes should have an opportunity fully to develop individual capacities.

I think there is an element of fear in the prejudice of Negroes, but I don't think this is the chief element. I think the real basis for this prejudice is a racial antipathy that is instinctive and fundamental in the white race. I imagine that in individual cases where this prejudice does not exist it is not because it was not there originally, but because it has been overcome by reason and education. It isn't unlikely that this prejudice is in the main grounded upon an instinct in the white race to keep its strain pure and strong.

It seems to me that it isn't isolation so much as it is contact that favors the development of race prejudice. If the Negroes had never been brought out of Africa, we wouldn't feel the prejudice that we do. Or, if they were restricted to one or two southern states, prejudice in other parts of the country would rapidly disappear. A community that has no Negro problem is relatively free from prejudice. It is when the two races come into contact that prejudices run riot and race conflicts result. My own opinion is that if you should scatter the Negro population throughout Chicago and its suburbs and put one or two Negro families in every block, race prejudice would increase enormously.

A minority of the population will not get complete justice at the hands of an overwhelming majority. But this is true of all minorities, whether racial, political, or religious. All we can do is to keep working for an approximation to ideal justice. A minority has the right to demand, and a majority should be willing to grant, substantial justice and that is all that can be expected in the present state of civilization.

C—

My opinion is that we must cling to the ideal of Lincoln—the right of every human being to equality in the real sense of the term. I have found, however, that Negroes are dull and sensitive. These opinions are based upon observation at Tuskegee and in this school—[the Lewis Institute]. Among my outstanding experiences is a visit made to Tuskegee and meeting Booker T. Washington. The visit showed great hope for the Negro. As a child I had no contact aside from living in the same city with them.

It has always been considered unwise in the circles in which I moved for whites and blacks to associate socially. I first became conscious of a race difference when a very small child—about three years of age.

Booker T. Washington, Cable, Dunbar, southerners and northerners who have traveled in the South are probably best fitted to speak for Negroes. I do inquire of both Negroes and whites for information. The only Negroes I know are working people. Robert Jackson, alderman, and Ed. Green, lawyer. Booker T. Washington's successor. I have read one Negro paper. It was insistent in a very fair way on the political rights of the Negro. Good. Lynchings, lying, stealing, and the attacking of little girls are the subject of discussion that most frequently lead to the Negro, and these occur principally among men who have seen Negroes socially and women who have hired them.

As a solution I would colonize them in Africa, and if they objected I would use all peaceable means to force them to go.

Regarding the propositions: Their education should be increased and the demands produced by education met.

Prejudice has its basis in race repulsion.   Unless the isolation is African colonization, there will be group prejudices.

Every man or group should demand and get complete justice.

D—

I assume that it is a fact recognized by science that Negroes are so different from whites that the two races cannot be amalgamated.   This fact interposes a barrier to social relationships.   I share in the general dislike of Negroes as neighbors or traveling companions on the street cars.   The white race is responsible for the existence of the Negro problem in America, and must submit patiently to the penalty for many years to come.   Lincoln's second inaugural is the best expression of this thought.   The Negro race is extraordinarily docile and easy to handle.   If surrounded by good living conditions and given a proper education they would be good citizens.   The progress of their race since slavery, considering their many handicaps, has been very creditable. The prejudice against them is probably the most deep-seated of all American prejudices, and must be reckoned with as one of the great factors in the problem.

In my opinion they are characterized by distinctly inferior mentality, deficient moral sense, shiftlessness, good nature, and a happy disposition.   I have in mind no special facts, authorities or sources of information on which I base my opinions.   I do, however, recognize the bearing of Christianity on the problem, and find it impossible to formulate a viewpoint which I can reconcile with the demands of Christianity.

We had a Negro family chauffeur some years ago who misconducted himself so seriously as to have caused a very considerable increase in the family prejudice against the race.   If he had been an Irish man our prejudice against him would not have extended to his race.   As a child I had no contacts with Negroes, excepting one or two fellow-pupils in public schools of whom I saw very little, and a few servants in the neighborhood who were of the old-fashioned type, of pleasant memory.

I can recall no early prohibitions of association with Negroes.   There were so few in my neighborhood that they constituted no real problem.   As to implied prohibitions, I suppose I understood at a very early age the existing social difference, although I remember no instances of this.

I cannot remember when I first became conscious of a racial difference, but I assume it was at a very early age.

I do not know that I can cite any friends, acquaintances, favorite authors or scholars well fitted to speak with authority on the question.   Lincoln's views always seemed true to me, while I have not been so favorably impressed by southern writers. Every southerner I have ever met, no matter how reasonable on other subjects, seemed to be incapable of looking at this question with an open mind.   His confidence that he knew all about the Negro and the problem seemed absolute, and therefore he was not in position to learn.   I occasionally inquire for information on this subject.

Naturally most of the men of whom I have made inquiries have been white, as I come in contact with very few Negroes. I have, however, talked with Negroes who have expressed their willingness to be segregated if the segregation was complete enough to rid their district of all whites, and give them fair living conditions. I cannot say that I know any Negroes, although there are a few with whom I have sufficient acquaintance to talk with them occasionally. As to their leaders in Chicago, I have assumed that their political leaders and their ministers were their leaders, the ministers having a larger place of leadership than ministers among white people. I used to come in contact occasionally with colored lawyers who were capable men, and I believe leaders of their race, and I understand that there is a colored physician, whose name I cannot recall, who is the real leader of the best Negroes in Chicago. Nationally I could not name any since the death of Booker Washington, whom I very much admired, excepting Du Bois whom I have heard speak, and with whose views I do not sympathize. I do not remember ever reading a Negro periodical.

As I live on the South Side the subject of discussion most frequently leading to the Negro is their encroachment on white residence districts. Two years ago my church was given up to a colored congregation, and the church into which we were transferred is seriously threatened by the same invasion. Property interests in a large part of the South Side bring up the question, as does the unpleasantness of meeting them on the street cars. I do not hear serious constructive discussion in any circle. The invasion is deplored in all circles, social, business, church and others.

I would not undertake to make any social adjustment on my present information, except segregation of the Negroes in a part of the South Side, and this only if it had the approval of their own leaders. I do not approve of "Jim Crow" street cars for Chicago, although I would not insist on their abandonment in southern cities where they are already used, and I would not favor any radical change if the better Negroes obstinately objected.

I believe in educating Negroes, even though I am not sure to what it will lead. I hope that as the race progresses the prejudice against it will be modified. Still this prejudice is so very great that I think it would be foolish for the Negroes ever to seek a high station through demands. Probably many of their demands should be granted, but they will make greater progress by reckoning with the prejudice, and continuing their present conciliatory attitude.

I do not believe that prejudice is based on fear. There is, of course, a well-founded fear of many individual Negroes, but I do not believe that the white race is conscious of any fear of the Negro race as such. I think the prejudice is based on the relative inferiority of the Negro race.

As a general proposition this is doubtless true that isolation fosters prejudice. As applied to Negroes, however, it is doubtful whether it would produce more conflict than the present system. I would feel more hopeful of the overcoming of the prejudice through more intimate contact with Negroes if the difference between Negroes and white men were not so fundamental.

As an abstract proposition the despotism of a majority cannot be justified. I would say it is a very bad doctrine to spread among a majority, but has in it a certain amount of practical truth which the minority would do well to bear in mind.

E—

Negroes do possess distinguishing traits of mentality and character. My opinions are based upon my personal observation.

As I knew the Negro in the South he was inclined to be indolent, shiftless and lacking in a high sense of honesty, though religious. His disposition is a happy one, and often his good will is shown in many ways of gratitude and faithfulness. These traits I have seen expressed in service as servants, in the cotton fields, in their homes, and on town streets. In Chicago, when the Negro has long been a resident here, having larger advantages in education and employment, I find the colored man honest in business and other transactions, diligent at work, and inoffensive, but firmly standing for his citizenship rights, and wanting to live peaceably. My Chicago experience has been principally as a physician visiting in Negro homes.

When a boy I worked in the cotton fields with Negroes, and I attended some of their religious meetings for the sake of amusement. It was a social law in the South that we must not eat at the same table with Negroes, and we were not to sit with colored people when riding on street cars or on trains. However, if a Negro was driver of a horse and buggy, the most beautiful and refined woman might sit on the same seat with the colored driver. White people visiting a colored church were given seats to themselves, usually front seats. Colored children could not attend white schools. At the age of six when I first saw Negroes, I became conscious of a race difference.

I regard Rev. John R. Hayworth as fitted to advise on the question. I have sought information from about twenty-five Negroes when in their midst as their physician. I am acquainted with at least a dozen Negro families but can give the names of only three. I consider Alderman De Priest, Mr. Lucas and Colonel Jackson leading colored men; Dr. George Hall is also well known. I have never read a Negro periodical.

In Chicago the subject of undesirable neighbors leads to the discussion of Negroes in our neighborhood improvement clubs.

Believing that both black and white people prefer to live separately, I would make agreeable provision for separate locations in which each might live and in so doing abide by the wish of the majority and enforce its dictates.

The Negro should be given the advantage of education, culture and good employment. We should expect to grant him better living conditions on account of such advantages.

Prejudice against the Negro has its principal basis in not understanding him, as well as fear and an inborn dislike for people of another race.

There never seemed to be any conflicts in the South because the whites and blacks occupied separate parts of towns. Colored people in the South seem to prefer to live in communities to themselves, because a bond of sympathy holds them together.

It is better for a minority to bear an injustice than for an overwhelming majority to bear an injustice.

F—

Negroes should have the same rights as we.

I know of no distinguishing traits.

My opinion is based largely on reading, as I never lived in the South. I had no early contacts. There were few Negroes near, and none in my schools. As authorities I would mention Professor Du Bois, Fannie B. Williams, Professor Graham Taylor. I know an able colored woman, a member of the Chicago Woman's Club and women who have worked in our home.

Occasionally I read a Negro periodical.

The discussion of lynchings and riots at home and church lead most frequently to the Negro.

Our schools, trades and professions should be opened to Negroes and they be permitted to take care of themselves. Let them follow their own bent so long as it injures no one else.

Of course, when you educate Negroes you increase their demands. Grant their demands.

Egotism and the jealousy that we whites are better are the basis of prejudice.

It is true that a minority has no right to expect complete justice from the majority, if Negroes reason from experience; but the colored race probably has idealists who hope for better future treatment.

G—

The trouble is with the whites; selfishness and pride have caused the situation and the regulation of the Negro according to faulty concepts of right will always fail. The Stock Yards riots gave proof of equality in passion, cowardliness, and unfairness between blacks and whites.

Negroes lag in evolution through hinderment. They may put reason above emotion as they develop mentally, as do cultured whites, but a better evolution may bring trained intuition from crude emotion.

My opinions are based upon short trips South, residence in Louisville and northern contacts, plus general reading.

My only contacts are on the streets.

Children's talk and the term "Nigger" just called my attention to a race difference.

I know a few highly educated Negro pastors. I never read Negro papers. The subject of interracial marriage leads to the discussion of the Negro.

As a solution they should be distributed without boundaries, among whites, as to residence, occupation and society. They would not object; it is what they fight for— equality.

Negro faults are the result of retarded mental growth. Why further retard them? The problem ceases to be as their mental level rises. Prejudice is the result of selfishness in whites. Your third proposition is absolutely true.

Injustice to the minority by the majority is unconstitutional, un-Christian and unwise.

H—

My opinion is that the Negro is entitled to life, liberty, and the pursuit of happiness as well as the white. The very fact that his skin is differently colored than mine is no reason why he should not be free to develop himself mentally, morally, and physically the same as I do. Observation is basis of my opinion. No contacts or warnings as a child. No friends particularly familiar with question.

I have given this matter some little consideration, and have discussed it with some Negroes as well as many white men. It is my opinion that the consensus of opinion among Negroes to whom I have talked is that they have no particular desire to mix socially with the white man, but that they do feel they should be given opportunity for development along those lines for which they are best fitted. I am not acquainted particularly with any of the leaders in this movement anywhere.

I read no Negro periodical. Racial equality is the subject that leads to the Negro.

In all circles where general subjects are usually discussed the question of the Negro arises.

Until the white man is ready to give the Negro a square deal, I would suggest that he be segregated, and given every opportunity for development possible under such segregation. If they objected I would insist upon majority rule.

Nothing is gained by keeping the Negro ignorant, any more than would be gained by keeping the white man ignorant. Education of all of our races will bring about the world's salvation.

Prejudice among white women has its basis in fear but not particularly among men. This is partly due to the publicity given to all acts against women by Negroes, in my judgment

The history of the world has proved that most of the races on earth tend to group themselves, which is the natural thing, because of the community of interest.

Until the Golden Rule is accepted unanimously majority rule will continue to be the human law and under our present world political arrangements, it seems to be about as fair as any arrangement could be.

I—

The Negro seems to me to be evolutionally handicapped, but possesses the qualities of children—imitativeness, affection, loyalty, receptiveness, lack of responsibility, carelessness, improvidence. They also seem to me to lack racial pride, for which their history in this country may well account. There are fine Negroes and those who are as worthless as "poor white trash." To judge them all by either the best or the worst would be manifestly unfair. I feel that they have, as a race, never had a fair chance for their finest development.

I have lived among them and practiced medicine in their families for ten years.

The most tender, loving service, beyond monetary recompense, of one Negro woman who worked in my family for ten years. Her intimate, gentle, faithful services to members of my family in health and sickness will always endear her to us and make us more conscious of the possibilities of members of that race.

The community in which I was raised had so few Negroes that there was no occasion for contacts or prohibitions to association. I suppose as a boy I first became conscious of race difference.

I have discussed this question with intelligent Negroes, have heard some fine sermons by Negro preachers, and am somewhat familiar with the writings of Booker T. Washington and Du Bois.

I do not read their periodicals.

Mention of the servant cited in a foregoing question, newspaper accounts of lynchings, house-bombings most frequently lead to discussion of Negroes among our personal friends.

I feel that Negroes would be happier if segregated in neighborhoods which allowed contact with the dominant race.   I feel that they are as unhappy to be isolated among whites as the whites would be to be isolated among Negroes.   I feel they should have the right to live under decent conditions, with those things which make life livable and enjoyable.   Probably part of my unwillingness to have them for neighbors lies in the fear of undesirable neighbors (bad citizens), in the fear of property depreciation which would follow, and because of the lack of interests in common that make for neighborly intercourse.   I suppose I am as inconsistent as others in this, for in my heart I have no prejudice of which I am aware, yet I believe I am infected with the universal indefinite prejudice, if I could but analyze it thoroughly.

Their education should not be curtailed, but enlarged.   Their demands should be granted if not incompatible with the common good.

It is probably true that prejudice is based on fear, a result of the abuse of female slaves by the whites in slavery time, and the resultant desire on the part of a few Negroes engendered during the reconstruction period by the carpet-baggers, to have social equality.   I have discussed this subject of "social equality" with intelligent, fine Negroes, and believe they meant what they said when they assured me that among decent Negroes there is no more desire for this than there is among the white people.   I feel that it is a bugaboo, useful in increasing fear and prejudice against the Negro.

By segregation, I did not mean isolation, but the natural grouping together of Negroes under wholesome conditions, but which permitted their contact through employment, through meetings for the common good, with the dominant race.

Even a minority has the right to expect and demand justice in opportunity to develop industrial, social and spiritual growth.   I recognize that education of both whites and blacks is necessary to overcome fear and prejudice and make this possible.

J—

My opinion, which is still open to conviction, is that the Negro race overlaps the white race throughout the bulk of the frequency curves of distribution of intelligence of the two races; but the average of the Negro race is probably lower than that of the white race, and among the extreme varieties the Negroes probably go lower and the whites higher than the similar varieties of the other race.   This refers to distribution of inherent capacity.   But I believe that many of them are modifiable and differ only in their average distribution from similar qualities in whites. Also that certain distinguishing traits may be so adjusted to the circumstances under which Negroes are educated and employed as to be distinctly advantageous, both to themselves and to society.

Aside from my conversation with southerners, I have made a special study of the Negro problem in connection with my undergraduate work, and again at the University of Pennsylvania.   I am familiar with a number of worth-while sources which can be listed on request.   I lived for four winters in St. Louis, where I saw a great many Negroes, but knew none.   Some excitement was caused there by an instructor inviting a mulatto school principal to address our sociology class.   There was no protest here in Evanston.   I also passed through the South, and stopped twice at New Orleans.

As a child in Portland, Oregon, I had two Negro nurses. At the age of perhaps seven or eight years, one of my nurses returned for a visit, and I was teased by companions for kissing her. That was my first consciousness of a racial difference.

My authorities and sources of importance are the N.A.A.C.P., Urban League, the Race Relations Commission, and certain Negroes. I might also mention the two Spingarns and Mr. Roger Baldwin. I know C. S. Johnson, T. Arnold Hill and the colored members of the Commission, together with the union leaders whom I heard. W. E. B. Du Bois, Haynes, Dr. Roman, J. W. Johnson, T. A. Hill, I regard as leaders among the Negroes.

I read the *Crisis*, and occasional newspapers. The *Crisis* is good except the fiction; the newspapers are rather poor.

Race relations, mob action, venereal disease, and housing questions lead to discussion of the Negro.

As a solution I suggest equal facilities, spontaneous segregation, spontaneous co-operation in common interest, education in matters of sex. In this program there would be no compulsion involved—unless possibly upon the whites.

Their education should be modified and their demands granted so far as they can be harmonized with the general good.

The main question involved in prejudice seems to me whether it is an interest or an instinct. If it is an interest then changes in social organization may with comparative ease abate the fear and the prejudice. If it is an instinct then we can only deal with it by repression and sublimation of a more deeply psychological character.

I question whether the prejudice is greater the greater the isolation. The word isolation should be analyzed into physical or economic on the one hand, and psychological on the other.

Plato asked, "What is justice?" The answer can never be final, and one's concept of it is usually colored by interest. A sociological definition of justice is in terms of harmony or harmonization of interests. Complete harmony never does exist, else we should have no thought and no progress, but harmonization of interests can be a continuous process, and is not irreconcilable with the existence of minorities and majorities.

K—

I have formed no definite opinions about Negroes. I am inclined to the opinion that generally the balance is found on the side of the white races. In general I believe they possess distinguishing traits of mentality and character. I find it very difficult, however, to define my opinion regarding this.

When I was in high school in Petersburg, Illinois, from 1895 to 1898, the school had an attendance of about forty. There were two Negroes, a boy and a girl. The boy's name was John Gaddie. I have the impression now that they both acted as though they were out of place. I found John a likeable boy. I think all of the members of the school liked him. I particularly liked him, so paid considerable attention to him, to which John reacted in a decided manner. He never forgot it. I do not like to shake hands with Negroes. I avoid it whenever I can, but I never had any hesitancy in shaking hands with John. After finishing school, I went to college and John went to work. His work was some sort of manual labor. From time to time when I went back to Petersburg I saw John, always spoke to him, shook hands with him and talked to him. John appreciated this very much and acted as though he regarded it a condescension on my part. I am not aware that I feel toward any other Negro as I feel toward John Gaddie.

I was first conscious of a racial difference when I first knew the Negro, which was when I was about fifteen years of age. In the small town of Petersburg (about 3,000 inhabitants) the Negroes there, as here in Chicago, lived in a segregated district. There were no clashes between the Negro and the whites but the racial difference was obvious enough.

I know very few Negroes. I know too little to be in a position to consider anyone as a leader among the colored people in Chicago or the United States. I never read a Negro periodical. The subjects most frequently leading to the discussion of the Negro are riots, housing problems, certain industrial problems, and, here in Chicago, politics.

The fact that the Negroes obstinately objected quite logically would not interfere with making any adjustment which seemed "wise." The social adjustment which seemed "wise" would have to be based on the possibility of objection on the part of the Negro. If the leaders were obstinate, some other solution would have to be worked out, but if the leaders saw that it was wise and for the best interest of the masses I would insist that the plan be tried out.

I do not comprehend what is meant by "demand." It may mean ambition for social standing in the sense of intermingling with the whites. It may mean other things. No matter what it means, I am not impressed, if the statement is true, that it is any reason for not educating the Negro. I am not impressed that it becomes necessary either to curtail or modify the Negro's education or to grant their demands whatever they may be.

I do not think it true that prejudice has its basis in fear.

So far as I am familiar with it there is naturally a very high degree of segregation of the Negro as to living quarters everywhere. I am not aware that the segregation which we now find of habitation brings about the development of special group prejudices. Undoubtedly, if there are or were such prejudices they would form the background of conflicts. It doesn't seem to me to follow that the greater the isolation the greater the prejudice.

There never is complete justice; but if a minority may not expect justice at the hands of an overwhelming majority it can expect no justice at all. The justice, if it comes at all, will be at the hands of an overwhelming majority. Theoretically, in this country all are entitled to justice. I know no reason why this should not be true in a practical sense. Furthermore, I see no reason why a minority may not only expect but demand, at the hands of an overwhelming majority, justice. It seems to me that if the overwhelming majority hoped to prosper, it would see to it that justice was dispensed to the minority. I do not find myself ready to place the Negro on an equal basis with the white in every respect, that is, socially and otherwise. I do not regard the failure to so place the Negroes as injustice to them.

L—

In general, I like the Negro, but I lament his presence in this country in large numbers. I have never heard a solution of the Negro problem. Their distinguishing traits are ignorance, good nature, mental weakness, and physical strength.

I have never heard of good arguments for extensive isolation.

M—

I have a strong prejudice, but it is undefined. For instance, the hair of Negroes always holds a peculiar fascination, but under no consideration could I touch it, but there was always a great curiosity about it. I was undecided whether or not I should shake hands or in any way touch a colored skin, but I am quite sure I would never do it from choice. The everyday contacts on street cars are the only personal experiences I have had. The fascination of watching them is constant.

When I was about two years old a family moved into the village bringing with them an old colored nurse. She was too old to work, and my childish remembrance is that she always sat in the corner near the fireplace with a pipe in her mouth. I did not know that the Negro could do anything else.

When I was about five years old a Negro came to the village and opened a barber shop. I remember my father telling mother about the Negro and how he took the three small children down to see "Snowball" as a matter of curiosity. My reaction was that the Negro was not a person such as I was accustomed to seeing, although there was no feeling of classing him as an animal.

The third contact came when I was half-grown. My father was prominent in politics and on election day the table was kept set so that anyone sent from the polls could have a meal. By some chance a Negro was sent and ate. After he had gone I remember seeing my mother take the plate and other dishes out in the yard and scour them with brick dust, evidently with an idea that something had rubbed off.

My information is largely taken from the books of Booker T. Washington. I admired Dunbar's poems when they were current in the newspapers and magazines. I have not seen any of them for many years but remember vividly, "When the Bread Won't Raise." I was naturally familiar with *Uncle Tom's Cabin*, both as a book and a play in Civil War days. I do not consciously seek for information on the subject of Negroes and do not personally know any Negroes. Outside of the names which appear in the press I do not know of any Negro leaders and could not be sure of correct information as to those who are well known.

I have never seen a Negro periodical and have so rarely heard Negroes discussed that no conclusions can be given. The Negro is rarely a topic of conversation in my circle.

As a solution they might be nationalized if possible, somewhere and somehow, like the Japs. Liberia is a failure largely because of white leadership and policy. Some portion of the earth should be set aside where the Negroes can be a nation, perhaps in Africa. They have a right to work out their own problems in their own ways.

All Negroes should be educated as highly as possible. They have a right to it because they are Americans. If demands follow this education, it is right they should be granted.

There is no personal fear of Negroes as a basis of my prejudice.

I agree with the third proposition as to isolation.

Majority's injustice to minority is always true in politics, religion, everyday dealings. Is not peculiar to relations between white and colored.

N—

My views are more impressions than opinions. I have a distinct aversion to close association with Negroes generally. On the other hand I have a distinct liking for particular Negroes whom I have been thrown with. Aside from the more educated ones, they seem to me to be of a sluggish mentality and of somewhat low moral character. They seem to have more of the animal in them. I am not sure that this is not an impression rather than an opinion.

I have no basis for my views except my own experience and what I have read in papers and periodicals.

I had two Negro classmates in college; I saw a good deal of Negroes as a boy; and I have known Negroes, some well educated, since I came to Chicago from the law school.

Although my contacts were largely casual, I particularly remember one very old Negro man whom I regarded as a sort of patriarch and of whom I was a little bit afraid. Then I recall vividly my impression of the filth and sordidness of "darky-town" in the small city in which I lived as a boy. I was never forbidden, so far as I can remember, to associate with Negroes. In public school there was no separation of the races. As a small boy, it seems to me my playmates in school were partly Negroes. Of course the Negroes, as is usual, lived in a separate part of the city. I should say that this seemed to me then to be a natural and necessary arrangement. Negroes were black and we were white. That was about all there was to it.

Very early I became race conscious, I should say along about the fourth or fifth grade in school, perhaps even before.

I regard as authorities on the question teachers or officers of Fisk University, Tuskegee Institute, those who have to do with criminals; employers of Negroes; persons who have dealt with Negroes as a class as well as individually. Booker T. Washington's writings should be an authority.

I have made very few inquiries for information. I know few Negroes in Chicago. Those that I do know are of the better educated type. Some of them, I think, have been at Fisk University. I do not know the leaders in the city, nor do I know the leaders in the country; but I should say they are the heads of the great Negro universities and colleges, like Fisk, Tuskegee, Lincoln Institute. Booker Washington was, of course, a leader. I do not know who his successors are.

So far as I know, I have seen only one Negro periodical, some years ago. The article I read in it I happened to be interested in because I was dealing with the subject of it, and it was undoubtedly a prejudiced article founded on misinformation and a rather wilful disregard of facts. As I recall the paper as a whole its main motive and purpose was an apparent hatred of the white race. I realize that this is not enough to base an opinion on.

The discussion of labor, politics, especially questions connected with southern politics, almost any question relating to the South, education, home missions, living conditions, the servant problem, crime, most frequently lead to the Negro.

It would hardly be feasible to send Negroes out of the country as a whole; they are needed in the industrial world, and it would not be a Christian act to deport them. Nor does it seem right or practicable or just to segregate them entirely. They need education and the help that comes from association with those who are further along in the polite amenities. On the other hand, unless they are somewhat segregated racial troubles are sure to arise when a Negro tries to settle, say, in the same block with upper class whites. I am not sure that it might not be a good plan if one or two of the southern states could be turned over to the Negroes, but if this is done they should be allowed to govern themselves and should be protected from exploitation from unscrupulous whites.

It seems to me that race prejudice is not based principally on fear, but rather on a natural aversion or shrinking from a man of another color. It is almost as elemental as fear. We fear any uneducated, ignorant and brutal man, whether he be white, red, black or yellow. We have an aversion, as I have said, to close association with any man of another color, even though he be educated. I do not know whether this aversion is curable by any method or not.

I am inclined to agree with the third proposition, and I suppose the fourth proposition is regrettably true.

The outstanding feature in the answers to the queries: "Have you formed definite opinions about Negroes?" and "Do Negroes, in your opinion, possess distinguishing traits of mentality or character?" is the great variation in opinions. As a race they are "shiftless," "childish," "docile," "evolutionarily handicapped," "undependable," "some of them good," "they have as a mass a lower level of inherent capacity," "disliked in the mass," "liked as individuals," "entitled to the same leniency and consideration as whites," "entitled to the same rights as whites," "lacking in racial pride," "loyal," "imitative," "affectionate," "improvident."

The feelings toward Negroes are as varied. There is aversion to close association, a distinct dislike, a desire that Negroes should have equal rights and privileges, a desire that they should have the same rights, a feeling that Negroes have been mistreated and exploited, a feeling that selfishness and pride of white persons have caused the present racial situation, and a conviction that present behavior toward the Negro is faulty and wrong. Lincoln is twice mentioned but with different meanings. The trend of sentiment, while unfavorable toward Negroes, maintains some sort of ideal. Although childish, they "must be trained," "although we dislike their presence, we must submit to our penalty for years to come," etc. Some are not sure of their opinions. Some call them impressions or regret a lack of knowledge. A general summing up would show a desire to be fair in spite of unfavorable opinions.

The questions regarding the disposition they would make of Negroes if they could entirely control the situation were put to get views uninfluenced by considerations of present practicability. The play of circumstances, opinion, ethical considerations, and difficulties were excluded from consideration. The trend of replies was toward segregation, even to the extent of colonization in Africa. There were curious anomalies, like segregation without Jim Crow and segregation for the Negro's own happiness. Others would distribute them without boundaries throughout the social system. When segregation is generally mentioned it is conditioned on the consent of Negroes.

Interesting answers are made on propositions (a), (b), (c), and (d), covering education, prejudice, isolation, and justice. In spite of unforeseen danger, it is pretty generally agreed that Negroes should be educated, even though their demands are thus increased. There is less agreement on granting demands. The analysis of prejudice brought a wide variety of opinions. Repulsion, natural aversion, social equality and the sex complex, selfishness of whites, egotism and inborn dislike, as well as fear, are accredited as forming the basis of prejudice.

The problem of isolation was essentially a problem of segregation. Strange to say, although the trend of some was toward isolation, there was a majority belief that isolation would increase conflict and friction. The ethical problem developed in general the opinion that there does exist a disparity between what is and what should be.

The unwisdom of an unjust course of social conduct is recognized, but is for the most part held to be warranted by the peculiar difficulty of present relations. Here, probably as nowhere else, the problem was compared with other general problems not involving race.

The experiences on which opinions are based divide into definite classes:

1. Experiences in the South.
2. Experiences with individual Negro servants.
3. Experiences with individual Negroes of intelligence.
4. General observation.

The actual basis of opinions as stated by the persons themselves provides an interesting question.

The question concerning early childhood experiences was put to draw out, if possible, impressions unconsciously insinuated or consciously obtained but perhaps discounted and forgotten through subsequent years of intermittent relations. It was successful in bringing to light incidents of striking significance. The answers, indeed, show striking elements in the heritage of racial consciousness. Impressions gained in early life require many facts to unsettle or remove.

Most important in considering the trustworthiness of information sources are the replies to the question: "Whom of your friends, acquaintances, favorite authors, scholars, etc., do you regard best fitted to speak with authority on the question?" There are mentioned seven Negroes and ten white persons. Of the four local Negroes mentioned, two might be regarded as well informed; one has been out of public life for fifteen years, and the other, although by no means an authority, probably could provide interesting information. Of the Negro national figures, Washington, Du Bois, and Dunbar are mentioned, Washington three times, Dunbar and Du Bois once. Booker T. Washington died in 1915. Paul Laurence Dunbar, the poet, died in 1906. Practically all of the white persons mentioned have been at some time connected with movements to improve conditions among Negroes. George W. Cable wrote for the most part stories of the Creole South.

It is strange, though, that in answering the question, "Who are the Negro leaders?" so many gave the names of politicians, who are not the real leaders of Negroes. About half of those who answered had never read a Negro periodical, and half of those who had read them considered their influence pernicious.

V. PUBLIC OPINION AS EXPRESSED BY NEGROES

The practice of "keeping the Negro in his place" or any modification of it in northern communities has isolated Negroes from all other members of the community. Though in the midst of an advanced social system and surrounded by cultural influences, they have hardly been more than exposed to them. Of full and free participation they know little. The pressure of the dominant white group in practically every ordinary experience has kept the attention and interests of Negroes centered upon themselves, and made them race conscious. Their thinking on general questions is controlled by their race interests. The opinions of Negroes, therefore, are in large measure a negative product.

It is probably for this reason that most of their expressions of opinion take the form of protest. This same enforced self-interest warps these opinions, giving exaggerated values to the unconsidered views of the larger group, increasing sensitiveness to slights, and keeping Negroes forever on the defensive. Extreme expressions, unintelligible to those outside the Negro group, are a natural result of this isolation. The processes of thought by which these opinions are reached are, by virtue of this very isolation, concealed from outsiders. Negroes by their words alone may often be judged as radical, pernicious, or fanatic. Without the background of their experiences it is no more possible for their views to be completely understood than for Negroes to understand the confessed prejudices of white persons, or even their ordinary feelings toward Negroes.

Negroes know more of the habits of action and thought of the white group than white people know of similar habits in the Negro group. For Negroes read the whites' books and papers, hear them talk, and sometimes see them in the intimacy of their homes. But this one-sided and partial understanding serves only to make the behavior of the whites more keenly felt. Until these differences, long held as taboo, are thoroughly understood and calmly faced, there is small chance of satisfactory relations.

The opinions of Negroes on this question are as various as the white opinions of the Negro. Their response may reflect the sentiment of the larger group; it may take a conciliatory turn, or, it may be exclusively self-centered in disregard, if indeed not in defiance, of the white group. The rapid growth of the Garvey movement[1] is a good example of this last type of opinion. There is harmony of opinion on ultimates, but on programs, processes, and methods there are differences among Negroes that reach the intensity of abusive conflicts.

No Negro is willing to admit that he belongs to a different and lower species, or that his race is constitutionally weak in character. All Negroes hope for an

[1] See p. 493.

adjustment by virtue of which they will be freely granted the privileges of ordinary citizens. They are conscious, however, of an opposition in the traditions of the country and actually meet it daily. Conflict arises from opinions as to methods of combating and overcoming the opposition with the greatest gain and smallest loss to themselves.

Thus we come to hear of different schools of thought among Negroes. Booker T. Washington is contrasted with W. E. B. Du Bois, and Du Bois is contrasted with Owen, Peyton, and Colson, and they, in turn are contrasted with Garvey. Among individual Negroes opinion is determined by experience as well as tradition. The Negro house-servant does not feel toward white persons as does a Negro common laborer. The independent professional man holds an opinion essentially different from the social worker. Yet they are all governed by those trends of sentiment protective of the Negro group, and in crises either act upon them or suffer the group's censure.

An instance of the strength of Negro group opinion appeared in a tragic by-product of the Chicago riot. A Negro prominent in local political and social circles was sought out as a leader, and asked for an interview by a reporter of the *Chicago Tribune* during the riot. In the published interview he was reported as saying: "This is a white man's country, and Negroes had better behave or they will get what rights they have taken away." This aroused a solid Negro sentiment against him; his life was threatened; for several weeks he had to have police protection; he was finally ostracized; and in less than a year he died. His friends asserted that he was slanderously misquoted, and that his death was due largely to the resulting criticism.

The more balanced opinions may be found among Negroes who have developed a defensive philosophy. Race pride and racial solidarity have sprung from this necessity. The term radical is used to characterize Negroes whose views and preachments are in advocacy of changes which to the general white public appear undesirable. It will be observed that most of the so-called radicals are southern Negroes now living in the North. They know by experience the meaning of oppression. Contrasts with them are sharper and the desire for change is more insistent, because they can appreciate differences.

Frequently this "radicalism" is no more than a matter of interpretation by white persons and possibly an oversuspicion. For example, Attorney-General A. Mitchell Palmer, in his report on the investigations of his department, referred to the bitter protests of Negro publications against lynching and disfranchisement as radical and incendiary documents. This report is headed, "Radicalism and Sedition among the Negroes as Reflected in Their Publications." It reads in part as follows:

There can no longer be any question of a well-concerted movement among a certain class of Negro leaders of thought and action to constitute themselves a determined and persistent source of a radical opposition to the government, and to the established rule of law and order.

Among the more salient points to be noted in the present attitude of the Negro leaders are, first, the ill-governed reaction toward race rioting; second, the threat of retaliatory measures in connection with lynching; third, the more openly expressed demand for social equality, in which demand the sex problem is not infrequently included; fourth, the identification of the Negro with such radical organizations as the I.W.W. and an outspoken advocacy of the Bolsheviki or Soviet doctrines; fifth, the political stand assumed toward the present federal administration, the South in general, and incidentally, toward the peace treaty and the League of Nations. Underlying these more salient viewpoints is the increasingly emphasized feeling of a race consciousness in many of these publications always antagonistic to the white race and openly, defiantly assertive of its own equality and even superiority. When it is borne in mind that this boast finds its most frequent expression in the pages of those journals whose editors are men of education, and in at least one instance, by men holding degrees conferred by Harvard University, it may be seen that the boast is not to be dismissed lightly as the ignorant vaporing of untrained minds. Neither is the influence of the Negro press in general to be reckoned with lightly. The *Negro World* for October 18, 1919, states that "there are a dozen Negro papers with a circulation of over 20,000, and scores with smaller circulation. There are half a dozen magazines with a large circulation and other magazines with a smaller circulation, and there are easily over fifty writers who can write interesting editorials and special articles, written in fine, pure English, with a background of scholarship behind them." Notwithstanding the clumsiness of expression of this particular assertion, the claim is not an idle one. It may be added that in several instances the Negro magazines are expensive in manufacture, being on coated paper throughout, well-printed, and giving evidence of the possession of ample funds.

In all the discussions of the recent race riots there is reflected the note of pride that the Negro has found himself, that he has "fought back," that never again will he tamely submit to violence or intimidation. The sense of oppression finds increasingly bitter expression. Defiance and insolently race-centered condemnation of the white race is to be met with in every issue of the more radical publications, and this one in moderateness of denunciation carries its own threat. The Negro is "seeing red," and it is the prime object of the leading publications to induce a like quality of vision upon the part of their readers. A few of them deny this, notwithstanding the evidence of their work. Others of them openly admit the fact. The number of restrained and conservative publications is relatively negligible, and even some of these . . . . have indulged in most intemperate utterance, though it would be unfair not to state that certain papers—I can think of no magazines—maintain an attitude of well-balanced sanity. . . . .

The *Messenger* for October is significant for one thing above all others. In it for the first time a Negro publication comes out openly for sex equality.[1]

It is the sentiment briefly sketched in the foregoing pages that summons attention. What are Negroes actually thinking? How are they being affected by what the general public is thinking? What do they want? Against what are their protests directed? What kinds of group sentiments are being devel-

[1] The *Messenger* is pronounced in its stand for woman suffrage.

oped and how significant are they as to subsequent relations between the two groups?

This report merely sets out examples of those views in the hope of showing the beliefs that control the conduct of Negroes in Chicago.

I. RACE PROBLEMS

Criticism of Negro leaders.—A Negro attorney said:

I have read numerous articles written by prominent colored men on the subject of Negroes moving North, and I have heard many of them speak. But few of them, in my opinion, will bear rigid criticism. They are wanting in genuine expression of true conditions. Those writers and orators who have some personal motive for their expression do not necessarily speak with absolute frankness.

A Negro worker said:

Our leaders are not interested enough in the welfare of the race. As soon as they reach some little place of fame they try to get off to themselves.

Contacts as basis for respect.—A Negro professional man said:

When in school in Oberlin my professor in debating and oratory was so prejudiced that he would not let the other colored boy and me be on teams together. We asked him repeatedly, but he always refused. We decided to work on a debate for all there was in it and compel him to recognize the fact that we could measure up to the other members of the class. When we finished he praised our work in the highest terms. After that he began to take an interest in me and finally told me that he did not know anything about Negroes and just felt that there was nothing worth while in them. He tried to persuade me to teach, and when I left he gave me one of the best letters of recommendation that I have ever seen. That shows what contact can do.

Not a race problem.—A Negro business man said:

There is no race problem; if the white people would only do as they would be done by we would not have need of commissions to better conditions. This won't be done, but an easier plan is to enforce the law. The laws are good enough but they are not enforced. Riots grow out of hate, jealousy, envy, and prejudice. When a man becomes a contented citizen there will be little chance of causing him to fight anyone. Give us those things that are due us—law, protection, and equal rights— then we will become contented citizens.

For better race relations in Chicago.—A Negro alderman said:

1. Pass a vagrancy law that will take the idle, shiftless and intolerant hoodlum off the streets. Put the burden of proof on the one so arrested.

2. Close all vicious poolrooms and dens of vice, and permit no boy under nineteen years of age to enter poolrooms.

3. Forbid loitering on the street corners, especially transfer points.

4. Prohibit vicious and race-antagonizing campaign speeches on the streets of the city and in public halls. Races must not be arrayed against each other.

5. Make more rigid the habeas corpus act, tighten up on the parole and probation laws and enforcement of the truancy law.

6. Stop the newspapers from referring to the territory occupied by the colored people as the "Black Belt."

7. Inciting and inflammatory headlines in the newspapers must be stopped.

8. Open the gates of employment to all races in our public utilities, such as street-car and elevated-road service, Chicago Telephone Co. exchanges, Peoples Gas Light & Coke Co., and the Commonwealth Edison Co.

9. Better housing for the colored people and improvement of the district in which a vast majority of them reside by turning certain streets into boulevards, building small parks and playgrounds, and let the city or South Park Commissioners build a bathing-beach equal to any other for the benefit and comfort of all races along the water front, between Twenty-ninth and Thirty-ninth streets. This without lines or thought of segregation and for the benefit of a neglected part of our tax-paying community.

10. Apprehend and convict the bomb throwers by placing in command of our police-stations officers who will do their duty and place patrolmen on duty who will not sympathize with this lawless element of our citizenry. Greater still, insist that the state's attorney do his full duty in prosecuting the people who are responsible for inciting these criminal acts.

11. Safeguard the rights of all races in our public parks and on the public highways.

12. Give us a man's chance in the field of labor, and we will prove that we are no burden to any other race of people.

2. THE EMOTIONAL BACKGROUND

An old settler.—The sentiment presented below is probably the unpolished feeling of a Negro who was born in Chicago before the fire of 1871, and has lived here since. His grandfather owned the property where the post-office now stands. He was at one time a member of the Central Y.M.C.A. (white). For two and a half years he was assistant bookkeeper in a white bank in Memphis, Tennessee. He said:

Prejudice has been on the increase in Chicago since 1893. Southerners came to the World's Exposition and many of them remained. They brought their prejudices with them. On the cars they would order colored people to get up and give their seats to them. This resulted in fights, and when the cases were taken to court colored people won as many cases as whites. I took my grandmother to the fair and on the street car I had an altercation with a white southerner who called her "Auntie." He tried to hit me, and I got out my gun to shoot him. A Columbian guard and detective grabbed me. When the case was called I was discharged.

Hyde Park is a nest of prejudice. These southerners moved out there. Southern clubs are established throughout the country. They get northernized and want straight-haired mulatto maids for their mistresses and call them typists. The southern white boys get jobs on newspapers in the North and work for nothing in order that they may write articles and editorials against Negroes and spread the doctrine of the South.

A good many years ago colored people lived in good homes and the Irish lived in shanties. They used to call them "flannel mouth," "mick," and "shanty Irish."

It used to be that only colored men of light complexion could secure jobs as porters on certain railroads. In 1908 the Archbishop of the Diocese of the Catholic Church issued an edict that white communicants should not worship at the Thirty-sixth and Dearborn streets church. The whites still go there, however. The very fact that the G.A.R. invited the Confederate veterans to march in the same parade on Memorial Day goes to show that prejudice against Negroes is increasing. They are combining. These southern societies in Chicago which foster race prejudice should be exposed.

Abyssinians.—During the summer of 1920 a group of self-styled "Abyssinians," in a spectacular demonstration,[1] killed two white men and seriously wounded two Negroes, one of whom was a policeman. Neither whites nor Negroes could give any further explanation of the affair than that it was an ignorant outburst of fanatics. Although the demonstration was announced as part of a membership drive in a "Back to Africa Movement," there was a definite racial sentiment in the appeals to unlettered Negroes. This sentiment was calculated to solidify the fanatic group, while, at the same time, by its anti-social dogma, it placed this group in opposition to the safety and well-being of the community. Meetings and speeches and anti-racial dogma, founded upon unusual interpretations of the Bible, gave their sentiments a religious fervor and a racial aim. Thus these sentiments grew, uncorrected by outsiders, and finally expressed themselves in criminal but significant conduct. The significance of these sentiments is apparent in the attitude of a sympathizer with the movement, expressed to one of the Commission's investigators several weeks before the outbreak made the movement unpopular. He is a shopkeeper, and most of his trade is among Negroes. His business with whites is wholly with wholesale dealers. In his treatment of those who came into his store during the interview he was rude and discourteous. He said:

I am a radical. I despise and hate the white man. They will always be against the Ethiopian. I do not want to be called Negro, colored, or "nigger." Either term is an insult to me or to you. Our rightful name is Ethiopian. White men stole the black man from Africa and counseled with each other as to what to do with him and what to call him, for when the Negro learned that he was the first civilized human on earth he would rise up and rebel against the white man. To keep him from doing this it was decided to call him Negro after the Niger River in Africa. This was to keep him from having that knowledge by the Bible, for his right name was Ethiopian. This was done so we could always be ruled by the white man. I will call your attention to the Bible. There is not one word of evil against the Children of Israel and Ethiopia written in it. Ethiopia came out of Israel and God said they are his people and he will be their God. He also says after the 300 years of punishment he will never go by [desert] Israel again and will be with him for ever and ever. We find by the Bible that he, the Ethiopian, is the only child of God.

The three hundred years of punishment are up, and this is the year of deliverance. It started in 1619 when we were stolen from Africa and made slaves. God is taking care of the black man. Some great destruction will take place, but God's chosen

[1] See p. 59.

people will be all right. White passers-by from other neighborhoods are the only people who trouble us. They will call you insulting names or try to annoy you in a hundred little ways. The white people in the neighborhood are all right. Two white men ran down an old pet rooster of mine this morning. They were on a motor-cycle and picked him up, carried him off, paying no heed to me, as I ran two blocks after them.

Ready for trouble.—A Negro ex-soldier said:

I went to war, served eight months in France; I was married, but I didn't claim exemption. I wanted to go, but I might as well have stayed here for all the good it has done me. . . . . No, that ain't so, I'm glad I went. I done my part and I'm going to fight right here till Uncle Sam does his. I can shoot as good as the next one, and nobody better start anything. I ain't looking for trouble, but if it comes my way I ain't dodging.

Agitation and discussion.—A Negro lawyer said:

Agitation by the press, both white and colored, does nothing but create dissension. The religious and political leaders have gone from one extreme to the other. Formerly the Negroes were cringing and ingratiating when dealing with the whites. Now they are trying to be radical in order to gain notoriety. There is nothing to be gained in either being servile or radical. I have had indignities heaped upon me by the white man. Why, my mother was ill when a white man in Georgia took every bit of our furniture from us, pulling the bed from under her. She screamed with pain each time they moved the bed, but they left her on the floor. I swore that I would kill that man and for many years held hatred against him. Now I know it is wrong and only hope that he has learned better.

A Negro and a mob.—How does a Negro feel when he is being hunted or chased by a mob? Few persons are able to analyze their emotions under such stress. It happens, however, that a Negro university student fell victim to the sportive brutality of a gang of white men in a clash in September, 1920, and after being chased and hunted for five hours and a half in an unfriendly neighborhood escaped uninjured. He recounted his experience in an effort at a purely objective study of his emotions.

While at work in a plant just outside Chicago he became ill and was forced to leave early. Unaware that a riot was in progress, he left a street car to transfer in a hostile neighborhood. As he neared the corner one of a group of about twenty young white men yelled: "There's a nigger! Let's get him!" He boarded a car to escape them. They pulled off the trolley and started into the car after him. His story follows:

The motorman opened the door, and before they knew it I jumped out and ran up Fifty-first Street as fast as my feet could carry me. Gaining about thirty yards on them was a decided advantage, for one of them saw me and with the shout "There he goes!" the gang started after me. One, two, three, blocks went past in rapid succession. They came on shouting, "Stop him! Stop him!" I ran on the sidewalk and someone tried to trip me, but fortunately I anticipated his intentions and jumped into the road. As I neared the next street intersection, a husky, fair-haired fellow weighing about 180 pounds came lunging at me. I have never thought so quickly in all my life as then, I believe. Three things flashed into my mind—to stop suddenly and let him pass me and then go on; to try to trip him by dropping in front of him; or to keep running and give him a good football straight arm. The first two I figured would stop me, and the gang would be that much nearer, so I decided to rely on the last. These thoughts flashed through my mind as I ran about ten steps. As we came together, I left my feet, and putting all my weight and strength into a lunge, shot my right hand at his chin. It landed squarely and by a half-turn the fair-haired would-be tackler went flying to the road on his face.

That was some satisfaction, but it took a lot of my strength, for by this time I was beginning to feel weak. But determination kept me at it, and I ran on. Then I came to a corner where a drug-store was open and a woman standing outside. I slowed down and asked her to let me go in there, that a gang was chasing me; but she said I would not be safe there, so I turned off Fifty-first Street and ran down the side street. Here the road had been freshly oiled and I nearly took a "header" as I stepped in the first pool, but fortunately no accident happened. My strength was fast failing; the suggestion came into my mind to stop and give up or try to fight it out with the two or three who were still chasing me, but this would never do, as the odds were too great, so I kept on. My legs began to wobble, my breath came harder, and my heart seemed to be pounding like a big pump, while the man nearest me began to creep up on me. It was then that an old athletic maxim came into my mind— "He's feeling as tired as you." Besides, I thought, perhaps he smokes and boozes and his wind is worse than mine. Often in the last hundred yards of a quarter-mile that thought of my opponent's condition had brought forth the last efforts necessary for the final spurt. There was more than a medal at stake this time, so I stuck, and in a few strides more they gave up the chase. One block further on, when I had made sure that no one was following me on the other side of the street, I slowed down to walk and regained my breath. Soon I found myself on Forty-sixth Street just west of Halsted where the street is blind, so I climbed up on the railroad tracks and walked along them. But I imagined that in crossing a lighted street I could be seen from below and got down off the tracks, intending to cross a field and take a chance on the street. But this had to be abandoned, for as I looked over the prospect from the shadow of a fence I saw an automobile held up at the point of a revolver in the hands of one member of a gang while they searched the car apparently looking for colored men.

This is no place for a minister's son, I thought, and crept back behind a fence and lay down among some weeds. Lying there as quietly as could be I reflected on how close I had come to a severe beating or the possible loss of my life. Fear, which had caused me to run, now gave place to anger, and a desire to fight, if I could fight with a square deal. I remembered that as I looked the gang over at Fifty-first and Ashland I figured I could handle any of them individually with the possible exception of two, but the whole gang of blood-thirsty hoodlums was too much. Anger gave place to hatred and a desire for revenge, and I thought if ever I caught a green-buttoned "Ragen's Colt" on the South Side east of State that one of us would get a licking. But reason showed me such would be folly and would only lead to reprisals and some other innocent individual getting a licking on my account. I knew all "Ragen's" were not rowdies, for I had met some who were pretty decent fellows, but some others—ye gods!

My problem was to get home and to avoid meeting hostile elements. Temporarily I was safe in hiding, but I could not stay there after daybreak. So I decided to wait a couple of hours and then try to pass through "No Man's Land"—Halsted to Wentworth. I figured the time to be about 11:30 and so decided to wait until 1:30 or 2:00 A.M., before coming out of cover. Shots rang out intermittently; the sky became illumined; the fire bells rang, and I imagined riot and arson held sway as of the previous year. It is remarkable how the imagination runs wild under such conditions.

Then the injustice of the whole thing overwhelmed me—emotions ran riot. Had the ten months I spent in France been all in vain? Were those little white crosses over the dead bodies of those dark-skinned boys lying in Flanders fields for naught? Was democracy merely a hollow sentiment? What had I done to deserve such treatment? I lay there experiencing all the emotions I imagined the innocent victim of a southern mob must feel when being hunted for some supposed crime. Was this what I had given up my Canadian citizenship for, to become an American citizen and soldier? Was the risk of life in a country where such hatred existed worth while? Must a Negro always suffer merely because of the color of his skin? "There's a Nigger; let's get him!" Those words rang in my ears—I shall never forget them.

Psychologists claim that it is in the face of overwhelming forces that man is prone to turn to the Supreme Being. I was no longer afraid, only filled with righteous indignation and a desire to get out of danger. But mingled emotions shook me, and a flood of tears burst forth. In the midst of it I found myself praying fervently to God against the injustice of it all, for strength and help to go through safely, and thanks for my deliverance from the gang which had chased me. Then relief came from all these pent-up feelings with the determination to get up and try to go through—and to fight, if necessary. I began to speculate on means. A freight train came along, and the impulse came to jump on it and ride out of town until the trouble was over, but the knowledge of only 15 cents carfare in my pocket compelled the rejection of this idea. I thought of phoning to a friend to come and get me in his car, but this was futile, for where could I find a phone and be safe in that neighborhood? Some clothes on a line in a yard across the field offered a disguise, but even dressed as a woman I'd need a hat, and that idea had to be abandoned. With resources at an end, I picked up four rocks for ammunition and started out.

For four blocks I glided from shadow to shadow, through alleys. A couple of dogs nearly "spilled the beans" when they barked just as an automobile came down the street. I dove for cover until the car had disappeared and then emerged. At Forty-ninth Street and Union Avenue I climbed up on the railroad tracks and cautiously walked along them in the darkness. All of a sudden a block ahead appeared what seemed to be about ten men standing on the tracks, so I dropped to the ground and made a pair of binoculars out of my hands. For what seemed like five minutes I watched these forms then decided they were uprights on a bridge and went on. Imagination and fear can play tricks, and this was one of them.

Finally I found myself at Thirty-seventh and Stewart streets, having been walking northeast instead of east as I thought. I climbed down to the street and walked through back lanes until I saw the Sox ball park. All was quiet, so I came out and crossed Wentworth Avenue. At State and Thirty-seventh I saw two colored fellows waiting for a car and ran up to them. Putting my hands on their shoulders

I said, "Gee! I'm glad to see a dark skin." Then I related my experience. They assured me the "fun" was all over, and I was thankful. It was twenty-five minutes to four, just five and a half hours after I had started for home from work. A white man came along, and my first impulse was to jump on him and beat him up. But again reason told me he was not responsible for the actions of a gang of rowdies, and he was as innocent as I had been when set upon.

Is such an experience easily forgotten? Recent events would prove to the contrary. I vowed that morning never to let the sun set on me west of Wentworth Avenue, and never to go into that section unprotected, even in daytime. On a recent Sunday the papers came out with an "Extra" about 11:00 P.M., announcing a "Big South Side Fight." I went to the door and hailed a boy. Just then an automobile with men standing on the running-board came around the corner. The possibility of another riot flashed through my mind and without looking at the paper I snapped off the light, closed the door, and prepared for trouble if it came my way. But the "Fight" had been a gunman's war. This is just indicative of the caution such an experience develops. It is not a fear, but a wariness in uncertainty.

3. DEFENSIVE POLICIES

To stimulate group morale and solidify the sentiments of Negroes for unified opposition to what they regard as oppressive measures of white people, many tactics are employed. The most common of these is that of interpreting the aims and ambitions of Negroes to white persons and of defending themselves generally against criticism. A selection of types of this "defensive" sentiment is given.

A Negro attorney said:

The only way to gain favorable public opinion is to create favorable press notices. A certain amount of agitation is necessary on the part of colored papers to educate the race as to what it is entitled to. The American white race has been very successful in its propaganda that colored people are not entitled to certain things. This has caused many Negroes to believe that they are not as good as the white people.

The press can be a source of evil or of good. It depends upon the point of view. The difficulty lies in the fact that the white press has the wrong attitude, usually. A great deal of harm is done by paid workers who will give interviews that will sustain the viewpoint of the papers. Others desirous of newspaper notoriety are guilty of the same offense. Usually those interviewed are not capable of giving exact opinions and viewpoints. Those capable of doing justice to the situation are not sought by reporters. During the time when there is more calm and people are in a position to give thoughtful consideration to the question, no effort is made to find out the attitude of substantial citizens. If this were done the papers would get somewhere.

A letter from a Negro thanking the editor of a northern paper for a fair editorial said:

The colored citizens realize fully the extent to which propaganda is spread against them in the average newspaper under the guise of news, and when they find someone who knows that too, and who is strong enough to help, as is the —— [newspaper], they thank him with all the strength of their hearts, although their lips may remain mute.

Negro sentiment regarding racial news in the white press.—A Negro weekly paper said:

Whatever be the cause or the motive there is apparently a well organized plan to discredit the race in America and to bring estrangement between fellow Americans. A short-sighted . . . . press is contributing to this estrangement by playing upon the passions of the undiscriminating and thoughtlessly by its glaring and sensational headings, emphasizing rumours of alleged crimes by Negroes.

Flattery as a means of promoting tolerance.—A popular Negro orator said:

I think that the great trouble with us already is that we have allowed the white people to settle too many things for us. The nation gave you constitutional freedom, but no man can make you truly free except you yourself. The white man hates nothing worse than a coward, and the American white man is the most remarkable human being the world ever knew. He is God's superman. As white and black have one destiny beneath the Stars and Stripes, so have we the common duties of citizenship. . . . .

Woodrow Wilson is my leader. What he commands me to do I shall do. Where he commands me to go I shall go. I had naught of ill will toward Von Bernsdorf until Wilson pointed him out as a national menace. Whom Woodrow Wilson cannot receive into fellowship, I cannot receive.

A Negro resident of Chicago for fourteen years, formerly of Louisiana, said:

I went to Wilson's last inauguration in Washington and tried to talk to the President. I got in the gate, but the guard would not let me go farther without a pass. I went into every place that men were allowed to enter and found no "Jim-Crowing" in any public place. The nearest approach to it was in the printing department of the government. There were several colored girls all working at the same table. In other departments I had seen white and colored together. I went into every washroom on every floor of one building and must have washed my hands twenty times.

Negroes, real Americans.—A letter from a Negro workman to Governor Lowden said:

Why is it that intelligent colored people, the real Americans and the most humble and purest nation that ever trod the soil of America since they have been here—we have never thrown any bombs; we have never written a black-hand letter and what disgrace and shameful things we do it was learned to us by our foreparents' masters down south because they taught them to steal and murder and do all other most disgraceful things. We have never bombed any white people's homes, but I cannot see into it why it is that all nations such as the Polish, Japan, Chinaman, Mexican, German and Russ and now you see what they have done to this country; they have done everything to overthrow this Government and have got the I.W.W. and the Red. Where have we done such dirty deeds? We have enriched this soil of America with our blood in every war for this country and then cannot live where we want to as an American citizen. We even shed our blood in France to save someone else money and their homes, and the thanks we got when we come back was a big race riot which I do believe was started by southern white men to put a disgrace on the North because the North do not lynch and burn as they do. Of course I know you cannot do anything by yourself. But if you can get enough men who have got a backbone to protect the ones who have always protected them this outrage could be stopped. I read a piece in the *Herald-Examiner* that it would be a riot here; that has poisoned the minds of so many people. So now I hope you will try to stop such trouble.

Defensive philosophy; silence does not mean contentment.—A Negro educator said:

Many white men of high intellectual ability and keen discernment have mistaken the Negro silence for contentment, his facial expression for satisfaction at prevailing conditions, and his songs and jovial air for happiness. But not always so. These are his methods of bearing his troubles and keeping his soul sweet under seeming wrongs. In the absence of a spokesman or means of communication with the whites over imagined grievances, he has brightened his countenance, smiled and sung to give ease to his mind. In the midst of it all he is unable to harmonize the teachings of the Bible which the white Christian placed in his hands with the practices of daily life. He finds it difficult to harmonize the fatherhood of God and the brotherhood of man, and his faith is put to the test in that "Providence" which enslaved his ancestors, corrupted his blood and placed upon him stigmas more damaging than to be a leper or convict by making his color a badge of infamy and his preordained social position at the bottom of human society. So firmly has his status been fixed by this "Providence" that neither moral worth, fidelity to trust, love of home, loyalty to country or faith in God can raise him to human recognition.

Votes for Negroes.—The *Crisis* for January, 1921, said:

The astonishing thing about the Bourbon South is its intellectual bankruptcy when it comes to the Negro. It continually assumes that the Negro is a fool. Some Negroes are fools, but the proportion among them is steadily decreasing, while that among the Bourbons seems to increase. When the average white Southerner faces the problem of racial contact he has absolutely nothing to offer except what he offered in 1861, namely: the Will of God, Force and Bloodshed, and, "The best friend in the world to the Negro is the Southern white man—the only one who truly loves him." We quote from our ever-delightful friend, the editor of the *Macon* (Ga.) *Telegraph.*

The tragedy of the situation is that this man believes what he says. He knows absolutely just the "place" for which God made "niggers"; but to support this sincere belief he spreads falsehoods. He says that the woman suffrage party by its secret machinations "probably" caused the blood shed in the Florida elections! He threatens murder for black men who want to vote, and almost weeps over the misguided Negroes who have left the Empire State of lynching and gone to Chicago.

There seems to be in this man's mind absolutely no conception of the tremendous, increasing, unswerving development of the Negro. To him all aspiration, unrest, and complaints of black folk are conspiracies of whites. For the blacks he has no program, no vision, except that they stay where they have always been, growing more content with "Jim-Crow" cars, lynching and disfranchisement.

It is inconceivable to the mentality of this section of the white South that such a program is absolutely impossible. That if, in the end, the price we must pay for aspiration to modern manhood is death, and death in the most horrible form of public torture and burning like that in Florida, if to live we must die, then the South will have us to kill. Any man who does not prefer death to slavery is not worth freedom. . . . .

The black man must vote. Every Southerner with brains knows this. The Negro is awaiting his enfranchisement with greater patience than the South has any right to expect. But he will not wait forever. If he sees gathering signs of sanity—a willingness to let the intelligent and thrifty vote, an honest effort to establish law and order and overthrow the rule of the mob, a desire to substitute honest industrial conditions in place of the organized and entrenched theft of black wealth upon which southern industry is based today—such a program, tardy and slow and inadequate though it be, may count on the infinite patience and long suffering of Ethiopia.

4. RACE CONSCIOUSNESS

Ancient Order of Ethiopian Princes:[1]

To My Kinsmen.—In a broad sense, the words "Negro" and "Nigger" have no historical significance. They are used synonymously in the white man's dictionary. "Negro" is a pure Spanish word meaning "black." The word "Negro," therefore, may be descriptive of a race, but not the name of it. In reality "Negro" is an alias, or nickname applied to us originally, in much the same contemptuous spirit as the black boy is called "Rastus" or "Sambo."

The white man writes his history for us to study, makes his scenario with his heroes and heroines for us to admire, and supplies our newspapers. Through these instrumentalities he almost entirely controls our thought.

Remember that "a word is the sign of an idea." The kind of an "idea" that the "sign" stands for depends upon our teaching. If we associate a word, then, with a noble or degraded idea, we have been taught to do so.

You can easily prove this by experimenting with certain words for yourself. After repeating each word tell what your idea is and what you see: (1) Roman, (2) Paradise, (3) Statesmen, (4) General. Is the idea or picture you get degraded? No. The White Press, history, reel and teacher have taken care of that.

Now take the following words: (1) Lynched, (2) Jim Crow, (3) Disfranchised, (4) Negro.

What is the result? The words "Lynched," "Jim Crow," "Disfranchised," are the signs of degraded ideas. Moreover, "Negro" is very apt to creep into each one of the three mind pictures and conversely one of the three into the "Negro" mind picture.

Do you understand? Now why is that? That is what Ethiopic culture teaches, through the "Ancient Order of Ethiopian Princes."

If we believe that we come from nowhere and have no history but that of a slave, our substance will be the charity of our oppressors, and our future handicapped by doubts and fears.

Ancient history knows no "Negro," but ancient history does know Ethiopia and Ethiopians. Change a family's name and in a generation you cannot tell whether

[1] Prospectus issued in 1921.

its foreparents were rogues or saints.   It is the same with a race.   You cannot trace
your ancestors through the name "Negro."

Take away our birthright, our ancient honorable name, "Ethiopian" and you
have stopped the very fountain of our inspiration.   If we are "Negroes" we are by
the same dictionary also, "Niggers."   The moment we realize, however, that we are
"Ethiopians," we can see the beams from the lamps of Ethiopian culture lighting a
pathway down the shadowy ages, and the fires of ambition are rekindled in our hearts,
because we know that we came from the builders of temples and founders of civilization.

Study this.

Contrasts of North and South.—An investigator's report on home conditions
of retarded children said:

The mother is eager to learn, and constantly talks of wanting to attend night
school if the opportunity ever offers itself.   She is eager for her girl to complete her
education and wants her to take a business course so she will be independent.   "A
white man can take everything from the colored man but his learning," Mrs. ——
said repeatedly.

In coming to Chicago she wasn't sure what she would find, but she had heard
that colored people had a show here.   She brought her child here to give her one.
Chicago seems like heaven to her now when she thinks of what she had been through
in the South.

When the investigator asked her about the church to which she belonged she
said: "Olivet. I goes every Sunday and Wednesday nights to prayer meeting just to
thank God that he let me live to go to a place of worship like that, a place where my
people worship and ain't pestered by the white men."

The Chicago riot provoked probably the first full expressions of sentiment
from Negroes in their own press.   Underlying them are attitudes toward present race relations.   There is a strong note of resentment, and the announce-
ment of the birth of a "New Negro."

The war is credited with bringing about this change.   More than 250,000
young Negroes, the pick of the race in health and intelligence, had returned
to the United States, presumably with changed ideas, and perhaps with growing cynicism as to promises of fair treatment.   Perhaps for the first time in
American history the Negro group fought in the 1919 riot as a body against
mob violence.   The idea that these disorders are a result of active opposition
to distasteful practices is prominent in practically every Negro discussion.
"The Negro race is facing about" is a familiar statement.   Said one Negro
newspaper:

It is the utter ignoring of the Negro in the community life that is responsible for
these outbreaks.   The controlling whites were absolutely out of touch with the
Negroes, and the races came together in a quarrel and there was no means by which
the trouble could be settled.

A monthly magazine, the *Favorite*, said:

If the white man thinks that the rights, privileges and ordinary pursuits of the Negro can now be annulled at this stage of the world's affairs, he certainly has "another thought coming." This Washington revolt is only the "handwriting on the wall." Don't squeeze the Negro too hard; if you do you squeeze him to the bursting point. The young Negro of today is far different from his foreparents, and will not be content with anything less than a fair deal.

The *New York American* said:

The dangerous enemy of his race is the colored man that advocates force as a remedy. There is such a thing as being outnumbered beyond any hope.

A Negro newspaper replied:

There is such a thing, too, as a noble preference of death to a life of slavery. Do Hearst and Arthur Brisbane think the sentiment of "Give me Liberty or Give me Death" belongs exclusively to a white skin?

A poem in the *Crusader* and republished in the *Messenger* and several other periodicals, carries this same idea:

IF WE MUST DIE

If we must die, let it not be like hogs
    Hunted and penned in an inglorious spot,
While around us bark the mad and hungry dogs
    Making their mock at our accursed lot.

If we must die—oh, let us nobly die,
    So that our precious blood may not be shed
In vain; then even the monsters we defy
    Shall be constrained to honor us, though dead!

Oh, kinsmen! We must meet the common foe;
    Though far outnumbered, let us still be brave,
And for their thousand blows deal one death-blow!
    What though before us lies the open grave?
Like men we'll face the murderous, cowardly pack,
    Pressed to the wall, dying, but—fighting back!

—CLAUDE McKAY

Defensive measures justified.—The general belief among Negroes is that resistance to violence is justified. Some view this display of counterviolence as simply defensive measures, some as retaliation, which in substance means the same.

The *Washington Eagle*, a Negro newspaper, commenting on the beginning of the Washington riot, said:

Notwithstanding the fact that these mobs, increasing in number and in violence each evening, were allowed to harass law-abiding colored citizens for three consecutive evenings, the colored citizens showed no signs of revenge or retaliation. But when the situation became so terrible that colored citizens could endure it no longer they rose up almost as one man, and, adhering to the first law of human nature, which says that self-preservation is the first law of nature, they armed themselves "to the teeth," to use the phrase of one of the local newspapers. It was only when they showed this disposition to fight back that the riot ceased.

The *Messenger*, a Negro magazine, said:

The world knows not that the new Negroes are determined to observe the primal law of self-preservation whenever civil laws break down; to assist the authorities to preserve order and prevent themselves and families from being murdered in cold blood. Surely, no one can easily object to this new and laudable determination.

Opinions of Negroes regarding the conduct of the police.—Negro condemnation of the police seems general. From a large selection of comments two are given. The *Favorite* said:

History proves that nearly all race riots are started by white policemen. East St. Louis, Houston and Washington, D.C., have had terrible cataclysms provoked by white bluecoats who in nine cases out of ten carry their prejudices with them whenever they enter black belts. Instead of acting in behalf of law and order white policemen usually act in behalf of some passion that tells them Negroes are convenient brutes. For the safety of the twenty-five thousand colored and ten thousand whites in the Second Ward of Chicago we ask that every white patrolman in the district be replaced by a colored bluecoat. Chicago must not be added to the list of American cities cut off from civilization by race riots, and it is up to Mayor William Hale Thompson and Chief Garrity to see that the honor of that city is preserved.

The *Washington Eagle* thought most of the trouble was due to the overbearing attitude of the police. It said:

Bishop Cottrell, wiring from Holly Springs, Miss., wants the President to call a conference of representatives of both races to consider the matter of mob law. We doubt if the President will take the trouble to do anything of the kind: while he is thinking it over the police in every place had better be instructed to have more respect for the rights and feelings of the Afro-American people. Most of the trouble is to be found in the insolent and overbearing attitude of the police.

Negro opinions regarding white newspapers.—It is asserted by numerous Negro papers that certain white papers spurred the rioters to greater lawlessness in the Washington outbreak, and in some cases settled the date and place of assembly for attacking parties. The *Afro-American* quoted from the *Washington Post* an excerpt headed "Mobilizing for Tonight," and reading:

It was learned that a mobilization of every available service man stationed in or near Washington or on leave here has been ordered for tomorrow evening near the Knights of Columbus hut on Pennsylvania Avenue, between Seventh and Eighth streets. The hour of assembly is 9 o'clock and the purpose is a "cleanup" that will cause the events of the last two evenings to pale into insignificance. Whether official cognizance of this assemblage and its intent will bring about its forestalling cannot be old.

The *Afro-American* added:

Commenting on this article Secretary Shillady of the National Association declares: "In view of the fact that the 'mobilization' announced by the *Washington Post* had not been ordered by any authority, military or civil, does not the passage show intent by the *Washington Post* to bring about such mobilization?"

Another Negro paper in Washington carried the criticism farther:

Editorials are supposed to concern those topics that are most important to the community in which they are written. No one can deny the importance of the race riots that disgraced the name of fair America's Capital during the present week; yet two of the leading daily papers of the city found everything to fill their editorial columns but the proper attempts to discourage mob violence and a disposition to place the blame where it justly belongs. The rioting, in itself, was a deplorable disgrace, but a greater disgrace is that the daily newspapers should have encouraged the rioting by the glaring, ugly headlines that they gave it, rather than discourage the riots in editorials.

The *National Defender and Sun* replied to an editorial of the *Chicago Tribune:*

In a recent edition of the *Chicago Daily Tribune*, which calls itself the world's greatest newspaper, in discussing the recent race riot in Chicago, it had this to say: "Can the two races continue to live in peace in Chicago without segregation? We have for some time criticized the South for its treatment of its black citizens. We believe since the race riot in Chicago that segregation, separate cars, will be the only cure to prevent race riots in the future." We are very much surprised at the statement of the *Chicago Tribune*. Does the world's greatest newspaper forget that Atlanta, Ga., Memphis, Tenn., Arkansas and Texas, had great race riots, and that all of the above-named states have their Jim Crow laws and segregated district?

The *New York Age* had this to say:

So much clamor and bad blood have been aroused by the repeated charge of assaults attempted upon women in the city of Washington, that more than ordinary significance attaches to a news item found tucked away in an inconspicuous position on an inside page of the *Washington Times*. It was headed: "Woman Now Denies She Was Attacked," and read as follows: "The case of an alleged attack on Mrs. Minnie Franklin, 1361 K. Street Southeast, by two Negroes near Fifteenth and H. Sts., Northeast, Thursday night, was closed last night when according to detectives, the woman said the story was a fabrication. Several headquarters detectives questioned the woman yesterday and then went over the ground where the alleged attack was supposed to have occurred, but could find no evidence of a struggle."

This reported case of "assault" had "scare" headlines at the time it was supposed to have occurred, and it looked as if the daily papers were trying to provoke another riot. Later, by the admission of the accuser, the police and the press, the charge was shown to be groundless. Time and again these charges of assaults have been shown to be "faked," and the most credulous should be brought to see the necessity of searching investigation before pronouncing the accused guilty. Hysteria, by newspaper suggestion, may be at the foundation of many a case of reported "assault."

Charges of southern propaganda in the North.—A wide distinction has been made by Negro observers between the Washington and Chicago riots, the former being called a typical southern, and the latter a typical northern, riot. Reasons for this are given in the different forms of incentive to rioting. The Washington reasons were largely sentimental and bore a striking resemblance to the Atlanta riot about 1906. Reports of attacks on white women, played up in the newspapers, were sufficient to set the current going. The sentiment of the South is said to have been behind this outbreak. Said the *Chicago Defender:*

It is easy to see that the southern white man is at the bottom of race riots in the northern cities to which we have migrated in recent years. . . . . It is idle to suppose that the black man was the only migrator from the South; every northern community is practically overrun with southern whites of both sexes. In many of the northern cities a majority of the white women employed as clerks and saleswomen in department stores, telephone operators and other fields of industry are from the South. In every place where men are utilized, including public officials, judges and prosecuting attorneys, some of them are also from the South.

Remedies.—The *Chicago Defender* said:

To emphasize the fact that no self-respecting citizen had anything to do with the disgraceful affairs recently witnessed here and in Washington, thousands of circulars have been distributed by our people and to our people filled with good, wholesome advice as to being good, law-abiding citizens. Our only salvation lies in harmony, and both elements must come to understand that each is necessary to the other, and that with all pulling together, democracy for America will no longer be a theory, but a reality.

The foregoing examples of sentiment by no means cover the varieties of Negro opinion. They are merely illustrative of different types. The peculiarities of group behavior which appear to be the attributes of the Negro group would doubtless show themselves in any other groups similarly placed in the social scale. There would at the same time be no more likelihood of their being understood. Situations develop which appear to the uninitiated white observer strange and even dangerous. That they do represent very definite and calculated programs of action within certain circles of the Negro group may be illustrated by a few examples.

At a garment manufacturer's plant thirty colored girls were employed in a separate unit. When a white girl was employed, the colored girls walked out. They explained that when they first began work in a plant employing white girls a precedent for this action was given. If white girls were too proud to work with colored girls, then colored girls should be too proud to work with white girls. It required much effort on the part of the Urban League to correct their viewpoints.

A short time ago there was considerable agitation among certain groups of Negroes over the appointment of a Negro principal for one of the elementary schools. His appointment was strongly opposed by Negroes. Although this may have seemed inexplicable to white people, the action was not wholly illogical from the viewpoint of Negroes. The school in question, near the Negro residential area, had an attendance of about 70 per cent Negro children. Negroes reasoned thus: If a Negro principal were appointed the white teachers would eventually resign or for one reason or another be transferred; the white parents then would withdraw their children because there would be no white teachers, and so the first step would be accomplished toward segregation of Negroes in the public schools. It was segregation that was opposed, although the advancement of one of their number must be sacrificed.

Marcus Garvey, a West Indian Negro, with a remarkable genius for organization, four years ago began a venture on a commercial basis and developed it into a definite racial movement. He conceived the notion of establishing trade relations with Africa, and accordingly organized a steamship line. It was a large undertaking. There were few large Negro investors, and if money was to be raised it had to come in numerous small amounts rather than in a few large ones. Again, if commercial relations were to be established, there must be intelligent Negroes at the African end. The effort grew into another "Back to Africa" movement. To increase interest it was necessary to campaign actively, using appeals calculated to arouse the great mass of Negroes. This Garvey did with such success that his "Back to Africa" slogans created a far larger movement than his original commercial proposition. The Universal Negro Improvement Association attracted more interest and members. The *Negro World*, a newspaper with a constant and powerful appeal to racial pride, racial solidarity, and racial independence, is the organ of the movement. During the summer of 1920 a great convention was held. A provisional president of the Black Republic was elected, and was acclaimed the recognized leader of the black people of the world. The women were organized into "Black Cross" nurses and it was planned to establish a "Black House" in Washington. The movement has been widened to include the black peoples of the British colonies and Africa. An alliance of sympathy has been declared with peoples similarly disadvantaged. Thus Ireland's contention for home rule is supported, in spite of the supposed general hostility between the Negroes and the Irish in the United States. The movement is credited with 4,000,000 followers in different parts of the world.

VI. OPINIONS OF FIFTEEN NEGROES ON DEFINITE RACIAL PROBLEMS

What are Negroes thinking? Few white persons know the intimate reactions of Negroes to problems which they face daily. Yet it is obvious that the conduct of Negroes in practically every phase of life is determined by these very sentiments, which for the white world remain a closed book.

It was with this in mind that a series of questions was put to seventeen Negroes whose intelligence and public-mindedness qualified them for critical self-analysis as well as dispassionate examination of racial issues as they affect the minds, behavior, and policies of Negroes as a group. Ten of these Negroes lived in Chicago and represented an ordinary type of the intelligent Negro. Five of them lived outside of Chicago. Included in this latter number were two Negroes whose writings have been widely read and who may be said to exercise some influence over the thinking of Negroes.

The fifteen whose replies are presented here included business men, physicians, ministers, school teachers, lawyers, and social workers. Two were women.

ARE RACE RELATIONS IMPROVING?

Question: Putting aside for the moment the question of right and wrong and the iniquity of the causes back of present relations, do you believe that the relations are becoming better or worse, or are they at a standstill?

Answers:

1. Better, decidedly better. If it becomes unprofitable to lynch Negroes, or unprofitable to shoot them up in riots, they will probably more and more be let alone. The riots in Chicago and Washington mean that not only Negroes will lose their lives. They also indicate to me that the Negro feels that his back is more and more to the wall, and he is bestirring himself. So long as he is satisfied, his case is hopeless. When he begins to force respect he will usher in the dawn of a new day. Again there is an increasing number of evidences that white people are waking up to the conditions. Negroes feel that some of the "Study Groups" are ineffective, but the fact remains that at one time the race question was not deemed worthy of study except by Negroes. When all is said, I would rather be living in 1920 than in 1870.

2. The relations are becoming worse. Relatively speaking, race relations in America have not kept pace with progress in many fields along other lines. The great desideratum is that the Negro change his point of view.

3. The present relations between the races seem more tense than formerly. This is due to the fact that Negroes have developed within the past few years a greater race consciousness, a great race respect. The immigration from the South which permitted him to enter into the industrial life of the North with very few hindrances, to partake of its civic life without an ever-constant reminder of race, was one of the main factors in increasing race consciousness and race respect. Another factor was the treatment as equals and fellow human beings of the Negro soldiers by the French soldiery and people. These things have caused the Negro to demand the respect which he is entitled to as a man and the privileges due him as a citizen. The whites at the present time still object to giving him these. This causes friction. I believe, however, that it will be lessened as soon as the whites realize that these demands

of the Negro will not be withdrawn but will continue to be made with greater insistence.

4. Better.

5. Much was gained through the war. However, at the present time things seem to be at a standstill.

6. Racial relations between all races were never more acute nor more keenly felt and resented than during the present day.

7. Conditions, I believe, are getting a little better.

8. I don't believe that consideration of right and wrong influences fundamental reactions. One's conception of advantage and disadvantage determines the character of every act. I believe that all social relations are in a state of flux and that with the improvement of mankind which is coming with the evolution of a sense of higher values there will be an improvement in human relationships.

9. Race relations on the whole are growing worse instead of better, and they are crystallizing in the wrong direction. The whites are adjusting their conscience to their conduct, and are consciously or unconsciously justifying violation of the Ten Commandments, the Golden Rule, the Sermon on the Mount, the Declaration of Independence and the Constitution of the United States at the behest of race prejudice.

10. They are becoming distinctly worse as each year solidifies the hatred and crystallizes the opinions of the whites which immediately subsequent to the Civil War were in a chaotic state.

11. The last year or so has shown that riots are more quickly started. In our opinion race relations are likely to get much worse, especially if the present flood of European immigration continues. But getting worse to become better is much like a boil which, after it gathers and breaks, leaves the body in a healthier condition. Negroes are becoming more and more determined to enjoy their constitutional rights.

12. I am in doubt.

13. I am an optimist. I believe relations are becoming better.

OPINIONS ON SOLUTION

Question: Do you believe that money and the acquisition of wealth make an appreciable difference in the degree of respect in which Negroes are held by their white neighbors, or in the treatment they receive?

Economic Progress*	1866	1919	Gain in Fifty-three Years
Homes owned....................	12,000	600,000	588,000
Farms operated..................	20,000	1,000,000	980,000
Businesses conducted.............	2,100	50,000	47,900
Value of church property..........	$1,500,000	$85,900,000	$84,400,000
Wealth accumulated..............	$20,000,000	$1,100,000,000	$1,080,000,000

* "Statistical Statement of Negro Progress in Fifty-three Years," from *Negro Year Book*, 1918-19.

Answers:

1. Yes, money and wealth are the root of all good and evil.   In North Carolina, a rich Negro, McCary, who, it was alleged, had been caught in intimate relations with a leading white woman, was sued for money damages instead of being lynched.   Money and wealth must be widely diffused enough to make an appreciable difference, however; isolated cases of wealth ordinarily engender friction and hatred.

2. No, because I personally know many who are highly respected and kindly treated in their communities though in very humble circumstances.

3. I believe that money or wealth causes more respect to be accorded within white people's hearts, but it is more likely to increase racial feeling than to lessen it.   The element of jealousy among poorer whites probably gives rise to such statements as keeping the Negro in his place.   The whites of better circumstances merely use these existing feelings to gain their own selfish ends.

4. Yes, and no.   Money is power.   The power over a man's subsistence is the power over his will.   The individual who has money is sought because he is in a position to confer advantages.   He is likewise hated because he can inflict pain.   Were race prejudice logical and based upon reason and not hysteria, the procurement of money and the consequent demonstration of basic equality would improve conditions.   However, the majority of persons do not think but are exploited.   Religious dogmas and racial antipathies being useful adjuncts in the process are sufficient to outweigh material or rational considerations.

5. Absolutely.

6. The possession of money causes whites to accord the Negro more respect and better treatment if the particular Negro can intelligently handle his affluent situation so as to demand such.

7. I think that money and the acquisition of wealth make an appreciable difference in the degree of respect in which Negroes are held by their white neighbors; not that the prejudice against the race is reduced considerably or possibly to any extent, but because men worship dollars, and if they are possessed by Negroes, Negroes fall in for additional respect as the holders of wealth.

8. I believe that the acquisition of wealth causes marked increase in respect, provided that a fairly large group of Negroes in that community respectively are the possessors; but for merely one or two persons to acquire wealth in a community is not likely to inspire respect.   It may cause its opposite.   I assume, of course, that a fair intelligence was necessary to secure the wealth.

9. Intelligence and wealth are necessary to the self-respect of the Negro.   I doubt not that in many instances they would increase racial friction for the time being; but the time must come and is now near at hand, when the white race must recognize that the whole is greater than any of its parts.   A community like Chicago, for instance, cannot be intelligent if the Negro is ignorant; it cannot be competent if the Negro is inefficient; it cannot be virtuous if the Negro is vicious; it cannot be healthy if the Negro is diseased.   Intelligence and wealth will not of themselves solve the race problem, but the problem cannot be solved without intelligence and wealth.

10. Money and wealth do make a difference in the amount of respect accorded to individuals, as they lessen the causes for class antagonism. The white man accords esteem to those who are able to secure good clothing, decent homes, education, and indulge in what are considered luxuries. These things, too, increase the respect the Negro has for himself and make him demand respect from others. The treatment accorded him is not likely to be changed as his advancement tends to increase hatred among the whites whom he rises above, and a desire not to treat him as an equal among those whose level he reaches.

11. Money, commerce, rule the world. The average white man is happiest when he sees the Negro down. But if the Negro has money he is willing to conceal his prejudice and trade with him. Money, in the possession of no matter whom, commands fear, which is the nearest most human beings get to having respect for others. While one rich Negro in a town, in most instances, would receive pretty much the same treatment as other Negroes, yet a hundred rich Negroes in that same town would certainly make a big difference. Apply this ratio to the nation. A rich Negro, even in Georgia or Mississippi, certainly has a far pleasanter lot than a poor white.

12. Yes.

13. Yes, it does for white people. To quote a friend, "It is easy for anybody to be respectful and courteous to a million dollars." This is especially true of Americans.

Question: Do you believe that if Negroes were 100 per cent literate it would make any great difference in race relations? Are general and higher education likely to widen the breach between Negroes and white persons, increase intolerance, resentment, sensitiveness to insults, or can a quieted process of adjustment or complete fusion of interests be expected?

Educational Progress*	1866	1919	Gain in Fifty-three Years
Per cent literate	10	80	70
Colleges and normal schools	15	500	485
Students in public schools	100,000	1,800,000	1,700,000
Teachers in all schools	600	38,000	37,400
Property for higher education	$60,000	$22,000,000	$21,940,000
Annual expenditures for education	$700,000	$15,000,000	$14,300,000
Raised by Negroes	$80,000	$1,700,000	$1,620,000

* "Statistical Statement of Negro Progress in Fifty-three Years," from *Negro Year Book*, 1918–19.

Answers:

1. Education will help decidedly, especially that kind of education which gives Negroes a command of some special accomplishment in any field of endeavor. Higher education will not in my opinion widen the breach if Negroes will consciously and deliberately set out to educate white people as to their ideals, ability and character, and at the same time labor to increase the spirit of self-help and self-confidence among their own group which will serve to decrease ignorance and irresponsibility among the less fortunate and untrained members of the race.

2. I conceive that literacy in itself is a cure for nothing except illiteracy. One-hundred-per-cent literate Negroes without proper use of their literacy may even make matters worse.   General and higher education may be expected to make matters better only if there is general and higher education among whites and the education on both sides is of the right kind.   In America, at present, education, where it touches race lines, appears to be more propaganda than education.   It is reported that some histories of reconstruction taught to Negroes by the state in parts of the United States emphasize and detail their shortcomings and omit their virtues.   Obviously such education is education for mistrust, unrest, conflict.   It educates the races apart, and its logical consequence is conflict.   I am ready to answer, then, that general and higher education which emphasizes likeness and passes over without undue attention unlikeness, education which aims to have men live in harmony and co-operation and does not aim to array classes against classes and races against races by omissions and emphasis, may be expected to better our race relations in the United States provided it finds lodgment in the school systems of both races.

3. If 10,000,000 literate Negroes were environed with 100,000,000 white men, the majority of whom were below their cultural level, the dominant minds among the whites would arouse ethnic antagonisms as an economic weapon to be used in promoting their selfish ends.   I believe that there is not a single force, ethical, religious, or of any type, sufficiently powerful to cause an individual to forego what he believes to be his highest advantage, and the appeal to group instincts is the easiest method of securing mass action.

4. If Negroes were 100 per cent literate they would certainly be more sensitive to insults and more resentful.   I should expect a great increase in racial differences, unless those Negroes imbibed a tendency to non-resistance· That, however, is far from likely.   With universal literacy, a larger acquaintance with current events and conditions, Negroes could immeasurably improve their living conditions, but their contacts with the whites would be far more unpleasant.

5. One hundred per cent literacy among Negroes would make a huge difference.   In the long run it would lessen the breach between Negroes and white persons, for Negroes would strive for equality.   The most essential thing is to produce a change in the mental equipment of the Negro.   The white man's mind will take care of itself.   What is needed is a more balanced and equal meeting of the minds.   But there would be bloodshed at the beginning.

6. Resentment and sensitiveness to insults will increase on the part of Negroes as they grow in intelligence, but as their spirits rebel more insistently and positively against insults, it cannot help but have its effect upon white men who ignorantly mistreat them, and if the respect growing out of love does not follow, the respect growing out of tolerance, as in the case of the Jews in America, will ensue and result in recognition of equal intelligence and culture.

7. Literacy must be 100 per cent on both sides to bring about a "complete fusion of interests" or a "quieted process of adjustment."   Intelligent Negroes among uneducated whites would aggravate the situation.

8. If Negroes were 100 per cent literate they would command more respect, because men always command more respect when they are intelligent.

9. I believe in education first, last, and always as a leveller and as a bulwark of defense. There is no race prejudice among broadly cultured people. Art knows no such distinctions.

10. (a) Yes. (b) Not, if at the same time the education of the whites is broadened and made more general. (c) Better education of both races will facilitate a fusion of interests, beginning probably in economic relations.

11. It would make them much more bitter, for (a) the Negro would be more sensitive to injustice and have more of the combative spirit which literacy usually gives, and (b) whites would be more jealous and anxious to show the Negro his place. I believe that such an intensification of the struggle is desirable and necessary, as I don't believe that the brilliant ideas necessary for solution of the race problem can come other than as the children of the most intense and bitter racial conflict. Of course it would defeat its purpose if such a conflict were bloody, as then we would have a long period of the nauseating burden such as America suffers with today, viz.: the North attempting to reconcile the South.

12. Literacy will make a difference also in race relations. The difference will increase in degree as literacy advances beyond the mere ability to read and write to a wider participation in every field of educational or intellectual endeavor. As far as I have been able to observe, the breach between whites and Negroes is widened as Negroes advance in education and culture. The educated Negro rarely comes in contact with the white man as a menial or laborer—the only point of contact which the great majority of white people want. He will respect the Negro teacher, lawyer, doctor, or business man who knows his work thoroughly and can do as well as he. He is not likely, however, to find any reason to co-operate with this class of Negroes, and the Negroes do seek such co-operation.

13. (a) Yes. (b) In slavery times whites made it a crime to teach Negroes to read. That desire, in up-to-date garb, remains in the breast of most whites today. To many white persons a Negro of superior talent and refinement is a more detestable production than the most pronounced rogue. Most white persons, even of the best quality, are secretly displeased at a Negro of this type. They were brought up to regard Negroes as being below them, and the sight is a blow to their vanity. (c) A dollar talks much more sweetly than Emerson or Shakespeare and even Christ to most men, therefore a process of adjustment or complete fusion of interests will be effected chiefly through trade relationship, not esthetics.

Question: If unrestricted suffrage were given Negroes throughout the United States, would matters be helped?

Answers:
1. Equal suffrage between the races in some parts of the country would doubtless precipitate a temporary disturbance, but it is not thinkable that under democratic institutions any group or class can be permanently or for a long while refused equal participation in the government under which they live and by which they are controlled. Shall we do evil that good may come?

2. Every appreciable increase in power among Negroes will be met with jealousy and repression by the whites. Unrestricted suffrage does not mean much when people have guns at the polls and dare other people to vote. Its

inception would mean acute racial trouble, I think, but if the Negroes used the same means and methods to register their vote as the whites do to keep them from registering it, and kept it up long enough, ultimately conditions would be very much improved where Negroes constitute about half the population of a unit.

3. Yes. Even though Negroes might not vote intelligently at the outset, they would tend to vote for their own welfare. The Negro does not feel wholeheartedly that he is a part of the American people. But with the vote he would be in a better position to work for common ends. Though voting for the capitalist parties would not mean much to the Negro, a vote for the money barons is better than no vote at all.

4. Unrestricted suffrage is a right as well as a privilege. It is essential for building up the sense of responsibility and loyalty among any group of people in a democracy founded on the ideals of the Declaration of Independence and the Constitution.

5. Yes, the ballot is a protection which the Negro now is intelligent enough to use and keep. In the present segregated condition of the Negro, the ballot has a genuine property value. Police protection, better lighted and better paved streets, I am convinced, must come to him through the ballot or else he does not get them.

6. Unrestricted Negro suffrage would help a great deal in securing for Negroes the things it is possible to secure through the use of the ballot. Political parties, as well as the Negro himself, would realize the power of Negro suffrage and would doubtless be inclined to cater to that vote. The exercise of such unlimited suffrage is likely to increase for a time the tenseness in race relations, as the whites would not readily give up the domination they have secured. The agitation in Ohio and in the Middle West over the exercise by the Negro of his suffrage shows how clearly the white man fears the power of the ballot when used by the Negro.

7. Other things remaining the same, it would not.

8. Not necessarily by that fact alone. The ultimate value of the right of suffrage is conditioned by the intelligence with which that right is used.

9. This goes without saying. In Chicago, Negroes exercise considerable influence in the city administration, because of their strong political power. The same is true of New York and Cleveland. Apply this to the nation.

10. Yes.

11. Yes, if we had a third party with racial cohesion.

12. Suffrage to be effective must be taken and not conferred. "Who would be free, himself must strike the blow." A man has no right that he can't protect and defend.

Question: How about religion as a solvent of racial difficulties and differences?

Religious Progress*	1866	1919	Gain in Fifty-three Years
Number of churches	700	43,000	42,300
Number of communicants	600,000	4,800,000	4,200,000
Number of Sunday schools	1,000	46,000	45,000
Sunday-school pupils	50,000	2,250,000	2,200,000

* "Statistical Statement of Negro Progress in Fifty-three Years," from *Negro Year Book,* 1918–19.

Answers:

1. Religion, if it ever becomes a vital force in the everyday affairs of people, will be one of the greatest forces in solving race difficulties. At the present time its influence is practically nil. The average church is still calling worn-out theology religion; those which have adopted a more modern and practical view of religion are too few to exert any influence in race problems.

2. Religion per se, to my mind, has failed, but Christianity, the spirit manifested by Jesus Christ in his life and which he commanded his followers to imitate, if adopted in its vital truth and simplicity by all professing Christians, could solve all the difficulties.

3. Religion might be helpful in solving racial difficulties if it were tried—but it has not been very largely tried yet.

4. Religion as a solvent of racial difficulties is necessary, but both groups will need to practice it to the same degree.

5. The religion of America, or of any other country, is merely an index to the national character. Religion expresses itself in the church, and the church is a capitalistic institution. Expressed religion in America, because its pecuniary existence largely depends upon the rank and file of the people who support it, will not rise above the prejudices and folkways of that rank and file. Religion will not solve many racial difficulties or differences.

6. Religion hardly touches the deeper motivations. It may regulate details, but usually the priest-craft succeeds by sophistry, emphasis or omission in avoiding certain fundamental issues in their religious exhortations. It often appears that the preacher is retained to idealize the crassness of the world, and unpleasant things are simply taboo. He must look to his salary.

7. It has no utility. It had no utility in the world war and so a fortiori could have no utility in our race problem where more bitter issues are involved.

8. Unfortunately religion has little sanction over the social conduct where interest and passions are involved. This was too sadly manifested in the world war. It is to be hoped, however, that there may arise a moral and spiritual renaissance under whose sanction religion may exercise controlling influence over the frictional relations among men.

9. Very much overestimated is religion as a solvent of racial differences. Neither Negroes nor whites have enough confidence in it to put it into practical application. No one thing will bring about the Negro's real emancipation. The fight must be carried on in every sphere where prejudice has vitiated relations.

10. Religion has failed to solve the racial difficulties and differences in America because its principles have never been practiced by the people. Religion has remained a beautiful theory. If the religious principles were practiced there would be no racial difficulties.

11. Utterly valueless. The average individual cannot think. He lives only in the concrete. Material advantages outweigh philosophical benefits. Deprive religion of the moving force of fear which its exponents engender, and it will entirely cease to be dynamic.

12. The religion of Christ will prove a solvent if men ever give it a trial.

13. Religion, in our opinion, has never settled any question. Nothing else contains so much the germs of strife. Mankind, throughout the ages, has never been able to agree on it. The history of Europe, Asia and Northern Africa is one long record of warring religions.

SOCIAL ADJUSTMENTS

Question: What are some of the most pronounced mental complexes experienced in adjusting your personal desires and expectations to the present social system ?

Answers:

1. A constant haunting feeling when in the presence of white persons that they desire to shun me because of my color; that they are eager to use me to further their ends under the guise of piety or patronizing the "good-feeling-toward-your-people" attitude. I suffer from time to time an acute embarrassment because of uncouth conduct in the presence of white persons on the part of uncultured Negroes. Such conduct embarrasses me generally, but the presence of white persons who are supposed to be inimical seems to be the dominant element in the situation.

2. The most pronounced mental complex which I experience in adjusting my desires and expectations to the present social system is not the "inferiority complex" with which most Negroes are.charged by the whites. I desire all that the social system affords; but as to expectation it is necessary for me to use auto-hypnotism to make myself expect it in order that I can present to the white man the front of optimism, the necessary air of expectancy to secure success. The shocks and disappointments which a Negro must constantly experience tend to get him in the attitude of expecting nothing.

3. I can't describe the mental complexes, but some are caused by situations such as these: I go to the library to get a book, and I am told that I must sit in a seat among dusty shelves of newspaper files at a table marked "For colored people"; in order to see a play I have to sit in the gallery. I submit to that and when I get to the theater, I am told that no seats are reserved for colored people. I go to a lecture by the Hon. Mr. So and So (white) and he discusses the Declaration of Independence and the Constitution, creating much enthusiasm among the unthinking and some of the thinking. Then the next morning I take up the paper of which the same gentleman is the editor, and read a sneering editorial on the race question, and so on.

4. Personally, I am able to impersonalize my relation to the situation, and experience no mental perplexities. I try to preserve a rational attitude in an irrational environment and objectify cruelty, injustice and wrong. I know that I as an individual am not Jim Crowed, or disfranchised or socially isolated; it is the race to which I belong. My only perplexity is how to remove these racial, not personal, disqualifications.

5. Determination to fulfill my personal desires in spite of the present social system; a loss of respect for the white man's sense of justice.

6. The arrogance of the poor ignorant white man and the snobbishness of the middle class. This is the stumbling-block for the future of our race to overcome.

7. Trying to get white persons, as employers, etc., to accept me as a man first of all, then to judge me on my merits, irrespective of my color. Trying to attain to the same degree of success and liberty of any other man of my training and experience in spite of the world in which I live.

8. Amused and almost cynical tolerance. A desire to reap the greatest possible advantages from the system, without permitting my intelligence to admit that it is right because it is personally advantageous.

9. My desires are never adjusted to the present "social system"; they are constantly out of harmony with the practices of our so-called democracy, as these practices relate to the Negro.

10. If this question means what I think it does, space will not permit an intelligent answer.

11. A hyper-sensitiveness in regard to the subject Negro; a tendency to see racial antagonism as a motive of conduct in every act of white persons when perhaps it is sometimes absent; a hesitancy about entering public places or approaching individuals for fear of rebuff or insult; a withdrawal into a Negro world in which almost every thought and act are colored by a racial aspect before a humanitarian one, are some of the mental complexes experienced in a greater or less degree by almost every colored person.

Question: Do you believe that Negroes are prejudiced against white persons?
Answers:

1. Some are, but the prejudice is due to nurture rather than to nature.

2. Prejudice means pre-judgment. Negroes come into the world to find most white persons disliking them. They grow up in an atmosphere where they find whites ready to insult them because of the color Nature saw fit to give them. Therefore, knowledge, not prejudice, causes Negroes to dislike whites. Human beings, and even dumb animals, love only those who love them. The average Negro is, however, quick to drop this defensive attitude when he meets a fair-minded white person. Perhaps too easily, as he is often taken advantage of by shrewd whites disguised as friends.

3. I do not believe that Negroes are inherently prejudiced against the white race. Personally, I have absolutely no such prejudice. I do not believe that the white race is inherently prejudiced against the Negro, but that it is wholly a feeling stimulated by social opinion which can be modified and controlled. I put in evidence the facts: First, when social pressure is removed, white women marry Negro men, and white men marry Negro women. Second, the superior always shows prejudice against the inferior, whether superiority is claimed on basis of wealth, culture, birth, or position. The prejudices of inferior against superior is never so pronounced as that of superior against inferior. Natural antipathy is mutually reciprocal. Third, some white persons are less influenced by it than others. Fourth, race antagonism as such is scarcely discernible where Latin civilization and the Catholic religion are in control. Fifth, it does not exist in the Mohammedan dispensation. Sixth, the experience of thousands of Negro soldiers in France proves its comparative absence. Seventh, race prejudice seems to be principally the vice of the Teuton and the Anglo-Saxon, which must be subject to ultimate control. It will not be quite so strong among Germans as it was before the war.

4. I do not believe that Negroes as a race are prejudiced against white people, although I am conscious of an increasing prejudice against white people on the part of many individual Negroes, especially educated colored women who live in the South and resent keenly the indiscriminate approaches of white men.

5. Many Negroes are cynical of all the professions of white men. They often express their hatred of white people openly. I think, however, that feeling is more prevalent among the younger Negroes than among the older ones.

6. Many pretend to be. Most of them are not.

7. Yes, 98 per cent of them are.

8. Not as individuals. They are affected by the spirit of mass hostility to dissimilar masses based upon the desire to appropriate and retain advantages. Racial prejudices are the products of the will of dominant individuals evoking responses from weaker intelligences and serving the purpose of the dominating mind.

9. If so, to a very slight extent. What feeling most Negroes have is created almost solely to offset the prejudice and antagonism of the whites. The prejudice of the whites I might describe as primary; that of the colored, secondary.

10. Yes; too much so among some groups.

11. Negroes in most cases are very much prejudiced against whites.

12. Yes. The difference lies in the degree. Prejudice is artificial. It is learned. The white boy and girl have been "taught" more prejudice than the Negro. Negroes seldom teach prejudice outright. When they learn it, it is inescapable. America is a school, I fear, at present where even the most backward learns something of prejudice whether he will it or not.

13. I believe there is a strong prejudice against white persons. This antipathy is, I believe, not based on racial unlikeness, but on resentment because of cruel treatment as an inferior.

Question: Are you ever conscious of a feeling of racial inferiority or even the desire to compensate for a supposed inferiority?

Answers:

1. I attribute inferiority and superiority alike to individuals, not race. I have every confidence that my race is capable of producing as great men, and proportionately as many of them, as any other race under the sun. I trace to environment the responsibility for not releasing their energy upon constructive work, but concentrating it upon gaining a living or a chance to gain a living. Many times I feel the desire to compensate for a supposed inferiority, because I believe in nailing a lie wherever possible.

2. I never have a feeling of racial inferiority or a desire to compensate for a supposed inferiority (with reservations). I am usually cognizant of the fact that most white people consider the Negro an inferior. This often causes the bristles to rise on my back.

3. Personally, at no moment of our lives. The Negro is really superior in stamina. His race is progressing, while the whites appear to be standing still. The white race has had seven thousand years or more of education and civilization, yet in this prosperous republic today the average white person is comparatively poor and possesses little education. The Negro, in spite of the oppressive handicap due to color, is progressing along all lines, commercial, professional and artistic.

4. I am never conscious of racial inferiority, but I am a firm believer in the theory that any human being will be whatever his environment and his heredity will make of him, regardless of the color of his skin or the form of his skull. One in considering this point of view should be sure not to confuse the words "inferiority" and "inequality."

5. No.

6. I feel no desire to apologize to the world because I am a colored woman; I had to be of some race, and here I am.
7. No. I believe that accidents of environment determine relative positions.
8. Decidedly no! I believe absolutely in my own worth as a man and as a Negro and defer only to wider experience, knowledge, or skill, whether possessed by white persons or Negroes.
9. No!
10. No.
11. I never have a feeling of racial inferiority or a desire to compensate for a supposed inferiority.
12. Personally, I am absolutely unconscious of any feeling of racial inferiority. I recognize the control of social forces and influences which may seem too strong to be overcome at present. I simply suffer it to be so now.
13. I have never felt any racial inferiority, though always when thrown in school work or business with white people the desire to do my work as well or better than they is very strong. This desire comes primarily from a desire to show that the Negro is not inferior in his ability.

NEGRO PROBLEMS

Question: Do you believe that there should be recognized leaders of Negroes? Are there such persons whom you regard as qualified for leadership? Discuss their merits and demerits.

Answers:

1. As long as the dominant power treats with us as with Negroes rather than as with American citizens, there will be need of recognized leaders; but these leaders should be chosen by the Negroes themselves, not chosen and imposed by others.
2. Yes and no. Theoretically and ultimately, no. Practically and immediately, yes. In any clearly differentiated group the spokesman should come from and grow out of conditions within the group. In a community in which there were cultural and not ethnic divisions there would be no need for Negro leaders. What was good for the hive would be for the good of each bee. However, in a community in which color is a target, defensive alliances under the best possible leadership are a *sine qua non*. I am too close to the problem to have sufficient perspective to attempt the discussion of personalities.
3. Logically, no. Practically, under present conditions it is imperative to have Negro leaders. Where people do not read much, do not study much, they are incapable of doing much thinking. Better a bad leader under such circumstances than no leader at all. The very clashes between rival leaders with their several points of view force the rank and file to attend to conditions and compare conflicting views. This often marks the beginning of interests in striving to improve conditions. The merits of leaders are considered in another place.
4. I do not think that it will be possible, or advisable, to attempt to appoint or elect leaders for Negroes. Naturally men and women of exceptional powers will be recognized by those of less developed powers as leaders of thought in various connections in their several localities.

5. There should be no recognized leaders of Negroes except those who are selected from groups or bodies of Negroes—selected by them for a particular purpose or a particular cause.   I do not believe in Negro leadership secured by members of the white race and then handed to our group as a leader without first having had the endorsement of the Negroes themselves.

6. Yes.   Emmet Scott, Dr. Du Bois and Mr. Grimke.   Mr. Scott has great executive ability.   Dr. Du Bois is a great philosopher and an ardent race rights advocate.   Mr. Grimke a scholar and wise counsellor.   This combination as Leaders' Council would, in my opinion, conserve our best interests. Mr. Scott is too much of an opportunist for an ideal leader, Dr. Du Bois is too radical at times, Mr. Grimke is too much of an intellectual recluse.

7. There should be recognized leaders of Negroes, recognized by Negroes because of their merits in their particular fields of endeavor.   There are Negroes qualified for such leadership today, but their affiliations with organizations largely or partly supported by philanthropic whites negative their usefulness.

8. I believe every community should develop its own leadership.   A great deal of our present leadership is too largely clerical and political and therefore not free, broad, and independent.   We need a leadership which is free, courageous, and which possesses a program and definite objective.

9. I do not approve self-appointed leadership or leadership bestowed by white friends because they can command funds.   If there are to be leaders, they should be chosen by selection so that there can be "solemn referendum." With this qualification, there are a large number of Negroes whom I would vote for as leaders.   The trouble now is that our so-called leaders are not responsible to those whom they are supposed to represent.

10. There should not be; as soon as one appears, destructive influences are brought to bear upon him both from within and without, making of him within a short period an extremely artificial and useless guide, but who is followed, nevertheless, by Negroes blindly to their own great injury.

11. I believe firmly in the capacity of the race for self-leadership.   Any people can govern themselves better than an outsider is apt to govern them, unless the alien is willing to become naturalized in the group he aspires to lead. The white race at present is unable or unwilling to become naturalized in the Negro group.

12. The basis of Negro leadership should rest on the ability to develop within the masses a desire and the power to obtain better homes, education and their privileges as citizens without belittling themselves or adopting the toadying attitude.   Any individual who is striving in a community to secure these things for his people should be considered a leader.   The mere ability to write a book, edit a magazine, or publicly express the cause of the Negro is not a sufficient qualification for leadership even though it does bring national prominence.

13. (a) Under the circumstances, yes.   (b) Useless to discuss this.   People usually choose as their leaders those who express most strongly prevailing sentiments.   (c) The followers are their own judges of merit and demerit.

Question: What, in your opinion, are some of the greatest mistakes of prominent Negroes in their policies or stand on racial issues?

Answers:

1. Most are honest, I think, but emphasize too much some one pet solution, such as "Get Property," "Industrial Education," etc. Many are insincere, using their influence to feather their own nests, letting the race go hang. An intolerance among Negroes themselves for those among their number who have different opinions as to the wisest courses in arriving at the better conditions which they equally are trying to bring about. Some characteristics possessed by most of the so-called leaders may be summed as follows:

    Don't bother and leave all in the hands of God.

    Overestimation of the Negroes' present attainments, eulogies instead of information.

    Oratory of denunciation only, raising prejudice against whites but offering no course of action or thought leading to improvement either of Negroes personally or individually, or as a race.

    A disinclination to tell the blunt truth when interracial conferences offer the opportunity for an exchange of views.

2. The greatest mistake that leaders usually make is that of failing to study the problems towards the solution of which they are working. They also are not willing to co-operate with leaders along other lines.

3. Selfishness and lack of moral backbone in the face of possible financial loss.

4. To accept that there is a purely racial psychology. And to think, act, or accept as a Negro and not as a man.

5. (a) Compromising attitude; (b) depending on support of white people financially and morally; (c) failure to co-operate freely with all cases among the Negroes themselves.

6. Lack of absolute frankness with white people about mind and feeling of Negroes; lack of absolute frankness with Negroes about their own shortcomings and failure. I believe that many men are overcoming this weakness.

7. Short-sightedness. They seem not to look ahead and see the consequence of their arrangements and concessions. Most of them, because of the manner of their selections, are unacquainted with history, sociology, etc. They see the present, not even the present generation. They fall into advices and concessions today which prove a noose tomorrow. There is lack of poise. Often they seem to know nothing of a means. There is no intermediate ground; it simply is or it is not. This absolutism inevitably leads to trouble. This of course does not apply to all of our leaders.

8. The greatest mistakes of prominent Negroes in their stands: A statesman is supposed to be the fusion of two necessary elements: (1) the theorist, such as we have in our college professors and most of our writers; and (2) the practical politician who can get things done. The main fault with most of our prominent Negroes in their policies and behaviour is that they never accomplish this fusion; all fall very definitely into either group one or group two, and either group by itself is helpless.

9. The greatest mistake of prominent Negroes, in my judgment, is that they pay too great a deference to the attitude of the white race rather than to the inherent demands of humanity. Jesus refused to defer to the arrogance of Pilate, although he exercised the power of life or death.

10. Faulty perspective due to improper training; failure to grasp the economic significance of race prejudice; and a tendency to preach the doctrine of non-resistance when they get rich and fat. The younger crop of Negroes, armed with modern scientific education are remedying the first two. Time will show whether they will prove more unselfish.

DEFENSIVE PHILOSOPHY

Question: If it may be assumed that there are conditions which are intolerable, or, at least, a constant source of irritation to Negroes, it is to be expected that some defensive philosophy is necessary to give poise, dignity, and self-respect. What is your philosophy? What basic philosophical considerations, even if not crystallized into dogma, support your outlook on life, or that of Negroes of your acquaintance and general point of view?

Answers:

1. I believe racial solidarity, as I conceive it, to be the defensive philosophy of many Negroes. My own philosophy, if I have one, is summed up in the belief that potentially the Negro has the same qualities making for success and usefulness as any other group. All he needs is an even break. I believe in an offensive program to teach pride in their achievements and prepare themselves for keen, hard competition all along the line. I believe in attacking the indifference and ignorance of white people which is largely the basis of prejudice, by educating them to respect and believe in the self-defending, non-favor-asking, justice-demanding Negro.

2. My philosophy rests upon two propositions. The first is borrowed from the Latin "I am a man; nothing human is foreign to me." The second is: A man is entirely the product of his environment. (Heredity is the sum of our former environments.) Given, then, an essential equality in all men, temporary advantages are the results of environment. Self-preservation and its corollary, the desire for the preservation of species, are fundamental traits, and the Israelites, killing those who said Sibboleth and not Shibboleth, have their prototype in those who make non-conformity in hair, color, speech or culture, a crime and inferiority stamp. It seems rational to suppose, however, that man may evolve sufficient mentality, and far enough away from the brute, to make differences in culture and not physical characteristics the basis of distinctions. Until then the pursuit of pleasure and advantage is the proper aim of life.

3. The Negro maintains his self-respect and dignity in the face of intolerable conditions because of his natural optimism and his hope for and belief in the approach of a better day. I teach my children that they should not seek companionship with any other children who reluctantly associate with them, not that my children should consider themselves in any way inferior or unequal, but that they should be possessed of too much personal pride to wish association with those who would not be pleasant and agreeable.

4. My philosophy is a pessimistic one. There is often a sense of hopelessness. To live in the white group makes it incumbent on me to overcome many presumptions on their part. On the other hand, to create mutual understandability is a phase of aggressive conduct I follow. To conduct one's

self in a more socially acceptable way, viz., to do a certain thing better than any member of the dominant group, is another excellent mode of enhancing social values. But the best way of all is to assume an offensive attack, and place the white group or individual on the defensive at all times. This can be accomplished only by a superior type of mind.

5. Never submit passively to unnecessary indignities. Keep alive the spirit of protest against all injustice from black or white. I am just as good or at least my right to decent treatment is as good as that of any other man. I am what I think and do, not what some other person does to me or thinks about me.

6. My experience with the segregation tendency has taught me to look down upon the system. It bristles with contradictions, being foolishly fastidious, fanatically unreasonable, and usually carried out by the uncultured element. Moreover, the promoters of the system are not ready to discuss the matter; it is simply taboo. The immoral forays of members of this super-sensitive "superior race" coupled with criminal economical advantages maintained by intimidation aside from being tragic lends a subtle hypocrisy which does not escape even the casual observer. Add to this the hysteria of the thing and you have a medley of the ludicrous hypocritical, illogical, and hysterical. Any man then who is honest and self-respecting easily comes to feel himself superior to the promoters of the institutions. One moves among these conditions with a feeling probably not unlike that of Socrates among the Athenians, although, if he chances to be a man of color, with far less freedom of conduct and speech.

7. My philosophy would be that by our conduct as a group we will be able to disprove the principles upon which the white man's intolerance is based; we should assert our rights and use propaganda to change the white man's point of view civically, morally and in the economic world.

8. I am firmly convinced that a dignified friendly attitude towards the white race is the wisest course for the Negro: education, industry, and good manners will win for us more real tolerance and consideration than continued. agitation and bitterness. Truth and justice will demand fair play in time, and sentiment must be molded by appeal to intelligence and finer sentiments through undisputable facts.

9. Cultivate a wholesome discontent with untoward conditions and use every lawful means to improve these conditions, so that it may not be said that we are satisfied with unjust discriminations. "The talent for misery is the fulcrum of progress."

SEGREGATION AND RACIAL SOLIDARITY

Question: What, to your mind, is the distinction, either in point of view or definite racial aim, between segregation and "racial solidarity"?

Answers:

1. Segregation implies coercion by the dominant group. Racial solidarity implies certain subjective tendencies of like-mindedness. Racial solidarity may be enhanced by segregation but it thrives best if its causes have their roots in the will to progress rather than the will to exist amidst oppression.

Though segregation may aid the tendency toward racial solidarity, neither segregation nor racial solidarity are to be advised in a modern civilization. Racial solidarity for protective reasons with strong limitations (never legal) may be advisable today in America.

2. The definite racial aim of segregation is to prevent the contact of races physically; to prevent Negroes from living with the whites in their neighborhoods and vice versa; to keep themselves separate as a group, thus making segregation of schools and other institutions a natural sequence. Whereas, the aim of racial solidarity is to focus the financial, economic, political and social strength of the group for the purpose of meeting the attacks of the white race as well as for the solution of group problems; for example, solid financial strength would mean Negro business houses of every description, banks, etc.; it would mean that the race as a unit would withdraw its patronage and support from any institution or business that discriminated against members of their group; they would boycott as a unit any brand of goods made by a firm dealing unjustly with colored patrons, etc. It means that politically the group would throw its strength to the party whose principles are in harmony with the welfare of the Negro.

3. Segregation presupposes a force from without which seeks to compel those of the same race or nationality or religious belief to remain among themselves, separated from those of another group supposedly superior. Grouping together either for purposes of living or of religious worship or for other purposes, with the idea of developing a group or race consciousness and thus to develop "pride of race," presupposes a force from within—that is a conscious desire of the people themselves to develop the latent powers within their own group through intensive application.

4. Negroes tend to flock together as do members of other racial groups. I do not regard this as segregation. When an effort is made from without to group them together, which carries along with it restrictions of movement, residence or activity, we have segregation. Racial solidarity seems to me to be the conscious or unconscious reaction to segregation. It is a doctrine of revolt.

5. Segregation means to me regulation of racial contacts by law or force between white and colored people. Racial solidarity is a natural development of massing because of race congeniality.

6. Segregation and racial solidarity differ fundamentally and essentially in the motive prompting the individual act to be discussed. Segregation is the forcing apart of any group into a less favorable environment in order that advantage or position may accrue to those in authority. Race solidarity represents the active part in the same rôle, and is the effort of individuals to utilize similarity of aims or of situation as the basis of an offensive or defensive alliance.

7. Racial segregation is harmful as a social aim. Racial segregation is the result of the attempt of a more powerful group to impose its ideas of racial inferiority upon a weaker group. The weaker group in its attempt to defeat this program rightly adopts racial solidarity as a definite aim in order to strengthen itself both to resist discrimination which usually follows segregation and to attack the vicious and narrow-minded motives of proponents of racial segregation.

8. Voluntary segregation is a step, consciously or unconsciously taken, toward racial solidarity.

9. It seems to me that segregation and racial solidarity differ in that the latter is merely a mental attitude whereas the former, though it includes a certain mental attitude, is chiefly characterized by a sort of hysterical physical separation. Racial solidarity obviously can exist among groups separated by considerable distance, as among Jews. When the mental attitude is not, or is felt not to be, adequate to effect the desired separation among races, then a sort of hysteria ensues and separation is one of the forms in which this hysteria expresses itself. On the whole we may have reason to doubt its efficacy, for it bears a relation to race solidarity akin to that which legal restraint bears to moral restraint.

It seems probable that both racial solidarity and segregation aim at the same thing. Segregation, it seems to me, in the long run must prove a poor means to the end, and it would not require a very imaginative person to think that in its crass forms it may destroy the very end it aims to achieve by creating a prejudice of a violent and consuming sort.

10. The term "segregation" in current discussion connotes legal compulsion, whereas "racial solidarity" implies voluntary union of the colored group under the compulsion of internal feeling or social influences.

11. Segregation, either voluntary or forced, is purely an objective situation, a setting apart in a definite location from one's fellows. Racial solidarity is subjective and is the feeling of cohesion between persons of the same race. Segregation is undoubtedly a factor in intensifying this feeling of the consciousness of kind.

12. The distinction between segregation and "racial solidarity" is in a point of view, viz.: racial solidarity concerns the interior of the Negro, his psychosis, as to its inclusion of a cohesive spirit; segregation concerns the exterior of the Negro, is looking at the situation from the viewpoint of the whites and relates to the barriers opposed by the whites to his unlimited expansion. Voluntary segregation may seem to point to the mind and viewpoint of the Negro rather than the whites, but voluntary segregation does not become a practical problem until the whites attempt to use it as a precedent, in which case it becomes after all a matter of the viewpoint of the whites.

13. It would appear that there is a very fundamental difference between segregation and racial solidarity as the terms are now used in the United States relative to the Negro. By racial solidarity it is generally understood that there is some sort of a physical separation which has been decreed by a law, as for example: the various residential segregation laws enacted some years ago and the segregation laws relative to the separation of races in public conveyances, etc. Racial solidarity, it may be said, is largely volitional, whereas segregation, as the term now is generally used, has back of it an enacted law or the idea of having an enacted law.

A still more fundamental distinction is that racial solidarity does not turn upon the receiving of benefits from privileges or things that are for all the public; segregation, on the other hand, has to do almost exclusively with the restriction of privileges relating to the free use of things that are for all the public, as for example, the free use of public conveyances, public places, the establishing of residences, etc.

14. Segregation aims to herd Negroes together in order that they may be cheated of the rights of citizenship the more easily. Racial solidarity urges Negroes to get together in order that they may fight segregation the more effectively. "National solidarity" is, to our thinking, a far better weapon. Negroes should endeavor to find out those whites who are their friends and ask them to join in the fight for the enforcement of the Constitution.

Question: A large number of Negroes are in agreement on the matter of separate colored churches with colored pastors, and, more recently, colored bishops. Yet this is an argument used by many exponents of the segregation idea, both whole and partial, for other separate institutions. Candidly, what is your opinion on the subject?

Answers:

1. Separate churches, etc., are but a part of the system of segregation inherent in the social fabric of America. This question is therefore not fundamental or basic enough. As a matter of logic and sociological analysis, since I do not favor legal or customary segregation, I cannot favor separate churches, which are but a reflex of enforced segregation. Therefore I do not favor other separate institutions. Yet, I at all times favor free assemblage and organization whatever the social system is or may be. If separate institutions are "desired" by the group and this "want" is not cramped by such considerations as factors like American public opinion, then separate institutions are in order. The test is the free and unimpaired development of the group.

2. The "colored" church is itself an anomaly. The very idea is logically ridiculous. From the practical standpoint it is the result of the un-Christian attitude of churches which preceded it and largely brought it into being. If I had to join a church now, I hope I should decide according to the doctrines and tenets rather than according to the race of the pastor and communicants. If any consideration should guide me rather than the doctrines, it would be to go where I could do the most good.

3. The idea of using the fact of the Negro's preference for his own church, governed by its own ministry, as a reason for segregation not only is absurd but is a weak reason for the manifestation of race prejudice. That Negroes prefer to be together in religious worship is a well-established fact; that they wish their church to be governed by their own ministers and bishops is equally well established; that such desire is natural and human, one must admit; but that this perfectly normal desire should become a reason for forcing upon the Negro other separate institutions is not justifiable. There is a fine distinction between the performance of one's religious rites and the activities necessary to maintain and foster these (which becomes social in character), and the business arrangements of getting an education, being conveyed somewhere, buying a meal, or paying to hear a world-famed artist. The former is part of one's private life and as such is a matter of choice and should be confined to those who are closest to him by race and spiritual conception. The latter are affairs of business wherein one wishes something and pays for it; and as

long as he has the necessary greenback, expects to be accorded the rights and courtesies given any citizen of the city or state. The French, the Italian, nearly every nationality, have their own churches, their own ministers, and worship in their own tongue. But no one ever hears anything about segregating the Frenchman or the Italian for that reason.

4. The latter plan, racial solidarity, is not at all inconsistent with the spirit of democracy even when it means the development of separate colored churches or the appointment of colored bishops for colored churches in the denominations where the color line is not so sharply drawn.

5. In my opinion, the Negroes as a whole are not in harmony and agreement on colored churches as such. It is a condition that has been pushed upon them; a means to the end. If Negroes were treated just as any other member of a white church, and given the same opportunity to advance to positions of honor within the church, ministers, priests, bishops, etc., regardless of color, there would be no Negro churches.

6. It is this universal spirit which causes Negroes to desire Negro churches and Negro bishops, because the dominant minds can more easily secure advantages when in an environment in which they conform to the majority pattern and are not parts of a clearly differentiated minority.

7. Separate colored churches in some degree are necessary in order to build up racial solidarity as described above. In other words, a strong defensive many times makes for an effective offensive.

8. Separate colored churches have never seemed to me to be necessary.

9. I am convinced that a limited race separation is not only desirable but unavoidable. There is a wide stretch of possibilities between absolute segregation and unlimited social communication. To argue that because Negroes have and want ministers and teachers of their own color, therefore they should want absolute segregation, strikes me as a bit absurd. There are at least two justifications: it may be thought that the Negro ministers and teachers understand our racial aspirations better and can better impart instructions leading to a realization of them.

10. Wherever Negroes find themselves segregated in schools and churches by choice or control, they should have teachers, preachers and overseers of their own race. Long distance leadership is neither desirable nor effective. This leadership will acquire requisite efficiency by survival of the fittest.

11. The motivation of any separate institutions should be the basis of its approval or disapproval. If Negroes of their own volition develop Negro churches, banks, clubs, stores or other organizations as a means of developing enterprise or initiative, or for providing better opportunities of work for young men and women of our race, I am in accord with such separation. If, however, such separation is forced on them especially in public places, such as hotels, restaurants, theaters and railroads, a separation which sets the Negro apart from the general public, I believe it should be condemned and fought against.

12. It is argued that if many of our leading Negroes agree upon the expediency of complete racial separation in church life, they are inconsistent in not applying it to all matters concerning the Negro. The answer to this is as follows: The highest end of the Negro is the same as that of the man of any

other race, viz.: complete self-expression and development of his individuality; in deciding upon what he shall accept or reject in any case this must be his guiding principle; between being a nonentity in the "white" church and partially expressing himself in a Negro church, he naturally chooses the latter, choosing it not as the *summun bonum*, but solely as the lesser of two evils; between having the Negro officers in the world war and having Negro officers who are trained in a separate camp, he considers the latter less injurious. But give the Negro a choice between a separate church where only partial self-expression can be possible, and a "white" church which would give him full opportunity for individual expression, and he would not hestitate a moment in choosing such a "white" church.

13. Separate colored churches, colored pastors and colored bishops represent more or less a voluntary action of colored people and are indicative of racial solidarity in just the same way as Jewish churches having Jewish rabbis represent Jewish solidarity.

14. As a slave the Negro was welcome to worship at the white church. As a citizen he is not. The white church is a semi-public institution, being more social than religious in its tone. Since Negroes are not wanted, their only recourse is to have their own churches. And if their own churches, why a white pastor or bishop, when Negro preachers quite as competent can be found?

OPINION-MAKING

Question: On what instruments ordinarily responsible for the making of public opinion do you rely for your opinions? With what reservations do you accept what you read in the white press? To what degree are you influenced by the opinions of colored persons?

Answers:

1. Of course I read daily papers, magazines and books and attend lectures and seek every possible means to learn the trend of thought and philosophy of life as it develops throughout civilization. However, whenever the Negro question is treated, I always approach with suspicion the arguments presented by white people. I always read expressions forecasting the approach of democracy with the knowledge that but few white writers and speakers think of the colored races in their utterances. The colored newspapers are much more fair than the whites, but even they, at times, are inclined to bias.

2. Magazines, colored and white papers, public speakers. I accept with great reservation what I read in the white press. I am influenced to a small degree by the opinions of the colored papers.

3. The daily papers, the *Nation*, the *New Republic*, the *Crisis*, the *Messenger*, the *Literary Digest*, the *Socialist Review*, the colored papers, and other scattered organs from here, there and everywhere. The dependence I put upon these white papers is hard to state in words. If in a white paper I see something favorable to the Negro on a question of fact, I take it at face value. On questions of opinion, I draw my own conclusions from my own study and experience, wherever possible. Likewise in a colored paper I

take at face value on a question of fact anything favorable to the white view. Otherwise I draw my own conclusions.

4. (a) Daily papers, lectures and magazines. (b) Always with reservations on any subject, especially on race records. (c) Not very much outside of a few good magazines.

5. Every article in white or Negro press is read with the idea that the bias of the writer must be discounted and that the conclusions cannot be accepted, but that one's conclusions must be made from the aggregate of the facts gleaned from every available source bearing upon the subject under discussion.

Leading New York newspapers: *Herald, Times, World, Tribune, Call.*

Leading American monthlies: *World's Work, American, Metropolitan.*

Leading American weeklies: *Nation, New Republic, Freeman.*

Leading American quarterlies: *Yale Review, American Journal of Sociology, Non-Partisan Review.*

Leading New York Negro weeklies: *New York Age, Negro World.*

Leading Negro monthlies: *Messenger* and *Crisis.*

I read all these papers with great reservations as to their truth and good judgment.

6. Newspapers, magazines, legislative action, personal contacts. The white press will always justify suspicion and the traditional grain of salt with reference to its news concerning Negroes. White news reporters know too few actual facts about Negroes and are too hemmed about by traditional prejudices to be reliable news gatherers in this field. Colored newspapers are, in my opinion, becoming increasingly more reliable in their expression of the thoughts and mind of Negroes, although many times they suffer from the same disease with reference to white people which besets white reporters.

7. History and observation. I habitually question unfavorable comment, because the prejudice and the training of the writers must be considered. Colored papers, unless paid to do otherwise, are more likely to exaggerate reports favorable to the Negro. Therefore some reservations must be made on account of the prejudice and the lack of training of many of the writers.

8. I believe that the information I get from the instruments ordinarily responsible for public opinion influences my opinion but little at any particular moment. I seem to have a theory of present-day tendencies in American institutions with reference to the Negro, and I accept items from these instruments merely as confirmations or negations of my opinions. Usually the negations are so few and far between that I can look upon them as sports or the "exception that proves the rule." Perhaps the *Crisis* figures most prominently in forming my opinion. At least when my opinion is formed, I am unable to account for it by any small number of books, or other publications. I read regularly the *New York Age*, the *Negro World*, and from time to time many other Negro newspapers; I read the *Crisis*, the *Messenger*, the *Century*, *Review of Reviews*, *World's Work*, *Outlook*, *Independent*, and various scientific articles bearing on

the Negro and such reviews of an even larger number of articles as appear in the *Psychological Bulletin* and similar publications from time to time.

Nearly always when I read, the white press items concerning the Negro are looked upon as carefully selected and shaped for propaganda. By a careful and studied system of emphasis and omission such items can be made to prove most any point. There are exceptions, such as the *Independent* editorials, etc. Colored newspapers influence my opinion little directly. The items of real news are accepted at face value, there being no appeal, and these are referred to a more or less stable theory of the situation. The theory changes so gradually that I am unable to tell what items exert the greatest influence.

9. I read the dailies and the *Crisis*, *Messenger* and *Amsterdam News*. I accept what all of them say with great reservation, though I naturally give more credence to report of Negro topics in Negro papers than in white papers.

10. I regret to say that the Christian church and the religious press, which should be the chief reliance in shaping public opinion in the moral direction, are all but negligible factors. More race prejudice will be shown in Chicago in the churches on next Sunday morning than in the schools on the following Monday. Religion failing, the chief reliance for the present must be upon the secular agencies such as science, politics, trade, business and the public press and platform. The Negro himself must shape and direct righteous public opinion. Moral reform comes through the public, who feel the need of it. The Negro press is greatly hampered by restrictive and controlling influences, but on the whole it is, perhaps, the most righteous voice in America now crying in the wilderness.

11. I rely on books, magazines and newspapers for facts on which to base opinions. With the exception of a few weeklies, and a few radical newspapers and magazines, I believe the white press is hostile towards the Negro. Whatever I read concerning him, in the daily papers especially, I take with a grain of salt. In matters of race problems the Negro papers usually present the facts of the case fairly. I am inclined to accept their views about such matters. Their opinions about other phases of life, in which race is not predominant concern, I take also with a grain of salt or not at all.

12. Personally we rely on facts, not opinions. Hardly anything in the white press regarding Negroes is to be believed. It rarely, if ever, mentions good about Negroes. The white press is the chief instrument used for fostering the exploitations of Negroes. Most of the news is cooked and doctored to fan race hatred. A few white editors would perhaps write more fairly were they free. Personally very little. Nearly every Negro newspaper that we know, though, aims sincerely to benefit Negroes. While the judgment of the Negro editor is often at fault, his heart is honest. It is infinitely safer for Negroes to accept the judgment of a Negro editor than that of a white one.

Question: Specifically what constitutes the offensiveness in the manner in which the subject "Negro" is handled in some of the local white papers and what sensitive spots do these methods of handling touch?

Answers:

1. There is a suggestion of inferiority and degradation in the usual handling of the subject "Negro" by the local white papers; they generally use the subject in connection with something evil or unlovely; seldom discussed with credit or praise. This affects race honor, race pride, and race love.

2. Withholding the titles Miss and Mrs. from the names of colored women.

   Crime headlines, parading Negro crime and criminals.

   Printing misstatements of facts but not the denials of them.

   Continual suggestions of "proper limitations upon Negro activity" along lines innocent where other races are concerned.

   A patronizing attitude toward the Negro and his activities.

3. I detest the use of the word "Negro" as it is spelled with a small *n*. I shrink from the feminine "Negress." "A colored American" is not distasteful to me at any time.

4. The realization that an inferior man whose face is white can, by appealing to white racial consciousness, outstrip his superior by the utilization of mass cohesion. My feeling is one of thwarted ambition rather than offended sensibilities.

5. Spelling of "Negro" with a small *n*.

   Negro caricatures—always a joke and easily handled.

   The Negro as criminal is the general view.

   Nothing said about the Negro on the progressive side.

   Negro naturally inferior. I need only refer to the Harding episode.

6. The assumption that all Negroes are intellectually and morally inferior. The implication that certain crimes are peculiar to the Negro. The application of opprobrious epithets, so common in some papers. The statement that the race is satisfied with the treatment it receives in public places.

7. Undue prominence and emphasis upon the social aspect of news which is purely personal. Evident failure to obtain or give expression to the Negro point of view.

8. The tendency in my community to connect the Negro in public print with some offensive or boorish or irresponsibly humorous incident is the most annoying use of the word "Negro." By careful emphasis and omissions, the word "Negro" comes to be associated with irresponsible, apish, or silly conduct on the one hand or criminality on the other.

9. Among the other things I take offense at the way the local white papers cannot report crimes committed by Negroes without a big headline, often on the front page, stating that "Brutal Negro Commits Outrage"; I object to the use of the word "Negress," to spelling Negro with a small *n;* and particularly I object to the sins of omission of these newspapers in that they never attempt any news which may construct better relations, e.g., such as could be obtained if they secured on their reportorial staff an intelligent Negro who knew the needs and aspirations of his people. My sensitiveness upon this results from two things: (1) it wounds my self-respect, and (2) I hate to see race struggle consciously and effectively fomented by the powerful press.

10. The white race as a whole seems to disregard the just sensibilities of the Negro race, and does not scruple to use offensive terms and epithets which would be violently resented by any other group of American citizens.   I have no objection to the term Negro used in a descriptive sense for the entire racial group.

11. The word Negro is still printed in many papers with a small *n*.   A general attitude to ridicule Negroes is sometimes evident.   Recently a baby contest was held in New York in which there were entered several Negro babes; some of them took prizes.   One paper spoke of them as "dusky belles." Very often when a colored woman is mentioned in the papers it is written in this manner: "Katherine Jones, a negress."   The recent discussion of Senator Harding's lineage showed that most of the papers considered it a "vile and contemptuous slander"; the possession of Negro blood seemed to be a polluting element which could only mean degradation.

12. The word Negro is wrong, altogether.   Prejudice is the only reason for its use.   Capitalizing might help, but does it modify the treatment?

The editor of the *Crisis*, whose opinions are read by millions of Negroes, was one of the five Negroes living outside of Chicago to whom the foregoing questions were put.   He sensed in them an insidious attempt to make Negroes confess that they preferred ill treatment, riots, segregation by proscription, and Negro Ghettos.   Acting upon this conviction, he warned the Negroes of the country to watch the white members of this Commission.   The article is given as it appeared in the January 1921 issue of the *Crisis:*

CHICAGO

We would advise our Chicago friends to watch narrowly the work and forthcoming report of the Interracial Commission appointed by the Governor of Illinois after the late riot.   The Commission consists of colored men who apparently have a much too complacent trust in their white friends; of white men who are too busy to know; and of enemies of the Negro race who under the guise of impartiality and good will are pushing insidiously but unswervingly a program of racial segregation.   They have, for instance, sent a "questionnaire" to prominent colored men, consisting of fifteen questions, which with all their surface frankness and innocence seek to betray black folk by means of the logical dilemma of "segregation" and racial "solidarity." By subtle suggestion these queries say: If you believe in colored churches, why not in colored ghettos?   Does not Negro advancement increase anti-Negro hatred? Are not Negroes prejudiced against whites?   Are not the mistakes of Negro leaders manifest?   And so on.

Indeed, if a professed enemy of black folk and their progress had set out to start a controversy so as to divide the Negroes and their friends in counsel and throw the whole burden of such hasty outbreaks of race hate as the East St. Louis, Washington, and Chicago riots upon them, he would have framed just such a questionnaire as has been sent out by this Commission.

The *Crisis'* view of the questions is presented in the following contrast:

The Questionnaire	The "Crisis" Version
What, to your mind, is the distinction, either in point of view or definite racial aim, between segregation and "racial solidarity"?	If you believe in colored churches, why not in colored ghettos?
A large number of Negroes are in agreement in the matter of separate colored churches with colored pastors, and, more recently, colored bishops. Yet this is an argument used by many exponents of the segregation idea, both whole and partial, for other separate institutions. Candidly, what is your opinion on this subject?	
Do you believe that if Negroes were 100 per cent literate it would make any great difference in race relations? Are general and higher education likely to widen the breach between Negroes and white persons, increase intolerance, resentment, sensitiveness to insults, or can a quieted process of adjustment or complete fusion of interests be expected?	Does not Negro advancement increase anti-Negro hatred?
Do you believe Negroes are prejudiced against white persons?	Are not Negroes prejudiced against white persons?
Do you believe there should be recognized leaders of Negroes? Are there such persons whom you regard as qualified for leadership? Discuss their merits and demerits.	Are not the mistakes of Negro leaders manifest?
What in your opinion, are some of the greatest mistakes of prominent Negroes in their policies or stand on racial issues?	

At the time of this article the Commission had made no report of its findings whatever, and there was no possible basis for the accusation of bias. When a Negro living in Chicago explained that the questionnaire was prepared by a Negro member of the Commission's staff, the editor of the *Crisis* replied that "whoever framed the questionnaire of which I speak in the *Crisis* or advised its framing had a bias against Negroes. Of that I have not the slightest doubt, and what I was doing was simply to warn the public of this bias."

CHAPTER X

PUBLIC OPINION IN RACE RELATIONS—*Continued*

B. INSTRUMENTS OF OPINION MAKING

I. THE PRESS

We cannot escape the conclusion that the press is the most powerful institution in this country. It can make men, it can destroy men. It can conduct crusades; it can put an end to crusades. It can create propaganda; it can stifle propaganda. It can subvert the Government; it can practically uphold the Government. It is at once the most powerful agency for good in the United States and the most dangerous institution known under our system of Government. More than all this, despite theoretical laws which restrain abuses of the Press, so determined are the American people that its freedom shall not be abridged that they have written into the Constitution of the United States (Amend. I) the express provision that "Congress shall make no law . . . . abridging the freedom . . . . of the press," and in practice the Press is free to destroy men, institutions and races, or to make them live, the power being limited only by the conscience and sagacity of the men who compose this powerful Fourth Estate.

—EDMUND BURKE

Sound opinions depend always upon accurate statements of facts. Upon the objective information which the press is supposed to provide, the public depends to guide its thinking. If the information source is polluted, pollution may be expected in the opinions based upon it. When the public is deluded by distortions of fact, one-sided presentations, exaggerations, and interpretations of fact controlled by definite policies of whatever sort, a situation is created which will inevitably accomplish great damage.

Race relations are at all times dependent upon the public opinion of the community. Considering the great number of delicate issues involved, the careful handling of this kind of news is a question of great concern and has been the subject of much comment and criticism both by Negroes and whites. These criticisms are frequent and vehement. Negroes in Chicago almost without exception point to the Chicago press as the responsible agent for many of their present difficulties. Throughout the country it is pointed out by both whites and Negroes that the policies of newspapers on racial matters have made relations more difficult, at times fostering new antagonism and enmities and even precipitating riots by inflaming the public against Negroes. For example, the Federal Council of the Churches of Christ in America, in its report on the church and social work, makes this comment: "We observe also with regret and deep concern . . . . the continuing incitement to riot by certain public officials and periodicals, especially the partisan press with its misrepresentation and inflaming spirit."

Said the *Survey* magazine, May 15, 1920: "The custom of newspapers to ridicule the efforts of colored people is a gratuitous insult that they have to meet on every hand."

The *New Republic* observes editorially: "Race riots within a week of one another occurred in Washington and Chicago. . . . . The press made a race question of individual crime, and the mob, led by marines and soldiers, took up the issue which the press had presented to them."

Negroes are loud in their condemnation of the press throughout the country. Says one Negro newspaper:

Whatever be the cause of the motive, there is apparently a well-organized plan to discredit the race in America and to bring estrangement between fellow-Americans. A short-sighted . . . . press is contributing to this estrangement by playing upon the passions of the undiscriminating, and thoughtlessly, by its glaring and sensational headlines, emphasizing rumors of alleged crimes by Negroes.

The Associated Negro Press accuses the Associated Press of fostering ill feeling and hatred between whites and Negroes. It says:

The Associated Press (white) . . . . always in its first paragraph. . . . . attributes the source of trouble to our people "molesting white women." That, the Associated Press knows, is always fuel for the fire of the fury. . . . . It arouses certain elements of whites to indignation by the thoughts of the ever "burly black brutes," and it stirs the people of our group to a state of fighting, mad by the folly of it.

The *Philadelphia Tribune*, a Negro paper, said: "Daily papers keep up mob sentiment. They continue to fan the riot flames into a destructive blaze."

The method of news handling now in practice in the Chicago Press, white and Negro, appears to contribute in effect to strained relations between the races. This condition prompts a more than casual inquiry into these methods.

A few examples will illustrate. On the night of July 20, 1920, following the demonstration of a group of Negro fanatics, the self-styled "Abyssinians," a prominent newspaper printed in large headlines: "Race Riot—Two Whites Slain." The paper was an extra and widely distributed. At Sixty-third and Halsted streets four Negro ministers returning from a church conference in Gary, Indiana, were set upon by a mob of whites who had merely read the report, and were beaten unmercifully.

On January 23, 1920, the following article appeared in the *Chicago Herald-Examiner*:

STUDENTS DEFY NEGRO TEACHER

Pupils' Strike Starts at Altgeld School over Substitute;
Parents Support Them

A revolt which threatened to require settlement by the Board of Education developed yesterday in the eighth grade of the Altgeld School, Seventy-first and Loomis streets. Two of the pupils have been suspended, others threaten a general walkout. Pickets are to be established about the school today, several students promised tonight to urge a general strike. The regular teacher was ill with influenza yesterday.

PUT NEGRO GIRL IN CHARGE

The only available substitute was a Negro girl, Effie Stewart, normal graduate and accredited eighth-grade instructor. She was taken to the schoolroom by Principal J. W. Brooks and given charge. As the principal left pandemonium broke loose. Disregarding the efforts of the teacher to restore calm, several of the boys arose and harangued the class to ignore the substitute. Half a dozen of the pupils left the room.

REFUSE TO OBEY HER

The teacher directed one of the pupils, Paul Brissono, to summon Principal Brooks to the room. Paul flatly refused. He walked out and reported the trouble to his parents at 1406 West Seventy-third Street. Genevieve Lindy, 6744 Laflin Street, next was told to go to the Principal's office for help. She declined and went home. Principal Brooks ordered both pupils suspended. He said the facts would be placed before the district superintendent, John A. Long. In the meantime many of the parents of eighth-grade pupils took a stand supporting their children.

The Commission sent investigators to check up the facts as a thorough test of a report which most whites believed and most Negroes did not believe. The Negro teacher in question, the school principal, the superintendent of schools, and some of the parents of white children in the school were interviewed. The following is the result of the Commission's investigation:

a) Every item noted by the press in this case was contradicted by the principal and teachers.

b) Principal Brooks stated that "the only part of the story that the newspapers gave straight was the color of the young lady teacher."

c) Superintendent of Schools Mortensen stated that there was no basis whatever for the story, and that no more trouble happened than often happened when mischievous boys took advantage of the absence of the regular teacher.

d) Miss Stewart, the colored substitute teacher involved, stated that she was assigned to the Altgeld School on Monday, to the Pullman School Tuesday, and back to the Altgeld Wednesday. On Monday she had charge of the eighth grade. About twenty-five minutes before recess five or six boys came to her stating that they had been appointed as monitors for that day and asked to be excused. This request was granted by Miss Stewart. Shortly afterward Miss Deneen, a white teacher, brought the boys back into the room, stating that they had been disorderly; she deprived them of their monitorship. One boy, Paul, mentioned in the article, resented this and was impudent to Miss Deneen. He was suspended by Miss Deneen to take effect the next day and to return only on condition that he made apologies for his conduct. He was present in the room on the same afternoon.

Miss Stewart first knew about the supposed strike when she read it in the morning paper. She stated that she had no trouble with any of the students during the entire day, and there was no occasion to call in the principal, Mr. Brooks. Miss Deneen also had some trouble with a girl in the same room. Miss Stewart had no trouble either with Paul or the girl mentioned in the case. Mr. Brooks at no time during that day was called into the room.

e) The parents of the children were incensed over the false publicity given them.

f) The suggestive effect of this report was immediate. At the Coleman School, according to the principal, the children were greatly excited over the account and looked upon it as a precedent which had not occurred to them. She thought that such publicity, even if true, could have no good effect upon the minds and conduct of the children.

The prominence given to the idea of "striking" also had its effect. Discussions of strikes for other causes followed in the Pullman School. Later, in February the students of the Crane Technical School threatened a strike because of the removal of a teacher from the junior staff to the high-school staff.

On June 18, 1918, a Negro organization expressed the views of Negroes on the *Chicago Tribune's* handling of a news article entitled: "Negro Benefit Carries Mammy to Pearly Gates." The occasion of the article was a musical recital given by Negro artists at the Auditorium and patronized by many cultured whites and Negroes. It was a benefit performance in aid of the families of Negro soldiers. The letter of protest to the editor of the *Tribune* read:

On Saturday, June 15, there appeared in your paper what purported to be an account of a meeting and concert at the Auditorium held for the benefit of Negro soldiers' families. Despite the fact that it was distinctly a patriotic affair, presenting on its program colored artists of unquestioned talent, and rendered in such a manner as to evoke the warmest praise from an appreciative and music loving audience, your reporter saw fit to tell of it by reciting what he knew or thought he knew about Negro "mammies."

The body of the article contains sixty-two lines. Thirteen of these are devoted to mention of the names of the colored artists, ten to a description of the crowd, which, by the way, was inaccurate, fourteen to another list of notables in attendance and twenty-five to an enraptured dissertation on "mammies." Not only is this reference grossly irrelevant, but to colored people it is positively distasteful as everyone should know by now.

The caption of the article "Negro Benefit Carries Mammy to Pearly Gates" could by no stretch of fancy be taken as the heading for an account of a musical concert. . . . . There is no complaint against the limited appreciations of your reporter, neither do we protest against his fondness for the adolescent idol of his black mammy; but as a news item the account is ridiculously improper and out of place.

The patriotic endeavors of the colored people of this city have more than once been discouraged by just such thoughtlessness and incomprehension. You would do a great service to colored people and to our government in the prosecution of the war if in such accounts as appear you cause to be eliminated such personal reminiscences and irritating irrelevancies as are calculated to make patriotism difficult and racial relationship unsettled.

1. GENERAL SURVEY OF CHICAGO NEWSPAPERS

It was assumed by the Commission that so far as the ordinary reading public is concerned the study of the three Chicago white daily papers with the largest circulation and the three Negro weekly papers most widely read would provide an adequate basis for a test of news handling, and for measuring the effect on the public of accounts of racial happenings. The papers selected are listed in Table XXX.

TABLE XXX

NAME OF PAPER	PUBLISHED	CIRCULATION*	
		Week Days	Sundays
White			
Chicago Tribune...................	Every morning	439,262	713,966
Chicago Daily News................	Every afternoon except Sundays	404,726	....
Chicago Herald-Examiner...........	Every morning	289,094	596,851
Negro			
Chicago Defender..................	Weekly	185,000	....
Chicago Whip.....................	Weekly	65,000	....
Chicago Searchlight...............	Weekly	10,000	....

* Circulation figures as of 1920.

For the two-year period 1916 and 1917 the Commission listed from the *Chicago Tribune*, the *Chicago Daily News*, and the *Chicago Herald-Examiner* 1,551 articles on racial matters. Of these articles 1,338 were news items, 108 were letters to the press, and 96 were editorials.

Table **XXXI** classifies these items according to subject:

TABLE XXXI

Subject	Number of Articles		Number of Articles
Riots and clashes..............	309	Migration.....................	45
Crime and vice	297	Personal	39
Soldiers	199	Special columns...............	33
Politics......................	99	Education	18
Housing......................	89	Meetings......................	17
Ridicule......................	63	Art	8
Illegitimate contacts	61	Business	5
Sports.......................	56	Total	1,338

These figures do not represent all articles appearing on racial issues during the two-year period. Many additional articles appeared in early editions and not in the editions examined.

Generally these articles indicated hastily acquired and partial information, giving high lights and picturing hysteria. Frequently they showed gross exaggeration. The less sensational articles, permitting a glimpse of the stabler side of Negro life, were less than seventy-five. The subjects receiving most frequent and extended treatment in these three papers were: crime, housing, politics, riots, and soldiers. In analyzing the articles themselves, under these specific headings, it appears that the appeal to the interests of the public is founded on definite assumptions in the public mind. It has come to be recognized by both whites and Negroes, but more especially by the latter, that crime is most often associated with the publication of Negro news in white newspapers.

Crime.—The University Commission on Southern Race Problems in a recommendation to the white college men of the South said:

Colored people feel very keenly about the way crime committed, or alleged to have been committed, by Negroes is played up in the newspapers. We never see the Negro's good qualities mentioned. As a rule, when a Negro's name appears in the newspapers he has done something to somebody, or somebody has done something to him. It may be true that the newspaper's attitude toward the Negro does not influence white public opinion as much as the Negro thinks, but it is bound to affect the point of view of those white people who do not know the Negro.

As between North and South this press handling of racial matter seems but a question of degree. For a public which depends upon newspapers for its information an inordinately one-sided picture is presented. This emphasis on individual crimes specifying Negroes in each offense tends to stamp the entire Negro group as criminal. The following headings in white newspapers will suggest the inference of the public as to whether or not Negroes are criminally inclined:

NEGRO ROBBERS ATTACK WOMAN NEAR HER HOME
Tear Open Her Waist in Search for Money, but Fail to Find $6 Which She Had

POLICE HUNT FOR NEGRO WHO HELD UP WOMAN
Scour Englewood District for Short Black Man Who Threatened
Girls with Revolver

NEGRO SLAYER ESCAPES FROM JAIL

AUSTIN WOMAN ATTACKED IN OWN HOME BY NEGRO

WOMAN SHOCKED BY NEGRO THIEF
Mrs. John W. Beckwith Surprises Black Burglar in Her Home

RESCUE NEGRO FROM MOB THAT THREATENED LYNCHING
Morgan Park Police Save William Shaw Who Attacked Woman from
Infuriated Crowd

NEGRO ATTACKS WOMAN. HER SCREAMS BRING HELP
Mrs. Joseph Westhouse Dragged into Dark Passageway on South Side Street

ARREST NEGRO SUSPECT. FIND MUCH IN POCKET
Earnest Wallace Identified by Three Men as Ku Klux Robbers Who
Held Them Up

MASKED NEGRO ROBS AS WHITE
Arthur Hood Learns to Disguise Voice in Prison; Uses Talent

GIRLS FLEE FROM NEGRO
Accused Wm. Brewere of Following Them

NEGRO TROOP RUNS AMUCK. THREE MEN ARE WOUNDED

NEGRO STANDS WITH KNIFE OVER SLEEPER IN PARK

NEGRO CAMP INTRUDER ARRESTED AFTER FIGHT

CORONER CLEARS POLICEMAN FOR KILLING NEGRO

NEGRO SHOT DEAD TRYING TO ESCAPE AFTER CRIME

NEGRO ATTACKS DANCER IN ROOM OFF LOOP STAGE
Purpose Robbery

SAILORS CHARGE NEGRO INSULTERS IN EVANSTON

The frequent mention of Negroes in connection with crime by the white press has the following effects:

1. It plays upon the popular belief that Negroes are naturally criminal.

2. The constant recounting of crimes of Negroes, always naming the race of the offender, effects an association of Negroes with criminality.

3. It frequently involves reference to sex matters which provides a powerful stimulant to public interest.

4. It provides sensational and sometimes amusing material, and at the same time fixes the crimes upon a group with supposed criminal traits.

The beliefs handed down through tradition concerning the weak moral character of Negroes and their emotional nature are thus constantly and steadily held before the public. Police officers, judges, and other public officials are similarly affected, consciously or unconsciously, by these beliefs and by the constant mention of Negroes in relation to crime. Arrest on suspicion, conviction on scanty evidence, and severe punishments are the results. A vicious circle is thus created.

Crimes involving only Negroes as offenders and victims receive little newspaper attention. It might be supposed that they are uninteresting because there is no element of race conflict. As long as crimes are committed within the group, and this group is regarded as an isolated appendix of the community, there is little public interest in them, and consequently little news value. When, however, a member of the isolated group comes into conflict with the community group, whether in industry, housing, or any relation, it assumes a wider significance, and the information appears to become news of importance in the judgment of the press.

Instances of purely Negro crime, which in the community at large would have a strong appeal to public interest, take on news value only when the ludicrous or grotesque can be pictured. For the most part, this type of article is written by a reporter with some reputation for wit. He inserts the expected Negro dialect, whether with or without warrant, and proceeds to make an amusing story.

Negro soldiers.—News interest in articles on Negro soldiers appears to be founded largely on sentiment. During the war Negro soldiers, especially from Illinois, were given unstinted praise by the public and the newspapers. Illustrative headlines follow:

CHICAGO SOLDIERS ARE READY
Col. Dennison Declared to Reporter That Regiment 1,038 Strong Ready
for Call to War

COLORED MEN SERVED IN THE COLONIAL ARMY
Washington Favored Their Enlistment, but for a Time There Was Opposition

TO TRAIN COLORED MEN FOR OFFICERS

COLORED TROOPS TO GO SOUTH
Baker Says the 8th Illinois Will Be Sent to Camp Logan

DRAMATIC FAREWELL TO COLORED TROOPS
Cheers of Crowd Show Chicago Loyalty to Men of 8th Infantry

COLOR LINE WORRIES EXEMPTION BOARDS
Negro District Officials Wonder How They Can Furnish 40 Per Cent All White

TOBACCO FOR NEGRO SOLDIERS
Texas Club Will Give Midnight Benefit to Aid Fund

NEGRO STEVEDORES TO FRANCE
Colored Workers Are Being Organized into Four United States Regiments

ARMY IGNORES COLOR LINE
Negro Troops Ordered to Every Cantonment Where Available.   War
Department Not Affected by Protest, Latest Ruling Shows

8TH REGIMENT IS ORDERED TO HOUSTON
Chicago Colored Infantry to Be Accorded Same Privilege as White Soldiers.
Overrule City's Protest

COLORED SOLDIERS HELP LOAN
Col. Dennison's Men in the 8th Infantry Are Enthusiastic

8TH REGIMENT READY TO BEGIN BOND DRIVE
Spirit Shown by Officers Insures Good Response from Colored Soldiers

ORGANIZE NEGRO LABOR UNITS
U.S. Army Will Soon Have 24 Companies of Colored Volunteers

Politics.—In politics the listed articles were confined almost exclusively to suggestions of corruption, unfavorable criticism of Negro politicians, and treatment of Negro political support of Mayor Thompson as blind, careless, and venal loyalty.

The following headings on listed news items will indicate the character of emphasis:

MAYOR'S RULE SCORED BY VOTERS' LEAGUE

Since Harding retired from Council, Moores has collapsed entirely.   In combination with his colleague, Oscar De Priest, colored, he has become a partisan, willing to go to any length in behalf of the politicians fighting the Council.

M.L.V. URGES DEFEAT OF MAYOR'S CLIQUE.   SECOND WARD, NEGRO
WARD, NO RECOMMENDATIONS

HOT ON TRAIL OF VOTE FRAUDS LETTER

E. H. Green's (Negro) Communication to Dr. Leroy N. Bundy (Negro)
May Reach Grand Jury
Alderman De Priest (Negro) Involved
All Interested in Rounding Up Colored Republican Voters Talk of Colonizing

FIVE IN HOT FIGHT IN SECOND WARD

It is said, however, that W. R. Cowan (Negro) and L. B. Anderson (Negro) have best chance.

COLORED MAN IN SENSATION
St. Louis Dentist Said to Have Revealed Election Fraud

EAST ST. LOUIS BRIBERS SAFE

Attorney-General Brundage says they are immune under law. These men were accused in confession of Bundy (Negro).

BLACK AND TANS WIN POINT

Will Have Half the Delegation from Louisiana to Republican
National Convention

DE PRIEST QUITS ELECTION RACE AT G.O.P. ORDER

Indicted Alderman Ducks Impending War in Second Ward

3,000 NEGROES CHEER ATTACK ON ROOSEVELT

NEW YORK ELECTS ITS FIRST NEGRO TO THE LEGISLATURE
Ed. A. Johnson

MAYOR LOSES BIG WARDS

In recognition of what the second ward did, the administration has made more Negro appointments than ever before in Chicago. Yesterday the City Hall forces were led by Alderman De Priest, Corporation Counsel Ettleman, Dr. A. J. Cary, and Edward Wright. Morris won by 4,050 over Bibb.

IMPORT NEGROES FROM THE SOUTH TO SWING MID-WEST

NEGRO LEADER EJECTED FROM HUGHES QUARTERS
E. H. Green Told to Move On When Authorship of Letter Is Traced

NEGRO VOTE MANIPULATION ALLEGED IN EAST ST. LOUIS

Housing.—The subject of the housing of the Negro is interesting because of its peculiar connection with: (*a*) segregation; (*b*) bombing; (*c*) neighborhood antagonisms; (*d*) alleged depreciation of property; (*e*) Hyde Park–Kenwood efforts to keep Negroes out of the district.

During 1917 the *Tribune* carried six articles on Negro housing. One was the mention of the purchase of a $75,000 lot by Mme. C. J. Walker, a colored woman living in New York. Two related to the efforts of white residents to keep Negroes out of white residence districts; two were devoted to the effort of white residents to put Negroes out of white districts; and one to a meeting of realty men at which, it was alleged, angry Negroes "blasted harmony on a housing plan." The plan in question was a segregated Negro district to which Negroes objected. Trends of subjects treated in news items are given:

ST. LOUIS VOTES TODAY ON NEGRO SEGREGATION

OFFERS HER HOME TO NEGROES ONLY
West Side Woman Adopts Novel Revenge in Row with Neighbors
Due to Spite Fence

NEGROES MAY BUY HOUSE ADJOINING SPITE FENCE
Owner of Property Will Sell to Colored People Only in Plan for Revenge

RACE QUESTION LEFT TO BLACKS
Negro Committee Given Power to Act in Morgan Park Feud

COMMITTEE REPRESENTING BOTH SIDES TO SUGGEST SOLUTION AT
NEXT MEETING
Com. L. T. Orr and Chas. R. Bixby, White, and G. H. Jackson, and
G. R. Faulkner, Colored

RACE QUESTION TAKEN TO COURT
Morgan Park Negro Alleges Conspiracy to Close His Building

NEGRO SUBURB PLANNED AFTER ENGLISH GARDENS
Dunbar Park, Prepared by Frances Barry Byone

OAK PARK NEGRO HOME SET AFIRE. SEES WHITE MAN
Shoots as Arson Suspect Stumbles over Hedge Screaming
Second Attempt at Blaze

NEGRESS BUYS LONG ISLAND LOT AMONG HOMES OF RICH
Mme. C. J. Walker $75,000 Lot

SEGREGATION OF NEGROES SOUGHT BY REALTY MEN
Plan Legislation to Keep Colored People from White Areas

ANGRY NEGROES BLAST HARMONY IN HOUSING PLAN
Bolt Meeting at Realty Board with Threats to Fight

NEGRO OWNER OF FLAT HOUSE TO WAR BACK
Eugene F. Manns—Property in Morgan Park

COURT BLOCKS NEGRO INVASION
Injunction to Halt Move until Improvements Are Put In

RACE SEGREGATION IS RENT BOOSTER'S AIM
Owners Hope to Prevent Encroachments of Either Colored or White Citizens

TRY TO KEEP NEGRO OUT OF BLACK BELT
Colored Organizations Do Not Want Newcomers to Go to Old District

URGE RACE SEGREGATION LAW
Members of Real Estate Board to Move to Save South Side

TAKE UP HOUSING OF NEGROES
Two White and Two Colored Realty Dealers Consider the Problem

The migration.—The migration provided a subject of sufficient interest to
stimulate a number of articles. Hordes of illiterate and impecunious Negroes
were pouring into the city, according to some reports, at the rate of forty carloads a day; they brought smallpox and low living standards, imperiled health,
and created a dangerous problem for the city. The combined estimates from
day to day in the press would give a number of arrivals in Chicago, equal to
or even more than the migration to the entire North. Thus the articles ran:

COMMITTEE TO DEAL WITH NEGRO INFLUX
Body Formed to Solve Problems Due to Migration to Chicago from South

WORK OUT PLANS FOR MIGRATING NEGROES
Influx from the South Cared For by the Urban League and Other Societies

OPPOSES IMPORTING NEGROES
Illinois Defense Council Moves to Stop Influx from South

2,000 SOUTHERN NEGROES ARRIVE IN LAST TWO DAYS
Stockyards Demand for Labor Cause of Influx

RUSH OF NEGROES TO CITY STARTS HEALTH INQUIRY
Philadelphia Warns of Peril, Health; Police Heads to Act

NEGROES ARRIVE BY THOUSANDS—PERIL TO HEALTH
Big Influx of Laborers Offers Vital Housing Problem to City

SEEK TO CHECK NEGRO ARRIVALS FROM THE SOUTH

City Officials Would Halt Influx until Ready to Handle Problem

NEGROES LEAVING SOUTH; 308,749 IN FEW MONTHS

DEFENSE BOARD WARNED AGAINST NEGRO INFLUX
Investigators See Peril Such as Resulted in East St. Louis

HALF A MILLION DARKIES FROM DIXIE SWARM TO THE NORTH TO
BETTER THEMSELVES

NEGROES INCITED BY GERMAN SPIES
Federal Agents Confirm Reports of New Conspiracy in South; Accuse
Germans for Exodus from South

NORTH DOES NOT WELCOME INFLUX OF SOUTH'S NEGROES
NEGRO INFLUX BRINGS DISEASE
Health Commissioner Orders Vaccination of Arrivals to Check Smallpox

Racial contacts.—Aside from the riots and clashes the most intensively
featured articles were those dealing with intimate racial contacts. They dealt
with intermarriage, positions of authority for Negroes, intermingling of the
races in resorts, and love affairs—in fact, the usual taboo themes and "forbidden" interracial practices. Some of these subjects are thus indicated:

WIFE VANISHES—HUSBAND SEEKS NEGRO

MAY PUT WOMAN ON TRIAL FOR PAYING NEGRO'S FARE
San Diego Case First Instance of Man Not Being Taken under Mann Act

LITTLE MARJORIE GAY, BUT AGED MAMMY MOURNS
Colored Woman Who Raised White Girl Says Officers Are Influencing Child

A STRANGE, TRUE STORY
On Frank Jaubert, manager of New Orleans City Belt Railroad, who was accused
of being a Negro. Reference to Marjorie Delbridge case.

MAMMY LOSES FIGHT TO KEEP DELBRIDGE GIRL
Girl Declared Incorrigible, Delinquent and Ward of Juvenile Court

DIXIE WOMAN TO GIVE MAMMY AND HER CHILD NEW HOME TOGETHER
Mrs. Brock Also Had a Mammy

ALL HER TROUBLES NEAR HAPPY END AS NEW HOME LOOMS WITH MAMMY

MAMMY KIDNAPS HER CHILD
Negress Seizes Delbridge Girl; Flees in Auto

MAMMY DENIES KIDNAPPING WARD
Search for Marjorie Delbridge Leaves Disappearance a Mystery.
Mrs. Brock Through

2. INTENSIVE STUDY OF CHICAGO NEWSPAPERS

A careful study of the three selected white daily papers was made covering 1918, the year preceding the riot, to note relative space, prominence, importance, and the type of articles on racial matters. During the year 534 articles appeared on racial matters distributed among the three papers as follows:

NEWS ITEMS ON RACIAL MATTERS—1918

	No. Items
Chicago Daily Tribune	253
Chicago Herald-Examiner	157
Chicago Daily News	124
Total	534

TABLE XXXII

CLASSIFICATION OF ARTICLES ACCORDING TO SUBJECT AND NEWSPAPER DURING 1918

SUBJECT	"TRIBUNE" No. of Articles	"TRIBUNE" Amount of Space in Inches	"HERALD-EXAMINER" No. of Articles	"HERALD-EXAMINER" Amount of Space in Inches	"NEWS" No. of Articles	"NEWS" Amount of Space in Inches	TOTAL Articles	TOTAL Space
Crime and vice	70	231	58	181	21	122	149	534
Soldiers, war work	33	136	21	88	28	196	82	420
Politics	21	78	12	28	14	63	47	169
Riots	15	80	5	19	2	3	22	103
Lynchings	24	57	15	43	4	21	43	121
Editorials	6	34	8	67	6	28	20	129
Organizations and movements	13	25	8	22	4	27	25	75
Housing	12	28	5	14	1	3	18	46
Personal and miscellaneous	15	35	5	16	5	33	25	85
Industry, labor	11	28	1	1	2	18	14	47
Athletic, sports	8	12	3	4	3	7	14	24
Letters to editor and "Voice of People"	13	107	9	30	21	34	43	171
Migration	2	4	0	0	9	126	11	130
Propaganda	0	0	0	0	1	6	1	6
Race relations	0	0	1	1	1	8	2	9
Radicalism	0	0	1	1	3	9	4	10
Guide post	0	0	4	59	0	0	4	59
Intermarriage	0	0	1	7	0	0	1	7
Education	3	8	0	0	0	0	3	8
Segregation	4	15	0	0	0	0	4	15
Social service	1	8	0	0	0	0	1	8
Theatrical	2	1	0	0	0	0	2	1

Most of the published information concerning the Negro and issues involving him magnifies his crimes and mistakes beyond all reasonable proportions. The Chicago public is aware of the sentiment against morons created by the newspaper practice of calling persons who attack women or girls morons—an unscientific classification, of course, since all who attack women are not morons. Negroes frequently say that if each crime committed by a "red-headed" man were listed as a crime committed by a "red-headed" man, a sentiment would soon be created sufficiently hostile to provoke prejudice against all red-headed men.

In 1918 there were more than 90,000 Negroes in Chicago. Practically all of the more serious crimes in this group, especially those involving whites and Negroes, were given publicity. This simple notation of crimes may be a part of the routine of journalism. It does not, however, explain the obvious appeal to passion found in many of them or even the prominence given to articles of a certain type. Crimes, riots, intermarriage, lynchings, and radicalism were the subjects of articles which, in their repetition and accumulative significance, presented a disproportionately unfavorable aspect of the Negro population.

The *Chicago Tribune* published, in 1918, 145 articles which, because of their emphasis on crimes, clashes, political corruption, and efforts to "invade white neighborhoods" definitely placed Negroes in an unfavorable light. Of this number, twenty-three appeared on the first page of the first section and twenty on the first page of the second section. It also published eighty-four articles dealing with Negro soldiers, sports, industry, and personalities, which, aside from flippancy in treatment, did not place Negroes in an unfavorable light. Of this number, two were on the first page of the first section and three on the first page of the second section. The relative length of articles indicates another possible effect on the public. The unfavorable 145 articles contained 487 inches of printed matter, while the less colorful items contained 223 inches.

Front-page space amounting to eleven inches was given to favorable articles, and 158 inches to unfavorable. Of the articles concerning Negro soldiers appearing on the first page, four of the eleven inches concerned a report that two Negro soldiers had been killed following a dispute at Camp Merritt between a white sergeant and a Negro trooper.

The *Herald-Examiner* published ninety-seven unfavorable and thirty favorable articles. Of this number, thirty-one unfavorable and six favorable appeared on the front page.

The *Chicago Daily News* devoted thirty-three articles to unfavorable publicity and fifty-one to publicity of a favorable sort. Of these, eighteen unfavorable and eighteen favorable appeared on the first page.

Bombing publicity.—The bombing of the homes of Negroes is an expression of lawlessness which in an orderly community should not be tolerated. The primary function of the newspaper is to report the facts. Upon this basis the public may then pass its judgment. In the case of a bombing it might be supposed that an orderly community would wish to know the persons involved, the damage effected, the motive, the action of the police and the result of efforts to capture the perpetrators of the act. Ordinarily this is done in most cases of lawlessness and in bombings not involving racial issues.

Of the forty-five racial bombings which took place in Chicago between July 1, 1917, and June 18, 1920, fourteen were not mentioned in any of the six large dailies of the city.[1] Of the remaining thirty-one, seven were reported in one paper, ten in two papers, nine in three papers, while five appeared in four papers. Not one of the forty-five cases appeared in more than four papers. Although there might have been a total of 270 news reports of these bombings only seventy-four actually appeared. Of the forty-five bombings the *Tribune* and *Herald-Examiner* each reported twenty, the *Post* fourteen, the *News* eleven, the *Journal* eight, and the *American* one. In all cases the reports openly recognized that these bombings were not the result of individual grievances but involved organized effort and activity on the part of groups or communities in the practice of throwing racial bombs. It was generally referred to as a "race bomb" or "race war bombs." Typical headings were:

Journal, April 7, 1919:
> RACE HATRED BOMB HURLS SIX FAMILIES FROM BED

Journal, November 19, 1918:
> BOMB HOME OF AGED NEGRO. EXPLOSION SEEN AS PROTEST BY WHITES

Journal, March 6, 1920:
> ATTRIBUTE BOMB TO SOUTH SIDE RACE WAR

Journal, March 31, 1920:
> ANOTHER BOMB IN RACE WAR. OWNER SELLS BUILDING TO NEGROES DESPITE OBJECTION OF NEIGHBORS

Herald-Examiner, May 25, 1920:
> NEGRO CLUB IS BOMBED. SOME BLAME POLITICS

Chicago Tribune, May 25, 1920:
> NEW RACE WAR WRECKS PORCH OF NEGROES' CLUB. THE CLUB IS COMPOSED OF 600 COLORED PERSONS

Herald-Examiner, June 13, 1920:
> TWO BUILDINGS BOMBED. RACE PREJUDICE BLAMED

Herald-Examiner, December 28, 1919:
> RACE WAR BOMB INJURES WOMAN

Herald-Examiner, September 24, 1918:
> POLICE SAID BOMB WAS INTENDED TO INTIMIDATE NEGROES WHO RECENTLY MOVED INTO THAT NEIGHBORHOOD

Herald-Examiner, April 7, 1919:
> A RACE WAR IS GENERALLY BELIEVED TO HAVE BEEN BEHIND A BOMB EXPLOSION EARLY THIS MORNING AT 4212 ELLIS AVE.

Herald-Examiner, April 4, 1920:
> RACIAL DIFFERENCE RESPONSIBLE FOR BOMB

Journal, March 20, 1919:
> BELIEVE BOMB THROWING CONTINUATION OF A FEUD CARRIED ON BY THE WHITES AND BLACKS IN THE DISTRICT WHERE NEGROES HAVE BEEN ALLOWED TO OCCUPY BUILDINGS FORMERLY OCCUPIED BY WHITE PEOPLE

In two instances a racial bombing was considered significant enough to occupy more than nine inches of one column. This space was given by the *Tribune* and the *Herald-Examiner*.

[1] This statement is based upon the available files. The February file of the *Chicago Herald-Examiner* for 1919 was unavailable at the time this study was made.

Jesse Binga, a Negro banker, was bombed five times. The article in the *Daily News* was five inches long. In the *Herald-Examiner*, April 20, 1919, there appeared an article, "Curious Boy Drops Bomb as It Explodes." The article covered eleven inches, of which eight inches were given to the story of a boy who picked up a bomb in the street and dropped it as a lady signaled him to drop it because it might be an explosive. At the end of this article were appended three inches containing a narrative of a racial bombing at 4722 Indiana Avenue where Wimes & Lassiter, Negro real-estate dealers, had an office.

The fifth bombing directed against Mr. Binga is treated humorously in spite of the serious damage done to his home.

The average length of racial bombing articles was about four and one-half inches. The explanations of motive offered were stereotyped in character and involved assumptions which it is not considered necessary here to analyze. It was explained that the person bombed was a Negro or that he had moved into a "distinctly white residential district," against which encroachment bombing had been instituted as an intimidating or expulsive measure. It was sometimes stated that the person was a real estate agent negotiating with Negroes concerning property in "restricted" districts. This sort of explanation was either stated in the headline or appended at the end in a brief sentence. The reports in the papers apparently undertook merely to notify the public that bombings had happened. The following are examples of press treatment of race bombings:

Herald-Examiner, May 25, 1918:
    This building was occupied by Negro families. . . . . The white residents objected to the Negroes.

Post, November 19, 1918:
        BOMB SHATTERS NEGRO HOME IN "WHITE DISTRICT"

Tribune, March 19, 1919:
        BINGA PROPERTY WAS WRECKED
    Binga is an agent for buildings. He is colored, and has been leasing apartments formerly occupied by white tenants to colored.

Post, March 20, 1919:
    Police are investigating whether the bombs were thrown by members of the Janitors' Union retaliating against Jesse Binga, colored real estate dealer who had been hiring non-union janitors, or whether intended as another warning to the colored people to keep out of residential districts that have been hitherto exclusively white.

Post, April 7, 1919:
        BOMB EXPLODES IN FLAT WHERE NEGRO MOVED IN

Tribune, April 7, 1919:
        BOMB SET OFF IN NEGRO FLATS
    White residents of the district had held indignation meetings because he had peopled his building with colored folks.

Herald-Examiner, April 20, 1919:
        OFFICE OF WIMES & LASSITER, NEGRO REAL ESTATE DEALERS,
                        WAS THE TARGET

Tribune, May 18, 1919:
NEGRO FAMILY ON GRAND BOULEVARD OBJECT OF BOMB

Post, June 13, 1919:
TWO BOMB BLASTS ON FRINGE OF NEGRO DISTRICT

Post, January 6, 1920:
BOMB DAMAGES HOME OF NEGRO ON GRAND BOULEVARD
Ernest Clark moved in recently. He is a Negro. All his neighbors are white.

Daily News, February 2, 1920:
WHILE A BOMB WAS EXPLODED ANOTHER BATTLE IN THE SOUTH SIDE RACE WAR OVER THE SEGREGATION OF BLACKS IN RESIDENTIAL DISTRICTS

Daily News, February 10, 1920:
BUILDING RECENTLY SOLD TO APPOMATTOX CLUB, A NEGRO ORGANIZATION

Daily News, February 13, 1920:
TWO BOMBS TOSSED
. . . . against encroachment of Negroes in white residential districts.

Herald-Examiner, March 11, 1920:
SOUTH SIDE HOUSE SOLD TO NEGROES BOMBED

Journal, March 24, 1920:
BOMB SHAKES BUILDING. DEAL FOR SALE OFF
The prospective buyer was talking with —— when there came a loud noise. [Buyer was colored.]

A typical example of newspaper reports of the bombings of Negro homes appeared in the *Herald-Examiner* of April 4, 1920:

BOMB BLASTS IN FRONT OF NEGRO FLAT BUILDING

A black powder bomb was exploded last night in front of the vestibule of a four-story flat building 423 E. 48th Place, occupied by Negroes. The building is owned by Robert B. Jackson, who lives on the second floor. He recently purchased it from Louis Cohen. The apartment is in the neighborhood peopled mainly by whites, and the police believe racial differences are responsible for the bomb. The explosion did slight damages. No one was hurt.

One of the typical shorter reports also appeared in the same paper May 25, 1918:

BOMB EXPLODES BEFORE HOME OF NEGRO FAMILIES

A bomb exploded in the front of 4529 Vincennes Avenue early this morning, wrecked the front porch of the structure and broke windows for a block around. The building is occupied by Negro families. White residents objected to the Negroes.

Similar language was used in all the articles.

Most of the articles carried a suggestion of a race war on the South Side. Many of the reports helped to contribute to popular anticipation of future trouble. For example, in the *Post* of January 6, 1920, page 1, column 3, a bombing was reported thus: "A bomb early today damaged the residence at 4404 Grand Boulevard which was said to have been a Negro 'sniping-post' during the race riot last summer."

The home at 4404 Grand Boulevard was owned and occupied by Mrs. Byron Clarke, and was not a sniping-post during the riot. It had been bombed four times, once while officers were guarding it. All papers used the expression, "No one was hurt." Property destruction was usually dismissed with statements like these: "All the glass was shattered"; "the front porch was demolished"; "about $—— damage was done"; or "the damages were slight." The *Daily News* was exceptional in using the word "outrage" three times.

Two reports gave accounts of arrests, and all others in which police activity was mentioned merely said, "The police are investigating." None of the articles gave the results of any such investigation, other than that the police generally attributed the "hurling of the bomb" to the occupants of a black touring-car. The articles contained no condemnation of the bombings as lawlessness or crime except in the case of a bombing at 3401 Indiana Avenue, where a child was killed May 1, 1919. The *Chicago Tribune* spoke of this death as an incident of that bombing.

One of the two arrests above referred to was that of a janitor who was not able to explain sufficiently his presence in or about a building which had just been bombed. He was taken into custody but was soon dismissed. The other arrest was that of the nephew of a prominent business man living in the neighborhood of the bombed property.

During the time from February, 1918, to February, 1919, prior to the Chicago riot, there were eleven bombings in the city. If each paper had reported each bombing there would have been sixty-six reports. Only seven reports actually appeared. During the six weeks immediately preceding the Chicago race riot, there were seven racial bombings. Of a possible forty-two reports, only four appeared, or two bombings in two papers. Thus violent and criminal expressions of hostility which might have been checked by arousing the public conscience silently continued. The resentment of Negroes increased, and the ignorance of the larger white public remained undisturbed. The articles were apparently written without much investigation. Upon the fifth bombing of Mr. Binga's home, the *American, Herald-Examiner*, and *Chicago Daily News* quoted Mr. Binga as saying, "This is the limit; I am going." Mr. Binga declares that he did not say this, that he did not even see a reporter, and that he had not moved.

During the nine months following the riot, publicity on bombings increased to several times the former amount. Beginning in March, 1920, the articles again showed slackened interest. The *Tribune* and *Herald-Examiner*, usually giving most frequent publicity to such matters, missed about every other one. The *Post* had no reports, the *Journal* two, the *News* four, and the *American* none. Seven bombings took place from March 1 to July 1.

The apparent indifference toward race bombings in the minds of editors, officials, and the public was indicated by the relative prominence given to a race bomb which threatened life and damaged property as compared with an "odor bomb" dropped in a moving-picture theater.

On the first page of the *Tribune* of February 11, 1921, under the caption "Crow Raid Opens Inquiry into Bombs," were seventeen inches of space reporting cases of "odor bombs" and emphasizing the determination of the state's attorney to make investigation. At the bottom of the adjoining column were four inches devoted to a dynamite race bomb which damaged a three-story apartment and involved menace to life. No reference was made to any effort by the state's attorney or the police to investigate. Similar prominence was given to the "odor bomb" in the *Herald-Examiner*.

An editorial in the *Tribune*, February 14, 1921, condemning bombing made no reference to the fifty-six race bombings of recent record, but did refer to other bombing aimed at white citizens. The editorial reads:

The Business of Bombing

Anthony D'Andrea, whose aldermanic campaign meeting Friday night was broken up by a bomb which injured seventeen persons, speaks with some indignation on the matter as indicating a bad moral slump in political methods. If it had been a union labor bomb, apparently, it would have been of no great importance.

"I'm a union man myself," he explains. "I wouldn't care if they threw a bomb at my house. That's all in the game."

On the latter point D'Andrea is right. It is "all in the game," but the game is one which gets out of control of the players. It is because bomb throwing has come to be accepted as "all in the game" of union labor warfare that it is now being extended to political warfare. The man, the gang, or the organization which sanctions or adopts bombing as a method of obtaining results in ordinary activities cannot expect to be able to restrict the use of such methods to one line of business.

Originally the bomb was a political weapon, as in the hands of the Russian nihilists. In late years it has grown popular with labor leaders of a certain class. Such bombings as the recent one at the Tyson apartments, ascribed by the police to labor troubles, and the repeated odor bomb outrages at movie theaters, are sufficient illustrations of its use by labor. The post-office bombing in 1918 and the numerous so-called race-bombs exploded on the South Side are illustrative of the widening use of bombs. In such progress D'Andrea should not be surprised that the bomb is being adopted by ward politicians. Properly applied, a good bomb can be expected to neutralize half a dozen or so precinct captains. Bomb throwing is becoming a business.

Friday night's bombing is a perfectly logical development. As a result several men may be cripples for life, if they do not die. It is time such logical developments are stopped. Among the scores of bomb outrages of the last few years, so far as we recall, there has not been a single case of punishment of the perpetrators. They are justified in believing that they are safe. As long as they retain that belief they will continue to extend the business of bombing. One thing will stop it. That is drastic punishment. Any person who throws a bomb is a potential murderer. Life in prison is none too severe a penalty. Good detectives can trap some of these men and good prosecution can send them to prison. It should be done and done now.

The Abyssinian affair.—The "Abyssinian affair" referred to earlier in this part of the report, was treated with remarkably good judgment by the press. It is to be believed that further clashes were avoided by the effective way in which the newspapers pointed out that the demonstration was the work of fanatics rather than a race riot.   Two days later, however, the *Chicago Tribune* published an article ascribing the Abyssinian murders to "racial reds."   The article ran:

"Abyssinian" Murders Bare Racial "Reds"
Leaders Lay Unrest to Du Bois Creed

Shocked by the fantastic violence of Sunday night, when a United States sailor and a citizen were killed by pseudo-Abyssinian zealots, thoughtful colored leaders began a determined effort yesterday to stamp out anti-white exploitation and to bring about better understanding. . . . .

This type of exploitation, they say, is aimed at the more ignorant among the colored masses.   It carries the same appeal as the glittering promises of the I.W.W. and the Communists to the illiterate and ignorant among the whites.

According to Negro leaders, this exploitation is based upon the theory of *social equality*.   Its motive can be seen, they say, in recent utterances and writings of Negro intellectuals, in which a high pitch of "social equality" fervor is established as a panacea for the ills of the race.   This theory, translated and exaggerated into ambiguous prophecies by the soap-box orator, is slowly being percolated through the masses of a race as yet generally unprepared by education to understand it.

Chief among the writers whose works have been of this intellectual caliber is Dr. W. E. B. Du Bois. . . . . His latest volume, a "best seller" entitled *Darkwater*, has been widely circulated.   It is a volume of almost super-intellectual caliber, and is bitter in tone.

In *Darkwater*, which is taken simply as a typical volume, are found the teachings, colored leaders say, which have been seized upon by those who, under the shadow of Dr. Du Bois' reputation among colored folk, would seek to incite and exploit.

The "colored leaders" quoted were F. L. Barnett, R. S. Abbott, and A. H. Roberts.   They did not impute any such danger to Mr. Du Bois' books.   Mr. Barnett, for example, mentioned the exploitation of the "Back to Africa" movement by Jonas and Redding, while Mr. Abbott and Mr. Roberts spoke of the lack of sympathy among Negroes for criminal types like Jonas and Redding.   The article then stated the "Du Bois Creed," saying:

The agitators have used considerable skill in exploiting the Negroes by use of doctrines which they have taken from Dr. Du Bois, as expressed in *Darkwater*.   Here are some of them:

"The world market most widely and desperately sought today is the market where labor is cheapest and most helpless and profit is most abundant.   This labor is kept cheap and helpless because the white world despises 'darkies.'"

This is given as the underlying premise for the late war.

"But what of the darker world that watches?" the author continues.   "Most men belong to this world.   With Negro and Negroid, East Indian, Chinese, and Japanese they form two-thirds of the population of the world.   A belief in humanity is a belief in colored men.   If the uplift in mankind must be done by men, then the destinies of the world will rest ultimately in the hands of darker nations."

The article quoted from *Darkwater* a chapter, which, by cutting the text, left a suggestion of sex intimacy between a colored bank messenger and a white girl very different from the intention of the author. The entire article was calculated, through its suggestion and insinuation, to rouse racial antagonism. It is doubtful whether the "Abyssinian" leaders, who were ignorant fanatics little known within the Negro group, had read Du Bois' books. With all its wildness and fatuousness the movement was directed away from America and from whites. A photograph of Du Bois was published with the caption:

KARL MARX OF NEGROES
Noted Colored Philosopher Whose Works Are Used by Agitators to
Stir Race Hatred

Miscegenation.—Similarly dangerous treatment is apparent in an article which appeared in the *Tribune* of November 6, 1920, under the heading: "Miscegenation is O.K.'d in New Constitution."

The article called attention to a proposed provision in the new state constitution of Illinois against public discrimination on account of color, which was intended to put into the constitution rights already guaranteed by state laws. According to the article this law was tentatively agreed upon "during the newsy days surrounding the Republican National Convention and escaped the notice of the public generally." The article said:

Under the basic law, if adopted, a colored man and woman will be entitled to buy vacant seats of a grand opera box, otherwise occupied by whites. A Mongolian—if a citizen—and a mesochromic bride cannot be denied a vacant flat in the most "exclusive" apartment building.

A law prohibiting the Japanese, as in California, from owning land, will be illegal. Two colored people may take two of the four seats in the Blackstone restaurant beside the wives of two packers.

A member of the convention said yesterday that it is as broad and comprehensive as it can be made. He claimed that this sentence in the constitution will prevent the Legislature from prohibiting in any way the colored citizen from getting all the rights and privileges accorded to other citizens. According to this constitutional delegate and lawyer the new constitution, as now worded, will prevent segregation of the Negroes, Jim-Crow cars, or special schools for the colored.

A Negro lawyer said that the Morris section only recognizes openly the rights of equality which were settled by the Civil War and enunciated in an amendment to the federal Constitution.

The remainder of the article dealt in brief with fifteen other decisions of the Convention. These decisions were merely stated and not commented upon.

Newspaper handling of the "back of the Yards" fire.—At the close of the Chicago riot fire was set to a large number of houses back of the Stock Yards. Since these were the homes of white persons, principally Lithuanians, it was generally assumed that it was an act of retaliation by Negroes. Articles in the newspapers strengthened the belief.   The *Chicago Daily News* article gave a full account of statements made by Fire Marshal O'Connor to the effect that Negroes were responsible.   It stated that the police and militia were combing the South Side for a band of eight Negroes, alleged automobile fire bugs. These men, it was said, were stalled in an automobile at West Fifty-fifth and South Wood streets ten blocks south of the fire; when the police reached Fifty-fifth Street the Negroes had repaired their car and fled.   John R. McCabe, Fire Department attorney, was reported as being positive that the fire was started by Negroes.

Investigation was made by the Commission to ascertain the facts concerning Negro responsibility for these incendiary fires.   The state's attorney declared that no records had come to his office implicating Negroes, and that he had no information, except rumors which he seriously questioned.   The records, he thought, were held at the Stock Yards police court.   Inquiry at this police station disclosed the fact that no Negroes had been apprehended on this charge, and the belief was expressed that the act was committed by white men with blackened faces.   The fire marshal's office had no record other than unsubstantiated rumors spread by persons living in the district.   The matter had been dropped for lack of evidence.

Negro revolt.—On January 4, 1920, during the general crusade against "reds" the *Herald-Examiner* published a two-inch headline across the top of the first page saying:

Reds Plot Negro Revolt
I.W.W. Bomb Plant Found on South Side

The article mentioned below alleged secret activities of Negroes and their plans to revolt against the government.   The bomb plant and many of their secret plans were reported to have been discovered by the state's attorney's office.   The article further stated: "In Chicago it was learned that the headquarters for Negro revolutionary propaganda are centered in these four organizations: The Free Thought Society, Universal Negro Improvement Association, Negro Protective League, and Soldiers and Sailors Club."

Each organization named was, as a matter of fact, open to the public, though patronized almost entirely by Negroes.   The Negro Improvement Association was by no means secret in its plans; it published a newspaper in which they were set forth.   The slogan of this organization was then and is now, "Back to Africa," and not "Down with the United States."

The Free Thought Society mentioned is the Chicago Free Thought Educational Society.   The following is a declaration of its principles:

In order to achieve a better understanding of the phenomena of nature, for ourselves and for such of our fellow-men as shall care to become affiliated with us, we do hereby bind ourselves by the following declaration of principles.

First: That the attainment of truth shall be the fundamental purpose of the work of this society and all its members.

Second: That truth shall be recognized as that body of conclusions which may be logically drawn from the facts of nature as evidence by the five senses, or may be demonstrated mathematically.

Third: That we abstain from all dogma, insisting upon a fair and impartial investigation of all subjects and at all times.

Fourth: That we do recognize a universal kinship binding together in one common band all members of the human society regardless of race, color or sex.

Among its members are W. E. Mollison, F. D. Summers, and among its honorary members are F. Percy Ward, lecturer for the Chicago Rationalist Society, and Clarence S. Darrow. The Negro Protective League is an employment office and day nursery. The full name of the organization is the Negro Equal Rights and Protective Association.

The Soldiers and Sailors Club is a community house located on the South Side and a branch of the local War Camp Community Service. It served during war time as a recreational and social center for returning soldiers, and in 1920 became the South Side Branch of Community Service, Incorporated. At the time of the article it was under the general supervision of the Chicago Community Service, of which Eugene T. Lies, formerly of the United Charities, was director.

Newspaper handling of the Waukegan riot.—Considerable excitement was occasioned by reports in all the Chicago daily papers of a race riot in Waukegan, about thirty-six miles north of Chicago. The first news reports gave the following versions:

THE BEGINNING OF THE RIOT

Chicago Tribune, June 1, 1920:

A group of Negro boys in Sheridan Road stood about stoning passing automobiles for several hours, finally shattering a windshield on the car of Lieut. H. B. Blazier and injuring Mrs. Blazier.

A throng of sailors and marines were passing when Mrs. Blazier was injured and they immediately chased the Negro boys. The chase led to the Sherman House, a rooming place for Negroes, and when the persons living there defended the boys and sought to drive off the sailors, there was a prospect of serious trouble.

Chicago Daily News, June 1, 1920:

According to the police a thirteen-year-old colored boy and his little sister had been in ambush near Sheridan Road throwing stones at passing automobiles. *One of the stones* struck the windshield of a car driven by a coal dealer, Chas. Bairscow, according to Assistant Chief of Police Thomas Tyrrell, and injured a woman occupant of the car. Another shattered the windshield of the car of Lieut. A. F. Blasier a naval officer. Mrs. Blasier was cut by flying glass. When he drove into the city Lieut. Blasier told several sailors of the affair and the news quickly spread. The town was alive with marines and sailors on "shore leave." They concentrated in the town square and upon a signal made an attack on the Sherman House, a hostelry occupied by Negroes.

CLASHES

Chicago Tribune, June 1, 1920:

For hours there were individual instances of attacks by both whites and Negroes in various parts of the town.

Chicago Daily News, June 1, 1920:

A general man hunt ensued. One group stormed the postoffice and tried to break open the doors, as it was thought a Negro was hiding there. Another made an attack on the house of Ike Franklin, colored. Ike had fled. Another group chased a Negro across the Genesse bridge in the center of the town. It had nearly captured him when the blue-jacket guards arrived in trucks. Under command of Provost Marshall Lieut. A. C. Fisher the town was quickly cleared. The police arrested the following six marines: Thomas Levinger, Charles Thrawle, John Smith, Burney Poston, Herman Blockhouse and Harold Denning.

RACE RIOTS AND THE POLICE

Chicago Daily News, June 1, 1920:

Acting Chief Tyrrell, after a cursory investigation, said that, as far as he could learn, Policeman Frank Bence, on whose beat the trouble started, was not in the vicinity at the outbreak. He said that if this proved true the man would be dismissed. The policeman said he was making a tour of alleys at the time of the stone throwing and knew nothing of it.

Inquiry by the Commission brought out the following facts: The first newspaper accounts of the riot indicated that Lieutenant Blazier and his wife were driving in one automobile, and that Mr. Bairscow was driving in another automobile. The story was that Mrs. Blazier was injured by glass from the windshield broken by stones, and that a woman occupant of the Bairscow car was similarly injured. Lieutenant Blazier and Mr. Bairscow were driving in the same car, the windshield of which was broken, instead of separate cars. There was no woman in the car and Lieutenant Blazier has no wife.

The story was telephoned into the *Tribune* by a member of the staff of the *Waukegan Sun*. This was the source of the report of the woman being injured.

The stoning occurred one block away from the Sherman House, occupied by Negroes.

Negro housing in Chicago.—The housing situation has frequently occasioned alarm on the part of whites and bitterness of feeling toward Negroes. Many newspaper articles, by their play upon racial fears, have increased the tension between the two groups. An example of this type of article is given:

WHITE TENANTS FEAR NEGROES WILL BUY BLOCK. FIRE CHIEF'S RESIDENCE ONE OF THOSE IN DANGER

Twenty-six houses on the old Chicago university campus in East Thirty-fourth Street, between Cottage Grove Avenue and Rhodes Avenue, are about to be sold to colored people, according to the tenants. . . . .

"I'm going to offer the houses to the present occupants at prices ranging from $6,000 to $7,000 on easy terms," Mr. O'Brien said. "Of course if they don't accept I'm going to do the best I can. I can't predict how things will turn out until the tenants have given me their reply. They'll be around tomorrow.

"Among the residents of the block are Fire Chief Thomas O'Connor, Dr. William E. Hall, and Dr. M. J. Moth.

"The tenants are all worried. Colored people have learned of this sale and for days have been walking up and down and pointing out houses, discussing, apparently, what they intended doing and where they planned to live. Unless every one of the twenty-six buys his house it will not remain a white neighborhood. And I don't believe we can get everyone to buy" [*Chicago Tribune*, February, 1920].

Inquiry by the Commission disclosed a situation similar to that underlying many discussions of "exclusive areas." The article was written by a member of the *Tribune* staff. It was learned at Mr. O'Brien's office that he had come to that office inquiring about the matter. A member of the O'Brien firm stated to him that he did not think the matter had any racial significance because the firm intended to sell the houses to present tenants, all of whom happened to be white.

Labeling fights as "riots."—Attention might be called to the suggestion in articles which treat trival disputes and street fights as race riots. On August 4, 1920, the *Evening Post* published an article headed: "Negroes Held to Grand Jury after Riot in Street Car."

The article related a dispute over a car seat ending in a fight in which one man was stabbed. The entire article is given:

Six Negroes were arraigned in the South Chicago court today, charged with having started a "near" race riot in a Cottage Grove Avenue car last night. They were: Isaac Nelson, 3256 South Park Avenue; Henry Broadnax, 3235 Calumet Avenue; Samuel Bound, 3127 Cottage Grove Avenue; Albert McMurry, 3027 Cottage Grove Avenue; Abe Mitchell, 3703 South La Salle Street and Walter McConnor, 538 West 45th Street.

McConnor, who was charged with assault with a deadly weapon, is said to have taken a seat which Herbert Douglas, 1637 East 78th Street, offered to a woman passenger.

In the scuffle which ensued, Douglas received a stab from a knife in the hands, it is alleged, of McConnor, and was taken to the South Chicago hospital. The Negroes were held on bonds of $400 to $3,500, pending jury trials.

In May, 1920, the *Tribune* gave eight inches to an article with the headline: "Race Riot and Labor Riot in New England." The item reported a fight between a Negro waiter and a Harvard student in one of the college dining-halls. To show how trivial the incident was the article said in part:

The trouble began when Mayer (a colored waiter) made a slighting remark to Wilson (a white student) and, grabbing him by the hair struck him in the face. Wilson, in an attempt to defend himself, grabbed a water pitcher, and as he raised it.

Mayer drew a revolver and pointed it at Wilson.   Immediately the student body was in an uproar and rallied to the defense of Wilson. . . . . The police are searching for Mayer.

The *Daily News* referred to a "riot" precipitated by a colored chef's remarks.   The incident referred to loud talking in the kitchen of a Greek restaurant and the chef's swearing at a cook which was overheard by a woman in the dining-room.   She objected, and the police were called.   Another such article appeared in the *Tribune* under the heading: "Women in Riot.   White versus Negro in Reformatory."   The article told of state troops, local police, and a chaplain having been mobilized to stop a "race riot."   The casualties given were one policeman bitten by a girl and several state troopers kicked and scratched.

An instance of undiscriminating news handling appeared in the *Chicago Tribune* of July 24, 1917.   During the race riot in East St. Louis, while the front pages of all the papers were filled with descriptions of the horrors, an article appeared in the fourth column of the first page, along with the East St. Louis riot news.   It occupied fourteen inches and bore the heading: "Whites Were Firing at Blacks near Scene of Murder.   Four Negroes Jailed after Slaying of Aged Man."   Of the fourteen inches, six were given to an account of the murder in Chicago of a saloon-keeper by a Negro in which mobs of Negroes were said to have flourished guns; four inches were given to a totally irrelevant report that two young white girls were chased through Washington Park by a Negro; three inches more to a further account of the first murder, and one inch to a report that a Negro was shot by a policeman.

On the second page was an eleven-inch article with the large headline: "Lawyer Warns Negroes Here to Arm Themselves."   Underneath was a five-inch report concerning a Negro held for trial on a girl's story of an attack. Nine inches were given in another article to a warning by Chicago labor leaders that "the influx of blacks" to replace the strikers in the plants was bringing a riot peril to Chicago.   Under this article was an account of the freeing of a policeman for killing a Negro; and beneath this an article from Orange, Texas, with the headline: "Negro Shot Down Trying to Escape after Crime."   Also on the same page nine inches were devoted to a condemnation of black politics in East St. Louis, and three inches to a minor clash in which a Negro was reported to have drawn a knife when attacked by six white youths.   Two inches were given to the account of a clash between Negroes and whites in New York City and seventy-two inches to accounts of the East St. Louis riot.

The emphasis was on the work of the mob and the fact that Negroes were replacing strikers in East St. Louis, and that this was responsible for the riot. Some of the reports of Chicago incidents proved to be inaccurate.   It developed that Charles A. Maronde, a saloon-keeper, who was supposed to have been killed by Negroes, his death precipitating a clash between Negroes and white persons, actually died of heart failure. There was no connection and no apparent reason for inserting the incident of the white girls being chased through the park by a Negro. This report was hearsay and was joined to the article in this manner: "About the time the Negroes were being fired upon, two young white girls were being chased by a Negro through Washington Park."

The item concerning the Negro held for trial on the charge of a white that he had attacked her, turned out to be the imaginings of a young girl, which involved a forty-three-year-old Negro, whose character had never before been questioned, and who, as the facts developed, was entirely innocent. Linked up in this article was an account of disciplining in the county jail; 150 prisoners had been locked in their cells and placed on bread and water because they were found shooting craps in the "bull pen."

Flippant treatment and ridicule of Negroes.—The "human-interest" newspaper story is undoubtedly one of the most effective means of gaining public attention. But it presents a single incident from which the reader is likely to apply characteristics vividly set forth concerning an individual to the group of which the individual is a member. It therefore leads to unfair judgments of the group when the characteristics are not representative of the group, even if they are representative of the individuals. It may be written with genuine humor and with the best of intentions, or perhaps only with thoughtlessness of the effect. But that does not obviate the sense of injury when the group involved feels itself misrepresented and held up to ridicule.

Newspaper flippancy concerning Negroes has found a sensitive spot among members of the race. Often there are suggestions and exaggerated descriptions that can be characterized as nothing else than ridicule. Negroes especially resent misrepresentation of Negro weddings, since no accounts are given by white newspapers of more representative weddings.

A Negro Wedding

"Yassah, I'se tuh git hitched up. I'se heighty-six and Emily's sixty-nine, but we done got license.

"Yassah, I am de man you is huntin'. Yes, suh, I'se agwine to git hitched with Emily Holland. De carryings-on are agwine to come off tomorrow night. Emily done got lonely like and I'se getting no 'count.

"I was in the wah wid de march to de sea, and I got fo' minie balls. One ob em took two ob my toes. I'se a-carrying de otha ball in my frame. Uncle Sam done provided fo me now wid a pension. It am enuf fo me an' Emily. It ain't too much, cause in de days ob de wah I done lay in trenches and fit all night in cold water."

BULLET IN HIS LAIGS

"I knowed how to bust bad coons in de army and I was p'moted to sahgent in Co. E, 60th Reg., U.S.A. Now comes the achings of bullets in my laigs and chest and I feel like I cain't walk no mo. Den it am de time when I wants a wife to look at me. Emily say she ain't ready fo to take on no mo 'sponsibility. Den I argufies with her.

"'How comes this heah 'sponsibility talk'? I say.

"'Taint no how come 'bout it,' she says, 'You is a ol' man.'

"'So is you a ol' woman,' I says."

IS YOU OR IS YOU AIN'T?

"Den we jaw aroun' about it for a long time. Yestiddy I say, 'Emily you all hab done been widout a husband fo' nigh onto 22 yeah.' She don't say nothin'. I talks 'bout it some mo', then I says, 'Emily, is you gwine to be my wife or is you ain't?' She says 'Yes' and den we get de license. Now we hab done got de ministah and it am all ready. I'se feelin' kinda sprightly like tonight and unless my misery comes on me thar sho'ly am agwine to be some 'spicious carryings-ons in dis abode tomorrow night" [*Chicago Tribune,* January 11, 1916].

During the war Negroes were as seriously engaged in battle and as freely sacrificing their lives as other soldiers. When deeds of heroism were cabled back to the United States, Negroes at home expected serious reports of the activities of the sons, husbands, and brothers whom they had given up to fight for their country. Exception was taken by them to newspaper treatment of a serious feat as merely ludicrous. For example:

BLACK YANK BAGS HUN; MAJOR WEARS CAPTAIN'S MONOCLE

Paris, Sept. 7 (Delayed). During the recent American advance out of Château Thierry, a Red Cross captain was looking about for suitable hospital sites, when he met an American Negro soldier marching along toward Château Thierry, following close behind a German major. The Negro had transferred his pack from his own back to the back of the German officer, and had also transferred the German major's monocle to his own eye. Thus equipped the black warrior was parading triumphantly down the road. As he passed the Red Cross captain he called out, "I say, look here what dis Niggah done got" [*Chicago Evening Post*].

The following is a news report, with dialect, which was supposed to have been cabled from Paris:

NEGRO STEVEDORE COMING BACK "BY WAY OF NEW OHLEENS"

August 17 (Delayed). George Washington Henry Clay Smith, Negro stevedore at one of the American base ports, expressed the feeling of a large part of the expeditionary force about ocean travel. "When dis heah wah is ovah," he said, "you-all will nevah see me goin' back across dat ole ocean. Ahm not goin' back to United States that away. Ahm goin' back by way of New Ohleens" [*Chicago Evening Post*, September 9, 1918].

"Crap shooting" is ordinarily regarded as the peculiar pastime and passion of Negroes. Popular expectation is fed by newspaper stories of these games, made even more humorous by dialect, and the frequent implications of levity in religious matters. Such stories would probably be enjoyed by Negroes if they did not have the effect of picturing this trait as an exclusively Negro form of gambling.

Or again, the newspaper plays up a supposed superstition of the Negro in such an article as appeared in the *Chicago Tribune* of January 1, 1920, under the heading "Negroes Driven to Jail in Big Black Hearse." Pseudo-serious newspaper reference was made to Negro street sweepers as the "official chamber maids" of the city in an article in the *Chicago Herald* of March 31, 1916, headed:

BLACK BIRDS AS WHITE WINGS

Negroes Supplant Sons of Italy as City's Official Chambermaids

Or again, a Negro saves a white man from a mob and is called a "darky" in the report of the incident:

DARKY PASTOR SAVES WHITE AUTOIST FROM NEGRO MOB

Newport News, Va., Oct. 27.—The attempt here today of a mob of Negroes to lynch Isadore Cohen after his automobile had run over a Negro child was frustrated by R. H. Green, a Negro preacher, who fought off the white man's assailants long enough to let him escape in the car. Cohen is held without bond [*Chicago Tribune*, October 28, 1920].

A Chicago colored boy is pictured at the Salvation Army Camp at Glen Ellyn. Under the picture is the title "Rastus." He has been given a piece of watermelon to complete the picture.

JOY SUPREME

"Come here, you Rastus, and git yo' pitcher took t' show how glad you are."

Rastus was glad and Rastus came hither, but he was so glad about going to the Salvation Army Camp yesterday with several hundred boys and girls from the poorer districts that he failed to register the smile his mammy demanded.

The annual camp of the Salvation Army at Glen Ellyn opened in the afternoon. In the morning the first group of children left over the Northwestern Railroad. Practically every nationality was represented [*Chicago Tribune*, July 3, 1920].

Another picture is given in another issue of a little Negro boy at the Juvenile Detention Home. It is headed "Losted," and carries the suggestion of loose family life:

LITTLE PICKANINNY WHO WAITS FATHER AND MOTHER TO CLAIM HIM

Who's lost a little colored boy about four years old? He's at the Juvenile Detention Home. He says his mother is "Mis' Brown" and his father "Mistuh Parsons."

He's got an inexpensive lavalliere for identification, a dime with a hole in it. He keeps the dime on his neck by means of a piece of string that runs through the hole [*Chicago Tribune*].

3. NEWSPAPER POLICY REGARDING NEGRO NEWS

The policy of a newspaper in handling racial news can be better determined by studying its articles and editorials than by asking the editors. In fact, when the editor of the *Tribune* was asked concerning this matter he referred the Commission to the columns of his paper. It would be difficult to find a definite policy on the race question stated and consistently followed out by any newspaper in all items affecting race issues. Ordinarily when misleading emphasis, misinterpretation, and distortions of fact occur, they are due to the ignorance concerning Negroes which is fairly general among white persons, rather than to any inclination to injure a disadvantaged group of people. Reporters and editors frequently use, doubtless unwittingly, terms unnecessarily irritating to Negroes. Individual notions of relations between whites and Negroes determine the character, color, and emphasis of articles and editorials.

A conference of editors of the white press was held to discuss these matters with the Commission. The white press was represented by Edgar T. Cutter, district superintendent of the Associated Press, W. A. Curley, managing editor of the *Chicago American*, Victor F. Lawson, editor of the *Chicago Daily News*, and Julian Mason, managing editor of the *Chicago Evening Post*. A brief questionnaire was filled out and returned by Joseph M. Patterson, editor of the *Chicago Tribune*.

A. EDITORIAL POLICY

Chicago American.—The *Chicago American* had recently adopted a policy of eliminating the racial designation, "Negro" or "colored," unless some special circumstance made the mention of race of particular news value. Said Mr. Curley:

There was a meeting at which newspaper men were gathered together with some representatives of the colored race down in a clubhouse on Grand Boulevard, the Appomattox Club, and we were informed then that there was a feeling among the Negroes that the newspapers emphasized in crime stories particularly the fact that a man was a Negro. Our publisher and I discussed it, and we decided that there was no more reason to emphasize that it was a Negro bandit than that it was an Irish or Jew bandit.

Our general policy has been that we must treat the Negro with the same consideration and tolerance as we give any other nationality. When he had those troubles here before [the riot of July, 1919] we had some editorials to that effect.

Since the date of the meeting mentioned, the *American* has consistently maintained this policy. Its editorials prior to that time had shown a spirit of tolerance and fairness. During the riot especially it published editorials designed to aid in the restoration of order.[1] It published perhaps the strongest of local newspaper editorials condemning the bombing of Negro homes.

Chicago Daily News.—The *Chicago Daily News* in its reference to Negroes used the expression "colored." Although it had sometimes published articles which were not representative, it had often given space and prominence to news concerning Negroes which presented them in a more favorable light. This was clearly manifested during the world-war. Its interest in a serious

[1] See p. 44.

treatment of Negro affairs was shown in two special series of articles, the first by Junius B. Wood, the second by Carl Sandburg, both published later as booklets. These articles were well received and gave a necessary balance to the more usual publication of stories involving Negroes only in crimes. In a special column of the *Daily News*, "The Human Side of Things," many articles have been published relating to efforts for social welfare among Negroes.

Concerning the use of the racial designation in reporting crimes, Mr. Lawson explained that he considered it appropriate to mention race, as, for example, in giving an account of a lynching or the bombing of a Negro home. The racial designation, he believed, gave significance to the article. This consideration, he believed, balanced references in other cases. He said:

The newspaper point of view is to use the national, or professional, or racial distinction, the word giving the distinction, wherever it interprets the news that is being printed. There are some places where the character of the thing that is being told naturally suggests the name Negro, or the word Presbyterian, or Jew or Gentile or German or English, or Irish, and the newspaper never stops to suppress that. On the contrary it puts it in as interpreting fully the character of the news that is being told.

Concerning news items unnecessarily provoking race antagonism, as, for example, reports of speeches by a candidate for governor of Illinois on "White Supremacy," he thought that most of the papers as well as his own "played it down."

The statements of Mr. Lawson on other questions of policy are quoted:

Mr. Lawson: We regard items describing constructive work by Negroes or items indicating their advancement as better news than articles indicating degradation or criminality on their part. The *Daily News* endeavors to appeal to all readers alike. Instructions in news handling comprehend the employment of fairness, conservatism, and candor; special instructions based on these principles are issued to cover special cases. The terms "darky," "nigger," "coon," "shine," "wench," and "negress" are not employed by members of the staff in writing news articles and are rarely admitted to any class of matter. The style of the *Daily News* for many years has been to speak of the Negro as a colored man and the Negroes as colored people. When "Negro" is used it is rarely capitalized.

Commissioner: Is it objectionable?

Mr. Lawson: No, simply the style of the paper; typographic styles of paper vary. Some papers capitalize more than others. Some papers always spell the word "Bible" with a capital *B*. We don't. It simply follows the style of the paper. Dialects are very seldom employed in the news stories. They are not used to ridicule any race or nationality. The *Daily News* recognizes the importance and delicacy of the race problems in Chicago in its news columns as elsewhere in the paper. It aims to assist constructive movements, eliminate sensationalism, and quiet prejudice, while at the same time presenting truthfully such facts as may be of interest and proper to the reading public as a whole. I think, perhaps, I ought to emphasize that last thought to this extent: the newspaper impulse is to print the news, that is the controlling, dominating purpose of the newspaper mind, to print the news. But circumstances will at times suggest some particular expression of that impulse. Many times, as Mr. Curley told you, we don't print the news, we suppress it in the public interest.

Chairman: But that is a difficult self-control.

Mr. Lawson: Yes, I think so. To err is human, to print the news is the natural impulse of newspaper people, but we do recognize—I know all newspapers recognize—a very definite responsibility that, in so far as it lies within a reasonable discretion and a reasonable ability to act, they must consider always the general public interest in any grave matter. I think Mr. —— struck a very important interpretative status when he said he didn't like to have the designation of the race in any respect used as an expression of ridicule. Of course, that goes without saying. No newspaper that is wise, let alone a newspaper that is fair, will deliberately inflict derision on any class of its readers. It is a foolish thing to do aside from anything else, and anything that would seem to suggest a deliberate intent to bring the Negro race into derision, every man in the room would resent and properly. But I think, as I said before, that at times a purpose of derision is imagined when there hasn't been any. I think that is true and I don't think that it is surprising. If I were a member of a race that was fighting its way all the time toward a square deal and a fair show, I presume I'd be supersensitive about some things.

Herald-Examiner.—The *Herald-Examiner's* principal handling of the race issue has been through the presentation of news items. The term of designation employed is "Negro." On several occasions the *Herald-Examiner* has made commendable effort to show in its columns that a friendly spirit exists between the two races. Most notable of these efforts was the picture of whites and Negroes fraternizing in an effort to restore order immediately after the "Abyssinian affair," in which two white persons were killed and several Negroes, including a Negro policeman, were injured. Some of its editorials on the Negro question were headed:

NEGRO EDUCATION
Education the Best Solvent for the Negro Problem (Based on the Report of
the Chamber of Commerce of the United States)

DISLOYALTY AND LYNCHING
East St. Louis Massacres Have Not Been Properly Published. A Gulf
Separates Governor Lowden's Denunciation of the Riot and
the Treatment Accorded Slayers

THE BLACK MAN STOOD PAT
On the Loyalty of Negroes

NO "PATRIOTIC" MOBS
A Condemnation of Mob Violence in Illinois

On the other hand, some of the most emphasized misrepresentations of Negroes have appeared in the *Herald-Examiner*, as, for example, the story of the "Negro revolt,"[1] and various riot articles.

[1] See p. 540.

Chicago Tribune.—The *Chicago Tribune* stated its policy of handling Negro news to be one of "fair dealing and recognition of the difficulties." The managing editor stated that the *Tribune* used dialect in cases of kindly human-interest stories, refrained from the use of terms like "darky," "coon," "Negroes," etc., and employed the term Negro, capitalizing the *N*. The last practice was begun at the instance of Negro leaders. During the threatened race riot the *Tribune* sought the aid of leading Negro newspapers in Chicago. There were no definite instructions regarding the handling of Negro news matter. The difficulties in race relations recognized by the editors of the *Tribune* are to be found in the following editorials:

WHITE AND BLACK IN CHICAGO

It is possible for whites and Negroes to live in peace in Chicago. They have done so for years, in normal conditions and in normal times. They have managed to live without much prejudice. There has been good feeling. The Negro has had political equality. There has been an attempt to give him a fair representation in public affairs and not to resent his presence there.

We admit frankly that if political equality had meant the election of Negro mayors, judges, and a majority of Negroes in the city council the whites would not have tolerated it. We do not believe that the whites of Chicago would be any different from the whites of the South in this respect. . . . .

We have been able to extend the essentials of citizenship to the Negroes freely because the whites are dominant in numbers. All the essentials are in the possession of the Negro. He is not Jim-Crowed by law. A line is drawn by usage. The law in fact forbids what actually is done. It is a futile law because it encounters instinct.

Legally a Negro has right to service anywhere the public generally is served. He does not get it. Wisely he does not ask for it. There has been an illegal, non-legal, or extra-legal adjustment founded upon common sense which has worked in the past, and it will work in the future.

The fact is that so long as this city is dominated by whites, whether because of their numbers without force or by their force if they were in the minority, there will be limitations placed upon the black people. They will be limitations which will not work an injustice to the black people, who have a right to their own development.

There is no objection to economic equality. There is a decided objection to the exploitation of black labor. During the war many Negroes were brought from the South. Thousands of them went into the Stock Yards. The war shut off the supply of common labor. The South supplied the want.

Thus the population of blacks doubled in war times. Concerns which brought the Negro here to exploit him damaged the community by throwing a race question upon it. Concerns which needed the Negro and put him upon an equal basis with the whites, without importing cheap labor to take the jobs of whites, were legitimately supplying their need for labor.

The race issue in California grew out of the fact that the Japanese were cutting under the price of white labor. That will produce race troubles as quickly as anything.

Concerns may have been derelict in not considering the housing problem. The imported Negroes could not live in the streets or vacant lots. They had to get under roofs, and in getting under roof they suddenly established new contact with white neighborhoods.

In this change there was bound to be trouble unless precautions were taken. In the present case there is no evidence of precaution and some of provocation. It is possible for that question to adjust itself. Such realty movements cannot take place without friction, but the friction need not lead to riots. The city is steadily shifting in residential character. Some of the people affected by the shifts do not like it, but in normal times the readjustment is not disturbing to the community. A spread of factories may change the character of a section. A spread of Negroes may do the same thing.

A writer once summed up the Negro question by saying, "The North has the principles and the South has the Negroes." We are coming to have the Negroes, and we want to keep the principles so far as they are applicable.

Industrial radicalism, expressed in the I.W.W. propaganda among the Negroes, will not help us to keep them. Thuggery will not help us to keep them. A rebellion by the Negroes against facts which exist and will persist will not help us to keep them, but we are confident that the situation in Chicago is susceptible of being handled in the fashion it always has been handled.

UNSETTLING THE RACE PROBLEM

. . . . Regardless of what may be considered the justice of the claims of the races, the fact undeniably is that white and black will not mix in quantity. For this reason —the reason reached by the jury—the remedy seems obvious: there must be a plane upon which the races can live socially distinct but industrially co-operative.

We are not disposed to think that the mass of the Negroes want social equality in the full sense of the term. The *Tribune* has had many intelligently composed letters from Negroes disclaiming any such desire. We believe the Negroes want an opportunity to develop their own society. If this is true there ought not be widespread objection to social segregation, directed by themselves and upon the theory of wholesome living conditions.

But against what we think is an inherent disregard for exact social equality there is appearing a very insidious propaganda among the Negroes. Whether it is being circulated as a radical irritant calculated to disturb political conditions or merely is the parlor philosophy of eager sociological transcendentalists, there is no means of determining.

The propaganda urging agitation for social equality may have every support under the law and under what ought to be human justice, but while fortified by what ought to be, it flies in the face of what is. . . . .

The blacks form less than 10 per cent of the population of the United States. They have less than one-tenth of a ghost of a show if the relations between white and black become bitterly hostile. The average black man and the average white man get along fairly well. Unless something happens to arouse their race prejudices and instincts they live by tolerance which may not be a solution of race difficulties, but it is a method of life and it is practical.

There is plenty of evidence just now that something is raising the race question. There is evidence, it is said, to support the story that agents had played on the imagination and ignorance of Negroes in Arkansas inciting them to arise against the whites and take their lands. Agitators have tried to excite the blacks. Some misguided sentimentalists have tried to organize whites and blacks for the compulsory recognition of social equality—a propaganda which is even more vicious than the red propaganda. There are numerous elements and factors of disorder, and the consequences already have been bad. . . . .

The position of the Negro is not a preferred one in American society. The Negro is at an economic disadvantage. He is needed in the South and has been brought into the North to meet labor emergencies, but he does not have an open field of work. These disadvantages cannot be removed by discussing them. They exist in race instincts and, along with the other disadvantages which the Negro meets, arise from causes not at the control of the reasoning faculties.

No sensible person imagines that he knows what to do about the race problem because he does not know a method of eradicating race instincts, and he would not want to eradicate them if he knew how. A person may know what will surely happen if the race instincts become inflamed and not have the slightest idea how to prevent contact from flaming into violent action.

We know that if it comes to violence the blacks will get the worst of it. We know that the situation as it exists now has many possibilities of danger. Both North and South have had enough violence. Both may have more. Communities may not be able to stop agitation or effectively to counteract it, but they can see that the processes of law are applied with severity.

Law strong enough to make the races live in peace will allow them to find their own ways of living in the same communities.

B. HANDLING OF NEGRO NEWS

Chicago Evening Post.—The *Post* is an afternoon paper. It does not carry a large amount of news on racial matters. The policy of this paper was thus expressed by the managing editor, Mr. Julian Mason:

We have always checked information very carefully because we have had a very close Negro sympathy for years and because we have had editorial writers who have had special contacts. For instance, during the race riots we were constantly in communication with a young Negro, Mr. Jackson, a Y.M.C.A. man, a fine man. We checked up with him every single day. We used to call up Mr. Barnett and some of the others.

We use the word "Negro" and the Negro dialect in what you call feature stories. I don't know why we should deprive American life of that flavor. We also use the word "darky" once in a while in a humorous sense, but not in news items.

The Associated Press.—Mr. Edgar T. Cutter, district manager, Western District, the Associated Press, said in his testimony before the Commission:

The Associated Press is a non-money-making, non-sectarian, non-political organization. It is made up of over 1,260 daily papers. It is a mutual organization, and it gets its news by an exchange among the members. Aside from that, in big cities like Chicago we have our own bureaus which collect news in certain events. In Chicago the Associated Press gets its news from the five daily papers that are members, and from the city news bureau. This city news bureau, by the way, is kept up by the Chicago papers and therefore is supervised by them and carries the same class of news.   Now on a big story such as the race riots, the Associated Press got its news from all these sources, and it also sent a staff man who was experienced in general newspaper work to the South to investigate for himself so we should get the absolute facts.   The Associated Press makes a practice of covering only news of general interest, and it has made its reputation on the covering of facts.   It never handles editorials, nor does it ever make a comment on any news.   If a piece of news is not of general interest, at least throughout the state, it doesn't attempt to handle it. It confines itself to news that is of general interest throughout the country, and therefore it covers these matters very briefly.

Question: Do you personally in your representative capacity handle any of the news from the southern states ?

Mr. Cutter: Only as it passes through here.   Each district passes on its own news, but we verify it if it ever appears to be incorrect.   But any item that reflects upon any person or upon any organization, even if we get it from our own newspapers, is first checked up to its source, if that is at all possible, and then if there is a matter of controversy and only one side has been stated, we always try to get a statement from the other side, from some head official.   In case of Negro news, we have many times had as our representatives leading Negroes.   Negro organizations have come into our office and we have solicited news from them. . . . .

In cases of lynchings and such things from the South, the Associated Press often has used twenty-five or fifty words and just let it pass with the mere fact.   Where we have covered crime in full, big cases, very often it has been upon the demand of the members of the organizations.

News concerning Negroes is handled just the same as any news of any nationality. We use the words, "Negro" and "colored."   And it is always the desire of the Associated Press and the attempt of the Associated Press not only not to injure any person but to show the proper respect to all religions, races, and all classes of society. It makes no difference whether we would capitalize the word "Negro" or not.   Our copy goes to the newspaper and, as Mr. Lawson says, they follow their own ideas in that. . . . .

In all of our services we attempt to suppress news that we think might stir up race relations involving Japanese, Mexicans, Negroes, or any others, and we follow the lead of newspapers.

Question: What is the extent to which news from these members of the Associated Press is verified when it comes from regions or localities where there may be prejudice ?

Mr. Cutter: Wherever there is any question of the news or wherever there are two sides, as in the labor question, we send a staff man out from headquarters who makes his reputation and that of the Associated Press upon covering both sides of the story equally.   He knows very readily that if he doesn't cover that with thorough fairness, he is going to hear from it later from one side or the other.

Chicago American.—Mr. William H. Curley, managing editor of the *Chicago American*, gave the following information:

Of course as to accuracy, we check that up the same as we do any item.   We find out where the item came from; if it is a police item we find out who is responsible for it and send reporters immediately to cover it and rely upon them for accuracy regarding the report.

Question: Let me ask whether you do that with the same care and precision that you do in the case of a white man that is involved.

Mr. Curley: Absolutely.

Question: That is no insinuation against the newspapers, but, for instance, it is said that in the courts, if a man is a colored man he doesn't have the same thoughtful care that a man has if he is a white man.

Mr. Curley: A good many items, of course, come from the City Press that supplies all the newspapers. If it is a matter that is trivial, of course a newspaper won't send a special reporter but relies upon the City Press for accuracy. In a crime story we eliminate the word "Negro" unless there is some reason for it. We don't use any of the terms, "darky," "nigger," "coon," "shine," "wench," or "negress."

Question: Do you get news unsolicited regarding Negroes any more than other persons?

Mr. Curley: We don't take any news that comes in over the telephone without checking it.

Question: Regarding items coming from the South, is there any particular care or checking used to see whether they are true stories, trustworthy or not?

Mr. Curley: You have to take that as it comes because that is your news service. In other words, they are supposed to use their care down there the same as we do here. We have to rely on that.

Chicago Daily News.—

Mr. Lawson: Sources of information are the same as in the case of other news, and in addition matter originally in Negroes' own publications, bulletins of welfare organizations, etc. Generally speaking, it may be said that more news on this subject comes from outside sources such as telephone tips and correspondence than from members of the staff. Perhaps 10 per cent comes from the Associated Press. This is an arbitrary estimate. The same methods are used to determine the accuracy of news concerning the Negroes that are used under other circumstances. The *Daily News* does not publish any news except after determining its accuracy to the best of its ability. No special reporter may be said to be assigned to news of Negroes, but owing to his special study of the conditions in Chicago, however, Carl Sandburg is on occasion called into consultation or assigned a topic for investigation. I may say that years ago the Negro poet Dunbar was a reporter on the *News*.

Negro news is received from the Associated Press in the same manner as other news. It is not often re-written, and then only when the subject-matter is local to Chicago. Headlines are written to conform to the text of the article. The *Daily News* is in touch with very reliable and well-informed Negroes in whom, because of long experience, it has confidence. It obtains information from them and seeks their viewpoint on serious matters. We regard items describing constructive work by the Negroes or items indicating their advancement as better news than articles indicating degradation or criminality on their part. The *Daily News* endeavors to appeal to all readers alike.

Chicago Tribune.—The following is taken from the replies in the question-naire returned by Mr. Joseph M. Patterson, editor of the *Chicago Tribune:*

The sources of Negro news are the same as sources of other news. Some comes from the staff; some from the City News Bureau. Some of the local news concerning Negroes comes from reporters. No news of any consequence is received by telephone or correspondence. The Associated Press treats it on the same basis as other news. To insure accuracy the usual methods of inquiry are employed. However, most of this news comes from responsible news bureaus. Articles are re-written but only for condensation. During the threatened race riot the aid of leading Negro newspapers was sought to check information on serious matters. Each item is judged on its merits.

4. THE NEGRO PRESS

Among the considerations which have been urged by Negroes as making necessary the establishment of the Negro press are:

1. The indifference of white newspapers to the Negro group, their emphasis on the unfortunately spectacular, and the consequent loss of items of interest among Negroes throughout the country.

2. The importance of developing the morale of the Negro group, creating a solidarity of interest and purpose for measures of defense, correcting the impressions created by general opinion, and centering the attention of Negroes upon themselves and their destiny. There has never been sufficient capital for the adequate development of the Negro press. The purpose, however, has been served of collecting items of interest from all sections of the country, although they lack the facilities of so efficient an agency as the Associated Press.

For a time practically all of the northern Negro newspapers fell under the condemnation of the United States Attorney-General's office.[1] They were accused of radicalism and incitation to violence. Frequent criticisms of the Negro press declare it dangerous to the interests of cordial race relations. Ex-President Taft in the *Philadelphia Ledger* said: "The editors of the colored press should be reasoned with to cease publishing articles, however true, having inciting effect."

Commenting on criticisms of this kind, Isaac Fisher, editor of the *Fisk University News*, said:

Since the Washington and Chicago riots, the colored newspapers have been bitterly arraigned in some quarters for being responsible for race hatred. But the singular part of the indictment is that these papers are not accused of "falsifying" the record, but of stating the grounds of the Negro's resentment; and there is growing up a school of thought which argues that the colored papers should refrain from publishing as news any facts, even though true, which serve to increase the bitterness of the colored people against the white people. The comments made by those who

[1] See p. 476.

charge the Negro press with being the cause of race antagonism are unanimous in interpreting as "incendiary" all statements of facts whose bare recital makes the Negro discontented with present conditions.

It should also be noted that the charge of inciting to race hatred is laid against the Negro press specifically for the period which has followed the end of the late war; whereas the charge of inciting white people to wrath against the Negro is an old one which has been repeated again and again during the past thirty years.

But, while the Negro press is not as old as the white press and cannot possibly be charged with having "been on the job" quite so long, it is true, nevertheless, that some of its members have cast all prudence to the winds since the signing of the armistice, and have entered a mad race with the most "yellow" of yellow white journals in vitriolic race attacks, in this case upon all white people, in the attempt to meet the "yellow" white press more than half way.

Whatever the relative degree of culpability, "yellow" journalism is as reprehensible when supported by a part of the Negro press as it is when upheld by a part of the white press. The Negro might just as well learn now the lesson which the white man must learn if he would save the civilization which he has been laboring so long to perfect, i.e., that one's color and race do not excuse wrongdoing. If it is wrong for a white newspaper to make white people hate colored people, how can it be right for a Negro newspaper to make colored people hate white people?

A. CLASSIFICATION OF ARTICLES

The news items in Negro papers show a bias in reporting the opposite of that of many white papers. They emphasize the Negro's view, frequently to the point of distorting fact. If anything, they might be said to provide a compensatory interpretation of the news. The three Negro newspapers selected for study mentioned and briefly characterized in the foregoing pages will show a classification of news items appearing during a forty-week period.

In addition to general news items concerning Negroes, the *Defender* gave one page to sporting news, one page to theatrical news, two pages to personal news items sent in by correspondents in other cities, and one page to local personal items. On its editorial page two and one-half columns each week were devoted to health articles by Dr. Wilberforce Williams.

The *Whip* gave one page to sports, one to theatrical news and organization articles, one to out-of-town personal news items and one to local personal items. Its editorial page devoted one column to "Legal Hints to Women," one-half column to "Health Hints," one column to "Legal Catechism," and two columns to editorials from other papers.

The *Searchlight* gave one page to theatrical, local personal news, and church notes. The editorial page contained two half-columns each week by "The Man about Town."

TABLE XXXIII

SUBJECTS	"DEFENDER"	"WHIP"	"SEARCHLIGHT"
	Local Articles		
Crime...............................	53	46	42
Racial clashes......................	6	....	1
Education..........................	2	9	11
Business...........................	4	26	14
General news not involving race issues..........	5	66	65
Vice...............................	14	8	10
Bombing...........................	5	10	10
Politics............................	26	60	61
Social work........................	6	9	17
Public meetings....................	2	16	13
Religion...........................	7	18	34
Science............................	2	5	4
Negro progress.....................	2	....	17
Negro soldiers......................	....	6	....
Courts.............................	4	24	2
Discrimination.....................	3	9	1
Race contacts......................	....	....	....
Lynchings..........................	....	....	....
Industrial relations................	8	10	1
Philanthropy.......................	....	2	....
Personal...........................	9	....	34
Jim Crow..........................	1	1	3
General local welfare...............	2	11	3
Art................................	....	3	1
General race relations..............	....	22	1
	Local Space		
Crime.............................	586	497	669
Racial clashes......................	42	156	16
Education..........................	21	52	46
Discrimination.....................	23	62	101
Business...........................	58	199	187
General news not involving race issues..........	23	555	441
Vice...............................	112	89	201
Bombing...........................	50	121	98
Politics............................	512	741	893
Social work........................	24	41	110
Public meetings....................	84	130	66
Religion...........................	59	238	257
Science............................	59	30	46
Negro soldiers......................	....	57	48
Courts.............................	19	130	9
Race contacts......................	....	116	....
Lynchings..........................	....	....	....
Industrial relations................	72	400	13
Philanthropy.......................	....	....	....
Personal...........................	113	45	176
Jim Crow..........................	6	8	98
Art................................	....	12	2
General local welfare...............	35	78	13
General race relations..............	....	273	156
South..............................	7	105	152
Africa.............................	4	....	....
Migration..........................	....	....	....

TABLE XXXIII—*Continued*

SUBJECTS	"DEFENDER"	"WHIP"	"SEARCHLIGHT"
	Out-of-Town Articles		
Crime	282	152	32
Racial clashes	19	18	4
Education	54	42	74
Business	31	10	14
General news not involving race issues	81	104	138
Vice	31	3	....
Bombing	....	....	2
Politics	27	46	85
Social work	12	6	42
Public meetings	14	12	8
Religion	36	23	....
Science	....	4	....
Negro progress	28	....	40
Negro soldiers	11	11	33
Courts	15	24	15
Discrimination	30	21	10
Race contacts	9	3	3
Lynchings	32	54	32
Industrial relations	8	16	22
Philanthropy	11	4	2
Personal	105	9	5
Jim Crow	6	6	2
Art	1	7	5
General race relations	15	60	44
South	38	50	5
Africa	1	12	4
Migration	2	3	5
	Out-of-Town Space		
Crime	1,082	833	191
Racial clashes	136	148	43
Education	174	223	421
Business	112	40	73
General news not involving race issues	216	434	538
Vice	154	7	....
Bombing	....	....	5
Politics	132	233	365
Social work	40	41	164
Public meetings	103	76	35
Negro progress	82	244	198
Soldiers	50	46	153
Courts	120	108	66
Discrimination	145	13	49
Race contacts	44	32	13
Lynchings	239	407	215
Industrial relations	29	67	119
Philanthropy	32	21	11
Personal	213	48	20
Jim Crow	36	21	13
Art	2	22	19
General race relations	124	382	308
South	202	42	69
Africa	21	55	18
Migration	6	8	26

NOTE.—A much smaller period for study for Negro papers is necessary since practically all items appearing contain some reference to race.

TABLE XXXIV

SUBJECTS	"DEFENDER"		"WHIP"		"SEARCHLIGHT"	
	Article	Space	Article	Space	Article	Space
General race relations...........	12	137	39	525	53	868
Propaganda...................	3	60	3	65	1	6
Constructive suggestions.........	11	168	15	306	5	92
Criticism of leaders.............	3	30	10	185	5	31
Criticisms of white persons or organizations.................	6	101	6	83	4	59
Political propaganda............	30	398	10	154	17	251
Discrimination.................	7	65	....	....	5	36
Industry......................	5	39	4	65	6	39
Education.....................	....	....	3	35	5	53
South........................	5	68	5	96	6	52
Negro progress.................	5	57	9	265	14	111
General news, etc...............	3	42	12	174	9	83
Housing.......................	....	....	....	....	1	6
Miscellaneous..................	3	39	....	....	....	....
Provoked by incidents inimicable to Negroes..................	1	9	1	15	....	....

Crime publicity.—Sensational news was featured in each of the papers, especially cases in which whites and Negroes were involved. The intention appeared to be to present the Negro's side of the story. A measurement of news interest on different types of crime articles is possible in Table **XXXV**, with space in inches.

TABLE XXXV

LOCAL AND OUT-OF-TOWN CRIMES COMBINED

NEGRO NEWSPAPERS	CRIMES INVOLVING ONLY NEGROES		CRIMES INVOLVING NEGRO v. WHITE		CRIMES INVOLVING WHITES v. NEGROES		CRIMES INVOLVING ONLY WHITES	
	No. of Articles	Space	No. of Articles	Space	No. of Articles	Space	No. of Articles	Space
Defender......	233	1,032	90	467	55	260	4	31
Whip.........	75	495	70	440	44	350	8	44
Searchlight....	26	121	37	440	11	67	1	2

The method of presentation of articles revealed the strongest characteristic of Negro journalism. In this connection a random selection of headlines is interesting:

CRIMES INVOLVING WHITE ASSAILANTS AND NEGRO VICTIMS

"Free White Woman Who Killed Attorney"

"Threatens Mother and Babes with Axe"

"Bowman Milk Driver Brutally Assaults Woman"

"Crime of Postmaster Starts Serious Trouble"

"Commits Suicide to Escape Mob"

"Baby Girl Assaulted by White Farm Hand"

"Maid Is Robbed by White 'Iceman'"

"Stepped on Man's Foot in Street Car; Shot"

"Wouldn't Say 'Mister'; Is Beaten to Death"
"Kills White Man for Girl's Honor"
"Convict White Man on Rape Charge"
"Protects Wife's Honor; Slain by Land-Owner"
"White Tenants Kick on Living in Same Building with Owner"
"White Woman Confesses Lies on Colored Men"
"Kills Negro Minister for Stepping on His Foot"
"White Confectioner Arrested for Refusing to Serve Trotter"
"To Pay $750 for Attack on Negro Woman"
"White Girl Robs Father's Bank; Elopes with Negro Taken in Rooming
House; Half of Stolen Wealth Recovered"
"Two Boys Shot; Crowd Blames White Man"

CRIMES INVOLVING NEGRO ASSAILANTS AND WHITE VICTIMS
"Laundryman Stabbed in Controversy over Price"
"Boy Pupil Rebels at Scolding; Shoots Teacher"
"Slayer Captured, Tried, Hanged, in 24 Hours"
"Quarrel over Price of Cotton; Farmer Is Shot"
"Hold Three for Murder of White Infantryman"
"Haunted by Man's Face He Killed; Surrenders"

CRIMES INVOLVING ONLY NEGROES
"Woman Who Took a Life to Die Herself"
"Mother Kills Self and Babe with Gas"
"Wife Slayer Must Serve 20-Year Term"
"Raids on Homes Net Pullman Goods"
"Woman Dynamites Jail to Free Her Lover"
"Bullet Strikes Brass Chain, Man's Life Saved"
"Girl to Die on Gallows; Slew Rival"
"Cost Girl Her Life to Stop Love Affair"

Definite differences of news value were noted, between articles appearing in Negro papers and those in white papers on the same topics. The items, for the most part, carried a specific appeal. Where the item was of general interest and appeared in both white and Negro papers, the facts usually corresponded.

The difference again lies in emphasis and prominence. Headlines for the same news, as shown in white and Negro papers, follow:

WHITE NEWSPAPERS	NEGRO NEWSPAPERS
"Jim Crow Law Is Upheld by U.S. High Court" [*Chicago Tribune*, April 20, 1920]	"Highest Court Upholds Jim Crow Law. Separate Cars for White and Colored People Declared Legal in Kentucky" [*Chicago Searchlight*, April 24, 1920]
"Miscegnation is O.K'd. in New Constitution. Negroes Given All the Rights of Whites" [*Chicago Tribune*, Nov. 6, 1920]	"Morris Gets Civil Rights into Constitution. Victory for Race Won at Springfield" [*Chicago Whip*, July 10, 1920]

"Phillips High School for Colored
Pupils, Principal Suggests"
[*Chicago Tribune.* March 8, 1920]

"Jim-Crow School Scheme Exposes
Attempt to Inaugurate Separate
Schools in Chicago—Discovered
and Opposed"
[*Chicago Searchlight*, July 31, 1920]

"Accuse Perrine of Color Line Ruling.
Principal of Wendell Phillips Openly
Attacked by Public. Who Saw
Children Jim Crowed at Com-
mencement; Ask His Removal;
Ministers Feared as Betrayers"
[*Chicago Defender*, July 3, 1920]

Group control.—Although the Negro population does not rely upon the Negro press for authentic general news it does rely upon it for news concerning Negroes. The *Chicago Whip* devotes two columns of the paper to a section called "Under the Lash of the Whip," the "You Know 'Em, Editor," and "Nosey Knows." Persons who become offensive to the principles supported by the *Whip* are put "Under the Lash." "Nosey Knows" and the "You Know 'Em, Editor" attempt to hold individual conduct of Negroes to conventional standards by the threat of semi-publicity, for example:

You know those new "loop hounds." I know them because they go to the loop for the purpose of visiting—no object of buying anything. Well, tell them it's alright to go to the loop, but they don't have to attract everybody's attention for blocks around with their loud talk, using their ignorant, non-sensical expressions. And should they get hungry while down there and feel like having lunch, don't stand outside the door of a restaurant with a surprised look on their faces—just tell them to walk right in, in an orderly and sensible manner and order what they want. They don't have to slip in like thieves.

You know the restaurants where those household insects known as flies are very prevalent. I know you know them, because they are all along State Street, Thirty-first and Thirty-fifth. Well, if you don't mind, kindly tell some of those proprietors that there is a way of ridding their places of such nuisances.

You probably don't know that lady who resides in a prominent building in the vicinity of Thirty-first Street and Indiana Avenue, and who tried to enveigle a young girl on the street car to her flat by telling her that she could meet some high class doctors and lawyers there. Well, you may not know her now, but if you watch the columns of the *Whip* you will know her because she is gradually working her way to the penitentiary by the route of the seduction law. Everybody will know her then.

The *Searchlight* carries a column by "The Man about Town" which is similar in character. Two examples of its criticism of Negro conduct were:

The gang that hangs around the "pillars of knowledge" in the county building every day at noon is becoming so obnoxious that they are attracting the attention of everybody who enters the building.

Politicians from every section of the city crowd there and shoot off their "hot air" in a loud tone of voice. They seem to think that the future of the country depends on what they say or do.

They have become so bold in their actions they have begun to stop some of our race women and engage them in conversation around that historic spot.

Now boys, cut out that "rough stuff" and take a walk around the block at noon and let the fresh air blow on your beautiful carcas; if you don't the sheriff will ask you to do so, or he may take some of you fellows to the North Side. Don't make yourself a nuisance around the city hall and county building. Hear me, boys.

Another thing that is very disgusting is the arrogance of the girl waitresses in some of these race restaurants. Instead of striving to please the patrons they act as though they were doing you a personal favor to serve you, and when you are through with your meal you must thank them for so doing and leave a piece of money at the cash stand for them. If you don't do that the very next time you go into that restaurant the waiter will not want to wait on you. The poor proprietor of the place, if he or she is one of the "brothers" or "sisters," is almost helpless in the matter because if he opens his mouth to one of these so-called waitresses about the mistreatment of their guests he is minus a waiter. Go down in the loop and see how the other folks attend to business and treat patrons. Awake, folks, from your slumber; you are fast asleep. Do you hear me?

A fight on vice in the Second Ward was begun by the *Searchlight* and finally given strong emphasis by the local daily papers.

B. NEGRO NEWSPAPER POLICY

Although Negroes for their general news depend upon the white press, with its superior facilities, they look to the Negro press for full and specific news covering the activities of Negroes. The editorial columns, as well as the arrangement of news items and writing of headlines, are aimed at building up the morale of the Negro group. Frequently an attempt is made to get these papers into the hands of whites to acquaint them with the Negro's point of view.

A conference was held by the Commission with several Negro newspaper men. The Negro press was represented by R. S. Abbott, editor and publisher of the *Chicago Defender;* Nahum D. Brascher, editor-in-chief, and Claude Barnett, director of the Associated Negro Press; Willis N. Huggins, editor of the *Upreach Magazine;* and R. E. Parker, editor of the *Chicago Advocate.*

Mr. Brascher, of the Associated Negro Press, said:

The colored newspapers have recently gotten up to the point where most of us are proud to have them seen in the hands of our white friends and it is only through them that they can really get our viewpoint. We cannot hope to have the daily newspapers give our viewpoint and the aspirations and struggles that we are making, and some of the things that we are suffering. I am very much interested in having the editorial feeling of the newspaper get to the white people. Sometimes they may be termed as radical. I found in recent months that some of the weekly papers published in the South are saying things editorially that I would question about saying even here in Chicago, and, as we say in common parlance, getting away with it I have in mind now one particular instance. In Houston, Texas, week before last, the entire circulation list of the *Houston Informer* was stolen out of its office. The theft was attributed to the new organization of the Ku Klux Klan. The daily papers of Houston came out condemning that move, and also condemning the idea of the Ku Klux Klan, and this young man has an editorial in last week's issue that is one of the strongest I have ever seen on the matter, backed probably by some of the strong things that have been said in the daily papers.

Now if we could have people of Chicago know just how the sentiment is changing in the South in favor of a square deal and mutual toleration, we could soon get to a point where there'd be no fear on either side of working out our salvation, you might say, along co-operative lines.

Another instance concerned the *Plain Dealer* in Birmingham, Ala. The Ku Klux Klan paraded the streets of that city about three weeks ago and in an editorial this paper came out and stated that if that was done to frighten the colored people, they had to do something different, because whenever they began to terrorize and came down into the neighborhood where colored people lived somebody there would be ready to meet them. That is a pretty strong statement for Birmingham, and they got away with it.

The *Chicago Defender* gives the greatest amount of space to criminal news of a sensational type in the field of racial happenings. It is a great favorite in the South with Negroes because it publishes news condemning the practices of the South in terms forbidden to southern Negro journals. Of a circulation of 185,000, two-thirds of which is outside of Chicago, it was largely responsible for stimulating the migration to the North.

The term "Negro" is used occasionally in the *Defender*. Its policy is to use the term "race" man, where it is necessary to distinguish Negro from other groups. Adopting the opposite policy from the white papers, it places "white" after persons not Negroes to mark the distinction. Concerning this, Mr. R. S. Abbott, editor of the *Defender*, said:

We use that as a bridge, as you might say, which we intend to blow up pretty soon. We are leading the people away from the word "Negro," especially in our papers. And in cases where white men are well known in the country we never even put "white" after their names. We never put "colored" after a colored man's name in this city.

The *Defender's* editorials are as a rule carefully written, balanced, and critical, at times in contrast with the popular appeal of the news articles. The *Whip's* editorials usually are on some aspect of the general race problem in the United States. They are characterized by strong pronouncements of the views of Negroes and violent criticism of practices alleged to be inimicable to Negroes. An editorial from each of the papers will indicate the trends of interests. The first is from the *Defender:*

JUST BETWEEN OURSELVES

Character is what we are; reputation is what other people think we are. We get only the respect we demand; no more, no less. One of the greatest barriers to our progress is the individual who attempts to curry the favor of the whites by whom he is employed by openly humiliating and insulting others of his same flesh and blood. Because sections of this country reek with color prejudice, must we lend a helping hand to those who foster segregation, discrimination and "Jim Crowism" in general? And yet that is just what many are doing.

In the railroad service as waiters and porters we have a monopoly, and those whose runs require them to cross the Mason and Dixon line are often confronted with situations that require good common sense in handling. In many states the law requires the blacks and the whites to be separated on transportation lines, dining-rooms, places of amusement, etc. There is no question as to whether these laws are just or unjust. They are at least temporary laws and must be obeyed. But there is something mentally wrong with the porter or the waiter who lends himself to such measures, whether under orders from his superiors or not.

Admitting that to disobey such orders means the loss of a job, there are other jobs that pay a better wage where a man does not have to sacrifice his principles to hold. What other group of people in the world have those that could be induced at any price to place their heel on the neck of even the humblest member of their race? Are we less human, less interested in the welfare of our race than they? Are we still puppets, still chattels, still ignorant of the fact that as we respect ourselves, so others will respect us? This matter is put squarely up to you, Mr. Porter; to you, Mr. Waiter. Will you play the part of a man and refuse to humiliate your people? Will you cease playing the part of a spy? Will you singly and collectively tender your resignation to employers who require you to "Jim Crow" one of your own? If you will do these things there is only one thing that can happen—a speedy repeal of the offensive legislation.

Recently a young woman who was able to "pass" entered the Washington (D.C.) railroad station café and was given a seat at a table with several other ladies. Soon there entered two refined, well-dressed, unmistakably colored, young women who took seats at an unoccupied table. Immediately a colored waiter rushed over to them and after a few minutes of whispered conversation the embarrassed patrons followed the waiter to a far corner of the café, where semi-screened off they were permitted to dine. So enraged was the first young woman that she boldly went to the desk where stood the white higher-ups and several waiters, and gave them a curtain lecture they doubtless will not soon forget, not failing to tell them her own nationality. This incident happened in Washington, the seat of our government, where the doctrine of democracy is preached but not practiced.

Things worth having are worth fighting for. We must make sacrifices. If it is the policy of certain business places to discriminate let us not be a party to the discrimination. Let it be firmly fixed in the mind that we are a vital part of this nation's life, that we are a necessary "evil," that our places cannot and will not be filled with whites, no matter how drastic is our stand, providing we have right on our side, which we undoubtedly have in this instance. This heart to heart talk applies to those engaged in other lines of endeavor as well as it does to those who follow railroading.

Many who run barber shops, for instance, display the sign, "For whites only." If we did not realize that these evils are the direct result of ignorance and lack of racial pride, it would indeed be discouraging. But, truly, we are still a child race. We must not be flattered by the tales of our marvelous advance during the last fifty years into dropping our oars and resting on our laurels, for we have barely started up the hill called success. When we have reached the first milestone on our journey—racial solidarity—the rest of the way will be comparatively easy. Success has come to the Jew and to the Japanese because they are clannish. Black isn't a bad shade; let's make it popular in complexions as well as in clothes.

This is from the *Whip:*

WHO'S AFRAID?

If the white races of the world are so sure of their inborn and inherent supremacy, if they are so sure that they are the salt of the earth and the born rulers of human kind, it appears to us as strange indeed that they should fear that their glory will be usurped, their power depreciated, and their world-wide domination seriously challenged.

As a general rule, the giant does not fear the pigmy, neither does man, the acme of civilization, fear that his civilization will be eclipsed by a new order of apes. Should the tribes and clans of the highest developed gorillas seek to overrun the accomplishments of humanity, no one would say, "Beware of monkey domination." Man, according to his own concepts, is only a little lower than the angels and the monkey just a little lower than himself. The white races claim that their darker brothers are lower in the graduated scale of their own making than themselves, yet they cry out, "Beware of the Yellow Peril and behold the Black Plague."

If the white races possess the keys to knowledge and the passwords to progress as well as the elixirs of strength, why should they fear danger of "Black domination" and "Yellow dictation"? The white man, even through the maze of his own conceit and out of the trance of his self-hypnotism, sees that "he and his heirs" shall not forever inherit the face of the earth.

The black and yellow races are breaking the white man's monopoly of organized brain and wealth. The white man sees this and in his own bigotry knows that these people are not his inferiors in latent abilities. He knows that the same fire of genius burns in the breasts of the black and yellow races as did in the dark and mediaeval ages. He knows that black and yellow men can unravel the mysteries of nature and the intricacies of science. He knows that creative and constructive ability has been beaten down by his might but yet it lives. The white races know that their present achievements are small in comparison with those which will be accomplished. It is feared that in the future, not in the mediate or immediate, but not far distant nevertheless, that the sleeping giant will awaken, shake off the listlessness of a thousand years and put into action again the powerful dynamo of his great reign and shake the world again.

We do not object to the cry of "Beware of the Yellow Peril and behold the Black Plague." It is the involuntary shriek of danger which is a part of man's reaction. White people know that they are not superior to the dark races. They know that the raillery about dark people being innately and inherently inferior is nothing more than the outcropping of race prejudice, color hatred and ignoble fear. They fear that should they lose the power of might and brute force, and equal opportunities are gained by the dark people, that they will be dethroned and surpassed. For this reason they warn of the unfitness and undesirability of their darker brothers. They ruthlessly declare that Japanese, East Indians and Negroes are not their equals and justify all of their tyranny upon this foolish subterfuge.

We are tired of subterfuge and evasiveness. If the white man wishes to maintain his power at the expense of the dark people of the world, let him cease his prattlings about charity, human kindness and benevolence. Let him admit that he is afraid of the rising tide of color and fear shakes his entire system. Let the world know that the cry of inferiority and unfitness is not conscientious and that apprehension clouds the brow of white humanity.

An editorial in the *Searchlight* read:

CLEANING UP THE "BLACK BELT"

"Death Corner" has a local reputation which bespeaks an abominable state of affairs. Nice respectable persons dare not visit it unless heavily escorted. The "East Side" in New York provokes a shiver by the very sound of the name. The "Black Belt" carries the same dark background of hovering evil. One is expected to regard black belts as isolated plague-spots full of lurking pitfalls for unsuspecting innocents. It is spoken of as "that Black Belt down there." Little girls go there and go wrong and you never hear of them again. When trouble is threatened in the city the police force is dumped into it with clubs and pistols and rifles, patrol wagons, flivvers and ambulances. For you can never tell what is likely to break out in a place with so many mysterious corners and vicious characters. When the morals of the city come under scrutiny the crusaders send up a howl of helplessness for the rampant vices in that "Black Belt down there." The entire city believes it to be a bad place. The neglect of it is a standing disgrace to the city, and yet the only means of cleaning it up and bringing it up to the standard of the community as a whole discovered so far is by keeping the handful of white persons out of it. The protests against the mixed cafés, by far the loudest and most severe, seem to represent the sole spirit and motive of the effort. No attention is paid to the iron circle tightening around this section and making it practically impossible for Negroes to move out. No attention is paid to the rundown schools in the district. No one is interested in providing recreation facilities for the thousands of colored children growing up in the streets. No one of these reformers and critics has suggested that a branch of the public library be made convenient. The Juvenile Protective Association, an association whose purpose is to prevent criminality, walks around the district and speaks about it as disparagingly as the rest. The old Committee of Fifteen had no representative there to detect the out-cropping of vicious places. It had been thus for the eight years of its existence. And yet epithets are hurled at the district, and it is called bad names and the city turns up its nose and goes on.

C. NEGRO NEWS SOURCES

Negro newspapers are published weekly because they cannot compete with the daily papers in providing any part of the public with news from day to day.

For out-of-town news, the news letters of correspondents and accounts of incidents by specially designated representatives make up a large portion of the reports. All the papers have the service of a clipping bureau. Items in local papers are noted and, when practicable, the newspapers telegraph to some responsible person in town to send a full account of the incident. Traveling men from Chicago and friends of the paper scattered throughout the country also contribute to the news supply. News letters containing personal items are still continued in the *Defender* and are said to be responsible for the first extension of its circulation. The *Defender* and the *Whip* have small staffs of reporters to cover local news. The objects of the Associated Negro Press were thus outlined by Mr. Barnett, a representative of that organization:

It is an organization of affiliated newspapers. We serve eighty-nine newspapers throughout the country, the total circulation of these papers as given to us for advertising purposes running a little in excess of 400,000. . . . .

We handle items only that are of national importance because we are a national news service. We gather all out of town items that we are able to gather for the same reason, if they are of national importance. As a news service we would not take any purely local item in Chicago unless it would interest readers in every section of the country. We also get service from a clipping bureau.

It all relates to the interests of the colored people. If there is anything which affects the country at large, which also has either an indirect or a direct influence upon our group, we feature it, but as a rule most of the news which we gather is about things which particularly affect colored people.

II. RUMOR

Rumors which significantly affect race relations consist largely of unfounded tales, incorrectly deduced conclusions, or partial statements of fact with significant content added by the narrator, all of which are given easy and irresponsible circulation by a credulous public during the excitement of a clash. Examples of this type of irritating untruth were found in the Chicago riot.

The number of Negroes killed during the riot (twenty-three Negroes and fifteen whites) has been magnified in popular accounts beyond all reasonable limits of credibility. It is popularly believed that more persons were killed than official records indicate. The exaggeration has not been confined to reports involving Negroes. For example, there was a report in circulation that more than seventy-five white policemen were killed during the riot. The rumor was traced to the half-jesting remark of a policeman that, as a member of a benefit organization, he had paid death dues on a number of policemen greater than the total deaths of the riot as popularly estimated at the time. This number was placed at seventy-five. The director of the Civic Bureau of the Seattle Chamber of Commerce, writing to a friend in Chicago, asked for authentic information concerning the number of Negroes killed during the riot. He sought the information because, he said, the industrial editor of the *Outlook* had told him that police officers said that "more than 2,000 Negroes were killed in the race riot," and that a certain labor report placed the number at 1,700. Suspecting that even the latter number was too large, although the police mentioned 10,000 wounded and killed, he wrote for information.

I. AN IMPRESSION STUDY

A special impression study was made with a class of forty-nine students in the University of Chicago, to measure the effect upon them of word-of-mouth rumor, gossip, and newspaper stories concerning the 1919 riot. Specific questions were asked concerning their understanding as to the number of whites and Negroes killed and their source of information. The students ranged in age from twenty to twenty-five years. Each was asked to indicate in the order of their influence upon him the sources of information which gave him his understanding of the magnitude of the riot. The following is a compilation from their statements.

Ten were out of the city at the time and got their information chiefly through newspapers published elsewhere. Their average opinion of the number killed was fifty-five. Thirteen were informed chiefly by second-hand stories quoting relatives who were in Chicago, policemen interviewed, and others, and their general impression of the number killed averaged 209. Thirty-three got their information from newspapers both in and out of the city, and their average impression of the number killed was 115. Twenty-four of those who were residing in Chicago got their information chiefly from newspapers published in the city, and their average impression was that 131 were killed.

A point of interest in comparison is that those who were out of town and read out-of-town newspapers believed seventy-three were killed, while those who got their information through local publications thought 131 were killed. One young woman made this interesting comment:

I think a very conservative estimate of the number killed would be about 450 or 500. My first source of information, newspapers. My father also told me of the affair and he is a medical director of an insurance company and therefore was in a more or less good position to know.

A young man said:

There were at least 200 people killed in the race riot. Sources of information: a policeman who was stationed at Forty-seventh Street and Wentworth, my own direct observations, and conversations with people who live in the Black Belt.

Another young man said:

About 200 were killed. Chief source of information a review of Carl Sandburg's pamphlet, and newspaper stories.

Another young woman thought that about 150 were killed. She said that her father maintained an office at Forty-third Street and St. Lawrence Avenue, which is in the Negro district. Another said:

If I remember correctly, about forty black and white people were killed and several hundred wounded, and there was a loss of several thousand dollars worth of property by fire. The chief information that impressed me was personal experiences. I witnessed one mob of 2,000 whites take a Negro on the West Side and burn him to death. The newspaper gave me my information of atrocities on both sides.

Another stated that he believed the number killed in the race riot in Chicago was about 275, and continued:

I base my guess on reports of the newspapers, i.e., the dailies of the city and particularly one weekly paper which in my opinion is entirely unbiased in such matters, the *Weekly Socialist*. I personally saw four Negroes lynched and shot to death.

It might be expected that a fairly balanced type of impression would come from university students. The effect of rumor stands out from the examination of this highly selected group. In exaggeration the word-of-mouth rumors led, followed by rumors circulated by newspapers and alleged first-hand accounts of eyewitnesses.

Rumors from policemen and relatives placed the average number of persons killed at 209, the largest average of the lot. This is significant when taken with the reports given in the foregoing pages which emananted from policemen. Undoubtedly their experiences were of such a nature as to make exaggeration easy and plausible. They were living in conditions far from normal, and their impressions were greatly magnified by the stress and the excitement of events. The out-of-town students were less affected by word-of-mouth rumor, and consequently their impressions showed the smallest average of persons killed.

Personal experiences show more vividly than anything else the unreliability of much of the testimony from observation that gives such frequent rise to rumor. One student said he saw a mob of 2,000 whites take a Negro on the West Side and burn him to death. Records show that only one Negro was killed on the West Side (Joseph Lovings). He was shot and stabbed many times, but not burned.[1] Another student "personally saw four Negroes lynched and shot to death." No Negroes were lynched in the riot.

2. THE BUBBLY CREEK RUMOR

A persistent rumor during the riot served to provide an explanation of the unaccounted deaths of the riot. It had plausibility and soon was accepted and even repeated on the floor of Congress in Washington as a fact. Bubbly Creek is a small branch of the Chicago River extending to the Stock Yards. Into it flows a great deal of waste from the slaughter houses. The surface of the water is thick with the scum of decomposed substances, hair, and trash. Bodies could be thrown into it and remain undetected for a long time. A rumor became current that bodies of riot victims were thrown into this stream. It became so persistent that efforts were actually made to discover them.

[1] See coroner's statement, p. 32.

Even when no bodies were found, the rumor did not weaken. Examples of how it cropped up in various ways are given:

A man told a friend of mine, I can furnish the name of that man; a man told him that he saw fifty-six bodies taken out of Bubbly Creek. [A juror in the coroner's inquest.]

I heard the story that 100 men had been taken out of Bubbly Creek. They used a net and a seine to drag them out. [A. L. Williams, attorney, before the coroner's jury.]

There is a story that was repeated on the floor of Congress that numerous colored people were caught down there [at the Stock Yards] and thrown in Bubbly Creek, and their bodies never recovered. A congressman from our district down there, representing our Stock Yards district, told me that on the floor of Congress it was recently stated that a man with a dumb-bell in his hand stood there at the big rock entrance of Exchange Avenue and knocked a half-dozen of these colored men on the heads as they passed through that rock door there. [A juror in the coroner's inquest.]

I hear they dragged two or three bodies out of Bubbly Creek. [A witness before the coroner's jury.]

A meat curer in the superintendent's office of Swift & Company said: "Well, I hear they did drag two or three out of Bubbly Creek—dead bodies, that is the report that come in the yards, but personally I never got any positive evidence that there was any people who was found there."

The *Chicago Daily News* of July 29, 1919, printed the subheading: "Four Bodies in Bubbly Creek." The article did not give details, but said: "Bodies of four colored men were taken today from Bubbly Creek in the Stock Yards district, it is reported."

In its final report the coroner's jury made a conclusive statement regarding the Bubbly Creek rumor which stamped it as pure rumor.[1]

3. RIOT RUMORS

The state of mind produced by rumors is manifest in other experiences of riot. The following is an example:

At Forty-fourth Street and Grand Boulevard, a corner on which the only Negro family in the block lived at the time of the riot, an elderly white man clad in a worn dressing-gown, carpet slippers, and a skull cap, excitedly rushed from his house to the curb and shouted to a crowd: "They're giving ammunition away to the niggers at the Eighth Regiment Armory!" The crowd became excited and finally threatened the house of the Negro family. A cry went up, "Hang the niggers! The niggers in the house are firing at every white man that passes!" The police searched the house and found an 1894 model rifle, ammunition, that would not fit, and a decorated sword. The six Negroes in the house were taken to the police station.

During the riot a white man was caught crawling beneath a house in which Negroes lived. In his pocket was found a bottle of kerosene. He

[1] See p. 33.

confessed that his mission was arson and justified his intended act by repeating a rumor then current that Negroes had set fire to the houses of whites back of the Yards.

One Negro said that a mob of white men knocked a colored woman down, cut her up frightfully, and then took her baby and dashed its brains out on the street-car tracks. He was of fair complexion and could easily be taken for white. He said:

I came upon the mob as they were laughing and shouting. Why I could have torn every one of the white cusses in a thousand pieces. Just think, they stood there laughing and shouting over what they had done. Why every drop of blood in my body boiled and at that momemt I swore to God in heaven that I'd kill some white man if I swung for it.

This report was not substantiated by wide and thorough inquiry by the Commission.

Rumor in the East St. Louis riot.—Under "Myths," hereinafter discussed, are given stereotyped sex stories circulated to produce antagonistic sentiment toward Negroes. Many rumors, however, which had no relation to sex crimes were circulated at the time of the East St. Louis riot. The following example taken from the testimony before one of the boards of inquiry pictures the effective use at East St. Louis of a rumor concerning an imaginary smallpox epidemic:

Mr. Tower: Other statements I heard were that people feared an epidemic of smallpox; that the County Hospital had been burdened for months with an average of thirty cases of smallpox. . . . . The whole County became fearful. You could hear the same discussions away from East St. Louis. People were inflamed, and their feelings were directed against the big employers of East St. Louis feeling that they were responsible for the great influx of Negroes.

4. RUMORS PREDICTING RIOTS

Rumors that persist usually have some plausibility. The series which follows contains elements of possible truth. Rumors predicting race riots in Chicago centered about fixed dates on which excitement often existed each year. Thus July 4, a holiday celebrated with fireworks and noise in which shots would not be noticed, was the date set in popular expectation for the Chicago riot that broke out almost three weeks later. Signs had been posted in Washington Park to the effect that Negroes would be driven out of the park on that date.

All this expectation undoubtedly caused preparation for trouble. It is conceivable that this preparation at least accentuated the violence of the riot which began on July 27.

Hallowe'en night, when ruffians could mask and take reprisals with less fear of identification or detection than ordinarily, was the next date in popular expectation. An official report to Washington by a governmental agency on "Radicalism among Negroes," carried the rumor thus:

. . . . A report was received at this office to the effect that an uprising of Negroes in Chicago has been planned for the night of October 31, 1919. This report came in a somewhat vague form, through children attending schools located in the colored districts. The Negroes were aroused over a report to the effect that the white residents of a certain South Side district were planning to drive out all colored inhabitants. The police were informed of the situation.

No riot occurred at or near that date.

May 1, 1920, was next rumored as the date when a riot would start surpassing in violence any that had yet occurred. Labor parades were planned in Chicago for May 1, 1920. It is also moving day, many residence leases then expiring. Thousands of Negroes, it was widely said, would be told to leave Hyde Park. Negroes, it was further said, had no intention of leaving and would oppose ejection even with force. This rumor was taken up and circulated by responsible authorities. As early as April 20, 1920, this article appeared in the *Herald-Examiner:*

U.S. SEES RACE RIOTS HERE MAY 1

Warning that race riots may occur in the South Side Negro districts May 1 was sent yesterday to John H. Alcock, first deputy superintendent of police, by the army intelligence department. The exact nature of the warning could not be learned and no information could be obtained as to the supposed source of the predicted trouble, but it is expected to arise when Negro families move into new homes in white sections of the South Side.

Numerous bombings have given strength to the belief that more trouble may develop this summer. Official notice to the police department is said to have been made by E. J. Rowens of the army intelligence staff.

No comment on the warning could be obtained from Chief of Police John J. Garrity or Superintendent Alcock. Capt. Michael Gallery of the Deering St. Station said that he believed such reports were absurd.

"I have been all through the Negro section of my district today," said Capt. Gallery. "All is serene and the Negroes are happy. I do not believe that there will be any trouble this summer."

Capt. Thomas Caughlin of the Cottage Grove Ave. Station in whose district the riots started last summer, said he was always prepared and on the lookout for trouble in his territory.

An inquiry based upon this "May 1" rumor came to the Commission. The manager of a West Side restaurant told the Commission that a Negro girl in his employ had asked him whether it would be safe for her to come to work on that day. Her sister had been warned in a friendly way by white fellow-waitresses in a downtown restaurant that she should not risk coming to work that day, "because there is going to be a race riot."

On May 1, as was to have been expected, thousands of persons were armed and ready for the anticipated clash.

No riots occurred. The report was later denied by the Army Intelligence Department.

Labor Day, 1920, was next set. Rumors flying fast were picked up by agents from the state's attorney's office. Reports by these agents from day to day show the persistence of the rumor. For example:

The U.S. Club which had planned to hold a meeting August 28, did not hold the meeting because they expected another race riot on Labor Day.

On August 28, Negroes in the barber shop on —— State Street were carrying guns. Many went to Gary and Hammond to stock up against Labor Day but found that hardware dealers would not sell.

On August 29 little else was talked about in the Black Belt outside the coming riot on Labor Day. The statement of Garrity [chief of police] that an extra cordon of police would patrol the Black Belt was taken as confirmation of the rumor August 20.

An averted clash.—Seeley Street on the West Side is a district where Negroes infrequently go. On the night of May 1, one of the dates scheduled in rumors and reports for a race riot in Chicago, the daughter of a pressroom foreman was returning home at night. As she passed an alley a man grabbed her by the arm and attempted to drag her into the alley. She managed to struggle away and ran home, reporting the incident incoherently to her father. Immediately he armed himself and went out looking for the assailant.

Near the alley where the incident occurred, a lone Negro was standing dressed in overalls. Across the street was a clubroom in which were a number of white men. When he saw the Negro his first impulse was to shoot. The Negro, however, gave no indication of being hunted, but reached into his pocket, looked at his watch, and continued to stand there.

It occurred to the father that he had not learned from the girl whether it was a white man or a Negro who had attempted to attack her. He went back home and asked, and she said it was a white man.

5. RUMORS CONCERNING NEGRO RADICALS

During the country-wide excitement over radicals caused by the activities of the Department of Justice in the fall of 1919, the Chicago office of the United States Army Intelligence Bureau sent to Washington reports concerning Negro organizations. These reports were founded upon scarcely anything more than suspicion due to lack of information and acquaintance with the Negro group. One section of a report made in October, 1919, read:

A convention of the colored organization known as the National Urban League was held in Detroit on October 15, 1919, at which Eugene Kinkle Jones, Negro agitator, presided. Mr. Jones has his headquarters at 127 East 23rd Street, New York City. Wm. D. Haywood was invited to speak at this convention.

The National Urban League is an organization of responsible Negroes and whites, with branches in thirty-one cities. It numbers among its executive officers L. Hollingsworth Wood, A. S. Frizzell, Robert R. Moton, Mrs. Julius

Rosenwald, George W. Seligman, and Mrs. Booker T. Washington. Its avowed purposes are:

1. Try to show social welfare agencies the advantage of co-operation.
2. Secure and train social workers.
3. Protect women and children from unscrupulous persons.
4. Fit workers for work
5. Help to secure playgrounds and other clean places of amusement.
6. Organize boys' and girls' clubs and neighborhood unions.
7. Help with probation oversight of delinquents.
8. Maintain a country home for convalescent women.
9. Investigate conditions of city life as a basis for practical work.

Concerning the reference to William D. Haywood and E. K. Jones, this statement was received by the Commission from E. K. Jones:

The National Urban League did hold its annual convention in Detroit, October 15, 1919. William D. Haywood was not invited to speak at this convention. Judging from the reference to Haywood the term "Negro agitator" as applied to myself connotes a most violently radical strain in whatever methods I might be using to bring about better conditions for the Negro.

Throughout my ten years' connection with the League, I have sought by courageous but practical methods to bring to the Negro an opportunity in American life and have urged Negroes to measure up in every way along lines of efficiency and be satisfied with nothing but a square deal and equal opportunity in our national life.

I have never suggested violence of any kind as a means toward this end, nor, in fact, has the idea ever arisen in my mind that this would be an effective means of attaining this end.

From the same Intelligence Bureau report this statement is taken: "Another recent report states that the National Association for the Advancement of Colored People with offices at 70 Fifth Avenue, New York City, is planning to flood the colored districts with I.W.W. literature."

The National Association for the Advancement of Colored People is a reputable organization of whites and Negroes numbering among its executive officers Hon. Moorfield Storey, Rev. John Haynes Holmes, Arthur E. Spingarn, Oswald Garrison Villard, Mary White Ovington, and Dr. Charles E. Bentley. It has no relation with the I.W.W. and has never planned any distribution of I.W.W. literature.

6. RUMOR WITHIN THE NEGRO GROUP

The *Chicago Advocate*, a Negro paper of an irresponsible, sensational type, published under large headlines a report of a run on the Lincoln State Bank. The reason alleged was indignation over the refusal of the white officials of the bank to lend money on Negro property in Hyde Park. The bank officials were accused of discrimination in favor of an organization of men in Hyde Park who were making every effort to keep Negroes segregated within the

"Black Belt." The Pyramid Building and Loan Association was said to have requested the loan. Since nearly 90 per cent of the depositors of the bank were supposed to be Negroes, the act was considered an insulting disloyalty to Negroes who supported the institution.

A number of Negroes, believing that their savings were in danger, rushed to the bank. Soon there was an actual run, and for several days long lines of depositors passed through the bank and carried away their savings. More than $243,000 was withdrawn. The report proved to be without foundation, and the three largest and most influential Negro newspapers aided in restoring normal business relations. The president of the bank charged the head of the Building and Loan Association and the editor of the newspaper that published the story with responsibility for this rumor.

7. RUMORS OF ATROCITIES

Of the type of rumor which has had effect upon the sentiments of Negroes concerning the Chicago riot, the following quotations from a pamphlet entitled *The Chicago Race Riots*, by Austin D. N. Sutton, a Negro, provide a good example:

In an investigation made personally by me, beginning about five o'clock Wednesday afternoon, July 30, until far into the evening, visiting the districts from Forty-seventh Street, East to Indiana Avenue, West to Wentworth Avenue, South to Fifty-fifth Street, I found a little short street between Forty-eighth and Fifth Avenue called Swan Street, that is not easily located, and very little known by the general public. Eye-witnesses said that men, women and children were being attacked and killed and thrown into the sewer, and no account of their whereabouts has ever been given.

I found about twenty refugees who had been run away from their homes on Forty-eighth, Forty-ninth and Fifth Avenue, also Wentworth and Princeton avenues. Their homes had been burned, and they were made to flee for their lives. I have the names and addresses of more than one hundred cases investigated, one more horrible case, where a young colored boy was gasolined and burned after having been killed and where colored women in the Stock Yards district were attacked and their breasts cut off. These things were perpetrated by the whites upon peaceful law-abiding blacks, some of whom had been residents for twenty-seven years in that neighborhood.

Thorough inquiries were made by the Commission into these alleged atrocities, and no evidence was found to show that anyone was "gasolined and burned" during the riot or that any colored women's breasts were cut off.

8. RUMORS AND THE MIGRATION

The rumors in circulation in the South at the beginning of the migration of Negroes to the North were responsible for the presence in Chicago of many who heard them. It is hard to conceive how the tale that the Germans were on their way through Texas to take the southern states could have been believed, yet it is reported that this extravagant rumor was taken seriously in some quarters.

On the outskirts of Meridian, Mississippi, a band of gypsies was encamped. The rumor gained circulation that the Indians were coming back to retake their land, lost many years ago. Further it was declared that the United States government was beginning a scheme to transport all the Negroes from the South to break up the Black Belt. Passed from mouth to mouth unrestrainedly, the tale became an established verity for many Negroes.

It was declared on the word of honor of "one in a position to know" that the packing-houses in Chicago needed and would get 50,000 Negro workers before the end of 1917. One explanation of the belief that the South was overrun with labor agents is the fact that Negroes at the South saw in every stranger a man from the North looking for laborers and their families. If he denied it, they thought that he was concealing his identity from the police, and if he said nothing, his silence was regarded as affirmation.

Hundreds of disappointments of prospective migrants were traced to the rumor that a train would leave on a certain date, sometimes after the presence of a stranger in town; they would come to the station prepared to leave, and when no agent appeared, would purchase their own tickets to the North. Wages and privileges in the North were greatly exaggerated. Some men, on being questioned, supposed that it was possible for any common laborer to earn $10 a day and that $50 a week was not unusual. The strength of this belief was remarked by several social agencies in Chicago which attempted to supply migrants with work. The actual wages paid, though much in excess of what they had been receiving, were disappointing. Similarly in the matter of privilege and "rights," it was later discovered by the migrants that unbounded liberty was not to be found in the North. Many cases of grotesque misconduct of newly arrived migrants in Chicago, against which more sober-minded Negroes preached, possibly had root in exaggerated reports of "freedom and privilege" in the North which had reached the South.[1]

III. MYTHS

There arise among groups of people various stories with little or no basis in fact, which, through repetition and unvaried association with the same persons or incidents, come to be regarded as true. These stories, when they persist through years and even through generations, are myths. They are usually the response to a prejudice or a desire.

In general they have some plausible and apparent justification. In turn they lend stability not only to the beliefs out of which they were born, but to themselves. Frequently they are the result of the assumption that because two things happen at the same time they are connected by the relationship of cause and effect. So long as these stories are uncorrected they hold and exercise a marked degree of control over personal conduct.

Myths are important in any consideration of the instruments of opinion-making. Fernand von Langenhove, a Belgian scientist associated with the

[1] Charles S. Johnson, *The Migration of Negroes to Chicago.*

Solvay Institute for Sociological Study at Brussels, has made probably the first researches in this field. He took as his material the reports spread in Germany by German soldiers concerning the Belgian priests. These myths, for the most part unfounded, began to spread and eventually were taken up by German authorities and given the stamp of official sanction. The reports were investigated and found to be false and libelous by German authorities themselves. The method by which these myths arose is thus described in his book *The Growth of a Legend:*

Hardly had the German armies entered Belgium when strange rumors began to circulate. They spread from place to place. They were reproduced by the press and they soon permeated the whole of Germany. . . . . Public credulity accepted these stories. The highest powers in the state welcomed them without hesitation and indorsed them with their authority. Even the Emperor echoed them and, taking them for a text, advanced in the famous telegram of September 8, 1914, addressed to the President of the United States, the most terrible accusations against the Belgian people and clergy.

. . . . It was the German army which, as we have seen, constituted the chief breeding ground for legendary stories. These were disseminated with great rapidity among the troops; the liason officers, the dispatch riders, the food convoys, the victualling posts assured the diffusion of them. . . . .

Submitted to the test of the German military inquiry these stories are shown to be without foundation. Received from the front and narrated by a soldier who professes to have been an eye witness, they are nevertheless clothed in the public view with special authority. Welcomed without control by the press, the stories recounted in letters from the front appear, however, in the eyes of the readers of a paper clothed with a new authority—that which attaches to printed matter. They lose in the columns of a paper their individual and particular character. . . . . The statements thus obtain a substance and an objectivity of which they would otherwise be devoid. Mixed with authentic news, they are accepted by the public without mistrust. Is not their appearance in the paper a guaranty of accuracy? . . . .

All these pseudo-historical publications are, however, only one aspect of the abundant literary production of the Great War. . . . .

So one finds in this literature of the lower classes the principal legendary episodes of which we have studied the origin and followed the development; accommodated to a fiction, woven into a web of intrigue, they have undergone new transformations; they have lost every indication of their source; they are transposed in the new circumstances imagined for them; they have usually been dissociated from the circumstances which individualize them and fix their time and place.

The evolution of myths concerning Negroes shows a striking resemblance to these mentioned by von Langenhove. In this category would fall the myths concerning Negro mentality, or the closing of the frontal sutures at the age of fourteen; the "rape myth," or the belief that some character weakness and inordinate sexual virility in Negroes make them rapists by nature; and the "insurrection myth," or the recurrent assertion and belief that Negroes are plotting the downfall of the government. These are general in their acceptance. They illustrate the tendency of authors observed by Langenhove in his study "to incorporate new ideas with the complex old ones and show that they are not surprising and that all earlier facts tend to prove it." The efforts of some recent writers on the Negro question may be noted.

In 1895 R. M. Bache[1] made one of the first experimental studies of the relative mentality of the white, Negro, and Indian races. His study was based on only ten Negroes. He began with an assumption of the inferiority of Negroes and was satisfied that he had proved it. In his tests the whites were slowest in reacting to the visual, auditory, and electrical stimulation, the Indians were quickest, and the Negroes about midway between. He deduced from this that the whites were superior, the Indians next, and the Negroes the lowest of the group. The Negroes he explained were slower than the Indians because they were of mixed white and Negro blood and had inherited the effects of slavery, while the Indians' mode of life compelled them to rely upon quick movement. Therefore he said the Indian was of a higher race than the Negro. Dr. Vogt, a German anthropologist, is responsible for the statement: "On examining the brain of a Negro I find a remarkable resemblance between the ape and the Negro, especially with reference to the development of the temperal lobe." He made this deduction from the examination of the skull of one Hottentot Negro woman.

A. T. Smith made association and memory tests and concluded[2] that the Negro child was psychologically different from the white child in power of abstraction, judgment, and analysis. He took a single Negro boy as typical.

For the purpose of studying myths pertinent to this inquiry instances were taken from the testimony in race riots, both in East St. Louis and Chicago. The excerpts which follow illustrate the tendency of myths to create and give currency to rumors:

NEGROES SECRETING ARMS

I returned in about an hour and learned from Col. Tripp that it had been reported that Negroes were forming and had large quantities of arms and ammunition at a saloon on the northeasterly corner of Nineteenth and Market Avenue; at the time the small detachment of troops remaining at the City Hall was loaded into an auto truck and Col. Tripp, Lieut. Col. Clayton, Chief of Police Ransom Payne and myself, in my automobile proceeded to the saloon and pool-room located at the northeasterly corner of Nineteenth Street and Market Avenue, where it was reported there were large stores of ammunition and arms.

We accompanied Col. Tripp into the building and found perhaps fifteen or eighteen Negro men; Col. Tripp ordered them to surrender arms and there being no ready compliance with the order, he thereupon ordered them searched and found one man who had a number of loaded shot-gun shells. [Testimony by Thomas L. Fekete, Jr., city attorney of East St. Louis, at East St. Louis Inquiry into Conduct of Militia.]

[1] "Reaction Time with Reference to Race," *Psychological Review*, II, 475–86.

[2] "A Study in Race Psychology," *Popular Science Monthly*, L, 354–60.

NEGROES PLANNING ATTACK

Question: Now what happened Tuesday ?

Answer: Well, Tuesday I spent most of my time in the City Hall except when we would be sent out on false alarms, calls from the different parts of the city. That was practically all of our work there then. There was no rioting on Tuesday, but they continued calling from different parts of the city that Negroes were forming and ready to attack, and we would send men, whenever they were available, out with squads, two squads of men to investigate, but invariably it was a false alarm. [Testimony by Major Wm. Klauser at East St. Louis Inquiry into Conduct of Militia.]

CONCEALING ARMS FOR INSURRECTION

We then searched the building, particularly the dwelling quarters above these rooms, for arms which it had been alleged Dr. L. N. Bundy had stored at this place. We found that Dr. Bundy had sent two cartons of his property to this place for safe-keeping and on opening the cartons, we discovered that they contained no firearms or ammunition, but contained automobile supplies and some stationery. [Testimony by Col. S. O. Tripp at East St. Louis Inquiry into Conduct of Militia.]

NEGROES ARMING AND PLANNING AN ATTACK

Then we commenced to get reports from different parts of the city that Negroes were arming, getting ready to attack. One of the persistent rumors was there were two hundred Negroes armed around Sixty and Bond streets some place there. That rumor was so persistent that Col. Tripp ordered me to take Company B down and investigate it and the police sent one policeman along to show us the way and show us the place where it was supposed to be. We got down there within probably three blocks of the place and the policeman told us we better not get too close without forming a line of skirmishers, which I did. I divided the company into two platoons. One platoon under the Company commander and the other under the first lieutenant, and we combed that district all through. The policeman deserted us as soon as we started out and we were all left alone. We combed all over for an hour or probably more.

Question: Who was the commander of Company B ?

Answer: Captain Eaton. We did not find a single thing except two Negroes who just came out of a house. We searched them and they were armed and we arrested them. We brought these back with us when we came perhaps an hour or an hour and a half later.

Question: Is there anything else that night ?

Answer: Yes, it was not very long until we got rumors that at about 27th and 28th and Tudor that the Negroes and whites were in a pitched battle. That is about two miles I think southeast, and they asked me to go out and look into the situation and take a squad of men with me . . . . we got to Eighteenth and Bond and we were perhaps a quarter of a mile ahead of the truck and we were fired upon. We stopped the car and Brown returned the fire. We could see smoke coming from a vacant lot and by that time the truck came up and we formed a line of skirmishers and went through and could not find a single thing.

The Chief of Police was advised, on rumor, that Negroes were forming in the Black Belt for the purpose of marching on the whites. In response to this rumor, the witness [Col. S. O. Tripp], the Acting Mayor [Fekete], and the military officials left for the seat of the purported mobilization of Negroes, but found that the report was untrue. The record shows that during this temporary departure of authorities, military and civil, acts of lawlessness were being exerted against Negroes in other sections of the city. [Testimony by Major Wm. Klauser at East St. Louis Inquiry into Conduct of Militia.]

ARMED AND MASSED ATTACKS BY NEGROES

. . . . As we got to 27th and Tudor I found a first lieutenant of the Missouri National Guard there. I afterwards found out his name was Crawley. He had one soldier with him. He called him his orderly. I think his name was Murphy. There they were perhaps a dozen young men, about eighteen or twenty, armed with rifles and were lined up at 28th Street there under trees, that is behind trees, at least it looked that way in the night, and perhaps a half a block more north it looked to me two houses were burning; it was a big fire; they were burning, and they claimed that the Negroes had been firing at them and they were returning the fire, and I guess that is where the report came from. He advised me that it was a little dangerous work up there and that we had better form a few men, form a line of skirmishers, and I sent one bunch to the east side of the fire to see what we could find in there. So I did that. I gave Capt. Easterday a bunch of men, one detachment, and Lieut. Brown another, one on each side, and then Lieut. Crawley and one private went right through the center of it, right next to the place seemed deserted and we could not find anybody and we waited for the other detachments to come out and they did not find anything and I walked around, it seemed on the west side of the block, between 27th and 28th Streets, and I saw a couple of fellows sticking their heads up over the fence, the fence of an old two story brick building, and I hollered. I thought perhaps it was Lieut. Crawley and waited for him and we found a bunch of Negroes in there, perhaps twenty-five of them. Lieut. Crawley and myself lined them up and searched them and there was not a Negro who had any arms or ammunition, and we asked if there were any more in the house, and they said this private came in and already had three of us. So Lieut. Crawley said if I guard the ones outside he would go inside and run the rest out, so in the neighborhood of one hundred fifty or two hundred came out, men, women and children and we searched all of them but did not find anything on them. [Testimony by Thomas L. Fekete, city attorney at East St. Louis Inquiry into Conduct of Militia.]

I. THE RAPE MYTH

It is the common belief among whites that Negroes are rapists by nature. In this belief are involved the "fear obsession" of Negro men, held by many white women, fear of the "social equality" bugaboo, condonings of lynchings, and repressive social restriction as well as attempts at legislative restraints. The persistency of these assertions and this belief point to an interesting peculiarity of popular opinion.[1] There have been cases of rape involving

---

[1] See "I. Primary Beliefs—Criminality," p. 440. In questionnaire, return to question: "What subjects of discussion most frequently lead to the Negro?" The reply is given: "Lynching, lying, stealing, and attacking of little girls."

In commenting on the proposition: "Prejudice has its principal basis in fear," the statement is made: "I believe this is true among women; not particularly among men. This is partly due to the publicity given to all acts against women by Negroes, in my judgment."

Negroes, but they have contributed no such preponderance as would justify the wholesale charge against the Negro race. The tendency is to stress Negro sex offenses as though they alone constituted almost the whole of revolting crime. The usual proportion of white sex offenses is lost in the general statistics of crime. In the South, where it was first persistently asserted that Negro men have an abnormal tendency to sexual crimes, each crime, or attempted crime, and in many cases even suspected crime, of this sort has registered itself in a lynching.

In the twenty-year period between 1883 and 1903 there were lynched in the South 1,985 Negroes. Rape was assigned as the cause in 675 cases. In 1,310 cases other causes were given. James Welden Johnson, field secretary of the National Association for the Advancement of Colored People, has prepared figures on lynchings and sex offenses charged to Negroes which point out the misrepresentation in easy but persistent charges and the unquestioning acceptance of them by the public. He says:

Whenever the Negro protests against lynching, nearly all southern newspapers and a great many northern newspapers call upon him to deprecate the crime which leads to lynching. The authentic statistics on lynching prove the falsehood on which this propaganda is based. In the past thirty-five years fifty Negro women have been lynched. In the twelve-month period, August, 1918—August, 1919 [when the statement was prepared] five Negro women were lynched.

LYNCHINGS

Years	Lynchings	Number Charged with Rape
1914–18*	264	28
1883–1903	1,985	675

* Does not include the Negroes killed in East St. Louis.

When the Congressional Committee on Immigration in 1911 made its study of crime in the United States, an investigation was made of 2,262 cases in the New York Court of General Sessions, and in that investigation it was found that the percentage for the crime of rape was lower for Negroes than for either the foreign-born whites or native whites.

NEW YORK COURT OF GENERAL SESSIONS*

1911	Rape
Native-born whites	.8 per cent
Foreign-born whites	1.8 per cent
Negroes	.5 per cent

* Congressional Committee on Immigration.

Contrast these records, bad as they may appear, with the records for New York County, which is only a part of New York City, and we find that in this one county in the single year of 1917, 230 persons were indicted for rape. Of this number, 37 were indicted for rape in the first degree.

INDICTMENTS AND LYNCHINGS FOR RAPE

Place	Year	Crime	Number
Number indicted by Grand Jury, New York County...	1917	Rape	230
Number of whites indicted by Grand Jury, New York County...............................	1917	Rape in first degree	37
Number of Negroes indicted by Grand Jury, New York County...............................	1917	Rape in first degree	0
Number of Negroes lynched in entire United States	{ 1914 1918 }	Charged with rape	28

That is, in just a part of New York City the number of persons indicted for rape in the first degree was nine more than the total number of Negroes lynched on the charge of rape in the entire United States during the period 1914–1918. Among these thirty-seven persons indicted by the New York County Grand Jury, there was not a single Negro. The evidence required by the Grand Jury of New York County to indict a person charged with rape must be more conclusive than the evidence required by a mob to lynch a Negro accused of rape.

In Chicago the statistics of sex offenses tell a significant story. Chicago judges in the criminal courts were questioned by the Commission on their experience to test the foundation of this belief. Their replies were practically unanimous. Some of them are given:

Judge Pam: You talk about sex cases. Whether you call them rape cases or crimes against children, I have more serious rape cases against white than I have against colored people. The most serious case I had was about ten days ago, and I sentenced the man to life imprisonment. I never had such a case involving a Negro.

Commissioner: We read a great deal in the papers about rape in the South. How does the colored man stand on that matter in comparison to the white man?

Judge Thompson: Practically the same.

Commissioner: You spoke about crimes involving sex. What is your experience with regard to whether they are committed more often by colored persons than whites?

Judge Trude: I don't think in Chicago they are committed more by Negroes than whites.

Judge Thompson: In my work with the criminal court I was astounded at the large number of crimes involving the sexual abuse of children, but I remember no case in which a colored defendant was charged with that crime. Almost all other races were represented, but I don't remember one colored man charged with the abuse of a child. . . . . I tried many of those cases, but never tried a colored man for that offense. I would say the majority of them were slavic or German; practically no Scandinavian.

Dr. Adler, State Criminologist: We had the same thing here in Chicago of a colored man sent to the penitentiary on a charge of attempted rape or something of that sort, where the identification was made by a child of six or eight years who picked him out in a crowd under suspicion. No such evidence ought to be accepted. We are perfectly sure, and everybody else agrees that such evidence is not sufficient to warrant the action.

2. THE SEX MYTH

East St. Louis riot.—The records of the Congressional Investigating Committee contain much evidence of the use of this myth in fomenting riots. Edward F. Mason, representing the interests of labor, gave a vivid account of the report that Negro men had committed vicious acts of assault against white girls in the East St. Louis streets. He stated further that 200 white women were among the 1,200 persons present at the meeting on the night of May 28, just prior to the riot, and that "we brought these girls along to see if we couldn't teach—we wanted to wake him [the mayor] up. He was in a trance. He couldn't see the thing like we did."

Alois Towers emphasized in his testimony the sentiment among the whites of East St. Louis just prior to the outbreak:

Mr. Chairman, yesterday I made the statement that the great influx of Negroes was responsible for the riot. I want to try and show some of the feelings that developed after this great influx of Negroes. It was a terrible feeling in the air. Everyone felt that something terrible was going to happen. On the street corners, wherever you went, you heard expressions against the Negro. You heard that the Negro was driving the white man out of the locality—by moving into the white neighborhood—that the whites were being forced out of their localities. Stories were afloat on the streets and on the street cars of the worst kind that would inflame the feelings. For instance, I heard one story so persistently that I commenced to think later on there might be some truth in it. First I thought it was just originated by some who might want to inflame the feelings of the people. I heard stories of this kind and I heard it no less than a dozen times on the streets of East St. Louis, that Negroes had made the boast that they were invited to East St. Louis; that great numbers of white people were taken away for war purposes; and that *there would be lots of white women for the Negroes in East St. Louis.* . . . . The whole country became fearful. You could hear the same discussions away from East St. Louis. People were inflamed and their feelings were directed against big employers of East St. Louis, feeling that they were responsible for the great influx of Negroes.

Of actual assaults against white women there was found no evidence. Testimony by the mayor before the Military Committee investigating the conduct of soldiers adds substantiation to this fact:

Q.: Now did you hear of any other complaints of these colored men from any source as to their conduct and behavior when they first came here other than being imported here to work in large numbers?

A.: Yes sir.

Q.: What do you know about it?

A.: Some complaints that they were sticking up people, holding up people at night time, and various other police violations.

Q.: Now were these complaints verified by the records, or otherwise?

A.: I think they were, they were arrested and locked up, got trial and punishment, the usual procedure of the Police Department and Courts.

Q.: You keep in pretty close touch with these Police Court Proceedings?

A.: Yes sir.

Q.: So you would say that there were more colored people arrested and convicted for such offenses as you mentioned than there were four or two years ago?

A.: I have not made that comparison, but I would think so.

Q.: Any other offenses except larceny and robbery?

A.: No.

Q.: Any sex outrages?

A.: No.

Q.: No complaints or prosecutions that white women were outraged by colored men?

A.: No sir.

[Board of Inquiry, East St. Louis, Ill.]

Washington riot.—The Washington race riot was precipitated by reports of alleged attacks upon white women by Negroes. These reports were featured in the daily newspapers with large front-page headlines, and suggestions were made that probable lynchings would follow the capture of the Negroes. The series of reported assaults totaled seven. In each it was claimed that a Negro had assaulted a white woman. When the fury and excitement of the riot had subsided and the facts were sifted, it was found that of the seven assaults reported, four were assaults upon colored women. Three of the alleged criminals arrested and held for assault were white men, and at least two of the white men were prosecuted for assaults upon colored women. It further developed that three of the assaults were supposed to have been committed by a suspect who at the time of the riots was under arrest.

Waukegan riot.—A story with the implication that a sex issue was involved was the significant feature of the riot between marines from the Great Lakes Naval Training Station, aided by citizens of Waukegan, and the Negro residents of Waukegan. It is entirely likely that the outburst was wholly precipitated by the entirely false report that "Mrs. Blazier, the wife of Lieutenant Blazier," was "attacked" by Negro boys.[1] Lieutenant Blazier, it developed, was unmarried and had no woman occupant in the car.

Chicago riot.—The most atrocious murder of the Chicago riot of 1919 was precipitated by a report involving an Italian girl. The story circulated that she had been killed by a Negro. Joseph Lovings, an innocent Negro, chanced into the neighborhood on a bicycle. He was set upon and murdered. The coroner found fourteen bullet wounds, many stab wounds, contusion of the head, and fractures of the skull bones and of the limbs. The report proved a myth, for no girl was killed by anyone during the riot. The Negro killed was innocent of any injury, and if a girl was injured it had not been learned by whom the injury was inflicted. There had been no previous rioting on the West Side, where the murder was committed, and no further clashes followed it. The usual report of the burning of the Negro which followed an assault was also circulated, and this was false and unfounded.

[1] See p. 541.

In the frenzy of the rioting in Chicago a report gained circulation that white women were being attacked by Negroes. Some reports picked up by newspapers asserted that women were being shot as the riot grew. The *Chicago American* during the riot pertinently made a plea for cool-headedness and intelligence in receiving reports. In an editorial it thus importuned the citizenry:

Don't circulate wild stories that tend to infuriate respectable citizens, both white and black. They are trying to suppress the hoodlums who have been responsible for all the rioting.

Don't believe every infuriating report you hear, and don't repeat them to others more credulous than yourself.

Depend on the *American* to tell you what happened just as accurately as careful, intelligent reporting will permit.

The most notable instance of inflammatory faking was observed in one newspaper (not the *American*) yesterday afternoon. It ran across its front page in big type the heading: "Women Shot as Riots Grow." It was based on an incoherent, unsubstantiated rumor which later investigation proved has no foundation.

The same information was received by the *Evening American* from the detective bureau, where the report was received. The *American* published a few lines announcing that the police had received such reports. Men were rushed out, but the report could not be verified, and this newspaper withdrew further publication of the unverified report.

At Chicago Heights a race riot was reported on August 7, 1920. It was said in the press that a Negro motor-cyclist had run down a Hungarian boy. The actual report circulated was that a Negro had struck an Italian girl. The latter report was not true; the first one, contrary to press reports, did not start a riot. In fact, there was no riot.

In the racial clash of September 20, 1920, the sex myth again arose.[1] Immediately after one of the Negroes had struck Barrett down, the trio ran. Few persons actually knew what had occurred. Excitement waxed high when the wild report flew about that a Negro had attacked a white woman. A mob of several thousand men, women, and children formed to storm the church in which they had sought refuge.

An investigator from the Commission, sent out immediately after the clash, picked up traces of this myth in the sentiments of white residents of the neighborhood.

There was a story which everyone in the neighborhood seemed to know concerning trouble on the street-car lines between Negroes and whites. A middle-aged Irish woman on Union Avenue, who had been with the crowd at the church, gave the following account of it: "Not long ago, a Negro knocked a white woman off the cars. It never appeared in the papers. I never go on the cars where they [Negroes] are. You couldn't get me to go on a State Street car line."

[1] See Barrett case, p. 64.

A barber at Forty-fifth Street and Emerald Avenue said:

There was some trouble the Saturday before Labor Day. A Negro gave the conductor a dollar bill, and the conductor said he hadn't change and told him to get off the car. As he was getting off, he knocked against a white woman, and seven men in an automobile who were right behind the car saw him and chased him. They brought him up to the alley right across the street, beat him up, and cut up his head something awful.

IV. PROPAGANDA

Both whites and Negroes have recognized the value of propaganda as an instrument of opinion-making. Both employ it, sometimes openly, sometimes insidiously. Its effects may be unmistakably observed in much of the literature about the Negro. It is the purpose here to give attention to certain forms of propaganda now in circulation, with a view to defining roughly their place in the manufacture of sentiment on the race question in Chicago. In spite of similarity it would be obviously unfair to lump all sorts of propaganda, good and bad, under one general classification. It is possible, however, to classify different types from the examples which came to the attention of the Commission, as follows: (1) educational, (2) radical and revolutionary, (3) malicious, (4) defensive.

1. EDUCATIONAL PROPAGANDA

Propaganda on the race situation with a true educational purpose seems to be confined largely to organizations composd of both whites and Negroes, who make joint appeals to both groups. An example is the publicity campaign of the National Association for the Advancement of Colored People. This Association definitely asserts that it can best accomplish its ends by reaching "the conscience and heart of the American people," and publicity is the weapon. The *Crisis* magazine is the principal organ of the Association, although the public is reached through various other channels.

From the report of the Association for 1919, the following figures covering the circulation of information is obtained: During that year 1,138,900 copies of the *Crisis* were sold; officers of the Association traveled 101,009 miles, delivered 286 addresses, including eleven in Chicago, and contributed nineteen special articles, not including special releases, of press material to magazines of wide circulation.

2. RADICAL AND REVOLUTIONARY PROPAGANDA

A broad basis of appeal to Negroes as a group is provided in their economic status. Placed by circumstances near the bottom of the industrial ladder, victims of exploitation, restlessly resentful of practices employed against them because of class as well as race, it might be reasoned that they would be vitally interested in a revolution, industrial if not social. The Industrial Workers of the World has reasoned after this fashion and, probably because class meant more to it than race, extended open arms to Negro workers. This appeal was even stronger in view of the attitude of partial exclusion adopted by many trades unions. To strengthen its organization, ally with it a restless group, 90 per cent of whom are laborers, while at the same time providing an unmistakable demonstration of its own disregard for race lines in its so-called struggle for "industrial freedom," the I.W.W. directed a definite propaganda toward the Negro group, and founded it upon a very human desire. Thousands of letters and pamphlets were addressed, "To the colored workingmen and women," calling them fellow-workers. Excerpts from one of them follow:

There is one question which, more than any other, presses upon the mind of the worker today, regardless of whether he be of one race or another, of one color or another, the question of how he can improve his conditions, raise his wages, shorten his hours of labor, and gain something more of freedom from his master, the owners of the industry wherein he labors.

To the black race, who, but recently, with the assistance of the white men of the northern states, broke their chains of bondage and ended chattel slavery, a prospect of further freedom or *real freedom* should be most appealing.

For it is a fact that the Negro worker is no better off under the freedom he has gained than under the slavery from which he has escaped. As chattel slaves we were the property of our masters and, as a piece of valuable property, our masters were considerate of us and careful of our health and welfare. Today, as wage workers, the boss may work us to death, at the hardest and most hazardous labor, at the longest hours, at the lowest pay, we may quietly starve when out of work and the boss loses nothing by it and has no interest in us. To him the worker is but a machine for producing profits and when you, as a slave who sells himself to the master on the installment plan, become old, or broken in health or strength, or should you be killed while at work, the master merely gets another wage slave on the same terms.

We who have worked in the South know that conditions in lumber and turpentine camps, in the fields of cane, cotton and tobacco, in the mills and mines of Dixie, are such that the workers suffer a more miserable existence than ever prevailed among the chattel slaves before the great Civil War. Thousands of us have come and are coming northward, crossing the Mason and Dixon line, seeking better conditions. As wage slaves we have run away from the masters in the South, but to become the wage slaves of the masters in the North. In the North we find that the hardest work and the poorest pay are our portion. We are driven while on the job, and the high cost of living offsets any higher pay we might receive.

The only problem then, which the colored worker should consider, as a worker, is the problem of organization with other working men in the labor organization that best expresses the interest of the whole working class against the slavery and oppression of the whole capitalist class. Such an organization is the I.W.W., the *Industrial Workers of the World*, the only labor union that has never, *in theory or practice*, since its beginning, twelve years ago, barred the workers of any race or nation from membership. The following has stood as a principle of the I.W.W., embodied in its official constitution since its formation in 1905:

"By-Laws. Article 1—Section 1

"No working man or woman shall be excluded from membership in Unions because of creed or color."

If you are a wage worker you are welcome in the I.W.W. halls, no matter what your color. By this you may see that the I.W.W. is not a white man's union, not a black man's union, not a red or yellow man's union, but a *working man's union*. *All of the working class in one big union.*

In the I.W.W. all wage workers meet on common ground. No matter what language you may speak, whether you were born in Europe, in Asia or in any other part of the world, you will find a welcome as a fellow worker. In the harvest fields where the I.W.W. controls, last summer saw white men, black men and Japanese working together as union men and raising the pay of all who gathered the grain. In the great strikes the I.W.W. has conducted at Lawrence, Massachusetts, in the woolen mills, in the iron mills of Minnesota and elsewhere, the I.W.W. has brought the workers of many races, colors and tongues together in victorious battles for a better life.

The foundation of the I.W.W. is *industrial unionism*. All workers in any division of any industry are organized into an *industrial union of all* the workers in the *entire industry;* these *industrial unions* in turn are organized into *industrial departments* of connecting or kindred industries, while all are brought together in *the central organization of the Industrial Workers of the World—one big union of all the working class of the world*. No one but actual wage workers may join. The working class cannot depend upon anyone but itself to free it from wage slavery. "He who would be free, himself must strike the blow."

When the I.W.W. through this form of *industrial unionism* has become powerful enough, it will institute an *industrial commonwealth;* it will end slavery and oppression forever and in its place will be a world of the workers, by the workers, and for the workers, a world where there will be no poverty and want among those who feed and clothe and house the world; a world where the word "master" and "slave" shall be forgotten; a world where peace and happiness shall reign and where the children of men shall live as brothers in a world-wide *industrial democracy*.

Another pamphlet published a hideous picture of a lynching in the South. In both of these pamphlets the appeal is about the same and may be summarized as follows:

The Negro is oppressed. He is subjected to the worst possible cruelties and indignities. The working men are oppressed. Negroes have left one slavery for another which is shared by white workers. Race hatred is played upon by capitalists to keep the two races apart and thus thwart their efforts at improving their condition. The I.W.W. union will unite all of the oppressed of all colors and all languages. One big union of defensive brotherhood, not only in America but throughout the world.

3. MALICIOUS PROPAGANDA

Anti-Negro propaganda is not wholly new in the North, but it has usually been carefully concealed. Recently there have been several conspicuous instances of open and organized effort to influence the minds of white persons against Negroes. The slogans, charges, and incriminations have included, with gross exaggeration, not only all of the actual but all of the fancied and rumored defects of Negro character. Ignorance and suspicion, fear and prejudice, have been played upon violently. A group of South Side real estate dealers and owners, anxious to preserve exclusively for whites sections of the city known as Hyde Park and Kenwood, formed themselves into an organization to protect property values on the assumption that the presence of Negroes depreciated real estate values. Since they did not own or control enough property to be in themselves effective, they sought to awaken the white residents to the "danger that menaced them." Funds were raised, meetings held, a journal started, bills and posters distributed, and many letters circulated. A bulletin was widely distributed with this heading:

YOUR RIGHTS AND MINE

A Short Symposium on Current Events as Applied to and Effecting Realty
Values in Kenwood and Hyde Park

It began by disclaiming any desire to foment or foster race antagonism, but stated its determination to work insistently and persistently along legal lines for the elimination of undesirables of whatever brand or color whose residence in this section lowered the value of real estate. The remainder of the bulletin, however, was devoted to a discussion of the Negro. A letter to Mayor Thompson from the president of the Association mentioned the vicious element of Negroes "haranguing about constitutional rights," aided by the Negro press, claiming social equality, and then attributed the riot to the scattering of Negroes in white residential sections. It spoke of a feeling that was rampant because the "legal rights of Negroes have been placed above his moral obligation to the white people." The *Chicago Tribune* was quoted twice and the Chicago Real Estate Board once on the desirability of segregation. The *Daily News* afforded a fourth quotation from an article in which three solutions were advanced—amalgamation, deportation, and segregation. As to amalgamation the article said: "Every white man would rather see the nation destroyed than adopt that method."

The *Property Owners' Journal* became so bitter in its utterances that the protests of whites forced its discontinuance. A few selections from the *Journal* picture the character of the campaign:

What a reputation for beauty Chicago would secure if visitors touring the city would see crowds of idle, insolent Negroes lounging on the South Side boulevards and adding beauty to the floricultural display in the parks, filling the streets with old newspapers and tomato containers and advertising the Poro-system for removing the marcelled kinks from Negro hair in the windows of the derelict remains of what had once been a clean, respectable residence.

THE NEW NEGRO

Negroes are boasting, individually and through the colored press, that the old order of things for the Negro is changing and that a new condition is about to begin. As a result of the boastful attitude, the Negro is filled with bold ideas, the realization of which means the overturning of their older views and conditions of life. The Negro is unwilling to resume his status of other years; he is exalting himself with idiotic ideas on social equality. Only a few days ago Attorney General Palmer informed the Senate of the nation of the Negroes' boldest and most impudent ambition, sex equality.

From the Negro viewpoint sex equality, according to Mr. Palmer, is not seen as the equality of men and women; it is the assertion by the Negro of a right to marry any person whom he chooses, regardless of color. The dangerous portion of their outrageous idea does not consist in the accident that some black or white occasionally may forget the dignity of their race and intermarry. That has happened before; doubtless it will recur many times. Where the trouble lies is in the fact that the Department of Justice has observed an organized tendency on the part of Negroes to regard themselves in such a light as to permit their idea to become a universal ambition of the Negro race.

As a corollary to their ambition on sex equality, it is not strange that they are attempting to force their presence as neighbors on the whites. The effrontery and impudence that nurses a desire on the part of the Negro to choose a white as a marriage mate certainly will not result in making the Negro a desirable neighbor. That fact alone is enough to determine the property owners of this district to declare to the Negroes that they must stay out. As neighbors they have nothing to offer. "They lived for uncounted centuries in Africa on their own resources, and never so much as improved the make-up of an arrow, coined a new word, or crept an inch nearer to a spiritual religion," and it is a certainty that their tenure of those unfortunate buildings now occupied by them will not be improved by a single nail if it is left to the Negro to provide and drive the nail.

Keep the Negro in his place, amongst his people, and he is healthy and loyal. Remove him, or allow "his newly discovered importance to remove him from his proper environment and the Negro becomes a nuisance." He develops into an overbearing, inflated, irascible individual, overburdening his brain to such an extent about social equality that he becomes dangerous to all with whom he comes in contact; he constitutes a nuisance of which the neighborhood is anxious to rid itself. If the new Negro desires to display his newly acquired veneer of impudence where it will be appreciated we advise that they parade it in their own district. Their presence here is intolerable.

As stated before, every colored man who moves into Hyde Park knows that he is damaging his white neighbor's property.

Therefore, he is making war on the white man.

Consequently, he is not entitled to any consideration and forfeits his right to be employed by the white man.

If employers should adopt a rule of refusing to employ Negroes who reside in Hyde Park to the damage of the white man's property it would soon show good results.

FOOD FOR THOUGHT FOR HYDE-PARKERS

Their solid vote is the Negroes' great weapon. They have a total vote in Chicago of about 40,000. This total vote is cast solid for the candidate who makes the best bargain with them. When both our principal political parties are split, and when each of them has two or more candidates in the field, this solid block of 40,000 becomes a possible power and might be able to defeat or elect a candidate.

This vote situation is the foundation of the Chicago Negro's effrontery and his evil design against the white man's property. He feels that he holds the balance of power and that he can dictate the policy of any administration that happens to be elected by his controlling black vote.

He therefore becomes arrogant, insulting, threatening. He abuses his rights and liberties and feels that he is perfectly safe in doing so for the reason that as he controls this block of votes he believes that he can practically dictate to the police department, the city administration and the courts. Consequently he is bold.

Now then, white property owners and voters, this vote situation must be corrected. It is time for you to think and ponder. Remember this, that this Negro vote power could not exist except for the fact that the candidate who caters to it is traveling on his belief that the white man will vote the ticket any way. The white voter is not supposed to think, nor to indulge in any investigations of a candidate to ascertain whether or not the candidate is favorable or inimical to his interests. No, the white voter is supposed to be a blind ass who has no care for his own interests, who does not know or care to know of the foul plots against him, who has no knowledge of what is going on around him, but who simply does as he is told and walks to the polls as in a dream, having eyes and seeing not, ears and hearing not, and religiously casts his vote for the ticket and against his own interests.

Wake up, white voters! Come out of your dream. Open your eyes and ears. It is high time that you realize what is going on. Hereafter in local affairs affecting your property and home interests, there should be only one test of a candidate and that one should be, "Will his election work for the betterment of Hyde Park or for its deterioration?"

The Negro should be consistent. As he segregates his vote and casts it all together in one block, so he should live together all in one block.

Some of the slogans of the organization were: "Our neighborhood must continue white"; "They shall not pass"; "Stay out of Hyde Park"; "We base our rights on priority, majority and anthropological superiority."

The sentiment was contagious.[1] Other literature of even more pronounced anti-Negro character followed. An unsigned card was distributed in large numbers throughout the district during the presidential campaign, showing a vicious looking Negro and words of warning for family protection.

The attempt still further to instil fear and bitterness was manifest in a pamphlet sent, by whom it is not known, to the wives of prominent white residents of the city and particularly of Hyde Park, entitled *An Appeal of White Women to American Womanhood*. It was a reprint from an article in the *New Times*, which in turn reprinted an appeal from the *German Women on the Rhine*. Although there could be slight connection between the conduct of colored French colonial troops on the Rhine and Chicago Negroes, its circulation in Hyde Park possibly helped to fan the flames of race feeling which had already been so deliberately kindled. The pamphlet detailed the "bestial ferocious conduct of Negroes against German women."

4. DEFENSIVE PROPAGANDA

Within the Negro group there are to be found many defensive programs designed for group protection. They rarely reach the point of organized effort for the control of opinion. The essence in all appeals is "protest," which is tacitly understood to be an effective sentiment to circulate. The most

[1] See discussion of this campaign in section on "Bombings," pp. 115–22.

striking illustrations of this type of propaganda are those which follow definite provocations. The appeal of the propaganda is directed first to Negroes as a means of cementing the group from within, and indirectly to the whole group by way of impressing it with the strength of solidified opposition to insults. One example of this type will suffice.

Following the bombing of Negro homes and the inauguration of a campaign of reckless propaganda against Negroes in the interest of exclusive white residence neighborhoods, Negroes organized the "Protective Circle of Chicago." The object of this organization was to "oppose segregation, bombing and the defiance of the Constitution." The admitted method of combating these objectionable practices was propaganda. The question on which certain white people living in Hyde Park were greatly wrought up was that of keeping Negroes out of "white residential districts." Negroes were classed as "undesirables," and the efforts of the whites in offensive propaganda were aimed at proving it. Fortunately for the Negroes, an article appeared in a real estate publication, the *Real Estate News*, presenting with unusual force an aspect of the neighborhood dispute favorable to the contention of the Negroes. This was seized upon by the Protective Circle, and the editor consented to elaborate it. Twenty-five thousand copies were distributed among Negroes and whites, residents of the district.

The heading "Solving Chicago's Race Problem," coupled with the fact that the article had first appeared in a real estate periodical published by whites, immediately attracted attention. The subheadings of the article read: "South Side Property Owners Warned against Perils of Boycott and Terrorism Being Promoted by Local 'Protective Associations,'" "Conspiracies Violating Civil Rights Act Bring Danger of Heavy Damages or Imprisonment," "A Complete Analysis of Chicago's Race Movement Proves It to Be Small Factor in Causing Great Changes in Residential Values," and "How Influence of Stock Yards, Railroads, Auto Industry and City Growth Force Big and Sweeping Changes on South Side of Chicago." One paragraph of the article, printed in italics, ran:

Any association formed in Chicago for the purpose of, or having among its aims, refusal to sell, lease or rent property to any citizen of a certain race, is an unlawful association. Every act of such an association for advancement of such an aim is an act of conspiracy, punishable criminally and civilly in the District Court of the United States. And every member of such an association is equally guilty with every other member. If one member hires a bomber, or a thug who commits murder in pursuance of the aims of the association, all in the organization may be found guilty of conspiracy to destroy property or to commit murder, as the case may be.

At a mass meeting held by the Protective Circle at which there were 2,000 Negroes present, $1,000 was collected to advance this propaganda. As the chairman of the meeting stated:

We wanted to get at the responsibility for these bombings and intimidations, and we intended to give publicity to the Negro's side of the story. Papers will not print the Negro's story. We wanted to get this survey of white and colored property owned, and whites and Negroes bombed, and send it to every white person living in Kenwood, and just as we were about to start on our task, there came like a flash out of the sky an article by the editor of the *Real Estate News*. It was a godsend. We have secured thousands of copies of this paper and are buying more as fast as we can get funds. We intend to send copies to every white person interested in this question.

v. CONCLUSIONS

The inquiries of this Commission into racial sentiments which characterize the opinions and behavior of white persons toward Negroes lead us to the following conclusions:

That in seeking advice and information about Negroes, white persons almost without exception fail to select for their informants Negroes who are representative and can provide dependable information.

That Negroes as a group are often judged by the manners, conduct, and opinions of servants in families, or other Negroes whose general standing and training do not qualify them to be spokesmen of the group.

That the principal literature regarding Negroes is based upon traditional opinions and does not always portray accurately the present status of the group.

Most of the current beliefs concerning Negroes are traditional, and were .cquired during an earlier period when Negroes were considerably less intelligent and responsible than now. Failure to change these opinions, in spite of the great progress of the Negro group, increases misunderstandings and the difficulties of mutual adjustment.

That the common disposition to regard all Negroes as belonging to one homogeneous group is as great a mistake as to assume that all white persons are of the same class and kind.

That much of the current literature and pseudo-scientific treatises concerning Negroes are responsible for such prevailing misconceptions as: that Negroes have inferior mentality; that Negroes have inferior morality; that Negroes are given to emotionalism; that Negroes have an innate tendency to commit crimes, especially sex crimes.

We believe that such deviations from recognized standards as have been apparent among Negroes are due to circumstances of position rather than to distinct racial traits. We urge especially upon white persons to exert their efforts toward discrediting stories and standing beliefs concerning Negroes which have no basis in fact but which constantly serve to keep alive a spirit of mutual fear, distrust, and opposition.

That much of the literature and scientific treatises concerning Negroes are responsible for such prevailing misconceptions as that Negroes are capable of mental and moral development only to an inferior degree, are given to an uncontrolled emotionalism, and have a distinctive innate tendency to commit crimes, especially sex crimes.

CHAPTER XI

SUMMARY OF THE REPORT AND RECOMMENDATIONS
OF THE COMMISSION

THE SUMMARY

I. THE CHICAGO RIOT

1. BACKGROUND

In July, 1919, a race riot involving whites and Negroes occurred in Chicago. For some time thoughtful citizens, white and Negro, had sensed increasing tension, but, having no local precedent of riot and wholesale bloodshed, had neither prepared themselves for it nor taken steps to prevent it. The collecting of arms by members of both races was known to the authorities, and it was evident that this was in preparation for aggression as well as for self-defense.

Several minor clashes preceded the riot. On July 3, 1917, a white saloon-keeper who, according to the coroner's physician, died of heart trouble, was incorrectly reported in the press to have been killed by a Negro. That evening a party of young white men riding in an automobile fired upon a group of Negroes at Fifty-third and Federal streets. In July and August of the same year recruits from the Great Lakes Naval Training Station clashed frequently with Negroes, each side accusing the other of being the aggressor.

Gangs of white "toughs," made up largely of the membership of so-called "athletic clubs" from the neighborhood between Roosevelt Road and Sixty-third Street, Wentworth Avenue and the city limits—a district contiguous to the neighborhood of the largest Negro settlement—were a constant menace to Negroes who traversed sections of the territory going to and returning from work. The activities of these gangs and "athletic clubs" became bolder in the spring of 1919, and on the night of June 21, five weeks before the riot, two wanton murders of Negroes occurred, those of Sanford Harris and Joseph Robinson. Harris returning to his home on Dearborn Street, about 11:30 at night, passed a group of young white men. They threatened him and he ran. He had gone but a short distance when one of the group shot him. He died soon afterward. Policemen who came on the scene made no arrests, even when the assailant was pointed out by a white woman witness of the murder. On the same evening Robinson, a Negro laborer, forty-seven years of age, was attacked while returning from work by a gang of white "roughs" at Fifty-fifth Street and Princeton Avenue, apparently without provocation, and stabbed to death.

Negroes were greatly incensed over these murders, but their leaders, joined by many friendly whites, tried to allay their fears and counseled patience.

After the killing of Harris and Robinson notices were conspicuously posted on the South Side that an effort would be made to "get all the niggers on

July 4th." The notices called for help from sympathizers. Negroes in turn whispered around the warning to prepare for a riot; and they did prepare.

Since the riot in East St. Louis, July 4, 1917, there had been others in different parts of the country which evidenced a widespread lack of restraint in mutual antipathies and suggested further resorts to lawlessness. Riots and race clashes occurred in Chester, Pennsylvania; Longview, Texas; Coatesville, Pennsylvania; Washington, D.C.; and Norfolk, Virginia, before the Chicago riot.

Aside from general lawlessness and disastrous riots that preceded the riot here discussed, there were other factors which may be mentioned briefly here. In Chicago considerable unrest had been occasioned in industry by increasing competition between white and Negro laborers following a sudden increase in the Negro population due to the migration of Negroes from the South. This increase developed a housing crisis. The Negroes overran the hitherto recognized area of Negro residence, and when they took houses in adjoining neighborhoods friction ensued. In the two years just preceding the riot, twenty-seven Negro dwellings were wrecked by bombs thrown by unidentified persons.

2. STORY OF THE RIOT

Sunday afternoon, July 27, 1919, hundreds of white and Negro bathers crowded the lake-front beaches at Twenty-sixth and Twenty-ninth streets. This is the eastern boundary of the thickest Negro residence area. At Twenty-sixth Street Negroes were in great majority; at Twenty-ninth Street there were more whites. An imaginary line in the water separating the two beaches had been generally observed by the two races. Under the prevailing relations, aided by wild rumors and reports, this line served virtually as a challenge to either side to cross it. Four Negroes who attempted to enter the water from the "white" side were driven away by the whites. They returned with more Negroes, and there followed a series of attacks with stones, first one side gaining the advantage, then the other.

Eugene Williams, a Negro boy of seventeen, entered the water from the side used by Negroes and drifted across the line supported by a railroad tie. He was observed by the crowd on the beach and promptly became a target for stones. He suddenly released the tie, went down and was drowned. Guilt was immediately placed on Stauber, a young white man, by Negro witnesses who declared that he threw the fatal stone.[1]

White and Negro men dived for the boy without result. Negroes demanded that the policeman present arrest Stauber. He refused; and at this crucial moment arrested a Negro on a white man's complaint. Negroes then attacked the officer. These two facts, the drowning and the refusal of the policeman to arrest Stauber, together marked the beginning of the riot.

[1] The coroner's jury found that Williams had drowned from fear of stone-throwing which kept him from the shore.

Two hours after the drowning, a Negro, James Crawford, fired into a group of officers summoned by the policeman at the beach and was killed by a Negro policeman. Reports and rumors circulated rapidly, and new crowds began to gather. Five white men were injured in clashes near the beach. As darkness came Negroes in white districts to the west suffered severely. Between 9:00 P.M. and 3:00 A.M. twenty-seven Negroes were beaten, seven stabbed, and four shot. Monday morning was quiet, and Negroes went to work as usual.

Returning from work in the afternoon many Negroes were attacked by white ruffians. Street-car routes, especially at transfer points, were the centers of lawlessness. Trolleys were pulled from the wires, and Negro passengers were dragged into the street, beaten, stabbed, and shot. The police were powerless to cope with these numerous assaults. During Monday, four Negro men and one white assailant were killed, and thirty Negroes were severely beaten in street-car clashes. Four white men were killed, six stabbed, five shot, and nine severely beaten. It was rumored that the white occupants of the Angelus Building at Thirty-fifth Street and Wabash Avenue had shot a Negro. Negroes gathered about the building. The white tenants sought police protection, and one hundred policemen, mounted and on foot, responded. In a clash with the mob the police killed four Negroes and injured many.

Raids into the Negro residence area then began. Automobiles sped through the streets, the occupants shooting at random. Negroes retaliated by "sniping" from ambush. At midnight surface and elevated car service was discontinued because of a strike for wage increases, and thousands of employees were cut off from work.

On Tuesday, July 29, Negro men en route on foot to their jobs through hostile territory were killed. White soldiers and sailors in uniform, aided by civilians, raided the "Loop" business section, killing two Negroes and beating and robbing several others. Negroes living among white neighbors in Englewood, far to the south, were driven from their homes, their household goods were stolen, and their houses were burned or wrecked. On the West Side an Italian mob, excited by a false rumor that an Italian girl had been shot by a Negro, killed Joseph Lovings, a Negro.

Wednesday night at 10:30 Mayor Thompson yielded to pressure and asked the help of the three regiments of militia which had been stationed in nearby armories during the most severe rioting, awaiting the call. They immediately took up positions throughout the South Side. A rainfall Wednesday night and Thursday kept many people in their homes, and by Friday the rioting had abated. On Saturday incendiary fires burned forty-nine houses in the immigrant neighborhood west of the Stock Yards. Nine hundred and forty-eight people, mostly Lithuanians, were made homeless, and the property loss was about $250,000. Responsibility for the fires was never fixed.

The total casualties of this reign of terror were thirty-eight deaths—fifteen white, twenty-three Negro—and 537 people injured. Forty-one per cent of the reported clashes occurred in the white neighborhood near the Stock Yards between the south branch of the Chicago River and Fifty-fifth Street, Wentworth Avenue and the city limits, and 34 per cent in the "Black Belt" between Twenty-second and Thirty-ninth streets, Wentworth Avenue and Lake Michigan. Others were scattered.

Responsibility for many attacks was definitely placed by many witnesses upon the "athletic clubs," including "Ragen's Colts," the "Hamburgers," "Aylwards," "Our Flag," the "Standard," the "Sparklers," and several others. The mobs were made up for the most part of boys between fifteen and twenty-two. Older persons participated, but the youth of the rioters was conspicuous in every clash. Little children witnessed the brutalities and frequently pointed out the injured when the police arrived.

3. RUMORS AND THE RIOT

Wild rumors were in circulation by word of mouth and in the press throughout the riot and provoked many clashes. These included stories of atrocities committed by one race against the other. Reports of the numbers of white and Negro dead tended to produce a feeling that the score must be kept even. Newspaper reports, for example, showed 6 per cent more whites injured than Negroes. As a matter of fact there were 28 per cent more Negroes injured than whites. The *Chicago Tribune* on July 29 reported twenty persons killed, of whom thirteen were white and seven colored. The true figures were exactly the opposite.

Among the rumors provoking fear were numerous references to the arming of Negroes. In the *Daily News* of July 30, for example, appeared the sub-headline: "Alderman Jos. McDonough tells how he was shot at on South Side visit. Says enough ammunition in section to last for years of guerrilla warfare." In the article following, the reference to ammunition was repeated but not elaborated or explained.

The alderman was quoted as saying that the mayor contemplated opening up Thirty-fifth and Forty-seventh streets in order that colored people might get to their work. He thought this would be most unwise for, he stated, "They are armed and white people are not. We must defend ourselves if the city authorities won't protect us." Continuing his story, he described bombs going off: "I saw white men and women running through the streets dragging children by the hands and carrying babies in their arms. Frightened white men told me the police captains had just rushed through the district crying, 'For God's sake, arm; they are coming; we cannot hold them.'"

Whether or not the alderman was correctly quoted, the effect of such statements on the public was the same. There is no record in any of the riot testimony in the coroner's office or state's attorney's office of any bombs going off during the riot, nor of police captains warning the white people to arm, nor of any fear by whites of a Negro invasion. In the Berger Odman case before a coroner's jury there was a statement to the effect that a sergeant of police warned the Negroes of Ogden Park to arm and to shoot at the feet of rioters if they attempted to invade the few blocks marked off for Negroes by the police. Negroes were warned, not whites.

4. CONDUCT OF THE POLICE

Chief of Police John J. Garrity, in explaining the inability of the police to curb the rioters, said that there was not a sufficient force to police one-third of the city. Aside from this, Negroes distrusted the white police officers, and it was implied by the chief and stated by State's Attorney Hoyne, that many of the police were "grossly unfair in making arrests." There were instances of actual police participation in the rioting as well as neglect of duty. Of 229 persons arrested and accused of various criminal activities during the riot, 154 were Negroes and seventy-five were whites. Of those indicted, eighty-one were Negroes and forty-seven were whites. Although this, on its face, would indicate great riot activity on the part of Negroes, further reports of clashes show that of 520 persons injured, 342 were Negroes and 178 were whites. The fact that twice as many Negroes appeared as defendants and twice as many Negroes as whites were injured, leads to the conclusion that whites were not apprehended as readily as Negroes.

Many of the depredations outside the "Black Belt" were encouraged by the absence of policemen. Out of a force of 3,000 police, 2,800 were massed in the "Black Belt" during the height of the rioting. In the "Loop" district, where two Negroes were killed and several others wounded, there were only three policemen and one sergeant. The Stock Yards district, where the greatest number of injuries occurred, was also weakly protected.

5. THE MILITIA

Although Governor Lowden had ordered the militia into the city promptly and they were on hand on the second day of the rioting, their services were not requested by the mayor and chief of police until the evening of the fourth day. The reason expressed by the chief for this delay was a belief that inexperienced militiamen would add to the deaths and disorder. But the troops, when called, proved to be clearly of high character, and their discipline was good, not a case of breach of discipline being reported during their occupation. They were distributed more proportionately through all the riotous areas than the police and, although they reported some hostility from members of "athletic clubs," the rioting soon ceased.

6. RESTORATION OF ORDER

Throughout the rioting various social organizations and many citizens were at work trying to hold hostilities in check and to restore order. The Chicago

Urban League, Wabash Avenue Y.M.C.A., American Red Cross, and various other social organizations and the churches of the Negro community gave attention to caring for stranded Negroes, advising them of dangers, keeping them off the streets and, in such ways as were possible, co-operating with the police. The packing companies took their pay to Negro employees, and various banks made loans. Local newspapers in their editorial columns insistently condemned the disorder and counseled calmness.

7. THE AFTERMATH

Of the thirty-eight persons killed in the riot:

Fifteen met death at the hands of mobs. Coroner's juries recommended that the members of the unknown mobs be apprehended. They were never found.

Six were killed in circumstances fixing no criminal responsibility: three white men were killed by Negroes in self-defense, and three Negroes were shot by policemen in the discharge of their duty.

Four Negroes were killed in the Angelus riot. The coroner made no recommendations, and the cases were not carried farther.

Four cases, two Negro and two white, resulted in recommendations from coroner's juries for further investigation of certain persons. Sufficient evidence was lacking for indictments against them.

Nine cases led to indictments. Of this number four cases resulted in convictions.

Thus in only four cases of death was criminal responsibility fixed and punishment meted out.

Indictments and convictions, divided according to the race of the persons criminally involved, were as follows:

	NEGRO		WHITE	
	Cases	Persons	Cases	Persons
Indictments............	6	17	3	4
Convictions............	2	3	2	2

Despite the community's failure to deal firmly with those who disturbed its peace and contributed to the reign of lawlessness that shamed Chicago before the world, there is evidence that the riot aroused many citizens of both races to a quickened sense of the suffering and disgrace which had come and might again come to the city, and developed a determination to prevent a recurrence of so disastrous an outbreak of race hatred. This was manifest on at least three occasions in 1920 when, confronted suddenly with events out of which serious riots might easily have grown, people of both races acted with such courage and promptness as to end the trouble early. One of these was the murder of two innocent white men and the wounding of a Negro policeman by a band of Negro fanatics who styled themselves "Abyssinians"; another was the killing of a white man by a Negro whom he had attacked while returning from work; and still another was the riotous attacks of sailors from the Great Lakes Naval Training Station on Negroes in Waukegan, Illinois.

8. OUTSTANDING FEATURES OF THE RIOT

This study of the facts of the riot of 1919, the events as they happened hour by hour, the neighborhoods involved, the movements of mobs, the part played by rumors, and the handling of the emergency by the various authorities, shows certain outstanding features which may be listed as follows:

a) The riot violence was not continuous hour by hour, but was intermittent.

b) The greatest number of injuries occurred in the district west and inclusive of Wentworth Avenue, and south of the south branch of the Chicago River to Fifty-fifth Street, or in the Stock Yards district. The next greatest number occurred in the so-called "Black Belt": Twenty-second to Thirty-ninth streets, inclusive, and Wentworth Avenue to the lake, exclusive of Wentworth Avenue; Thirty-ninth to Fifty-fifth streets, inclusive, and Clark Street to Michigan Avenue, exclusive of Michigan Avenue.

c) Organized raids occurred only after a period of sporadic clashes and spontaneous mob outbreaks.

d) Main thoroughfares witnessed 76 per cent of the injuries on the South Side. The streets which suffered most severely were State, Halsted, Thirty-first, Thirty-fifth, and Forty-seventh. Transfer corners were always centers of disturbances.

e) Most of the rioting occurred after work hours among idle crowds on the streets. This was particularly true after the street-car strike began.

f) Gangs, particularly of young whites, formed definite nuclei for crowd and mob formation. "Athletic clubs" supplied the leaders of many gangs.

g) Crowds and mobs engaged in rioting were generally composed of a small nucleus of leaders and an acquiescing mass of spectators. The leaders were mostly young men, usually between the ages of sixteen and twenty-one. Dispersal was most effectively accomplished by sudden, unexpected gun fire.

h) Rumor kept the crowds in an excited, potential mob state. The press was responsible for giving wide dissemination to much of the inflammatory matter in spoken rumors, though editorials calculated to allay race hatred and help the forces of order were factors in the restoration of peace.

i) The police lacked sufficient forces for handling the riot; they were hampered by the Negroes' distrust of them; routing orders and records were not handled with proper care; certain officers were undoubtedly unsuited to police or riot duty.

j) The militiamen employed in this riot were of an unusually high type. This unquestionably accounts for the confidence placed in them by both races. Riot training, definite orders, and good staff work contributed to their efficiency.

k) There was a lack of energetic co-operation between the police department and the state's attorney's office in the discovery and conviction of rioters.

The riot was merely a symptom of serious and profound disorders lying beneath the surface of race relations in Chicago. The study of the riot, therefore, as to its interlocking provocations and causes, required a study of general race relations that made possible so serious and sudden an outbreak. Thus to understand the riot and guard against another, the Commission probed systematically into the principal phases of race contact and sought accurate information on matters which in the past have been influenced by dangerous speculation; and on the basis of its discoveries certain suggestions to the community are made.

II. The Migration of Negroes from the South

During the period 1916–18 approximately 500,000 Negroes moved from southern to northern states. Some cities of the North received increases in Negro population of 10 per cent to 300 per cent. The Negro population of Gary, Indiana, increased from 383 in 1910 to 5,299 in 1920, an increase of 1,283 per cent.

Chicago was in direct line for migrants from the South, especially along the Mississippi Valley, and received approximately 65,000, who constituted a large proportion of the increase of 148.5 per cent in its Negro population in the last decade. These migrants definitely accentuated existing problems of race contact and brought new problems of adjustment and assimilation. Southern Negroes with southern manners, habits, and traditions, and mostly from rural districts, became part of a northern urban community. Knowledge of the causes of this movement of Negroes will make easier an understanding of the difficulties following it. These causes were economic as well as sentimental.

The South was paying to Negroes wages which varied from 75 cents a day on a farm to $1.75 a day in certain city jobs. For two seasons the boll weevil, a destructive pest, had been making heavy ravages upon the cotton crops, ruining thousands of farms and throwing out of employment many thousands of Negro workers. Lack of capital to carry labor through a period of poor crops and over the normal intervals between planting and harvesting largely increased Negro unemployment. Unsatisfactory living conditions, on plantations and in segregated quarters of southern cities, stimulated unrest. School facilities for Negro children, described as lamentably poor even by southerners, increased dissatisfaction with conditions in the South. The Negro illiteracy in fifteen southern states was 33.3 per cent as compared with 7.7 per cent for whites. The appropriations for teachers in the schools of these states on a per capita basis was $10.32 for each white child, and $2.89 for each Negro child.

On the other hand, the North was for the first time on a large scale opening up opportunities for Negroes to earn a livelihood. The cessation of immigration due to the war and the drawing of workers into military service created a great demand for labor; and the opening of new industries and the extension of old ones to meet the demands of the war provided still greater opportunities. At the same time, these industries were paying laborers from $3 to $8 per day, and offering shorter hours and the opportunity for overtime work and bonuses. The North also offered living accommodations which, although below standard for city dwellers, were a vast improvement over most of the plantation cabins and frail frame dwellings of the South. There are no segregated schools in the North, and Negro children are offered identical school privileges with white children.

Other causes of the migration, as stated by the migrants and otherwise confirmed, were: lack of protection from mob violence, injustice in the courts, inferior transportation facilities, deprivation of the right to vote, "rough-handed and unfair competition of 'poor whites,'" "persecution by petty officers of the law," and "persecution by the press."

Between 1895 and 1918, 2,881 Negroes were lynched in the United States, and more than 85 per cent of these lynchings occurred in the South. The *Atlanta Constitution* declared that the heaviest migration of Negroes was from those counties in which there had been the worst outbreaks against Negroes.

How the migration began.—The migration began early in 1916. Hard-pressed industries in the East, principally in Pennsylvania, imported Negroes from Georgia and Florida. During July of that year, 13,000 were carried to Pennsylvania by one railroad company alone.[1] They wrote back for their families and friends. Reports of high wages and good treatment, aided by the hysteria of a mass movement, accomplished the rest.

The migration was first noted in Chicago in 1917. It had been rumored in the South that the Stock Yards needed 50,000 men; the city had been regarded by Negroes as a future home since the World's Columbian Exposition in 1893; it was the great city of mail-order houses, the home of the *Chicago Defender*, a widely circulated Negro newspaper, the "end of the railroad line," and the "top of the world" for Negroes. Negro newspapers gave up their columns to migration news and urged southern Negroes to go North. The movement soon became a mass movement; with standards, songs, and watch-

---

[1] *The Negro Migrant in Pittsburgh*, published in 1918 under the supervision of the School of Economics, University of Pittsburgh; U.S. Department of Labor Bulletin, *Negro Migration in 1916–17*, published in 1919.

words the migrants began arriving in the city faster than they could be absorbed into the population.

The arrival in Chicago.—Prior to the migration, the majority of Negroes in Chicago lived in a fairly limited area on the South Side, principally between Twenty-second and Thirty-ninth streets, Wentworth Avenue and State Street, and in scattered groups east of State Street to Cottage Grove Avenue. This area adjoined the old vice area, and many houses of the vicinity had been abandoned by older Chicago Negroes. Shortly after the migrants began to arrive, practically all available houses had been taken and filled to overcrowding. On a single day the Chicago Urban League found 664 Negro applicants for houses with only fifty-five dwellings actually available for use by Negroes. At the same time rents for Negroes were increased by from 5 to 50 per cent.

Meeting actual conditions of life in Chicago brought both exaltation and disillusionment to the migrants. These were reflected in the schools, in public amusement places, in industry, and in the street cars. The Chicago Urban League and the various Negro churches and newspapers assumed the task of making the newcomers "city folk." The difficulty of adjustment showed itself in the great differences in habits of life and employment. Craftsmen had to relearn their trades when thrown amid the highly specialized processes of northern industries; domestic servants went into industry; professional men had to re-establish themselves in a new community.

Many Negroes sold their homes in the South and brought their furniture with them. Reinvesting in property frequently meant a loss; the furniture brought was often found to be unsuited to the tiny apartments or the large abandoned dwellings that they were able to rent or buy.

Change of residence carried with it in many cases change of status. The "leader" in a small southern community when he came to Chicago was immediately absorbed into the great, struggling mass of unnoticed workers. School teachers, male and female, whose positions in the South held commendable prestige, had to go to work in factories and plants because the disparity in educational standards would not permit a continuation of their profession in Chicago.

The migrants visited by the Commission investigators, however, for the most part gave evidence of satisfaction with their change of home, and were pleased with the opportunity of voting, of sending their children to schools, and of higher wages, and with the privilege of participation in community life. Others felt the pressure of high rents and bad living accommodations and complained against certain discriminations.

The fact is, however, that few Negroes have returned to the South, even in response to insistent invitations and offers of free transportation and better home conditions made by southern states that were left badly in need of laborers as a result of the migration.

III. The Negro Population of Chicago

1. Distribution and Density

The Negro population of Chicago, as reported by the Federal Bureau of the Census, was 44,103 in 1910, and 109,594 in 1920. The increase during the decade was, therefore, 65,491, or 148.5 per cent. Negroes constituted 2 per cent of the city's total population in 1910 and 4.1 per cent in 1920. The increase in the white population during the decade was 450,047, or 21 per cent, bringing the number up to 2,589,104 in 1920. Counting 3,007 Chinese, Japanese, and Indians of whom there were 2,123 in 1910, Chicago's total population in 1920 was 2,701,705.

This growth of the Negro population did not bring into existence any new large colonies of Negroes, but merely expanded and increased the density of areas in which they already lived. The areas of Negro residence are listed under designations arbitrarily given for convenient reference.[1]

1920

SOUTH SIDE

Roosevelt Road–Fifty-fifth St.; Wentworth Ave.–Cottage Grove Ave.
Population: total, 376,171; Negro, 92,901.

Woodlawn

Sixty-first St.–Sixty-seventh St.; Eberhart Ave.–Grand Blvd.
Population: total, 8,861; Negro, 1,235.

Lake Park Avenue Area

Fifty-third St.–Fifty-seventh St.; Harper Ave.–Lake Park Ave.
Population: Negro, 238.

Ogden Park Area

Fifty-ninth St.–Sixty-third St.; Halsted St.–Loomis Blvd.
Population: total, 38,893; Negro 1,859.

NORTH SIDE

North Ave.–Chicago Ave.; State St.–Larrabee St.
Population: Negro, 1,050.

Ravenswood

Lawrence Ave.–Montrose Ave.; Sheridan Road–Ashland Ave.
Population: Negro, 175.

WEST SIDE

Austin Ave.–Washington Ave.; Morgan St.–California Ave.
Population: Negro, 8,363.

MORGAN PARK AREA

107th St.–115th St.; Loomis St.–Vincennes Ave.
Population: Negro, 695.

[1] These do not embrace the whole of each area commonly included under such designations. The population figures are those of 1920.

2. NEIGHBORHOODS OF NEGRO RESIDENCE

The South Side.—While the main colony of Chicago's Negro population is located in a central part of the South Side, Negroes are to be found in several parts of the city, ranging from less than 1 per cent to more than 95 per cent in proportion to the total population. In some of these neighborhoods whites and Negroes have become adjusted to one another; in others they have not. One of these adjusted areas is the so-called "Black Belt." Because 90 per cent of the Negroes of Chicago live there, it is usually assumed that the area is 90 per cent Negro. The fact is very different. The most densely populated section of the South Side area, between Roosevelt Road and Thirty-ninth Street, Wentworth Avenue and Lake Michigan, has a population of 54,906 Negroes and 42,797 whites. There has been no noticeable friction in this area; and even during the riot few whites living or engaged in business there were molested by Negroes. Most of the whites killed or injured there came from other sections of the city. The many large apartment houses and family hotels occupied by whites are apparently little affected by the presence about them of many Negroes. Relations in Woodlawn, where the Negro increase has been relatively large, are for the most part friendly. No clashes have been reported except in the one instance of a group of white boys who threw stones at a building in which they saw Negroes. When they were arrested it developed that they had come from another neighborhood. Following the stirring up and organization of anti-Negro sentiment in Hyde Park, an attempt was made to organize white Woodlawn property owners against the "invasion" of the district by Negroes. This organization was not a very great success. There have been no bombings in this district, and no concerted opposition to the presence of Negroes as neighbors. Long, amicable residence together and the good character of the Negroes as well as the whites are probably important reasons for the absence of friction. And it also should be said that in the Woodlawn district the proportion of Negroes is so small that there has been no occasion for much controversy over an alleged depreciation of property values on account of Negro occupancy.

The West Side.—On the West Side there has been a settlement of Negroes for many years. Houses are cheaper there than on the South Side; and although the general level of ordinary workingmen's homes compares favorably with that on the South Side, there are few abandoned residences formerly occupied by wealthy persons now available for Negroes. There has been little friction within this area, in which 9,221 whites and 6,520 Negroes live. West Side Negroes, laborers for the most part, are generally home-loving, hard-working people, desirous of improving conditions for their children. Older settlers among them have been able to make their adjustments without great difficulty, meeting with no serious antagonism from white neighbors.

The North Side.—On the North Side, Negroes live among foreign whites and near a residential area of wealthy Chicagoans. The appearance of the first Negro residents there occasioned little notice or objection. They were for the most part house servants living near their work.

This neighborhood has experienced several complete changes in population. It was first occupied by Irish, then by Swedes, then by Italians, who are the present neighbors of Negroes. Friendly relations exist between the Sicilians, who predominate, and their Negro neighbors. Some Negroes live harmoniously in the same tenements with Sicilians. Their children play together, and some of the Negro children have learned Sicilian phrases so that they are able to deal with the Sicilian shopkeepers. Elsewhere on the North Side the feeling between Italians and Negroes is not so cordial.

Non-adjusted neighborhoods.—In other sections the failure of Negro and white neighbors to adjust themselves mutually has produced the most serious phases of the Negro housing problem. A general housing shortage may be relieved by the opening of new neighborhoods or the availability of houses in various parts of the city, but for Negroes there is less opportunity for thus relieving the housing shortage because of the hostility of many white neighborhoods to the presence of Negroes.

White residents immediately south of the old West Side Negro residence area objected to the moving in of Negroes, sending numerous threatening letters to the newcomers and otherwise annoying them. In certain sections of the North Side, Negro residents have been molested. On one occasion shots were fired at their homes, and at other times warning signs with pictures of skulls, crossbones, and coffins were posted. In the Lake Park Avenue area on the South Side, Negroes are limited to a few blocks, are not permitted to buy, and are discriminated against in practically all restaurants and amusement places.

West of Wentworth Avenue, adjoining the South Side Negro residence area, few Negroes live. The residents here are largely Irish working people and distinctly hostile to Negroes, even to those merely passing through the neighborhood. This area has many organized gangs and "athletic clubs," and its racial antagonisms appear to be traditional.

In Park Manor and Wakeford, between Sixty-ninth and Seventy-ninth streets, Cottage Grove and Indiana avenues, excitement was created in a new white settlement by an advertisement in a local paper addressed to Negroes offering them houses there. The name of a white real estate dealer living there was given. A demonstration followed, meetings were held, and the real estate man was asked to explain. He asserted, and it seems to have been the case, that the advertisement was the "spite work" of an enemy.

Kenwood and Hyde Park: The neighborhood between Thirty-ninth and Fifty-ninth streets, State Street and Cottage Grove Avenue, just south of the Negro residence area, has been termed a "contested neighborhood," because of the recent influx of Negroes. The "Black Belt" was already overcrowded, and its occupants were seeking relief from deteriorated and insufficient housing. The coming of thousands of Negroes from the South made it overflow. With Lake Michigan flanking the east, encroaching industry the north, and overcrowded, hostile neighborhoods the west, the overflow inevitably went south into the west portion of Hyde Park and Kenwood. Scattered through the South Side were numerous houses and apartments that had been vacant for many years; and sales were gladly made to the Negroes, many of the recent southern migrants having considerable funds. In 1919, of the 3,300 owners of property in the region embracing parts of Kenwood and Hyde Park and adjacent territory, 1,000 were Negroes. Already a popular agitation against the Negroes had been begun by real estate men who formed the Kenwood and Hyde Park Property Owners' Association. They increased and organized the prejudice against the Negroes in a campaign "to make Hyde Park white." They held meetings, published a weekly newspaper, and called upon property owners and other real estate dealers to pledge themselves against renting or selling to Negroes. In carrying out their program, they resorted to vilification, ridicule, and disparagement of Negroes, accusing them of destroying property values and robbing white people of their homes.

Outlying neighborhoods.—Few outlying places welcome Negroes as residents. Morgan Park, however, has offered homes for Negroes, and the Negro population there has increased from 126 in 1910 to 695 in 1920. They live for the most part on one side of the town near their own churches; they own their homes and keep them attractive. School accommodations are poor, many children leaving school early for that reason.

Robbins, another suburb, is entirely Negro, having a Negro mayor. The town is difficult to reach, unattractive, and uninviting. About 400 hard-working Negroes occupying seventy houses are trying to develop a town against the handicaps of lack of capital, swampy lands, and inaccessibility.

Depreciation of property.—One of the strongest influences in creating and fostering race antagonism in Chicago is the general belief among whites that the presence of Negroes in a neighborhood inevitably and alone depreciates the market value of real estate, and this belief is commonly accepted as a valid reason for unfriendliness toward Negroes as individuals and as a race. Therefore the Commission felt that it was important to learn what basis there is for this belief.

The principal influence of Negroes upon property values in a neighborhood is psychological, due to the deep-seated and general prejudice of whites against Negroes, which begets and sustains the belief that Negroes destroy property values wherever they go. The facts as ascertained by the Commission show that Negro occupancy in a neighborhood is more often due to a prior depreciation of the property there than the depreciation is due to Negro occupancy; and that it is unfair to place the entire responsibility for loss of property values in a neighborhood upon Negro occupancy. In other sections of the city, where there are no Negroes, depreciation of property values has been produced by contacts between populations differing in race, religion, or social standards. Race prejudice produces the present conditions of social injustice toward the Negro, and uses the depreciation of property which it causes, as a new ground for such racial prejudice.

In virtually every neighborhood in Chicago where Negroes now live they were preceded by two or more distinct groups of occupants, and an earlier and often long-continued depreciation of property values is one of the explanations of their presence. This depreciation of values has come from several causes, such as natural physical deterioration, vacation of old and large houses through the death of their original occupants or their removal to new neighborhoods, or the encroachments of vice, or business, or factories, and the like. In this way Negroes have found an opportunity to rent or buy at figures that were comparatively low and within their limited means.

The extension of Negro occupancy into the district between State Street and Lake Michigan and Thirty-first and Thirty-ninth streets followed such an earlier depreciation; and later, similar conditions had similar consequences in the district between State Street and Cottage Grove Avenue and Thirty-ninth and Sixty-third streets, where there has been the most active opposition to the Negro influx.

In the first named of these two districts there are now about 20 per cent more Negroes than whites. During the eighties and nineties this area embraced the most fashionable residence district in Chicago, and almost the entire Negro population lived in the adjoining area on the west—from State Street to Wentworth Avenue and north of Thirty-fifth Street. When the fashionable people of this district began to move to the North Side, the deserted section began to depreciate, and costly houses recently occupied by wealthy owners were thrown upon the market and began to pass through the hands of real estate dealers and into the possession of people belonging to a different social class. Physical deterioration also played its part. Between 1900 and 1910, when the first Negroes moved into Wabash Avenue—one street nearer to the old fashionable district—the houses were at least twenty years old and many of them much older. Real estate men estimate the natural depreciation of such buildings at from 2 to $2\frac{1}{2}$ per cent per year; so that in many cases property once exclusive and of a high class had depreciated at least 50 per cent before there was any prospect of Negro occupancy.

In 1912 the old vice area west of State Street and northwest of this exclusive area was broken up. The inmates, numbering at that time more than 2,000, moved into the nearest large houses available where they could ply their trade clandestinely. They could afford high rents, and owners and agents profited accordingly. Cabarets, cafés, and saloons sought the side streets, and buffet flats were opened. Raids and prosecutions called attention to the changed character of the neighborhood, and property values sank still lower.

Many buildings affected by this decline were bought up by real estate speculators and sold to Negroes who were eager for housing. One speculator bought more than 1,400 such houses.

Then came the automobile industries with their showrooms, gas stations, manufacturing plants, and accessory shops, even invading the boulevards, and the desirability of adjacent residence property still further declined.

After the coming of the Negroes the depreciation continued. It was clear that the character of the neighborhood had definitely changed. Negroes were frequently unable to make the needed extensive repairs while they were paying for their property. There are other instances in this area where property not owned by Negroes declined in value chiefly because of its neglect by landlords.

In the district west of Cottage Grove Avenue, adjacent to Hyde Park proper, depreciation had proceeded in much the same manner. This neighborhood was temporarily congested in the period of the World's Columbian Exposition in 1893, and hotels and apartment houses were built far in excess of normal needs. Real estate men of that district have made much of this point, stating that many of the houses there had been vacant as long as fifteen years. The first "undesirables" were not Negroes, but other national or racial groups of whites who were objectionable to the original residents. Several factors have combined to make this section less and less desirable for residence purposes. It is close to the Stock Yards, with their offensive odors; and railroads flank it on both sides, with their smoke and noise. The coming of the automobile industries, the opening of boarding-houses, the southward movement of the vice element, all had their adverse effect on property values before Negroes moved east of State Street.

The widespread and deep-seated racial prejudice among whites against Negroes, heretofore mentioned as a psychological basis for the belief that the presence of Negroes is disastrous to property values, is directly reflected in the unwillingness of whites to buy property close to that occupied by Negroes and in their desire to sell, even at a sacrifice, when Negroes move into the immediate neighborhood. While frequently the demand for property among Negroes financially able to buy has not been large enough to absorb realty offered for sale because of the reasons given here, there are, on the other hand, some neighborhoods where the Negro demand has provided a market for property that had long been unmarketable, and in these neighborhoods there has been some increase in the value of such property. It should be noted that the understandable bitterness of feeling on this question of Negro entrance into white residence districts has been intensified in some cases through exploitation, by both white and Negro real estate operators, of anti-Negro prejudice and fear of loss on account of Negro occupancy.

In brief, Negro occupancy depreciates the value of residence property in Chicago because of the social prejudice of white people against Negroes, and because white people will not, and Negroes are financially unable to buy at fair market prices property thrown upon the market when a neighborhood begins to change from white to Negro occupancy; nevertheless, a large part of the depreciation of residence property often charged to Negro occupancy comes from entirely different causes.

Financial aspects of Negro housing.—One difficulty of Negroes in handling their own housing problem is the attitude of real estate mortgage and loan concerns with respect to property tenanted or likely to be tenanted by Negroes. Such property is assumed to be a bad risk, and, as a consequence, Negroes are charged more than whites and find it difficult to secure mortgages to assist in purchásing and are greatly handicapped in their efforts to improve property. This situation has its basis in various beliefs concerning Negroes that are often unwarranted. It developed from the inquiries of the Commission that mortgage brokers were influenced to a large degree by opinions of prospective buyers of Negro mortgages, and these prospective buyers in turn were influenced by beliefs for which there was little basis. It was assumed, for example, that Negroes were unreliable in business dealings. Conferences were held by the Commission with the real estate men who handled the greatest portion of Negro property, and many other real estate men were interviewed by the Commission's investigators. Their testimony indicated a buying capacity far beyond what was expected and showed that Negroes had a good record for meeting their obligations. One real estate man who has made a large number of sales to Negroes, stated that in the whole of his experience there had been but two forfeitures, and neither of these was due to negligence or carelessness. An increasing tendency to buy was noted. This was easily explained by other facts gathered by the Commission which indicated that it was easier for Negroes to buy than to rent property, that during the period of the migration hundreds of dwellings were offered for sale to Negroes on long-term payment plans, and that many migrants who had sold their homes, farms, and belongings in the South came to the city prepared to make substantial payments on property. Many Negroes now own houses valued at from $10,000 to $20,000, and in one instance $30,000.

Regarding Negro habits of saving, inquiries were made at all the principal banks of the city's business section and of the neighborhood where Negroes live. Those who were able to check up on Negro depositors reported large sums deposited and invested. One trust and savings bank had Negro deposits of $1,500,000 and another of $1,000,000; one state bank had $650,000 and another $150,000. A large banking institution in the "Loop" district had 4,000 Negro depositors.

Opportunities for using their own capital to relieve their housing problems were limited by lack of opportunities for obtaining business experience. All the concerns questioned regarding the practicability of employing Negroes in such institutions were of the opinion that it would not meet with the favor of the other employees and patrons.

Bombings.—The antagonistic sentiment attributable to the Negro housing situation both incited and condoned the fifty-eight bombings of homes committed between July 1, 1917, and March 1, 1921. In these bombings two persons, a Negro girl and an infant, were killed, many whites and Negroes were injured, and damage done to property amounted to more than $100,000. Negroes who purchased or rented property and whites who sold or leased it were bombed. Thirty-two bombs were exploded within the area bounded by Forty-first and Sixtieth streets, Cottage Grove Avenue and State Street. Although Negroes in some cases were warned of the exact dates on which they were to be bombed, and policemen were sometimes on duty at the places where bombs were exploded, only two arrests were made. One of those arrested was immediately released and the other was never brought to trial. Protests to the authorities from Negroes have been without effect, and a strong feeling of insecurity and resentment has developed among them. It appears from evidence presented to the Commission that bombings have been systematically planned. Many white residents, objecting to the violence suggested and used to keep out Negroes, withdrew from the neighborhood protective organizations, fearing that they might be held responsible for the resulting lawlessness.

These protective associations have denied responsibility and declared that they used only legitimate methods, such as foreclosure of mortgages and refusal to deal with Negroes. During the summer of 1920, they stated, sixty-eight foreclosures were effected.

3. THE NEGRO COMMUNITY

The Negro community in Chicago is virtually a city within a city. It affords opportunity to observe how it is accomplishing its own adjustment to the larger community, and how it attempts to function in its own behalf and for the betterment of the community at large.

Negroes have lived in Chicago since its founding. In fact, the first settler, in 1778, was a Negro, Jean Baptiste Point de Saible. There were Negro property owners at the time of the city's incorporation in 1837. Before the Chicago fire in 1871 they lived near what is now the "Loop" business district, north of Harrison Street on Clark and Dearborn streets and on Lake Street on the West Side. Their homes were burned in 1873, and after that they settled in the territory adjoining what later became the "red light" district near Roosevelt Road.

Organization of the Negro community.—Partly from necessity and partly from choice, Negroes have established their own churches, business enterprises, amusement places, social agencies, and newspapers. The number of their business places increased from about 1,200 in 1919 to about 1,500 in 1920. There are 651 places of business operated by Negroes on South State Street, and 549 on the principal cross streets. The majority of these places are those rendering personal service—barber shops, restaurants, hair-dressing parlors, and undertaking establishments. There are also two banks.

Organizations for social intercourse are numerous, consisting principally of churches, fraternal societies, and social clubs. There are 170 congregations holding services in church edifices and in "store-front" churches. Olivet Baptist Church has more than 10,000 members, the largest Negro church membership in the world. It employs sixteen paid workers, and during the last five years has raised more than $200,000. These churches are the principal center for "face-to-face" relations and aid greatly in the process of adjusting Negroes to civic responsibilities. Forty-nine of these congregations own property valued at fully a million and a half dollars.

The social and civic agencies are expressions of the group effort to adjust itself to the community. There are in the Negro community distinct organizations of this kind designed especially for Negroes, and branches of general agencies located conveniently for use by Negroes. Of the former type the Chicago Urban League is the most notable example. This organization is a clearing-house for social work among Negroes, and its activities include social investigations, an industrial bureau, and child welfare. It has an executive board and officers composed of both whites and Negroes, and a highly efficient staff of Negro workers. During 1920 more than 25,000 Negroes were assisted through this organization. Provident Hospital is another example of this type.

Of the latter type the Wabash Avenue Y.M.C.A. is an example. It is a branch of the city Y.M.C.A., and has adjusted itself to the peculiar social problems of its membership and community. Other agencies are the Community Service, Wendell Phillips Settlement on the West Side, Butler Community Center on the North Side, Phyllis Wheatley Home for Girls, Home for the Aged and Infirm, Indiana Avenue Y.W.C.A., Elaine Home Club, Julia Johnson Home for Girls, Hartzell Center, and Illinois Technical School for Colored Girls (a Roman Catholic institution).

Of the general social agencies with branches convenient for Negroes are the American Red Cross, United Charities, Municipal Tuberculosis Sanitarium, Abraham Lincoln Center. Although some of these branches are poorly supported and undermanned, they represent efforts of the community to care for itself. During 1920 six social agencies and twenty-seven churches raised among Negroes $445,000 for social-welfare work.

IV. Racial Contacts

The problems arising out of various occasions, both voluntary and enforced, for race association in Chicago, have, for convenience, been included in this report under the general classification of "racial contacts." Attention is given to contacts in the public schools, in public recreation places, on transportation lines, and in other relations exclusive of industry and housing which require special treatment. Negroes in Illinois are legally entitled to all the rights and privileges of other citizens. Actually, however, their participation in public benefits in practically every field is limited by some circumvention of the law.

I. CONTACTS IN PUBLIC SCHOOLS

The public schools furnish one of the most important points of contact between the white and Negro races because of the daily association of thousands of Negro and white children at an impressionable age. The Chicago Board of Education makes no distinction between the races and keeps no separate records. Certain schools, therefore, with white American, Negro, and white foreign-born preponderances, were selected for special study.

Physical equipment of schools.—Twenty-two schools located in and near areas of Negro residence were selected and visited. Of these only five, or 23 per cent, have been built since 1900, and four of these five schools are in regions where the Negro population is smallest. The ten schools serving the largest percentage of Negroes were built, one in 1856, one in 1867, seven between 1880 and 1889, and only one after 1890. Of the 235 schools attended almost wholly by whites, 133, or 56 per cent, were built after 1899. The old buildings will not accommodate modern equipment and cannot be enlarged. The absence of modern buildings is in part due to the old residence areas in which Negroes must live. The gymnasiums in fifteen of these twenty-two schools of predominant Negro attendance are poorly equipped, and in the other seven schools there are none. Playground space is about the same in all the schools, and there was no exceptional overcrowding in schools attended largely by Negroes except in one case where by the "shift" system a double attendance was made possible. In the schools of mixed attendance one instance was conspicuous: Fuller School—a branch of Felsenthal which is well equipped, and under the same principal, who is an advocate of segregation—is in a neighborhood where the percentage of Negroes is the same as that around Felsenthal, but it has no playground, is run down, and neglected. Yet it has 90 per cent Negroes, while Felsenthal has 38 per cent. Unmanageable white children are sent to Fuller.

Retardation.—The question of retardation[1] of Negro children is of serious concern in race relations, since this fact is urged by advocates of separate schools as an unnecessary handicap for white children and a reason for segregation. Twenty-four schools were selected, with the aid of the Board of Education: six attended mainly by Negroes, six mainly by white Americans, and twelve mainly by children of immigrants. Of a total of 34,593 children there were 18,230, or 53 per cent, retarded—the same percentage as in the entire city; 10,250, or 30 per cent, normal; and 5,910, or 17 per cent, accelerated. In the schools attended mainly by white Americans, 49 per cent were

---

[1] The standard in Chicago is Grade I for children six years of age.

retarded; in those attended mainly by children of immigrants 49 per cent; and in those attended mainly by Negroes 74 per cent. The percentage of retardation in schools attended mainly by Negroes ranges from 57 to 80 per cent; in schools attended mainly by children of immigrants from 32 to 71 per cent; and in schools attended mainly by white Americans from 40 to 62 per cent.

Predominating causes of this retardation of Negro children, according to the Board of Education's classification, are: ."late entrance to school," "family difficulties," "fathers or mothers working," "lack of education in parents." The majority of retarded Negro children are southerners, and their retardation can be readily understood when the gross inadequacies of southern schools for Negroes are considered.

Among the whites, late entrance, inability to speak English, ill health, backwardness, and low mentality are the various causes. It is interesting to note that while it is often maintained that Negroes are mentally weak and incapable, classification of retardation figures according to causes does not bear out that theory. Negro children retarded from "late entrance" have made excellent records in attaining a normal rating, some completing three grades in a year.

One hundred and sixteen Negro children were picked at random for an intensive inquiry by the Commission into causes of retardation. Of these, 101 had been in school before coming to Chicago; and of the 101 children, eighty had lived in the South and had gone to southern schools; those born and educated in the North showed no greater rate of retardation than the whites. For much of the retardation the school facilities for Negroes in the South appear to be responsible. In Mississippi, for example, only eighty days' schooling is required in counties that do not absolutely reject the compulsory-education law. Other causes found were inadequate care and instruction at home due to the ignorance of parents, mothers working out, poor parental discipline, and the physical condition of homes.

Contact problems.—A wide variety of opinions was found among principals and teachers concerning the relations of white and Negro children. Several principals were distinctly antagonistic to Negroes, and in their schools the race relations of the pupils were not cordial. The most important factor in determining the attitude of teachers as well as of pupils was the attitude of principals. Kindergarten teachers found a natural, pleasant relationship existing between the young white and Negro children. As children grew older they became more race conscious, and in the high schools friction frequently arose from race groupings in class and social organizations. Negro teachers are assigned to schools attended by both Negroes and immigrants, and apparently have no difficulties with pupils or parents. Difficulties and bad feeling have been provoked by the disposition of certain white teachers to adapt their instruction in accordance with their assumptions concerning

Negroes' mental and emotional characteristics, putting stress on singing and handicraft instead of on basic studies in arithmetic and grammar.

2. RECREATION

In its investigation of recreation places, the Commission listed 127 parks, playgrounds, recreation centers, and beaches under the supervision of the Municipal Bureau of Parks, Playgrounds, and Bathing Beaches, and of the South Park, West Park, and Lincoln Park commissions. Of these, thirty-seven are in or near Negro areas. Though this figure represents a fairly adequate distribution, it is not an accurate picture. Twenty-three of these places are playgrounds attached to schools, fourteen being in, and nine near, Negro areas; and only thirteen have more than 10 per cent use by Negroes. Three bathing-beaches are within, and two near, Negro areas, while only one has more than 10 per cent use by Negroes. There are seven recreation centers near Negro areas, none within, and only one with more than 10 per cent use by Negroes. Armour Square, for example, is a recreation center bordering on the area of the largest Negro population; but the hostility of whites, especially gangs of hoodlums, attacks on Negro children, and the indifferent attitude of the director render attendance by Negroes extremely hazardous. Of a daily attendance of 1,500, less than 1 per cent are Negroes, despite the fact that over 50 per cent of the immediately surrounding population is Negro. Natural barriers of distance, unofficial discrimination of officials, and the hostility of neighborhood groups are largely responsible for the lack of participation.

The beaches have presented the most difficult problems of race control. The riot of 1919 began at the Twenty-ninth Street Beach, and since the riot numerous smaller clashes have occurred there. At Thirty-eighth Street, also on the edge of the largest area of Negro residence, Negroes are entirely excluded, the policeman on duty and the attendant in charge assisting in this exclusion to prevent clashes. In neighborhoods with a small Negro population, attendance at the recreation places is always much below the percentage of Negroes to the total population in such neighborhoods, this being due to the hostility shown by whites, especially of the hoodlum element, and also to the reluctance of Negroes to go where they feel unwelcome.

Contacts.—Most difficulties in parks and playgrounds have not been caused by the behavior of Negroes there. Such complaints against Negroes as have come from these contacts have concerned groups of rough or domineering children at the playgrounds rather than adults. Two playgrounds on the South Side make such complaints.

Race relations of the children.—Lack of racial antagonism was reported at a large number of playgrounds. Apparatus was used by both groups without friction. Negro and white children mingled freely in their games and in the swimming-pools, and both Negroes and whites played on baseball and athletic teams. The occasional playground fights usually lack any element of racial antipathy. "There might be personal misunderstandings and disagreements between a white and a black just the same as between two whites," said the director of Union Park, "but I wouldn't lay it to race prejudice. They work together and play together and seem to harmonize in most instances." When this director came to Union Park a year ago he found a tendency among Negroes and whites to separate into race groups, but steps were taken to bring them together in games of various kinds, and toward the end of the season the director felt that they "harmonized better and worked together more cordially than they did before." When the Commission's investigator visited Union Park Playground he saw small children of both races playing together on the same pieces of apparatus—a Negro child on one end of a teeter ladder and a white child on the other. Occasionally there is a disturbance, usually starting from a dispute over the apparatus; but on the whole the children play together peacefully.

Voluntary racial grouping.—Voluntary racial grouping appears to be more characteristic of the large parks and beaches which adults frequent than of the playgrounds, which are used mainly by children. One instance of voluntary grouping among children was found at Copernicus Playground. The playing space is in the shape of an "L," one end intended for boys and the other for girls, but by common consent the children divide along race lines rather than sex.

In the general use of Lincoln and Washington parks the Negroes and whites stay in separate groups. There has never been any difficulty, according to the Lincoln Park representative, arising from the fact that Negroes have taken possession of a spot desired by whites for a picnic or other amusement. No part of either park is especially set aside for the use of one race, and groups of both Negroes and whites are seen everywhere in the parks, but they do not mingle.

Some directors attempt to regulate these contacts to avoid any mingling of groups. At the Municipal Pier, for example, an investigator learned that when Negro couples went on the dancing-pavilion floor the floor manager informed them that they were not dancing properly and took them to one side to acquaint them with the approved style of dancing; no matter how well they danced, they were to be prevented from going on the floor by the manager's judgment of their dancing. More recently, however, Negroes have reported that they have been able freely to use this dance floor.

Clashes in the various recreation places as early as 1913 were found to have been started mostly by gangs of white "roughs." On one occasion, for example, the secretary of boys' work of the Wabash Avenue department Y.M.C.A. (for Negroes) conducted a party of nineteen Negro boys to Armour Square. They had no difficulty in entering the park, but on leaving they were assailed by crowds of white boys. Some of them were tripped, trodden upon, and badly bruised. They took refuge in a neighboring saloon, where they remained for a half-hour, when a detachment of police scattered the white gang. On another occasion a group of boys from the same institution were driven from the lake at Thirty-first Street. In 1915 Father Bishop, of St. Thomas Episcopal Church, took a group of Negro boys to Armour Square to play basket-ball. The entire party, including Father Bishop, were beaten by white boys and their sweaters taken from them. In the same year an attempt was made by a Negro boys' club director to take seventy-five Negro boys through the Stock Yards. They had received tickets of admission to the stock show. In spite of the presence and efforts of four adult leaders, these boys were struck by sticks and other missiles while passing from one section of the show to another. Police assistance was required to get them from the pavilion to the street cars.

Gangs of white boys, sixteen and seventeen years of age, from the neighborhood of Fifty-ninth Street and Wentworth Avenue frequently interfered with Negro participants in baseball games in Washington Park, especially during the spring and summer of 1918 and 1919. They also annoyed Negro couples on the park benches. Where the Negro showed fight, minor clashes resulted. Park officials have not been able to restrain the ill feeling which these conflicts engender.

Clashes were noted in Ogden Park as early as 1914 and frequently since that time. A Negro playground director testified that he and other Negroes had been slugged while attending band concerts or attempting to use shower baths after a game in the park. At the boathouse in Washington Park, in the early summer of 1920, there were numerous clashes between Negroes and whites. In the following year, however, considerably fewer instances of friction were reported. Playground directors are of the opinion that friction is likely to occur where groups of Negro children for the first time come into parks theretofore exclusively used by whites. Adjustment is likely to follow after this period. In some cases, however, when the proportion of Negroes has grown larger than that of whites, a Negro director has been placed in charge of the park with the unofficial understanding that it should be turned over to Negroes.

The two causes of neighborhood antagonism back of the friction in the parks most commonly cited are the housing and sex problems. The playgrounds and parks usually share in a general way the sentiments of the mixed neighborhoods in or near which they are located.

One source of racial disorders is lack of co-operation between park and city policemen. The park police stop a fight between white and colored children and send them out of the park. When the fight is renewed outside the park they have no power to interfere. Spectators may then get into the fight, and serious clashes may be well under way before the city police can be summoned.

The most important remedies suggested to the Commission for the betterment of relations between Negroes and whites at the various places of recreation were: (1) additional facilities in Negro areas, particularly recreation centers which can be used by adults; (2) an awakened public opinion which will refuse to tolerate the hoodlum and will insist that the courts properly punish such offenders; (3) selection of directors for parks in neighborhoods where there is a critical situation who have a sympathetic understanding of the problem and will not tolerate actions by park police officers and other subordinate officials which tend to discourage Negro attendance; and (4) efforts by such directors to repress and remove any racial antagonism that may arise in the neighborhood about the park.

3. CONTACTS IN TRANSPORTATION

The study of contacts between whites and Negroes in street cars and other public conveyances was prompted by a usually unexplained emphasis on apparently trivial incidents connected with public conveyances, together with the observation that the greatest disturbances during the riot of 1919 commonly occurred along transportation lines and at transfer points.

Although many clashes and other instances of racial friction on the street cars were not serious enough to be reported to the newspapers or to be made the subject of complaint, information obtained by investigators for the Commission showed that the attitude of both Negroes and whites toward each other was being affected by contacts on the cars.

As affecting attitudes on race relations, transportation contacts, while impersonal and temporary, are significant for several reasons. Many whites have no contact with Negroes except on the cars, and their personal impression of the entire Negro group may be determined by one or two observations of Negro passengers. Unlike contacts in the school, playground, and workshop, transportation contacts are not supervised, and if there is any dispute among passengers the settlement usually rests with themselves. Suspicion or prejudice on either side because of the difference in race accentuates any misunderstanding. And transportation contacts, at least on crowded cars, involve physical contact between Negroes and whites, which rarely occurs under other circumstances and sometimes leads to a display of racial feeling.

The Commission's investigators, white and Negro, men and women, made many trips for observation on the twelve lines carrying the heaviest volume of Negro traffic and therefore involving the greatest amount of contact. Counts of passengers, Negro and white, were made, behavior and habits were noted, and passengers and car crews were drawn into conversation. Officials of surface and elevated lines, starters, and station men were interviewed. Instances of friction which came to the attention of the Commission were noted and the circumstances studied.

Traffic counts made by the Chicago Traction and Subway Commission in 1916 showed 3,500,000 surface-railway and 500,000 elevated-railway passengers carried in a twenty-four-hour day. Negroes constitute 4 per cent of the city's population and probably about that percentage of the city's street-car traffic. Negro traffic, however, instead of being scattered over the city, is mainly concentrated upon twelve lines which traverse the Negro residential areas and connect those areas with the manufacturing districts where Negroes are employed. Because of this concentration the proportion of Negroes to whites on these twelve lines is much higher than 4 per cent, and on such lines as that on State Street, the principal business street of the South Side Negro residence area, it often happens that the majority of the passengers are Negroes.

There is no "Jim Crow" separation of races on street cars in Chicago. Contacts of Negroes and whites on the street cars did not provoke any considerable discussion before the period of migration of Negroes from the South, when occasional stories of clashes began to be circulated; and even then, such friction as developed did not come prominently to public attention. Only one incident involving a clash was reported in the newspapers. Even since the migration began, there have been very few complaints based upon racial friction. The Elevated Railroad Company, whose South Side line has the largest Negro traffic of any elevated line, replied to inquiries that, except during the riot of 1919, when a few cases of racial disorder were reported, there had been no complaints from motormen or trainmen since 1918, when a trainman was cut by a Negro. No complaints from white passengers had been received since the spring of 1917, when white office workers objected to riding with Stock Yards laborers, mainly Negroes, on the Stock Yards spur of the elevated. White laborers in the Stock Yards mostly live within walking distance of their work, but Negroes found it necessary to use car lines running east to the main area of Negro residence. The Chicago Surface lines replied that complaints due to racial friction were negligible.

Many of the migrants are laborers who must use these lines going to and from work, and many of them are rough-mannered and entirely unfamiliar with standards of conduct in northern cities. Another serious factor is the recent entrance of Negroes into industry. Before the war the great majority of Negroes gainfully employed were engaged in some form of personal service which did not require use of transportation lines in their working clothes to and from the manufacturing centers. The migrants, many of them coming to a city like Chicago with no "Jim Crow" segregation, felt strange and uncertain as to how they should act. In fact, peculiarities of conduct on the part of these were noted by Negroes of longer residence in Chicago, and it has been remarked by whites and Negroes that they could tell a Negro migrant by his uneasy manner and often by his clothing. Conspicuous points of behavior of migrant Negroes before they became urbanized, which many whites noted and commented on were: "loud laughter and talking," "old and ill-smelling clothes," "roughness and his tendency to sit all over the car." These are easy to understand when one considers the background of the southern Negro. There are, on the other hand, exceptional cases where Negroes have walked miles rather than take a car, thus avoiding possible embarrassment. A Negro who has been in Chicago for a long time is not self-conscious about sitting near white persons. Negroes who get into trouble with whites about insisting on their right to a seat often belong to the class of suspicious and sensitive Negroes who fear that an attempt is being made to segregate them, and sometimes they are simply "greenhorns."

Soiled and ill-smelling clothing was found to be an objection applying to white as well as Negro laborers. These complaints came, for the most part, from clerical workers who objected to physical contact with persons who might "rub off." A difficulty involving this feature was adjusted by one packing company by dismissing its clerical workers and its laborers at different hours. A frequent source of misunderstanding has been a situation in which it appeared that Negroes had taken seats intended for white women. In several such cases thoroughly examined by the Commission's investigators the difficulties were found to have resulted from misunderstood actions.

Most of the difficulties in transportation contacts reported and generally complained of seem to have centered around the first blundering efforts of migrants to adjust themselves to northern city life. The efforts of agencies interested in assisting this adjustment, together with the Negro press and the intimate criticisms and suggestions for proper conduct of Chicago Negroes, have smoothed down many of the roughnesses of the migrants, and as a result friction from contacts in transportation seems to have lessened materially.

4. CRIME AND VICIOUS ENVIRONMENT

Many students of the race problem look upon public crime records as a register of the failure of Negroes to adjust themselves to the social fabric. Study of infractions of law by Negroes, of provocation to lawlessness, and of the history of their crimes would indeed reveal an interesting background of their present behavior in relation to whites, if such a study were possible from present records. The Commission carried its investigations into this field and found no means of determining how great a proportion of the city's crimes is committed by Negroes.

The prevailing impression that Negroes are by nature more criminal than whites and more prone to commit sex crimes has restricted their employment, increased unfair measures of restraint, and blackened the name of the entire Negro group. Two important facts were apparent from the Commission's study: (1) the danger inherent in the vicious environment in which Negroes are forced to live, and (2) the misrepresentative character of the statistics of Negro crime.

Environment.—The limitations imposed on Negro residential areas have provided undue cause and occasion for crime. The entire population, good and bad, is thrown together, exposing children to the sight and temptation of vice and immorality. Ninety per cent of the Negro population has always lived near the city's former segregated vice districts, partly because white sentiment excluded them from other neighborhoods, partly because rents in the neighborhood of vice were low enough to meet their meager economic resources, and partly because their weakness made their protests against the proximity of vice less effective than the protests of whites. When the vice districts were broken up and the inmates scattered, they entered the better neighborhoods of Negro residence and clandestinely plied their trade. In fact, according to the report of the Chicago Vice Commission in 1911, at one time prostitutes were promised immunity by the police if they confined themselves to a certain area in which Negroes predominated. The spread of the Negro population has always been accompanied by the spread of clandestine prostitution. The Vice Commission's report said:

The history of the social evil in Chicago is intimately connected with the colored population. Invariably the large vice districts have been created within or near the settlements of colored people. In the past history of the city every time a new vice district was created downtown or on the South Side, the colored families were in the district moving in just ahead of the prostitutes. The situation along State Street from Sixteenth Street south is an illustration.

So whenever prostitutes, cadets, and thugs were located among white people and had to be moved for commercial or other reasons, they were driven to undesirable parts of the city, the so-called colored residential sections.

Most of the vicious resorts in the "Black Belt" are owned and operated by whites and are not interfered with by the authorities. Protests from Negroes have never succeeded in removing them. Opportunities for wholesome recreation in the Negro districts are limited, and commercial amusements, though probably no worse than in some other sections of the city, are of a distinctly inferior type and carelessly supervised. In such an infective environment it is not unnatural that many criminals should be developed.

But the study of crime statistics, aside from showing the unreliability of records due to careless methods of obtaining and presenting data, revealed that Negroes suffer gross injustice in the handling of criminal affairs. The general inaccuracy of criminal statistics is shown by the fact, for example, that the police reported 1,731 burglaries, or persons arrested for burglary, in 1919, while the Chicago Crime Commission reported 5,509 burglaries during the first eleven months of that year. The evidence at hand indicates that Negroes are debited with practically all their crimes, while others are not. It further appears, from the records and from the testimony of judges in the juvenile, municipal, circuit, superior, and criminal courts, of police officials, the state's attorney, and various experts on crime, probation, and parole, that Negroes are more commonly arrested, subjected to police identification, and convicted than white offenders; that on similar evidence they are generally held and convicted on more serious charges, and that they are given longer sentences. This bias, when reflected in the figures, serves to bolster by false figures the already existing belief that Negroes are more likely to be criminal than other racial groups.

V. THE NEGRO IN CHICAGO INDUSTRIES

Out of Chicago's Negro population of approximately 110,000 in 1920, it is estimated that 70,000 were gainfully employed. The opportunity for engaging in industry in large numbers came to Negroes following the outbreak of the world-war. With the enormous demand from the belligerent countries for American goods, existing establishments were enlarged and new ones created. As an example of the increased demand for workers, one of the packing-plants in the Chicago Stock Yards increased its force during the war from 8,000 to 17,000. Immigration was almost wholly cut off. The labor shortage became acute after the entrance of the United States into the war in 1917. The migration of Negroes from the South during that period was mainly in response to this demand.

Prior to the beginning of the war in 1914, Negroes had been virtually limited to personal and domestic service in almost every city in the North. In 1910 more than 60 per cent of those gainfully employed were so engaged, 15 per cent in manufacturing, and 3 per cent in clerical occupations. The Commission's inquiries covered 136 establishments reporting five or more Negroes. In these were employed 118,098 whites and 21,987 Negroes—12,854 in manufacturing and 9,133 in non-manufacturing industries.

1. INCREASE IN NEGRO LABOR

Between 1915 and 1920 there was a remarkable increase in the number of Negroes employed in industries which before 1915 had either employed them in small numbers or not at all. In a total of sixty-two such plants there was an increase from 1,346 in 1915 to 10,587 in 1920, or more than 1,000 per cent. Labor shortage, or inability to obtain competent white workers, was the reason given in practically every instance for the large increase in Negro employees.

Frequent complaints have been made that large employers, particularly the packers, imported Negroes from the South and were thus responsible for the difficulties that followed. Definite effort was made to determine the facts, but the Commission found no basis for the statement.

2. CLASSIFICATION OF NEGRO WORKERS

Absence of standards of classification for skilled, semi-skilled, and unskilled work invalidated the Commission's effort to classify Negro workers. In sixty-six industries with definite divisions in grades of work, it was found that out of 12,529 Negroes employed, 927 were skilled, 267 semi-skilled and 11,335 unskilled workers. In other returns, not capable of full classification, ten establishments reported 304 Negro molders; there were thirty-one Negro molders in 1910. Twelve factories reported 382 machine operators; in 1920 the census reports showed only twenty-eight.

Wages of Negroes in the branches of employment where they were permitted to work were generally the same as for white workers. There were instances, however, of discrimination in placing or keeping Negroes at work on processes in which they could not earn as much as in processes on which white men were engaged. Also there were instances of discrimination in piece-work, the foremen invariably giving Negroes only the jobs yielding a low rate. For common labor the average wage was 45 and 50 cents an hour for an eight-, nine- and ten-hour day for men; $15 to $20 a week for women, and an average of $15 a week, with room and board, for domestics were the going wages.

3. EMPLOYERS' EXPERIENCE WITH NEGRO LABOR

Whether or not the Negro will be able to hold the position in industry made possible for him by the war depends much on employers' attitude toward him as a worker. Common explanations given before this period as a reason for not employing Negroes more were that they were lazy, shiftless, irresponsible, and inefficient. Generalizations of this sort demonstrate their weakness in the fact that employers were not speaking from their own experiences. To reach a fair conclusion employers of Negroes in large numbers were interviewed by the Commission's investigators.

Employers drew a distinction between northern and southern Negroes; they thought that the latter had shortcomings when they first began work, but that this was due to former habits of work and familiarity with only simple industrial processes. Many of these southern workers were irregular at first in reporting for work and frequently drew their wages before pay day, thus confusing the bookkeeping. They were soon forced, however, to abandon these habits.

One question asked of all employers was: "Has your Negro labor proved satisfactory?" Of the 137 establishments employing five or more Negro workers, 118 reported that Negro labor had proved satisfactory; nineteen reported that Negro labor had not proved satisfactory. The 118 establishments reporting Negro workers as satisfactory employed 21,640 Negroes, while the nineteen reporting them as unsatisfactory employed 697. Comparing the efficiency of Negro and white workers, seventy-one employers interviewed (thirty-four manufacturers and thirty-seven non-manufacturers) considered the Negro equally efficient, twenty-two employers (thirteen manufacturers and nine non-manufacturers) considered the Negro less efficient. The seventy-one establishments included almost all the large establishments. A few gave the Negro a higher rating than the foreigners because of his knowledge of English.

Regarding reliability, ninety-two employers gave opinions. Sixty-three (thirty manufacturers and thirty-three non-manufacturers) believed that Negroes did not require more supervision than white workers, while twenty-nine (sixteen manufacturers and thirteen non-manufacturers) thought they required more supervision. Of the employers interviewed, fifty-seven expressed the opinion (twenty-three manufacturers and thirty-four non-manufacturers) that "absenteeism" among Negro workers was no greater than among whites, while thirty-six reported it was greater.

One plant employing 2,084 Negroes stated that the better living standards and ambitions had brought up the rating of Negro workers during the war period.

4. LABOR TURNOVER

Of the thirty-two employers giving figures on relative labor turnover, twenty-four (eleven manufacturers and thirteen non-manufacturers) reported the Negro turnover to be the same as the white, and twenty–eight (eighteen manufacturers and ten non-manufacturers) believed the turnover to be greater. Closely connected with the labor turnover among Negroes is the question of "hope on the job," as one Negro expressed it.   When Negroes are not allowed to advance to better positions in a given plant, or are discriminated against by foremen underrating their efficiency, the turnover in the plant is high.

5. NEGRO WOMEN IN INDUSTRY

Before the war Negro women were even more definitely restricted than Negro men in choice of occupations.   Two-thirds of those gainfully employed were in two occupation groups: "servants" and laundresses, not in laundries, and domestic servants.   Of the 137 establishments studied, forty-two had no Negro women employees, forty-five kept no separate records, and fifty reported a total of 3,407 Negro women workers.   Although this study does not include all industries employing women, the total given represents a large increase over the figure of 998 Negro women enumerated by the 1910 census as engaged in all industries in Chicago.

Many of the establishments in question had employed large numbers of Negro women as an experiment and had found them satisfactory.   One mail-order house employed as many as 650 girls for clerical work.   When the plant was investigated in 1920, there were 311 girls, 75 per cent of whom were high-school graduates, while 12 per cent had had two or more years in college. These employers said the girls felt that they were making history for the race and were, if anything, a little over-zealous.   They were thought to be excitable and suspicious of the actions of the white girls.

Millinery establishments, manufacturers of clothing, lamp-shades, gas-mantles, paper-boxes, and cheese makers reported satisfactory experience with Negro women. Of twenty laundries employing Negro workers, satisfactory or unsatisfactory, four did not keep separate records.   Twelve with 409 Negro women reported their work satisfactory, and four with 134 Negro women reported it unsatisfactory. The chief complaint was unwillingness to work overtime or on Sundays. In both instances, however, employees interviewed complained that the hours were long (nine hours a day) and their treatment by the management harsh and inconsiderate.

Of 865 Negro employees interviewed, less than 1 per cent complained of disagreeable treatment by white workers and less than 50 per cent complained of conditions of work. Others expressed themselves as glad of the opportunity to earn good wages. Complaints against conditions of work were found in the iron and steel mills, Stock Yards, and dining-car and sleeping-car service.

6. INDUSTRIES EXCLUDING THE NEGRO

Several important industries have not opened their doors to Negroes except as janitors and porters. Among these are the traction companies, elevated and surface, the State Street department stores, and the taxicab companies. Employers in these establishments express the belief that the public would object to Negroes.

Attention has been called to the waste involved in the limitations of Negroes in industry. Men with college training are forced to work as waiters and porters, and young-women college graduates are frequently forced to work as ushers in theaters and as ladies' maids. This condition helps to account for the ease with which 1,500 Negro girls with more than average schooling were recruited in less than two months for the mail-order houses.

7. RELATIONS BETWEEN WHITE AND NEGRO WORKERS

Through working together friendliness between white and Negro workers has been increased, according to prevalent views. Information concerning relations was secured from all the 137 plants studied. Two reported that race friction was a disturbing factor in the plants. Minor instances of friction have occurred, but it appeared that as a rule the workers reflected the attitude of the management. The setting up of partitions separating the races developed an antagonistic sentiment, and in some instances this antagonism was removed when the partitions were taken down. Of 101 establishments visited eighteen, or 11 per cent, with 2,623 Negroes, maintained separate accommodations. This constituted a continuous source of dissatisfaction for Negro workers, who felt themselves "Jim Crowed." In the remaining 89 per cent, employing 19,714 Negroes among more than 100,000 whites, all accommodations were used in common by both races.

8. THE PERIOD OF INDUSTRIAL DEPRESSION

Following the war's inflation of industry a slump came in the winter of 1920–21. Common labor was reduced in all the large plants from 20 to 50 per cent. Negroes, mostly common laborers, suffered most from this reduction. At one period there were as many as 15,000 Negroes unemployed in Chicago. They were cared for during their enforced idleness by the Urban League and Negro churches and by popular contributions from working Negroes. The reduction of labor was usually carried out by employers with some system, and few instances of gross race discrimination were reported.

9. ORGANIZED LABOR AND NEGRO WORKERS

Clashing interests have manifested themselves conspicuously in the relations between union labor organizations and Negro workers, and this antagonism has been carried over into the relations of whites and Negroes generally. The efforts of union labor to promote its cause have built up a body of sentiment not easy to oppose by workers unsympathetic toward the labor movement. Circumstances have frequently made Negroes strike breakers, and thus centered upon them as a racial group all the bitterness of the unionist toward strike breakers as a class.

On the other hand, Negroes have often expressed themselves as having little faith in the union labor movement because the unions have manifested prejudices against permitting them to share equal benefits of membership; and again they have gained their first opportunity in a new industry frequently through the desire of a strike-bound employer to keep his plant running when his white employees have walked out.

From its beginning the American Federation of Labor has declared a uniform policy of non-racial discrimination, but this policy has not been carried out in practice by all its constituent or affiliated bodies. At several of its conventions resolutions have been passed embodying the official sentiment of the federation, but no means has yet been discovered to effect a uniform policy of fair dealing throughout all its affiliated bodies. Aside from those unions in which the membership privilege for Negroes is modified, eight of the 110 national or international unions affiliated with the American Federation of Labor explicitly bar the Negro by provisions in their constitutions or rituals. These unions are: Brotherhood of Railway Clerks, Brotherhood of Railway Carmen of America, International Association of Machinists, American Association of Masters, Mates, and Pilots, Railway Mail Association, Order of Railroad Telegraphers, the Commercial Telegraphers' Union of America, and American Wire Weavers' Protective Association.

The general exclusion policy of the railway brotherhoods and several unions of the Railway Department of the American Federation of Labor has created a feeling of bitterness among Negroes, many of whom are employed in branches of the railway service. As a protest against this policy there has been formed the Railway Men's International Benevolent Industrial Association with seventeen locals in Chicago and a local membership of 1,200. Mr. Mays, president of this organization, stated that its purpose was merely to safeguard the ranks of Negro workers, and said that it was ready to merge itself into the general unions as soon as they were ready to accept them without discrimination and accord the same privileges as white railway workers.

The Commission obtained information from local unions in Chicago with a membership of 294,437, of whom 12,106 were Negroes. On the basis of policy toward the Negro, unions in Chicago may be divided into four classes or types:

A. Unions admitting Negroes to white locals
B. Unions admitting Negroes to separate or co-ordinate locals
C. Unions admitting Negroes to subordinate or auxiliary locals
D. Unions excluding Negroes from membership

Wherever and whenever Negroes are admitted on an equal basis and given a square deal, the feeling inside the union is nearly always harmonious. Examples of type A are the Amalgamated Meat Cutters and Butcher Workmen of the World, Hodcarriers, Flat Janitors, and Ladies' Garment Workers. In some of these organizations Negroes hold office.

Unions of type B give as reasons for organizing Negroes into separate locals, first, preference of Negro workers for locals of their own, and, second, unwillingness of white workers to admit Negroes to white locals. The Negro Musicians' Union belongs to this type and has the same wage scale as the white union. There appears to be little difficulty here because there is no conflict in contracts for work in the city. The painters, however, have had difficulties which have "hung fire" for more than a year; after being given a temporary charter they still were unable to work.

Unions of type C, admitting Negroes to subordinate locals, are few in number, apparently because Negroes strongly resent this form of affiliation. There is, however, one example of this type which permits Negro helpers in a certain trade to be organized as an auxiliary under the jurisdiction of the white local unions having jurisdiction over their district. By constitution it is provided that their minutes be submitted to the white locals and their grievances placed before the white locals. The constitution also provides that there shall be no transfer of colored helpers to any except Negro auxiliaries, and that Negro helpers shall not be promoted to skilled trades or to helper apprentice, and shall not be admitted to shops where white helpers are employed. These Negro locals are represented by delegates selected by the white locals in their districts.

Unions of type D, excluding the Negro from membership, do so either in conformity with the laws of their national unions or in the exercise of local option. In addition to the eight internationals which exclude the Negro by constitutional provision, there are other locals which are known to reject Negro applicants. The Machinists' Union, for example, although complying in its constitution with the American Federation of Labor policy of no racial discrimination, still effectually bars the Negro by a provision in its secret ritual. With the Machinists' Union must be grouped such unions as the

Amalgamated Sheet Metal Workers' International Alliance, the Electrical Workers, and the Plumbers and Steam Fitters.

Some Negro leaders, in view of these practices, have been strong in their advocacy of non-affiliation with union organizations, holding that the employers, after all, offer for Negroes the fairer terms, and that they have, in fact, given Negroes their first opportunity in industry. However, certain other Negroes have taken advantage of the rift between employers and labor unions to exploit Negro laborers. They have played upon racial sentiment to establish separate unions for Negroes, both in lines of work where they are admitted to the general unions and in lines of work where they are excluded. This type of leadership has been irresponsible and dangerous; it has made ridiculously generous promises, and has addressed its appeal to the less intelligent classes of Negro workers. Its literature has in turn provoked extreme bitterness among labor union members and officials, who have mistakenly accepted it as representative of the sentiment of all Negro workers.

Interviews with Negro workers outside of the unions reveal an attitude of indifference or suspicion which is attributed by both white and Negro labor leaders and union men to the following reasons: (1) the usual treatment of Negroes by white men, (2) traditional treatment of Negroes by white men, (3) influence of racial leaders who oppose unionism, (4) influence of employers' propaganda against unionism. Many of them, it was learned, have a distorted view of the purposes and principles of unionism, and many others, while sympathetic with the movement, object to the practices of the locals. An experience frequently referred to was the waiters' strike in 1911, when Negro union men walked out with white union men and were replaced by white girls, while the white union men returned to their jobs; since that time Negro waiters have been out of the more desirable hotel jobs.

The explanations by labor leaders of the practices of local unions are to the effect that while the general public race prejudice might be expected in organizations of white workingmen, the unions, as a group, are fairer to the Negro than other groups; that unions are blamed for conditions which are really due to general public opinion. They cite as an example the fact that Negroes are not employed in Chicago as motormen or conductors on the surface or elevated lines because of public objection, and that they cannot be organized until they are in positions. Views were also expressed in condemnation of the exclusion policy of one local. These union officials believe that the unions will eventually be the most powerful agencies in the removal of race prejudice.

VI. Public Opinion in Race Relations

A. Opinions of Whites and Negroes

The "Negro problem" is deeper and wider than the difficulties which center about the more specialized problems of Negro housing, Negro crime, and industrial relations involving Negroes. All such special studies conducted by the Commission left a baffling residuum of causes of racial discord, deep rooted in the psychology of the white and Negro groups in contact. The beliefs and attitudes, firmly fixed and accepted prejudices of the one race as to the other, grouped under the term "public opinion," thus became the subject of a novel but most interesting inquiry.

Public opinion with respect to the Negro forms a body of sentiment so definite and compact as to make it an excellent laboratory case for analysis and study; but the Commission's aim in investigating it was merely to make apparent and objective its place and importance in race relations; to indicate some of the ways in which it has developed; how it expresses itself; how it affects both the white and Negro groups; how, in its present state, it is strengthened, weakened, polluted, or purified by deliberate agencies or even by its own action; and finally how it may be used to reduce, if not prevent, racial unfriendliness and misunderstanding.

Public opinion is regarded here as a phase of the social mind, but nevertheless as a definite reality. For purposes of examination, therefore, its study gives attention to that body of sentiments, beliefs, attitudes, and prejudices which, taken together, give to public opinion its content and meaning.

To present this subject intelligently, the following plan has been employed:

1. Beliefs and sophistications regarding Negroes, which exercise so great an influence in determining the conduct of white persons in relation to them, are described as they apply in the local environment, and in origin and background are traced suggestively to their responsible sources in literature and circumstance.

2. Types of sentiment which, in Chicago and similar northern communities, are variants of these basic beliefs are presented with a view to making them intelligible and classifying them according to resolvable factors of misunderstanding.

3. Since personal attitudes and beliefs are molded by traditions and heritages apart from the exclusive influence of literature, more significant material collected through intimate inquiry is presented objectively to describe the processes by which they appear to be created and grow. Replies to a searching questionnaire on attitudes and opinions are, in the instances quoted, the result of painstaking self-analysis.

4. The opinions and sentiments of Negroes on these same issues are described and illustrated with a view to making them understandable, and their interpretations of current white sentiment are explained as far as possible.

5. The report then turns to the agencies by which these opinions are made and perpetuated and the individual attitudes created. The chief of these are: (a) the press, (b) rumors, (c) myths, (d) propaganda. The conscious and unconscious abuse of these instruments of "opinion making" is pointed out and explained.

6. Finally, the study is intended to suggest means by which public opinion, where it is faulty, may correct itself and employ its own instruments in the

creation of wholesome sentiments among Negroes with respect to whites, and among whites with respect to Negroes.

1. BELIEFS OF WHITES CONCERNING NEGROES

The conduct of individuals is largely determined by their attitudes toward a subject and their general beliefs concerning it   Definite beliefs concerning Negroes may be found in the North as well as in the South, varying with the individuals who hold them, according to degrees of contact with the Negro group and the individuals' traditional background.   These may be divided according to their character and effect into two general classes: (*a*) primary beliefs or those fundamental and firmly established convictions which have, all around, the deepest effect on the conduct of whites toward Negroes and are pretentiously supported by statistics, authorities, and scientific research; (*b*) secondary beliefs, or modifications and variants of important assumptions as to cardinal attributes.

a) Primary beliefs.—Among these primary beliefs are the following:

1. Mentality: That the mind of the Negro is distinctly and distinctively inferior to that of the white race.   Some believe that this is due to backwardness in ascending the scale of civilization; some that the Negro belongs to a different species of the human family.

2. Morality: That Negroes are not yet capable of exercising social restraints common to white persons; that they are unmoral as well as immoral.

3. Criminality: That Negroes possess a constitutional character weakness, and a consequent predisposition to sexual crimes, petty stealing, and crimes of violence.

4. Physical unattractiveness: That physical laws prompt whites to avoid contact with Negroes.

5. Emotionality: That Negroes are highly emotional and for that reason are given to quick, uncalculated crimes of violence as easily as to noisy and emotional religious expressions.

b) Secondary beliefs.—As continued repetition of any plausible statement without correction of its error eventually gives it credence, these secondary beliefs have rooted themselves deep in the public mind.   Among other things it is believed that Negroes are: (1) lazy, (2) "happy-go-lucky," (3) boisterous, (4) bumptious, (5) over-assertive, (6) lacking in civic consciousness, (7) addicted to carrying razors, (8) fond of shooting craps, (9) flashy in dress and like gaudy, brilliant colors, especially red.

2. BACKGROUND OF PREVAILING BELIEFS CONCERNING NEGROES

Soon after the first emergence of Negroes from slavery their illiteracy and general behavior in response to the novel experience of freedom created situations which appeared to justify judgments concerning their group traits. Scholars rationalized and tried to explain these apparent traits: If they were illiterate as a group they must be incapable of learning, and if they committed crimes, they must be fundamentally lacking in social restraints.

Dr. Jeffries Wyman, of Harvard, Professor A. H. Keene, author of *Man Past and Present*, Dr. J. C. Nott, author of *Types of Mankind*, and almost all the other anthropologists of that period, gave the stamp of scientific authority to the view that Negroes were of a different species and could never reach the level of the Caucasian. Even more recently mental tests were carried out on the same assumption and were made to prove it in some instances where the facts were unexpectedly contrary. Students of the race problem in the South continued to generalize about Negro character from selected specimens, other more popular writers and speakers, with their anecdotes, stories, and jokes, all of which went uncorrected, tended to strengthen this body of beliefs to a point where any difference of views was intolerable. Although the status of the Negro has changed, the beliefs remain the same, and have led to bitterness and resentment among Negroes, with consequent misunderstandings and friction.

In Chicago sentiments collected from a wide variety of sources and involving the views of several thousands of white persons indicate the persistence of these archaic beliefs and fears, so deep set and of such long standing that they are assumed by many persons to be instinctive.

To secure definite information upon the traditional background of beliefs concerning Negroes, fifteen white persons with no special interest in Negroes were selected at random from professions, business, and other vocations and submitted to a careful and searching inquiry. They were asked eighteen carefully prepared questions to draw out the raw material of their unqualified reactions on the question of the Negro and, as far as possible, the background in their early experience. They were asked for their opinions concerning Negroes, whether or not they believed that they possessed distinguishing traits of mentality and character; their attitudes were solicited by questions and propositions designed to provoke an expression of attitude. Questions were put regarding instances and experiences involving Negroes in their early experience; their first consciousness of racial differences; their first contacts; and information was sought on the definite sources of their knowledge or opinions concerning Negroes.

All the persons questioned had clear-cut opinions and thought that Negroes possessed distinguishing traits ranging from "affectionate loyalty" to "mental and moral handicaps imposed by evolution." An abolitionist's son, for example, thought that "Negroes should desire segregation"; a man who had observed Negroes at Tuskegee and Lewis institutes would increase their education and meet the demands produced by education. One whose only contact had been with his "black mammy" thought that the Negroes were "affectionate and loyal, but lacking in racial pride, though evolutionarily handicapped, possessing the qualities of children." Another who had had an unfortunate experience with his Negro chauffeur thought that Negroes were characterized by "distinctly inferior mentality, deficient moral sense, shiftlessness, good-natured, and a happy disposition." They knew little about the activities of Negroes, their leaders, their papers, or their problems, and the sources on which they relied for their information, except in two instances, were undependable.

3. NEGRO OPINION

Negroes, although exposed to various forms of social contact, have been intellectually isolated from the white group. They have not participated fully and freely in community and cultural activities. The pressure of the white group in practically every ordinary experience has kept their attention and interest centered upon themselves, and they have become race conscious. Their thinking, therefore, on general questions, whether they involve race relations or not, is conditioned and largely controlled by the relation of these questions with group interests. The opinions of Negroes, therefore, on race relations are largely negative. White persons know very little about what Negroes are thinking, because they are not familiar with their experiences; they frequently do not accredit them with the sensibilities that they do possess; and are not acquainted with the processes of thought by which the opinions of Negroes are formed. Thus it is that many of the statements and expressions of feeling of Negroes are unintelligible to persons outside of their group. Similarly, many statements and expressions of feeling by white persons are unintelligible to Negroes. But in the understanding of white persons Negroes have the advantage, because they do read their papers, see them in the privacy of their homes, and are forced constantly to interpret their actions.

Among Negroes there may be found a group control as strong and binding as among white persons. One striking instance of the operation of this group control was the complete ostracism of a prominent Negro lawyer who was reported to have made a public statement contrary to the views and aspirations held by his group. When this Negro was reported in the press to have said, "This is a white man's country, and Negroes had better behave or they will get what rights they have taken away," he was first snubbed, then his life was threatened, and for several weeks he was forced to go about under police protection. He was seriously criticized and finally ostracized. In less than a year he died. His friends declare that he was slanderously misquoted.

The sentiments of Negroes fall into somewhat the same classification as those of whites, but with one or two notable exceptions: there is (1) more discussion of race problems, more criticism of the conduct of leaders, more discussion of the practicability of programs of action; and (2) a great deal of literature and other expressions concerning the development of a defensive philosophy. In this latter are included various defensive policies, the stimulation of race pride, the explanation of behavior, and the struggle for status. There might also be included frequent evidences of the development of race consciousness.

The emotional background, class consciousness, and the influences of group control are as evident in the sentiments of Negroes as of white persons.

A wide selection of views was obtained from Negroes and presented under the classifications in which they appeared naturally to fall. To get a more precise statement of views, a questionnaire was sent to Negroes representing a class intellectually able to subject themselves to self-analysis and to discuss various confusing angles of the race question. They were asked concerning interracial problems; whether or not race relations appear to be growing better or worse; whether the acquisition of wealth, or 100 per cent literacy, or unrestricted suffrage could affect race relations; they were asked questions concerning their adjustment to the present social system, their most pronounced mental complexes experienced in adjusting personal desires to the present social system; whether they were prejudiced against white persons; whether or not they were conscious of a feeling of race inferiority, or of a desire to compensate for a supposed inferiority. Concerning Negro problems they were asked whether or not there should be recognized leaders of Negroes; their criticisms of the policies of Negro leaders. Their racial philosophy was solicited. They were asked the distinction that they made between segregation and racial solidarity, and information was sought on the agencies responsible for their opinions. A most interesting array of views was secured, ranging from suspicion and abuse of the questions themselves to dispassionate analysis.

The war has produced a new type of sentiment. It not only brought disappointment and disillusionment for Negroes led into a new hope by the promises that accompanied the manifest efforts to stimulate patriotism, but actually gave to Negroes new experiences. Following the return of Negro soldiers from France, measures of restraint were increased, and from the usual lawlessness of the period of reconstruction they probably suffered more severely than others because they are to a much larger extent dependent upon law enforcement for security and comfort. Race riots, which are an expression of both loose machinery of community control and the development of a more determined resistance on the part of Negroes, grew more frequent in number and more serious in consequences. A new note was sounded in radical Negro literature, which appeared to carry a very popular appeal.

B. FACTORS IN THE MAKING OF PUBLIC OPINION

I. THE WHITE PRESS OF CHICAGO

Aside from the agencies ordinarily responsible for providing the individual with his views, there are others equally as powerful in developing and influencing opinions. Most important of these is the press. For that portion of the public which depends upon the press for its contact with the Negro group and its information concerning it, this agency holds a controlling hand.

Throughout the country it is pointed out, by both whites and Negroes, that the policies of many newspapers on racial matters have made relations more difficult, at times fostering new antagonisms and even precipitating riots by inflaming the white public against Negroes. A study was made of the three principal white daily newspapers of Chicago, covering a two-year period. Included in this study were 1,347 news items, 108 letters to the press, and ninety-six editorials on the Negro.

As an example of the type of publicity given to racial news concerning Negroes and the types of articles considered to have good news value, of the 1,338 articles published, 606, or nearly 50 per cent, dealt with riots, crime, and vice. Each of these articles specifically identified the persons involved as Negroes.

Constant identification of Negroes with certain definite crimes could have no other effect than to stamp the entire Negro group in the public mind as generally criminal. This in turn contributes to the already existing belief that Negroes as a group are more likely to be criminal than others, and thus they are arrested more readily than others. Publication of their names with race identification and with the crimes alleged against them keeps up a vicious circle. The unfortunate emphasis on sex offenses involving race, the subtle fanning of latent animosities by innuendo and suggestion, attaching the crime not only to the individual but to the race, direct a current of fear, intolerance, and ill will against the whole Negro group. An apt illustration, frequently cited by Negroes, is that if each time a crime was committed by a red-headed man, he was so described in telling of his crime, a popular fear and prejudice would soon develop against all red-headed men.

Crimes involving Negroes alone receive little attention. As with the Italians, as long as crimes are committed within the group, and this group is regarded as an isolated appendix of the community, they hold very little news value. When, however, a member of the isolated group comes into conflict with the community group, whether in industry, housing, or any relation, its representative significance is thus established, and the information becomes news. Publicity on housing, for example, stresses the conflict with other neighborhoods, the "invasion" of white districts, and plans for segregation. News items on politics involving Negroes get more space and prominence when they describe graft and corruption. In the list of articles studied are included sixty-three articles particularly ridiculing the Negro group.

Incidents occurring during the activities of the Commission were checked up with reports of them appearing in the papers, and serious misrepresentations of the Negro group were revealed. One example was an article in the *Herald-Examiner* on January 4, 1920, with two-inch headlines across the entire first page: "Reds Plot Negro Revolt," "I.W.W. Bomb Plant Found on South Side." The article mentioned the alleged secret activities of Negroes and their plans to revolt against the government. The bomb plant and many of their secret plans were reported to have been discovered by the state's attorney. The article further said: "In Chicago it was learned that the headquarters for Negro revolutionary propaganda are centered in these four organizations: the Free Thought Society, Universal Negro Improvement Association, Negro Protective League, and the Soldiers and Sailors Club." The article and the reported "discoveries" of the state's attorney's office are evidence of the absurd ignorance frequently manifested by members of the white group concerning the activities of Negroes. Each of the organizations named was known to the Commission and visited by its representatives on numbers of occasions. All of their meetings are open to the public, though attended almost entirely by Negroes. The Universal Negro Improvement Association publishes all of its plans in its newspaper, the *Negro World*. Its slogan is "Back to Africa" and not "Down with the United States." The Free Thought Society mentioned is an organization designed to provide a medium of expression for persons who seek the "attainment of truth." Its discussions concern religion and philosophy, and it numbers among its members prominent Negro and white professional men. The Negro Protective League is an employment office and day nursery. The full name of the organization is the "Negro Equal Rights and Protective Association." The Soldiers and Sailors Club is a community house located on the South Side and a branch of the local War Camp Community Service. Eugene T. Lies, formerly of the United Charities, was its director. The occasion of the publicity in question was a convention of a national Negro Greek-letter fraternity, which held its meetings in the auditorium of the Soldiers and Sailors Club. This fraternity, like all others of its kind, excluded non-members and by so doing aroused the suspicion of the newspaper's informants. No correction appeared in the paper, and to date no further "discoveries" have been made.

Articles of this type illustrate the possible effect on the public mind of such misrepresentations of the Negro. One newspaper has abandoned its policy of identifying Negroes with reports of incidents, in recognition of the gross unfairness of the practice.

2. THE NEGRO PRESS

The development of the Negro press was stimulated by several necessities important among which were:

a) The indifference of the white press to the Negro group; its emphasis on the unfortunately spectacular, and the consequent loss of items of interest about Negroes throughout the country.

b) The importance of developing the morale of the Negro group, creating a solidarity of interest and purpose for measures of defense, correcting the impressions created by general opinion, and centering the attention of Negroes upon themselves and their advancement.

Three of the most important local Negro weekly papers were studied. Their news items showed bias in reporting just the reverse of that which characterizes the reports of many white papers. They emphasize the Negro's view and may be said to provide a compensatory interpretation of the news. When, for example, the *Chicago Tribune* reports the approval in the Illinois Constitutional Convention of a civil-rights bill with the headline: "Miscegenation Is O.K.'d in New Constitution; Negroes Given All the Rights of Whites," the *Chicago Whip*, a Negro newspaper, headlines the same incident: "Morris Gets Civil Rights into Constitution; Victory for Race Won at Springfield."

The most important function exercised by the Negro press is its control of the Negro group and of their education in conduct. All of these papers give considerable space to such popular education.

3. RUMOR

Rumor, if unchecked, can do incalculable damage to race relations. Included under the term "rumor" are those unfounded tales, incorrectly deduced conclusions, partial statements of fact with significant content added by the narrator, all of which are given wide circulation and easy credence by the public. Other forms of rumor are tales of unheard-of brutality and of plots and plans which are either fabrications or partial statements of fact and serve only to stimulate resentment, fear, and a desire for retaliation. Of the rumors predicting riots, one example will illustrate: During the riot a white man was caught in the act of crawling beneath a house in which Negroes lived. In his pocket was found a bottle of kerosene. He confessed that his mission was arson and justified his act by repeating to the police the current rumor that it was known that Negroes had set fire to the houses of whites "back of the Yards."

A persistent tale circulated during and for a long time after the riot was to the effect that the bodies of hundreds of Negroes were taken from Bubbly Creek where they had been thrown after being killed by white rioters. The story was so frequently repeated that it was accepted and even repeated in Congress. It caused an intense feeling among Negroes. Investigation by the coroner, Police Department, and other agencies showed that no bodies had ever been thrown into Bubbly Creek or recovered from it.

A rumor given official sanction and carried into the files of the Department of Justice illustrates other possible dangers of this kind. This rumor concerned two prominent and highly accredited organizations for Negroes. Rumors connected them with "I.W.W. plots and plans to overthrow the government." These reports were founded upon scarcely anything more than suspicion due to lack of information and acquaintance with the Negro group. The National Urban League, for example, an organization of responsible Negroes and whites with branches in thirty-one cities, was reported to have asked William D.

Haywood, head of the I.W.W., to speak at its convention in Detroit. This report grew out of the misreading of the name of William Hayward, a United States district attorney in New York, who is a member of the executive board and whose name appears on the stationery of the organization. The National Association for the Advancement of Colored People, also a reputable organization of whites and Negroes, was reported to be "planning to flood the colored districts with I.W.W. literature." This was entirely false, but the reports went to the Department of Justice headquarters secretly and could not be corrected by the persons most affected.

4. MYTHS

Group myths, like those about the American Indian, the Oriental, and the Jew, are very common. Usually they are the expression either of a wish or of fear, which sociologists call a negative wish. Mythical stories and anecdotes about Negroes, accepted by whites, are usually popular. Many of them may have had a reasonable origin, but as a matter of fact have long outgrown it. So long as they are uncorrected they hold and exercise a marked degree of control over personal conduct.

In the category of myths fall the popular beliefs of whites concerning the mentality of Negroes, and the more definite myth that the mind of the Negro child ceases to develop when he reaches the age of puberty. The sex myth is always in evidence. It involves the fear obsession of Negro men held by many white women, fear of miscegenation, the condonation of lynchings, repressive social restrictions, as well as attempts at legislative restraints. Negroes are by these myths shown to have a predilection for sex crimes. This sex myth has been stressed in almost every riot. It precipitated the Washington riot; it provoked the most brutal murder of the Chicago riot, and it was responsible for the brutality of the Omaha and Tulsa riots. Always resident in the background of popular consciousness, it shows the same head and features in almost every clash of races.

5. PROPAGANDA

Conscious control of public opinion by propaganda has been used with tremendous effect by social, political, and religious organizations seeking popularity and support for their movements and reforms. Both Negroes and whites employed propaganda, sometimes openly, sometimes insidiously. Racial propaganda has probably a more powerful appeal than any other type because it is based upon the instinct of race and race differences, rivalry and jealousy. The most common forms of propaganda may be classified into the following types: (a) educational, (b) radical and revolutionary, (c) defensive, (d) malicious.

The activities and programs of the National Association for the Advancement of Colored People fall under the classification of educational propaganda;

this propaganda is directed to the white public principally and is intended to change public opinion by providing a foundation of actual facts for the public's judgment.

The more striking examples of the radical and revolutionary propaganda are the appeals sent out by the Industrial Workers of the World to Negroes, carrying their doctrines and extending open arms to Negro workers and offering them what most other organizations refuse—the privilege of association and membership on the basis of brotherhood.

Defensive propaganda is more apparent within the Negro group and is usually designed for the purpose of combating aggression and injury to their purposes and aspirations from without. The appeals of this propaganda are directed first to Negroes as a means of cementing the group from within, and indirectly to the white group by way of impressing them with the strength of solidified opposition to insults. The Protective Circle of Chicago, organized to "oppose segregation, bombing, and defiance of the Constitution," admitted employing propaganda to accomplish its purpose.

Malicious propaganda is by far the most dangerous because it is founded upon race antagonism. In the appeal to the emotions facts are soon lost. Anti-Negro propaganda is not wholly new in the North, but when employed it has usually been done insidiously because "Negro-baiting is considered in bad taste." Recently, however, there have been conspicuous instances of open and organized efforts to influence the minds of whites against Negroes. Ignorance and suspicion, fear and prejudice, have been played upon deliberately. The stated purpose of the propaganda was to unite white property owners in opposition to the "invasion" of other residential areas by Negroes, but in the actual carrying out of the propaganda it was extended to all Negroes, and many methods were employed which could have no other effect than to arouse bitterness and antagonism leading to clashes. The *Property Owners' Journal*, the organ of an association of real estate men, became so violent in its preachments that the protest of whites forced its discontinuance. Appeals were made not only to the instinct of race but to the sex instincts and the protective instincts of white men. A pamphlet sent to the wives of prominent residents in that neighborhood, entitled *An Appeal of White Women to American Humanity*, recounted the "horrible conduct of French Colonials on the Rhine and the abuse of German white women," although there was little apparent connection between the conduct of Chicago Negroes and that of the black soldiers in the French Army of Occupation on the Rhine. This pamphlet, however, served to increase the fears of Negro men by white women and to arouse the resentment and hatred of white men.

THE RECOMMENDATIONS OF THE COMMISSION

Many of our citizens who were appalled by the rioting and murders of 1919, feeling the need of a solution of the problem dealt with in this investigation, have hoped that this Commission might suggest some ready remedy, some quick means of assuring harmony between the races.

Careful consideration of the facts set forth in this report shows that no such suggestion is possible. No one, white or Negro, is wholly free from an inheritance of prejudice in feeling and in thinking as to these questions. Mutual understanding and sympathy between the races will be followed by harmony and co-operation. But these can come completely only after the disappearance of prejudice. Thus the remedy is necessarily slow; and it is all the more important that the civic conscience of the community should be aroused, and that progress should begin in a direction steadily away from the disgrace of 1919.

Each member of this Commission feels that he has more understanding and less prejudice than before its work began. Therefore we recommend the thoughtful examination of the body of this report, so that all who read our recommendations may weigh for themselves the evidence upon which they are based.

Having in mind the basic facts in the problem of race relations and the conclusions from a careful study of the various phases of these relations in Chicago, the Commission presents for the consideration and action of state and local authorities, and of the social agencies and citizens of Chicago, the following recommendations and suggestions.

To the Police, Militia, State's Attorney, and Courts:

HANDLING OF RIOTS

1. We recommend that the police and militia work out, at the earliest possible date, a detailed plan for joint action in the control of race riots.

2. In accordance with such a plan, and in the event of race rioting, we specifically recommend: (a) that the militia, white and Negro, be promptly mobilized at the beginning of the outbreak; (b) that police and deputy sheriffs and militia, white and Negro, be so distributed as adequately to protect both races in white and Negro neighborhoods and to avoid the gross inequalities of protection which, in the riot of 1919, permitted widespread depredations, including murder, against Negroes in white neighborhoods, and attacks in Negro neighborhoods by invading white hoodlums; (c) that the police and militia be stationed with special reference to main street-car lines and transfer points used by Negroes in getting to and from work; (d) that substantial assurance be given of adequate and equal protection by all agencies of law enforcement, thus removing the incentive to arm in self-defense; (e) that in the appointment of special peace officers there shall be no discrimination against Negroes; (f) that all rioters, white and Negro, be arrested without race discrimination; (g) that all reports and complaints of neglect of duty or participation in rioting by police, deputy sheriffs, or militia be promptly

investigated and the offenders promptly punished; (*h*) that all persons arrested in connection with rioting be systematically booked on distinct charges showing such connection, in order to avoid the confusion and evasions of justice following the riot of 1919.

3. We recommend that, without regard to color, all persons arrested in connection with rioting be promptly tried and the guilty speedily punished.

BOMBINGS

4. We recommend prompt and vigorous action by the police, state's attorney, and courts to suppress the bombings of Negro and white houses, these acts being criminal and likely to provoke race rioting.

5. The testimony of court officials before the Commission and its investigations indicate that Negroes are more commonly arrested, subjected to police identification, and convicted than white offenders, that on similar evidence they are generally held and convicted on more serious charges, and that they are given longer sentences. We point out that these practices and tendencies are not only unfair to Negroes, but weaken the machinery of justice and, when taken with the greater inability of Negroes to pay fines in addition to or in lieu of terms in jail, produce misleading statistics of Negro crime. We recognize that these practices and tendencies are in a large degree the unconscious results of traditional race prejudice. We recommend to the police, state's attorney, judges, and juries that they consider these conditions in the effort to deal fairly (and without discrimination) with all persons charged with crime.

6. We recommend that, in order to encourage respect for law by both Negroes and whites, the courts discountenance the facetiousness which is too common in dealing with cases in which Negroes are involved.

VICIOUS ENVIRONMENT

7. We recommend that the police, state's attorney, and other authorities promptly rid the Negro residence areas of vice resorts, whose present exceptional prevalence in such areas is due to official laxity.

POLICING OF PARKS AND BEACHES

8. We recommend better co-operation between the city and park police in and near parks, bathing-beaches, and other public recreation places, especially where there has been or is likely to be race friction; and in the speedy punishment of persons guilty of stoning houses, molesting individuals, or committing other depredations calculated to arouse race antagonism.

"ATHLETIC CLUBS"

9. We recommend that the police pay particular and continuous attention to the so-called "athletic clubs" on the South Side, which we have found to be a fruitful source of race conflict, and that when race conflict arises or is imminent the members and meeting places of such clubs be searched for arms and that, if deemed necessary, such clubs be closed.

THE BARRETT MURDER

10. We commend the police for the prompt and effective action in the Barrett murder case, September 20, 1920, which allayed public alarm and averted a serious clash.

To the City Council and Administrative Boards, the Park Boards and the Municipal Bureau of Parks, Playgrounds, and Bathing-Beaches:

CONTROL OF FIREARMS

11. We recommend that the most stringent means possible be applied to control the importation, sale, and possession of firearms and other deadly weapons.

SUPERVISION OF "ATHLETIC CLUBS"

12. In order to facilitate police supervision of so-called "athletic clubs," we recommend that all such clubs be required to file with the city clerk statements of their purposes and, at stated intervals, lists of their members and officers, with their addresses.

SANITATION

13. We recommend that the authorities exercise their powers to condemn and raze all houses unfit for human habitation, many of which the Commission has found to exist in the Negro residence areas on the South and West sides.

14. We recommend better enforcement of health and sanitary laws and regulations in the care, repair, and upkeep of streets and alleys and the collection and disposal of rubbish and garbage in areas of Negro residence, where the Commission has found these matters to be shamefully neglected.

RECREATION CENTERS

15. We recommend that the park and other proper authorities (a) put an end to the present gross discrimination by white persons which practically bars Negroes out of certain recreation centers near their own congested residence area; and (b) that a recreation center of adequate size and facilities be established for the use of both whites and Negroes in the principal Negro residence area of the South Side; and (c) that steps be taken to secure more adequately trained, competent, and intelligent playground and recreation-center directors, white and Negro, who shall be held responsible for racial clashes arising in places under their direction and shall be required to interest themselves in reducing and avoiding racial friction in their neighborhoods; and (d) that proper equipment and supervision be provided at the Twenty-sixth Street Bathing-Beach, where they are now almost wholly lacking; and (e) that, in co-operation with the city police, the park police adequately protect all citizens, without regard to color, in going to and from parks, recreation centers, and playgrounds.

To the Board of Education:

MORE SCHOOLS IN NEGRO AREAS

16. We recommend that in the areas where the main part of the Negro population lives, and where elementary-school accommodations are notably deficient, buildings, equipment, and teaching forces be provided which shall be at least equal to the average standard for the city, in order that the present conditions of overcrowding, arrangement of pupils in shifts, and the assignment of too large classes to teachers may be remedied.

NIGHT SCHOOLS AND COMMUNITY CENTERS

17. We recommend the establishment of night schools and community centers in sections of the city not now adequately provided with such facilities.

COMPULSORY EDUCATION

18. Having found that many Negro children who quit school at an early age, as in the case of similar white children, appear later as criminals and delinquents, we urge strict enforcement of regulations as to working permits for such children, and we especially recommend that truant officers give attention to school attendance by the children of Negro families migrating here from the South.

ATTITUDE OF PRINCIPALS AND TEACHERS

19. Since the attitude of principals and teachers vitally influences the relations of white and Negro children in the public schools, we recommend that special care be exercised in appointing principals and teachers who have a sympathetic and intelligent interest in promoting good race relations in the schools.

STUDENT ACTIVITIES

20. We recommend that public-school principals and teachers encourage participation by children of both races in student activities as a means of promoting mutual understanding and good race relations in such schools and in the community.

To Social and Civic Organizations, Labor Unions, and Churches:

PROMOTION OF RACE HARMONY

21. Being convinced by our inquiry that much of the antagonism evinced in the areas of marked hostility toward Negroes is founded upon tradition which is itself without foundation in fact or justice, we recommend to schools, social centers and agencies, churches, labor unions, and other organizations in these areas, and to public-spirited citizens, white and Negro, that they endeavor to dispel the false notions of each race about the other and promote mutual tolerance and friendliness between them.

22. We recommend that both white and Negro churches seek and use means to improve race relations, and that these means include the finding of

frequent occasion for having their congregations addressed by representatives of both races on the subject of race sympathy and tolerance.

SOCIAL AGENCIES IN NEGRO COMMUNITIES

23. We commend the course of such agencies as the United Charities, Illinois Children's Home and Aid Society, and American Red Cross in extending their work to the Negro community, and recommend that other agencies whose work is similarly useful extend their work in like manner.

24. Recognizing and commending the practical efforts of the Interracial Committee of the Woman's City Club, the Public Affairs Committee of the Union League Club, and the Chicago Urban League, in promoting better race relations, especially in the summer of 1920, when racial friction was deemed imminent, we recommend that other organizations of the same kind undertake like activities.

25. We recommend that the appropriate social agencies give needed attention to dealing extra-judicially with cases of Negroes coming before the morals and juvenile courts; also to cases of Negro children dropping out of school too early in age.

OPPORTUNITY FOR RECREATION TRAINING

26. We recommend that Negroes, as well as whites, be given opportunity for training for service in the city's public recreation facilities.

To the Public:
INTERRACIAL TOLERANCE

27. We are convinced by our inquiry: (*a*) that measures involving or approaching deportation or segregation are illegal, impracticable and would not solve, but would accentuate, the race problem and postpone its just and orderly solution by the process of adjustment; (*b*) that the moral responsibility for race rioting does not rest upon hoodlums alone, but also upon all citizens, white or black, who sanction force or violence in interracial relations or who do not condemn and combat the spirit of racial hatred thus expressed; (*c*) that race friction and antagonism are largely due to the fact that each race too readily misunderstands and misinterprets the other's conduct and aspirations.

We therefore urge upon all citizens, white and Negro, active opposition to the employment of force or violence in interracial relations and to the spirit of antagonism and hatred. We recommend dispassionate, intelligent, and sympathetic consideration by each race of the other's needs and aims; we also recommend the dissemination of proved or trustworthy information about all phases of race relations as a useful means for effecting peaceful racial adjustment.

28. Since rumor, usually groundless, is a prolific source of racial bitterness and strife, we warn both whites and Negroes against the acceptance or circulation by either of reports about the other whose truth has not been fully estab-

lished. We urge all citizens, white and Negro, vigorously to oppose all propaganda of malicious or selfish origin which would tend to excite race prejudice.

29. We commend race contacts in cultural and co-operative efforts as tending strongly to mutual understanding and the promotion of good race relations.

30. We condemn the provocation or fostering of race antagonism by associations or organizations ostensibly founded or conducted for purposes of patriotism or local improvements or the like.

PERMANENT RACE-RELATIONS BODY

31. We recommend as of special importance that a permanent local body representing both races be charged with investigating situations likely to produce clashes, with collecting and disseminating information tending to preserve the peace and allay unfounded fears, with bringing sound public sentiment to bear upon the settlement of racial disputes, and with promoting the spirit of interracial tolerance and co-operation.

To the White Members of the Public:

RACE ADJUSTMENT IN MIXED NEIGHBORHOODS

32. We call to public attention the fact that intensity of racial feeling is not necessarily due to the presence of Negroes in a neighborhood, either in the majority or minority, and that such feeling is not the rule but the exception; and we cite as a conspicuous example the peaceful conditions that have long obtained in the area between Roosevelt Road and Thirty-ninth Street from Wentworth Avenue to Lake Michigan, in which the Negro population in 1920 numbered 54,906 and the white population 42,797.

BETTER NEGRO HOUSING WITHOUT SEGREGATION

33. Our inquiry has shown that insufficiency in amount and quality of housing is an all-important factor in Chicago's race problem; there must be more and better housing to accommodate the great increase in Negro population which was at the rate of 148 per cent from 1910 to 1920. This situation will be made worse by methods tending toward forcible segregation or exclusion of Negroes, such as the circulation of threatening statements and propaganda by organizations or persons to prevent Negroes from living in certain areas, and the lawless and perilous bombing of houses occupied by Negroes or by whites suspected of encouraging Negro residence in the district.

We therefore recommend that all white citizens energetically discourage these futile, pernicious, and lawless practices, and either co-operate in or start movements to solve the housing problem by constructive and not destructive methods.

DEPRECIATION AND PROPERTY RISKS

34. Testimony before the Commission and investigations made by it show two important facts: (*a*) that depreciation of residence property generally

charged exclusively to the presence of Negroes in a neighborhood is often largely due to other factors; (b) that many Negroes of this city meet their obligations in such a manner as to make their home-building and home-owning investments seem a more desirable risk than has been generally supposed. We therefore recommend that these facts be taken into consideration in connection with loans on Negro property.

ADVANCED RENTS FOR NEGROES CONDEMNED

35. We condemn and urge the discontinuance of the practice of property owners who arbitrarily advance rents merely because Negroes become tenants.

INFORMATION ABOUT NEGROES

36. We recommend that white persons seek information from responsible and representative Negroes as the basis of their judgments about Negro traits, characteristics, and tendencies, and thereby counteract the common disposition, arising from erroneous tradition and literature, to regard all Negroes as belonging to one homogeneous group and as being inferior in mentality and morality, given to emotionalism, and having an innate tendency toward crime, especially sex crime.

To the Negro Members of the Public:

RACIAL DOCTRINES

37. We recommend to Negroes the promulgation of sound racial doctrines among the uneducated members of their group, and the discouragement of propaganda and agitators seeking to inflame racial animosity and incite Negroes to violence.

SUPPORT OF SOCIAL AGENCIES

38. We urge Negroes to contribute more freely of their money and personal effort to the social agencies developed by public-spirited members of their group; also to contribute to the general social agencies of the community.

SPECIAL PROBLEMS

39. We recommend that the Negro community, through the extension or establishment of the necessary social agencies, undertake to supply means and encouragement for leisure activities, and undertake work among Negro boys and girls along the lines of prevention of vice and crime; also that it provide institutional care of dependent Negro children.

40. We particularly urge that Negroes vigorously and continuously protest against the presence in their residence areas of any vicious resort, and that they join in and support all efforts to suppress such places.

ADJUSTMENT OF MIGRANTS

41. We commend the important work done by the Chicago Urban League, the Negro churches, and other organizations in facilitating the adjustment of

migrant Negroes from the South to the conditions of living in Chicago and urge its extension. We also commend the work already done by Negroes through community associations in bettering the appearance and sanitary condition of housing and recommend its further extension.

RACE PRIDE

42. While we recognize the propriety and social values of race pride among Negroes, we warn them that thinking and talking too much in terms of race alone are calculated to promote separation of race interests and thereby to interfere with racial adjustment.

To Employers and Labor Organizations:

ATTITUDE TOWARD NEGRO WORKERS

43. We have found that in struggles between capital and labor Negro workers are in a position dangerous to themselves and to peaceful relations between the races, whether the issues involve their use by employers to undermine wage standards or break strikes, or efforts by organized labor to keep them out of certain trades while refusing to admit them to membership in the unions in such trades. We feel that unnecessary racial bitterness is provoked by such treatment of Negro workers, that racial prejudice is played upon by both parties, and that through such practices injury comes, not alone to Negroes, but to employers and labor organizations as well.

We therefore recommend to employers that they deal with Negroes as workmen on the same plane as white workers; and to labor unions that they admit Negroes to full membership whenever they apply for it and possess the qualifications required of white workers.

NEGRO AND WHITE WORKERS

44. We commend to the attention of employers who fear clashes or loss of white workers by taking on Negro workers the fact that in 89 per cent of the industries investigated by this Commission, Negroes were found working in close association with white employees, and that friction between these elements had rarely been manifested.

INDUSTRIAL AND BUSINESS OPPORTUNITIES FOR NEGROES

45. In view of the limited field of employment within which Negroes are restricted we recommend that employers in all lines enlarge that field and permit Negroes an equal chance with whites to enter all positions for which they are qualified by efficiency and merit. In this connection especial attention is called to the fact that opportunity is generally denied to Negroes for gaining experience in business methods through service in responsible positions in business houses. Such opportunities, if made available for them, would not only be of benefit to Negroes in the development of sounder business methods

among them and the building up of their resources, but would also be a gain to the business establishments and the community at large.

46. We have found that Negroes are denied equal opportunity with whites for advancement and promotion where they are employed. As a measure of justice we urge that Negroes be employed, advanced, and promoted according to their capacities and proved merit. We call to the attention of those concerned the high qualifications of many Negro workers in sleeping-car and dining-car service, and recommend that when they deserve it and the opportunity offers, they be made eligible for promotion to positions as conductors and stewards.

TEMPORARY EMPLOYMENT OF NEGROES AS STRIKE BREAKERS

47. We point out as an injustice and a cause of racial antagonism the practice of some employers who having hired Negroes as strike breakers discharge them when the strike is settled to make places for former white employees.

NEGRO WOMEN WORKERS

48. We find that employment of Negro girls at a smaller wage than white girls and the denial to them of apprenticeship opportunities are a cause of racial antagonism. We therefore recommend that the employment of Negro girls be based on merit, with equality of wages, piece rates, and apprenticeship opportunities with white girls; we also recommend that Negroes in domestic employment rendering the same quality of service as whites be paid at the same rate as white domestics.

RACIAL PEACE IN INDUSTRY

49. Realizing that the common welfare is involved in the employment or non-employment of Negro workers, and seeking means to preserve racial peace in industry, we recommend: (a) that where Negro employees are dismissed for unsatisfactory service other Negroes, recommended by reliable Negro organizations, be given an opportunity to replace them; (b) that in times of industrial depression, employers reduce their forces in such a manner that the hardships of unemployment may not be disproportionately severe on Negro workers; (c) that where Negroes are employed with whites at the same tasks they be given equal pay for equal work and equal opportunity for piecework and overtime work; (d) that Negro workers be given opportunity for advancement and promotion according to merit and efficiency and without race discrimination; (e) that Negro workers be afforded the opportunity to learn and engage in the skilled processes of their employment; (f) that superintendents closely supervise the relations of foremen with Negro workers and see that there is no racial injustice or discrimination; (g) that employers generally deal with Negroes, whether engaged in, or seeking opportunity to engage in,

manual labor or clerical work, without discrimination as to race, and apply to them the same tests and conditions as to white employees.

SEPARATE LABOR UNIONS

50. We strongly condemn the efforts of self-seeking agitators, Negro or white, who use race sentiment to establish separate unions in trades where existing unions admit Negroes to equal membership with whites.

To Negro Workers:
RELATIONS WITH UNIONS

51. We recommend that qualified Negro workers desiring membership in labor organizations join unions which admit both races equally, instead of organizing separate Negro labor unions.

RELATIONS WITH EMPLOYERS

52. We recommend that Negroes completely abandon the practice of seeking petty advance payments on wages and the practice of laying off work without good cause.

LEARNING TRADES

53. We recommend that Negroes avail themselves wherever possible of opportunities in apprentice schools and classes.

54. We recommend to all Negroes dependent on manual labor the learning of some skilled trade even though there is no present opportunity to engage in it.

To the Street-Car Companies:

PROTECTION OF PASSENGERS

55. In view of the large number of racial assaults on persons riding in street cars, we recommend that conductors and motormen be specially instructed concerning protection of passengers, white and Negro, and be rigidly held to the discharge of this duty.

OVERCROWDING

56. We recommend that at all loading-points where whites and Negroes board cars in large numbers, starters be employed and overcrowding be prevented as far as possible.

To Restaurants, Theaters, Stores, and Other Places of Public Accommodation:
EQUAL RIGHTS IN PUBLIC PLACES

57. We point out that Negroes are entitled by law to the same treatment as other persons in restaurants, theaters, stores, and other places of public accommodation, and we urge that owners and managers of such places govern their policies and actions and their employees accordingly.

To the Press:

HANDLING OF NEWS INVOLVING NEGROES

58. In view of the recognized responsibility of the press in its general influence upon public opinion concerning Negroes—especially important as related to the suppression of race rioting—we recommend: (*a*) that the newspapers generally, including the foreign-language press, apply the same standards of accuracy, fairness, and sense of proportion, with avoidance of exaggeration, in publishing news about Negroes as about whites; in this connection special attention is called to the fact that emphasis, greatly out of proportion to that given their creditable acts, is frequently placed on the crimes and misdeeds of Negroes, who, unlike other groups, are identified with each incident and thus constantly associated with discreditable conduct; (*b*) that the manner of news treatment be no different in the case of Negroes than in that of whites, to the end that there shall always be the unwritten assumption that the same responsibility for equal consideration of the rights of the one by the other rests on whites and Negroes alike, in respect of the matter involved in the publication; (*c*) that, in consideration of the great ease with which the public is influenced against the whole Negro group by sensational articles and headlines, the press should exercise great caution in dealing with unverified reports of crimes of Negroes against white women, and should avoid the designation of trivial fights as race riots; (*d*) that in recognition of the dangers of racial antagonism on the part of the ignorant, the unthinking, and the prejudiced of both races, publication be made, as opportunities offer, of such matters as shall in their character tend to dispel prejudice and promote mutual respect and good will.

We specially recommend more frequent publications concerning: (1) creditable achievements of consequence by Negroes; (2) their efforts toward a higher cultural and social life, and (3) their improvement of the physical conditions of their own communities; (4) the common obligation of all citizens of all races to recognize in their interrelations the supreme duty of strict obedience to the law, in spirit as well as in deed; (5) verification, so far as practicable, of all news concerning Negroes and their activities by reference to recognized Negro agencies or responsible representative Negroes.

We further recommend the capitalization of the word "Negro" in racial designation, and avoidance of the word "nigger," as contemptuous and needlessly provocative.

HANDLING OF NEWS INVOLVING NEGROES AND WHITES

59. To the Negro press we recommend greater care and accuracy in reporting incidents involving whites and Negroes, the abandonment of sensational headlines and articles on racial questions, and more attention to educating Negro readers as to the available means and opportunities of adjusting themselves and their fellows into more harmonious relations with their white

neighbors and fellow-citizens, and as to the lines of individual conduct and collective effort which will tend to minimize interracial friction, promote their own social and economic development, and hasten interracial adjustment.

CHICAGO, December 6, 1921

ROBERT S. ABBOTT
EDGAR A. BANCROFT
Chairman
WILLIAM SCOTT BOND
EDWARD OSGOOD BROWN
GEORGE C. HALL
GEORGE H. JACKSON
HARRY EUGENE KELLY
VICTOR F. LAWSON
ADELBERT H. ROBERTS
JULIUS ROSENWALD
FRANCIS W. SHEPARDSON
Vice-Chairman
LACEY KIRK WILLIAMS

GRAHAM ROMEYN TAYLOR
Executive Secretary
CHARLES S. JOHNSON
Associate Executive Secretary

APPENDIX

A. BIOGRAPHICAL DATA OF MEMBERS OF THE COMMISSION

ROBERT S. ABBOTT, Editor.

Born, Savannah, Georgia; graduate, Hampton Institute; graduate, Kent College of Law; owner and publisher, the *Chicago Defender*.

EDGAR ADDISON BANCROFT, *Chairman*, Lawyer.

Born, Galesburg, Illinois; graduate, Knox College; graduate, Columbia Law School; ex-president, Chicago Bar Association, Illinois State Bar Association; trustee, Knox College, Carnegie Endowment for International Peace, and Tuskegee Institute; Senator of Phi Beta Kappa.

WILLIAM SCOTT BOND, Real Estate Dealer.

Born, Chicago, Illinois; graduate, University of Chicago; graduate, Kent College of Law; member, real estate firm William A. Bond & Company; trustee, University of Chicago.

EDWARD OSGOOD BROWN, Lawyer.

Born, Salem, Massachusetts; graduate, Brown University; graduate, Harvard Law School; for ten years judge of the Illinois Appellate Court, First District; for some years president, Chicago Branch of National Association for the Advancement of Colored People,

GEORGE CLEVELAND HALL, Physician and Surgeon.

Born, Ypsilanti, Michigan; graduate, Lincoln University; graduate, Bennett Medical College; trustee, Provident Hospital; vice-president, Chicago Urban League; orator at dedication of Booker T. Washington memorial monument at Tuskegee, 1922.

GEORGE H. JACKSON, Real Estate Dealer.

Born in Canada; graduate, Cincinnati Law School; former member, Ohio Legislature; president, Pyramid Building and Loan Association.

HARRY EUGENE KELLY, Lawyer.

Born, Des Moines, Iowa; graduate, State University of Iowa; former member, Colorado Legislature; for some years United States district attorney for Colorado; former president, Denver Bar Association; attorney for Interstate Commerce Commission; regional counsel at Chicago for Director General of Railroads.

VICTOR F. LAWSON, Editor.

Born, Chicago, Illinois; graduate, Phillips Academy, Andover, Massachusetts; owner, editor, and publisher, *Chicago Daily News* since 1876; ex-president and now a director, Associated Press; founder, Daily News Fresh Air Fund and Daily News Free Lectures; called "father of postal savings bank in America."

EDWARD H. MORRIS, Lawyer.

Born in Kentucky; for two terms representative in Illinois General Assembly; member of Illinois Constitutional Convention, 1920–21; for eleven years Grand Master of the Colored Odd Fellows of America.

ADELBERT H. ROBERTS, Lawyer.

Born in Michigan; student, University of Michigan; graduate, Northwestern University Law School; for two terms representative in Illinois General Assembly.

JULIUS ROSENWALD, Merchant.

Born, Springfield, Illinois; president, Sears, Roebuck & Company; philanthropist, stimulated construction and contributed $325,000 toward total cost of Y.M.C.A. buildings for Negroes in thirteen cities; contributed over $1,000,000 toward rural schools for Negroes in fourteen southern states; trustee, Tuskegee Institute, University of Chicago, Rockefeller Foundation.

FRANCIS WAYLAND SHEPARDSON, *Vice-Chairman*, lately Director of Registration and Education, State of Illinois, under Governor Lowden.

Born, Cincinnati, Ohio; graduate, Denison University; postgraduate, Yale University; former professor of history, University of Chicago; Senator of Phi Beta Kappa.

LACEY KIRK WILLIAMS, Minister.

Born, Eufaula, Alabama; graduate, Arkansas Baptist College; pastor, Olivet Baptist Church, Chicago, since 1916 (largest Protestant Church in America); president, Illinois General Baptist State Convention; vice-president, Colored National Baptist Convention.

B. THE STAFF OF THE COMMISSION

In selecting the staff to assist in carrying through the investigation and the preparation of the report careful effort was made to find persons well qualified by educational background and practical experience in social work. The staff averaged fifteen in number during the eighteen months of its existence. In all, thirty-seven people, twenty-two white and fifteen Negro, were engaged, some of whom served throughout the entire period and others for varying briefer periods. The personnel was as follows:

Exeutive Secretary

GRAHAM ROMEYN TAYLOR. A.B., Harvard, 1903; resident, Chicago Commons Social Settlement 1904–12; member, editorial staff, the *Survey* magazine 1905–16; special agent, United States Census Bureau, 1910; author, *Satellite Cities, A Study of Industrial Suburbs*, 1915, and many magazine articles; special assistant to American ambassador to Russia, 1916–19.

Associate Executive Secretary

CHARLES S. JOHNSON. A.B., Virginia Union University, 1916; Ph.B., University of Chicago, 1917; graduate student in social science at the University of Chicago; special investigator of migration of Negroes from the South for the Carnegie Foundation for International Peace; director of the Department of Research and Records of the Chicago Urban League.

INVESTIGATION

Investigators with Supervisory Duties

MADGE HEADLEY. New York School of Philanthropy 1910; assistant secretary, Tenement House Committee, Charity Organization Society, New York City, 1910–15; made studies of housing conditions in Providence, Rhode Island, New York City, Sullivan and Ulster Counties, New York; of rural juvenile delinquency in Ulster County, New York, for Federal Children's Bureau; and of industrial and garden cities in England; served with American Red Cross in France housing and feeding refugees, 1917–19.

ALBERT E. WEBSTER. Ph.B., Alfred University, 1909; graduate student, University of Chicago, 1909–12; Anti-saloon League investigator, New York state, 1906–7; United Charities, Chicago, 1911–16; unemployment study, Calumet district, 1914; supervised Red Cross relief work in Indiana flood disaster, 1913; assisted in supervising relief work in Eastland disaster, Chicago; directed various surveys in Chicago 1918–20; assistant superintendent and field secretary, Juvenile Protective Association, Chicago.

Investigators

H. H. ALLEN. Teacher of sociology three years, Northern Texas Normal School; newspaper experience; graduate student University of Chicago, studying for Ph.D.

RUTH ARNETT.   University of Illinois; volunteer girls' workers, War Camp Community
Service; investigator for Red Cross, East St. Louis riot relief.

ELSIE BALL.   Attended Leander Clark College two years; Chicago School of Civics and
Philanthropy one year; resident director, District Neighborhood House, 1915–17; American Red Cross, 1917–20.

ELIZABETH BENHAM.   Teaching experience; worked on Federal Census, 1920; resident,
University of Chicago Settlement; secretary, Inter-racial Committee, Chicago Woman's
City Club.

ELLA G. BERRY.   Enumerator in Chicago for Federal Census, 1920; Chicago School
Census, 1918

ANGELINE BROCKMEIER.   A.B., University of Illinois, 1917; Chicago School of Civics
and Philanthropy, 1918; Federal Children's Bureau, 1918–20; study of infant mor-
tality in Gary, Indiana; study of courts and children's cases; statistical experience.

JOSEPH H. COLLINS.   Business course, Central Y.M.C.A., Philadelphia, 1904–5; inspector, Railway Audit and Inspection Company, Philadelphia, 1907–16; assistant industrial
secretary, New York Urban League; welfare worker, Bush Terminal Company, New
York City, and American International Shipbuilding Corporation, 1918–19.

ESTHER FULKS.   Carnegie Technical Institute, Pittsburgh; special courses in social
science, University of Chicago, New York University, and Hampton Institute; National
Training School, Y.W.C.A., New York; supervisor of physical training, public schools,
Charleston, West Virginia; industrial secretary, Y.W.C.A., East St. Louis, Illinois; made
surveys of industrial opportunities, educational and recreational facilities, and social
agencies for Negroes in East St. Louis.

HENRY W. HAMMOND.   A.B., New York University, 1909; secretary, Goff Street branch,
Y.M.C.A., New Haven, Connecticut, 1911–13; boys' work secretary, Wabash Avenue
branch, Y.M.C.A., Chicago, 1914–16; probation officer, juvenile court, Chicago, 1916–20·

DAN H. KULP.   Graduate student, University of Chicago; investigated recreation
facilities, Providence, Rhode Island, and prepared statistics; investigated industrial and
racial conditions in China; general director, Yangtsepoo Social Center, Shanghai.

KATE F. MARKOVITZ.   Assistant matron, Montana State Orphan Asylum, 1911–12;
Chicago School of Civics and Philanthropy, 1913; officer, Chicago Juvenile Protective
Association, 1913–16; director, jail division, Cook County Bureau of Social Service,
1916–18; overseas secretary, Y.W.C.A., 1918–19; volunteer, Hull-House, 1912–20.

LUCIUS L. McGEE.   Teacher, four years, Virginia Union University; experience investigating Negro conditions, Richmond, Virginia; graduate student, University of Chicago,
studying for Ph.D.

EDITH W. RIDDLE.   A.B., Vassar, 1898; assistant superintendent, Illinois Children's
Home and Aid Society, 1905–6; resident, Hull-House; boys' school and farm work,
Michigan, 1907–10; club organization, Goodrich Social Settlement, Cleveland, 1913–17;
Federal Children's Bureau, 1918; Association for Crippled and Disabled Children, Cleve-
land, 1919.

PHILIP SHERMAN.   A.B., Carleton College, 1919; one year Harvard Law School; campaign auditor, Y.M.C.A. Building Fund, Sioux Falls, 1919.

ALONZO C. THAYER.   A.B., Fisk University, 1904; experience as reporter, manager,
and editor of newspaper, also experience in real estate; assisted in industrial work of the
Chicago Urban League.

CHARLES H. THOMPSON.   A.B., Virginia Union University, 1917; M.A., University of
Chicago, 1920; field work, neighborhood study, Richmond, Virginia, 1917; comparative educational study, Moseley School, Chicago, 1920.

Assistants in Compilation of Data

LUCIEN V. ALEXIS. A.B., Harvard, 1917; assistant organizer, colored work, War Camp Community Service, Trenton, New Jersey, 1919–20; director of education, South Side Division, Community Service, Chicago, 1920.

HENRY A. RABE. University of Wisconsin, 1903–5; business experience, Chicago, 1905–19; student, University of Chicago, specializing in economics and sociology and investigating industrial conditions in Chicago.

OLIVE H. RABE. Business experience, eight years; graduate, Northwestern University Law School, 1916; practiced law three years; student, University of Chicago, two years, specializing in economics and sociology.

WINIFRED RAUSCHENBUSH. A.B., Oberlin College, 1916; organization work, Ohio Suffrage Association, 1917; graduate student, sociology, University of Chicago, 1918; prepared material for book on foreign-language press by Professor Robert E. Park, University of Chicago, 1918–20; prepared maps and graphs for book by Professor W. I. Thomas, 1919.

NORMAN L. RITCHIE. Newspaper work, twenty years, New York, Chicago, Cleveland, Pittsburgh, Saratoga, and Plattsburg, New York; editorial writer, *Chicago Daily News*, nine years; director of education and information, Community Service, Chicago, 1920.

FLORENCE TAYLOR. A.B., Vassar College, 1921; publicity, research, and field studies, National Child Labor Committee, New York City, 1913–18; personnel-management study, Collegiate Bureau of Occupations, Chicago, 1920.

ELIZABETH WAGENET. A.B., University of California, 1914; investigator, California State Commission on Social Insurance; investigator, California Industrial Welfare Commission, having charge of cannery investigation; assistant, department of economics, Washington State University under Professor Carleton Parker; on staff of War Labor Policies Board, Washington, D.C.

Clerks

GERALDINE DISMOND. A.B., University of Chicago, 1915; teacher, Chicago public schools; special work for Chicago Urban League.

MARCELLE V. LAVAL. A.B., University of Illinois, 1920; editor, State Water Survey Division, Department of Registration and Education, State of Illinois, 1918–19.

JOSEPHINE TAYLOR. A.B., Smith College, 1920; volunteer, social service department, Cook County Hospital, Chicago, summer of 1919.

C. EPITOME OF FACTS IN RIOT DEATHS

I. Deaths due to mob violence, and in which the coroners' jury recommended members of the unknown mob be apprehended and held to justice, and in which none of the members were so apprehended. The cases listed in this category do not include all those due to mob violence, but only those qualified as stated:

1. Eugene Williams

Race	Negro
Date of death	July 27
Approximate time of death	Probably 4:00 P.M.
Place where death occurred	Lake Michigan at foot of Twenty-ninth Street
Manner in which death occurred	Drowning

Quarrel arose on beach between Negroes and whites in regard to the use of the beach. Many stones were thrown on both sides. Williams, in the water, was prevented from landing because of stone-throwing and drowned as consequence.

2. John Mills

Race	Negro
Date of receiving death wound	July 28
Time of receiving death wound	5:35 P.M.
Place of receiving death wound	Normal Avenue, 150 feet south of Forty-seventh Street
Manner of wound	Skull fracture; beating

Mob of 300 or 400 white people, all ages, attacked east-bound Forty-seventh Street car, pulled the trolley from the wire, stopped the car. White passengers alighted, Negro passengers hid under seats. From twenty-five to fifty white men boarded car and beat the Negroes with bats, clubs, bricks. Driven out from the refuge of the car, they ran for their lives, chased by the mob. Mills ran from Forty-seventh Street into Normal Avenue. A brick hit him in the back, halted him, and before he could run again a young white man hit him on the head with a scantling. He was left unconscious. Four other Negroes from this car were beaten but not fatally.

3. Oscar Dozier

Race	Negro
Date of receiving death wound	July 28
Time of receiving death wound	5:55 P.M.
Place of receiving death wound	Thirty-ninth Street and Wallace Avenue
Manner of wound	Stabbing; external violence

Dozier worked for the Great Western Smelting and Refining Works. The foreman warned negroes not to try to go home till adequate protection could be furnished. In spite of the warning Dozier was seen to crawl over the fence around the works at 5:45 P.M. He was next seen breaking away from a mob of 500 to 1,000 white men at Thirty-ninth Street and Parnell Avenue. He ran west on Thirty-ninth toward Wallace, the crowd throwing stones. Halfway down the block he fell. When rescued by the police immediately afterward he was found to have a stab wound two inches long over his heart.

4. Henry Goodman

Race	Negro
Date of receiving death wound	July 28
Time of receiving death wound	7:30 P.M.
Place of receiving death wound	Thirty-ninth Street and Union Avenue
Manner of wound	External violence

Goodman, with other Negroes was returning from the Stock Yards on an east-bound Thirty-ninth Street car. A truck stalled across the track at Thirty-ninth Street and Union Avenue brought the car to a stop and allowed white men to force an entrance through the front door and beat the Negroes off the rear of the car. The chief weapon was the iron lever used for opening the front door of the car. The Negroes tried to run east to Halsted Street where there were police officers. The crowd pursued, knocked Goodman down, and beat him. Apparently Goodman recovered from the violence, but a week later it was necessary to remove him to the hospital, where a skull fracture, with a small pebble imbedded in the wound, was discovered. He died of tetanus on August 12. The wound was first treated by Dr. William W. Bradley on the evening the deceased was injured. The coroner's jury said, "Tetanus would probably not have developed had the wound been thoroughly examined and properly cleaned."

5. Louis Taylor

Race	Negro
Date of receiving death wound	July 28
Time of receiving death wound	9:40 P.M.
Place of receiving death wound	Root Street and Wentworth Avenue
Manner of wound	Scalp wounds; skull fracture due to external violence

Taylor, employed by the Chicago & Great Western Railway Co., had just come off his run and was returning home on a south-bound Wentworth Avenue car. Cars, both north and south bound, were attacked at Root Street and Wentworth Avenue by a mob of 100 white people armed with clubs and bricks. Taylor was found unconscious on the sidewalk, his watch and suitcase missing, when the police arrived. He died August 1.

6. B. F. Hardy

Race	Negro
Date of receiving death wound	July 28
Time of receiving death wound	11:30 P.M.
Place of receiving death wound	Forty-sixth Street and Cottage Grove Avenue
Manner of wound	External violence

Hardy was the only Negro passenger on a north-bound Cottage Grove Avenue car crowded with white people. At Forty-seventh Street some of these alighted. A mob of whites in the street saw the Negro and jerked the trolley from the wire. The car came to a stop at Forty-sixth Place. White passengers in a panic demanded to be let off. When the front door was opened Hardy tried to hide in their midst and leave the car. He was seen by the waiting mob, knocked down, and pounded with fists until unconscious. He died the next day.

7. John Simpson

Race	Negro
Date of receiving death wound	July 28
Time of receiving death wound	7:30 P.M.
Place of receiving death wound	Thirty-first Street between Wabash Avenue and "L" alley
Manner of wound	Bullet wound

Several accounts have been given of the killing of Simpson. The coroner's jury says: ". . . . Thirty-first Street near the said elevated station, being well filled with a rioting and disorderly mob, mainly colored people, a white man being pursued east on Thirty-first Street, at that time, and that deceased was a police officer of the City of Chicago, and was engaged as a police officer in preserving the peace in and about the point indicated, and that a number of shots were fired from revolvers held in hands of men unknown to this jury." Another account says Simpson was shot by the Negro keeper of a poolroom on account of a previous quarrel. Simpson did not regain consciousness after being shot.

8. Henry Baker

Race	Negro
Date of receiving death wound	July 28
Time of receiving death wound	10:00 or 11:00 P.M.
Place of receiving death wound	544 East Thirty-seventh Street
Manner of wound	Bullet wound in skull

The bullet which caused Baker's death was one of a number fired on the streets at the time. Baker was not on the street but in a second-story window. It is not known whether this shot was one fired by white men from a passing automobile or by one of a crowd of Negroes at Thirty-seventh Street and Vincennes Avenue. The majority of witnesses gave the time of the shooting of Baker as 11:00 P.M., but the coroner in his report names 10:00 P.M. as the hour.

9. David Marcus

Race	White
Date of receiving death wound	July 28
Time of receiving death wound	9:30 or 10:00 P.M.
Place of receiving death wound	511 East Thirty-seventh Street
Manner of wound	Bullet

Only one eyewitness, a white companion of Marcus, testified. He said a Negro walked up to Marcus and shot him. The witness stopped to pick up his friend, was advised by Negroes to get out of danger, but when he persisted in lifting the wounded man, he himself received a bullet wound in the arm. A bullet also pierced the window of a laundry at this time. The coroner gives the time of shooting as 8:45, though most of the testimony seems to indicate that it occurred about fifteen or twenty minutes after the first shooting from automobiles which occurred at approximately 9:15 to 9:30. The police report gives 10:45 as the hour.

10. Eugene Temple

Race	White
Date of receiving death wound	July 28
Time of receiving death wound	5:30 P.M.
Place of receiving death wound	3642 South State Street
Manner of wound	Stab wound

Temple, owner of a laundry at the above address, left his place of business to enter his automobile which stood at the curb. His wife and another young woman accompanied him but were the width of the sidewalk from him when he was attacked by three Negroes, robbed, and stabbed. The murderers escaped in the crowd of Negroes which immediately gathered. It was testified that Temple employed both Negroes and whites and had never had any difficulties of a racial nature with his workers.

11. William J. Otterson

Race	White
Date of receiving death wound	July 28
Time of receiving death wound	7:10 P.M.
Place of receiving death wound	Thirty-fifth Street and Wabash Avenue
Manner of wound	Skull fracture due to external violence

A mob of about 500 Negroes at Thirty-fifth Street and Wabash Avenue was stopping cars, beating white people, and throwing bricks. An automobile bearing Otterson as a passenger turned from Thirty-fifth Street to go south on Wabash Avenue. One of the stones and bricks hurled at the motor car hit Otterson on the head, and he immediately became unconscious. He was seventy-four years old and a plasterer by trade.

12. Stefan Horvath

Race	White
Date of receiving death wound	July 28
Time of receiving wound	9:00 or 9:35 P.M.
Place of receiving death wound	Root and South State streets
Manner of wound	Bullet wound

At the time Horvath was shot, there was a crowd of fifty to seventy-five Negroes on the sidewalk, but only about three on the corner where the shooting occurred. The only eyewitness who testified was a policeman who saw the shooting from a distance of 400 feet. The three Negroes ran after firing the shot, and could not be found later.

13. Edward W. Jackson

Race	Negro
Date of receiving death wound	July 29
Time of receiving death wound	9:00 A.M.
Place of receiving death wound	Fortieth and Halsted streets
Manner of wound	Shock and hemorrhage due to beating

Jackson had started to walk to work. At Fortieth and Halsted streets he was attacked by four or five white men and beaten. He ran to Thirty-ninth Street, where he was found by the police. No further information could be obtained in this case.

14. Samuel Bass

Race	Negro
Date of receiving death wound	July 29
Time of receiving death wound	Between 7:00 and 9:00 P.M.
Place of receiving death wound	Twenty-second and Halsted Sts. or Union Ave.
Manner of wound	External violence

Samuel Bass, on account of the street-car strike, was walking the five and one-half miles from his work to his home when a gang of white men knocked him down three times, and cut gashes in his nose and cheeks with their shoes. Bass hid behind freight cars till a Jewish peddler took him in his cart to State Street. A doctor was visited, but when he learned that Bass had no money, he turned him away without treatment. He was picked up by a passing patrol and taken to the hospital, where his treatment was cursory. Apparently he recovered, but in two weeks gave evidence of a hemorrhage on the brain from which he died September 5.

15. Joseph Lovings

Race	Negro
Date of receiving death wound	July 29
Time of receiving death wound	About 8:00 P.M.
Place of receiving death wound	839 Lytle Street
Manner of wound	Bullet wound, stab wounds, skull fracture

Lovings, returning home from work on a bicycle, rode through an Italian neighborhood whose residents were much excited because it had been said earlier in the evening that a Negro employee of a mattress factory near-by had shot a little Italian girl. A mob filled the streets when Lovings was sighted. He tried to escape by running down an alley between Taylor and Gilpin streets, and then jumped back fences and hid in a basement. The mob dragged him out, riddled his body with bullets, stabbed him, and beat him. It was afterward rumored that his body had been burned after being saturated with gasoline. This was proved not to be true.

II. Deaths due to circumstances creating no criminal responsibility:

1. Nicholas Kleinmark

Race	White
Date of receiving death wound	July 28
Time of receiving death wound	About 6:58 P.M.
Place of receiving death wound	Thirty-eighth Place and Ashland Boulevard
Manner of wound	Stab wound

Scott, Brown, and Simpson, Negroes, were returning by street car from work in the Stock Yards when the car was boarded by a mob of white men who attacked the Negroes with clubs and bricks. Scott defended himself with a pocketknife, while Kleinmark tried to beat him with a club. One of the blows with the knife went home, and Kleinmark staggered from the car mortally wounded. Scott was jailed and charged with murder. The coroner's jury commented as follows: "It is the sense of this jury that the conduct of the police at the time of the riot at this point, during the subsequent investigation, and at the preliminary hearing at which Joseph Scott was bound over to the grand jury without counsel, was a travesty on justice and fair play."

2. Clarence Metz

Race	White
Date of receiving death wound	July 28
Time of receiving death wound	11:30 P.M.
Place of receiving death wound	Forty-third Street between Forrestville and Vincennes avenues
Manner of wound	Stab wound

Metz was one of an assaulting party of whites which roamed the streets from Forty-third to Forty-seventh streets and from Grand Boulevard to Cottage Grove Avenue on the night of the twenty-eighth. Three Negroes, one of them Lieutenant Washington, U.S.A., were returning from a theater with three Negro women by way of Forty-third Street. At the place mentioned they were attacked by a mob of whites and beaten with fists and clubs. One of the Negroes was shot in the leg. Lieutenant Washington, threatened with an ax handle, defended himself with his pocketknife. Metz was stabbed as a result. The coroner's jury said: "We find that the group of colored people, en route to their home, were acting in an orderly and inoffensive manner, and were justified in their acts and conduct during said affray."

3. Berger Odman

Race	White
Date of receiving death wound	July 29
Time of receiving death wound	8:30 P.M.
Place of receiving death wound	Sixtieth and Ada streets
Manner of wound	Bullet wound

This shooting occurred just inside the Negro neighborhood near Ogden Park. One of the numerous mobs threatening this neighborhood began to move into it from Fifty-ninth and Sixtieth streets and Racine Avenue. The vanguard, composed of young boys, went a few feet inside the Negro area and fired directly at a Negro named Samuel Johnson. He returned the fire with a rifle. Other Negroes also fired in the direction of the boys. One of the latter, Odman, was fatally wounded. The coroner's jury said: "We believe and find that the action of Samuel R. Johnson was fully justified and recommend his discharge from police custody."

4. James Crawford

Race	Negro
Date of receiving death wound	July 27
Time of receiving death wound	6:00 P.M.
Place of receiving death wound	Twenty-ninth Street and Cottage Grove Avenue
Manner of wound	Bullet wound

A mob of about 1,000 Negroes congregated at Twenty-ninth Street and Cottage Grove Avenue, whence they had chased Officer Callahan, supposed to have refused to arrest the alleged slayer of Eugene Williams. Other policemen attempting to disperse the mob were assaulted. James Crawford, Negro, fired a revolver directly into the group of policemen. They retaliated and Crawford ran. A Negro policeman followed Crawford, attempting to stop him by firing. Crawford was wounded and died on July 29. The coroner's jury asserted: "We further find that the shooting was justifiable on the part of the police officer."

5. Thomas Joshua

Race	Negro
Date of receiving death wound	July 29
Time of receiving death wound	7:00 or 7:30 A.M.
Place of receiving death wound	Fifty-first Street and Wabash Avenue
Manner of wound	Bullet wound

About 7:30 A.M., July 29, Lieutenant Day of the Police Department, his son and daughter, and Policeman Mitchell rode down Fifty-first Street in an automobile. As the automobile reached Wabash Avenue a colored boy pointed a gun toward it. Day sprang out, drawing his pistol. It is said that the boy fired and Day returned a shot. The boy ran, and Day fired two more shots. A crowd of Negroes running from State Street came upon the scene. The police escaped in a Yellow taxicab. Joshua was shot by Lieutenant Day. While the testimony was a mass of contradictions, the coroner's jury said: "We are of the opinion that Thomas Joshua came to his death from revolver shots fired by the police officer in the discharge of his duty."

6. Ira Henry
   Race — Negro
   Date of receiving death wound — July 30
   Time of receiving death wound — 1:30 A.M.
   Place of receiving death wound — 4957 South State Street
   Manner of wound — Bullet wound

Policeman Keal and Sullivan were accompanying three Jewish families from their residence on South State Street to the Fourth Precinct police station. As the party passed 4957, Officer Sullivan saw a Negro in an alley. He ran back to search him and received a bullet wound. He returned fire. Keal ran to his assistance and fired other shots. Henry was killed instantly. A Negro woman who was with Henry testified that the first shot was fired by Sullivan, but this was not substantiated. The coroner's jury said: "We are of the opinion that the officers were fully justified, owing to the circumstances, in shooting the deceased."

III. Deaths due to the Angelus riot as to which no recommendations were made by the coroner's jury:

1. Joseph Sanford
   Race — Negro
   Date of receiving death wound — July 28
   Time of receiving death wound — 8:00 P.M.
   Place of receiving death wound — Thirty-fifth Street and Wabash Avenue
   Manner of wound — Bullet wound

2. Hymes Taylor
   Race — Negro
   Date of receiving death wound — July 28
   Time of receiving death wound — 8:00 P.M.
   Place of receiving death wound — Thirty-fifth Street and Wabash Avenue
   Manner of wound — Bullet wound

3. John Walter Humphrey
   Race — Negro
   Date of receiving death wound — July 28
   Time of receiving death wound — 8:00 P.M.
   Place of receiving death wound — Thirty-fifth Street between Wabash Avenue and the "L"
   Manner of wound — Bullet wound

4. Edward Lee
   Race — Negro
   Date of receiving death wound — July 28
   Time of receiving death wound — 8:00 P.M.
   Place of receiving death wound — Thirty-fifth and State streets
   Manner of wound — Bullet wound

The Angelus riot centered at the intersection of Thirty-fifth Street and Wabash Avenue, the location of the Angelus apartment house, occupied at the time by whites; Thirty-fifth Street was crowded all the way to State Street. It was at Thirty-fifth and State streets that a secondary riot occurred, an aftermath of the Angelus riot, yet almost simultaneous with it. The crowd of Negroes on these corners had been growing during the afternoon, and stone-throwing had been prevalent. The rumor which raised the mob to riot pitch was that a Negro boy had been shot by a white tenant of the Angelus building. A search by the police failed to produce a culprit. By eight o'clock a mob of about 1,000 to 1,500 Negroes massed on the streets. To cope with the mob were between sixty to 100 policemen on foot and about twelve mounted officers.

About eight o'clock a Negro either threw some missiles or fired a shot at a policeman. Immediately there followed a massing of the police at the north of the intersection of the two streets. Evidence of an order to fire was not produced, but simultaneously with the massing came a volley. During this fire Sanford and Taylor were killed while trying to escape into the entrance of the Angelus building. Shots followed at Thirty-fifth Street and the "L," where a large number of the Negroes ran for protection. Several were wounded, and Humphrey was killed. Almost at the same time shots were fired at Thirty-fifth and State streets, where Lee received his death wound.

The Lee case is the only one in which suspicion of deliberate shooting rested upon anyone. Atrus Lee, brother of the deceased, accused Mounted Policeman Brooks of firing directly at his brother. Brooks said that shots were fired at him from north of the intersection, and that he fired in the air and ran east. Drs. Anderson and Teffner, white, who saw the shooting from Dr. Anderson's office windows, bore him out. The corner's jury concluded: "We find that deceased was wounded by one of the shots fired at Officer Brooks."

IV. Deaths in circumstances which seemed to involve specific persons named by the coroner's jury for further investigation, but as to which no indictments followed:

1. Joseph Schoff

Race	White
Date of receiving death wound	July 30
Time of receiving death wound	5:00 or 5:30 P.M.
Place of receiving death wound	4228 South Ashland Avenue
Manner of wound	Stab wound

Schoff, walking on Ashland Avenue, accosted Jose Blanco repeatedly, "Are you a Negro?" Receiving no response he swung at Blanco with his fist. The latter stabbed Schoff under the heart, then walked on. As he was about to enter the house of a friend the police arrested him. He admitted that he had stabbed a man, but said he had done it in self-defense. The coroner's jury reported: "We, the jury, are unable to agree as to whether the accused, Jose Blanco, should be held to the grand jury upon a charge of manslaughter. . . . . We recommend that the coroner present this evidence to the grand jury for consideration and determination."

2. Samuel Banks

Race	Negro
Date of receiving death wound	July 30
Time of receiving death wound	11:00 P.M.
Place of receiving death wound	2729 Dearborn Street
Manner of wound	Bullet wound

At 11:00 P.M., July 30, three policemen patrolling State Street at Twenty-eighth Street, heard a shot on Dearborn Street. At Twenty-sixth Place they met about a dozen Negro ex-soldiers acting as police reserves under doubtful orders and asked them to accompany them. They all went into Dearborn Street. Sixteen-year-old Sam Banks saw them and ran for refuge, dodging under the house steps at 2729. His running was taken as evidence of guilt. The officers halted in front of the house. One Francis, a Negro, also believing that because the boy ran he was guilty, opened his door and pointed out the hiding-place of young Banks. The boy ran into the passageway between the houses. A shot fired by one of the officers took effect. Suspicion rested upon Patrolman O'Connor of the Police Department and two of the ex-soldiers, Adams and Douglas. The coroner's jury stated: "The jury is unable to determine whether one or more individuals of the group was acting criminally and is not able to determine which individual fired the shot. . . . . We find that two of said volunteers, Ed. Douglas and Charles Adams, are held on a charge of murder in connection with the death of deceased. We find there is evidence of the presence of Ed. Douglas, but no satisfactory evidence of the presence of Charles Adams at the scene of the shooting. We recommend the discharge of Charles Adams from police custody on the charge of murder."

3. Theodore Copling

Race	Negro
Date of receiving death wound	July 30
Time of receiving death wound	10:00 P.M.
Place of receiving death wound	2934 South State Street
Manner of wound	Bullet wound

A gang of Negro boys passing 2920 South State Street saw the white man and came back. A Negro, one Partee, was sitting outside the store. He warned the watchman to get inside. Almost immediately shots were fired. The only person injured was young Copling, who apparently was not in the crowd but on the outskirts as a sightseer. Suspicion rested upon four persons—Baker, Negro, leader of the gang; Partee, Negro, who warned the watchman and was opposed to the gang; Torcello, white watchman; and Graise, Negro, step-father of Copling, who had on previous occasions threatened to kill the boy because of disagreements between them. The coroner's jury said: "We recommend that the said Hanson Baker, and the said Norman Partee, and the said Dan Torcello, and the said Louis Graise be held to the grand jury on a charge of murder until discharged by due process of law."

4. George Flemming

Race	White
Date of receiving death wound	August 5
Time of receiving death wound	9:00 or 9:30 P.M.
Place of receiving death wound	549 East Forty-seventh Street
Manner of wound	Wound (inflicted by bayonet)

The coroner's jury report said: "We find that deceased, in company with several other young men, was at Forty-seventh Street and Forrestville Avenue when they were ordered to move away by a police officer and that they obeyed and were walking east; that the group were followed by one Edgar D. Mohan, a soldier, armed with a rifle, bayonet fixed; that said Mohan commanded the young men to move faster, accompanying the command by twice stabbing and wounding one Thomas J. Fennessey in the right hip and scrotum; and that he immediately after plunged the bayonet into the back of deceased, the bayonet penetrating through the body. We recommend that the said Edgar D. Mohan be held to the grand jury upon a charge of manslaughter, until discharged by due process of law.

"Being informed by the attorney general of Illinois that the military authorities of the state of Illinois have jurisdiction over acts of the said Edgar D. Mohan while in the military service, and have in fact assumed jurisdiction, a court martial being now in progress, we, the jury, hereby amend the last paragraph of our verdict of September 12, 1919, to read that 'Edgar D. Mohan be held to a court martial' instead of 'Edgar D. Mohan be held to the grand jury.'" The court martial exonerated Mohan.

Statements made in the office of the state's attorney show that Flemming was implicated in attacks in the neighborhood upon Negroes earlier in the riot period and was known as the leader of an unruly group who made a certain poolroom their hangout.

V. Deaths for which specific persons were subsequently indicted by the grand jury:

1. Casmere Lazzeroni

Race	White
Date of receiving death wound	July 28
Time of receiving death wound	4:50 P.M.
Place of receiving death wound	3618 South State Street
Manner of wound	Stab wound

The defendants were four Negro boys, Charles Johnson, eighteen; Frank Coachman, sixteen; John Green, fourteen; and Walter Colvin, sixteen. Lazzeroni, a sixty-year-old Italian peddler, driving a banana wagon on State Street, was pursued by boys throwing stones who overtook him, jumped on his wagon, and stabbed him with pocketknives. All except Johnson were alleged to have confessed, and the confessions were given before the grand jury by Policeman Deliege as he remembered them. They were not read. The boys who confessed implicated the one who did not, Johnson. Mrs. Dolly Herrmann identified all of the boys as being implicated.

The four boys were indicted and tried and on September 19, 1919, a verdict of guilty was rendered against Colvin and Johnson. They were sentenced to the penitentiary for life on December 17, 1919; the cases of Green and Coachman were stricken off with leave to reinstate.

2. Joseph Powers
Race	White
Date of receiving death wound	July 29
Time of receiving death wound	6:00 A.M.
Place of receiving death wound	Root and Emerald streets
Manner of wound	Stab wound

A Negro, William Henderson, was walking west on Root Street on the morning of July 29 going to work at the Stock Yards. He was overtaken by another Negro whom he did not know, but who accompanied him down the street. As they crossed Emerald Avenue they were met by two white men walking east. One of these was Joseph Powers. He walked slightly behind the other white man, whose identity was never discovered. It was not known whether Powers was with this man or not. As the unknown white man passed the two Negroes he struck out at them. The unknown Negro walking with Henderson struck back, evidently with a knife in his hand, and hit Powers, who was then abreast of the group, mortally wounding him. All the participants ran except Powers. Henderson was the only one overtaken. He was chased through alleys and brought down with stones and bricks and severely beaten. From the description of the second Negro given by Henderson, and the fact that another had been found wounded near this spot, it was supposed at first that the second man was one Henry Renfroe. The coroner's jury said: "We believe that William Henderson was guilty of no wrong doing, and that if the unknown colored man should prove to be Henry Renfroe, that he was acting in self-defense. We recommend their immediate discharge from police custody. We further recommend that the white men guilty of assault on William Henderson and his companion be apprehended and punished."

Later Judge Tate, Negro, was identified as the companion of Henderson. Both Negroes were indicted by the grand jury. On December 13, 1919, a verdict of not guilty was returned against Tate and the case of Henderson was nolle prossed.

3. Walter Parejko
Race	White
Date of receiving death wound	July 29
Time of receiving death wound	7:30 A.M.
Place of receiving death wound	Fifty-first Street near Dearborn Street
Manner of wound	Bullet wound

4. Morris I. Perel
Race	White
Date of receiving death wound	July 29
Time of receiving death wound	8:15 A.M.
Place of receiving death wound	Fifty-first and Dearborn streets
Manner of wound	Stab wound

The same three defendants appear in both these cases, three young Negro boys, Ben Walker, William Stinson, and Charles Davis.

There were no eyewitnesses in either case except the defendants involved, and they did not appear in person before the coroner's jury, but statements by them were either read or repeated by officials in charge. Davis and Stinson declared that Walker shot Parejko. When the statements were read to Walker, who had so far refused to make a confession, he said Stinson stabbed Perel.

Parejko and his friend Josef Maminaki, laborers on the Grand Trunk Railway, were going to work. According to Stinson the boys were sitting on a bread box in front of a store when they saw the two white men. Walker said, "Let's get this guy." Stinson answered, "Not me." Walker said, "Stand aside now, boys; I will do my stuff." He fired and Parejko was mortally wounded and Maminaki slightly wounded. Walker denied the shooting. However, he told where the weapon could be found, and it was brought before the coroner as evidence.

Perel was walking to his place of business going west on Fifty-first Street. Near Dearborn Street four or five Negro men or boys jumped on him and stabbed him. When he was found, it was discovered that his gold watch had been forcibly severed from the chain and was missing. Someone said a crowd of boys had been seen running south. According to the statement of Ben Walker, "Fat Stinson jumped on him and stabbed him and hit him with a club at the same time. . . . . After he stabbed and hit him the whole gang jumped on him." Afterward Stinson is reported by Walker to have said, "I surely hit that guy," and to have displayed a pearl-handled knife.

The coroner's jury said in the Perejko case: "We recommend that the said Ben Walker, the said William Stinson, and the said Charles Davis be held to the grand jury upon a charge of murder until discharged by due process of law." In the Perel case the jury said: "We recommend that the said William Stinson be held to the grand jury upon a charge of murder until discharged by due process of law."

They were indicted by the grand jury, and on January 9, 1920, a verdict of not guilty was returned in each case.

5. Harold Brignadello (see p. 27)

Race	White
Date of receiving death wound	July 29
Time of receiving death wound	10:30 A.M.
Place of receiving death wound	1021 South State Street
Manner of wound	Bullet wound

Harold Brignadello was one of a crowd of white men who wandered south on State Street and halted at No. 1021 and stoned the house. It was not brought out whether the stone-throwing was done because Negroes lived in the house, or was provoked by taunts from Negroes in the second-story window. A Negro woman and two men appeared at the window, and when the throwing did not stop, the woman raised her arm. A shot was fired into the crowd, fatally wounding Brignadello. Police officers found in the flat and arrested Emma Jackson, Kate Elder, John Webb, Ed Robinson, and Clarence Jones. The coroner's jury recommended that they be held to the grand jury upon a charge of murder until discharged by due process of law, and that members of the unknown white mob be apprehended. The five Negroes named were indicted, and on September 20, 1919, a verdict of not guilty was returned as to each.

6. G. L. Wilkins

Race	White
Date of receiving death wound	July 30
Time of receiving death wound	1:30 P.M.
Place of receiving death wound	3825 Rhodes Avenue
Manner of wound	Bullet wound

Wilkins, an agent for the Metropolitan Life Insurance Company, on his rounds collecting, entered the house at 3825 Rhodes Avenue where several Negro families live. While he was inside three young Negro men approached one of the tenants who was sitting on the front porch, and one of them asked who the white man was. This youth is alleged to have said,

"We don't want no damned insurance man here. What money we have got we want to keep it." When Wilkins appeared, two of the youths stood on the curb, and one went between two houses which Wilkins had to pass. As he went by he was shot. It was said that Spurgeon Anthony and Willis Powell were the two who stood at the curb, and John Washington was the one who went between the houses. The coroner's jury recommended that the three be held to the grand jury upon a charge of murder, and the grand jury indicted them. On December 16, 1919, a verdict of not guilty was returned as to Powell, and Washington was found guilty and sentenced to twenty years in the penitentiary.

7. Paul Hardwick

Race	Negro
Date of receiving death wound	July 29
Time of receiving death wound	5:00 A.M.
Place of receiving death wound	Wabash Avenue and Adams Street
Manner of wound	Bullet wound

A mob of white civilians, soldiers, and sailors, who had been chasing Negroes through the "Loop" district for the previous two or three hours, beating and robbing them, and destroying property where Negroes were not found, entered one of Thompson's restaurants where Hardwick was breakfasting. Another Negro, one King, was also in the restaurant. The mob set upon them, throwing food and dishes. Hardwick dodged into the street and King hid behind a dish counter, where he was wounded with a knife. Failing to catch Hardwick as he fled down Adams Street, one of the rioters stepped to the curb and fired a revolver at him, bringing him down. Several of the crowd robbed the corpse. At the time of the coroner's jury hearing the only one of the mob identified was Ray Freedman, aged seventeen. He was apprehended and charged with murder, malicious mischief, and inciting to riot, but was not indicted Later Edward Haines was connected with the case, indicted, and on February 21, 1920, sent to Pontiac.

8. Robert Williams

Race	Negro
Date of receiving death wound	July 29
Time of receiving death wound	6:15 A.M.
Place of receiving death wound	At or near State and Van Buren streets
Manner of wound	Stab wound

The murder of Williams was the second riot killing in the heart of Chicago's business district on the morning of July 29. Before Williams died he said he had been assaulted by white men at State and Van Buren streets. An eyewitness, a Negro, said he saw Williams running west on the car track on Van Buren Street, followed by a mob of about 200 white men. One of them, whom he positively identified as Frank Biga, stabbed the deceased twice, but Williams continued to run for a distance after that. A white man who saw Williams picked up at Harrison and State streets also identified Biga as a man who all during the morning had led gangs chasing Negroes. A woman went to a policeman and pointed out Biga as the leader of riot mobs. The coroner's jury recommended that Biga be held to the grand jury upon a charge of murder. At the time of the identification of Biga by the woman the policeman arrested him, found a broken razor in his possession, and had him booked for disorderly conduct, for which he was fined $5 and costs in the boys' court and sent to the House of Correction. The next day he broke out of the House of Correction and was not again apprehended until he was implicated in the murder of a shoe merchant, Fred Bender, on August 8, 1919. He killed Bender with a blow on the head from an iron pipe. On February 18, 1920, Biga was sent to the penitentiary for life.

9. William Dozier

Race	Negro
Date of receiving death wound	July 31
Time of receiving death wound	7:15 A.M.
Place of receiving death wound	Stock Yards, Exchange Avenue about Cook Street
Manner of wound	External violence

Dozier, Negro, approached a meat curer employed in the superintendent's office of Swift & Co. to ask if the Negroes were not going to have protection in the Yards that morning. A white worker stepped out of the crowd and struck at Dozier with a hammer. Dozier dodged and caught the blow on the neck. He started to run east on Exchange Avenue. As he ran he was struck with a street broom and shovel and other missiles; near the sheep pens a brick felled him. The meat curer above mentioned and an assistant identified one Zarka as the man who wielded the hammer. Joseph Scezak was identified as the man who used the broom. The coroner's jury recommended that these two be held to the grand jury on a charge of manslaughter and also that the unknown participants be held upon the same charge. Zarka and Scezak were indicted for murder, and on May 6, 1920, a verdict of not guilty was returned as to each.

D. TABLE SHOWING NUMBER OF PERSONS INJURED IN CHICAGO RIOT, BY DATE AND BY RACE

DATE	RACE			TOTAL
	White	Negro	Unknown	
July 27	10	31	5	46
28	71	152	6	229
29	55	80	4	139
30	20	20	2	42
31	10	9	0	19
Aug. 1	0	1	0	1
2	1	3	0	4
3	1	1	0	2
4	1	0	0	1
5	1	0	0	1
6	1	0	0	1
7	2	0	0	2
8	0	1	0	1
9	1	0	0	1
Date unknown	4	44	0	48
Total	178	342	17	537

INDEX

DATE		
MAR 2 8 '73		
MAY 3 73		
GAYLORD		